THE STEWARTRY OF KIRKCUDBRIGHT AND THE COUNTY OF WIGTOWN

". . . by Statistical is meant . . . an inquiry into the
state of a country for the purpose of ascertaining
the quantum of happiness enjoyed by its inhabitants
and the means of its future improvement."

SIR JOHN SINCLAIR, BART.,
1798

THE THIRD STATISTICAL ACCOUNT OF SCOTLAND

The 'Third Statistical Account of Scotland' is compiled and edited by the four Scottish Universities, each University being responsible for the county volumes in its own region. Tribute must be paid to the Scottish Council of Social Service under whose aegis the work is being published and to the Local Authorities throughout Scotland for contributing towards costs of publication.

The complete list of volumes is as follows:

1. The County of Ayr*
2. The County of Fife*
3. The County of East Lothian*
4. The City of Aberdeen*
5. The City of Glasgow*
6. The County of Dunbarton*
7. The County of Aberdeen*
8. The County of Lanark*
9. The County of Argyll*
10. The County of Banff*
11. The Counties of Renfrew and Bute*
12. The County of Dumfries*
13. The County of Ross and Cromarty
14. The Counties of Kirkcudbright and Wigtown*
15. The City of Edinburgh
16. The County of Inverness
17. The Counties of Moray and Nairn
18. The Counties of Stirling and Clackmannan
19. The Counties of Caithness and Sutherland
20. The Counties of Orkney and Zetland
21. The County of West Lothian
22. The County of Midlothian
23. The Counties of Berwick and Roxburgh
24. The Counties of Peebles and Selkirk*
25. The City of Dundee
26. The Counties of Kincardine and Angus
27. The Counties of Perth and Kinross

* *Already published.*

THE THIRD STATISTICAL ACCOUNT OF SCOTLAND

THE STEWARTRY OF
KIRKCUDBRIGHT

EDITED BY

John Laird and D. G. Ramsay

AND

THE COUNTY OF
WIGTOWN

EDITED BY

M. C. Arnott

vol. 14

COLLINS

144 CATHEDRAL STREET, GLASGOW, C.4.

1965

FIRST PUBLISHED 1965 X

THE THIRD STATISTICAL ACCOUNT OF SCOTLAND

GLASGOW UNIVERSITY REGION

*COUNTY OF AYR, *J. Strawhorn* and *W. Boyd*
*CITY OF GLASGOW, *J. Cunnison* and *J. B. S. Gilfillan*

SUBSEQUENT VOLUMES UNDER THE GENERAL EDITORSHIP OF
GEORGE S. PRYDE

*COUNTY OF DUNBARTON, *Margaret S. Dilke* and *A. A. Templeton*
*COUNTY OF LANARK, *George Thomson*
*COUNTY OF ARGYLL, *Colin M. MacDonald*
*COUNTIES OF RENFREW, *H. A. Moisley* and *A. G. Thain*
    BUTE, *A. C. Somerville* and *W. Stevenson*
*COUNTY OF DUMFRIES, *G. F. B. Houston*

VOLUMES UNDER THE GENERAL EDITORSHIP OF
J. B. S. GILFILLAN

*COUNTIES OF KIRKCUDBRIGHT, *John Laird* and *D. G. Ramsay*
    WIGTOWN, *M. C. Arnott*
COUNTIES OF STIRLING, *R. C. Rennie*
    CLACKMANNAN, *T. Crouther Gordon*

* *Already published.*

© WILLIAM COLLINS SONS & CO., LTD. 1965
PRINTED IN SCOTLAND BY
COLLINS CLEAR-TYPE PRESS

CONTENTS

THE STEWARTRY OF KIRKCUDBRIGHT

	page
PREFACE	15

Part One: THE COUNTY

1. THE NATURAL BACKGROUND	17
2. HISTORY	25
3. THE ECONOMY	32
4. GOVERNMENT AND PUBLIC SERVICES	41
5. THE COMMUNITY	56

Part Two: THE PARISHES

6. ANWOTH by the Rev. John Turnbull	67
7. BALMACLELLAN by the Rev. William Peebles	78
8. BALMAGHIE by the Rev. John W. T. Dickie	85
9. BORGUE by the Rev. William Moore	98
10. BUITTLE by T. L. N. Hogg	108
11. CARSPHAIRN by the Rev. Wilfrid R. Sievewright	121
12. COLVEND AND SOUTHWICK by the Rev. James D. Duff	125
13. CROSSMICHAEL by the Rev. James A. Fisher	137
14. DALRY by the Rev. M. G. Mullo Weir	146
15. GIRTHON & BURGH OF GATEHOUSE by James Anderson Russell	158
16. KELLS & BURGH OF NEW GALLOWAY by the Rev. W. Bruce Young	169
17. KELTON by the Rev. Donald M. Henry	178
BURGH OF CASTLE-DOUGLAS by J. F. Robertson	184
18. KIRKBEAN by the Rev. A. Dickson	193
19. KIRKCUDBRIGHT (PARISH & BURGH) by the Rev. J. E. Mothersill	201
20. KIRKGUNZEON by Alan W. Lindsay	215
21. KIRKMABRECK by the Rev. C. V. A. MacEchern	220
22. KIRKPATRICK-DURHAM by John Edwards	226

CONTENTS

		page
23.	KIRKPATRICK-IRONGRAY by the Rev. W. B. Aitken	233
24.	LOCHRUTTON by John Hyslop	245
25.	MINNIGAFF by Dr. A. Kellie Brooke	255
26.	NEW ABBEY by Douglas Walker	263
27.	PARTON by the Rev. G. D. Summers	274
28.	RERRICK by the Rev. Alexander H. Christie	279
29.	TERREGLES by J. M. Hutcheson	290
30.	TONGLAND by the Rev. George Tuton	297
31.	TROQUEER by the Rev. J. L. Mangles	305
32.	TWYNHOLM by the Rev. John Good	309
33.	URR by the Rev. George G. Campbell	313
	BURGH OF DALBEATTIE by R. M. Halliday	324
ACKNOWLEDGMENTS		331
BIBLIOGRAPHY		332
APPENDIX I. Motor Licences.		509
APPENDIX II. Parish Populations, 1901-61.		510
INDEX		511

THE COUNTY OF WIGTOWN

PREFACE		337

Part One: THE COUNTY

1.	THE BACKGROUND	339
2.	THE ECONOMY	353
3.	GOVERNMENT AND PUBLIC SERVICES	366
4.	THE COMMUNITY	378

Part Two: THE PARISHES

5.	WIGTOWN by the Rev. Gavin Lawson	389
6.	PENNINGHAME by the Rev. John Ross	401
7.	KIRKCOWAN by the Rev. Hugh Tolland and A. E. Truckell	407
8.	KIRKINNER by the late Mrs. Grace Christison	412
9.	SORBIE by the late Rev. N. Elliot	416
10.	WHITHORN by the Rev. John G. Scoular	420
11.	GLASSERTON by the Rev. John G. Scoular	427

CONTENTS

page

12. MOCHRUM by the late Rev. James Thomson   431
13. OLD LUCE by the late Rev. David Galloway   437
14. NEW LUCE by the Rev. F. J. Chambers   441
15. INCH by the Rev. Harry Galbraith Miller   445
16. STRANRAER by M. C. Arnott   456
17. KIRKCOLM by James G. Littlejohn   476
18. LESWALT by J. S. Boyd   480
19. PORTPATRICK by John Muir   484
20. STONEYKIRK by the Rev. Archibald L. Melrose   491
21. KIRKMAIDEN by the Rev. J. I. Andrews   499
ACKNOWLEDGMENTS   507
BIBLIOGRAPHY   508
INDEX   519

ILLUSTRATIONS

THE STEWARTRY OF KIRKCUDBRIGHT

TEXT FIGURES

		page
1.	Population of county	57
2.	Population of burghs	58
3.	The Parishes	59
4.	Age distribution by quinquennial age groups	61

PLATES

		facing page
1.	Dundrennan Abbey	128
2.	Sweetheart Abbey	128
3.	Galloway Bull Show	129
4.	Whitepark Farm, Castle-Douglas	129
5.	Dundeugh Forest, from the East	160
6.	Timber Extraction at Thinning Stage	161
7.	The Old Kirkcudbright Harbour	256
8.	*Shell Fitter*	256
9.	Clatteringshaws Dam	257
10.	Kirkcudbright Academy	288
11.	The Stewartry Province Bonspiel	289
12.	Sandgreen	289

THE COUNTY OF WIGTOWN

TEXT FIGURES

		page
1.	Contrasts in the rainfall at different parts of the Shire	341
2.	The geology of Wigtownshire	344
3.	Land Use	354
4.	Variations in the price of milk	355
5.	Farm cheesemakers	356
6.	People in employment during 1960	363

ILLUSTRATIONS

		page
7.	Variations in the number of unemployed during 1960	371
8.	School Leavers	375
9.	Population Distribution	380

PLATES

		facing page
1.	Mull of Galloway Lighthouse	352
2.	Dunskey Castle	353
3.	Isle of Whithorn	353
4.	Castle Kennedy	353
5.	Stranraer	384
6.	Portpatrick	384
7.	The Cree Bridge and Weir, Newton Stewart	385
8.	Penninghame Open Prison, Newton Stewart	385
9.	Galloway Creamery, Stranraer	448
10.	Cheesemaking at the Galloway Creamery	448
11.	A Thatched Cottage near the Mull of Galloway	449
12.	New Housing, Glenluce	449
13.	Last of the Portlogan Lifeboats	480
14.	The Portpatrick Lifeboat	480
15.	The First *Princess Victoria*	481
16.	T.S.S. *Caledonian Princess*	481

THE STEWARTRY OF
KIRKCUDBRIGHT

PREFACE

THE writing of the Third Statistical Account for the Stewartry appears to have coincided with a period of change in the county parishes. Not all of the ministers originally invited found it possible to complete the task, and although most of the parish accounts were submitted within a few years, several were written in response to invitations given some years later. As a result, the writing of the parish accounts covered a period of over ten years.

This posed a difficult problem for the county editors. To bring up to date the facts and figures in the parish account would have invalidated some of the opinions and conclusions of the parish writer. Each parish account accordingly gives the date on which it was completed and the facts and figures are correct as at that date.

The chapters dealing with the county were written during the years 1961 and 1962, and parish statistics, where repeated, have been brought up to date.

The account for the Stewartry, a social history at community and sometimes even family level, is not heavily weighted with statistics in the modern sense; such a treatment was not thought to be in keeping with the personable and friendly way of life so characteristic of this part of Galloway. The writing nevertheless made heavy demands on the time and goodwill of so many people that individual acknowledgement is not possible.

In the only way open to them the parish writers and county editors here offer grateful thanks to all who contributed directly or indirectly to the account.

Particular mention must however be made of the assistance of Rev. J. W. T. Dickie, who after completing the account for Balmaghie parish, showed such continuing interest in the whole project that he became in fact an associate editor and gave invaluable help in the editing and contributed the section on the early history of the Stewartry.

It is a matter of sincere regret that Dr. G. S. Pryde did not live to see this task completed; his enthusiasm for Scottish history did much to inspire all concerned with the account.

We are indebted to Sir George Laidlaw for his expert guidance on all business matters and to Mr. J. B. S. Gilfillan for the help given in bringing the work forward to the stage of publication.

JOHN LAIRD
D. G. RAMSAY

Castle-Douglas,
March, 1964.

Part One

THE COUNTY

CHAPTER 1

THE NATURAL BACKGROUND

KIRKCUDBRIGHT, often referred to as the Stewartry because of its former jurisdiction by a Royal Steward, is one of the lesser Scottish counties; it ranks only 23rd in terms of population, though 9th in terms of area (28,000 persons, 900 square miles, 1961). Together with its smaller but equally populous neighbour, Wigtownshire, it forms the Galloway district of south-west Scotland, as well known for its unspoiled coastal and upland scenery as for its black beef cattle and dairy produce. Its associations with Bruce's opening victory in the seven-year campaign which culminated at Bannockburn in 1314, and with the novels of S. R. Crockett, are less well known outwith Scotland. Crockett's works contain fine descriptions of the region, particularly of the wild and lonely uplands, the recreational and economic value of which has been recognised by the creation of the Glen Trool National Forest Park, named after the scene of Bruce's victory.

GEOLOGY

Foundation Rocks. The Stewartry lies in the western part of the Southern Uplands, wholly south of the Southern Uplands fault. Its foundation rocks, like most of the rocks of the Southern Uplands, are therefore Lower Palaeozoic in age and belong to the Ordovician and Silurian systems. They consist of a great accumulation, thousands of feet in total thickness, of muds, shales, silts, sands, and pebble beds that were laid down some 400 to 300 million years ago in a former sea that covered the greater part of what is now Britain. Many of the strata contain an abundance of fossils—graptolites, trilobites, corals, shells.

At the close of Silurian times this pile of sediments was folded and puckered by intense mountain-building movements into chains of magnitude comparable with the Alps and the Himalayas, running in a general north-east and south-west direction—a direction still preserved in the geological 'grain' of the area. The enormous earth-pressures involved compacted and toughened the muddy sediments into hard slates and the sandy sediments into greywackes, such as are now exposed over most of the Stewartry.

Igneous Rocks.   Shortly after the mountain-building movements, hot molten lava-like materials moved upwards from deep-seated reservoirs and penetrated the Ordovician and Silurian strata to form large emplacements where they slowly cooled and solidified as crystalline granite. Three large blunt cylinders of such granite now form the Criffel-Dalbeattie, the Cairnsmore of Fleet, and the Loch Doon masses; and a fourth smaller one forms Cairnsmore of Carsphairn.   The close interlocking crystal mosaic of these igneous rocks allows them to be worked in massive blocks, and, combined with the attractive appearance of the stone, contributes to the success of the quarry industry.

Much smaller in size, but much more numerous, are narrow wall-like dykes of igneous rock that cut the Lower Palaeozoic rocks and sometimes run across country for several miles.   There are swarms of them particularly on the east flank of Wigtown Bay, between Kirkcudbright and Castle-Douglas, and between Dalry and Carsphairn.

Renewed Sedimentation.   For perhaps 40 or 50 million years after the mountain-building movements and the intrusion of the igneous rocks, the Stewartry was a rugged land area subjected to intense weathering and erosion.   The mountain summits were worn away until only the mountain roots remained; and in the process the deep-seated granites were bared of their covering of sediments to be exposed at the land surface.

The subdued landscape moulded by erosion then underwent subsidence, and along the south-western margin of the Stewartry a sea advanced and partly submerged the Silurian rocks and some of the exposed Criffel granite.   In this sea were formed the rocks of the Carboniferous system, now seen in a narrow outcrop along the Solway Firth between the Nith estuary and Abbey Head.   The Carboniferous rocks are shallow-water marine sands and muds, with some highly fossiliferous limestones containing well-preserved corals and shells.

A Desert Interlude.   In its turn Carboniferous sedimentation was interrupted by renewed earth-movement, and the Stewartry was again converted into a land area. Erosion was continued under desert conditions, the deposits of the period—the New Red Sandstones—being composed partly of rock-scree, partly of wind-blown sands, and containing etched and polished pebbles.   These red beds, which form excellent building stone, are to be seen in the Nith valley along the western flank of the Dumfries basin.

The Landscape.   For nearly 200 million years after the deposition of the New Red Sandstone the record of the rocks in the Stewartry is almost a blank.   During that long interval the form of the present landscape was sculptured, the river systems established, and the coast delineated.   Most of the large valleys are aligned from north-west to south-east, that is to say, across the geological grain of the country; thus the system of rivers which carved these valleys appears to have been superimposed on the rocks. This must have taken place at some period, not only long after they were deposited, but also long after they were folded and faulted into their present form, i.e. in the latter part of 200 million years since the formation of the New Red Sandstone.

The evolution of the river system, and, therefore, of the physical landscape, has been studied scientifically by W. G. Jardine.[1] He believes that the river system originated in mid or late Tertiary times, that is, about 15 million years ago, when this part of Scotland began to emerge from the sea. This emergence continued in an irregular fashion. The general slope of the emergent land was from north-west to south-east and on this slope the initial rivers commenced to flow; during relatively stable phases coastal and river plains began to be formed, only to be abandoned as the land rose again further out of the sea.

Consequently the modern landscape consists of a series of platforms, rising like a staircase above the present coast. The lowest platforms have emerged most recently and are best preserved; in particular those at about 200 feet, 450-500 feet, 600-700 feet, 750-850 feet and 1,000 to 1,100 feet are readily recognisable. At higher levels the old platforms are much dissected by streams and are less perfectly preserved.

Glaciation. Landscape evolution by the development of river systems was interrupted during the last million years or so by another geological agent, ice, which left its mark all over the county. The gouging and scouring effects of large glaciers are strong in the Merrick and Kells ranges, where many mountain lochs occupy corries and almost every valley is to some extent U-trenched, and only to a less degree along the east wall of Cairnsmore of Fleet; and the upland rocks are everywhere scraped by ice to leave little soil and barren country. In the lowlands the moundy sweeps and loops of moraine, left behind by the melting glaciers, are evident in all the larger valleys and provide the rich soils to which the highly successful agriculture of the Stewartry is due.

Thus the physical landscape of Kirkcudbright ranges from wild, almost mountainous, uplands such as Merrick (2,764 ft.) and the Rhinns of Kells (2,000-2,600 ft.), with which are associated many attractive lochs, through lesser hills and uplands with broad, fertile valleys between, to a coastline of alternating cliffs and sheltered coastal bays. It is a landscape less rugged (and less well known) than that of the Highlands, but, in its own way, no less attractive.

CLIMATE AND WATER RESOURCES

In the low-lying, mainly coastal, areas the climate is equable and mild. Maritime influences preserve the most populous, low-lying, districts from all but the most penetrating winter frosts. By the same rule summer days are seldom excessively hot, the less so because of the relatively high incidence of cloud. Inland, and particularly in the upland districts, summers are even cooler and more cloudy, whilst with increasing altitude

[1] 'River Development in Galloway', *Scottish Geographical Magazine*, 75:2, 1959, pp. 65-74

comes an increasing incidence of frost and snow. Such a climate is not well suited to arable cultivation, least of all to cereal production, and it is largely on this account that livestock production of one sort or another has long been the mainstay of farming in the Stewartry.

The rainfall is fairly evenly distributed throughout the year, with a slight tendency for the spring and early summer period (i.e. March or April to June or July) to be less wet than the rest. August tends to be a cloudy, wet month, but September is often drier. Such dry periods tend, also, to be the sunniest. These are generalisations and cannot be relied on from one year to another, though they are true over a period of 30 years or so.

The combination of westerly situation and high altitude results in a particularly heavy accumulation of precipitation (rain and snow) in the uplands. Because of proximity to the coast the upland streams and rivers are short, steep and swift flowing. They are given to sudden spates which not infrequently lead to inconvenience and destruction along their lower reaches. Nevertheless the high upland rainfall is something of an asset both as a source of public water supplies and as a means of generating electricity: the Galloway hydro-electric scheme has been operating since 1936.

FLORA

The floral character of the county is primarily due to its geographical position, and to the continuing action of past and present climatic factors of rainfall and temperature upon its physical structure. But this character has been profoundly modified by the hand of man. His grazing animals, cropping methods and plantations of conifer restrict botanical variety. However, the coast and hills provide cliffs and ravines where grazing is reduced, and the many low-lying pockets of ground, which are difficult to drain, are occupied by lochs and bogs.

A narrow strip of carboniferous strata along the coast adds nutriment to the rock, and the heughs of Colvend and Orroland are clothed with variety of colour and kind. The yellow of Rock-rose, the white of *Rosa spinosissima*, the blue of Sheep's-bit and the red of *Geranium sanguineum* form a backcloth for the occasional occurrence of less common species as *Lychnis viscaria, Minuartia verna, Astragalus glycyphyllos, Orobanche alba* and *Carex punctata*. Proceeding westwards, Raeberry, Borness and Ravenshall Rocks, all have their specialties, including *Vicia Lutea, Astragalus danicus, Crithmum, Ligusticum* and *Scilla verna*.

At the foot of some sea cliffs are watery places where Phragmites may be joined by the Giant Horsetail and Fleabane, both uncommon in this area. In certain spots the rare Holy-grass pleasantly scents the air. Parts of the coast are fringed by salt-marsh, where *Halimione, Limonium humile, Ruppia, Scirpus tabernaemontani, Blysmus compressus* and *B. rufus, Schoenus*, the *Carices distans* and *extensa*, and *Parapholis strigosa* mingle with the commoner *Spergularias, Suaeda*, and *Salicornias, Aster tripolium* and *Triglochin*.

Sand and shingle are less frequent but in favoured botanical localities like Mullock and Brighouse Bays some locally uncommon plants such as Yellow Horned-poppy, Seakale, Isle of Man Cabbage, Sea Radish and Sea Holly maintain a precarious existence among more abundant but less colourful grasses and Oraches, Sow-thistles and Scentless Mayweed.

Turning inland, deciduous woodland is not plentiful and, where it does occur, it is more remarkable for the Spring-flowering beauty of its floor of Primrose and Wild Hyacinth with Gean and Bird Cherry above, than for uncommon species. The rising ground bordering the vales of Nith, Fleet and Cree is clothed with oakwood. Some dells have a delicate drapery of the tender Oak and Beech Ferns. *Pyrola minor* and *Melica nutans* are scarce in shady ravines.

Stewartry hedgerows have the usual Umbelliferous species in succession and other common plants. The variety is likely to be reduced still further by the prevalent blanket spraying of verges. War ploughing programmes have disturbed much pasture but hilly fields may have such species as *Meum, Gentianella campestris* and *Helictotrichon pubescens.* Damp meadows are favoured by the Butterfly Orchids (both species), Twayblade, Spotted Orchid, Northern Marsh Orchid and their hybrids.

Many kinds of plant are found in the extensive marshy or boggy ground. They range from widespread Bogbean, Marsh Cinquefoil, Whorled Caraway, Bog Asphodel and Cotton-grasses to plants of more restricted distribution. The Greater Spearwort and March Stitchwort at Carlingwark Loch, *Hypericum elodes* especially in Colvend, *Andromeda* well seen in the Nature Conservancy's Kirkconnell Flow but occurring sparingly in many other mosses, *Anagallis tenella, Pinguicula Lusitanica* to the west of the county, the carnivorous Bladderworts and long-leaved Sundews, *Scutellaria minor* and the uncommon *Carices limosa* and *paupercula* are among these local plants. In places where the percolating water is fairly base-rich the Grass of Parnassus, Knotted Pearlwort, *Eriophorum latifolium, Eleocharis quinqueflora* and the *Carices diandra* and *lepidocarpa* are characteristic.

The Yellow and White Water-lilies float in the surface of many lochs accompanied perhaps by stands of Bulrush and Reedmace. The loch floor may be dotted with plants of Shoreweed, Water Lobelia, Awlwort and Quillwort and thence arise the stems of various species of *Potamogeton* and *Sparganium.* The elusive *Najas flexilis* fruits freely in Loch Kindar and fragments break off and float about with stems of *Callitriche autumnalis.*

On some river banks, notably by the Ken and the Cree, extensive beds of sedge occur. Kenmure Holms have a rich flora including *Calamagrostis canescens* and *Carex elongata.*

Much of the high hilly ground has a granite foundation and large areas are covered with *Molinia, Nardus, Scirpus* and *Calluna,* but where the surrounding sediments are metamorphosed some less common species such as *Potentilla crantzii, Saussurea, Oxyria* and *Asplenium viride* occur on the rocks. The Blaeberry, Cowberry, Cranberry, Crowberry and Cloudberry (rarely) frequent the hills, where the air may be redolent of Bog Myrtle or Lemon-scented Fern.

The Stewartry, in view of its western position with a large mountainous mass and associated deep ravines within its confines, is rich in bryophytes. Rock exposures are plentiful, but chiefly of acid rock and the moss flora is correspondingly rich in acidophil species. Among hepatics pride of place goes to the Atlantic species, numbering no less than 21 in the county, though many of them are extremely scarce. *Lophocolea fragrans* has several stations, the tiny but striking *Colura* and the moisture-loving *Jubula* very few.

FAUNA

Within modest borders the Stewartry contains a rich variety of animal habitats. Red deer, descended from introduced stock, range widely over the hills and into the forests. The more sedentary Roe deer is plentiful and has recently been closely studied in Forestry Commission land with a view to combining essential control with conservation. Although outlawed, foxes remain common. Badgers are scarce, but otters are found from the highest lochs to the sea, while Red Squirrels occur in most woodlands. Both Brown and Blue Hares have prospered since the decline of the rabbit from myxomatosis; the range of the Blue, or Mountain Hare, now overlaps that of the Brown and hybrids occur. Small herds of feral goats, the males with impressive horns, may be seen threading their way across the crags in the north and west of the county.

A more tolerant attitude has helped the Golden Eagle to return in recent decades, but lack of seclusion in the nesting season is a threat to this and other fine birds. In addition the steeper crags provide scope for breeding Peregrines, Ravens and Buzzards, the last two species also descending to nest in trees along the fringes of the hills. Ring Ousels add enchantment to many a cleugh by their haunting song, while Wheatears nest even up to the summits, where, as on Carlin's Cairn, man has unwittingly provided a site. The shores of the hill lochs are too rugged to attract many birds, but Common Sandpipers, Pied Wagtails and Dunlin often feed along the little bays of sparkling sand, although drainage and afforestation have banished the Dunlin from some moorland breeding haunts. The large Gullery of Black-headed Gulls at lonely Loch Enoch is one of the highest in Britain, while there are small colonies of Common Gulls on several lochs. In the past 20 years tree-nesting Goosanders have been a notable addition to the breeding birds of the hill country. The larger swift-flowing burns are shared by Dippers and Grey Wagtails.

Extensive afforestation of moorland is making a deep impact on the fauna. Where young trees grow among heather, Stonechats and Grasshopper Warblers are often found, while everywhere the young plantations are attractive to Whinchats. At first some true moorland species such as Meadow Pipits, Red Grouse and Curlew remain while Merlins enjoy a temporary abundance of prey and nesting cover. Local 'plagues' of field voles bring Short-Eared Owls and Kestrels in their wake, while the Owls find the thick ground cover ideal for nesting as well. The growing trees provide a new habitat for warblers such as Chiffchaffs and White-throats, and continue to attract Blackgame for some years, but so swiftly do the conifers eliminate other vegetation that in 20 years the interior of the forest becomes somewhat dark and quiet except for the clap of Wood-Pigeons' wings, the screeching of the Jays and the shrill notes of the Goldcrest and Coal-Tit. On summer nights the ceaseless calling of Tawny Owls and the intermittent scream of a Barn Owl from distant marsh or meadow reveal that these two species are our commonest nocturnal owls, while the Long-Eared is now chiefly to be found in old, isolated plantations.

Yet the bird life of the maturing forest can become rather more varied with the advent of cone-bearing, Crossbills remaining to breed after invasion years, while larch seeds are a favourite food of Siskins, Redpolls and Goldfinches. Should a less highly specialised forest emerge, interesting additions to the bird population can be expected; but whether these will compensate for the widespread loss of birds like the Curlew, Golden Plover, Skylark and Merlin, whose presence and voices are the essence of spacious moorland, is doubtful. The stronghold of many woodland birds such as Woodcock, Redstart and Wood Warbler lies in the oak and birch woods of the finest glens. Indeed Pied Flycatchers, Great-Spotted and Green Woodpeckers have spread through the hard-woods this century. The mixture of willow, alder, birch and blackthorn, typified in the swampier parts of the Ken valley, supports a rich community, of which Long-tailed and Willow Tits, Bullfinches and Redpolls, Sedge and Willow Warblers, are characteristic.

As a winter haunt of wildfowl the Ken and Dee valleys are unsur-passed. Between New Galloway and Castle-Douglas it has sometimes been possible to find all the British Grey Geese. While the Grey-Lag is currently the most widespread, the 5-600 Greenland White-fronts ranging between Dalry and Threave form one of the few outposts of this race on the British mainland. The small flock of Bean Geese returning to the environs of Castle-Douglas between November and March are almost the last sizable, though declining, group of their kind in Britain; with them the rare Lesser White-front has lately been detected.

The marshy bays south of the Loch Ken viaduct are much favoured by dabbling duck including Pintail, Shoveler and the rarer Gadwall, while Carlingwark Loch, remarkable for its confiding Whooper Swans, is outstanding among many lowland lochs frequented by diving duck, especially Goldeneye, Tufted Duck, Pochard, Goosanders and Smew. Loch Arthur is one of several lochs where the display of Great Crested Grebes may be seen.

The western flank of the Nith estuary, with its mudflats and mussel-beds, attracts thousands of wintering duck, particularly Scaup, and waders, such as Oyster-catchers, Curlew, Redshank, Knot and Dunlin. Chiefly at times of passage, regular visitors include both Godwits—the

Black-tailed has increased—Greenshank, Whimbrel, Green Sandpipers and Spotted Redshanks.

The smaller estuaries are favoured by Widgeon and many waders in winter and by breeding Sheld-Duck and Mergansers. In summer the cliffs and rocky islands are dominated by the clamorous Herring-Gulls with a sprinkling of both black-backs. Since the late 1940s Fulmars have bred sparingly, and Guillemots, Razorbills and Cormorants occupy suitable sites. Jackdaws and Rock-Doves, the latter much interbred with feral pigeons, occupy caves and crevices, while at Portling there are cliff-nesting House-Martins. A few pairs of Ravens and Peregrines are faithful to coastal sites. In some years there are fine colonies of Common and Sandwich Terns on the islands. Spectacular flocks of gulls, mainly Common and Black-headed, gather in winter to roost in the estuaries, often feeding far inland.

In so brief an account only a few of the more striking features of the changing wild life can be mentioned, but in conclusion may be added the spread of inland nesting by Oyster-Catchers, the long-term decline of the Corncrake and the disappearance from some former haunts of the Nightjar and Kingfisher.

CHAPTER 2

HISTORY

EARLY TIMES

T HE story of Galloway, properly so called, does not begin until early in the tenth century, when the region was occupied by the Gallgaidhil, from whom it derives its name. Only the briefest sketch of its earlier history can be given here.[1] It was twice occupied by the Romans, and during the period when Rome held South Britain our area was inevitably much influenced by Roman civilisation, and latterly by Roman religion, Christianity, through the work of St. Ninian and others. Hence when Rome finally withdrew from South Britain, Galloway, like the rest of what we now call the Lowlands, was ruled by British kings who regarded themselves as in some sense heirs of Rome and defenders of Roman civilisation and the Christian religion against pagan invaders, the most formidable of whom were the Angles. This phase lasted about two hundred years, till the middle of the seventh century, when Galloway, like its neighbours, came under the sway of Northumbria, itself now Christian.

Anglian suzerainty lasted some two centuries, but Northumbria in turn collapsed under Danish attacks and early in the tenth century our region seems to have been overrun by a host of Norsemen from the Isles, who had acquired the Gaelic language there. The Irish and Scottish Gaels called them the 'foreign Gaels'—Gallgaidhil. They gave their name to Galloway, possibly through the Welsh form, Galwyddel; and their language, too, for Gaelic in time replaced the old British, or Welsh, speech, and itself remained the language of Galloway for about six hundred years. The Gallgaidhil apparently owed allegiance to the powerful earls of Orkney, who also held the earldom of Galloway. The greatest of these was Thorfinn the Mighty, whose daughter or widow, Ingibjorg, married Malcolm III, King of Scots, who thus acquired a claim to Galloway. Malcolm later married the pious and formidable Margaret, and her sons, not Ingibjorg's, eventually succeeded their father; wrongfully, as many Galwegians, and Scots too, thought. This was the cause of much trouble in years to come.

THE LORDSHIP OF GALLOWAY

David, the greatest of Margaret's sons, who became king in 1124, had spent much of his youth at the English court, where he became imbued with Norman and feudal ideas. Fergus, a native chieftain of the Galwegians, was also at the English court and, like David, married an

---

[1] Some notes on the archaeology of the Stewartry are given in an Appendix.

Anglo-Norman. The two men became friendly, David afterwards creating Fergus Lord of Galloway. Fergus moved his seat from Whithorn to near Kirkcudbright; the place is still called Lochfergus. He introduced feudal customs into his lordship, and founded great churches where the rule and rites of the Roman Church were followed, superseding the old Celtic religious system. The division of the land into parishes began at this time. These changes were resented by the native people, and the history of Galloway for the next century or so consists very largely of a struggle against the imposition of feudalism. In 1234 Alan, the last native lord, died, leaving three daughters, all married to Anglo-Norman nobles. The men of Galloway, bitterly resenting the passing of the lordship into alien hands, reacted in their usual way, by a rebellion, which was crushed by Alexander II. Feudalism was thus at last firmly established.

THE STEWARTRY

On the death of Alan's youngest daughter, the territory was divided between the husbands of her sisters. One, de Quenci, earl of Winchester, received western Galloway (now Wigtownshire), and the other, John Balliol of Barnard Castle, husband of the great Devorgilla, was allotted the part east of the Cree (now the Stewartry). Happily the Balliols proved good rulers, and indeed in the struggle against England, so soon to follow, Galloway was at first hostile to Bruce. Even as late as 1332 the people of Galloway took up arms for Edward Balliol. After his downfall the lordship was given by David II in 1369 to Archibald 'the Grim', later third earl of Douglas. He appointed a steward to administer eastern Galloway, and this is said to be the origin of the name Stewartry. But the stewardship may have already existed, perhaps from the time of Bruce.

Archibald Douglas was loyal, but some of his descendants proved as high-handed, and as dangerous to the throne, as any of the ancient Galwegian chieftains. James II finally succeeded in crushing the Douglases in 1455, their immensely strong fortress of Threave holding out to the bitter end. The lordship of Galloway was assumed by the crown, and so ended the virtual independence of the old province. Eastern Galloway, however, continued to be administered by a steward on behalf of the crown, the office becoming hereditary under the Maxwells. When heritable jurisdictions were abolished in 1747 a steward-depute was appointed, the equivalent of a sheriff-depute, but the distinctive title was eventually dropped. So ended 'The Stewartry' as an official name, though it remains as the familiar local name of the modern county; a more euphonious and evocative name, surely, than the cumbrous official 'Kirkcudbrightshire'.

REFORMATION AND COVENANTS

The Reformation, with its consequent changes, was accomplished quietly in Galloway, but the atmosphere of mutual tolerance which characterised this period was unhappily absent in the controversy of the seventeenth century between Episcopalian and Presbyterian parties within the reformed church. Instead there was mounting bitterness, leading to persecution and bloodshed, as the many local martyrs' memorials testify. Relief came first with James VII's Indulgence of 1687, and then finally with the Revolution. In 1690 the Church of Scotland was established on a Presbyterian basis, but the Covenants were quietly dropped.

THE POST-UNION PERIOD

Whatever the individual interest and appeal of its early history there is no doubt that developments since the Union of 1707 have largely shaped the county of to-day. Local opinion supported rural Scotland's opposition to the Union, four separate petitions being submitted, but the outcry was at least part-protest against a depressed economy and prevailing wretchedness—the products of Galloway's geographical isolation, the Killing Time's uncertainty, and the 'ill-years' of the 1690s. The expansion which followed was slow to take effect within the Stewartry; potatoes (introduced 1725) and shell marl (1730) were only gradually appreciated; smuggling's demands on human and animal labour hampered the work of 'improvers' like Craik of Arbigland (1703-98), who toiled on stony ground in more ways than one; even the improvement in the cattle trade meant enclosure, distress and the activities of the levellers of 1724. Nevertheless, better communications (Dumfries-Portpatrick military road, constructed 1760, improved 1800) and the financial assistance of the ill-fated Ayr Bank brought results, and two enduring features of local agriculture took shape—the increased raising of black cattle for droving to England and the grazing of blackfaced sheep on the uplands.

ECONOMIC ADVANCE

A real surge forward came with the agricultural boom which accompanied the wars with France (1793-1814) and the progress of this period survived the post-war depression, to be followed by the introduction of fertilisers, turnips for fodder, and deep tile drainage. The benefits were measured in the increased cattle trade, 20,000-30,000 being exported annually around 1840, still by droving, but more through the Galloway ports to Liverpool and Glasgow. Coastal shipping further reflected the expanding economy. At the Union, Kirkcudbright had lost much of its earlier importance: in 1692, its shipping consisted of one small boat of eight tons 'for carreing their coals but she hath never as yet been imployed'. (Report to Convention of Royal Burghs, 1692.) Trade improved sufficiently for the port to be separated from Dumfries for customs purposes about 1740 and the *Old Statistical Account* records 28 ships, 'two in foreign trade'. By 1840 this had risen to 54 ships and in 1835 regular steamer sailings between Kirkcudbright and Liverpool and Glasgow were begun. This revival brought with it shipbuilding and allied trades, notably at Kirkcudbright.

INDUSTRIAL DEVELOPMENT

The depressed years of the mid-eighteenth century had brought hopes that the Stewartry might share in the industrial developments beginning elsewhere. Great store was set by known mineral deposits, and a traveller of 1760 records the disappointment felt over the apparent failure to exploit lead near Minnigaff, iron ore at Auchencairn and coal at Rascarrel. Hopes died hard, for in 1792 the Rerrick minister indicates that the district still looked to these same deposits for its economic salvation. Granite quarrying at Creetown and Dalbeattie, begun in 1800, was to grow and survive, the latter's growth owing much to Victorian demand for solidity in building as in all else. The Woodhead lead mines at Carsphairn seemed a permanent prospect at their opening in the 1840s.

The Stewartry was to share in the rise in cotton manufacture dating from the 1790s. Although local tradition in textiles was lacking, water power attracted, and spinning mills were set up at Gatehouse and Twynholm. Gatehouse enjoyed a boom that lasted 50 years, bringing burgh status, a deepened harbour and by 1841 close on 2,000 inhabitants. By mid-century the coming of the railway was eagerly anticipated. The 1851 census was to mark the population at its highest (43,121), but already the emigration of young people caused concern. It was thought, however, that a rail link might bring in the manufacturing industries necessary to widen the economy. Eventually 1858-62 saw the construction of the Dumfries-Portpatrick line, with a later branch to Kirkcudbright. It served to transport the increased agricultural produce but did little for local industry, and it weakened the coastal trade; as a result the once active harbour of Kirkcudbright was filled up in 1908. By-passed by the railway, the mills at Gatehouse failed to recover from the cotton slump of the '60s. With the railway (and a well-established market) Castle-Douglas was strengthened as the commercial centre at the expense of the county town. The main banks set up branches there, and the county's newspaper began its long history there in 1858 as the *Kirkcudbrightshire Advertiser and Galloway News*.

AGRICULTURAL CHANGES

The arrival of the Ayrshire cow in 1850 was to be much more decisive than the coming of the railway, and the period 1850-75 brought a marked turnover from store to dairy cattle with a corresponding increase in arable farming to meet feeding demands. Reliance on live stock brought some escape from the slump of the 1870s and by 1914 Stewartry agriculture had settled in the definite pattern of dairy farming, stores, sheep farming and arable for feeding which characterises it to-day. The Ayrshire had come to dominate in dairying, but the Galloway and Beltie held their own safely, if unspectacularly, as stores. Shakespeare's 'Galloway Nags' had almost disappeared by the time of the *New Statistical Account*.

The inter-war years saw Stewartry agriculture continue to adapt itself progressively to changing times, although it did not escape the post-war depression and paid the penalty for over-dependence on dairying.

Creameries at Kirkcudbright, Tarff and Dalbeattie encouraged over-production. Local co-operatives failed to cope and recovery did not come till the Milk Marketing Board and road transport gave efficient distribution. The latter, however, finally killed the coastal trade. Further attempts to introduce industry, notably motor engineering and, later, textiles at Tongland, were unsuccessful, while the existing ones barely held their own.

POLITICAL EVOLUTION

Politically the Stewartry has remained stable since the Union. Although several Jacobite proprietors 'came out' in 1715, the people generally were hostile and provided several hundred men for the defence of Dumfries against Kenmure's attack. The '45 little affected the area despite the Pretender's occupation of Dumfries. Parliamentary representation was that laid down by the Scottish Estates in 1707. As royal burghs, Kirkcudbright and New Galloway were members of the Dumfries and Wigtown Districts respectively, while the county had its own member. This remained substantially unaltered till 1918 (the Wigtown Burghs disappearing in the Reform of 1884-5) when the Dumfries Burghs lost separate representation and the present Galloway division was created. Since the 1832 Reform Act the Stewartry's political complexion has conformed to rural Scotland's, Whigs and Liberals dominating till 1924, with consistent Conservative representation since 1931. Labour has never presented an effective challenge and in 1959 the Liberal tradition was twice strong enough to force Labour into third place. For over a century all the county M.P.s have had strong Galloway connections.

The famous Act of 1747 abolished local regalities and the hereditary Stewardship and opened the way for effective local administration. Castle-Douglas (1792), Creetown (1792), Gatehouse (1795) and Maxwelltown (1810) were erected burghs of barony and, with the exception of Creetown, they all adopted one or other of the nineteenth century Police Acts, as did Dalbeattie in 1858. Creetown's status disappeared by the 1892 Act's non-recognition of the surviving burghs of barony. The unrelated tangle of statutory bodies of county administration was cleared away by the creation of the elected county council in 1889; further revision in 1929 cost the Stewartry its largest burgh, Maxwelltown, which went to help Dumfries qualify as a 'large burgh'.

THE STEWARTRY TO-DAY

Thus has the modern Stewartry evolved. Consistent agricultural progress and the extension of rural electrification, pioneered locally since the 1930s, form the post-war story. Forestry and tourism are important parts of the economy, while Kirkcudbright's coastal trade shows revival. And yet the 1961 population census reveals an overall drop of 6 per cent. Local initiative, however, has brought new industry and prospects to Dalbeattie; enterprise of this kind offers a future consistent with the Stewartry's separate identity as a beautiful and historic county.

ARCHAEOLOGY OF THE STEWARTRY.[1]

That this area was inhabited in Mesolithic times (5,000-4,000 B.C. approx.) is indicated by the finding of a deer-horn barbed fish-spear at Cumstoun, on the Dee near Kirkcudbright. Other remains of the period are scanty.

The picture is very different when we come to the time of the Neolithic farmers (4,000-3,000 B.C.). This period is prolific in remains. There are 42 polished stone axes, mainly from the Langdale Pike factory, but including three Jadeite axes from Brittany. The Cree basin is notable for its group of at least seven Clyde-Carlingford courtyard cairns, those at Boreland (Minnigaff) and Cairnholy being specially notable. In the north, Cairnavel seems to be of this type. There are two large passage-graves at Bargrennan. Neolithic pottery and flints at Cairnholy extend from 'Secondary Neolithic' to 'Beaker'. Beaker pottery also comes from High Banks, Kirkcudbright, and from a cist with burial and bone ring at Mains-riddle. A flint blade of "Secondary Neolithic" from Rockcliffe suggests accultura-tion of a fishing and hunting community on the estuary of the Urr. The circular 'fort' at Drumcoltran (Kirkgunzeon) may be Neolithic.

The Bronze Age is represented by at least 33 perforated stone axes, showing, like the Neolithic axes, a concentration on the Dee estuary. There are 73 medium to large cairns likely to be of Bronze Age date, 26 of which are in the Cree basin. There is another concentration in the Deugh and upper Ken valleys. Seven of the 13 stone circles are in the Cree basin and one in the Carsphairn cairn group. Of Bronze Age date, too, are the remarkable crop-markings at West Logan, near Castle-Douglas—circles, and linear and horseshoe markings. There are a few barbed tanged flint arrowheads; and other Bronze Age weapons, including a Middle Bronze rapier, and a Late Bronze leaf-sword from New Abbey, and a hoard from Drumcoltran; a bronze dagger from Carlingwark Loch and more bronze implements from a small cairn at MacNaughton, Kirkpatrick-Irongray. High Banks cairn yielded two Food Vessels; an 'incense-cup' and urn were found at Whinnieliggate; urns too at Cairngill, Redbrae, and Garrochar, and several in the western outskirts of Dumfries. The Fleet Bay area, and the east side of the Dee area, show an extraordinary concentration of cup-and-ring markings of the Food Vessel period.

There are 66 Iron Age forts, concentrated in the coastal belt between Fleet and Urr. There are seven promontory forts, probably occupied in the Iron Age; 'raths' at Crossmichael and Kirkpatrick-Durham; and free-standing circular farm-houses at Croft's Burn and Arkland, both in Kirkpatrick-Durham. At least ten crannogs are to be found in the county, most of them in Carlingwark Loch. Two are in Milton Loch, of which one was excavated by Mrs. Stuart Piggott in 1953. The hill-fort at Trusty's Hill has been partly excavated, and shows a vitrified rampart, a hut-circle, a strong circular guardroom, and a rock-cut ditch. The cave sites at Torrs (Kirkcudbright) and Borness have yielded Iron Age 'B' material, and the curious semi-broch at Castle Ha'en seems to have Iron Age 'B' affinities. Iron Age finds also include the notable horse-hat and drinking-horn terminal from Torrs (Castle-Douglas); the Plunton armlet; the Balmaclellan hoard of mirror, plaque, and diamond-twill tweed cloth; a quern with La Tène ornament from near this site and the huge Carlingwark hoard of over 100 tools and weapons in a bronze cauldron. This hoard shows affinities with the Roman-occupied area of south-east England.

The large Flavian and Antonine fort at Glenlochar, and the small, probably Flavian, fort near Gatehouse, are the main Roman sites. There are some indications of a small site near Buittle Mill. The principal road so far found is that running east-west from Carzield and Dalswinton in Dumfriesshire, via Castle-Douglas, Gatehouse and, probably, near the Corse o' Slakes Road. A possible line, too, exists up the Dee valley, and a pony-track has been traced from the upper Shinnel across the Ken, and over the hills to Ayrshire. Loose Roman finds are a metal jug-handle from Cairnholy, a harness-ring from Milton Crannog, a Samian ware fragment from Torrs cave; and a thin scatter of coins.

The remarkable group of 'nucleated' or 'courtyard' forts in Rerrick parish and up over the Screel-Bengairn ridge to the Urr estuary would tie in chronologically

1. Contributed by Mr. A. E. Truckell, Dumfries.

with the 5th-7th century trading site at Mote of Mark across the estuary. This site has yielded imported Frankish ware, sub-Roman ware, Merovingian glass, one fragment of possible Middle Eastern origin, and many moulds for interlace work brooches. The fort at Stroanfreggan is a courtyard fort, with two nearby chapel sites. It is likely that some Iron Age forts were re-occupied without major alterations; the Pictish symbols carved at the entrance to Trusty's Hill fort, a fort only slightly modified, suggest this.

The St. Constantine dedications around Dalbeattie seem to be connected with the mission of St. Kentigern's disciple about 575 A.D. He was sent there 'because he was a Briton', i.e. a Welsh speaker. There are indications that Welsh died out about 700 A.D., perhaps through Anglian influence, as shown in such names as that of the river Fleet. The Anglian period lasted roughly from after 600 to about 900. The coastal Norse names, too, probably date from about this time; and the introduction of Gaelic by the Gallgaidhil may be dated after 920.

Objects of Dark Age type, other than crosses, are few. They include a Celtic handbell case (Monybuie); the Talnotrie hoard of ornaments; the local or imported Frankish material from Mote of Mark; spindle-whorls; Anglo-Saxon coins; a penannular ring and iron finger-ring from Castle Ha'en; the Barr of Spottes bronze flask; and a Viking double-handed sword, bronze pin, bead and glass linen-smoother. Some of the coastal promontory forts were probably occupied in Viking times.

The traditional site of Fergus's 'palatium', near Kirkcudbright, deserves excavation, as it might clear up many of the problems of the 11th and 12th centuries, when it would seem that Galloway dominated much of Southern Scotland.

The Middle Ages come in with 25 mottes, mainly in the Dee and Fleet basins though the most notable is an out-lier, the Motte of Urr, built in the 1130s and rebuilt in the 1170s. There are five 'Homestead Mottes'; and most of the 'earthworks' recorded belong to the medieval period, as does also the crannog in Lochrutton.

The ruinous Edwardian castles at Buittle and Castledykes (Kirkcudbright) are important; and Palace Yard (Girthon), which may have begun as an Edwardian camp, houses the palace of the last pre-Reformation bishop of Galloway.

CHAPTER 3

THE ECONOMY

AGRICULTURE

FROM the agricultural angle the Stewartry of Kirkcudbright presents some unusual features. A narrow belt of really good and generally arable land lies round the Solway coast, but inland the soil is thinner with a great deal of rock outcrop, usually the preferable whinstone, but sometimes granite. To the west and north-west are the Galloway uplands, merging with the counties of Dumfries, Ayr and Wigtown. It is an area of high rainfall, otherwise it could not be so productive, but winters are mild, which lets cattle and sheep lie dry. This is one of the territory's assets as a stock raising area.

Out of a total acreage of 524,000, the area under crops and grass is about 162,000, the remainder being heather or hill grazing. The main grain crop is oats and the acreage figures available show a remarkable consistency—in 1854, 32,000 acres; in 1872, 32,000; in 1921, 26,000; but in 1960, 16,700 plus 2,500 of barley, which has become more popular of recent years as a source of stock feeding. These figures point to the conclusion that cropping in the Stewartry is really ancillary to stock raising and to the supply of winter fodder and feed, and in a measure is part of a system of renewing grassland. In general, grain crops cannot be grown in competition with the richer arable districts of Scotland. Yields are lower, costs are higher and the nature of the land makes the full economic application of mechanisation more difficult.

It is a popular misconception that the county is almost entirely devoted to milk production. This is very far from being so, but over many decades this industry has been growing. In the time of people still living, many farms, now carrying large milking herds, were breeding and/or feeding beef cattle. The development of the Argentine beef trade forced change and this coincided with the movement of Ayrshire farmers into the county, where their industry and skill had a marked and beneficial influence. In the early days, with poor transport facilities, farm cheese-making was the rule, but in the last decade this industry has declined to a shadow of its former self and most of the milk is transported and processed by factories in spring and summer. In winter some of it finds its way to the large centres of population.

In 1924 there were 449 registered milk producing herds, in 1950 the number was 563 and in 1960, 526, but it would not be safe to deduce a fall in the size of the milk producing industry. Some small herds have gone out of business; many others have been increased in number. So it is that the total production of milk is larger than ever before, as is the yield of the cow. In 1939, the average number of cows in a herd was 36, in 1960, 48. The Stewartry was one of the first counties in Scotland to eradicate tuberculosis from dairy herds and, as the rest of the country began the same process, a large and lucrative outlet for animals surplus to local needs was created.

The county used to be a very important area for breeding beef cattle, mostly of the hardy Galloway type. This industry, so suited to the higher lying land, fell away from 1920 onwards, but thanks to a wise Government policy which guaranteed a reasonable beef price, there has been a great and wholesome upward movement. An estimate to-day might put the number of beef breeding cows at 7,550 as against 28,000 milk producing cows, each class showing a threefold increase since 1870.

The sheep breeding and feeding industry has always been important, with the heavy breeds on the lower ground and chiefly black-faced ewes on the hills. In 1854 it is estimated that there were 172,000 breeding ewes; in 1958, 207,000; a movement which argues well for the profitability of this branch. The lamb crop is largely fattened for export to the southern markets, but considerable numbers are bought by farmers from other parts of the country. Naturally, in this territory, a market for the sale of animals is essential, and for generations Castle-Douglas has been a very important centre of this kind; never more so than now. Large numbers of cattle and sheep are sold annually, many from neighbouring counties, and there is always a good attendance of buyers from south of the border, attesting to the quality and reputation of the stock exposed.

Farming here as elsewhere, and as with other businesses, has seen many vicissitudes. From 1880 onwards the price level declined consistently and disastrously. Improvement set in about 1900 till 1914, when war, as always, made values rise. A decline began in 1921 and from 1929 to 1939 farming was a very unprofitable business, the financial consequences being serious. The organisation of the Scottish Milk Marketing Board in 1933 helped to improve the lot of the dairy farmer, coinciding as it did with the improvement of transport facilities, which brought the city markets for milk within reach of more distant producers. The second world war brought price control and price guarantees, which are still with us, in one form or another, and provide a bulwark against low values created by dumped foreign produce. One marked consequence of better economic circumstances has been the improvement in housing and equipment generally. The signs of prosperity are obvious and the policy which made them possible has been fully justified on social grounds alone. Rural transport, however, remains a problem which improved housing and living conditions have never completely offset.

While the past 40 years have seen many minor changes, no fundamental change has taken place in the basic form of the industry. Milk production, sheep and cattle breeding and feeding, and the cropping system geared to that economy; so our forefathers understood the business and so it is carried on to-day, but there have been great developments in method. The milking machine, and recently the system of

collecting milk by tanker, the replacing of horses by tractors, the introduction of electricity, the innovation of the hay baler and combine
harvester, all these have lightened labour and added to the amenity of
country life. Inevitably, mechanisation has meant a fall in the number of
agricultural workers. The figures speak for themselves: in 1947, 3,339;
in 1958, 2,788; a drastic, perhaps regrettable, but certainly an inevitable change.

For many years, and until quite recently, agricultural land values
changed very little; the rental level of £1 an acre for the better farm was
the average figure, but recent new legislation resulting in a freer market
has led to a considerable upward movement. Many rents have doubled
or more while the saleable value of land in the better cases has certainly
trebled; a recognition of the capital factor represented by houses and
buildings and other considerations which cannot be dealt with here.

A feature of the county is the very large number of occupying-owners;
few large estates remain. Farms have been bought consistently by tenants
since the end of the first war and the process still goes on. Fifty years
ago the real farmer who was not a tenant was a rarity indeed, but it is
now thought by many people that ownership coinciding with active
operation is the soundest social system. That policy has been put into
effect by many land-owners, who no longer let a vacant farm, but farm it
themselves. Since the last review, many changes have thus taken place
and signs of progress are to be seen on all hands.

PRIVATE FORESTRY

The privately-owned woodland area in the county was given in the 1954
census of woodlands as follows:—

High Forest ...	...	...	9,249	acres
Scrub	...	...	4,052	„
Felled	...	...	4,500	„
			17,801	„

Thus nearly a half of the total was unproductive. In former times a large
part of this woodland area was devoted to growing Oak, which was
managed as coppice or coppice with standards, the bark being used to
produce tannin, and the timber largely for fuel. Many of these Oak
woods are now derelict, or have reverted to unproductive scrub, which
is costly to clear and re-stock with economic timber crops.

Private estates have, since the last war, made considerable progress
in bringing their woods back into good condition, and at the same time
the areas newly planted have been increasing each year. Thirty four
estates, with a total of 13,680 acres of woodland, have entered into
Dedication agreements, and a further one, with 120 acres of woodland,
has come within the Forestry Commission's Approved Woodland Scheme.
On smaller estates and farms there has also been a renewed interest in

planting, 855 acres having been planted or replanted since 1954 under the Commission's Small Woods Planting Grant Scheme.

Much, however, still remains to be done. The county generally has a favourable climate and suitable soil for timber production and produces high quality crops of both coniferous and broad-leaved species. There is a high proportion of rough, rocky land of low agricultural value, which offers further scope for the extension of conifer production.

STATE FORESTRY

The Forestry Commission began operations near Dalbeattie in the spring of 1921, and there has been planting at that forest every year since, resulting in a total of 5,781 acres of plantations to date. Even larger forests were started at Cairn Edward, near New Galloway, in 1922, the planted area now amounting to 17,458 acres; and at Glentrool in 1947, where already there are 14,178 acres of new plantations within the Stewartry. The very beautiful forest of Kirroughtree, near Newton Stewart, was started in 1931, and 7,048 acres have now been planted. There are other extensive forests near Gatehouse-of-Fleet, and between that town and New Galloway; on the roads radiating from Dalry; at Mabie, near Dumfries; and round about Twynholm and Kirkcudbright. The total area of State plantations within the county is now 65,119 acres; it is expected that this figure will be increased by a further 25 per cent. within these forests by 1968, although the greatly accelerated rate of planting since the war is now tending to level out at about 3,000 acres each year. Only a very small proportion of these areas is, or can be successfully, afforested with hardwoods, since it is seldom that the more fertile and sheltered strips of countryside become available to the Commission.

Nine of the twelve forests have already begun to yield timber, which from the age of 15-20 years, with most common conifers, is taken out in the form of thinnings and has been used almost entirely for pit wood and fencing material. The annual yield is now of the order of 17,000 tons; this will increase by 50 per cent. within the next few years. After 1967, however, as a result of the large post-war afforestation, the output will begin to rise much more quickly to something like 80,000 tons by 1975, and 150,000 tons, by 1990, of which nearly half will be of a size for sawmilling.

QUARRYING AND MINING

The granite massifs near Dalbeattie and Creetown provide ample and easily accessible supplies of excellent quality granite. Creetown granite because of its good texture and colour has been widely used for memorials of all kinds. Dalbeattie granite, which has a tinge of pink, has been used in many important public buildings and óther structures, examples being the Embankment in London and the George V Bridge in Glasgow. In the past the fortunes of this industry rose and fell with the prosperity of the building industries. Nowadays, however, it is used for roads in the form of tar-macadam and as chips for top dressing and crushed for granolithic work. More recently the development of reinforced concrete as a load-bearing frame for buildings and bridges has led to a steady demand and the establishment of a pre-cast concrete industry at Creetown. This process has now been applied to the manufacture of an ever-widening range—garages, walls, floor beams and smaller items such as troughs, flower pots and cycle stands. Whin quarries throughout the area are used as local supplies of road metal. Tongland quarry has been developed and mechanised by the county council as their main source of supply for their extensive road-making operations.

Other mineral resources (formerly worked)—lead at Carsphairn and Stronord, barytes at Auchencairn—are not available in quantities which would make for economic working at the present time. Mining operations in any general way ended about the turn of the century.

Recently the discovery by prospectors of uranium ore in Colvend parish raised hopes of profitable working of this mineral, which was in short supply throughout the world and much wanted in early experiments in nuclear fission. The world supply, however, has been increased and use has probably decreased so that the prices may fall below the level at which its extraction would be economic.

MANUFACTURING

The only large-scale unit of industry is the I.C.I. factory at Drungans, which is occupied by two divisions—Nobel and Plastics. Imperial Chemical Industries have been associated with the Stewartry since 1939, when the Nobel Division, on behalf of the Ministry of Supply, built and operated, on the Drungans Farm site, one of a group of wartime factories in and around Dumfries. The Dumfries factory continued to operate after the war, producing acids and nitrocellulose; the latter being used in the manufacture of paints, lacquers and leathercloth.

In 1949 the Nobel Division of I.C.I. purchased the Dumfries factory site from the Ministry of Supply and in the intervening years it has developed into the main centre for the manufacture of the chemical products of the division. In addition to the wartime nitrocellulose plants, new plants have been erected for the production of cellulose derivatives, namely Cellofas and Methofas, and Pentaerythritol. The demand for these products has been such that extensions have already had to be made to the original works. Full engineering services, including steam and electricity supplies, to maintain and operate these modern chemical plants have also been provided.

A plant to produce Ardil protein fibre was also erected but was not a commercial success and the project was abandoned in 1957. In 1959, however, the buildings were taken over by the Plastics Division of I.C.I. and re-equipped, and in March 1961 they were opened for the production of Melinex polyester film, a new transparent film made from the same basic raw materials as Terylene and used widely in the electrical industries for recording tapes, for drawing office materials, and in the decorative and packaging fields. Currently, increasingly large quantities of this product are being despatched from Dumfries all over the world.

Construction of a new Plastics Division plant to produce Polypropylene film started at the end of 1961 and completion is expected by mid-1963. Polypropylene film has excellent clarity and surface lustre, and it is expected to have wide application in the packaging industry.

Currently the combined Nobel and Plastics Division activities on the site cover an area of 115 acres and employ a total of 570 people. It is expected that when the Polypropylene film plant is fully occupied it will increase the factory strength to a total of about 750 people.

Of the small-scale factories in the Stewartry, mention can be made of two recently founded industries at Dalbeattie, one making welded steel radiators for central heating and the other denim overalls and other items of protective clothing. The last surviving bobbin mill in the Stewartry also operates in Dalbeattie.

ECONOMIC ORGANISATION

In general the business units are small family firms and maintain good relationships with their workers. In return the workers give, by modern standards, good value for money and often develop a strong loyalty to their employers and remain with them throughout their working lives. For these and other reasons Trades Unions and Employers' Federations do not occupy a prominent place in the industrial life of the community.

For the first time since the war, unemployment rose to problem dimensions in 1959. Dalbeattie burgh was seriously affected and the town council took active, and fortunately, successful steps to introduce new industries.

The Dumfries and Galloway Development Association have worked hard over the post-war years in publicising the south-west with the aim of introducing new light industries to the area. One interesting aspect of their work is the publication of an attractive quarterly magazine *The Quest*. The popular belief is that only the introduction of small units of new industries will stem the depopulation which continues slowly but relentlessly as the years go by.

FARM INDUSTRIES AND SERVICES

The land is basic to the economy of the Stewartry, agriculture and forestry being the main industries. Ancillary to agriculture is the milk product industry, processing of milk, butter and cheese-making in the creameries at Kirkcudbright, Twynholm and Dalbeattie, and the milk powder factory at Kirkcudbright. Bacon curing and sausage making are also carried on in a small factory in Kirkcudbright. Granulation of artificial fertilisers, to secure an even and economic spread, has just recently been introduced in a local factory at Dalbeattie. The 'smiddy', at one time a meeting point in almost every village, has disappeared except in a few centres, although a revival of interest in riding and pony-trekking has kept alive the craft of shoeing. Welding has been added to the blacksmith's skills and he supplements the repair of implements and tractors with the making of field and ornamental garden gates and sometimes attractive farm signs. Generally, however, the repair of farm machinery is now largely centralised in Castle-Douglas, where the suppliers offer maintenance and repair services. Of importance to the agricultural industry over a region extending far beyond the county boundaries is the market, Wallets Marts. one of the largest markets in Scotland for Galloways and attested Ayrshires. Seed fertilisers and feeding stuffs for the farms are supplied mainly from local family firms in Dalbeattie and Castle-Douglas, firms which would develop from small beginnings as meal mills. Farmers' co-operatives at Dumfries and Tarff also share this market, as does I.C.I. through a subsidiary. A post-war development has been the mechanical spreading of lime, fertiliser and selective weed-killer, often on a contract basis. The extending use of the combine harvester has also given rise to the need for grain-drying facilities, a need which has been met by the local firms.

FISHING

Fishing on a commercial scale is only of minor importance in the economy but it is an interesting carry-over from an earlier way of life. Salmon are caught in stake nets in all the main estuaries and Solway salmon is said to command the highest price in the London markets. Lobsters, shrimps and prawns locally caught are much in demand. The rivers and lochs have been developed for angling and good rents are charged. The catches of salmon and sea trout on the Dee have been very much smaller since the construction of the dams and power stations. Where lochs require restocking, supplies of fry are available from the Solway Hatcheries near Kinharvie.

TIMBER PROCESSING

Even now forestry is the second industry in the Stewartry and it is still expanding steadily. Ancillary industries have not yet developed beyond the permanent or semi-permanent sawmills established at convenient points throughout the county, but as the output from state forest and privately-owned woodlands increases it is likely that the raw material will be processed locally. An active branch of the Scottish Woodland Owners' Association has been encouraging private planting and the use of improved methods of extracting timber.

HORTICULTURE

Market gardening has been practised only to a limited extent, no doubt because of the distance from the large markets. Nevertheless, experimental nursery plots at Glenald established by the West of Scotland College of Agriculture carry out research work and provide demonstrations through the advisory service. Threave House, which some years earlier had been taken over by the National Trust, became in 1960 the centre for Threave School of Gardening. This interesting experiment in technical education is designed to give a thorough grounding in all aspects of horticulture to young men, as a qualification for promotion to important gardening posts or for further study leading to the Diploma of Horticulture.

TRANSPORT

Up to 1864 the only railway in the Stewartry was the main Dumfries-Stranraer line. In January of that year the branch line from Castle-Douglas to Kirkcudbright was completed. Further lines were contemplated but, in fact, since that date there has been no further extension of the railway system. With the development of road transport the railways have carried a diminishing share of the total passenger and freight trade. A special feature of road transport in recent years has been the increasing number of heavy vehicles on the roads. Examples of such traffic are haulage of timber to sawmills, transport of milk in tankers, and heavy floats for the carrying of live-stock. As a consequence, droves of cattle and sheep seldom hold up the steadily increasing flow of transport.

Recently there has been a notable change in the distribution of petrol and fuel oils. The harbour has been re-opened at Kirkcudbright and oil tankers carrying up to 800 tons call every second week and discharge oil by pump into storage tanks which have been built farther up the river. From there the different grades of oil are transported by heavy road tankers throughout south-west Scotland. As a result of these developments, in addition to ordinary contracting, the driving of heavy vehicles employs quite a number of men throughout the area.

More and more private cars come into use each year and as a result fewer passengers are carried by the railway and omnibus services. Consequently, rail services have been pruned severely and some of the local bus companies have gone out of business. With the prospect of still more owner-drivers the future of public service transport is not bright.[1]

DISTRIBUTIVE AND SERVICE TRADES

The organisation of the distributive trade follows the normal pattern for rural areas: gradually the smaller family firms are having to face competition from local branches of large multiple firms. The burghs and larger villages have adequate shops which, in effect, extend into the country around by the use of vans and, more recently, large mobile shops. In this way, too, the Co-operative Society covers most of the Stewartry.

Excluding the specialised demands of agriculture, already referred to, the service trades are those mainly required in connection with building and the maintenance of property, the sale and repair and servicing of motor vehicles, and with electrical installations, electric motors and equipment and the many and varied electrical appliances now in common use in most households.

THE PRESS

The *Galloway News*, which celebrated its centenary in 1958, is a fine example of the provincial weekly newspaper which maintains the intimate

(1) See Statistical Table, Appendix I, p. 509.

and friendly style so much valued by country readers. Printed in Castle-Douglas, it has increased in size and circulation and its proprietor now prints also, as a separate newspaper, the *Dumfries News*. Together, weekly circulation at present exceeds 15,000 copies. In addition, general and colour printing is undertaken by the firm, and orders are obtained from London and other centres in the face of keen competition.

PROFESSIONS

The three larger burghs provide the services characteristic of small towns serving as business centres for an agricultural area. Castle-Douglas, which has some claims to be the business centre, has a branch of all the Scottish joint stock banks. All three offer, however, a wide range of professional services—banking, the law, dentistry, veterinary surgery, accountancy and the ministry.

TOURISM

The Stewartry, one of the most beautiful counties in the south of Scotland, is a natural centre for tourism and is well supplied with excellent hotels. Immediately after the war there was a rapid expansion of the hotel trade, made possible, during a time of building restrictions, by the availability of large country mansions. In all, ten such houses were in varying degrees converted for this purpose, but they were difficult and expensive to run and maintain, and after some years only a few continued in business. The number of visitors, however, continues to grow and a few guest-houses have been opened. In the past few years there has been a marked increase in the number of private houses which offer 'bed and breakfast' to the passing motorist. The rapid rise over the past ten years in the number of caravans and tents used by holiday-makers as mobile homes has led to an ever-growing demand for caravan and camping sites offering the facilities required by public health regulations. Numerous sites have been developed, privately or by the burghs, and these have the effect of adding substantially to the visiting population during the season, with resulting benefits not only to the owners of the site but also to nearby traders.

The great increase in tourism since the war owes much to the work of the Galloway Publicity Association, which deals with enquiries and sends brochures and advertising material to many parts of Britain.

CHAPTER 4

GOVERNMENT AND PUBLIC SERVICES

PARLIAMENTARY REPRESENTATION

THE Stewartry and Wigtownshire together form the constituency of Galloway, which returns one member to the House of Commons. For long a Liberal stronghold, it changed to Conservative between the wars and appears now a very safe seat. The people are not politically minded and even at a general election it is difficult to arouse them from their apathy; probably the pleasant, and for many, the prosperous way of life, lulls any feeling of urgency for political thought or action.

LOCAL GOVERNMENT

There are in the Stewartry twelve local authorities—the county council, the town councils of the five burghs and six district councils. Of these, only the county council and the town councils have power to impose and levy rates. The district councils, covering between them the whole landward area and with very limited statutory functions, obtain any required rate income by means of a requisition from the county council, who in turn levy within each district concerned a rate sufficient to meet the requisition. None of the Stewartry burghs is a 'large burgh' for local government purposes and, accordingly, the functions of the town councils are in the main restricted to housing, water supply, drainage, sewage, street lighting, parks, unclassified roads and streets, regulation of buildings and various public order functions under the Burgh Police (Scotland) Acts. Broadly similar functions are exercised by the county council in the landward area. Throughout the whole area of the Stewartry, including burghs, the county council is the authority for education, classified roads, fire brigades, environmental health and welfare services, mental health, police, registration of births, etc., valuation, electoral registration, town and country planning, and welfare of children. As a result of recent legislation, certain of these functions are now administered over areas embracing several counties by joint committees to which the county council appoints members, e.g. the South-Western Fire Joint Committee embracing the Stewartry and the counties of Ayr, Dumfries and Wigtown; the Dumfries and Galloway Joint Police Committee, embracing the Stewartry and the counties of Dumfries and Wigtown; the Dumfries and Galloway Valuation Committee, embracing the Stewartry and the counties of Dumfries and Wigtown; and the Solway River Purification Board, whose area of operation includes all rivers or streams draining eventually into the Solway from the Scottish side.

The county council has 33 members, of whom 22 represent the landward area and 11 represent the burghs in the following proportions— Kirkcudbright, Castle-Douglas and Dalbeattie three each, Gatehouse and New Galloway one each. The landward members are elected triennially by the local government electors in the landward area; the representatives of the burghs are elected, also triennially, by the respective town councils. The council meets at the County Offices, Kirkcudbright, five times a year.

Of the five burghs, Kirkcudbright and New Galloway are royal burghs, with charters dating back to 1455 and 1630, respectively. New Galloway is the smallest royal burgh in Scotland. The burghs of Castle-Douglas, Gatehouse and Dalbeattie were incorporated in 1792, 1795 and 1858, respectively. At the 1961 census the populations of the burghs were: Kirkcudbright, 2,448; New Galloway, 327; Dalbeattie, 3,104; Castle-Douglas, 3,253; and Gatehouse, 820. Town council elections are held annually, one-third of the members retiring each year.

The landward area is divided into six districts. Glenkens district includes the parishes of Carsphairn, Kells, Dalry, Balmaclellan and Parton; Castle-Douglas district the parishes of Kirkpatrick-Durham, Kelton, Crossmichael and Balmaghie; Kirkcudbright district the parishes of Kirkcudbright, Rerrick, Tongland, Twynholm and Borgue; Western district the parishes of Anwoth, Girthon, Kirkmabreck and Minnigaff; Dalbeattie district the parishes of Urr, Colvend and Southwick, Kirkgunzeon, Lochrutton and Buittle; and Eastern district includes the parishes of Troqueer, Kirkpatrick-Irongray, Terregles, Kirkbean and New Abbey. At the 1951 census the populations of the districts were: Glenkens, 2,251; Castle-Douglas, 2,970; Kirkcudbright, 3,846; Western, 3,208; Dalbeattie, 3,712; and Eastern, 2,938. Members elected to the county council for landward electoral divisions become *ex officio* members of the appropriate district council. In addition, each landward electoral division or ward thereof elects one district councillor. District council elections take place triennially in conjunction with the county council elections.

The Stewartry, in common with the rest of Scotland, suffers from apathy in local government affairs and while the percentage poll in contested elections is rather above the national average, there is often considerable difficulty—particularly in the case of district councils—in securing candidates for all the available seats. National politics play very little, if any, part in local administration in the Stewartry and none of the local authorities is organised on party lines.

LAW AND ORDER

The Stewartry is included in the Sheriffdom of Dumfries and Galloway for sheriff court purposes, including ordinary, criminal and small debt courts and commissary work, the portion to the east of the River Urr being included in the eastern division of the sheriffdom, while the remainder is included in the western division. In the eastern division there is a resident sheriff substitute at Dumfries where courts are held twice weekly during session. There is also a resident sheriff substitute in the western division who holds courts at Wigtown once weekly, at Stranraer once fortnightly and at Kirkcudbright once weekly. There are police courts in each burgh and the Justice of the Peace Court has periodic sessions.

The High Court of Justiciary does not sit within the Stewartry. Serious criminal cases are heard either in the High Court at Edinburgh or at Dumfries, which is one of the circuit towns.

The probation service is administered by the Stewartry of Kirkcudbright probation committee, who employ one full-time probation officer. Although full use is made of this service by all the courts concerned, the case-load is never large—usually in the region of 36. The work of the probation officer cannot, however, be assessed merely by reference to the case-load at any given time. Much of the merit of the service is derived from the numerous pre-trial investigations and reports to the courts on the background of offenders, which are not fully reflected in these figures.

HEALTH

The first County Medical Officer for the county was appointed in 1891. Environmental hygiene was his chief concern, and most of his time was taken up trying to ensure that there was an adequate and satisfactory supply of water, and adequate drainage. In addition, he was occupied to a large extent in investigating epidemics of the zymotic diseases which were prevalent at the time. It was not until 1903 that suitable hospital accommodation for the isolation of infectious diseases became available in Castle-Douglas.

By 1907 he was able to change the emphasis from environmental hygiene and infectious disease to the study of deaths from infectious disease and tuberculosis, which in the years 1898-1907 was responsible for no less than 525 deaths. Until 1924, when Lochmaben hospital was extended, there were no beds in the area for the treatment of tuberculosis. A child welfare scheme was started in 1926, and there were seven district nursing associations employing seven district nurses.

From 1929 until the outbreak of the second world war one problem was the inadequate provision of hospital beds for maternity cases, and it was not until 1940 that satisfactory maternity accommodation was provided at Cresswell Hospital. The war years saw the introduction of schemes of immunisation against diphtheria, and schemes for the supply of welfare foods for infants and young children.

By the introduction of the National Health Service Act, the county council became the local health authority and the welfare authority on 1 July 1948. Though no longer responsible for providing hospital accommodation for infectious disease, tuberculosis and maternity cases, it was made responsible for a district nursing service, a health visiting service, a home help service and a domiciliary midwifery service. It was also made responsible for preparing and adopting schemes of vaccination and immunisation against diphtheria, whooping cough, poliomyelitis, and B.C.G. vaccination against tuberculosis.

As welfare authority, provision was made for the care of all handi-capped persons—including blind persons, and deaf and dumb, and residential accommodation was provided for old people at Carlingwark House, Castle-Douglas. Meals on Wheels schemes have been provided for old people living at home, and chiropody treatment has also been provided.

In 1948 the Children Act made provision for the establishment of a Children's Committee and the appointment of a Children's Officer. The act placed on the local authority the responsibility of providing for all children under 18 who appeared to them to be in need of care and atten-tion. A children's officer was appointed in 1949 and since that date the average number of children in care has been 39.

The Adoption Acts of 1950 and 1958 empowered local authorities to make arrangements for the adoption of children and prohibited such arrangements by any body or persons other than a local authority or a registered adoption society. The local authority was made responsible for the supervision of all adoptions in the area during a probationary period.

HOUSING

The concept that housing might be regarded as an essential social service was beginning to emerge after the first world war, and Parliament made the county and burgh councils responsible for this service under a series of statutes. The backlog of housing required, already considerable, increased dramatically after the second world war because of an almost complete cessation of civil building, the continuing deterioration of existing housing and the increased demand for housing because of improved standards of living and the trend towards earlier marriage. Priority was accordingly given after 1945 to housing programmes as soon as material and labour became available. Over the last ten years the building of new houses has been supplemented by giving grants to owners for bringing existing houses completely up to modern standards. A new system of grants, for bringing up to certain minimum standards houses which might thereby serve for another 15 years, has been in operation now for two years and already 53 houses in the landward area have been improved. The improved housing position illustrated by these figures has had far-reaching effects on social conditions and in the general well-being of the population. A measure of this improvement can be shown from the fact that in 1931 a population of 30,341 were accommodated in 7,655 houses; in 1961 the comparable figures were 28,877 people living in 9,478 houses—an overall reduction from 4 to 3 persons to each inhabited house, and, of course, a much greater percentage of the population are living in houses which come up to the relatively high modern standards. Local authorities in the Stewartry have gone some way towards solving the housing problem and the stage has now been reached where the policy is to deal with overcrowding and to replace condemned properties. A part of this policy is to build small (two-roomed) houses for single people and elderly couples; the houses of more than two rooms thus vacated are then made available for larger households.

TABLE I
NEW HOUSES—1945/59—LANDWARD

Parish	County Council Houses	Forestry Commission Houses	Agricultural Houses	Private Dwellings	Total
Anwoth	—	2	1	4	7
Balmaclellan	4	2	10	—	16
Balmaghie	30	3	4	4	41
Borgue	8	—	15	3	26
Buittle	28	—	2	6	36
Carsphairn	—	—	1	2	3
Colvend & Southwick	—	—	5	38	43
Crossmichael	46	—	13	8	67
Dalry	24	—	2	14	40
Girthon	—	—	8	2	10
Kells	—	24	2	2	28
Kelton	24	—	15	2	41
Kirkbean	8	—	8	4	20
Kirkcudbright	—	—	6	17	23
Kirkgunzeon	20	—	9	7	36
Kirkmabreck	86	—	4	7	97
Kirkpatrick Durham	2	—	4	3	9
Kirkpatrick Irongray	14	—	7	4	25
Lochrutton	26	—	8	5	39
Minnigaff	77	51	2	14	144
New Abbey	34	—	6	3	43
Parton	—	—	2	7	9
Rerrick	26	—	11	5	42
Terregles	16	—	—	12	28
Tongland	10	—	13	5	28
Troqueer	28	2	3	19	52
Twynholm	96	6	8	3	113
Urr	66	2	8	8	84
TOTALS	673	92	177	208	1150

TABLE II
NEW HOUSES—1945/61—BURGHS

	Town Council Houses	Other Building	Private Building	Total
Castle Douglas	267		32	299
Dalbeattie	228		33	261
Gatehouse-of-Fleet	64		5	69
		Forestry Comm.		
New Galloway	6	19	1	26
		Army		
Kirkcudbright	145	25	48	218
	710	44	119	873

TABLE III
IMPROVEMENT SCHEMES—1951/61

Landward Area	638
Castle Douglas	68
Dalbeattie	86
Gatehouse-of-Fleet	29
New Galloway	—
Kirkcudbright	51
	872

During the latter half of the nineteenth century there was a certain amount of progress in sanitation and most of the towns in the county had a reasonable water supply, but the villages had to depend for their supply on the village pump and only a few houses had the benefit of water-borne sewerage systems, the others depending on the dry closet. Between 1895 and 1900 the villages of Creetown and New Abbey were amongst the first to introduce piped supplies of water, and from then until 1914 many other villages followed suit and improved their supplies in this way. Supplies by water main were a distinct improvement on the old pump supply and brought great benefits to the householders who could afford to introduce water into their properties. Older people especially appreciated having water on tap, so that they were saved the tedious task of carrying from the well every drop of water they used. Most of these supplies had their origin in nearby springs or a local burn but, unfortunately, these sources were not always very reliable, especially during dry spells of weather. The county council had to consider whether it was possible to improve these supplies and at the same time provide a similar service to those areas which did not have any supply at all except a well.

Apart from Dalry, which in 1901 had taken a supply from Lochinvar, the first large water scheme to use as a reservoir one of the many natural lochs in the county was the Lochenkit scheme, which was commenced in 1934 and completed in 1937. This scheme covered an area extending from Kirkpatrick-Durham to Sandyhills, supplying *en route* Springholm, Crocketford, Haugh of Urr, Kippford, Rockcliffe and Portling, as well as augmenting the burgh supply to Dalbeattie. The second world war put an end to work of this nature but with the passing of the Rural Water Supplies and Sewerage Act, in 1944, there was a resumption in the interest of the ratepayers about water supplies and, as government grants became available for approved schemes, the county council took full advantage of these facilities. From 1946 onwards many schemes were designed and completed by the County Engineer and his staff. These included the improvement of the Dalry and Balmaclellan supply from Lochinvar; the extension of pipe-lines from the Loch Whinyeon scheme to supply Twynholm, Borgue, Bridge of Dee, Rhonehouse, Crossmichael, Ringford, Gelston, Dundrennan, Whinnieliggate, and Laurieston; the New Abbey scheme which improved the supply to that village and extended to Beeswing, Kirkgunzeon, Kirkbean, Mainsriddle and Caulkerbush. As water mains were extended by these schemes a network was gradually built up which covered the central part of the county. Apart from the benefit to villagers, farmers and proprietors of isolated houses quickly realised how essential it was to have a plentiful supply of excellent water and they took full advantage of the service when available.

In order to enjoy the full benefit of a piped water supply a water-borne sewerage system is required, and in spite of the difficulties caused by out-crops of rocks in many of the villages, which made the laying of the sewers a much more expensive operation, certain areas pressed forward with schemes. Between 1890 and 1900 special drainage districts were formed at Dundrennan, Dalry and Creetown and many other villages followed this example at varying intervals of time, so that by the end of the second world war only a few villages had not been dealt with.

Generally the sewerage systems adopted in the Stewartry were comparatively straight-forward and treatment of the sewage was usually by means of septic tanks or settling tanks. Only in a few cases was it necessary to instal more elaborate sewage works, where the effluent could not be discharged into a strongly flowing river which could give excellent dilution. Indeed a number of the towns and villages were able to discharge the effluent into the tidal waters of the Solway.

Although there was practically no pollution of any of the watercourses in the area, the passing of the Rivers (Prevention of Pollution) (Scotland) Act in 1951 caused the drainage authorities to review their standards and to improve on these wherever necessary. In 1954 the county council renewed and enlarged sewage works at Twynholm, in order to treat satisfactorily the greater volume of sewage from the village with its increased population. After consultation with the Solway Rivers Purification Board, Castle-Douglas Town Council decided to instal new sewage works to replace their old ones, which had become somewhat out of date and overworked. This was the first activated sludge plant to be installed in the Stewartry and it was put into commission in March 1961, at an estimated cost of £40,000.

GAS

Gas, which was first used for street lighting, gradually became the main source of heat and lighting for domestic purposes in the three larger burghs. In 1948 the Scottish Gas Board assumed responsibility for a service which for years had been yielding ground to a rapidly developing electricity service. Gas has now been largely replaced for lighting and power but is still much used for cooking and gas-fired boilers for central heating are increasing in popularity.

The local gas undertakings, although unlikely to be integrated into any national or regional grid scheme, continue to serve the public despite the difficulties of small scale production in an area distant from the coalfields.

HYDRO-ELECTRIC POWER

The Galloway Hydro-Electric Scheme was constructed between 1930 and 1936 under an Act of Parliament—the Galloway Water Power Act (1929)—and utilises the catchment area of the river Dee and its tributaries together with 50 square miles in the south-west corner of Ayrshire, a total of 396 square miles, with an annual average rainfall of 60 inches. The scheme cost £3,000,000 and involved the construction of five power stations, nine large dams, four tunnel systems, two seasonal storage reservoirs, five daily storage reservoirs and various associated works.

In the north-west, Loch Doon, in the county of Ayr, one of the main reservoirs, had its level raised 27 feet by constructing a dam at the outlet to give a storage capacity of 2,400,000,000 cubic feet. By tunnelling the adjoining hills water can be diverted into, or out of, the reservoir from the top reaches of the Deugh watershed by means of the Deugh-Doon tunnel system. By means of a valve on the side of the tunnel at the lowest point on this tunnel system, the water thus stored in Loch Doon can be let down under control to the Kendoon daily reservoir, together with the normal run-of-river water to the scheme's top station—Kendoon—which has a capacity of 24,000 kilowatts. It is a manually operated station with a hydraulic head of 150 feet, and generates an average of 42,000,000 kilowatt-hours yearly.

After the water reaches Kendoon power station it passes down the river Ken to Carsfad reservoir, where it generates 12,000 k.w. under a head of 65 feet, with an average annual output of 20,000,000 k.w.h. a year. The water then discharges into the headpond of another automatic station—Earlstoun—which has an output of 14,000 k.w. and an average annual output of 25,000,000 k.w.h., being discharged into the original river bed and flowing eventually into Loch Ken. These latter two stations are automatically controlled from the high head station—Glenlee (24,000 k.w.)—which is supplied with water from an artificial loch built on the upper reaches of the Blackwater of Dee. The water is conveyed through a tunnel, $3\frac{1}{4}$ miles long, to the station and is discharged into the river Ken above Loch Ken which forms the main reservoir for Tongland power station (33,000 k.w.) situated at the head of the estuary of the river Dee, near Kirkcudbright, the county town.

The most noteworthy feature of this hydro-electric scheme is the use of hydro stations to give peak load support to the national grid. Various alternative developments were investigated, but it was found that the most economical development was on a peak load basis.

The scheme was actually designed for an annual load factor of about 20 per cent, but as the rainfall has been found to be greater than was originally estimated when preparing the scheme, a load factor of about 25.8 per cent has been obtained. This has enabled the scheme to be operated to give greater maximum support to the steam stations connected to the grid at times of peak load. The maximum demand on the national grid occurs during the six months of autumn and winter and during those months the Galloway scheme can give the maximum help, as about two-thirds of the rainfall occurs then, and only one-third during the rest of the year.

The Galloway scheme has been an unqualified success. It was constructed at the cost estimated; it has done everything that was expected of it and, as regard units generated, has produced more than was expected.

OUTPUT FROM THE GALLOWAY HYDRO-ELECTRIC SCHEME SINCE THE FIRST COMPLETE YEAR OF OPERATION IN 1937

Parliamentary estimate	181·0 million units
Maximum annual output (1954)	320·0 million units
Minimum annual output (1941)	163·1 million units
25 years' average output (years 1937 to 1961 inclusive) ..	225·8 million units
Capital cost for each kw. installed	£29 approx.

COSTS

	Operating Costs	Capital Charges	Total
Cost for each unit sent out in 1961 on output of 236·8 million units	·0918d.	·095d.	·187d.
Comparison with south-west Scotland steam stations, 1961	·6820d.	·0625d.	·7445d.

ELECTRICITY DISTRIBUTION

The County Council of the Stewartry of Kirkcudbright had the unique distinction of being the first local authority in the United Kingdom to undertake the distribution of electricity over the whole county area. Moreover, at that time the population density, at thirty to the square mile, was lower than in any other similarly developed area and there were no large towns or industries to provide a substantial background for development.

Following the establishment of the Central Electricity Board under the 1926 Act and the Galloway Water Power Company in 1929, the way was prepared by the creation of the South of Scotland Grid and the hydro-electric stations for the development of a local distribution system. Under a Special Order in 1932, the county council commenced supplies in the burgh of Kirkcudbright and powers were granted to extend supplies to the whole of the county in 1933. In the same year, five small non-statutory undertakings at Castle-Douglas, Dalbeattie, Gatehouse-of-Fleet, Dalry and Twynholm, supplying approximately 1,000 consumers with D.C. supplies, were purchased by the county council and later inter-connected through the county H.V. system.

To encourage the use of electricity, assisted wiring facilities and hire purchase schemes were introduced. Substantial progress was made until the second world war restricted normal development. On nationalisation in 1948, the county became part of the Dumfries and Galloway area of the South-West Scotland Electricity Board, reconstituted in 1955 as the South of Scotland Electricity Board.

Since 1950 rural development has been an important aspect of board policy and 1,047 farms (or 97 per cent) were connected by the end of 1960. The board were instrumental in assisting with the pioneering

D

within the county of the first Bulk Milk Collection Scheme in the United Kingdom in 1954.

Ninety-five per cent of the habitable homes within the county were connected by the end of 1960. There are showrooms at Kirkcudbright, Castle-Douglas and Dalbeattie.

DISTRIBUTION OF ELECTRICITY 1933-1960

Year Ending	No. of Consumers	Units Sold (Thousands)	Average Charge a Unit (Pence)	No. of Farms Supplied
May 1933	104	11	5·34	—
,, 1936	2,786	1,914	2·29	64
,, 1939	4,449	4,356	1·80	217
,, 1942	5,127	7,400	1·70	319
,, 1945	5,367	9,144	1·59	372
March 1948	6,514	13,008	1·47	461
,, 1951	7,414	23,021	1·24	644
,, 1954	8,788	27,386	1·43	829
Dec. 1957	9,742	37,114	1·47	942
,, 1960	10,441	44,876	1·55	1,047

ROADS

During the nineteenth century, in common with other parts of Great Britain, residents of the Stewartry did not take a very great interest in roads until the coming of the motor car. About 1900, our roads, which had never been constructed to carry this type of traffic, were becoming a serious problem and there was public outcry at their condition. In wet weather the surfaces became veritable seas of mud, and in dry weather every vehicle raised great clouds of dust, to the discomfort and danger of all persons using the roads or living alongside them.

In 1909 a petrol tax was introduced to enable the government to pay grants to road authorities for the improvement of road surfaces, and in 1913 roads were classified in three categories depending on the traffic importance of each, class I, class II and unclassified. The first world war interrupted the work which had been started, and by 1920 the condition of the roads was causing so much anxiety that the government set up the Ministry of Transport and arranged to pay grants of 50 per cent towards the maintenance of class I and 25 per cent towards class II roads. The rates of grants and the classification of roads were altered from time to time, and just before the second world war the government accepted full responsibility for trunk roads established at that time. In 1961 the mileage of highways in the Stewartry totalled 794, made up of trunk roads (50 miles), class I (182 miles), class II (60 miles), class III (229 miles) and unclassified (273 miles).

Because of the undulating and rocky nature of the ground many of our roads were very tortuous in character, and along with the improvement of the road surface many schemes for widening and straightening had to be carried out. Prior to 1939, a start had been made to improve the important section of the trunk road between Dumfries and Castle-Douglas, where the number of dangerous bends was unusually high. Since the end of the second world war this work has been continued, the completion of the diversion at Southpark immediately south-west of Springholm being a notable example. Many other schemes have been planned, but financial restrictions have slowed up progress and no starting date has yet been fixed for such schemes as the by-passes at Twynholm, Gatehouse, Creetown and Carsluith.

Improvement schemes have also been carried out on many of the other important classified roads and considerable attention has been paid to the surfacing of carriageways. The policy of providing an impervious bituminous surface has extended to our unclassified roads and the mileage which has not been dealt with is now negligible. The introduction about 1945 of the mechanical spreading machine for the laying of tarmacadam and asphalt has greatly assisted in this work and has provided more regular running surfaces than is possible with hand-spreading. The roadmen skilled in hand-spreading work are fast dying out and it is only on small isolated jobs that one now sees this operation in progress.

NATIONAL ASSISTANCE

The National Assistance Board have now taken over all the public assistance and most of the social welfare duties formerly undertaken by the local authorities. Their task is to see that no one is left in need and to achieve this they supplement pensions or other payments where necessary to bring them up to the level prescribed by regulations.

EDUCATION—HISTORICAL DEVELOPMENT

'A school in every parish', one of the ideals enunciated by John Knox in his *First Book of Discipline* 1560, was not fully realised until the passing of the Education (Scotland) Act, 1872, made education compulsory. Successive attempts by parliament in the seventeenth and eighteenth centuries to enforce the provision of parish schools failed in the Stewartry as elsewhere in Scotland, although there are records at times of early successes, at other times of schoolmasters without schools, and on occasion of schools which operated only when a master could be appointed. The position over a period of some three centuries was that the church, assisted by the more enlightened members of the community, sought to force the establishment of a school in every parish against the wishes of heritors who generally were unwilling to be rated. The pattern was uneven, as continuity was exceptional, and yet few parishes had a completely negative record. At times private venture schools competed with the parish school or claimed to fill the vacuum where none existed.

The Royal Burgh of Kirkcudbright, with a Grammar School founded before 1576, almost certainly led the way in the Stewartry; the records of 1696 show the establishment of only two more, at Dalry (the result of a generous endowment) and Minnigaff. The years immediately before and after 1872 were eventful so far as school building was concerned.

To accommodate all the children of school age a few schools were enlarged, but in most parishes one new school, and in some cases two or even three, were needed. In relation to the resources available the programme of building at that time probably surpassed anything achieved even in the boom of recent years.

To begin with, the aim of education was to teach the '3 Rs' and it was later that 'higher class schools' developed into secondary schools. Broadly, over the present century, the decline in population has resulted in decreasing primary rolls in all but the burgh schools. On the other hand, by centralising post-primary pupils, more highly organised secondary courses were made possible, and the teaching has been increasingly done by graduate and other teachers, who are specialists in their subjects. Nevertheless, secondary rolls increased slowly until 1947, when the school leaving age was raised from 14 to 15. This sudden increase in secondary population was followed (note the order of events) by an emergency building programme. Over the last decade the high birth rate of 1946 and 1947, and an increasing tendency for pupils to remain at school beyond leaving age, have brought about a slow growth in secondary numbers, despite the falling population, a growth which will be further encouraged by the introduction of the Scottish Certificate of Education (Ordinary grade) at the fourth year level.

The most important growing point over the post-war period has accordingly been the development of secondary education appropriate to an age of science and technology. The problems of staffing during a time when the shortage of teachers has been critical, and of school building in a period marked by recurring economic crises, have remained the continuing preoccupations of administrators.

THE PRESENT SCENE

Primary education, defined as progressive elementary education in the prescribed subjects from about 5 to approximately 12 years of age, is provided in 45 primary schools and in 4 primary departments of larger schools. The needs of a small population widely scattered over a large area are reflected in a pattern of provision which is common throughout rural Scotland to-day.

PRIMARY SCHOOLS IN THE STEWARTRY OF KIRKCUDBRIGHT

	No. of Schools	Range in Roll
One teacher	10	9-24
Two teachers	19	25-56
Three teachers	13	57-90
Four teachers	2	91-140
Five teachers	1	141-175
Seven or more teachers	4	200-400
	49	

Special classes for slow learners have been established in the three largest centres of population, and in a child guidance clinic children are given help in overcoming learning difficulties.

The placing of schools by the School Boards after 1872 was based on the proposition that a primary school could serve an area of some three miles radius—the distance a small child could reasonably be expected to walk to and from school. The development of modern transport has changed the picture completely and it is not surprising that some of the more remote schools have been closed. The high cost of providing modern schools and the shortage of teachers will combine to ensure that this process will continue in districts where population is not maintained.

SECONDARY EDUCATION

There are seven secondary schools, all of which offer a range of courses designed to educate children according to age, aptitude and ability, including courses leading to 'O' Grade of the Scottish Certificate of Education. Kirkcudbright Academy alone offers courses leading to 'H' Grade. Pupils taking certificate courses remain in the local secondary school for four years or transfer at the appropriate stage to the 'H' Grade course. The other pupils follow general courses and many leave after reaching leaving age.

In their secondary school organisation the Stewartry Education Authority's policy has been to build up the local schools and centralise only at the more advanced stages of the secondary courses; as a consequence, the vast majority of pupils complete their education at the local secondary school.

SCHOOL MEALS SERVICE

The modern service, introduced during the period of war-time rationing of food, was in a sense anticipated by the voluntary soup-kitchens established much earlier in many Stewartry schools. This earlier provision of hot soup at mid-day was a natural development in an area where homes were often remote from schools. Of the central kitchens built during the war only four now remain, the rest having been replaced as a kitchen is incorporated in every new school. Half of the Stewartry schools now have kitchens, and about 3,500 meals are produced each day, by a staff of 15 full-time and 112 part-time workers. A further 20 people are employed part-time in the transport of meals to schools which are still without kitchens. In a year total expenditure is approximately £78,000 and purchase of food alone amounts to £38,000.

FURTHER EDUCATION

As is usual in a rural area, there is little demand for technical education. The only full-time course is a one-year pre-vocational commercial course which trains shorthand-typists and clerk-typists. Evening classes provide, in the three largest centres, commercial courses and the early stages of the national certificate courses in electrical and mechanical engineering. For advanced courses in these and other subjects students have to attend classes elsewhere.

A wide variety of classes of a recreative or utilitarian nature are held in local schools throughout the county.

In recent years, in association with the local education authority, the Glasgow University Extra-Mural Committee have each year offered an interesting programme of adult classes in the larger communities. Despite the difficulties inherent in an area of small and scattered population there has been an encouraging development of Youth Service activities.

Each year a summer school offering tuition by local artists and craftsmen in painting, weaving and pottery is organised by the local education authority. About 80 people are attracted, including, on occasion, visitors from overseas.

LIBRARIES

For some years now the library service for the burghs as well as for the landward area has been administered by the education authority. The general pattern is of static collections in the burghs and four of the larger villages, the rest of the area being served by regular visits from a mobile library which goes daily on its rounds with a collection of some 2,000 books. The total stock is approximately 66,000, composed of 13,000 juvenile, 25,000 fiction, 28,000 non-fiction. While television appears to reduce total reading slightly, it has nevertheless increased the demand for travel and other non-fiction works.

The library service is well used and very popular with a public which generally is far removed from places of mass entertainment. As a consequence, registered readers (12,000) form a significantly high proportion of the total population.

MUSEUMS AND ART COLLECTIONS

Kirkcudbright Museum, which was reorganised in 1956, now offers a very adequate and ordered display of items of local archaeological and historical interest.

Broughton House, left in trust to the people of the Stewartry by the late E. A. Hornel, one of the most distinguished artists of the Glasgow School and a founder of the Kirkcudbright Group, contains many examples of his own paintings and in addition what is thought to be one of the most complete private collections of the work of Robert Burns, as well as manuscripts and published works of other Scottish writers. Considerable use is made of this collection as source material by professors of literature and students, sometimes from overseas. The original Broughton House was the seventeenth century town house of the Murrays of Broughton but most of the present building belongs to a much later period. It contains many interesting pieces of furniture, not all of which are in period with the house.

Harbour Cottage, an interesting old house on the water-side near the harbour, was saved from demolition and reconditioned with the help of the National Trust for Scotland. It now serves as a picture gallery and has regular 'shows' of the works of Kirkcudbright artists and, on occasion, other loan collections.

Castle-Douglas has a picture gallery of two small rooms which contains a permanent collection of the works of the donor, the late Mrs. Bristowe, Craig, Balmaclellan. By arrangement with the Trustees, loan collections are occasionally on show.

CHAPTER 5

THE COMMUNITY

POPULATION—THE COUNTY

I N 1851, the year of the first census after the publication of the
New Statistical Account, the population of the whole county was
43,121 and this was the highest recorded at any census.   Since that
date the population has fallen with almost monotonous regularity
and only during the periods 1871-81 and 1931-51 were there slight
reversals of the general downward tendency.   In 1901 the population had
dropped to 39,383, while in 1931 and 1951 the figures were 30,341 and
30,725 respectively.   The latest census (1961) shows a further fall to
28,877.

In considering this decline in population, which is characteristic of
rural Scotland, we must note one or two factors which during recent
years have helped in this county to make the change more marked.   In
1929 the burgh of Maxwellton was transferred from the Stewartry to
the county of Dumfries and the loss in population in consequence of
this transfer was 6,094.   Again in 1938 and 1948 areas comprising parts
of the parishes of Kirkpatrick-Irongray, Terregles and Troqueer were
incorporated in the burgh of Dumfries with a resultant loss to the
Stewartry. In spite of the latter transfers, however, the 1951 census
showed a slight increase of 384 over the previous twenty years.

This general trend downward has been pronounced in the landward
parts of the county.   In the burghal areas the population has on the
other hand grown very steadily, although there have been occasional
deviations from the general pattern.   One such occurred when
Maxwellton was ceded, a decrease which of course affected the burghal
population.   Figure 1 shows graphically the population trends in the
county as a whole, in the landward portion and in the burghal section.
It will be noted that the increase recorded in 1951 was accounted for
by a rise in the town population.

THE BURGHS

It is interesting to examine how the individual burghs have behaved and
Figure 2 shows how the population of the six burghs, including
Maxwellton up to the 1921 census, has moved since 1841.   The year
1841 is taken here instead of 1851, as there is no recorded figure for
the population of Dalbeattie in the latter year.   It will be observed that
Maxwellton grew rapidly, apart from one drop at 1861 and another
at 1921.   The population of Kirkcudbright has not altered very materially

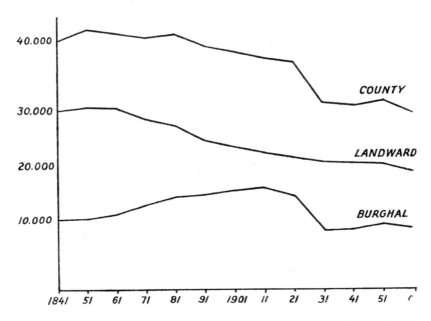

Fig. 1. Populations of county as a whole, of landward portion and
burghal portion.

over the hundred years—a gradual decline to the low water mark of
1921 and since then a steady but unspectacular growth. The mounting
importance of Castle-Douglas during the period is reflected in the almost
unbroken increase in the population from 1,847 to 3,322. The graph
for Dalbeattie shows some remarkable fluctuations. In 1841 the
population was 1,430 and in 1881 it had increased to almost 4,000, a
figure comparable with that of Maxwellton. The late Dr. Frew in *The
Parish of Urr* remarks 'The vicissitudes of the staple industry are
reflected in the variations of the population from the middle of the
nineteenth century to the present day. So long as the granite boom lasted,
it (Dalbeattie's population) rapidly increased; being 1,736 in 1861 and
rising to 3,865, the highest point it has so far reached, in 1881. The
period of depression which ensued between 1881 and 1891 saw the
population fall to 3,149, but since then there has been a considerable
recovery.' The population of Gatehouse was only 15 fewer than that
of Castle-Douglas in 1841 but the number has steadily declined from
1,832 to 877 with one slight increase of 19 at the 1911 census. During
the early years of the period New Galloway more than held its ground
but since 1861 the number has diminished each year, in some cases
almost imperceptibly.

Reference has been made to the drop in the population of
Kirkcudbright at the 1921 census. A similar drop may also be observed
in the curves of Castle-Douglas and Dalbeattie and to a lesser extent

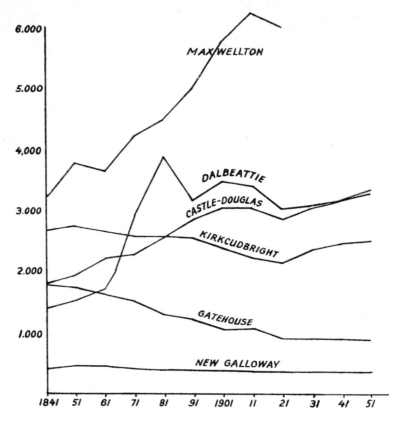

Fig. 2.   Population of burghs.

in that of Gatehouse. This of course is the period immediately following the first world war, when unemployment was rife, and doubtless migration to other parts of the country and emigration overseas in search of employment may account for the loss of population at this time.

THE PARISHES

During the period from 1851 to 1951 the population of most of the parishes has decreased, either naturally or through movement of population or in consequence of boundary alterations.   In only four has an increase been registered: Urr (1,119), Crossmichael (369), Kelton (210), and Twynholm (26); and of the others one only, Kirkcudbright, has decreased by less than ten per cent.   In seven the decrease in population is between ten and thirty per cent., while in the remaining 16 the decreases range from 30 per cent. to more than 80 per cent.   It is significant that the five parishes with increases and the minimum

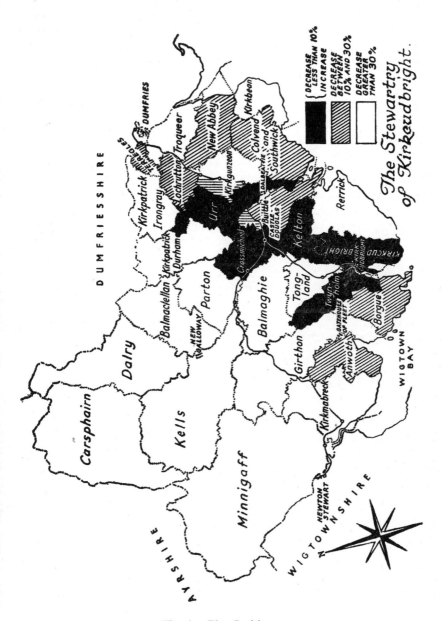

Fig. 3. The Parishes,

decrease are connected with the three large burghs of the county,
Dalbeattie being situated in Urr, Castle-Douglas in Crossmichael and
Kelton, and Kirkcudbright being in the parish of the same name and
fringing on Twynholm, which contains the county council housing
scheme of Mersecroft on the opposite side of the river Dee from
Kirkcudbright. (See Figure 3).

AGE DISTRIBUTION

The age distribution by quinquennial age groups for the year 1901 is
compared with that for the year 1951 in Figure 4.   The ratio of the
number of persons in each quinquennial age group to the whole
population has been calculated as a percentage. It will be seen that, as
was to be expected, the proportion of young people in 1901 was greater,
and that of older people less, than in 1951. The point at which there is
parity lies between 30 and 35 years of age.

An interesting fact was revealed by the 1951 census with regard
to the age of the population.   The percentage of the population in each
of the four main age groups in the landward area and in each of the
burghs has been tabulated as follows:—

	0-4	5-14	15-64	65 and over
Landward	9.2	16.5	63.1	11.2
Castle-Douglas	8.8	13.2	65.7	12.3
Dalbeattie	9.6	16.3	62.7	11.4
Gatehouse	7.6	13.3	63.5	15.5
Kirkcudbright	8.2	14.8	64.3	12.6
New Galloway	5.6	9.5	61.3	23.6

It would appear that in New Galloway, and to a lesser extent in
Gatehouse, a considerable proportion of the inhabitants have chosen
these attractive burghs as suitable places for retirement.

MIGRATION

It has been calculated that during the period 1931-51 the number of
births in the county exceeded the number of deaths by 2,640 and that
the increase in the resident population was 425.   This indicates that
there has been a loss of over 2,000 from the county in consequence
of the balance of movements of people *out* of the county over the
movements of people *into* it.

In 1901 the population of the county was 39,383, of whom 13,488
persons were born outwith the county; in 1951 the corresponding figures
were 30,725 and 14,586.   The incomers accordingly have increased in
those fifty years from 34.2 per cent. to 47.5 per cent., or from slightly
more than one third to almost half of the population.   Of the 14,586
born elsewhere, England accounts for 2,176, Ireland (North and South)
266, and the rest of Scotland 11,424, mainly Dumfriesshire (4,433),
Ayrshire (1,246) and Wigtownshire (1,791).   Two world wars, especially
the second with its massive evacuations of civilian population to the
Stewartry, have undoubtedly helped to increase this influx.   The growth

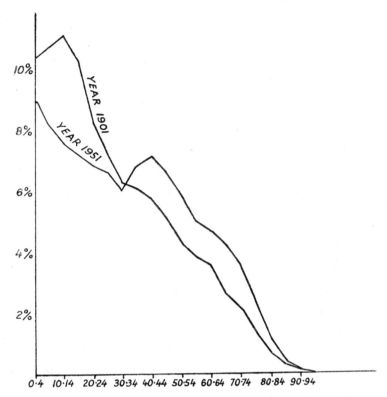

Fig. 4. Age distribution by quinquennial age groups. Comparison of years 1901 and 1951.

of the nationalised industries, which of recent years have caused a circulation of population over the whole country, has probably contributed to the same result, while tourism too has played its part. All these factors in a greater or lesser degree have tended to bring the Stewartry, which was previously rather remote and apart, more into the main stream of national life.[1]

THE CHURCH OF SCOTLAND

In the changing circumstances of a troubled era the witness of the Church has continued and congregations have remained faithful and generous when sacrifices have been asked.

Important ecclesiastical milestones have had their repercussions in the Stewartry—notably the Disruption of 1843, the Union of the Church of Scotland and the United Free Church in 1929 and the quatercentenary of the Scottish Reformation in 1960. From the Disruption, in many parishes, the Free Church stood in proximity and rivalry to

(1) For Table of Population, 1901-1961 (Parishes and Burghs), see Appendix II, p. 510.

the Parish Church, manse over against manse. There were tensions, financial anxieties and sometimes strained relationships.

Since 1929 there has been reunion and recovery to the great advantage of the Church. It seems incredible that, in the lives of many who are still active members of the Church of Scotland, two ministers laboured in each of the following parishes: Carsphairn, Corsock, Dalry and Balmaghie — to name only four typical rural parishes.

Along with the problem of readjustment is that of ministerial manpower — a problem that has caused much anxiety. So acute has been the manpower situation in the church that linking of congregations (rather than union) has been found desirable. One minister is thus responsible for the spiritual oversight of two parishes and the identity of each congregation is preserved. Such linkings have taken place and others are pending. The process of readjustment is slow but congregations have responded patiently and sympathetically. Linking is not necessarily a permanent arrangement and the church has never favoured readjustment merely for its own sake. Where it has been imperative, the Church of Scotland in the Stewartry has responded to the demands of an age of transition and reorientation.

The claims of the ministry of the church as a calling are continually being brought before our young men. It is disappointing, therefore, to record that on average in this county only one student in each decade has been licensed as a probationer of the Church of Scotland by the presbytery of Kirkcudbright.

One important matter must be mentioned, the Church Property and Endowments Act of 1925, which affects many parishes. By this Act, which paved the way for the Union of 1929, the heritors were relieved of the upkeep of parish churches and manses. Without exception, all Stewartry congregations have responded to this challenge. The maintenance of the ordinances of religion, with a minimum stipend that has more than doubled since 1929, has become a crucial problem for church finance. So far as the Stewartry is concerned, each year sees less aid being drawn from the Maintenance of the Ministry Fund, and congregations contributing to the support of a minister as never before.

The Church of Scotland, with an average for the Stewartry of approximately 12,000 members and 350 elders (during the last decennium), has been alive to the challenge of a nuclear age. In spite of depopulation in certain rural areas and the departure to the large cities of many of the younger members, there is no decline in membership. The church is alive to the problems confronting it at the present day. In 1960 generous contribution was made towards the extinction of a large debt in the Church Extension Committee. There is deep concern for refugees, and annual contributions are made for their aid. Many subjects affecting church and nation are debated in presbytery with goodwill and deep sincerity.

Like many things in 1961, the church in the Stewartry is changing. Ministers are faced with greater tasks — the greatest, perhaps, the proclamation of the Gospel in an atomic age. Territorial responsibility for many has increased, and further increases are pending. The members of the church, too, are faced with greater responsibilities. New avenues for service have been opened to the laity, and the conduct of public worship by lay readers, when necessary, is much appreciated. The church is being called to contribute more than ever before to the annual maintenance of religious ordinances and is responding magnificently to the call. There are abundant signs that the church is not reluctant to change: times of public worship have been altered willingly; ministers are glad to act, and are welcomed, as school or hospital chaplains; the special needs of youth are recognised, and the young are in evidence in Bible class, study group and Youth Fellowship.

OTHER DENOMINATIONS

In addition to the Church of Scotland, members of the Episcopal Church in Scotland, the Roman Catholic Church and the Congregational Church complete the picture of church life in the Stewartry. There are also groups of Brethren—meeting chiefly in the towns. In comparison with the national church, the aforementioned denominations are small in numbers but the members are loyal to their traditions and ecclesiastical disunity is less noticeable than in some other parts of Scotland. The relationship between the Episcopal Church in Scotland and the Church of Scotland is closer than for many years. The Episcopal Church in Scotland has suffered from the extinction of many of the larger county mansion-houses and has become more dependent on members of the Anglican Church who have crossed the border because of employment in the Stewartry.

In the past century the faith of our fathers has been preserved in the Stewartry of Kirkcudbright, the Gospel has been devotedly proclaimed in peace and war and it is evident that many sincere men and women are anxious to use wisely a new day for the church — a day of unparalleled difficulty and entrancing opportunity.

VOLUNTARY SERVICES

The State has now made itself responsible for a wide range of services, such as health, education, and care of the aged, but in spite of these far-reaching State activities there is still room for voluntary and philanthropic organisations to supplement the work of the State and to fill in the gaps where it does not operate. The work of a number of these organisations is carried on enthusiastically by many people in this county.

The Stewartry, bordering on the Solway and having a life-boat station at the mouth of the Dee, naturally supports a strong branch of the Royal National Lifeboat Institution. Many of the villages as well as the burghs have their committees and by means of whist drives, flag-days and collections considerable sums are raised in support of this cause.   A similar organisation is the British Sailors' Society, which receives active support in various parts of the county.   Recently a local committee was formed to arouse interest in, and gain financial aid for, the Cheshire Home, established some time ago at Carnsalloch in Dumfriesshire.   The British Red Cross, of course, is known to all and needs merely to be mentioned.   The Women's Voluntary Services have an enviable reputation for self-sacrificing effort since their foundation. One very worth-while service which they give is the provision of meals for aged and housebound people, under what is known as 'The Meals on Wheels' scheme.   Meals prepared in the school kitchens of the Education Authority are conveyed to the homes of these people, who in this way receive much-needed attention.   This is but one of the various forms of social helpfulness for which this organisation has made itself responsible.

Many devoted voluntary workers, interested specially in young people, form the leaders of Boy Scouts, Girl Guides and youth clubs The vital importance of such work can scarcely be over-emphasised. especially among the 'teenager' group, some of whom at times unfor- tunately go to excess at public dances.   Recently a Youth Council under the auspices of the Education Committee was formed, comprising members of the Education Committee and representatives of various youth organisations.   It is hoped that this council, by arranging dances under supervision and establishing youth clubs, may be able to give the young people entertainment and pleasure under wholesome conditions and help to a certain extent to combat an evil which is all too prevalent in the community.

ENTERTAINMENT AND RECREATION

R. L. Stevenson, referring to the South Sea Islander of his day, wrote that 'in a climate and upon a soil where livelihood can be had for the stooping, entertainment is a prime necessity.'   In a harsher climate and in a land where strenuous labour is required to wrest a livelihood from the soil, entertainment or at least recreation is felt to be just as necessary, though perhaps for a different reason.

For many people recreation means sport, whether they are onlookers or active participants.   The association football enthusiasts may attend the matches of their local clubs or may travel to Dumfries or farther afield for Scottish League fixtures.   Strange to say, rugby football has little following.   Some 30 years ago an attempt was made to establish a Stewartry Rugby Club, but it soon died through lack of support. Now it is only at Kirkcudbright Academy that this game is played in the county.   Cricket has its devotees in the summer months, especially at Gatehouse, while golf, bowling and tennis are popular where the facilities for these games exist.

As befits a county with many lochs and streams, angling claims many devoted followers.   A sport which has become very popular lately is sailing, and vigorous clubs have been formed at Kippford and

Kirkcudbright. The winters are generally not severe enough for open-air curling but the relative nearness of the artificial ice rink at Ayr enables this sport to be enjoyed with little difficulty. Indoor winter games are carpet bowling and badminton, played in community centre or village hall. Motor cycle rallies, pony trekking, and pigeon fancying deserve mention, as does water-skiing, a sport which of late has been growing in popularity. Quoiting, however, which used to be popular in the country villages, seems to have disappeared, or may it just be dormant?

The Stewartry, with its wild mountainous regions containing the giants of the Southern Uplands such as the Merrick and Corserine, is bound to foster a love of mountaineering and hill-walking, and many dedicated hill-climbers are to be found throughout the county. Again the sandy bays and beaches of the Solway have become very popular with tourists in the summer months, but the local people are just as appreciative of the joys of the seaside as the visitors. In the long summer evenings and at week-ends the well-known shores of Sandyhills, Rockcliffe, Sandgreen, Carrick or Mossyard are thronged with young and old alike.

Forms of recreation other than sport attract many. Horticultural societies flourish in town and village, and shows of flowers and vegetables at the appropriate time form the highlight of the season. As befits a community largely engaged in and dependent on agriculture, shows, sheep dog trials and ploughing matches are arranged and occasionally the experts in dry stone dyking give an exhibition of their skilled, but unfortunately dying craft.

The presence in Kirkcudbright, and elsewhere in the county, of painters and artists with a national and even international reputation has had its influence on the community. Dramatic and musical societies have revealed and encouraged much talent which otherwise might have remained hidden. The success of choral societies and drama groups at festivals is evidence of the keen interest in these activities and the high standard achieved. Mention should also be made of the Audience Club of Kirkcudbright and similar societies elsewhere which co-operate with the Arts Council in producing concerts of high quality. The Royal Scottish Country Dance Society does an important work in fostering and encouraging country dancing classes throughout the county, and a feature of the social life of the farming community is the Young Farmers' Club, a vigorous organisation whose activities embrace public speaking competitions, lectures and demonstrations.

The Way of Life

The numerous bus services, and of late years the increasing number of private cars, have in a very definite manner promoted the mobility of the population. These means of transport have altered greatly the way of life of the community. Places, which a generation ago were isolated,

E

are now within reasonably easy reach of large towns such as Dumfries and Ayr.   A residence at some distance from the place of employment does not present the problem which it did at one time.   Country folk are able to travel to the local centre to attend a concert or the cinema.

Here, as in other parts of the country, certain factors operate to deprive the home of the position of importance which it once occupied. Young people are able to earn more money than formerly and tend often in consequence to become more independent of home.   Again the mother frequently has to engage in whole or part-time employment and this in some cases may result in the weakening of the home influence.

Interest in public affairs is shown at general elections.   For the rest, it is fair to say that the apathy which characterises local government elections in other parts of the country is not unknown in the Stewartry.

The place of the Church in the community has been discussed in the preceding pages. Suffice it to say here that church attendance is no longer what it used to be, nor is the Sunday observed as it was in the past.   On the other hand it must be said that when the need or call arises, as in the case of the sinking of the *Princess Victoria* on 31st January, 1953, the springs of human kindness overflow with abounding practical help for the stricken.

Part Two

THE PARISHES

CHAPTER 6

THE PARISH OF ANWOTH

by the REV. JOHN TURNBULL.

Boundaries and Extent

These have not changed since the time of the *New Statistical Account*.
The parish is bounded on the west and north by Kirkmabreck; on the
east by Girthon; on the south-east by Fleet Bay; and on the south by
Wigtown Bay. Its eastern border is traced by the river Fleet. About
7¼ miles in length from north to south, the parish varies in breadth
between 1½ and 4½ miles, and has an area of 12,861 acres. It contains
the Fleet Street suburb of Gatehouse, which is divided by the river
between the parishes of Anwoth and Girthon and is the only town in
the district. (For an account of Gatehouse, see Parish of Girthon).

Communications

One or two important changes in the lines of communications are
worthy of mention. In the year 1844, in order to stimulate commerce,
Mr. Murray of Broughton and Cally constructed a canal of approximately 1,400 yards in length, at a cost of around £3,000. This
straightened the course of the River Fleet and deepened its channel
towards the Firth, thus enabling vessels of heavier tonnage to bring their
wares right into the harbour. Approximately 1,200 tons of exports
were handled annually in those early days, and imports in the form of
coal, manure and agricultural goods were brought to the stores which
were erected at convenient stages. A few of those stores still stand
and are in quite good condition. Mr. Belford, who is now in his 81st
year, well remembers the busy scenes of loading and depositing. His
family has been in the coal trade for over a century. Efforts are being
renewed to revive coastal trade in this area. Kirkcudbright has made
a successful revival, but it remains to be seen if Gatehouse can utilise
her own natural waterways and so help to solve one of her most urgent
and vital problems.

While the men were cutting the canal they discovered two large
rocks. The engineers used them for the foundation and pillars of the
draw-bridge, which was built almost directly opposite the old Cardoness
Castle. This bridge is now in decay and in disuse, though the actual

foundations are in good condition. Boats ceased to operate about 30 years ago; the draw-bridge has been out of action for about 20 years. Horse-brakes used to carry people from Gatehouse to Sandgreen over the bridge.

Earlier Accounts noted the common highway from Carlisle and Dumfries to Portpatrick as passing through the middle of the parish, just by the kirk. Nowadays the main trunk road, A.75, by-passes the Old Clachan and virtually skirts the shore from Gatehouse, bordering the old Castle and Ardwall. Modern motor coaches have replaced the picturesque and leisurely mail-coach.

The railway-line from Dumfries to Castle-Douglas was opened in 1859, and the line was continued to Portpatrick, being completed in 1861. Dromore was recognised as the station for Gatehouse. Horse-brakes were used in the early days to link up with the station and carry passengers and goods to and fro. Later, motor vehicles replaced them, under the auspices of Messrs. W. and A. Campbell.

Recently there was a serious set-back to the transport system of the area in consequence of the decision by the Railway Executive of British Railways to close down Dromore as the station for Gatehouse and district. There has been a great deal of public agitation to get the station re-opened, particularly in view of the remoteness of the inhabitants in that region, especially the shepherds and their families. The town of Gatehouse is six miles distant. Colonel F. Rainsford-Hannay, County Councillor, and Mrs. E. Murray-Usher, Murrayton, are doing all in their power to safeguard the interests of the community in this important matter of transport and communications. Now that the Dromore station has closed, Messrs. Campbell's coaches ply to Kirkcudbright as the centre. A few of the local merchants make Tarff station their depot, particularly for coal, fish, fruit and such commodities; others, especially those in the west side of the parish, utilise Creetown as their base for transport. Evidently, a slight concession has been made by the authorities in that the local residents at Dromore on the British Railway staff are allowed to embark and alight at the old station as an 'unofficial halt.'

A few years ago, before the nationalisation of the railways took place, the company generously provided the community with a disused carriage. This was erected on the verge of the roadway which serves as a boundary line between Kirkmabreck and Anwoth Parishes. It is used as a social, recreational and cultural centre. Religious services are held monthly with unfailing regularity, conducted jointly by the respective parish ministers.

Cardoness Castle and Ardwall

These two places are connected with the family of Ardwall. The first record of this family is of Gilbert McCulloch of Cardoness, who died in 1468. From him was descended Agnes McCulloch who married Duncan Crawford of Nether Skeldon. Their daughter Isobel married

David McCulloch of Ardwall. This formed the link between the two families. From Gilbert was also descended Marie McCulloch, who married William McCulloch of Myreton. Their grandson Alexander obtained a Nova Scotia baronetcy in 1664. His son was Sir Godfrey McCulloch who became involved in a dispute with the Gordon family regarding ownership of Cardoness. This culminated in the murder of his neighbour William Gordon, of which he was convicted. He was the last man to be executed on the 'Maiden', a Scots form of guillotine. With Sir Godfrey's death the connection of the Cardoness McCullochs with the parish came to an end. The Ardwall estate descended in the male line from William, who obtained a charter of the lands in 1587, to Walter who died unmarried in 1892. He was succeeded by his niece, Christian Brown, who married Andrew Jameson, Lord Ardwall, a Senator of the College of Justice.

The Maxwells of Cardoness descend from the Maxwells of Calderwood, of which family William Maxwell, minister of Monigaff, was a younger son. He was one of the displaced ministers of the Covenant and was forced to leave his charge in 1662. His son, also William, studied medicine in Edinburgh and was a strong adherent of the Earl of Argyll. When Argyll was sentenced to death in 1685, Maxwell obtained permission to visit him in prison, sat with him the night before his execution, and boldly accompanied him to the scaffold. The present owner of Cardoness, Dorothea, the younger daughter of the fourth baronet, in 1910 married Captain (now Colonel) Frederick Rainsford-Hannay.

Education

At the time of the publication of the *New Statistical Account*, education was still in the hands of the church. On the heritors fell the financial obligations entailed in maintaining a school and in remunerating the schoolmaster. The minister and kirk session shared in the supervision of parochial proceedings, interviewing and appointing scholastic candidates.

In 1845 Anwoth possessed two schools. The first of these, the official parish establishment, was where it had stood from olden times, directly across from the Rutherford Church. The master was John Thomson, who was elected the previous year. Two years later he was succeeded by Robert Shaw, from Tongland. Robert Stark, member of a well-known local family, reigned for a lengthy period, continuing service elsewhere in the parish with the passing of the Education Act of 1872.

It was in 1844 that the heritors took cognizance of 'the inadequate manner in which the teachers are supported' and also decided to place the 'side' school at Laggan on the 'footing of an additional parish school.' This involved the division of the total salary available, and to the new school was apportioned the value of one chalder of oatmeal (currently £17 2s 2d). The master appointed was David Shennan. He was the only master ever appointed to Laggan School, for he served until the school's closure under the Education Act of 1872.   Both masters received a well-deserved increase in salary in 1861, when Mr. Stark was advanced to an annual £45, Mr. Shennan receiving £25 (these amounts being supplemented by school fees).

The year 1873 proved most significant for Gatehouse district as regards education.   A joint school was set up for the two parishes. In place of Laggan a new and more conveniently situated school was opened at Skyreburn, which has since remained as a teaching centre. The first head teacher appointed to Skyreburn was Mr. Stark, who remained until his retirement.   Then followed John Pritchard, who also taught over a lengthy period stretching to almost forty years, and whose name is still revered.   The little school at Anwoth was closed. Now in the hands of Mr. George P. H. Watson, it is used as an artist's studio; quite a number of famous artists and pupils make use of this centre of art.   A new establishment was built on the Anwoth side of the Fleet, known as Fleetside School, and it continued as such until 1923 when it was subject to a scheme of reorganisation.   At Fleetside the first master was David Clark, who rendered excellent service until his retirement in 1906.   His successor was George Salmond, who in 1920 was appointed to Kirkmabreck.   This change enabled William Learmonth, who had been master at Girthon, to assume control of both establishments.

From 1911 it was customary to transfer the senior pupils to Girthon School for a more advanced education, among the subjects taught being Latin, French, mathematics, agriculture and domestic science.   Thus the school board recognised the demand for secondary education When Mr. Learmonth retired in 1923, opportunity was taken to amalgamate the two schools of Girthon and Fleetside.   Mr. Learmonth, besides being an inspiring tutor, acquired national fame as a geographical scholar and historian, compiling the admirable *Kirkcudbrightshire and Wigtownshire* volume in the 'County Series' of the Cambridge University Press.   A number of his pupils have attained eminence in several fields.   It is worthy of note that his son, Professor Sir James Learmonth, became a world-famous surgeon and medical adviser to King George VI.

The present headmaster, A. A. Stewart, was appointed in 1925. Until 1927 he continued to run the school in separate buildings at different ends of the town, but in that year a fine new suite of buildings was erected at Fleetside and centralisation took place, with the adoption of the name Gatehouse School.   For 28 years Mr. Stewart has rendered notable service to the burgh, and he became Provost in 1941.

At present Gatehouse Secondary School has a roll of 250 pupils; the teaching staff consists of the headmaster and nine other teachers, with two visiting teachers.   Skyreburn School is a primary school, dealing with pupils under 12 years of age.   It has about 20 pupils on the roll and is a one-teacher school.   Pupils at the extreme western edge of the parish, for example from Mossyard, Auchenlarie, and environs, are now transported by the Education Authority to Carsluith school in Kirkmabreck parish; some 12 pupils travel thither for education.

Local Ballads

Galloway has a theme song of its very own. It is sung at all social gatherings and is a most pleasing and haunting melody. The author of the song, George G. B. Sproat, was a prominent agriculturist who took a leading part in all that pertained to the parish. His publication entitled *The Rose o' Dalma Linn and other Lays o' Gallowa'* appeared in 1888. This work was composed while he was farming High Creoch in Girthon parish. An excerpt from 'The Rose o' Dalma Linn,' based on an old Galloway legend, was set to music by George Faed Hornsby and is known as 'Bonnie Gallowa'.'

Afforestation and Woodlands

There is a hostel in Garden Street called the Fleet Hostel under the auspices of the Forestry Commission. Usually around twelve residents are accommodated. Afforestation in the parish, however, is largely in the hands of the estates, Cardoness, Ardwall, Kirkclaugh and Rusko.

The woodlands contain both hardwood and softwood varieties, though cultivation of softwood is far more extensive since it yields a quicker return from the viewpoint of economics. Much of the hardwood is coppice; most of the softwood is made up of larch and spruce and Douglas firs. The woodlands are not being cut *en bloc* owing to state restriction on sales, supervision and control. Thinnings, however, at prescribed intervals, are marketed with timber merchants.

Agriculture

Three types of land are found in the parish. 1. Moorland or marginal hill land; average yearly rental is roughly 5s an acre. 2. Arable land; average yearly rental is 15s to 25s an acre. 3. Woodland, of both hardwood and softwood types.

Most of the land consists of mixed farms. During the century there has been a tendency for a number of the farms to change to dairy farming with Ayrshire stock. All such farms are now attested and subject to periodic scientific tests. Since almost 80 per cent. of the land is moorland, sheep farming is extensively carried on. The sheep stock is mainly blackfaced with occasional cross-breds.

As regards cattle the parish is chiefly a stock-raising one. There are several breeders of black Galloway cattle, with well-known pedigree stock of high marketable value. There is a famous herd of belted Galloways reared by Mr. G. Faed Sproat in Boreland of Anwoth. Quite a number of the belted Galloways have been exported to New Zealand and U.S.A., and others are awaiting shipment to South Australia. In order to achieve maturity of stock as early as possible, a few of the stock-breeders go in for double-crossing of the Galloway cow with white Shorthorn bull and then in turn with an Angus bull, thus arriving at a fine specimen of stock-breeding known as 'Blue-Greys.'

A few dairy farms are to be found on the better type of land. These deal in fresh milk provided by herds of attested and largely pedigreed Ayrshire cows.   The milk is cooled, put into containers and collected daily by trucks of the Scottish Milk Marketing Board.

The system of husbandry has not changed much over the years, apart from the general tendency towards mechanisation of equipment, which has taken place locally during the last 20 years.   Tractors have replaced horses for the most part, and improved types of machinery have reduced the manpower problem.   A large part of the fertilisers put on the land now consists of lime and chemicals.

The Way of Life

The wages of the agricultural worker during the last 20 years have risen from about £2 to over £5 a week.   Most of the farm cottages have water laid on, with indoor and modern conveniences.   Children of the shepherds and land workers are transported to the nearest school for their education.   The land worker now expects a greater degree of entertainment and amusement.   Radio sets are well-nigh universal. Every week considerable sums are spent on travelling to neighbouring towns to attend the cinema and football matches.   With all these attractions, entertainments and amusements it is doubtful if the craftsmen or agricultural workers are happier than they were in earlier times; certainly they seem less serene and less contented.

Housing

Apart from cottages annexed to the various farms and gradual improvements and modernisation according to the standards of the periods, there has been little extra building in the parish until comparatively recent years.

A magnificent new housing scheme has been built on the banks of the Fleet from Blackloch Farm to the Bridge of Fleet.   It is a most attractive colony, built in the form of a crescent with a fine roadway running throughout, and an excellent panorama is afforded to all the occupants.   The scheme was planned by the famous architect, Sir Frank Mears.   It consists of 12 bungalows of four apartments, 4 cottages of five apartments, 26 houses of four apartments, and 10 houses of five apartments.   It is well laid out with attractive garden plots verging the Dromore road.   All are more or less of the standard and traditional type.   No house gives access to the main road.   At the time of writing, plans have been submitted for the erection of a bungalow-type of nurse's home, complete with garage, reception room and all modern conveniences on a site in the aforementioned scheme.

Altogether 88 houses have been built since 1918 (52 of them since the end of the last war, 1945) and another ten houses are under consideration at present.

Mention was made in the last Account of two inns in Fleet Street. There is only one hotel in Fleet Street now: it is famed as the Anwoth Hotel, or Ship Inn, which keeps its link with past history and tradition. The owner has completely renovated, modernised and refurnished the place. He has also converted a piece of waste land opposite the hotel and made a beautiful garden sloping down to the water's edge just below the Fleet Bridge. Anglers come from far and wide and reside at the hotel. Several lochs in the district have been rented and stocked for angling enthusiasts and visitors. Another addition to the hotel has just been completed, in the form of a modern hall with all conveniences. This will serve as a catering centre for the large number of motor-coach travellers who tour Galloway during the summer season, and thus leave the hotel exclusively for residents. It is well booked all the year round. The new hall will also be used as a recreational centre for carpet bowling, the local darts club and other winter activities.

It is worthy of note that an artificial loch has been created at Ornockenoch, this being an ideal setting for fishing. It supplies power for the private hydro-electric scheme of Rusko estate, generating a quarter of a million units per annum, and supplying the mansion-house, Pulcree farm, the cottages and sawmill. A boathouse has also been constructed which houses the boats for the anglers.

The mansion-house of Ornockenoch is now occupied by Mrs. Buchanan, who has transformed the grounds, and has been successful in planting some rare Oriental shrubs in the policies. The view from the front door, with its natural setting, the loch in the immediate foreground, the Fleet slightly ahead and the hills beyond, is one of the most picturesque to be found anywhere.

Clubs and Organisations

Anwoth has an excellent curling club as a means of fostering goodwill, companionship and keen sportsmanship. It is the oldest curling club in the Stewartry. Curling is by far the most popular winter pastime with the men and appeals to all sections of the community. Rarely has a bonspiel been arranged in recent years owing to the lack of outdoor facilities and the nature of the weather. Matches are normally played on Ayr Ice Rink. The club is justly proud that two of its popular skips, J. Faed-Sproat and Tom Hamilton, were chosen for the Scottish Team which played in Canada and the United States of America in 1950.

The curling club was instituted on 30 December 1830. The old Minute Book carries the motto *Nunquam non paratus* meaning 'Never unprepared'. In the first minute it is recorded that 'curling was an ancient, honourable and manly game.' The centenary dinner of the club was held in the Town Hall, Gatehouse, on 2 January, 1931.

The Women's Rural Institute has a flourishing branch which meets monthly in Skyreburn School. Its membership averages 30. The programmes follow the official pattern of crafts, domestic science and allied feminine interests. Under the auspices of Anwoth Church a branch of the Woman's Guild meets monthly, usually in the library, Gatehouse, and occasionally at the manse, in a social capacity. Their programme is on devotional lines and stimulates interest in the Church's schemes, as well as greatly benefiting the fabric fund of the church. The membership of the guild is around 30.

A flourishing horticultural society exists jointly for the two parishes. Last year a splendid show was held in Gatehouse. The lairds and their gardening staffs give every encouragement to such ventures and this largely accounts for its popularity and its appeal to professional and amateur gardeners alike.

Another joint-association is the British Legion branch. This movement is very active, playing a magnificent role in all charitable appeals, and is specially concerned about the welfare of ex-service men. They have a keen body of officials. Colonel David Agnew, Anwoth Cottage, is president of the branch, which has 80 members. Organisations such as the Red Cross and Civil Defence are also well supported.

Churches

In a former report it was stated that there was a dissenting chapel in the parish near the Fleet Bridge. This has now become the church designated St. Mary's, Gatehouse-of-Fleet, under the Scottish Episcopal Church. Services are held monthly and according to the special festivals of the Christian year. The church is growing in numbers and has great prestige. It has a membership of approximately 35, who come from all the neighbouring parishes.

As far as can be estimated there are approximately 20 members of the Roman Catholic Church in the parish.

The church of Anwoth along with the Chapel of Culenes (*sic* for Cardoness) was granted to Holyrood Abbey by David I, confirmation being given by John, Bishop of Whithorn, 1189-1200, according to the Holyrood Charter. The existing Rutherford Shrine dates from 1627, but it was probably erected on the site of an older foundation. The first known owner of Cardoness was one David, son of Terr — probably one of the Anglo-Normans who crossed the Solway into Galloway and received grants of land for services rendered, leaving evidence of their residence in the remaining motehills. The site of this David's residence would likely be the Green Tower Mote at the back of Boreland farm. The chapel would be attached to his residence and the church in all probability would be on the site of the old Rutherford Church. There is no mention of Anwoth Church until the coming of Samuel Rutherford some 400 years later. He was appointed to the Parish of Anwoth in

1627 at the invitation of John Gordon of Lochinvar, Viscount Kenmure, who, at that time, resided at Rusko.

Mention was made in the last Account of the building of the new church and manse. The centenary of the church was commemorated in 1928. The church continues to be well supported by all members of the parish; its contribution to the life of the community is respected and appreciated. There is a Sunday school at Anwoth of around 20 members and one at Cardoness of about 15.

War Memorial

The War Memorial for the parish is in the Anwoth Church. Another one for the men of the two parishes was erected in Gatehouse around 1920, the names of the fallen in the second world war being added on side panels on the granite memorial.

As the bronze plate in the Anwoth Memorial was showing signs of deterioration, it was resolved by the church to remove the plate and instal a block of Sicilian marble to blend with the surround and the other memorials in the sanctuary. Thus the one marble memorial contains the names of the fallen in the two world wars. It was dedicated on 24 October 1948. The G.O.C. Lowland Division, Major-General E. Hakewell-Smith, gave an appropriate address, and the Convener of the County (Rev. J. A. Fisher) also took part. A former minister of the parish, the Rev. Frank William Saunders, who enlisted as a private in the first world war, became a lieutenant in the Argyll and Sutherland Highlanders, served in Palestine, and was killed in action 1 August 1918. His plaque was on the original memorial but was cut out and framed, and is now placed in the vestry gallery of portraits.

Political Parties

There is a very strong branch of the Conservative Party in the district, several of its leaders and officials being from this parish. Among the craftsmen and agricultural workers there is a semblance of support for the Labour Party. As far as can be ascertained there is no official organisation, certainly not in the parish. Local affairs are kept free of party politics and it is only at a time of a general election that one notices any sign of definite party allegiance.

Shops

There is now only one trading grocer's shop in the parish, next to the Anwoth Hotel. It is run by the Misses Dunning, members of an old business. The Co-operative Society operates from Gatehouse and employs a fleet of vans in the nature of travelling shops, which cover the entire parish. There is evidence of a marked growth in their trade and custom.

Dry Stane Dyking

The land of this parish is fenced almost entirely with dry stone dykes. Many of these are 200 years old and are still in good condition. Certainly they require periodic examination and systematic attention, but far less so than other forms of boundary lines. The dykes of Galloway were famous all over Scotland when enclosures were first undertaken. Samuel Smith, minister of Borgue, wrote a full description of the craft for the Account of 1842, when among the terms of reference for every parish was that of 'Enclosures'. James McTaggart, a rural poet, compiled the *Galloway Encyclopaedia*, and in that volume there appears an eighteen verse poem to 'Davie the Dyker', which depicts the art and craft of dyking. Col. F. Rainsford-Hannay, Cardoness and Kirkdale Estates, has been a great enthusiast for the craft and has arranged regular courses of instruction as well as many practical demonstrations all over the country. He has contributed many articles on the subject to the appropriate journals; he has also published booklets on the same theme.

Electricity

Electric light was installed in Gatehouse Town Hall on 30 January 1931. Most of the farms have electric lighting and power for driving farm machinery and operating the milking machines. There are, however, still a few farms without it. A number of the farms have their own generating plants, in some cases petrol engines, in others diesel, which are usually more powerful. The hydro-electric plant on Rusko estate is the only private scheme on a big scale.

For domestic purposes those farms and houses without electricity have installed insulated cookers, which have the great advantage of burning wood, coal or peat.

Notes on Game

Black Game appear to have vanished since 1919 and grouse have almost disappeared. The land has become 'sheep-sick', and the sheep have to be vaccinated from time to time for various ailments. A great deal of damage is still done by rabbits, but steps are being taken to deal with this menace to crops and grazing. Foxes have increased during the last five or six years. Roe deer are fairly plentiful, and a few can be seen quite regularly in front of the manse. Red deer have been observed in the Cardoness estate. Pheasants are still in good supply; a few golden pheasants can occasionally be seen.

Population

The population of the parish does not vary a great deal. However, there is a tendency for a reduction of staff in the mansion-houses, and also on the farms, owing to the high cost of wages, and the increasing mechanisation. On the other hand, there has been a considerable increase in the population with the establishment of the new housing colony by the banks of the Fleet.

Figures of the population of the parish are as follows:—

1801	637
1851	900 (maximum ever recorded)
1901	651
1911	688
1921	611
1931	555
1951	658

Quite a number of the newer residents have come from the south, and have settled in the larger houses as they became available for sale; most of these newcomers, however, are in the retired group. Generally speaking the residents have roots in, or affinities with, Galloway and these factors normally determine choice of settlement.

1951

CHAPTER 7

THE PARISH OF BALMACLELLAN

by the REV. WILLIAM PEEBLES

Physical Features

Balmaclellan is situated in the northern part of Kirkcudbrightshire and is one of the four parishes comprising what is known as Glenkens. The prefix, *bal*, is from the Gaelic word *baile*, meaning a town; the remainder was the surname of one, John Maclellan, who obtained a charter from King James III of the lands and village in 1466; thus the name signified the town or manor of the Maclellans.

The parish is irregular in outline, and in dimension is roughly twelve miles long by seven miles broad. It is mostly rough and mountainous; Blackcraig is 1,332 feet, Troquhain, 1,200 feet, and Wallace's Rigg, 875 feet above sea level; there are several small lochs which provide good fishing.

The parish is bounded by the rivers Ken on the west and Urr on the east; while the burns Craig and Shirmers mark the southern boundary and Garple Burn, the north. There has been a great decrease in the quantity of game in recent years. Grouse have become very scarce, as also have black game. Partridges, never very numerous, have not varied so much. Wild pheasants are fairly numerous but none have been reared since before the second world war. In the last few years the entire district has been disfigured with molehills, because, no doubt, of the scarcity of trappers.

A feature of Balmaclellan is the hump-back shape of so many of the fields, 'drums' as they are called in this part of the country. Fortunately, the advent of the tractor has somewhat alleviated the burden imposed upon both man and beast in the cultivation of the land.

The village stands high in the north-west of the parish and commands a magnificent view of the Ken valley and the long range of rugged hills in the west stretching from the neighbouring parish of Kells to beyond Carsphairn.

History

It is hard to believe that this parish, presenting as it does to-day such a perfect picture of rural peace, should be associated with persecution, torture, and bloodshed, and yet these are facts of history. The Holy Linn, a beauty spot near Barscobe Farm, sheltered congregations of Covenanters assembled for worship during the Persecution, and the 'outed' minister of Balmaclellan baptised children at a natural font in the waters of the Garple Burn. When Sir William Bannatyne came into Galloway after the Pentland Rising, his soldiers searched for David MacGill in this parish. The Covenanter escaped, dressed as a woman, but his wife was tortured and died as a result. Elspeth MacEwan, who was tried for witchcraft in 1698, lived in a solitary little house on Cubbox farm land. Following her arrest she was imprisoned, tortured for two years, condemned and burned near Kirkcudbright.

'Old Mortality', made famous by Sir Walter Scott in his book bearing that title, had close associations with Balmaclellan. While he travelled far and wide through Galloway in his self-appointed task of restoring and preserving the graves of Covenanters, his wife supported their family by school teaching in this parish. A stone monument, depicting 'Old Mortality' mounted on his white pony, stands in the grounds of Holme House, home of Viscount and Lady Templetown. In the kirkyard, a tombstone bears the following inscription—'To the memory of Robert Paterson, stone engraver, well-known as Old Mortality, who died at Bankend of Caerlaverock, 14 February 1800 aged 88'.

In the beginning of the sixteenth century the church was annexed to the Chapel Royal at Stirling and served by a vicar pensioner. At the time of the Reformation the prebend was held by Sir George Gray, who let the parsonage and vicarage tithes to Robert Gordon of Shirmers.

A standing stone on Dalarran Holm is understood to mark the spot where a Danish warrior of position fell in battle between the Danes and the Scots.

A round stone, measuring about four inches in diameter and three-quarters inch thick, with a half inch diameter hole off centre forming an eccentric, was found by Mr. Thomson, Shirmers, while ploughing one of his fields last year. This has been identified as a fine example of a stone-age spinning whorl.

The old castle ruin beside Shirmers farmhouse is believed to have been destroyed by fire on 16 June 1568 by the Regent Moray, as chastisement for the owner who had sided with Queen Mary. Kenmure Castle, on the opposite side of the river Ken, was burned at the same time.

Balmaclellan has never lacked men and women possessed with the spirit of enterprise and the desire to serve country and community. A simple but stately memorial, on the Dumfries road overlooking the village, bears the names of local men who made the supreme sacrifice during the two world wars. Two of them gained the Military Medal. The names of all men and women who served during the second world war are inserted in a Book of Remembrance which lies in the church.

Mrs. Ethel Bristowe, Craig House, though advanced in years, is an accomplished artist and the author of several well known books dealing with Biblical research. She and her husband, the late Sydney Bristowe, provided a fine playground for the children of the parish; it is situated in the village and equipped with swings, chute, horizontal bars and sand

pit.   In 1940 they gave a small hall completely fitted and furnished
to the local branch of the Women's Rural Institute, Mrs. Bristowe herself being its first President.

The Church and community have been ably served by their
ministers, and in this connection an unusual feature may be noted, that
no less than three members of one family have ministered in the local
parish church:—

Rev. George Murray of Troquhain, 1837-81.

Rev. George Murray of Troquhain, son of above, 1914-20.

Rev. T. K. Johnstone, son-in-law of above, 1921-32, now
minister at East Kilbride, near Glasgow.

Population

1801	554
1851	1,145
1901	634
1911	559
1921	557
1931	627
1951	550

The census figures show that the parish population, after a two-fold
increase in the first half of the nineteenth century, has now declined to
a lower level than in 1801.   It has not varied greatly, however, over
the past 50 years.

Water and Drainage

Outwith the village, water supplies are still almost exclusively private.
The village and immediate neighbourhood have a public supply which
until 1949 was drawn from a storage tank situated on a hill above the
village.   In that year, however, the water of Lochinvar was piped to
the existing village mains, giving a much more satisfactory service.   A
new reservoir is at present being built.   The village is supplied with an
adequate sewage system.

Electricity

The Galloway Water Power Scheme, situated in the neighbouring parish
of Dalry, has proved a great boon to the whole county.   Electric power
was available through the national grid system *via* Kirkcudbright County
Council's electricity lines before the Galloway Hydro-Electric Scheme
commenced generating power in March 1935.   The Glenlee Power
Station utilises the water catchment area of the Galloway Dee—345
sq. miles, with the addition of 50 sq. miles of the Loch Doon area.
Maximum output of the scheme is 103,000 kw. per annum; the average
is in the region of 30,000 kw. per annum.   Balmaclellan is supplied
from a main feeder from the Glenlee Station and electric power has
been introduced into almost every house in the village and near neighbourhood.   Many of the surrounding farms have been connected, and
it is anticipated that within a few years power mains will cover the
whole parish.   On many farms milking is done by electrically operated

machines, and the wide range of domestic appliances now available for lighting, heating and cooking by means of electricity add to the comfort, health and efficiency of the householders.

Gas

In many homes, particularly the more remote cottages, 'rural gas' is used, and these installations are regularly serviced by an agent from New Galloway.

Halls

Until the end of the first world war the village school was the only building suitable for social functions. In 1919 a commodious hall was erected in the village. This building is in process of being enlarged and having a new kitchen, committee rooms and toilets added. The hall is managed by a local committee. In 1940 a small hall known as 'Craig Room' was given to the W.R.I. by Mr. and Mrs. Sydney Bristowe of Craig. This building, beautifully fitted and furnished, has proved a great asset to the community.

Transport

Roads are in very good condition. The main Ayr/Castle-Douglas road passes within one mile of the village and is serviced by double-decked buses. A local bus service between Dalry and Dumfries is convenient for both village and country travellers. The nearest railway station is at Mossdale, some five miles from New Galloway, although the station at Parton is more conveniently situated on the Castle-Douglas bus route.

Health Services

One doctor resident in New Galloway and a District Nurse in Dalry serve all the Glenkens, although several people are patients of doctors practising in Castle-Douglas. The National Health Service provides first class facilities for the sick and suffering. There is the Cottage Hospital at Castle-Douglas, the Royal Infirmary and Cresswell Maternity Hospital at Dumfries.

Education

There is one primary school in the village, and children are transported daily from and to their homes in the more distant parts of the parish. There are 56 scholars on the roll at present. The staff consists of the schoolmaster and one lady assistant. Fourteen children from Balmaclellan attend Dalry Secondary School, where two ladies from Balmaclellan are teachers. The nearest senior secondary school is at Kirkcudbright. Three girls and one boy from this parish, who are scholars at Kirkcudbright Academy, stay during the week in the Hostel or in lodgings.

F

Voluntary Organisations

The following organisations function in the parish: Boys' Club; Girl Guides; Badminton Club; Junior Agricultural Society; Youth Fellowship (the latter, with the Sunday School, comes under the jurisdiction of the church); Woman's Guild; Women's Rural Institute; Musical Association; Dramatic Club; Curling Club; Football Club; Carpet Bowling Club; Handicrafts Class; and the local branch of the British Legion.

The Church

The parish church is situated in the village and is a good building, capable of seating about 300. Heating and lighting are by electricity. There are 216 communicants and six elders. The Session Clerk, Mr. Charles Robinson, has held office for 40 years. The present minister was ordained and inducted to the charge of Balmaclellan in October 1949.

Housing

There are 150 houses in the parish, of which seven are large. Nearly all of them are substantially built, roomy, sanitary and well situated. A great many of them have water and electric light. Some of the farm houses have been recently modernised. There are 12 council houses, 2 with two rooms and kitchenette, 4 with three rooms and kitchenette and 6 with four rooms and kitchenette. Four of the four-room houses are made of steel, covered with rough cast, and were built early in 1949; the remainder are 15 years old. In the 150 houses there are 685 rooms, so that with a population of 651 the average is slightly more than one room to a person. Almost every house has its garden, and the people take great delight and pride in growing both vegetables and flowers.

Agriculture, Industries and Commerce

This is wholly an agricultural district. At one time there were two threshing mills, one at Ironmacannie and the other at Grennan; these are not now used, and mobile mills visit the farms in turn. There have been great changes in farming methods in the past decade. The introduction of power-driven machinery has transformed not only the methods employed, but the whole life of the agricultural worker. The use of tractors, double, and even quadruple hydraulic ploughs, and innumerable complex implements allows the farmer to work more quickly and to cultivate more land. Science has brought a new knowledge of the land and by means of fertilisers and manure compounds has shown how best to obtain maximum results from it.

Drovers no longer take sheep and cattle on foot to the market. Nowadays all animals are transported by road in commodious and comfortable trucks that ensure their being fresh and in good condition on the day of the sale. Most farmers have their own motor car. Castle-Douglas, which is 13 miles from Balmaclellan, is now recognised as one of the most important cattle market centres in the country. Ordinary sales are held on Mondays and attested cattle sales on Thursdays.

There are 49 farms in this parish, 14 of them being owned by the farmers themselves. Rent is approximately eighteen shillings an acre. Farms are of average size. Only three farms have not changed hands during the past 30 years. One farm, Highpark, has been occupied by generations of the Shaw family for 150 years.

The past ten years have seen a decided change in this district from beef stock to dairy farming. This is shown in milk returns of the Marketing Board: in 1950 the milk returns from Balmaclellan were 289,486 gallons, whereas in 1940 they amounted to only 90,847 gallons. Many farms have lately been modernised in order to bring them up to the required standard for accommodating attested cattle. Sheep reared in this district are mostly of the black-faced variety. Live stock in the parish is made up as follows: Horses, 105; cattle, 2,186; sheep, 15,111; pigs, 51; poultry, 8,180. Apart from what was used for local consumption, the packing station at Dumfries accepted 173,052 dozen eggs from poultry keepers in this parish during 1950.

The scarcity of butcher meat during and after the war created a great demand for rabbits, and Balmaclellan's seven trappers were kept busy. Upwards of 60,000 rabbits were trapped in this parish in one season, most of them being sent to large centres in England such as Leeds, Sheffield and Birmingham.

An area of 1,921 acres has been taken over by the Forestry Commission in the north-east part of the parish. Of this, trees have been planted on 771 acres and the remainder is in course of preparation.

There are two shops in the village, both of them general provision stores. There is a blacksmith's shop, joiner's shop and post office with a postmistress, one spare-time postwoman and two spare-time postmen. Many of the farmers now have private telephones installed.

Butcher meat, fish and groceries are supplied to the village by vans which come from Dumfries, Castle-Douglas and New Galloway. The vans also supply the farms and distant houses regularly, usually twice weekly. Coal is delivered by a merchant from New Galloway and an agent from the mining district of Dalmellington.

There is no resident policeman in the parish. There is a policeman at New Galloway and an office and resident police sergeant at Dalry.

The Way of Life

The general standard of life in the parish is good. The inhabitants are kindly, hospitable and industrious. Family life is well maintained, and an intimate community spirit is manifest. The people are proud of their district and its past achievements, its associations with the Covenanters and its close proximity to Dumfries and Ayr with all that these places mean to lovers of Robert Burns. They are very sociable, and love nothing better than an evening's entertainment where local people are taking an active part; for some years back a special feature each winter has been the successful production of a pantomime by the minister and the headmaster.

Radio plays a large part in the people's lives, keeping them in touch with current events of world-wide interest. An inter-community spirit of friendly rivalry is maintained through a common love for amateur dramatics. Each small community has its own dramatic club and single and three-act plays are produced during the winter months, culminating in the county dramatic festival held each year. The national press has a wide circulation in the parish, as also have the provincial papers, the *Dumfries Standard* and the *Galloway News*.

Winter amusements are dancing, music, handwork, amateur dramatics, carpet bowling and curling (enthusiasts for the 'Roarin' Game' travel to the indoor rinks at Ayr and Glasgow). Older people enjoy whist drives, and these are a common means of raising funds. During summer the farmers are busy and social life is somewhat restricted, but for those who have the time and inclination good fishing and golf are available.

Church attendance is not what it was 50 years ago, but the people are interested in church life and affairs. Indeed, to-day there is a new and encouraging consciousness of the reality of religion in everyday life. In this parish the work of the minister is as much community as it is congregational. Parents are reluctant to bring their children to church for baptism, but prefer the minister to observe the Sacrament in their homes, and on such occasions the relatives of both parents are invariably present. It is indeed a celebration.

Another fine feature of this parish is mutual sympathy in times of trouble. A farmer incapacitated through accident or illness can always count on help from his neighbours. At a funeral, the men folk attend from far and near; at such times the house service is usually held out of doors in order that all may take part.

Men and women are aware of the vital part agriculture plays in the life of the nation. They are willing, indeed eager, to make a worthy contribution to the world's need, and given the opportunity and support they can be counted upon to serve the common good. They believe in the future prosperity of Scotland and are prepared to give, and if need be to sacrifice, in order that their children may inherit the fruits of their toil and service.

1951

CHAPTER 8

THE PARISH OF BALMAGHIE

by the REV. JOHN W. T. DICKIE

Boundaries and Extent

Balmaghie is an inland parish of the Stewartry of Kirkcudbright. It is bounded on the north by Kells, the Black Water of Dee separating the two parishes. On the east, the river Dee divides Balmaghie from Parton, Crossmichael and Kelton. On the south, the march is with Tongland and Twynholm, and on the west, with Girthon. The greatest length, north and south, is over seven miles; the greatest width, east and west, about five. The area is 21,059 acres.

Natural Features

East, along the river, the land is about 150 feet above sea-level. It rises gradually westwards, reaching at the Meikle Dornell hill a height of some 500 feet. It dips again to the valley of the Laurieston Burn and Woodhall Loch, and thence rises steeply to hilly moorland country which continues to the Girthon march. Some of the hills here reach a height of over 900 feet.

The rocks are mainly Silurian, with some granite in the north-west, where the parish boundary touches the fringe of the Cairnsmore granite mass. There are considerable sand deposits near Laurieston.

The scenery is varied, and much of it is gently beautiful, especially near the lovely Woodhall Loch. There are some fine woods, but a great deal of timber was felled during the second world war, and since. The oaks and beeches cut in the Laurieston area were a great loss to the amenity there—a loss scarcely replaced by the conifers of the Forestry Commission.

There are two villages. Laurieston, near the centre of the parish, has 43 houses, with 123 inhabitants. Bridge-of-Dee, at the extreme southern tip, has 27 houses, with 65 inhabitants. There are two other small groups of houses—Glenlochar (six houses, 20 people) and Shankfoot (six houses, 17 people).

History

That the area was inhabited in Neolithic times is indicated by the discovery of two stone axe-heads at Hensol. One of these is a work of art so perfectly proportioned and finished as to suggest that it was intended only for some ritual or magic purpose. The early history is quite obscure until the fourteenth century. There are earthworks at Duchrae, popularly, but improbably, known as 'The Roman Camp'.

The recent discovery of a larger, indubitably Roman, fort a few miles away at Glenlochar (but on the Crossmichael side of the Dee), makes the possibility of the Duchrae 'camp' being Roman a shade less unlikely than it would otherwise be. It *could* perhaps be some kind of outpost.

There are remains of Iron Age forts at Craig and Edgarton, and also a fort at Dinnance which may be a mote of the Anglo-Norman settlement. On the strength of a place-name near Laurieston (Quintinespie), it has been precariously suggested that here was the scene of the reconciliation between the rebel lords of Galloway and King William the Lion in 1174. 'When the Galwegians came to meet the King, some Scottish bishops stepped in between them and through their mediation they were reconciled.' (Fordun). Quintinespie would in that case mean 'the bishops' battle' (*cointin easbuig*).

Much the most striking and interesting relic of olden times is the ruin of Threave Castle, on an island in the Dee. It was built by Archibald, Earl of Douglas, in the fourteenth century, on the site of an earlier fortalice built by Fergus, first Lord of Galloway, in the twelfth century. The story of Threave has often been told and need not be repeated here. It was finally ruined by the War Committee of the Covenanters in 1640. At a meeting on the spot in that year, the Laird of Balmaghie was charged with the duty of dismantling it.

A description of the above-mentioned antiquities may be found in vol. 2 of the Royal Commission's *Report on the Ancient Monuments of Galloway*.

Balmaghie was involved in the disturbances connected with the Levellers, early in the eighteenth century. The Levellers' rising was an active protest against the enclosures of land by the lairds. The story of the Levellers may be found in several books on Galloway. Their last stand was made at Duchrae in this parish in 1724.

Church History

The old parish church stands on a low hill above the Dee, near the site of an older church of which only a fragment remains. The present structure dates from 1794. It is a beautiful church, with a little tower of distinctive charm. The original church was one of those bestowed by Fergus, Lord of Galloway, on Holyrood Abbey, and was dedicated to St. Andrew. The full story of 'The Kirk above Dee Water' is contained in the book of that name by Professor H. M. B. Reid, who was minister here from 1882 until his appointment to the chair of Divinity at Glasgow in 1904. Dr. Reid was also the author of *A Cameronian Apostle*, the story of the most famous of Balmaghie ministers, the Rev. John McMillan. He became minister here in 1701, and was deposed—for doctrinal reasons—in 1703. In defiance of the presbytery, and with the enthusiastic support of the great majority of his parishioners, he continued to occupy the pulpit, and manse, until 1727, when he left voluntarily, and joined the United Societies, which later became the Reformed Presbyterian Church.

Mention should be made of the Rev. Samuel Martin, minister here from 1769 to 1776, who was the author of the 12th paraphrase.

In the churchyard are the graves of three Covenanting martyrs. Two of the same name—David Halliday—lie in the same grave, which is marked by a table stone with an inscription in quaint but vigorous rhyme.

Samuel Rutherford Crockett, the novelist, a native of the parish, is buried here in the family burying-ground.

The parish War Memorial (1914-18) is a tablet of hard freestone built into the wall, outside, near the door. It records 20 names. Though many from the parish served in the second world war, happily no names had to be added to the Memorial.

The church possesses some fine communion plate, particularly two beautiful cups of silver, dating from about 1617.

After the Disruption, a church was erected in Laurieston in 1845, by those who adhered to the Free Church. This too, though small, has a modest dignity of its own. The first 'placed' minister was the Rev. John Johnstone, who was the author of an ingenious rhyming history of the Church of Scotland from the earliest times to the Disruption.

At the union of the Church of Scotland and the United Free Church in 1929, the parish was divided for church purposes into two parts, the minister of Balmaghie having his sphere of work in the eastern half, and the minister of Laurieston in the western. This arrangement worked well, and lasted until 1949, when the minister of Balmaghie retired, and the two congregations united under the minister of Laurieston, who thus became minister of Balmaghie—the whole parish. This has proved a very harmonious union. Both buildings continue to be used. They are some four miles apart. There is a church hall at Bridge-of-Dee, where services are held monthly; also a church hall at Laurieston, used for week-night activities. It was originally the Free Church School, which S. R. Crockett attended in his childhood. The congregations were about equal in size at the time of the union. Present membership of the united charge is 218.

Some of the old church records appear to have been lost before 1888, but the following exist, and are (at present) in the custody of the minister; Balmaghie Session records, 1768-77, and 1839 to the present day; Laurieston Session and Deacons' Court records, 1852-1949. The following are with the Registrar-General: Balmaghie Church, Record of Births 1768-1854 (except 1770-1804); and Record of Marriages 1805-54 (except 1838-9).

The Stewartry War Committee of the Covenanters met occasionally in this parish in 1640 and 1641. Their records have been printed and published (J. Nicholson, Kirkcudbright, 1855). The Presbytery of Kirkcudbright also met here from time to time in the eighteenth century, at Clachanpluck (now Laurieston).

Distinguished Natives

The best known is Samuel Rutherford Crockett, the novelist (b. Little Duchrae, 1859). His books had a great vogue, and some are still popular. He drew many of his characters from life; and whatever his faults of sentimentality and over-emphasis, which he shares with the rest of the 'Kailyard School', now so much blown-upon, he could tell a good tale, and depict with skill certain racy Galloway types such as may still, though perhaps decreasingly, be found in the locality. He died in France in May 1914. A monument was erected to his memory at Laurieston in 1932.

The following also deserve mention.

William Neilson (b. Dornell, 1772). His epitaph says 'his days were spent with care and industry in his native land and in America, being ever a zealous advocate for civil and religious liberty. He left a donation of five pounds per annum for the education of poor children'.

The Hon. John Neilson (Dornell, 1776), a member of the Executive Council of Canada.

John Johnston (Barnboard Mill, 1781), became 'merchant prince' in New York, travelled widely, and was a benefactor to his native parish.

William Hepburn (Bridge-of-Dee). He died in 1950 at the early age of 59. He became Director of Education for his native Stewartry, and held the same office for Lanarkshire at the time of his death. He was a pioneer of modern educational methods, and the initiator of a survey of the intelligence of Scottish children—the first national enterprise of its kind.

Place-names

The parish offers plenty of scope for those who want to play this dangerous game. Most of the old names are Gaelic, as one would expect since Gaelic was the language of Galloway from the ninth century when it superseded Welsh (or Brittonic, the ancestor of modern Welsh) and only died out, it is said, in the seventeenth. A Brittonic name survives in one important instance in the parish—Threave (W. *tref*, house). The old name of the parish itself was Balmakethe, the last syllable of which looks suspiciously like the old Welsh word for 'wood' (cf. Dalkeith), in modern Welsh *coed*. But the rest of the word is Gaelic, with the familiar *bal* (house or farm). The modern form of the name, 'Balmaghie', is a personal name meaning MacGhie's house. In 1478 a William Macge is styled 'of Balmage'. Gaelic names are themselves sometimes replaced by English ones. For example, the old name of Laurieston was Clachanpluck,—*clachan*, village, and *ploc*, lump or clod, referring either to the nature of the soil or to the numerous hummocks of ground in the vicinity. 'Laurieston' is derived from the name of an eighteenth century laird. Another instance of a change from a Gaelic name to an English one is that of the largest loch in the parish. At one time its name, like that of the house beside it, was Grenoch. The name of the house was deliberately changed, by a former owner, to Woodhall, and the loch has come to be called by that name too. It seldom gets its older name now. Grenoch may mean either 'sunny place' (*grian*), or 'gravelly' (*greannach*).

Plant and Animal Life

Trees will be dealt with under the section on Afforestation. Other plants hardly call for special mention, as there are no rarities, and none peculiar to the parish. Bracken is all too plentiful, but the use of bracken-cutters helps to check it.

Of animals, roe deer are fairly common. Red deer are rare visitors from the hill-country to the north and west. Foxes seem to be increasing in numbers. Badgers are rarely seen. Rabbits are everywhere. Hedgehogs seem unusually plentiful. Adders are common and have been known to find their way into houses, and even, on one occasion, into church, to the alarm of the lieges.

Amongst the rarer bird visitors or residents recently seen are the hen-harrier, marsh-harrier, peregrine, bittern, smew, greater spotted woodpecker, and pied fly-catcher. The lapwing, formerly very common, is now much scarcer. The corncrake, after having been unheard for about twenty years, was heard this year in several places. Grouse and blackgame declined during the war but seem to be on the increase again. There are many owls of different kinds. There are at least four kinds of goose, and all the commoner species of inland duck, including the goosander.

Two interesting facts may be worth recording. On 14 November 1950 a Greenland Whitefront goose was shot on Livingston estate, to which was attached a ring showing that it had been ringed at Kangiussack, West Greenland, on 27 July 1949; and, whereas fifty years ago on Balmaghie estate they used to shoot 400 to 500 partridges a year, and practically no pheasants, now the average is nearer 50 partridges a year, and from 200 to 300 wild pheasants.

Afforestation, as might be expected, is affecting bird life. Amongst the trees, whaups, stonechats, and wheatears give way to thrushes, tits, warblers, and pigeons; with a mixture of woodland and moorland types on the forest fringes.

As for fish, brown trout are plentiful in the burns and some lochs; pike and perch in others. There are salmon in the Dee. A pearl-bearing mussel is obtained in the upper reaches of that river, and pearls of good quality are occasionally found.

Agriculture

This industry employs, directly or indirectly, about 90 per cent. of the working population of the parish. There are 48 farms, 21 owner-occupied Approximate acreage is 5,790 arable; 13,475 rough pasture; and 242 meadow. The maximum acreage capable of cultivation is thought to have been attained. Because of the Government's policy of self-sufficiency during the second world war, far more ground is cropped now than ever before. On the farms on the low ground, the proportion of ploughed land is approximately two-fifths. Farms vary in size from holdings of a few acres to large hill-farms of over 1,000 acres; the average for arable farms is about 150 acres; and for hill-farms, 400. Rent varies greatly with the type of land, the average being 25s for arable, and 7s 6d for hill-land. The usual length of lease is 15 years. By far the largest number of low-ground farms are now devoted to milk production from Ayrshire cows. The milk so produced is collected by motor-lorry and conveyed to Kirkcudbright for transmission to the large industrial areas, or for manufacture. Complete freedom from bovine tuberculosis ('attestation') has been almost attained. Most farmers are improving their stock, and are achieving entry in the records or pedigree books of the various societies. Regarding sheep: on the high ground Black-face lambs are still produced, but on the marginal land crosses between the Border Leicester ram and the Black-face ewe are bred; and on the pure arable land considerable numbers of top-grade cross Suffolk Down-halfbred lambs.

The soil is fairly light. It is said that Balmaghie needs a wet day once a week to keep it in good order. The average yearly rainfall is 50 inches.

Methods of farming have changed greatly during the last 15 years. The number of workhorses is rapidly decreasing. Many farms are now without horses; others keep only one pair where formerly large numbers were employed. Their place has been taken by tractors, which carry out the work more quickly, though not so neatly. Shortage of labour during the war speeded up the change.

Farms generally are in a good state of repair, though there is still a balance of repairs to be done; the legacy of the war years. Cottages are being modernised, but the cost of building, and the absence of piped water, necessarily slow down the work. The majority of farm-workers still live in cottages provided on the farm by the employer. Dry stone dykes are still much in evidence, though when they fall into disrepair, post and wire tend to replace them. The craft of dyking has by no means died out however. There are indeed signs of a revival of interest in this fine craft—partly it may be because of the high cost of fencing material.

Afforestation

Very little has been done by private owners in recent times, though this aspect of cultivation is receiving attention at the time of writing. The Forestry Commission however is planting large areas in the north-west of the parish—the 'Laurieston Forest'. This forest, extending to 4,405 acres, was formed in 1938. New plantations extend to 1,100 acres and consist mainly of Sitka and Norway spruces, Japanese and European larches and pines, with some promising small stands of Douglas Fir, Grand Silver Fir, and Western Hemlock. Only six of the forestry staff reside in the parish at present, mostly in Forestry Commission houses.

The forest will eventually, however, employ about 50 men and women, and it is hoped that most of these will live in Forestry Commission houses to be built in Laurieston. Opinion varies much on the question of taking over sheep country, with its food and wool producing potentialities, for planting. But afforestation will go a long way in the arrest and reversal of rural depopulation. For example, Laurieston will be doubled in size if the hopes expressed above materialise. Moreover, forestry brings work to local tradesmen, and trains new men in the crafts of the woodman—crafts which were slowly dying out. It is hoped that in due course a new prosperity will develop about the forest areas.

Other Industries

There are three joiners in the parish, one each at Laurieston, Glenlochar, and Bridge-of-Dee. Two sandpits at Laurieston employ a few men. The average output is 300 tons a month for each pit. A mason and builder's business at Laurieston, mainly a family affair, gives some employment. Some half-dozen men work at present with timber-felling firms, cutting and sawing timber in neighbouring parishes, to which the men are conveyed by lorry. There was a blacksmith's shop at Laurieston, which closed down a few months ago, and is not likely to be reopened. A father and son run a haulage and contractor's business. There are two small general shops, with post offices, one at Laurieston, the other at Bridge-of-Dee. There are small nursing and domestic staffs at Laurieston Hall Hospital. A number of elderly retired people live in the villages.

Housing and Social Services

Housing on the whole may be said to be fairly good as rural parishes go. At least there are no shockingly bad instances, though of course there is plenty of room for improvement. Overcrowding is not a serious problem. Many farms and cottages have been modernised in recent years, and the process is still going on. Most farms, and nearly all the village houses, have electricity. Laurieston street is lit with electricity. This village has also a fairly good gravitation water supply. There are water-taps in the street, and 19 of its houses have a water supply laid on, with indoor sanitation. Under a county scheme, water is being brought to Bridge-of-Dee, and ultimately this will come to Laurieston also, to augment or replace the present supply. A sewage scheme is also planned for each village. Septic tanks are used at present. No county council houses have been erected so far. Some are promised for the villages. The sooner they come the better, as there is a demand for houses. Probably we shall have to wait for the houses until the new water and drainage schemes materialise; and this applies to the projected Forestry Commission houses as well. Four new houses have been erected already in the area.

Gardens as a rule are well cultivated, mostly for utilitarian rather than for decorative purposes.

Lack of housing accommodation on an adequate scale probably accounts for the fact that comparatively few summer visitors come to the parish in spite of its many attractions. There was at one time a hotel at Lochenbreck, on the uplands above Laurieston, with a chalybeate well said to have tonic properties. This was a popular resort 50 years ago, but is now a ruin. There are no hotels, or boarding-houses, in the parish; nor any public house, either, though there were four or five a hundred years ago. The last closed down some 30 years since.

A county scavenging scheme was instituted a few years ago, refuse being removed weekly, by motor dust-cart, from the villages and places *en route*. The parish is visited frequently by tradesmen's vans, mainly from Castle-Douglas, but also from Kirkcudbright and New Galloway.

Castle-Douglas is the main shopping centre, and there is a considerable exodus from Balmaghie to the town on Monday, the market day. The nearest doctors are in Castle-Douglas. So are the banks, the fire brigade, the police, and the most convenient, if not actually the nearest, railway station. In fact it is our metropolis. When we speak of 'the town' that is where we mean. A bus runs from it five times on Mondays and Saturdays, and four times on Wednesdays, to Mossdale and back *via* Glenlochar and Laurieston (no service on other days), and this, except for private transport, forms the main means of communication with the outside world for the largest part of the parish, which is therefore rather isolated. The main Galloway highway, Dumfries to Stranraer, crosses the extreme southern tip of Balmaghie near Bridge-of-Dee, which village therefore, with its immediate neighbourhood, has a good service of buses each way daily. The Castle-Douglas to Kirkcudbright branch of the railway also passes through this southern tip, and there is a station at Bridge-of-Dee, but it is now used for a limited inwards goods traffic only.

Most, if not all, of the farmers have cars and so have several others. Besides the fraction of the main road already mentioned, the parish is traversed by two through roads, which cross at Laurieston. One, leaving the Castle-Douglas to Ayr road in Crossmichael parish, enters Balmaghie at Glenlochar bridge, goes westward to Laurieston, and thence, through fine scenery, to Gatehouse-of-Fleet. The other is part of the Kirkcudbright-Ayr road, and runs here northward from the march with Tongland to that with Kells. There are several minor roads. All public roads are excellent.

Schools

There are two schools, both primary. Laurieston has a headmaster, a lady assistant, and 41 pupils. Glenlochar school has a headmistress, a lady assistant, and 20 pupils from Balmaghie, but it serves part of Crossmichael also and has as many pupils in addition from that parish. Further, eight children from the Bridge-of-Dee area attend Rhonehouse school in Kelton, as being the nearest. Similarly six children from the north of the parish attend Mossdale school in Kells. Children over twelve are transported by bus to Castle-Douglas High School (a three-year comprehensive secondary school). There are 20 of these. There is one pupil at Kirkcudbright Academy. The school population therefore at the time of writing is 96. In 1873, when the School Board was formed, and a census of children taken, it was 198.

Dinner is provided at school for the children.

Until a year ago the schools also served as libraries, boxes of books being sent quarterly from the county library in Castle-Douglas. This service is still continued for the children, but tor adult readers has been superseded by a better one. At fortnightly intervals, a large and luxuriously appointed library caravan visits the villages with a good selection of books. It stops for half an hour or so, allowing time for leisured choice, and has proved popular. Fiction is the commonest choice but general literature is not neglected. The Stewartry was the first, and, until recently, the only county in Scotland to have this admirable service.

Population

The following census figures show the changes in population during the past 150 years.

1801	969
1831	1,416 (highest ever recorded)
1851	1,217
1901	802
1911	770
1921	764
1931	650
1951	681 (341 men, 340 women)

The decline during the century 1831-1931 was no doubt due to the cumulative effect of a variety of causes; the grouping of small farms into larger ones; lack of opportunity for the more ambitious; increasing mechanisation of farms; smaller families; in fact, the social and economic factors which affected the whole country. The 1951 figures show a small but gratifying increase. The ebb tide may have turned. The increase will be due partly to prosperity in the farming industry, and partly to forestry requirements. Of the adult population it is doubtful if 50 per cent. will be natives. Of the rest, the majority will have come from other parts of the Stewartry; some from neighbouring counties in the south-west; and a few from farther afield.

Estates and Mansion-houses

The following are the principal estates and houses with their present occupants.

1. Balmaghie—Mrs. Hutchinson.
2. Livingston—Mr. H. L. Lockhart Mure.
3. Slogarie—Major Milner Gibson.
4. Hensol—Marquess and Marchioness of Ailsa. The older name of this estate was Duchrae, still preserved in the farm name, Mains of Duchrae.

5. Dornell—Lt.-Cmdr. G. R. Muir (R.N.)
6. Netherhall—Col. W. J. M. Ross.
7. Laurieston—This estate was sold and broken up about twelve years ago. The house, Laurieston Hall (earlier Woodhall, earlier still Grenoch) was bought by the county council and used as an infectious diseases hospital. It is now under the Dumfries and Galloway Hospital Board and is used as an overflow from Lochmaben sanatorium. At the moment there are 15 patients, but there is room for more than twice that number. Its future is uncertain.

Community Life

Owing to the way the population is grouped round widely separated village centres, there is not much sense of community *as a parish*. One organisation which does represent the parish as a whole is the church, including an active branch of the Woman's Guild, with 40 members. Another is the curling club (24 members) which is a redoubtable one, and has five times carried off the Queenshill Cup, the county championship. Another comprehensive parish function was the annual ploughing match, but it is now in a state of suspended animation, if not actually dead. Apart from these, social life generally centres round the villages already mentioned; while the northern area finds its focal point in Mossdale village, just across the water, in Kells. Thus there are three branches of the W.R.I. These are at Laurieston (60 members), Glenlochar (40), and Bridge-of-Dee (50). In the north, the womenfolk attend the Mossdale branch. There is a football club at Laurieston with 19 members. Bridge-of-Dee united with Rhonehouse in Kelton to form another. Bridge-of-Dee has also a badminton club (30). Laurieston club, founded 1922, claims to be the pioneer badminton club in the county. Laurieston carpet bowling club, still older, has 40 members, and uses the church hall. Bridge-of-Dee club has 43 members. Carpet bowling is the most popular game amongst the men, and some of the younger women also join in. These carpet bowling clubs seem to survive the vicissitudes that commonly overtake rural clubs, better than any others. Laurieston has a dramatic club which varies in size from year to year. The plays produced are mostly 'kitchen comedies'. Some really beautiful nativity plays have been produced in church by the children of the Junior Guild, a church organisation of great vitality.

A 'Mutual Improvement Society' was formed about the beginning of the century, but after some success it died of inanition some 20 years ago. The same fate overtook the outdoor bowling club. It failed to attract the rising generation. The green has now reverted to nature, so that unfortunately any resuscitation of this pleasant game, though sometimes mooted, is improbable within the foreseeable future. A once-popular quoiting club too is now no more. Football and the motor-cycle killed it.

Laurieston and Mossdale unite in a branch of the British Legion.

There is a pipe band of 14 members, young people of both sexes. The popularity of the bagpipes has had a curious result. Thirty years or so ago, young folk musically inclined 'took up' the fiddle, the traditional instrument of rural Scotland, in the Lowlands at least; and that instrument, with the piano, was used at dances. To-day when a boy or girl turns to a musical instrument, it will most likely be to the bagpipes or the piano accordion. For dances, a band is usually imported from town, with a remarkable assortment of instruments. The volume of sound is certainly greater than formerly. At small homelier occasions of the kind, wedding celebrations for example, the piano accordion as a rule supplies the music.

The mention of weddings recalls an odd custom. On the eve of his wedding day the prospective bridegroom is kidnapped by his friends. After blackening his face and feet with soot or the like they push him through the street on a barrow, sometimes preceded by a piper, to the unabashed delight of the younger element of the populace, and the mildly scandalised amusement of their elders. A folklorist might perhaps see in this a survival of some ancient pre-nuptial rite.

Whist drives and dances are very popular. They are usually promoted by some of the clubs to raise funds for themselves or for some charitable purpose. Concerts are less popular; lectures still less, though illustrated travel talks will always draw a number. Of Further Education classes, arts and crafts, and country dancing have proved successful. More academic subjects have not.

Indoor recreation at Laurieston has been much hampered by the lack of a good public hall. The old one, poor at best, gradually became derelict, the feeling being that it was not worth spending money on. It was demolished this year. Plans had been prepared, and money raised, to build an adequate and seemly hall on the site, with an extra piece of ground generously given by the proprietors. Owing to the economic situation this plan has been abandoned meantime. Happily, through the good offices of the Scottish Council of Social Service and the Stewartry Education Committee, a prefabricated temporary building has been obtained and is about to be erected. Bridge-of-Dee acquired a war-time canteen hut, and erected it as a hall there. It is commodious and well-equipped.

Other influences have affected local social activities; such for instance as radio, and motor transport facilities which enable people to go much farther afield for intercourse and entertainment, for example to 'the pictures' in Castle-Douglas, and to plays and concerts there. Motor transport has indeed wrought a revolution in country life. In many respects the effect has been good. Interests have been extended, horizons widened, corners rubbed off, narrow views broadened. There is another aspect however. Local initiative is adversely affected; local crafts too. The result in the case of various societies and clubs has already been indicated. Individualities and eccentricities such as gave a distinctive tang to the older Scottish rural life are apt to be ironed out. Opinion on the question whether in the aggregate the gain or the loss is the greater will be determined largely by the enquirer's own temperament. Probably those who feel the loss most are those who in earlier days had sufficient leisure, means, and education to give them the wider outlook and set them free from the limitations of the older life, while still enjoying its simplicity and peace. Such may be pardoned a nostalgic attitude towards the old order. The vote of the many would be for the modern ways, and on the whole they are probably right; for if much that was good has gone, so has much that was bad; and after all it will take a long, long time and a lot of ironing before the distinctive Galloway type and ethos are completely levelled. In one sphere at least—language—it is indeed taking a long time. Whilst English is the language of church, school (but not playground), and public occasions generally, Scots remains the folkspeech of the parish; and that in spite of occasional efforts on the part of parents to change it ('Mary, don't say "Ay", say "Yes"'). It is true many old words have died out, and some will say that the old tongue is dying. Perhaps it is, but if so it is a lingering death. Indeed it has of late received an injection that has given it a new lease of life, in the form of the vernacular plays that are so popular.

Religion

In Bridge-of-Dee there are some half-dozen Roman Catholic households, a long-established though not ancient little community. There are few Episcopalians in the parish, and not of the soil. Of the rest, the great majority would doubtless claim to belong in some sense to the Church of Scotland, though the connection in many cases is tenuous in the extreme. There are 218 communicant members on the roll of the parish church. Of a good many of these it may be fairly said that their membership is passive rather than active. There remains none the less a substantial element of really interested members.

It is difficult to say how much of the apparent apathy of a considerable proportion of the people is due to sheer indifference and how much to unawareness on the part of people living decent orderly lives—as the great majority do—of any challenge to their accepted beliefs. Such take their religion for granted, and do not feel that it requires more than conformity and respectability; using the latter term in its proper sense, and not in the disparaging sense employed by supercilious intellectuals.

Church attendance is good by present-day standards in the village centres, but at Balmaghie Church it is poor, as this church stands in what is now a remote and thinly populated part; and since the 1929 union it has suffered from the fact that denominational differences no longer exist, as families who formerly would have resorted to Balmaghie as the parish church now attend nearer places of worship.

This is a law-abiding community. Serious offences are unknown. Standards of behaviour have risen greatly, in such matters as drinking habits and sex relationships, during the last century. Family affection is strong, and children almost without exception have a well-cared-for appearance, and good manners. We have, happily, plenty of mischievous small boys and girls, but no 'juvenile delinquency'. It would be wrong of course to paint too idyllic a picture. Neighbours sometimes quarrel; gossip is not always kindly; young people don't always behave as they should; gambling, while not obtrusive, has a hold, especially 'the pools'. Nevertheless it remains true that Balmaghie is a very pleasant place to live in. People are neighbourly, kind, and hospitable. They have a dry humour; are somewhat conservative, though not necessarily in the political sense; and have in plenty that feature of character which in its good form appears as loyalty to principle, and in its less pleasing aspect shows itself as dourness; in which respect at least, if not in religious fervour, they resemble their covenanting forefathers. Which leads to the reflection that possibly, after all, the changes catalogued earlier are, many of them, but superficial—mere adaptations to the times—and that the Galloway character remains fundamentally unchanged: which is satisfactory, for it is fundamentally sound. So that, given peace in the world, we in this corner of it may face the future with a sober optimism.

1951

CHAPTER 9

THE PARISH OF BORGUE

by the REV. WILLIAM MOORE

It was noted by the Rev. James Bell Henderson in his short history of the Parish of Borgue, written in 1898, that Scotland was divided into parishes around the beginning of the twelfth century, 'the parishes being made identical with the estates of the different lords of the manor, who for the benefit and instruction of their vassals and dependants built churches and endowed them.' At this time the parish was owned by Sir Hugo de Morville, Constable of Scotland, who built and endowed the first parish church. The site of this church is supposed to be about the centre of the older part of the present churchyard. Sir Hugo also founded Dryburgh Abbey, to which he transferred Borgue Church about 1150 A.D.

Boundaries and Extent

The boundaries of the parish are unchanged since the *New Statistical Account* of 1843, when it was described as having the figure of a triangle, of which the Solway forms the base, the parish of Girthon with a small portion of the river Fleet one of the bounding sides, and the parish of Twynholm with three miles of the estuary of the Dee the other boundary line, the vertex of the triangle being inserted like a wedge between these parishes. The greatest length is ten miles, the greatest breadth seven, and its area may be computed at 25 square miles. The present parish boundary encompasses three of the original parishes, Senwick, Borgue and Kirkandrews. In 1618 Senwick and in 1657 Kirkandrews were suppressed as separate parishes and were absorbed under the name of Borgue.

Name

The origin of the name Borgue was attributed by the Rev. Samuel Smith in 1792 to 'the Gaelic *burg* signifying a small hill', which in his own words 'is certainly very descriptive of the situation of the church, which is placed on a beautiful eminence in the middle of the parish, or of the general appearance of this district of land, which is remarkably unequal in its surface'. Sir Herbert Maxwell, writing in 1887, prefers to attribute it to **borg** (a fort) in the Icelandic, which, he states, of all the modern Scandinavian dialects represents most nearly the Old Norse spoken by the Norse and Danish marauders of the eighth and ninth centuries.

Antiquities

Scattered throughout the parish are many fortified sites and places of archaeological and historical interest, many of which are listed in the *Fifth Report and Inventory of Monuments and Constructions in Galloway.* These include the medieval castles of Plunton and Balmangan, cup and ring marks at Clauchendolly, Senwick and near Auchenhay, and forts such as Castle Haven near Kirkandrews.

Flora and Fauna

A few notes may be given of the flora and fauna of Borgue. It is said that such plants as the *crithmum maritimum* are fast disappearing. The wholesale cutting of trees is also bound to have an effect on many of our woodland flowers, which owing to the shallowness of the soil will soon disappear in this now almost treeless parish. On the other hand, during the past years, the movement of sheep from the hills to these lush pastures has helped in the distribution of plants to this district.

On the cliffs are to be found odd pairs of nesting ravens and at least one pair of peregrine falcons. Black grouse formerly nested occasionally but are now very rare. Green plovers (lapwings) have decreased to a remarkable extent since 1914. The exact reason is uncertain but several factors have probably contributed, such as the killing of the birds for food and the sale of their eggs during the wars, several cold winters during the 1940s, and the change-over from horses to tractors in farming operations. Corncrakes are now extremely rare. This decline is not merely local and may be the consequence of modern methods of farming. The lack of gamekeepers has led to an enormous increase in the number of stoats, weasels and hedgehogs. Foxes are now more common. Roe deer are less frequently seen than formerly, probably because of the felling of trees. Otters are not unusual and an occasional seal is seen.

There is hardly any fresh-water fishing in the parish. In recent years there has been little sea-fishing, though some years ago there were stake-nets off Knockbrex and Carrick. Boats from Kirkcudbright catch large quantities of lobsters off Muncraig haughs and near Barlocco and Ardwall Isles.

Agriculture

Borgue is pre-eminently an agricultural parish. Contained within it are 39 farms, of which 24 are owner-occupied and 15 rented. The principal land-owners are Major Basil D. Hope Dunbar of Senwick House and Mr. J. Douglas Brown of Roberton and formerly of Knockbrex, both being resident in the parish. Five farmers farm two farms each in the parish, one farms three, and six (including four of the above-mentioned) farm land outwith the parish in addition to their holdings here. Thus may be seen the great change which has occurred over the last hundred years in the nature of land tenure. On average the farms are composed as follows:—

237 acres arable land; 25 acres permanent grass; 25 acres rough grazing;
total, 287 acres.

There are two types of farming practised in the parish, dairy farming
and beef farming, and, because the dairy farms have all been established
since the time of the *New Statistical Account*, they deserve special
mention here.

The dairy industry was first introduced to Borgue during the latter
half of the nineteenth century and such has been its influence that to-day
there are in the parish only eight farms not engaged in dairying, four
of these being engaged in breeding beef-cattle.   To begin with the main
product of the dairies was cheese, with butter-making a minor trade.
Most of the dairies were let under the old 'bowing' system to bowers
who contracted to pay the farmer an agreed rental varying from 16 to
20 stones for each quey or cow.   The farmer supplied an agreed
quantity of feeding stuffs, turnips, hay and straw, and stipulated that
so many quey calves should be reared for stock, that he should receive
so much butter and milk weekly and that his workers should have milk
at fixed prices.   The dairyman or bower, who supplied all his own
labour usually from a large family, received any cheese produced above
the quantity required as rent, and the whey which was a by-product of
the cheese-making was used by him to feed pigs, of which he might
fatten 200 or so during the season.   In the case of the bower not being
able to pay his cheese rent the farmer had power by his lease to seize
the dairyman's pigs as security.   The system seemed to work very
profitably for both parties and most of the dairymen in time rented
farms for themselves.

In the 1930s cheese-making declined and there remain to-day only
five farms in the parish where cheese-making is still carried on—
Cairniehill, Chapelton, Culraven, Ingleston and Ross.   The opening in
1923 of the creamery in Kirkcudbright, which ten years later was taken
over by the Scottish Milk Marketing Board, accelerated the change-over
from cheese-making to the sale of liquid milk.   This trend was further
encouraged by the payment of extra prices for clean milk (Grade A),
for milk from tuberculin tested stocks and for milk from newly established dairy stocks.   Where the bowing system was not practised, the
dairyman undertook to 'work' for a fixed sum for each cow.   With the
advent of the liquid milk trade this arrangement became more common,
the sum being around £12 for a cow.   The share system, as it is termed,
originally designed to encourage production, is gaining favour at least
with the dairymen.   By this system the dairyman receives one-sixth of
the monthly milk cheque and £2 for each quey calf reared, the value of
the milk required to rear a calf being estimated at £12.   With a good
farm and stock the dairyman's return should be about £20 and has been
known to be as much as £23.   This year (1952) there seems to be a
desire on the part of some farmers to reduce the dairyman's share to
one-seventh.

The dairy cows are all Ayrshires and practically all the young stock on the dairy farms is pure-bred. In the past dairy farmers were in the habit of crossing their cows with Angus, Galloway or Shorthorn bulls, the progeny going to beef-feeders or dairies working with a flying stock, but since the 1930s this trade has declined rapidly owing to the greatly expanded dairy industry and since then it has been mainly pure-bred heifers that have been reared. The latest signs show a tendency to go back to the original system of rearing cross calves.

On the beef-farms the stock is mainly pure-bred Galloway cattle or Galloway crosses. There is a herd of pure-bred Belted Galloways at Roberton, while at Borness there is usually a number of 'Belties' to be seen grazing.

In the parish of Borgue in June 1950 the number of cattle was as follows:—

dairy cows and heifers used for breeding and milking—2,282
beef cows and heifers used for breeding — 123

The sheep stocks in the parish are mostly Cheviot flocks breeding half-bred lambs by crossing with Border Leicester tups. What is now a separate breed from other Cheviots, namely the North Country Cheviot, is the unanimous choice here for the trade. A few farms of lower fertility or poorer quality run flying flocks of black-faced ewes, crossing them with Border Leicester tups, to produce grand fattening lambs called Crosses, while a few of the richer and heavier farms carry half-bred ewes, crossing with Suffolk tups, which results in a heavier type of fattening lamb, the Down Cross or Black-headed lamb.

The leases existing are mostly of 14 years' duration, though leases of 19 years exist. The rents are very low compared with other parts of the country and may be reckoned to average 16s an acre, which compares with 8s to £1 an acre (*Old Statistical Account*) and 17s an acre (*New Statistical Account*).

The land of the parish is extremely uneven of aspect and varied in quality, lying mainly in irregular patches among rocky outcrops or knowes. Although most of the knowes, which range in size from 40 to 50 square yards, are covered with a sole of grass, the soil on them is of no appreciable depth and cannot be cultivated. There are, however, some 30 'drums' and a small area of coastal flats to be found in the parish. The soil for the most part is a kindly sharp loam, but in some drummy and low-lying parts it is of a colder and stiffer nature. There are also certain areas throughout the parish of flatter, richer, dark loams, which from their situation and nature appear to be the drained remains of by-gone bogs, extending in most instances to two or more acres.

The general nature of the land gives rise to two main agricultural disadvantages, burning and waterlogging. Regarding the first, because the soil is mostly thin and sharp lying on rock, in hot spells there is a serious danger of the crops and grasses droughting and while steady rain will mostly repair the damage in ten days or a fortnight, it does happen that in some years the harm done is lasting. As an example, in the exceptionally dry summer of 1949 grassfields suffered to the extent that they assumed a most remarkably brown and wasted appearance. The phenomenon is locally termed 'burning'. In some cases that year fodder had to be carted to the cattle in the month of July and in many cases farmers had to send their young stock to hill grazings in the northern parts of the county. Regarding waterlogging, in some places owing to rock formation the soil is naturally inclined to be boggy, but as a result of the constant work of past generations it is now practically all drained and free from this defect. Many of these old drains are of the type known as 'stone drains'; although they were laid 100 or 150 years ago, they remain to-day in a fully efficient state.

There has been an increase since 1843 of almost 1,000 acres of arable land in the parish. Since at the present time the farmers have been striving towards the greatest degree of self-sufficiency attainable, it is extremely unlikely that this present acreage of arable land will be increased. By nature and climate this is a stock-rearing district, and attempts to bring more land under the plough would certainly not be economical and would in most cases be impracticable. The general system of cropping pursued is based on a six or seven year rotation.

1. Ley Oats; 2. Roots; 3. Sown out oats; 4, 5, 6, 7, Grass Ley.

Hay is cut on meadows and from one or other of the grass leys. Silage is not made to any great extent, farmers relying mainly on turnips, hay and straw for winter feeding, plus bought-in concentrates for winter milk-producing cows and fattening cattle. The uses of artificial manures are now fully realised and are standard practice, while extensive liming has been carried out during the past decade. The lime comes mainly from Cumberland, all the old marl pits in the parish being in disuse. Farmyard manure still plays a most prominent part in the fertilising scheme. As a result of this use of manures the fertility of the land is high, but since 1939, when labour began to become really scarce, the land has suffered from a lack of meticulous weeding and cleaning operations to which it had previously been accustomed, and to-day weeds of all kinds, particularly thistles, dockens, couchgrass, whins and bracken are in greater evidence than our forefathers would have tolerated.

The work on the land is carried out by 185 regular workers and 30 casual workers, assisted by 117 working horses and 40 tractors. Labour is now scarce and the bands of Irish and contracted haymakers and harvesters so familiar in pre-war days are now unknown. Farmers have now to rely on their own staff with the help in many cases of machinery. Some of the larger farms are almost entirely mechanised: some employ both tractors and horses. Of the latter there are two schools of thought, one ploughing and cultivating with horses and mowing, reaping and hauling with tractors, the other doing everything possible with tractors and leaving only the odd work for the horse. The few who depend on horses alone seem to be at no disadvantage either as regards quality of crops or speed of handling. This year, at least, these farmers finished harvest first. One mechanised farmer avers that the horse men on the old·fashioned system make more efficient use of their labour force. With men working horses each is an independent unit requiring help from the others only in exceptional circumstances. Where workers and large machines are used, however, the whole labour force is thrown idle by a break-down. Be that as it may, it is undoubtedly the case that farmers are coming to rely on the use of up-to-date machinery.

Practically all the workers' houses are tied with the exception of a block of houses at Chapelton Row erected for agricultural workers by the county council. The lack of response among farm workers to tenant the latter has been very noticeable and it may be deduced that tied houses are more convenient for farmer and farm worker alike. The difference in rent is approximately 13s a week; this no doubt is a deterrent to prospective tenants. On owner-occupied farms the houses are generally of a good and up-to-date character, a high proportion having an inside water supply, although in some cases with no water closet. A few houses, however, mainly on rented farms, are of a less satisfactory type but these are gradually being brought into line with present-day standards.

Trades and Commerce

Living and working in the parish are three blacksmiths, one each at Chapelton Row, Clauchendolly and Bridgend of Auchenhay. There are three joiners at Borgue village, Chapelton Row and Ivy Cottage respectively. In the centre of the village is a garage attending to the needs of car, tractor and bicycle and providing a hiring service. It is of interest to note that there are 81 private cars in the parish. In the village are two general stores, one of which is the post office.

There are two boarding-houses in the parish and one hotel in Borgue village but no licensed premises. Fishing is no longer pursued for a livelihood, though a few gather whelks in the season. There are two game-dealers who also catch rabbits and there is a mole-catcher. Two sawmills, both of recent establishment, operate in the parish, one at Mill Haugh Glen and the other at Black Briggs. Timber felling has been extensive in the parish of recent years, as it has been throughout the country. Much of the felled timber lay in neglected woodlands and in sparsely planted grasslands and it is a happy fact that a fair proportion of this area is either being replanted or being cleared for grazing. None the less, some areas of felled woodlands are being left in a most unsightly and useless state and throughout the parish there is much need for proper afforestation work. The Forestry Commission do not own any woodlands in Borgue, which does not contain any area of a magnitude likely to attract them.

Boundaries are marked by dykes, hedges and fences, and it is regretted that the dry stane dykes, the most common and at the same time the best type of boundary, are in many places in only moderate repair and do not receive the full attention that they deserve. A few dykers still work in the parish and the fault does not lie with them but with the land-owners who often do not make full use of the labour and material at their disposal.

Water and Electricity Supply

The parish is watered by springs and burns from spring sources, cottages and houses for the most part drawing water from wells through pipes led into the houses. In the last year, however, a mains water supply has been introduced and is at present in the final stages of completion. This will be of great benefit to the parish which has long felt the need for such a supply. The water originates from Loch Whinyeon.

The parish is extensively supplied with electricity and few houses are not now connected to the mains. This electricity was formerly generated by the Galloway Power Company and distributed by the Stewartry County Council, but the whole service is now nationalised and the supply is linked to the national grid.

Population

The population of the parish is as follows:—494 males; 448 females; total 942. Twenty-one persons are over 70 years including one aged 91. There are 310 persons under 15 years of age including 94 under five. These people live in 229 houses. As may be seen from the following figures, the nation-wide shift of population from country to town has shown its effect in the parish of Borgue.

1755	697
1793	771
1801	820
1851	1,043
1861	1,162
1901	1,045
1911	1,023
1921	990
1931	990
1951	936

Village of Borgue

With regard to Borgue village itself, until about 20 years ago little change had been made in its appearance since the fifties and sixties of last century when a number of two-storey houses had been erected in and around the village, mainly on ground feued from the proprietors on 99 years lease. In 1931, however, the cottages belonging to the Borgue House Estate were renovated and changed from the traditional style to red-tiled roofs and half-timbered porches. A public hall was erected in 1932 by the efforts of the parishioners. A memorial to commemorate the fallen in the first world war consists of a Celtic Cross in the middle of the village together with a striking clock placed in the church tower. The two blocks, each comprising four houses, erected at Chapelton Row by the county council in 1950 represented the first considerable increase in the number of houses in the parish for many years.

Schools

Borgue Academy, endowed by Thomas Rainy in 1802, reached perhaps its greatest fame about 1843 under Rector Poole, known significantly to the older generation of Free Kirkers as the 'Martyr'. Until the end of the century boarders came from far afield when the curriculum included navigation. Until 1947 a certain amount of secondary education was provided: now, however, all pupils who have completed the primary stage of their education travel to Kirkcudbright Academy. The staff consists of a headmaster and three assistants. A soup kitchen maintained by voluntary effort was in operation for a period of some 70 years before the provision of the School Meals Service by the Education Committee; of this service most of the pupils, who number in all about 100, take advantage. Few children walk any considerable distance to school; motor transport is provided for children from the outlying parts of the parish, while those residing to the west of a line from Tonguecroft to Barharrow go to Gatehouse. The public hall is used as a gymnasium for physical culture, but there are not wanting those who say that by the time the children have walked two or three miles they have had sufficient exercise and ought to devote their whole time and remaining energies to the study of the three Rs.

For some time after the Disruption there was in the village, in a building still standing, a day school belonging to the Free Church, while in Swinedrum a private school was also carried on.

Churches

Except for a change in handwriting and sederunt the records of the Established Church in 1843 ignore any untoward event, but the minister and the session clerk with a large proportion of the congregation had seceded. A church was built and a separate congregation continued to worship there, though in gradually lessening numbers, until a successful union was effected in 1933.

Although the two congregations failed to see eye to eye in many things, it was with remarkable unanimity that they effected changes in custom and fabric, and the history of both is very similar. In the Parish Church the old system of celebrating communion with relays of tables in the church (and, we presume, preachings by neighbouring ministers from a tent in the churchyard) was continued until 1874 when the number of tables was reduced to two. In 1879 it was enacted that communion should be observed simultaneously. Six months later the use of tokens was discontinued and communion cards were issued for the first time. In the same year the Scottish Hymnal was introduced, and in 1886 the session agreed that the moderator at an early opportunity should request the congregation during worship to stand at the celebration of praise to God and kneel or sit during prayer, a reversal of the former practice. Instrumental music was introduced into the Free Church in 1891, and after much discussion, and with the heritors' consent, into the Parish Church in 1894. The Parish Church was considerably extended and a session house and vestry added in 1899. There have been few complaints of lack of seating accommodation since that time. The Free Church was remodelled and renovated about the same period. The practice of holding services on the Fast Day, the Thursday before the Sacrament, continued at least until the end of the century. The preachers were usually visiting ministers, a survival of the 'Holy Fair'.

Six years after the union of the two churches the Free Church manse at Pringleton was sold. The former Free Church is now a church hall, and improvements including the provision of water and sanitary arrangements are at present in progress.

In 1845 the writer of the *New Statistical Account* stated that 'no very marked and observable progress has taken place in zeal about religion and in personal holiness'. If he wrote this about the flock that followed him into the wilderness in 1843, one hesitates to claim any advance in merit for the generations who have succeeded them.

Way of Life

The way of life has changed during recent years. Two contributory factors to this result are the establishing of bus services in the parish and the popularity of its shores with summer visitors from all over the country. The improved means of transport have brought the bigger shopping centres within easy reach of the people and have made it possible to travel for employment outwith the parish. Brighouse Bay has been discovered as an ideal place for a camping holiday and during the summer months it is thronged with caravans. Yachting is popular here and many boats use the old harbour—quite a change from long ago when the coal boat from Maryport was the only one to be seen, and that very occasionally. Incidentally this boat served the farms in the east end of the parish and also Ross Bay and Kirkandrews. Water ski-ing is also practised on the waters of the bay. Carrick Shore (partly in Girthon and partly in this parish) with its sandy stretches and grassy slopes is a favourite place for sea-bathing and picnicking, and scores of cars are to be seen here on a summer day.

The majority of the farmers in the parish attend Castle-Douglas market each Monday, while only half a dozen or so keep up the old market in Kirkcudbright on Friday, which has now become more or less a meeting for discussion and debate. The women of the parish owe much to the W.R.I. movement. They meet once a month for demonstrations and lectures and great talent has often been revealed amongst the members. In the winter, thanks to the Stewartry Education Committee, this organisation has the use of the school for a choir which meets once a week and competes in a festival in Castle-Douglas. Under the auspices of the same movement the young people receive tuition in country dancing. Football in a field near the village and a successful flower show are among the season's activities, while in the winter months the young people play badminton in the public hall and the older men have carpet bowling in their own hall, which was presented to the parish by that grand old man, Sir William Gordon, the Balaclava hero. The curlers too when conditions are favourable enjoy outdoor curling on Earlston Loch.

It will be seen therefore that the people of this lovely parish may have a full and interesting life. Within the parish they have a satisfying social life depending on their own resources and initiative, and when occasion arises they have the facilities for going farther afield for cultural and social activities.

1953

CHAPTER 10

THE PARISH OF BUITTLE

by T. L. N. Hogg

Name

The parish of Buittle (pronounced Bittel) takes its name from Buittle Castle which lies within the parish. This castle was the principal seat in Scotland of Devorgilla, wife of John Balliol, and in the code of statutes which she drew up in 1282 for the guidance of Balliol College, Oxford, the name is given as Botel. The word *Botel* is Anglo-Saxon and means 'house' or 'dwelling place' though in the case of Buittle Castle it probably meant a walled house or fort which must have stood on the site of the castle in Anglo-Saxon times.

Boundaries and Natural Features

To the north the parish is bounded by the parishes of Crossmichael and Kelton; to the east by the parishes of Urr and Colvend; to the west by the parishes of Kelton and Rerrick; while the River Urr and its estuary form the boundary to the south. The parish is about ten miles in length and about three in breadth. It is divided in local speech into the 'high end' and the 'low end', the 'high end' being formed of the outcroppings of the Southern Uplands where they terminate in the narrow coastal plain of the Urr estuary, which constitutes the 'low end'. The upper reaches of the parish present an undulating upland appearance; the lower reaches are flat and hemmed in on one side by the sea; and on the other by a series of craggy hills and knobbly hummocks which form the edge of the plateau. The climate is mild, the severities of winter being largely tempered by the nearness of the sea, and for the same reason rain is fairly abundant. The only village in the parish is Palnackie, which stands on the Urr in the 'low end' of the parish.

History

A full list of the historical monuments within the parish may be found in *The Fifth Report and Inventory of Monuments and Constructions in Galloway, Volume II*, published by the Stationery Office in 1914. Perhaps the most important monument within the parish is Buittle Castle, though only vestiges of the foundations and traces of its ditches now remain. It is, as already mentioned, associated with the Lady Devorgilla, wife of John Balliol, and daughter of Alan, the last Lord of Galloway, and Constable of Scotland. Through her mother she was related to William the Lion, King of Scotland. Buittle Castle was Devorgilla's principal seat in Galloway, probably because it was the nearest of her castles in Galloway to the main road and sea routes to England, for Balliol, her husband, held large possessions there as well as in France.

The castle stood in a strategic position, in the neck of a narrow side valley running from the broader Urr valley, and guarding directly the route which ran up this narrow valley to Castle-Douglas and Western Galloway, and by its flank position it guarded the direct route up the Urr valley into Middle Galloway. It stood on the west bank of the Urr in a position of considerable natural strength, with the Urr behind it and its protective ditches in front. It was of the Edwardian type with curtain walls and round towers at the angles of the walls, and wherever extra defensive strength was needed. It also probably stood at the point on the River Urr which a sea-going vessel could most conveniently reach on the tide, for in those days the sea must have reached much farther up the river, for Furth-head or Frith-head is about two miles above its present reach.

The old castle of Botel was a stronghold of the Lords of Galloway and figured prominently during the Wars of Independence in the thirteenth-fourteenth centuries, but is now best remembered for its associations with Devorgilla. Devorgilla and her husband, besides being petty sovereigns in Galloway, took part in many of the great events of the time. Perhaps the most important of these to us now was the founding of Balliol College, Oxford. This arose out of a boundary dispute between John Balliol and Walter Chirkham, Bishop Palatine of Durham. Balliol had much the better of the quarrel so long as only the temporal powers were involved, but once Chirkham had invoked the power of the universal church Balliol found himself in the unpleasant position of kneeling as a penitent before the doors of Durham Cathedral. Chirkham was not satisfied with his splendid victory, but insisted that some major act of charity should be performed by his helpless victim. Accordingly John Balliol endowed a hostel for 16 poor students in Oxford, and from this small beginning Balliol College sprang. The real credit, however, of consolidating the status of the college lies with Devorgilla, who not only aided it with substantial sums of money, but in Buittle Castle caused to be drawn up the code of statutes by which the college is governed.

On the death of her husband, Devorgilla had his heart embalmed and placed in a specially made casket. This casket was with her during the twenty-one years she survived her husband and was finally buried with her before the high altar of Sweetheart Abbey, which she raised as a memorial to him.

Perhaps the next most interesting relic in the parish is the old church at Buittle, which lies adjacent to the new church. It is now in a ruined condition and encrusted in parts with ivy, but the walls and gables stand intact. There is no documentary evidence to show when it was first built, but the nave which is the older part of the church was probably erected in the latter part of the twelfth century. Its name was then the

Church of St. Colmanel. The chancel, which was added later in the thirteenth century, is wider than the nave, and is probably contemporary with Devorgilla. It may have been built at her instigation for the church is within a mile and a half of her castle at Buittle. The earliest reference to the church is contained in a Charter of 1381 by Bishop Thomas of Galloway bestowing it on the monks of Sweetheart Abbey.

Architecturally the church shows evidence of frequent repair. The western gable has a round-headed doorway with flattened lintel inside, a round-headed window and a plain belfry, but curiously enough these features are asymmetrical. The side windows are surmounted by pointed arches which are cut from solid blocks of sandstone, and the chancel is separated from the nave by a single pointed arch with chamfered mouldings springing from shafts of pointed section with moulded caps and bases. The chancel itself has two side doors, but in the eastern wall, which is pierced by three slender and beautiful lancet windows topped by flattened arches, another door has been broken through, and a plain slab of stone now acts as a lintel and supports the stonework of the central window. Tradition suggests two reasons why there should be a door at each end of the church. The first is that it was done by the Covenanters who in their eagerness to overthrow the old papal ways made a complete reversal of everything in the church. The other, and more probable tradition, is that during the Reformation, the church was used at the same time by both Catholics and Protestants, each worshipping in their own particular half of the building—a tribute to the sound common sense which to-day is still a marked feature in the parish.

The church is a perfect example of a medieval church but is not cared for by the Ministry of Works. Instead, it is included with the churchyard which is under the care of the District Council.

Orchardton Tower, near the bay of Almorness, is cared for by the Ministry of Works. It is a circular fifteenth century keep with the remains of a range of buildings on its south side among which is a vaulted cellar now in a ruined condition. The tower had three storeys and a store-room underneath, but since the flooring in the upper storeys was of wood no trace of it now remains. The present entrance to the tower was once a window, for the original doorway was on the south side and connected by stairs to the buildings which lie on that side. No trace of this stair remains except the first two or three steps of the lower reaches. Beside the fireplace in the main room there is an arched ambry, with piscina, let into the wall, indicating that this room was once used as a chapel. A circular stair let into the thickness of the wall leads from this apartment to the walk round the battlements, access to which is gained through a small gabled cape house. The ruin is in a good state of preservation.

Other fragmentary remains are found within the parish. There are the remains of a vitrified fort on the lands of Castlegower. It is surrounded by a system of ramparts and ditches and it is only at a small part of the summit wall on the eastern side that vitrification can be seen. Near Almorness, on Castle Hill, are the ruins of a stone built fort, which local tradition connects with Orchardton Tower, though no positive data can be found on this. On Camp Hill, at Meikle Knox, there can be seen vague traces of an ancient hill fort and both at Ernespie and Milton Park are further fragmentary remains of camps, but so slight as to give little clue as to what they were like.

Agriculture

The parish of Buittle has 40 farms within its boundaries. In size they vary from over 400 acres to small holdings of little more than 20 acres. The average for farms taken all over the parish is just over 200 acres.

The principal type of farming is dairy farming combined with dairy stock rearing and practically the only breed handled is the Ayrshire. Up to about twelve years ago most of the dairy farms went in for cheese-making, but nowadays the milk is sent daily to the Milk Marketing Board's creameries at Dalbeattie and Castle-Douglas, and probably for this reason the making of cheese locally has ceased. The Milk Marketing Board is regarded as a great boon by the farmers, as they receive a guaranteed price for their milk, and their money comes to them monthly from the Board.

All the dairy herds in the parish are attested, and each farm keeps its own bulls, although there is an artificial insemination centre at Castle-Douglas. Quite a few of the herds are pedigree and several local farmers have done well in the show ring over the years. Since the milk attesting scheme was introduced into the parish in the 1930s the improvement in dairy premises has been considerable in order to comply with the recommendations suggested under that scheme, and the dairy premises in the district can stand comparison with any in Scotland. All steadings are lit by electricity, and milking is done by machines. Every stall is supplied with its own water bowl in the byre, while one farm has a mechanical bucket and rail system for bringing feeding stuffs from the stores to the stalls. Feeding of stock and cleaning out the byre, however, are still done by hand.

The crops which are grown depend very much upon the type of farming in operation. Most of the farms grow root crops as cattle feed, and this has the benefit of tradition behind it, but in recent years cropping for silage has been making headway in the parish, since among its other advantages it requires less labour in handling the crop. Silage, however, has not been established long enough to be fully accepted by all the farmers in the area, and the farmer who sticks to the old ways feels perhaps that so much of the land has to be used every year to make silage that in time the land may become impoverished, and adopts a wait-and-see policy accordingly.

The root crops grown are swede turnips, mangolds, rape and kale, all of which except rape are used as cattle feed. At one time potatoes were grown extensively, but now it is unusual to see any potatoes in the fields at all. The main grain crop is oats which are crushed and used as winter feed. Wheat is occasionally grown for sale in the market; beans, because of their high protein content, are likewise occasionally grown as an addition to the winter feed. Hay is a main crop, and consists of the normal grass mixtures with clover. Crops are grown in a seven-year rotation, including the grazing of the field for three or four years depending upon whether a crop of hay has been taken from it or not.

Not all farms in the parish are dairy farms. There are a few stock farms raising cattle for beef. Sheep are reared as well on most farms if any suitable hill pastures form part of the farm lands. The flocks are cross-bred, either from a Blackface-Suffolk, Leicester cross, or from a Cheviot-Suffolk strain. Breeding is also done from the first cross. Lambs are fattened on turnips and rape, and the sheep sold for slaughter. Small numbers of pigs may be found on most farms, though pig rearing is never on a large scale. Poultry flocks are found on all farms, though they are decreasing slightly because of the high cost of feeding stuffs. The hens may be allowed to range in the open fields but of late the deep litter system has been making headway.

Farmyard manure is the main stand-by for fertilising the fields, but large quantities of artificial manure are used as well, perhaps more so on farms which grow crops for silage than on the root crop farms. Artificial manures were at one time landed at Palnackie Harbour and distributed directly in the parish, but these last 30 years or so the artificial manures have come by road and rail and are now distributed from Dalbeattie. It is only very occasionally that a ship with artificial manure now docks at Palnackie.

The farms in the parish are highly mechanised, all ploughing being done by tractors, though some farms still keep a pair of horses for general purposes. Balers and threshing mills are common, it being customary to thresh part of the crop in the threshing mill installed in the steading and to have the travelling mill in later on in the season to thresh the remainder of the ricks. Hay elevators and triangular rick lifters are necessary adjuncts on most farms, but the combine harvester is not much used, perhaps because there is not a sufficient acreage under corn to make its use profitable. Most of the land is boggy and far from flat, conditions which are not suited to operating a combine harvester, and the binder is still the most used in handling corn crops within the parish. Two types of manure spreader, in addition to hand spreading, are in common use, one for spreading artificial manure, and the other for farmyard manure, while corn is no longer sown broadcast but by means of dibbler sowers which bury the seed two or three inches under the surface of the soil. Dutch barns are of modern construction and kept at a high standard of maintenance. Generally speaking, steadings and farmhouses present a trim and pleasing appearance.

The social life of the farming community has altered out of all recognition in the last 50 years. Farmhouses are lit by electricity, have hot and cold water installed, bathrooms, electric washing machines and refrigerators. Even the farm cottages are electrically lit and most have been renovated and brought up to date with interior sanitation and baths. The farmers' wives now have leisure, and since their husbands have cars, they go on shopping expeditions to Castle-Douglas and Dumfries. Having cars permits of a great deal of visiting in the evening among the various farms. The evening may be spent socially in talk or in playing cards. The Monday cattle mart in Castle-Douglas is the main meeting place of the farmers, however, and here news and gossip are exchanged. A curling club has been in existence for some years in the parish and long trips are made by cars to Glasgow and Ayr to curl on the indoor rinks there. Some farmers are keen football supporters and travel to the football matches in Dumfries on Saturday afternoons.

Farmers are more prosperous than they have been for many years and their standard of living is high. Their occupation gives them certain advantages in the food line, and to taste real cream in the sponge cakes is one of the pleasures of having tea in a farmhouse in Buittle parish. The interiors of the farmhouses are decorated with taste and the carpetings and plenishings are substantial. The farm labourer's lot has improved also in material respects. The open fires which were so prevalent in the early decades of this century in the farm workers' cottages have now been replaced by enclosed fires. At that time it was not unusual for people to sleep and eat in the same room, but that is very infrequent now. In these early decades people ate meat once a week. After the first world war their diet was soup, potatoes, scones and porridge, with meat every day. Following the second world war their diet, especially the meat, was controlled by what quantity was available for rationing. Farm labourers no longer keep cows of their own, though potatoes are still grown on the land for them. They work regular hours, as tractor drivers, for instance, and some of them do not even live on the farms where they work, but in villages such as Palnackie, which are convenient to the farms.

Most farms in the 'high end' of the parish are owned by the farmers, or are the property of trusts or firms such as I.C.I.; in the 'low end' Major Robertson of Almorness is the most extensive landowner, though some of his land has only recently been sold. Kirkennan and Munches, the properties of the Maxwell family, run to about 1,500 acres between them. £1 an acre is the average rental or valuation on which tax is paid, being somewhat higher on the good land of the low ground, and lower on the thinner soils of the uplands.

Woodlands

A casual survey of the parish shows it to have a well-wooded appearance, but much felling of timber has taken place during the first half of this century. In this respect the rapid disappearance of hedgerow trees is a feature of note. This is due to the difficulties they present to a farmer who wants to plough the extreme limits of his fields, while to a dairy farmer they seem a natural harbouring place for flies which at the least distract his cattle, and at the worst may spread disease among the herd. The planting of trees is carried out by the Forestry Commission and by private land-owners. To the private land-owner it offers certain advantages, because the taxation on woodlands is very small, and it is a good investment which, while it may not mature in his lifetime, certainly will in that of his son. The types of trees planted are quick growing conifers such as Japanese Larch, Picea Sitchensis, Spruce and Douglas Fir, and they are planted on the rough grazing land on the sides and tops of the hillocks. Hardwoods are not much planted at present for there is no demand for that type of wood. The Forestry Commission have woods at three places in the parish—North Glen, Lochhill and adjacent to the Doach Burn. Kirkennan and Munches have 500 acres of woodland between them. This is well managed because there is a family tradition of good management behind it, the previous members of the family taking an interest in personally supervising their estates when such things were more commonly left to factors and grieves.

Planting of woodlands is nowadays impossible without surrounding the area to be planted with wire netting to keep out rabbits. One hundred and thirty years ago the ladies in a shooting party at Munches were called out onto the lawn in front of the house to see a strange animal which had just been shot. This turned out to be a rabbit, which was a rarity in those days. Now it has grown into the dimensions of a pest, causing great damage throughout the parish. Bracken is another pest which has increased tremendously on rough hill grazings these last 40 years. Little can be done to combat this insidious invader except laborious cutting, which requires great labour if it is to be effective, and bracken has now assumed the proportions of a serious problem.

Quarrying

The quarry at Craignair Hill is the only one now operating in the parish. It is owned by Improved Road Constructions of Dalbeattie and now produces crushed granite and tarmacadam for surface dressing of roads, most of its output being taken by the county council. The only dressed stone now produced is for tombstones and memorials, though at one time dressed stone was the main production of the quarry. The last big job for which this quarry supplied the stone was the building of the King George V bridge in Glasgow, though the beautiful grey granite can be seen in the Thames Embankment, Liverpool Docks and in many public buildings throughout England and Scotland. The quarry now employs about 60 men.

Population

The figures of population since 1801 are:—

1801	863	1911	825
1851	1,042	1921	799
1861	1,165 (maximum ever recorded)	1931	778
1901	879	1951	766

As the figures show, the population of Buittle has remained fairly static over the last 50 years. The small but steady decline is probably due to the increasing mechanisation on farms which lessens the need for labour, and to the smaller number in the average family. Movement of young people into the towns is negligible, most of them finding work locally, though this may mean travelling as far as Dumfries. The population is mainly native stock, born either in the parish or in the county.

The Church

The present church of Buittle has no architectural features of interest. The previous statistical survey gives us the information that it was built in 1819 at a cost of £1,000, but the church was much renovated in 1903, the old high pulpit being removed at that time and replaced by a much lower edifice more acceptable to the ministers of the church. The church stands on an elevated knoll, and has a neat and pleasing appearance. At present, owing to the death of the late incumbent, it has no minister.

Communion is celebrated in the old style. Two beautiful silver cups, bearing the inscription *Ex dono pastoris, 1766,* are used at the service. The silver paten was presented to the church in 1858 by James Robb Grant, the then pastor. The flagon is of pewter and bears no markings.

Until the union of 1929 the salary of the minister was paid by tithes, but in that year the choice was given of either remaining on tithes or accepting a standard salary. The latter was chosen, and a year or two after 1929 the stipend was fixed at £512, plus the glebe, plus £8 per annum for Communion elements. At the next vacancy the presbytery recommended a salary of £400 plus glebe, the surplus from the teinds to be devoted to helping needier parishes adjacent to Buittle. This was fought successfully by the kirk session, and the stipend was fixed finally at £450 plus glebe. It has now been amended this year to bring the total stipend paid to the minister up to £500.

In the village of Palnackie there is a small mission hall which was built in 1877 largely at the expense of the same James Robb Grant who presented the silver paten to the church, and this is used for evening services and by the Palnackie Sunday School which has a membership of about 40. The other Sunday school, which has a roll of about 20, meets in the manse on Sunday mornings.

The congregation has remained steady with a roll fluctuating between 250 and 280. At the moment the roll contains the names of 261 members. Most church-goers arrive by car, for the church is set near the centre of this scattered parish. A bus runs every Sunday for the convenience of the 'high end' people, and once a month from Palnackie. The average congregation on Sunday is from 30 to 40.

The farmers, especially in the 'high end' of the parish, are staunch supporters of the church, but from Palnackie support is only lukewarm. The decline in the influence of the church among those under forty is as marked in this parish as it has been all over Scotland in the preceding half century, and none of the youths or young men from Palnackie ever attend the church. It would be pretentious to try to ascribe causes for this. Certainly it is not just indifference for people who do not attend church still send their children to the Sunday school. It may be laziness to make the effort to get to church; it may be that the Sunday newspaper makes a stronger call than the church; it may be a feeling that the church has little help to offer in times such as we live in; it may be that church going is now looked upon in a derogatory fashion by youth, and it takes a very bold young man to suffer the laughter of his fellows; it may be that materialism or religions of social equality have taken its place—or a combination of all of them. Guesswork, of course, but in the absence of a long study of the problem no true answer is possible. At the moment there are as many answers as there are people.

In church matters the women of the parish are more alert than the men, and there is a flourishing and live Woman's Guild with a membership of 42. They form the real backbone of the church, and by sales of work and other means give practical help when financial difficulties in the church have to be overcome. Talks and lectures are arranged by the Guild, and it is a real social and cultural influence in the parish.

Education

There is now only one school in the parish, and this is at Palnackie where the only concentration of population is to be found. It serves Palnackie and the surrounding district up to a radius of about two miles. It is a two-teacher primary school, secondary education requiring the pupil to travel by school bus to Dalbeattie for the three-year course, and eventually to Kirkcudbright for the completion of the five years' course. This break in the scholastic career is not too popular with parents who are anxious for their children to go on to the Scottish Leaving Certificate stage, but works well enough in practice. Pupils leave Palnackie School at the age of 12 though it was the practice not long ago to keep pupils in the local school until they had attained the leaving age. The large increase of technical and scientific subjects in the last 20 years has meant that the old village dominie no longer has the required knowledge to teach all subjects at the secondary level, for even a university graduate is only qualified by his degree to teach certain subjects at secondary level, that is, English or languages or science or mathematics but not all of them. This has led to the centralisation of specialist teachers in convenient towns to which the pupils can be taken from the primary schools.

The roll of Palnackie School at the moment is 55 and still rising. The school is well equipped and tastefully decorated inside. It has three rooms, two of which are classrooms, the third classroom now being a dining centre for the children, who pay for their dinners 7d, 6d or 5d a day on a sliding scale depending on the number in the family. Forty-eight children take dinners here every day. The dinners are brought in heat-retaining containers from the central kitchen at Dalbeattie by the same van which brings the children's free milk in the morning. A mobile library van which comes from the library in Castle-Douglas issues from 120 to 140 volumes every fortnight in Palnackie village alone, and also brings quarterly a complete library for both the pupils in the school and the members of the Youth Club in the village. These books are retained in the school for issuing. The school has an asphalt playground, and a slightly larger grass playing field adjoining it. It stands about 200 yards along the Auchencairn road on the side road leading to Almorness.

Land-owners

The oldest landed family in the parish is that of the Maxwells. Their family seat is Munches where Commander D. Herries Maxwell, R.N. (Ret.) resides, but Kirkennan House is owned by Major-General A. Maxwell, also of the same family. The family has been resident in Buittle since 1630, and was originally a strong Catholic family who changed to Protestantism after the Reformation to fall in line with the feelings of their tenantry. Mass, however, was said at Munches for many years after this, a fiddler on Dumfries Bridge giving the signal as to which house was to be chosen for the mass by means of a musical code, though the writer has been unable to find out which tune was assigned to Munches. Munches itself was rebuilt in 1850, burned in 1858 and rebuilt, but eventually pulled down in 1939 and rebuilt as a modern and smaller house. The estate has greatly shrunk in the last 50 years. Eleven farms within the parish and seven outwith have all been sold. This has been caused by the increased income tax and death duties and also by the fact that the rent of land is so low while repairs and maintenance have risen to such a high figure that the one no longer pays for the other. Land-owning is now only economic if the land-owner manages his own estates.

Palnackie

Palnackie village, which stands on one of the lower bends of the Urr, has a population of just under 250. Up to 20 years ago it was a thriving port, but now hardly a ship calls except an Admiralty vessel unloading ammunition for storage at Dalbeattie, or an occasional vessel with a cargo of fertiliser. The older houses in the village are mainly of two storeys, a survival from the time when lodgings had to be found for the sailors who came in on the ships docking in the small harbour cut out of the bank of the Urr. The introduction of road haulage, however, finished the coasting vessels as carriers of goods, and the houses are now private dwellings.

Between the wars these houses had no water supply apart from the water of Gardenburn, which flowed through the village, and several wells sunk in the vicinity of the houses. Since the war, water has been piped into the village from the county council reservoir at Lochenkit and, to begin with, spigots were erected in the street so that people could draw their water from them. These spigots were abolished when the water was piped into the houses. Now only five houses in Palnackie have no interior water supply. Bathrooms and sculleries have been built on to some of the older houses in the village, but these are about the only structural alterations which have taken place in these houses.

All new housing in the village, except for two bungalows which were built privately in the 1930s, is post-war. Twenty-eight new houses have been built, four of which, steel built, are for agricultural workers, the remaining 24 being for let by the county council to people who work in the vicinity. They are four-roomed houses of a good type and are equipped with all modern fittings. The rent is £36 per annum, which together with the rates works out at about £1 a week.

Although there have never been more than two shops in Palnackie, and the post office is the centre of life in the village, yet Palnackie is a semi-industrial village. Economically it is dependent on timber and road haulage. It has three sawmills which produce pit props, mainly for the south west coalfields of Scotland and the coalfields of northern England. Planking is made for railway waggon repair and construction work, and wooden rollers for the jute mills of Dundee. There is also a large seasonal trade in firewood with the north of England. The timber is bought locally by the sawmillers, sometimes involving purchase of the land on which the trees stand, and felling and haulage to the mills is done by the millers themselves. Permits, of course, are required before the trees can be cut down. The prices paid for a single tree can vary from £5 to upwards of £30.

There are six garages in the village, including one British Road Services Depot. Before the nationalisation of road transport, carrier runs were made by local hauliers to both Glasgow and Edinburgh, but these had to be abandoned under the Act as the hauliers were limited to operating within a specified radius. Milk and timber are the main commodities handled by the contractors, but general haulage work is accepted as well. The garages are well equipped and each contractor undertakes the maintenance of his own vehicles.

Community Life

The main family names in the village are Halliday and Paterson. Inter-marriage has taken place between two families, and now the relationships between the bearers of these two names are so involved that only a senior wrangler could adequately sort them out. A village hall was given to the village by one of the saw-millers, and now forms the focal point of village life. It is under the care of seven trustees who are elected as occasion demands, but is run by the secretary and treasurer, which is one of the extraneous duties which fall to the village schoolmaster. In this hall meets the Women's Rural Institute, which is perhaps the most flourishing of all the social institutions in the village. It has from 60 to 70 members and provides lectures, talks, competitions, cookery demonstrations, parties and social evenings for its members and friends. These are a source of great enjoyment. There is also a smaller W.R.I. in the 'high end' of the parish. The men are catered for by a carpet bowling club which meets on two evenings a week, though it must be admitted that the village inn plays just as big a part as a focal centre. An amateur dramatic club also uses the village hall for rehearsals and performances. It has about 20 members and what may be lacking in polish in their performances is made up for by their enthusiasm.

Like any large city Palnackie has its youth problem. A social consciousness and sense of responsibility are not too well developed amongst some of the young people. Minor outbreaks of hooliganism crop up from time to time, but there is nothing vicious behind them, and if handled properly the young lads are quite amenable. A youth club and the Girl Guides meet once a week in the hall. There are about 15 members in each, and they are run by the teaching staff of the local school. In the youth club lack of equipment is a drawback, as all apparatus has to be bought by the members of the club themselves. A playing field lies on the edge of the village, and is used by the men's football team in the summer and by the village children all the year round.

Incidentally, one of the games played by the village girls is new to the writer, and would have delighted the author of *The Golden Bough.* The game is called 'Pancakes'. The children pick a Mother, a Witch and a Maid. The Witch goes off and hides. The Mother and the Maid take the other children into 'a house', the other children being known as pancakes. The Mother goes for a walk, telling the Maid to look after the pancakes well. The Witch now comes to the door of the house and asks the Maid to get her something from the kitchen and while her back is turned the Witch steals as many 'pancakes' from the house as she can and carries them off. When the Mother returns, she counts the pancakes, and, finding some missing, everyone falls to and beats the Maid. The terms Witch, Maiden and Mother can be found in Frazer's *The Golden Bough*, abridged edition, page 403, as terms applied in Scotland to the last sheaf of corn cut, and it seems likely that the game 'Pancakes' is an old Corn-mother festival tricked out in modern guise as a children's game.

While dealing with such trivia, it might be as well to mention one house whose name has an amusing origin. This house stands high on the hill above Palnackie and commands a view down the Urr estuary, to the open sea. It was used as a lookout post by the smugglers in the days when Palnackie was a port, and lights in the windows were arranged so as to inform the vessels which were standing off and on in the Solway when it was safe to come up the river. This house still bears its old name of Glowrowrum, which if read in Scots will explain its function.

Modern transport has produced tremendous changes in the life of a country community. The ubiquitous bus now takes people wherever they wish to go; shopping in Dumfries, to drama festivals in Castle-Douglas, the cinema, football matches, social meetings and outings, school trips and even on holiday. Twenty or more years ago the roads of the parish were thick with white dust. Returning from church in the pony and trap days it was a point of politeness that no driver of a high-mettled pony passed a slower equipage, for fear that the occupants of the slower vehicle should have their Sunday clothes spoiled by the clouds of dust that were stirred up in the passing. Nowadays roads in the parish and in the surrounding area are in first-class condition, bus fares are reasonable and leisure is more abundant so that everything leads to an abandonment of the old isolation in which country communities lived. Villages such as Palnackie have become semi-urbanised without losing in any way their sense of community, and influenced by the towns their way of life is more comfortable and congenial than of old. Most houses in the parish are electrically lit, and the new houses in Palnackie might be those in a housing scheme in any city. The wealthier people have television sets and washing machines and a standard of living which city people might envy. And yet their life is more peaceful. There is the clash and buzz of village life, it is true, but it is all very harmless, and there is none of the bitter political faction which is so prevalent these days. Politically the people are Conservatively inclined, but politics are hardly ever a subject of discussion and largely pass the parish by. In the main the parish is prosperous and happy, and, as long as farming and timber and road haulage remain as remunerative as they are just now, will so continue.

1952

CHAPTER 11

THE PARISH OF CARSPHAIRN

by the late REV. WILFRID R. SIEVEWRIGHT

Name

The name of the parish of Carsphairn is probably derived from the Gaelic, *carse* and *fearna*, the plain of the alder trees.

Extent and Boundaries. The extent and boundaries have not changed since the time of the *New Statistical Account*. The parish is bounded on the north by the parishes of Dalmellington and New Cumnock; on the east by the parish of Dalry; on the south by Kells; and on the west and south-west by the parishes of Straiton and Minnigaff. The parish of Carsphairn is almost circular. It extends from the north-west to south-east about ten miles, and from the north-east to south-west about nine miles, and contains about 88 square miles.

Agriculture

The large estate of Craigengillan, which owned a considerable part of the land of Carsphairn at one time, was broken up about 1922 and some of the farms became the property of the occupiers. Unfortunately the farms in some instances are owned by farmers who reside outwith the parish, to the loss of the community life of the district.

The land is hilly and in consequence it is used extensively for the grazing of sheep. The Forestry Commission, however, have entered the parish and have planted trees on the farms of Muirdrockwood, Marscalloch and Dundeugh. Other farm lands which reared a good class of sheep will shortly be planted.

An interesting feature which should be noted is that, since the second world war, cattle now graze on the hills. In the opinion of the writer this change, by tearing up the grass and weeds and varying the manure, should do much to better the condition of the hill land and so contribute to the food stock of the country. Too long have sheep grazed on the hills, which may in some measure account for the periodic recurrence of certain types of disease among sheep. Subsidies granted to farmers should enable them to treat their lands with lime and other chemical manures, which should add to the growth value and the sweetening of the grass lands of the hills. More could certainly be done along this line for the benefit of grazing and agricultural prosperity, upon which so much depends at the present time.

During and since the war, ploughing has been revived in the parish because of the necessity to produce more cattle fodder for local consumption. Although the extent of ploughing is small in comparison with other rural parishes, there are four farms with tractors; and the other farms can hire tractors and implements either from the appropriate government department or from a tractor owner in the neighbouring parish of Dalry. The acreage under cultivation is unknown but should be in the region of 50 to 70 acres. The hills are grass to the top but a considerable amount of bracken remains uncut to the detriment of hill grazing.

As a result of the acquisition of large areas of land by the Forestry Commission for the planting of trees, good farms are being denuded of sheep at a time when production of live stock is absolutely necessary to provide food for the people of the country; whether this is sound economy, time alone will tell.

NAMES OF FARMS

Farms marked O = *Owner-occupier*
S = *Inhabited by shepherd in employment of owner*
T = *Tenant farmer*
F.C. = *Forestry Commission*

S	Muir of Deuch		Shiel (uninhabited)
S	Brownhill	S	Castlemaddie
S	Waterhead		Polquhanity (house let)
S	Eriff (Loch Muick)	S	Carminnow
S	Meadowhead	T	Knockgray
S	Lamford	S	Marbrack
S	Drumjohn	S	Furmiston
O	Lamloch	F.C.	Marscalloch
S	Woodhead	F.C.	Muirdrockwood
O	Brockloch	S	Smeaton
T	Holm of Daltollachan	S	Craigengillan
T	Garryhorn	S	Strahanna
O	The Crofts	O	Holm of Dalquhairn
T	Carnavel	S	Upper Holm
O	Bardennoch	F.C.	Dundeugh

Population

Unfortunately, as in other rural communities, there is the story of depopulation. Young people must find employment outside the parish; in consequence, the number of young people in the parish is small. Again the children from the age of twelve have to travel for their education to Dalry Secondary School, or to Kirkcudbright Academy. This leaving of the parish at an early age may be good educationally but it also engenders in the young mind an outlook which prefers the stir of town life to the quiet of the country, to the loss of that enthusiasm for things rural so necessary for the good of the country and a parish like Carsphairn. Twenty-five years ago Carsphairn had two teachers; now it has no schoolmaster, only a lady teacher with 16 pupils. The population of the parish at the census of 1951 was 250, a big reduction from the 1931 census figure of 355.

Public Services

Carsphairn village is fortunate in being up-to-date in every way. It has a good water supply and sanitation. Electricity supplies light and power to all the houses except two.

The houses and farms in the parish are well provided with a telephone service; and the local post office deals with money order business. Most houses have the wireless, and in winter when weather is bad and snow covers the roads to the exclusion of transport and news-papers this form of amusement and news service is a great boon and a blessing.

The parish is served by two doctors, one from New Galloway and the other from Dalmellington. The children are examined by a school doctor and dentist. In general the people enjoy good health, and longevity is happily the rule and not the exception.

Up to 1949 Carsphairn had the services of a policeman who resided in the village, but in that year, in the interests of economy and efficiency, the constable was withdrawn and the police station sold. This change may have led to an economy, but it is doubtful if the new arrangements are as satisfactory or efficient. The nearest police station is in Dalry, ten miles distant.

Voluntary Organisations

Before the outbreak of the second world war Carsphairn could boast of a Girl Guide company, which later ceased to exist owing to lack of numbers. A Women's Rural Institute is in a flourishing condition with a membership of over 40. Under the aegis of the Education Authority of the Stewartry of Kirkcudbright, further education has played an important part in the life of the community; classes in drama, singing, country dancing, sewing and leather work have been held with profit. But the stringency of the times and the cost of maintenance make it doubtful if the provision of these classes will continue. A carpet bowl-ing club and a badminton club are strong and attract quite a number of the shepherds, the former more so than the latter. A public hall was given to Carsphairn by a visitor, Major Wright, and is of great value to the communal life of the parish.

The Church

The only church in the parish is that of the Church of Scotland. Up to 1930 the parish had two churches, but in that year both agreed to unite under the present minister. There is a Sunday school which is not over strong in attendance owing to the small number of children in the parish and the distances which must be travelled. A service and Sunday school are held at Stroanfreggan in the parish of Dalry; here more children attend the Sunday school than at Carsphairn.

The church, erected about 1815, has undergone two major alterations. When first built the church was half hexagonal at the west end; later this was squared and a gallery erected to accommodate the miners who worked at the leadmines in the parish. In 1931-2 the gallery was removed, the ceiling raised and a chancel added to the east end; also in the reconstruction scheme a vestry and vestibule were built and a pipe organ was installed. This scheme has greatly added to the beauty of the building, which is much admired by the great number of visitors who frequent it throughout the year. The old communion table, which runs up the centre of the church, was retained as a feature of the building, much to the satisfaction and pleasure of the inhabitants. In 1949 the Woman's Guild installed electric light and erected a stone font, which greatly enhance the dignity of the church. At the present time there are six elders and a Woman's Guild of 30 members.

The glebe, which extends to about 18 acres, was until 1946 a golf course, but war conditions made its retention as a golf course difficult and expensive; in consequence, it was given up and is now farmed by a retired postman, who has reaped good mixed crops.

Housing

In general housing conditions are good. Nearly all houses in the village are owner-occupied. The former United Free Church was bought by the county council and converted into two commodious and substantial houses for the local roadmen. Few houses in the parish are in a state of disrepair and the village of Carsphairn is perhaps the tidiest and best kept in the county.

Occupations

The parish has no industry other than agriculture. Even the farrier, the tailor and the shoemaker have departed owing to the decline in the population, the introduction of the ready-made article, and the greater transport facilities which allow people to travel longer distances cheaply and shop in town.

At one time the village had two carpenters—now there is only one; the parish used to boast a dry-stone dyker—now no one follows that occupation. Three public houses used to cater for the inhabitants—now there is only the Salutation Hotel; three carters brought the merchandise from Dalmellington—now no one follows this calling. Two merchant shops still look after the dwindling custom of the people, while co-operative and multiple store vans serve at one's door. Two fish vans and two butcher vans also make their rounds in the parish.

War Memorials

In grateful remembrance of the men who fell in the first world war a memorial suited to the nature of the district was erected in 1923, and unveiled by Colonel Wm. H. Clark Kennedy, V.C., a native of Carsphairn who served with the Canadian Army. There are 13 names on the memorial. A brass tablet, on which there are three names, was placed in the church in 1946 to commemorate those who gave their lives in the second world war.

CHAPTER 12

THE PARISH OF COLVEND AND SOUTHWICK

by the REV. JAMES D. DUFF

Situation, Boundaries and Extent

Irregular in shape, and in surface, and of great beauty throughout, the parish of Colvend and Southwick lies in the Stewartry of Kirkcudbright immediately to the east of the Urr estuary; it contains some 23,472 acres and is bounded on the north by the parishes of Urr, Kirkgunzeon and New Abbey, and on the east by Kirkbean. The tides and sands of the Solway Firth are its boundary on the south.

Appearance and Attractions

The Colvend shore has provided an attraction for several generations; its caves and inlets hidden beneath lofty cliffs harboured the smugglers of whose exploits many stories are still told locally; its sands and kindly climate drew the 'sea-bathers', a word still in use amongst the older inhabitants, of Victorian days; and at the present time the lovely Bay of Sandyhills and the picturesque village and shore of Rockcliffe are crowded during summer week-ends and holiday periods with sightseers, bathers, picnickers, till parking space for motor cars and buses is difficult to find. This is indeed the 'Scottish Riviera' where beauty, mild climate and a very moderate rainfall conspire to provide ideal conditions for seaside rest.

Colvend is the westerly part of the united parish, and its beauty is of a rugged cast; outcrops of granite make natural rockeries everywhere, and scarce is a field to be seen without the rock either actually showing through, or causing islands to be left untilled because it lies just beneath the surface. But the local farmers have a very high opinion of the soil that lies in between the rocks, although at times they may refer to their beloved parish as 'the riddlings of creation'. Southwick lies to the east, and in its southern parts the beauty is softer; here down on the Merse begins the rich farming land that runs eastwards through Kirkbean.

Changes in Appearance

Physically the parish would appear very much as it is described in the earlier accounts, save that the main roads, maintained by the county council, are now very good and very busy; but the roads leading to the farms are often very rough, while many of the tracks formerly used by pedestrians are overgrown and almost forgotten. One would notice too that many of the crofts and smaller farms of the hillsides have been swallowed up by larger units; many of the but-and-bens and steadings of earlier days are in ruin, sometimes showing little more than their turf-covered outlines. Dr. Fraser, re-editing W. R. McDiarmid's *Handbook of Colvend and Southwick,* notes in 1895: 'within the last fifty years sixty such dwellings in the parish have been allowed to go to ruin and the families from sheer necessity have been obliged to seek the means of living elsewhere'. With the passing of these upland crofts, less of the actual hill ground is under cultivation than was at one time the case, and acres that once supported families provide now but a rough summer grazing. Only their names, lovely names like Craigieknowes, Croftmarill, Tarlillyan, are remembered affectionately by a generation that is growing thinner in its ranks.

Another change which would forcibly strike the eye is the carpet of green which has fallen over some of the hills and fills the higher valleys, a carpet of young and grown coniferous trees planted by the Forestry Commission. The beauty of it is apt to be monotonous, but it provides work and timber and uses much otherwise waste ground. There are local complaints that it gives shelter to many pests; to foxes, which are on the increase in the district; to rabbits, which are always with us here; to grey squirrels, pigeons and carrion crows.

But perhaps the most striking change of all in the appearance of the district is the increase in the size of Kippford, or, as the older people prefer to call it, the Scaur, and the rise of Rockcliffe as a village; in both places many private residences of considerable size and beauty, set in well-kept grounds and gardens, have been built. At Sandyhills too a number of residences look out over the bay to the lofty mountains of Cumberland, while clustered along the shore, and on both sides of the road leading to Dalbeattie (the Moss road where the peats were at one time gathered) there is a great number of huts and caravans, which disfigure the landscape at times, but provide welcome holiday accommodation for many, within easy reach of the sands. These dwellings, like many things in life, are a source of worry and sometimes annoyance to those who do not live in them, but a great source of joy and recreation to those who do.

Population

Little physical change would be noticed in Southwick, but there, as in Colvend, very few of the people belong to families which have been 'Co'en and Soothick' folk for generations. A very high percentage of the population has come in from outwith the parish. In the *New Statistical Account* the population was given as 1,495; that year, 1841, was a peak period; thereafter the population began to decline as the railways began to undermine the coastal trade upon which Kippford's prosperity had depended; also the farms had begun to grow in size and decrease in numbers and many natives sought their fortunes in the cities, on the high seas, in America, or in the Colonies.

Past population figures are as follows:—

1801	1,106
1841	1,495 (maximum ever recorded)
1851	1,398
1901	1,171
1911	1,143
1921	1,430
1931	1,128

At the time of the census in 1951 the population was given as 1,024, of which 446 were males, and 578 females.

The largest centre of population is Kippford, or the Scaur, with some 70 homes, including the houses at Rough Firth. Rockcliffe follows with some 60 houses. Approximately 50 per cent. of the houses in Kippford and Rockcliffe have been erected comparatively recently. The Portling and Portowarren area has some 20 residences; Sandyhills and Douglas Hall together account for 18; Barnbarroch has some 17; Mainsriddle about 12, and Caulkerbush half-a-dozen. It is impossible to give accurate figures as many of the houses in Kippford and Rockcliffe have annexes in the grounds, some inhabited in summertime, others lived in all the year round in these days of housing scarcity; again in all cases it is not easy to say where a village or hamlet begins or ends; and in some cases houses are in process of falling into disuse and ruin.

A considerable proportion of the inhabitants of Kippford and Rockcliffe are retired people, with a consequent scarcity of children and young people in these areas; but in other parts of the parish the distribution of age and youth is normal.

Agriculture

The principal occupation of the people of the parish is agriculture. Great changes have taken place in farming methods since the last account. Colvend and Southwick have moved forward with the general advance in agriculture throughout the country, but the following local changes are worthy of note. In the *New Statistical Account* we are told that 'the cattle are almost all of Galloway breed'. To-day there are still Galloways to be seen, but Ayrshire cows far outnumber them, and it is on the Ayrshires and their milk that the present prosperity of the farms in the parish is founded. A hundred years ago this was a poor parish; the majority of the farms were small, and the occupiers were glad to eke out a livelihood by working out on larger farms, trapping rabbits, fishing, labouring, and the like, if the size of the croft were insufficient to support a family. Crops of barley and oats were grown, with hay and turnips for winter feeding; milk was frequently made into cheese, the whey being fed to pigs; a coveted acquisition was a milk-round, for it paid well while the summer season lasted; calves were reared to be sold outside the parish. In winter the milk supply fell, but it scarcely mattered, for the customers too had gone till summer brought them again. But the returns were distressingly small; bulk milk, for instance, would sell at 5d a gallon. Writing in 1894 Dr. Fraser notes that 'the cultivation, even of good land, will hardly pay the labour and the outlay, not to speak of the rent'. Things on the land were black, and it was in these days that many left the parish to seek a fortune elsewhere.

The first world war brought relief to farming here as elsewhere, but conditions deteriorated again until the coming of the Milk Marketing Board. With the arrival of an assured market, bringing in steady returns, came the means of producing milk all the year round, the making of silage, the growing of more root crops, the feeding of concentrates. Farmers were not slow to adopt these new methods, which were costly but paid grand dividends. To-day there is scarcely a farm or croft in the parish which has not its milk churns full and ready for the milk lorry to collect.

Now the farms that were once uneconomic to cultivate are well cropped; not that the farmers of to-day are better than those of a generation or two ago, but they can now afford to take advantage of the improved methods. The following statistics will give an indication of the present state of agriculture in the parish:

Number of agricultural holdings in Colvend and Southwick	—	82
Gross rental as at 4 June 1952	—	£6,351
Acres under tillage	—	1,429
„ „ rotation grasses	—	1,864
„ „ permanent grass	—	2,200
„ „ rough grazing	—	7,915

Catering for Summer Visitors

The population increases greatly between June and the third week of September, when large numbers of holiday makers visit the parish. Some come from elsewhere in Scotland, but many are from the north of England. There are three licensed hotels, one each in Kippford, Rockcliffe and Southwick; there are also unlicensed hotels in Kippford and Rockcliffe; there are also several guest houses, and in many houses throughout the parish accommodation may be had, with or without attendance. There are also numerous huts, annexes, and houses to let by week or month during the holiday season. The beaches are splendid playgrounds for children; there are golf courses at Sandyhills and Kippford; there is yachting on the Urr estuary, and everywhere are delightful walks.

Forestry

In 1922 the Forestry Commission began planting coniferous trees in the parish, and at that time eight or ten men were employed; to-day the Commission employs around 60 workers, and has planted out 3,300 acres, about half of which is now in production for pit props and other purposes.

Quarrying

Granite was quarried at Barnbarroch around the middle of last century, and to some extent this industry compensated for the loss of employment

Plate 1. DUNDRENNAN ABBEY (the Old Abbey)

Plate 2. SWEETHEART ABBEY (the New Abbey)

Galloway News

Plate 3. GALLOWAY BULL SHOW
Parade preceding the Annual Sale at Castle-Douglas.

Dairy Supply Co., Edinburgh

Plate 4. WHITEPARK FARM, CASTLE-DOUGLAS
Modern dairy with refrigeration tank, designed for milk collection scheme.

caused by the cessation of shipbuilding and repairing at Kippford, following upon the decline of the coastal schooner trade, and also for that produced by the closing of the Millstone Quarries on the Glenstocking shore. In more recent days a quarry has been active at Kippford, but there is now no quarrying carried out in the parish.

Fishing

There are stake nets for salmon fishing at Portling, and fishermen from Kippford are engaged in mussel-gathering at the mouth of the Urr.

Local Trades

Another change which has taken place in the life of the community since the writing of the last account is the disappearance of the local boot and clog makers and tailors. Clogs were extensively worn some years ago but are now the exception. The unmistakable sound of clogs can still be heard, but these dry and cosy articles of footwear are disappearing quickly, before the advance of the much less hygienic wellington boots wherever it is damp underfoot.

Tweed is woven at Barnbarroch, but this is a recent introduction, not a continuation of the weaving of earlier days which was carried on in many homes throughout the parish. Some very beautiful work is being produced.

There are still three blacksmith's shops within the bounds of the parish, at Sandyhills, Caulkerbush and Auchenskeoch; the repairs effected at the smiddies are now more often to tractors and their implements than to horses. There are also three joiners and builders and one firm of masons.

Grocer's shops are four, one each in Kippford, Rockcliffe, Sandyhills and Caulkerbush, and in addition the district is well served by butcher's, baker's and grocer's vans from Dalbeattie and New Abbey. A great deal of the weekly shopping is done on market days in Castle-Douglas, Dalbeattie and Dumfries. Such large stores of meal, flour and other foods are not kept in the homes as was once the case; this was noticeable in the great storm of 1947 when the roads leading out of the parish were blocked. Most people nowadays are not prepared to withstand a prolonged siege.

Postal Service

Mail is now delivered throughout the parish fairly early in the day; the postman rings the manse bell at 7.15 a.m. Gone are the days when the pony and trap brought the mailbags from Dalbeattie to the local post offices whence the letters and packages were delivered by 'walking posts'. Now vans from Dalbeattie in the west and from Dumfries in the east make their way up the farm roads, or else the mail is left in boxes provided for the purpose at the 'road-ends'. The last two 'walking posts' covering rural areas retired this year, but in the village of Kippford there is still a delivery on foot. In Rockcliffe the 'postie' uses

I

a cycle. There are four local post offices—at Kippford, Colvend, Rockcliffe and Caulkerbush. Newspapers are either delivered by post, or else are thrown out from passing buses at the appropriate road-end and garden gate.

Water Supply

Formerly each house had its own supply, either from a well or by gravity from a spring on the hillside, or there might be such a supply for a group of houses. But now a county council supply is piped to Kippford and Rockcliffe and the houses and farms on the route. Throughout the rest of the parish water supply is either private or communally serves a group of houses.

Sewerage

A unified sewage disposal system throughout the parish would be quite impossible. However the proximity of tidal water in many parts of the parish makes the outflow from cesspools simple; in other parts the outflow simply percolates the soil; in many places water has no part in the system at all.

The ashpits which were once expected in every country garden have largely disappeared; the refuse is now collected weekly by a county council motor-lorry.

Electricity

For almost a quarter of a century the parish, in parts, has enjoyed the benefit of electric light; and the supply is reaching out to more rural areas. At present the South-West Scotland Electricity Board is taking cables north from Caulkerbush to serve a large area. One noteworthy gap in the provision of electricity is the area between the Manse and Barnbarroch Schoolhouse.

Besides lighting, the electric current is extensively used to operate milking and other machines on the farms, and electric welding has made its appearance in one of the smiddies. There is no street lighting, and in wintertime meetings, concerts and public functions are often timed to coincide with the full of the moon.

Education

There are three schools in the parish, two in Colvend and one in Southwick. Barnbarroch School, with one lady teacher, serves the Kippford and Barnbarroch area. It is the oldest school building in use in the parish, and at one time last century had an excellent name for turning out boys well equipped mathematically to become officers and captains in the merchant navy. The school at Colvend (Lochend) serving the Rockcliffe, Sandyhills, Portling area is also a one-teacher school. Both these schools have around two dozen pupils on the average. After the age of eleven-twelve the pupils attend the secondary school at Dalbeattie; if they attend the senior secondary school at

Kirkcudbright, it necessitates residence away from home. Southwick School has a headmaster and one lady teacher with an average of around 40 pupils.

Tales are still told of the distances walked by children to and from school, often over rough hill tracks; three miles to school in the morning and three back in the evening was no uncommon thing. Now the children from the more remote parts are driven to school in the school bus, which also takes the pupils from the parish to Dalbeattie school. Some young children in the north and central districts of the parish attend Dalbeattie school, and the children from Mainsriddle area travel by bus to Kirkbean school.

Midday meals are provided in school; at Southwick these are cooked on the premises; to Barnbarroch and Colvend they are brought in vacuum containers from Dalbeattie. They are greatly enjoyed by the children and are a great improvement on the 'piece eaten in the shelter of the dyke' of which the older folk tell. One noteworthy feature is the happy eagerness with which the children attend school; they no longer 'creep like snails unwillingly to school'; it says a great deal for the teachers and methods of the present day.

Evening classes are also held for adults in sewing and other crafts; these are well attended. Up till 1950, branches of the rural library were installed in the local schools, but since that date the Kirkcudbright County Council Education Committee's rural library van, a library on wheels, pays a welcome call weekly, remaining on certain recognised sites until the readers' books have been changed.

Health Services

There is one doctor in the parish, resident at Mainsriddle. Others from Dalbeattie and New Abbey attend patients in the district. Patients requiring hospital treatment are taken to the Dumfries and Galloway Royal Infirmary in Dumfries, or to the Castle-Douglas and district hospital in Castle-Douglas. This makes the visiting of patients by their friends somewhat difficult.

Those in need of nursing attention at home are visited by a district nurse from Dalbeattie or Kirkbean; there is no Queen's nurse resident in the parish. Many of the babies are born at home, but perhaps almost an equal number first see the light of day in the Cresswell Maternity Hospital, Dumfries, or in other nursing homes.

People seem to enjoy good health in the district, and most pass peacefully away in their own homes from no other ailments than those to be expected in extreme old age; no doubt the leisured tempo of life and the comparatively gentle climate have much to do with it.

Police

There is a police constable resident in the parish, at Mainsriddle. The rest of the area is covered by the officers from Dalbeattie. But fortunately there is no great requirement for their more stern duties. There is little crime, and though drinking is by no means uncommon, there is little drunkenness or disorder.

Women's Organisations

Colvend, Southwick, and Drumstinchall each have a branch of the Scottish Women's Rural Institute; monthly meetings with varied programmes of interest to women are held; the meetings and other activities are well attended and greatly appreciated by the members.

Branches of the Church of Scotland Woman's Guild hold monthly meetings in Colvend, and in Southwick; these are also well attended; the programmes concern the work of the church at home and abroad, and throughout have a very pronounced spiritual emphasis, they complement the activities of the 'Rural'.

Youth Organisations

There is a company of the Girl Guides in Colvend and another in Southwick; a pack of Brownies meets in Southwick House. Some time ago there was a troop of Boy Scouts in Colvend, whose numbers were greatly increased at the time of the evacuation during the second world war. It has since fallen into abeyance.

Sports

Carpet bowls are keenly played in Colvend Public Hall, in Bridgend Hall, Sandyhills, and in the church hall, Mainsriddle. Badminton is played in Colvend Public Hall and in Redbank Hall, Mainsriddle. There is a lawn tennis court at Southwick, and another in course of construction at Colvend. There is a splendid nine-hole golf course at Sandyhills, and another at Kippford attached to the Pines Hotel. At Kippford are the headquarters of the Solway Yacht Club, founded in 1904 with an ever growing membership and fleet of yachts; at present there are some 50 boats. Races are held throughout the season and an annual regatta in July draws many spectators. Many of the members travel long distances to sail on the Urr at week-ends, and these find the comfortable clubhouse, conveniently situated opposite the race starting line, a great convenience. Football is played with great enthusiasm on rather rough pitches at Sandyhills and Southwick.

Halls

For over 20 years now the Public Hall at Colvend has provided very convenient accommodation for meetings, concerts and recreation. It was erected by public subscription and by money raised by the W.R.I., under the leadership of the late Dr. Morris of Baron's Craig. It is capable of holding 300 people and is an invaluable asset in the life of the parish. There is also a hall at Mainsriddle under private ownership; it was formerly the U.P. Church building. The old United Free Church Hall at Mainsriddle is also still in use, but is rapidly falling into decay. There are smaller halls at Bridgend, Sandyhills and at Drumstinchall, while at Colvend Manse and at the Church of Southwick there are small church halls for congregational purposes.

Politics

The political outlook of the parish is predominantly Conservative, though many have a hankering after the former glories of Liberalism; some others see in Socialism the future way of hope for our country, and there is reputed to be a Communist. There are also several interested in the activities of the Scottish Covenant Association.

Transport

At the time of the last Account the easiest approach to the parish from a distance was by sea; coasting schooners traded between Liverpool, and the ports on the English coast of the Solway, and Kippford, Palnackie, and Dalbeattie. Passengers, coal and lime were introduced in that way, and the produce of the area—barley, corn, stone—was shipped out in the same manner. The coming of the railway to Dalbeattie in 1859 made the parish easier of access; prior to that the journey inland towards Dumfries, if not by water, was by horse-drawn vehicle, or on horseback, or on foot, a distance of 20 miles. The return journey on foot was by no means uncommon, and it is still narrated how at times a 'gird' (a hoop of ¼in. iron some 30 ins. in diameter steered by an iron 'cleek', similar to that used by children a generation ago) was used to encourage the walker to keep up a brisk trot for long mile after weary mile.

Now one walks most often to get exercise, very seldom to get anywhere. There is a good number of private motor cars in the parish; almost every farmer owns one; at a rough count the writer can think of 130 cars garaged all the year round in the combined parish. More careful counting would certainly reveal a larger number.

A very useful bus operated by Messrs. A. C. Penman plies between Dalbeattie and Rockcliffe and Sandyhills. It not only conveys passengers but acts as carrier also. Its driver most obligingly shops for those unable to visit town, and succeeds in carrying a bewildering assortment of requests in his mind and fulfilling them all to the letter; he has driven this bus for very many years and is a much beloved member of the community. The same bus also conveys worshippers and Sunday School children to Colvend church on Sundays. The Western S.M.T. Co. operates buses between Dumfries and Kippford *via* Dalbeattie, while Mr. J. Carruthers, a New Abbey bus proprietor, runs buses between Dumfries and Rockcliffe by the coast road.

There is no longer any traffic by sea between Colvend and the parts of England on the south side of the Solway. Small motor and steam coasters still from time to time make their way up the winding River Urr at high water to Palnackie, picking up a Kippford pilot, but no vessel now uses the pier at Kippford.

Churches

For the second time the ecclesiastical parishes of Colvend and Southwick are united under one minister. On 29 June 1950 the present incumbent was inducted to the united charge by the Presbytery of Dumfries. Previously the parishes had been joined in the reign of James VI; on 21 September 1612 David Hope was presented to the vicarage of Southwick and Cowen by the King.

The parishes remained united until the proprietor of Southwick estate, Sir Mark J. Stewart, M.P., had the new church of Southwick built in 1891. This lovely little church is in the Norman style. The cost was met by Sir Mark with some assistance from the Home Mission Committee of the Church of Scotland, the Baird Trust, and the Ferguson Bequest Fund, and approached £3,000. The result is a most worshipful sanctuary, unusual in its beauty and atmosphere of repose. There are in the belfry three bells—Faith, Hope and Charity—but, through some error, the least of these is inscribed 'Charity'!

Prior to 1891 the people of Southwick had to make their way to Colvend Church, up to eight miles distant; they did not frequently do so, except at Communion season. It was this which prompted the erection of the *quoad sacra* parish of Southwick.

Before the earlier joining of the parishes in 1612 Southwick Church was situated in the heart of the parish, in the small rocky glen of the Back Burn. The ruins of the building stand in the churchyard, which is still the burial place of the people of the eastern end of the parish. The first mention of the church is in the wardrobe accounts of Edward I; on 23 August 1300 he devoted a small sum to our Lady of Southwick. The old church was in occasional use for worship as late as 1743, in which year there is notice of an offender being rebuked before the congregation in Southwick church. There are tombstones in the churchyard bearing the date 1660 and onwards; one small stone bears the apt inscription *Hodie mihi Cras tibi*.

The church at Colvend in pre-Reformation times belonged to the Benedictine Nunnery of Lincluden, and subsequently to the Collegiate Church there. Annexed to Colvend Church was the Chapel of St. Lawrence at Fairgirth. The present church of Colvend stands in the old burying ground, and on the site of two known earlier churches. A new building was erected in 1771, and was in use until the first Sunday of October 1910 when Communion was held in it for the last time; it was thereafter taken down, the people worshipping meantime in Colvend school. The present church was built after a design by P. McGregor Chalmers, in the Norman style. It was opened on 27 July 1911.

Colvend church is well attended; Southwick church less so, for the members there are scattered over a wide area, and they have not the convenience of a church bus as at Colvend. The children of both districts attend Sunday School well. An interesting feature of the worship is that in Colvend shortbread is used as one of the elements at the

Communion service; the common cup is used there; at Southwick individual cups are used.

The majority of the parishioners are members of or adhere to the parish church, but there is a considerable flock belonging to the Scottish Episcopal Church, or to the Church of England. This latter group is not so much native to the parish as due to the numbers of incomers to the district, many from south of the border; some of these attend worship in the parish church; others naturally prefer their own form of worship and attend Christ Church, Dalbeattie. There are one or two Roman Catholic families.

Antiquities

In the district are several traces of fortifications; in the former accounts the forts on Castle Hill and the Mote at Rockcliffe receive mention. Since that account was written, subsequent study has suggested that these are not Danish as had been thought, but more probably belong to the Norman period. There are also fortifications at Portowarren and on the Moyle Hill at Barnbarroch.

Of similar period are the remains of fortified dwellings at Colvend on the right hand side of the Boreland Farm road, and at Southwick on the north side of the main road almost opposite the farm of Brough.

Hut circles and a considerable stone cairn are to be seen on the hillside above Boreland of Southwick.

In the Barean Loch in Colvend is a small island near the south end; at a time of dry weather in 1865, when the water was exceptionally low, the island was explored by members of the Dumfriesshire and Galloway Antiquarian Society, and it was found by oak piling and flooring to have been a crannog; previously two copper pots had been found on the island.

The ancient Church of Southwick is at present being excavated by Mr. Oliver H. Haslam, of Cairngill. He has not yet any discoveries to publish.

Fairgirth House, the residence of Mr. George Sloan, is probably the oldest inhabited house in the parish; it has been extensively modernised, but the charm of earlier days has been retained; the smoke-mellowed beams, the large fireplace occupying almost the whole west wall, the delightfully decorated aumbry on the north wall, the aged studded door leading to a winding stair in the oldest part of the house, all combine to make the lounge hall most attractive. At the head of the winding stair is a little attic room on whose walls carvings can be seen, but they lie almost hidden beneath many coats of paint and have not yet been investigated. This part of the house may have formed the dwelling of the Priest in Charge of St. Lawrence's Chapel, and also the rest house for ecclesiastical personages travelling between Dundrennan Abbey, New Abbey and Lincluden. The remains of the chapel form part of the wall of the present garden.

The ruins of Auchenskeoch Castle are of interest architecturally in that it is said to be the only example of castellated structure with a Z type ground plan in this part of the country; that is, a castle with a rectangular keep with circular towers at two opposite corners. The castle was the home of the Lindsays who were Master Falconers to the King from 1420 onwards; there was a deadly feud between the Lindsays of Auchenskeoch and their cousins, the Lindsays of Fairgirth.

Origin of Names

The origin of the names Colvend and Southwick has been disputed. What is certain is that from 1145 to 1179 Gospatrick was Lord of Workington in Cumberland; his son Thomas is styled Thomas de Culwen; either Thomas or his father had received a grant of the Lordship of Culwen from one of the Lords of Galloway; a younger son of Gospatrick is styled Gilbert of Suthayk. (*History of the Curwen Family* by J. F. Curwen).

From this it would seem that the names Culwen and Suthayk were already in use. The residences of these branches of the family were in all probability the mote hill at the Brough in Southwick, and the fort at Boreland of Colvend—where there is still the name Boreland, or the 'serf's place'. Culwen may be a form of Cell of John, but that is by no means certain; as regards pronunciation, the natives still call the place 'Coen'. The ancient spelling Suthayk seems to indicate that the meaning of the word has nothing to do with a 'wick' or creek, although the river does wind to the Solway like a creek, but, as has been suggested, it is probably connected with 'ayk' or oak; perhaps it comes from the Norse words meaning a 'blasted oak,' for the name also appears as Suithayk in old manuscripts. Certainly oaks have at one time been very plentiful.

Bird Life

The physical features of the countryside of the parish are immensely varied—hills, lochs, woodlands, a river estuary, a tidal island, tracts of rough uncultivated land, coastal cliffs and tidal flats—and the birds of the parish are correspondingly varied. Rough Island, lying in the estuary off Rockcliffe, is now a bird sanctuary and during the summer is the home of terns, gulls, oyster catchers, lapwings and ringed plovers. Special mention should be made of the migrant wild geese which come in their thousands to the mudflats and pastures near the shore. Recently the fulmar has nested frequently on the sea cliffs. Often, especially in calm winter weather, the sea off the shores may be seen to be streaked with long, dark lines and patches, the immense flotillas of a salt water duck, the scaup.

1953

CHAPTER 13

THE PARISH OF CROSSMICHAEL

by the REV. JAMES A. FISHER

Name

It is accepted that the name of the parish is derived from the Cross of St. Michael although no tradition or trace of the site of the cross exists. The pronunciation of the older men and women of a former generation would seem, however, to lend support to a view advanced by a recognised authority on Galloway history, traditions, and place names, to the effect that the true name of the parish is Cross-Meikle. Dr. Reid in his book *The Kirk above Dee Water* refers to this form of the name.

History

Of the estates in being at the date of the *New Statistical Account* only three, comprising more than two farms, exist to-day. The remaining estates were broken up after the first world war and were purchased in the main by the tenants. As an indication of the character of the change in ownership which has taken place, it is worthy of note that there were 28 heritors in the parish at the date of the former Statistical Account. In 1914 there were 16. To-day the number is 54.

The parish was well wooded and although considerable felling of trees has taken place during the war and later, it has been done with discrimination and consideration for the amenities, with the result that the beauty of the natural scene has not been seriously impaired.

Up to the passing of the Local Government (Scotland) Act, 1929, the parish was administered by a parish council, but is now administered by Castle-Douglas District Council exercising functions delegated by the County Council of the Stewartry. One representative from the parish is elected to the district council and has, as colleague, the local member of the county council. The member of the county council is also a member of the Castle-Douglas Area Education Sub-Committee. There is one Justice of the Peace in the parish, *ex officio* as Convener of the county council.

Prominently situated 200 yards east of the village is a beautiful memorial in the form of a Celtic cross, on the base of which are inscribed the names of men from the parish who gave their lives in two world wars, 36 in the earlier and eight in the late war.

Stipend and Glebe

In 1815, the teinds being exhausted, the stipend was fixed at £269 15s 10d and remains at that figure. Approximately one half of the glebe was purchased in the present century by the Galloway Power Company to provide for flood contingencies; the remaining portion is rented at £22 per annum. In 1815 the author of the *Old Statistical Account* of the parish, the Rev. John Johnston, erected a stone on the glebe with an inscription to mark the point to which the river rose during a time of exceptional flooding. In 1872 the then minister of the parish, the Rev. J. D. Stewart, recorded a slightly greater height on it. When the engineers for the hydro-electric project were formulating their plans, these figures, the only ones existing to show the extent of possible flooding, proved of the greatest value as basic data. The stone is now nationalised, being the property of the British Electricity Authority.

McLellan Trust

The kirk session, which has five elders, administers the McLellan Trust funds which provide a sum of money to assist a candidate studying for the ministry of the Church of Scotland or the mission fields of the Church, preference being given to a native of the parish. The trust also provides £25 annually for distribution to deserving females in sums of £1; this distribution is locally known as 'the Christmas pounds' and yearly stimulates speculation.

Notable Men

Of men who have achieved marked success beyond the parish, notable instances are the three Stewart brothers, sons of the Rev. J. D. Stewart, a former minister of the parish. The eldest, J. Douglas Stewart, became a partner in the shipping firm of James Gardner & Sons, Glasgow. In the course of the first world war he joined the Anglo-Persian Oil Company, became a member of the Board of Directors, and at his death at the early age of 53 was Deputy Chairman of the Company. William A. Stewart, after a successful business career in Glasgow, joined the firm of British Tankers Limited. During the war he was engaged by the Admiralty, and his very efficient services were recognised by the award of the O.B.E. Mitchell B. A. Stewart proved a successful India merchant, and on retirement purchased the estate of Nunland in the county. He entered the county council and became a prominent figure on that body. For some years before the passing of the National Health Service Act he was Chairman of the Dumfries and Galloway Joint Sanatorium Board, which was administered jointly by the county councils of Dumfries, Wigtown and the Stewartry, and the burgh of Dumfries.

Boundaries and Population

The boundaries of the parish remained the same as in the *New Statistical Account* until 1861. Thirty-seven acres of the parish were incorporated in the Burgh of Castle-Douglas. Since then the parish has been divided into two areas for administrative purposes, the landward and the burgh. Changes in the population are shown by the following figures. In 1841 the population of the undivided parish was 1,320; in 1931 the landward population was 1,023 and the burghal part 137; in 1951 the landward population was 1,079 and the burghal part 652. The population of the parish at the 1951 census, including both areas, was 1,731 as compared with the figure of 1,320 in 1841.

Up to the completion of occupancy of county council housing schemes the population, with few exceptions, was native born.

The age structure has changed greatly. There has been a marked increase in the number of old people absolutely and in proportion to other age groups. In the old village of Crossmichael the great majority of the houses are occupied by people over pensionable age.

Crossmichael has had its centenarian in the person of Mary Duff, who died at the great age of 104 years in 1926. On her hundredth birthday she was the amazed recipient of a telegram of royal congratulations. She had pride in speaking of an aunt who, she claimed, had been present on the battlefield in the evening of the day of Waterloo. The aunt was the wife of a sergeant in one of the units engaged in the battle.

Occupations

At the end of the nineteenth century there were two innkeepers, one pumpmaker, three blacksmiths, four shopkeepers, one stone mason, two millers, two shoemakers, two tailors, two joiners and one engraver. These have now been reduced to two joiners, two haulage contractors, and the owners of three shops, one public house and two mansionhouses adapted as hotels fully licensed. The major occupation is agriculture. There are many rich dairy farms, efficiently worked by progressive occupier-owners, following the most approved modern methods of mechanisation in farm management. Farming of the character pursued in this parish is a matter of high finance. It is estimated that a capital sum of £15,000 to £20,000 is necessary to purchase, stock and equip an average size dairy farm of 200 to 300 acres in size.

In the *Old Statistical Account* under the heading 'Implements and Operations of Husbandry' there is an inventory of the parish, namely, 80 ploughs, 120 carts, and 218 horses. To-day an inventory would reveal that while the number of ploughs and carts or their equivalent remains constant the horse has been displaced by the tractor, a prototype of which was operative on the farm of Culvennan in this parish as early as 1912. The attachment of plough, harrow, drill, pick-up baler, binder, mechanical elevator, and other devices to the tractor does the work formerly done by the horse and numerous labourers. Most of the dairy farms are provided with milking machines, sterilisers, and refrigerators, powered by electricity. These installations enable two persons to do the work formerly done by six.

Water Supply

In 1880 certain water rights were acquired by the burgh of Castle-Douglas in one of the lochs mentioned in the former Statistical Account

—Loch Roan. This loch was utilised to provide a piped supply of water to Castle-Douglas. The main passed along the watershed of the parish and piped supplies were made available to the farms and other residences *en route,* including the village of Clarebrand. Otherwise, up to the beginning of the present century, water was obtained from wells and other private sources. Early in the century Mrs. Stewart of Culgruff provided a supply of water to the village of Crossmichael, serviced through stand-pipes. Gradually the privately owned houses were given permission to instal water from these sources, but with the increase in the number of houses following the second world war this water supply proved wholly inadequate. In 1949 the county council received approval by the Department of Health for Scotland of a scheme to institute a piped supply of water on a county basis. Under this scheme the source of the water supply to Crossmichael is Loch Whinyeon. The six-inch main from this source enters the parish of Crossmichael from the neighbouring parish of Balmaghie at Glenlochar. It passes due east, supplying on the way the area of Abbeyyard, Townhead of Greenlaw, and adjoining residences. At Townhead of Greenlaw it turns northward to Crossmichael village, connections being made to farms and residences on the way, including the village school. At the centre of the village it runs eastward to a local storage tank capable of holding 50,000 gallons, sufficient for at least one day's supply to the village. In Crossmichael village at the date of the first world war there was no interior piped supply of water; to-day, out of a total of 102 houses, only three are without such a supply.

Drainage

When the county council's housing schemes at Old Ferry Road and St. Michaels were extended and completed and a total of 52 houses were built in the area it became obvious that the existing sewers in the village were totally inadequate to deal with the increased flow of sewage. It was necessary, therefore, to lay approximately 340 yards of twelve-inch diameter sewer to connect with a septic tank on the banks of the river Dee. At the same time it was necessary to modify the existing septic tank so that it would act as a storm water overflow to discharge the rain water direct into the river Dee. The sewage, of course, passes straight into two new septic tanks which are constructed alongside the existing tank and after attention and digestion in these tanks the effluent flows into the river Dee through an extended outfall pipe. This scheme was completed in June 1952. At Townhead of Greenlaw there is a small local drainage scheme to deal with new county council houses there. Unfortunately it was not possible in this scheme to make provision for the adjoining privately owned houses.

Electricity

On the completion of the Galloway Power Company's Hydro-Electric Scheme, bulk supplies of electricity were made available to the county council who, under the Stewartry of Kirkcudbright Electricity Special Orders 1931 and 1932, became undertakers for the distribution of electricity supplies within the county.   In 1934 the supply system was extended to Crossmichael parish and advantage of it was speedily taken by the farming community for power and lighting.   Owners of houses in the villages of Clarebrand and Crossmichael were also quick to avail themselves of the new scheme.   (In Crossmichael village there are only four houses without electricity).   In 1946 the village of Crossmichael was formed into a Special Lighting District and eleven lamps have been provided, leaving two to be supplied to complete the scheme.

Education

There are two primary schools in the parish, in the villages of Crossmichael and Clarebrand.   Crossmichael is a three-teacher school with 60 pupils and Clarebrand a two-teacher school with 34 pupils.   The number of pupils receiving secondary education either at Castle-Douglas High School or at Kirkcudbright Academy is approximately 20.

Libraries

The Parochial Library mentioned in the *New Statistical Account* continued until the advent of the County Library service in 1922 when the schools became the library centres.   On 26 May 1949 the Education Authority introduced a mobile library service, the first of its kind in Scotland, and the first call was to the village of Crossmichael when 65 books were issued.   This service continued and the number of books issued in the parish during 1951-2 numbered 4,585.   These are additional to books borrowed directly from the Central Library in Castle-Douglas.

Health Services

The parish is served by five doctors from Castle-Douglas and by two district nurses, in the employment of the county council, stationed in Castle-Douglas.   In 1903, adjoining Castle-Douglas, an Infectious Diseases Hospital was erected to accommodate 14 beds.   These served the needs of the population till 1940, when Laurieston Hall in the adjoining parish was adapted as an Infectious Diseases Hospital with accommodation for 40 beds.   The first hospital buildings were then used for the purposes of (a) evacuation, (b) agriculture, and (c) food distribution.   At the end of the war these buildings, with the exception of one retained by the Ministry of Agriculture, reverted to the county council and were organised as the offices of the Health Department of the county.

There is a well-equipped hospital of 37 beds in Castle-Douglas. Provision is made in it for the various clinics necessary for the efficient support of the hospital services.   The central hospital for the south-west of Scotland is the Dumfries and Galloway Royal Infirmary, Dumfries. The maternity hospital used by many expectant mothers in this parish is Cresswell Maternity Hospital, Dumfries, and increasing use of this institution is being made. Of the eleven infants baptised by the minister of this parish in the year 1952, nine were born in Cresswell.

Housing

The housing situation is good. New housing schemes have solved the problem of overcrowding, and houses unfit for habitation are rapidly disappearing.

Housing (Rural Workers) (Scotland) Acts, 1926-42

During the period of operation of these Acts 55 houses in the landward area of Crossmichael parish were modernised with the aid of grants authorised by the Acts. The total amount of subsidies granted was £5,346.

Housing (Agricultural Population) (Scotland) Act, 1938

Fifteen new houses have been erected with the aid of grant at farms in the parish to replace unsatisfactory farm cottages. The total amount of grants paid was £3,600.

Housing (Scotland) Acts, 1950 and 1952

Two houses in the parish have been modernised with the aid of grants amounting in all to £483.

Between 1926 and 1951 65 houses have been built by the county council in the landward area of the parish. In Crossmichael village there are two housing schemes—at Old Ferry Road and St. Michaels. Old Ferry Road is a pre-war scheme consisting of 18 houses of two in a block, one-storey cottage type. The houses are of two and three apartments. At St. Michaels, where there are 34 houses, and at Townhead of Greenlaw, where there are eight houses, they are of the four room type with accommodation comprising living room, 180 square feet, scullery with tub and sink, electric washing boiler and cooker, fuel store and larder, three bedrooms, 143 square feet, 125 square feet, and 110 square feet each respectively, with built-in wardrobes, bathroom, linen cupboards, and a large entrance lobby with accommodation for pram. The total superficial area of each house is 870 square feet. There are four houses at Old Bridge of Urr. These are two-storey, four in a block type, built to the design of Atholl Steel Houses Limited. The accommodation is similar to the other four-apartment houses but the total superficial area of each house is 900 square feet. In the pre-war years Castle-Douglas Town Council built 28 houses in the burgh area. and in the post-war years 132 houses. A house for the headmaster of Castle-Douglas High School was built in the burgh portion of the parish, comprising five apartments.

Antiquities

Joseph Train, the friend and antiquarian correspondent of Sir Walter Scott, writing for the *New Statistical Account*, states: 'There are in no other part of the Stewartry of Kirkcudbright so many vestiges of remote antiquity to be seen in the same space as in the parish of Crossmichael'. He goes on to mention that a few years earlier the head of a caparisoned warhorse in bronze, evidently of Roman manufacture, had been turned up by the plough near Glenlochar Bridge in the parish of Crossmichael. During the century which followed this find nothing of note was unearthed near Glenlochar and indeed no serious thought was given to it since it was held by experts that Galloway was the district 'neglected by Rome'. There was, however, a persistent tradition of organised work in the district. The adjoining area has the name of Abbeyyard and this seemed to imply the existence of an Abbey, but the name probably relates to Sweetheart Abbey, to which the Church of Crossmichael was transferred by Devorgilla, daughter of Alan of Galloway and mother of John Balliol. In the long dry summer of 1949 Dr. St. Joseph, Curator of Aerial Photography at Cambridge, was flying up the river Dee when suddenly he saw clearly outlined in the dry earth the shape of a Roman camp near Glenlochar Bridge. This was a discovery of the greatest archaeological importance, and in 1952 Professor I. A. Richmond of Durham University with Dr. St. Joseph carried out an excavation of the area. The dig revealed that there had been a large camp on the site, that troops had occupied it in the Antonine and Flavian periods and that the garrisons numbered the same as at Birrens, a cohort of 1,000 with probably 200 cavalry. The site will probably be excavated fully at some later date, but the fact of this incidence changes all previous ideas about the nature and extent of the Roman occupation of south-west Scotland.

Church

The church was built in 1751. Notable gifts in recent years are the Communion Table and the electric lighting installation given by Mr. J. H. Mackie, M.P., whose family have had a long association with the church, which contains several memorials, including two windows, to various members of the family. The baptismal font was placed in the church in memory of Miss Duncan of Daneville who had rendered invaluable service as voluntary organist and Sunday School teacher over a period of 60 years. The church was renovated and re-decorated in the late twenties of the present century.

The National Church is the only church in the parish. In the *New Statistical Account* mention is made of 'A Chapel in connection with the Relief Synod'. This building, marked on the 1853 Ordnance Survey map as the United Presbyterian Church, has disappeared, its members having, presumably, been absorbed into the new U.P. Church of Trinity, Castle-Douglas.

The bell in the tower is the oldest extant feature. It was hung in 1611, the year of the publication of the authorised version, and was re-hung in 1881, the year of the revised version, the former date being inscribed on the bell.

Crossmichael has its martyr grave. A tombstone in the churchyard has been erected to the memory of William Graham, who was shot by Claverhouse's Dragoons, and the inscription reads as follows:—

> 'Here lyes William Graham who, makeing his escape from his Mother's house, was pursued and taken and instantly shot by a party of Claverhouse troops for his adherence to Scotland's Reformation Covenants National and Solemn League, 1682.'

The earliest date inscribed in the kirkyard is 1629, on the tomb of Gordon of Airds.

The church, being situated at the north-west corner of the parish, is no longer used by the whole population of the parish for whom it was built. New churches in Castle-Douglas attract a considerable number of members from the families residing near the burgh. The population generally is connected actively or nominally to the Church of Scotland, either to the parish church or to the churches in Castle-Douglas. There are a few Episcopalians, whose church is in Castle-Douglas, and a few Roman Catholics, with a church also in Castle-Douglas.

There has been a decrease in attendances at public worship, not unusual in the evening of a long ministry, but at times of Holy Communion and the festivals of Christmas, Easter, and Harvest there are still large attendances. The family pew, however, has ceased to be a marked feature in the life of the congregation. There is more than a suspicion that listening-in to a broadcast service is accepted as a reasonable substitute for attendance at public worship. There are two Sunday Schools and Bible Classes which are well attended by the majority of those within convenient reach of them. The Woman's Guild has a relatively large membership; the church choir has a long and noteworthy history, frequently competing successfully at Musical Festivals.

Manse

The manse was built in 1744. Since that date it has been enlarged and in 1913-14 it was modernised, water and plumbing being introduced. It is a gracious building attractively situated on the banks of the Dee, but its size and the obligation of maintenance of the grounds impose a disproportionate burden on the occupier.

Voluntary Organisations

In the period under review there have been Boy Scouts, Girl Guides, Girls' Guildry, youth clubs and football clubs. A very popular game, quoits, was played on the former bleaching green, but was suspended during the first world war and has not been revived. There are two branches of the Women's Rural Institute, and two dramatic clubs, Crossmichael and Clarebrand. The Crossmichael Club has been successful at county and provincial festivals, and in 1948 gained the Outram Shield, the highest award in the south-west division of Scotland. In the same year the club provided guest artists at Bangor (Ireland) Festival and at the Edinburgh International Festival. There have been choral societies and a tennis club. Several of the youth organisations are in suspense at present owing to a dearth of suitable youth leaders. The Curling Club has had a long and successful career, celebrating its centenary in 1938.

Halls

There is a small guild room used by the Woman's Guild, a church room at Townhead of Greenlaw used for church purposes; largely attended functions such as concerts, parish meetings, whist drives, and dances have been held up to the present in the schools at Clarebrand and Crossmichael. (A Parish Memorial Hall is in process of erection and will meet a great need and serve as a centre for communal interests and activities). A hall built for the specific purpose of carpet bowling exists and is administered by a committee of the Carpet Bowling Club.

The Parish at War

Parishioners have always been ready to respond to the call for public service. A striking instance of this was the recruiting of 107 men, including eight out of a membership of nine in the kirk session, for the Home Guard in 1940 in the space of 48 hours.

Of the 13 bombs dropped on the Stewartry during the second world war by enemy aircraft, two fell on the farm of Chapelerne in this parish without injury to person or property; two rabbits, each claiming a bomb, were killed.

Transport

There is a railway station in Crossmichael village on the Stranraer/ Castle-Douglas line, but decreasing use is being made of it as there is a fully adequate bus service operating within the system of the Scottish Motor Traction Company Limited.

Way of Life

There has been a marked advance in the standard of living since the first world war: better housing; secure income; wireless and television; leisure, following the reduction of working hours, for hobbies, games and recreational activities; private motor cars and greatly improved travelling facilities. Clubs such as Young Farmers' Clubs and dramatic interests, increasing appreciation of the wealth and beauty of the natural scene, have created conditions such that a native of the parish could gratefully subscribe to the sentiment 'The lines are fallen into me in pleasant places; yea I have a goodly heritage'.

1953

K

CHAPTER 14

THE PARISH OF DALRY

by the REV. M. G. MULLO WEIR.

Physical Features

'The village is the handsomest in Galloway. Its situation is superb'.—
Dr. A. Trotter (*East Galloway Sketches,* 1901). Dalry village is at the
centre of the four 'Glenkens' parishes, said originally to have formed
one. The parish is over 15 miles in length, and from approximately
one and a quarter to seven and three-quarters miles in breadth. The
village, which is about two miles from the southern extremity of the
parish, is 200 feet above sea level at its lower end, rising to approximately 400 feet at Townhead. The highest hill is Lorg Hill, 2,100 feet.
The name Dalry is generally accepted as signifying royal dale (*Dal righ*)
but P. H. McKerlie (*Lands and their Owners in Galloway,* vol. 3)
suggested the dale of the ford, for which a case could be made. No
change has taken place in the boundaries since former accounts.

Natural History

Chief rocks are granite and trap. There is also blue slate, the quarrying
of which ceased many years ago. Principal lochs are Lochinvar,
Knocksting, Regland, and Knockman. Knocksting and Knockman have
excellent trout of good size; Regland moderate; Lochinvar more plentiful, but smaller. Carsphad dam and the river Ken from Boatweil to
Boatknoll are stocked with brown trout by Dalry Angling Association.
Formerly a good salmon river, the Ken has yielded few since the
establishment of the power scheme. Improvements in the 'ladders' at
Tongland may help. The loch was once stocked with sea trout, but
there is no record of any catches. Earlstoun Linn (formerly a noted
salmon leap) and other beauty spots were submerged by the dams,
although the lochs formed have a beauty of their own.

Forestry schemes come right to the boundaries at Dundeugh,
Corriedow and Muirdrochwood, but do not actually anywhere enter
this parish. There are woods at Earlston, Milton Park and other places
on the lower ground. The aged Earlstoun ('Queen Mary's) Oak is still
growing, but the large branch has been propped for over 20 years.
Trees are very scarce on the higher ground. Most common and some
less common wild flowers are found. Of rare varieties, the Wintergreen
Pyrola Secunda has been noted. The pink-coloured *Claytonia
Alisinoides* (Sibirica) is found in several places.

Pheasants were hand-reared in considerable numbers in Earlstoun
and Milton Park prior to the second world war. Since then they have

been less plentiful. Grouse, very scarce for many years, have recently increased. Large numbers of rabbits are trapped and marketed annually. Rabbits at Milton Park, which are white with dark markings, were at one time cross bred with tame varieties. Roe deer are occasionally seen. Foxes have multiplied with the proximity of afforestation. Bird life is very varied. Included are Jay, Kingfisher, Great Spotted Wood-pecker, Pied Flycatcher, Corncrake, Long-tailed Tit, Redstart, Lesser Redpoll, Blackcap, Garden Warbler, Gold and Bull Finches, Ring Ouzel, Peregrine Falcon. Montague's Harrier has been identified. There are water fowl in considerable variety. Until 20 years ago there was a heronry at Mackilston. Among butterflies, Peacock and Painted Lady may be mentioned, as well as both Tortoise-shells.

Antiquities

A list of the more important antiquities and archaeological remains may be found in the *Fifth Report and Inventory of Monuments and Constructions of Galloway*, vol. 2. These include pre-Reformation church, Earlstoun Castle, Lochinvar Castle, Dalry Mote, Mote on Lochrinnie farm, Hill Fort at Stroanfreggan, Stroanfreggan cairn, White cairn at Corriedoo, Holed Stone at Lochrinnie, Cairn at Culmark Hill, Chapel at Lochrinnie Hill, and Chapel at Bogue Farm.

No mention is made there of the ancient stone known as St. John's Chair. This stone was hidden for a time after an apparent attempt to remove it for Sir Walter Scott's collection. The origin and history of the stone, which is mentioned in the *Old Statistical Account*, cannot be traced, but it remains 'The Dalry Heirloom'.

Covenanting Associations

These are numerous. The Pentland Rising ('Rullion Green'), in 1666, originated at Midtown in Dalry village. In the same year fines of £9,500 were imposed on 43 families in the parish. John McMichan, parish minister, was imprisoned in Edinburgh in 1662; was deposed, and sub-sequently restored. In 1680 a Dalry weaver, John Malcolm, appears to have been executed at the Grassmarket, Edinburgh, for his part at Airdsmoss. There is a tombstone to three covenanters who were buried in Dalry churchyard.

The Gordons of Earlstoun suffered greatly for covenanting sym-pathies. William Gordon was fined £35,000 in 1662 and banished. Returning after Pentland, he was killed on his way to Bothwell Brig. Alexander Gordon, 'the Bull of Earlstoun', fought at Bothwell Brig, escaped, fled to Holland, returned, was captured, tortured, condemned to death, reprieved, and imprisoned on the Bass Rock and in Blackness Castle. In 1689 he was released and had his properties restored.

Literary Associations

The home of Wm. Douglas, author of *Annie Laurie*, was at Fingland, Dalry. J. G. Barbour, born at Gordonstone 1775, was a member of an old Dalry family, and published *Unique Traditions of West and South West Scotland*, and *Tributes to Scottish Genius*. A descendant, James Barbour, of Bogue, wrote various antiquarian articles. His daughter, Miss M. Barbour, Glendarroch, is the present oldest inhabitant.

Rev. A. McGowan, writer of the *Old Statistical Account* of the parish of Dalry, was master of Dalry Free Grammar School, 1772-82, and parish minister, 1783-1826. Rev. David Landsborough, born at Dalry c. 1779, wrote standard works and text books on seaweeds and zoophytes; some of the latter bear his name 'Landsburgii'.

Dr. R. Trotter, member of an old Glenkens family, who resided and practised in Dalry from 1864 till 1875, wrote *Lowran Castle* and *Derwentwater*. His five sons, all doctors, included Alex., author of *East Galloway Sketches*; R. de Bruce, author of *Galloway Gossip*; and James, who wrote *The Clachan Fair* (Dalry).

Prominent Residents

Several artists have been prominently associated with the parish, including H. J. Dobson, R. S. W., who married Jean Cowan, Dalry, and whose sons, Cowan and Raeburn Dobson became well-known portrait artists. Mr. R. Curtis-Hayward, Creaganfois, has painted excellent pictures of the district, and Mr. Donald Watson, the bird artist, has his home and studio at Barone in the village. Recent prominent residents have included the Rt. Hon. The Lord Sinclair, M.V.O., Knocknalling, who has represented the parish on the county council for many years. The late W. R. Gourlay, C.S.I., C.I.E., who had a distinguished career in the Indian Civil Service, resided at Kenbank from 1924 to 1938. He gave valuable service on the Stewartry Education Authority, particularly on the Library Committee, and improved the village of Dalry by modernising a number of cottages. Dr. Frances Melville, the first woman B.D. in Scotland, former Principal of Queen Margaret College, University of Glasgow, retired to Kirkstyle, Dalry, and made her home there from about 1930 until the post-war years. She gave valuable service among the girls and women of the district.

Local Sayings and Traditions

An old saying has survived from days when men gathered at 'news Knowe', the site of the present bowling green, to hear market prices, read by 'Cutler': 'The sun and the moon may vary but Cutler's clock will not'. Another was the prediction that there would be continuous rain when 'Paik's Hole's fu'.'

Lochinvar Castle, once the home of Scott's Young Lochinvar, and now a ruin, stands on an island in Lochinvar in the parish of Dalry. It is claimed locally that Robert Burns based 'Tam o' Shanter' on the tale of Adam Forrester, of this parish. There are many stories of ghosts and witchcraft. Extracts from official records show that Elspeth McEwen, or McCowen, who appeared before Dalry Kirk Session on witchcraft charges in 1696, was burned at the stake in Silver Craig Park,

Kirkcudbright, on 24 August 1698. Dalry was on the pilgrim route to Whithorn. The records show that money was paid by the King's Chamberlain in the reigns of James IV and V to the parish priest for the poor, and payments were also made for being ferried over the Boatweil, beside the church, on journeys to Whithorn. The ferry remained in use until 1800, when Allangibbon Bridge was built. Knights Templar associations are attributed to St. John's Town of Dalry. These are now difficult to trace, but former chapels at Bogue and Lochrinnie may be noted. There is a tradition that standing stones once surrounded Dalry Mote, and that the mote was inhabited by a white snake. Ancient religious worship is suggested.

Population and Housing

Population has tended to decrease, but not alarmingly so. Employment for young girls may become a problem. Regular domestic employment is practically a thing of the past. Two or three girls with commercial training travel daily to employment in Castle-Douglas. Two or three are employed in shops in the district and in forestry work. Some marry young and leave the district. The 1951 census (775) is the lowest recorded. There was a considerable rise between 1801 and 1831, possibly due to increased feuing and land improvement. The peak years were 1840 to 1880, when there may have been over-population, and a trek to the industrial areas, to the south, and emigration began. The pattern of population changes, typical for the whole of rural Scotland, applies also to Dalry parish.

Dalry has always been a pleasing village to the eye, as noted by Heron even in the eighteenth century. In recent years the interior comfort of the houses has come steadily nearer to the external attractiveness. Well into the present century there remained cases where inhabitants kept a pig in the rear of the dwelling house. Even in 1930 there were still many cottages in the village where conditions were primitive. In some cases there was overcrowding. Eight modern cottages of the bungalow type were built by the county council at Underhill after the first world war, and about 1930 three blocks of two-storey houses (12 dwellings) were added. Though quite up-to-date internally, the latter were unpopular, and were christened locally 'Barlinnie'. Aesthetically, they are out of keeping with the rest of the village. Many of the smaller houses were modernised during the 'thirties'. Some of these are now owned by the occupants. Between the wars several excellent houses were built privately, and recently a few old dwellings have been remodelled. Since the second world war, 16 quite pleasing one-storey houses have been built by the county council, forming Townhead Crescent. These make a total of 36 council houses in the village. Eight more are soon to be built. A large percentage of agricultural workers' and shepherds' houses have been modernised or new houses built. This has been a greatly needed improvement. Fifteen houses were built for employees at Kendoon by the Galloway Power Company in the 'thirties', and one was added later.

Water Supply and Sanitation

There is a good water supply. Prior to 1900 water was drawn by pump from wells, but in that year a special water district was formed. Supply was brought over four miles by three-inch pipes from Lochinvar Loch to serve the village. The supply, originally adequate, later was found insufficient and was replaced in 1945 by a modern and efficient scheme Sewage is efficiently dealt with by filter tanks below the village.

A special scavenging district was formed in 1930, and rubbish has since been collected twice weekly. In the post-war period collection has come within the county scheme and the Dalry rubbish 'toom' has been squared off and closed. There are no street scavengers, but the streets are always clean.

Electricity

Prior to 1926 the village was lighted by oil lamps. In that year the parish council was responsible for the formation of a local Electricity Supply Company. Twenty-one registered subscribers took up £1 shares in holdings varying from five to 500. Many had electricity installed and 11 electric lamps were introduced in the streets. With the advent of the Galloway water power scheme the village company was bought over in 1933, and electricity supplied by the county council. At that time there were 105 consumers. After recent nationalisation, supply has been by the South West Scotland Electricity Board. Most houses in the village have electricity, as have several outlying farms. The town hall clock is electrically lit.

Health

Earlier in the century there were resident doctors both in Dalry and New Galloway. Later, the four Glenkens parishes were served by one. Under the recent National Health Scheme, the area is served by a doctor, presently residing in New Galloway, with an assistant doctor and a district nurse, both in Dalry. Nearest hospitals are Castle-Douglas and Dumfries.

Police

Headquarters for the Glenkens parishes are at Dalry, with a resident sergeant and a constable in New Galloway.

Communications

Dalry is served by A roads to Glasgow (*via* Ayr) and Edinburgh (*via* Thornhill and Dalveen Pass). Dalry is served by New Galloway railway station, some eight miles distant. In 1888 it seemed a certainty that a Glenkens railway, Castle-Douglas to Dalry, would be built, with

probable extension later to Dalmellington. The advent of motor transport ruled out this projected scheme. There are six buses daily to and
from Castle-Douglas, a good service. Since 1929 there have been four
buses daily to and from Ayr, thence Glasgow. For some years there
was a through bus (Castle-Douglas/Glasgow), express between Glasgow
and Ayr. This is now discontinued and passengers must change at
Ayr. All heavy goods are delivered efficiently by motor transport. In
addition to railway carrier a private carrier has run once weekly for
many years between New Galloway and Glasgow.

Local Government

Prior to the 1929 Act there was an elected representative to the county
council (as now). In addition there was an elected parish council, an
active and competent body, which also appointed a county council
member, and created considerable local interest. The replacing of the
parish council by a district council, having one member for each parish,
with virtually nominal powers, dealt a death blow to local interest.
The experiment of a community council, with representatives from all
local organisations, was tried. Not having official powers, and being
unfavourably regarded by the bodies which *had*, as well as by the
inhabitants, it soon went into abeyance. This was a pity. For special
duties (e.g. coronation celebrations) meetings of inhabitants elect committees, a system which gives excellent results. Provision for the poor
was formerly in charge of the parish council, and after 1929 passed to
the county council, and later still to the National Assistance Board.
There are few real poor in the parish.

Education

Mention is made in the *Old Statistical Account* of the Endowed Free
Grammar School at Dalry, opened in 1668, an important school in its
day. It is dealt with also in Dr. J. A. Russell's *History of Education
in the Stewartry*, published in 1951. For many years the income from
the endowments was used for competitive annual bursaries within the
district, for higher education. In 1933 the administration passed to the
Stewartry Educational Trust, with a Glenkens Committee. In the early
part of the century education was in the hands of a local school board;
after 1918, of the County Education Authority, with a local School
Management Committee. After 1929 control passed to the county
council's education committee. The complexities of modern developments made this necessary. The country school at Corseglass was
closed soon after this change, the children being brought daily to
Dalry. The small school at Stroanfreggan remains. Free transport
has been a blessing to outlying children, as has the introduction in recent
years of the school meals service. Dalry School was built about 1878
and replaced the old Free Grammar School at Creaganfois. A new
primary department was built in 1931. The school was given secondary

status after the second world war, and two additional temporary buildings were erected. There is to-day also a modern kitchen, electrically equipped, which serves Dalry and sends hot meals, by motor, to schools in the neighbouring parishes. The school has a whole-time staff of ten, including headmaster, four being male, six female. There is also a gymnastic and sports instructor, a homecraft teacher and a whole-time janitor. The parish minister is school chaplain. Approximately 200 children are in attendance, 110 primary and 90 secondary pupils, who come from five parishes. A course with French is offered, and practical courses offer classes in woodwork and metalwork, technical drawing, rural subjects and homecraft. A wide range of continuation and adult education classes is offered. A reasonable number of pupils progress to senior education at Kirkcudbright; several in recent years have advanced to graduation at Glasgow or Edinburgh Universities. In sport the Stewartry Schools Athletic Championship for small secondary schools has been won by Dalry for the past three years.

Trades and Shops

There are family concerns covering painting, plumbing, building and slating, as well as a branch of a larger building firm. There are also two joiners. The total number normally employed in these trades will be fully 20. Till quite recently there was a contracting and coal agent's business, but coal is now delivered from New Galloway and Dalmellington. There is an agricultural implement maker. There are several rabbit trappers and a mole trapper. Ten shops, all family concerns and excellent, include a tailor and suppliers of the usual household necessities. Meat, fish and some chemist's goods are supplied regularly by van. Several men are competent barbers and there is a trained ladies' hairdresser. Approximately 20 persons are occupied in the shopkeeping business. There are three garages, of which two hire cars, one also having two commodious motor coaches for private hire. Dalry has a sub-post office under Castle-Douglas.

Agriculture

Much marginal land was brought into profitable cultivation during the second world war. Some has been returned to pasture, but manuring, cultivation and re-sowing with selected grasses have improved fertility and stock-carrying capacity. The occasional repetition of such treatment would give paying returns. Liming has long been practised on the better farms, and has been encouraged by subsidies. Phosphates have been used for about 30 years. One instance of improved methods may be found in the farm of Milnmark. Some years before the war this farm, which at one time carried a dairy herd of 20-30, was in poor condition and carried none. Dysentery also caused heavy losses among sheep. To-day, after drainage and treatment with cobalt, phosphates and lime, it is a good average arable farm. During the war it again carried a dairy herd of about 30, recently changed to black Galloway cattle. Dysentery among sheep has been fully controlled. Sheep generally are now inoculated against dysentery, lambs only where disease is prevalent. The bracken menace has been largely controlled during the past 10-15 years by cutting to bleed, a bracken cutter having been invented and manufactured locally.

There are herds of black Galloway cattle on several farms. The number of these seems likely to increase. Liquid milk other than local supply is sold to the Milk Marketing Board. This seems a pity, as prior to the second world war about 17 tons of excellent cheese was made locally each year. Butter also was produced in moderate amounts. All cows were officially declared tuberculin free by the early 1940s. Milk yields have greatly increased by recent improvements in stock and pasture.

Pigs are reared on some of the farms, but none now at the rear of dwelling-houses in the village. There are no large hen-farms, but smallholders have experimented with attested poultry and egg-production. Deep litter is being tried, as well as battery production. The eggs of open-range fowls remain definitely superior in quality, if fewer in number. The higher cost of feeding stuffs has greatly discouraged domestic keepers, who deserve more encouragement.

Commercial breeding of Clydesdale horses was practised at Newfield before the second world war. Two horses from this stud, 'Lochinvar' and 'Transformer', had the uncommon distinction of winning the senior and junior Grand Championships at the same international horse show at Guelph, Ontario, in 1937.

Silage crops have not so far been popular. Experiments have been made, but experience is lacking. The motto followed has been that good hay is better than bad silage. On higher ground, in particular, where hay is late, silage might be developed with profit, since cutting can be done when wet, and it is rich in protein. Barley is little grown to-day, but was once popular. Half the old teind was barley, and half meal. Oats are the main crop; wheat is not grown. There are no 'combines' for harvesting. Reaping machines with five-feet cutting bars are used. Milling is done by travelling mills. Formerly there were mills at Gordonstone and Grennan. The miller received his payment in meals—his 'mooter'. Turnip crops have been improved by treatment with D.D.T.

A Young Farmers' Club for the Glenkens district has given opportunities of studying farming methods over a considerable area. Interest has for the present dwindled. Tractors have been in general use since the second world war. Work has been speeded up by 100 per cent., and more new ground broken. Some horses are still retained, particularly on difficult ground, and where tractors bring down the soil. The number of agricultural workers has greatly diminished, e.g. one farm which formerly employed 12 men and boys now employs only three men. Some work is contracted out. Dry stone dykes remain in general use, but good dykers are very scarce.

Housing of farm workers and shepherds, until recently often poor, is now mainly good. New houses have been built or old modernised. There are few dealers to-day, the market being the dealer. With good farming, afforestation should be unnecessary. The completion of a road to the hill farm of Knocksting, modernisation of the house and buildings, and manuring, all subsidised, suggests that similar methods might have saved much ground throughout the country for food production, and in many cases proved a cheaper and better short and long-term policy than planting with trees. The subsidising of stock produced ought to be unnecessary.

Wages of outdoor workers, and labouring classes generally, averaged £2 to £2 10s before the second world war. To-day they average £5 to £6. In relation to decreased money values workers are rather better off.

Church Life

The parish church, St. John's Kirk of Dalry, was built in 1831, on the site of its predecessor of 1770. Adjoining are the remains of an older church of 1564. The church is approached by a fine avenue of lime trees, planted in 1828, at the cost of 2d a tree. The bell is inscribed 'Dalry 1754' and is mentioned in the records as made in the parish. A pipe organ was installed in 1920; various church furnishings were added more recently. Very old 'box-ladles' are still retained for uplifting offerings. There are marble wall memorials to Gordons of Lochinvar and Kenmure, and others. In 1949 a union of congregations was achieved with 'St. John's' (until 1929 St. John's U.F.), under the writer, minister of the old parish church since 1927. The last-named church is the regular place of worship. The former United Free Church was itself the product of a long series of unions. It has beautiful memorial windows, which seem likely in time to be transferred to the regular place of worship. The churchyard has some interesting old stones; one, possibly the oldest, of which the history is not known, has two children holding reaping hooks, in carved relief. There is a stone to three covenanters, and there are also graves of members of the Black Douglas family. The war memorial is at the churchyard entrance.

Almost all parishioners have some association with the church. There are 338 full communicants. About 65 children attend Sunday school, with an additional ten at a small Sunday school at Kendoon. There is also a mixed Bible class of 30, and a Woman's Guild with a real membership of 100. Church life is vigorous; attendance reasonable. Christian liberality has greatly increased, but commitments are correspondingly heavier. Since 1929 the congregation has been required to maintain its own properties. The church is respected even by non-supporters and is the leading influence in the parish. There is a handful of Roman Catholics, occasional services being held in the town hall by a Castle-Douglas priest. There is a very small Episcopalian sprinkling, and two or three agnostics or atheists, professing rather than actual.

Social and Cultural Organisations

The Town Hall, built in 1858, is the main social centre; the town clock was given by Mr. Alexander of Mackilston in 1890. There is a Scout troop of 25, as well as Girl Guides and Brownies. Youth club efforts have varied and fluctuated over a considerable period. There have been mixed and separate church and village clubs, and a 15-18 youth group, in turn. In 1937 a girls' club sewed a handsome 'Coronation Banner', depicting historic places in the district, which was on view at the 1938 Empire Exhibition, Glasgow. It is now in Dalry town hall. There are 125 members in the W.R.I., and 100 in the Church of Scotland Woman's Guild; both bodies are active and influential. There is a country dancing class of 30. For over 25 years until the second world war there was a musical association, with many festival successes; it has been in abeyance since the death of its conductor, Mr. T. Crozier. A male voice choir continues. A dramatic club has had good, but sporadic, productions. In recent years the church has done most to maintain the traditions in both these fields, with productions by children and adults. Musical appreciation has been fostered by British Arts Council visits, but some are still too prejudiced in favour of Scottish songs.

A village library was formed in 1845, and maintained a very high standard. In 1946 it was succeeded by a branch of the county library. The peak years were those which immediately preceded the transfer, when 2,000 to 3,000 books were issued annually. Literary societies have gone out of vogue. For some 50 years a Mutual Improvement Association flourished. Attempted revivals in recent years have been discouraging. Radio has usurped its place.

There has been a curling club since 1843, which has at present a membership of 20. The club was admitted to membership of the Royal Caledonian Curling Club in 1952, and competes in indoor Stewartry competitions at Ayr and Glasgow. A green bowling club was founded in 1912, and has a membership of about 40. The club has reached the Scottish 'Finals' at Queen's Park, Glasgow, in single-handed and rink, and was the second club to win in 1952 the new Stewartry Championship Banner. A ladies' section has recently been formed. For many years there was a nine-hole golf course, given up about 1932, after some of the ground had been lost in the building of council houses. Dalry Angling Association was formed about that time and has some 50 members. Carsphad dam and the river Ken are stocked with trout. There has been a badminton club of 30 members since 1931. A tennis club was formed in 1954 through the courtesy of Milton Park Hotel, and has at present 25 members. British Legion membership is 100. At the Men's Institute, carpet bowling and billiards are popular on winter evenings. Table tennis and darts are played in winter and in summer. The lads have a football club.

There is a Unionist Association and a Labour Party Committee. The former has much the larger following, some of whom are Liberal and leftist in certain points of outlook, but conservative in vote. There are few, if any, extremists in either party and probably no Communists in the strictest sense.

The local annual days include collie dog trials, ploughing match, clay pigeon shoot, and, on a district basis (every third year at Dalry) the Glenkens Society's Horticultural and Poultry Show. A mounted sports gymkhana has been held for the past two years at Dalry. There are also W.R.I. events, school children's sports, and day bus trips by various organisations. For many years, until the middle or late 1930s, Dalry Show ('The Clachan Show'), with poultry, pigeons, horticultural exhibits, highland dancing and sports, attracting entries from a wide area, was the great annual event. It was held on the first Friday in July. Every house was painted or whitewashed, and every visible weed removed for this occasion, perpetuating the tradition of smartness. This day is missed by older inhabitants. At one time the show was also something of a market for cattle and other stock. This is referred to in the poem, now scarce, called 'The Clachan Fair'. Co-operative efforts with the neighbouring parishes have tended to increase. They include Glenkens Agricultural Society; Glenkens Society; mounted sports; National Bible Society Auxiliary (since 1855); joint church choral and Woman's Guild efforts; British Legion and Masonic interests; secondary school sports and other activities. War-time civil defence was on a four parish basis.

Way of Life

The inhabitants find interest and satisfaction in life as they live it. They are industrious and excel in practical work. The background of the men is manual, and adult educational classes, apart from woodwork, have not attracted them. Many men spend their winter evenings at home with radio, reading, and the like, a number in company at the hotel bars, where moderation is mostly shown. They enjoy whist drives and local entertainments. There is less inclination than formerly for sustained community efforts among the men, but they will share readily in particular efforts. Football pools coupons are much in favour, and spectating at Division A football matches at Dumfries is popular with males on Saturdays. Young men, and a few older, attend the Men's Institute. Twice-weekly badminton, dancing and weekly cinema are favoured by the young. On summer evenings several men give assistance in outdoor work and gardens. Most house-fronts and gardens are well kept and attractive. Available sports have their devotees, but few games in or out of doors appear to be enjoyed by the men and lads to-day unless prizes or 'sweeps' are involved.

This is not the case with the women and girls. The women are of a good type, well domesticated, and make excellent wives. They work better together than the men, and are happier in community effort. Both in and out of the home they do most things with distinction. Many married women engage in part-time or occasional domestic employment and find pleasure in it. Like the men, they are more practical than 'intellectual', but appreciate cultural influences. W.R.I., church guild, country dancing, whist drives, are all enjoyed. A few take classes in needlework, rugmaking and other crafts. The girls and young women are mostly bright and attractive. They dress more tastefully than in former days and are more self-reliant. They are conscientious in duty. As with the lads, they enjoy dances, and the weekly cinema. They are readier to join in choral, dramatic and kindred activities. Summer recreations have been lacking for them; it is hoped that tennis will help.

Sundays are spent quietly and decorously by most of the inhabitants, but the church attendance of many is spasmodic. Good use appears to be made of Sunday radio services. Sunday newspapers are popular, as are walking, nature study, and visiting friends. A few men work in their gardens. There may be a little gambling, but it does not obtrude. The village has benefited by proximity to country estates (an influence rapidly ceasing), and also from talented 'incomers' and summer visitors. To the services of the former, in particular, it has owed much. There are no class distinctions in the city sense. Social merit is acknowledged. The village is much of a family, as is the small Kendoon community; the outer parish slightly more apart. Relatives of local families are scattered far and wide, many in good positions, and the majority have an outlook and interest broader than parochial. Local gossip is seldom lacking, but the wise treat it lightly, and Dalry is regarded generally as a friendly place to all who are friendly.

1954

CHAPTER 15

THE PARISH OF GIRTHON AND BURGH OF GATEHOUSE

by JAMES ANDERSON RUSSELL

Name

The form of the parish name appears invariably in the older records as Girton, as with the Cambridge women's college. Girthon is of Celtic origin, being an abbreviation of *girth-* (or *garth-*) *avon*, the garden or enclosure on the river (Fleet). Fleet itself has the significance of water, identically with London's now covered-over river. The name is here applied to the whole valley of the river, and the new state forest at Cally takes the name of Fleet.

Gatehouse-of-Fleet is in the somewhat anomalous position of being divided by the river between the parishes of Girthon and Anwoth, the stories of which inevitably overlap at many points. It is the only town, or even village, in the virtually double parish and most probably derived its name from being literally the house at the gateway to Cally House and demesne.

Extent and Boundaries

Girthon is bounded on the east by Borgue, Twynholm and Balmaghie, on the north by Kells and Minnigaff, on the west by Kirkmabreck and Anwoth, and on the south by Wigtown Bay. Its greatest length, from Water of Dee to Fleet Bay, is 16 miles. On account of the great irregularity of shape of the parish, the breadth varies from two miles at the south to five miles towards the north.

Topography

In appearance the parish is of almost infinite variety. The major part is mountainous, with bleak moorland stretches. Only in the south is there any intensive degree of cultivation. Even here the land is nowhere flat, though pleasantly undulating. The shores of Fleet Bay and Wigtown Bay are generally sandy or alluvial, though occasionally rocky; properly speaking, there are no headlands. Agriculturally, this coastal strip is rich and fertile, capable of producing excellent crops. It is here that dairy farming is chiefly carried on, the area being one of the regular supply centres of milk to the Glasgow market.

In the parish are several fresh-water lochs. The largest is Loch Grannoch, which is nearly three miles long with an average breadth of about half a mile. Also in the northern sector are Loch Fleet and Loch

Skerrow. To the east, on the borders of Twynholm, lies Loch Whinyeon, from which Kirkcudbright derives its water supply.

Climate

The climate varies with soil, surface and situation. Conditions are naturally more cold and severe in the higher lands; in the lower parts they are generally mild and agreeable. The prevailing winds are south-west and bring fairly constant rain from the sea. This accounts for the comparative mildness of the district but to this may also be traceable the fact that the chief personal complaints are of diseases of the rheumatic order. A change of wind to the north or north-east brings drier but harsher conditions, but such spells do not last long; snow is infrequent. In the main it is fair to say that the climate is healthy, conducive to longevity, as the rising age of the population testifies.

History

As the history of the parish is told with considerable detail in the two previous Statistical Accounts, earlier aspects need not be repeated here. In passing, it may be remarked that Girthon is lucky in having produced its native historian, Dr. Thomas Murray, whose *Literary History of Galloway*, published in 1822, has much in it of general interest.

Within the last century no event seems to warrant mention as peculiar to Girthon. Undoubtedly, the greatest upheavals to parochial life and economy, a reflection of events on the national plane, have been caused by the first and second world wars, raging respectively from 1914-18 and 1939-45. Eloquent testimony to the sacrifice of the men of the district in the cause of freedom is to be found in the many names recorded on the panels of the War Memorial, occupying a prominent position at the head of the town, where the Kirkcudbright and Laurieston roads meet. The memorial serves both Anwoth and Girthon. It is of Creetown granite and is in the form of a Celtic cross. For the first world war there are inscribed 88 names and for the second 14 names. On Remembrance Day a special service is held here, in which the British Legion and other official bodies take part.

Since we have mentioned Dr. Thomas Murray as a prominent native character, we may fittingly conclude this section by giving the names of others who have made their mark beyond the confines of the parish which bore them. The painter, John Faed, born at Barlay Mill, may again be mentioned, for though already of sufficient eminence to be referred to by the parish minister, the Rev. George Murray, in compiling the *New Statistical Account*, his life continued through the remainder of the century (to 1902) and his fame endures well into this. Otherwise probably the names of most outside significance are those of the medical men, Sir James Learmonth, formerly Professor of Surgery in the University of Edinburgh, surgeon to H.M. The Queen, and Professor John McMichael, holder of a chair of medicine in the University of London.

Land-owners

At the time of the *New Statistical Account* in 1845 the sole heritor in the parish was Alexander Murray of Broughton and Cally, M.P. for the then constituency of the Stewartry of Kirkcudbright. Originally this family hailed from Moray but settled in Wigtownshire whence came the name Broughton. To this was added the title of Cally, when, in 1763, that stately mansion was built as a family residence in Girthon. This was a fitting acquisition, as Richard Murray, great-grandfather of Alexander Murray, had married the heiress of Cally, or Kalecht as it was known in former times. The earliest proprietor of the estate was named Stewart, descended from the illustrious family of the High Steward of Scotland, the sixth holder of which office married Marjory, daughter of Robert Bruce, and so founded the historic House of Stewart.

After two centuries the line of the Stewarts of Cally passed to the female side, and the marriage of Elizabeth, only daughter and heiress of Sir John Stewart, to Donald, son of the Earl of Lennox, introduced a new family, hitherto designated as of Lennox-Plunton in the parish of Borgue. On the marriage of Richard Murray of Broughton to Anna, daughter of John Lennox, seventh holder of the Cally Estate, the various titles were conveyed to him by his father-in-law, who renounced all right to them.

It was James Murray who built Cally and acquired the complete heritorial rights in the parish, obliging him, for instance, to sole assessment under the Act of the Scottish Parliament of 1696 for the maintenance of a parish school. He also it was who obtained the charter for the foundation of Gatehouse in 1795 as a burgh of barony, his purpose being to establish it as a centre of the cotton industry. Already, in 1790, the Yorkshire firm of Birtwhistle had been encouraged to set up two mills, and these continued to operate with a fair degree of prosperity until 1840, when the upper mill was destroyed by fire. The mill was rebuilt, with improvements, but transport difficulties coupled with the distance from coal supplies brought about the closure of the whole activity. Robert Burns, a visitor to Gatehouse in both 1793 and 1794, refers to 'Roarin' Birtwhistle', meaning the noise of the machinery. The name of the enterprising firm is still commemorated in Birtwhistle Street, long known colloquially as the 'Whustle Raw'. These events are dealt with in detail in the Old and New Statistical Accounts. The tannery, brick manufactory, and brewery mentioned in the New Account have long closed down, though the name 'Brewery Brae' survives colloquially, as the Boat-Green keeps the memory of Gatehouse as a small port connected by a canal with Wigtown Bay. Until just before the second world war a bobbin factory was carried on in the old Birtwhistle mills, but the buildings now stand in ruins beside the Fleet.

There are to-day no collateral descendants of the Murrays of Broughton or the Lennoxes of Cally, these families being represented on the female side by Mrs. Elizabeth Murray-Usher. Cally House has been converted into a hotel and the grounds have been acquired by the

Forestry Commission

Plate 5. DUNDEUGH FOREST, FROM THE EAST

Showing also part of the Ken Valley flooded by the hydro-electricity dam above Kendoon Power Station.

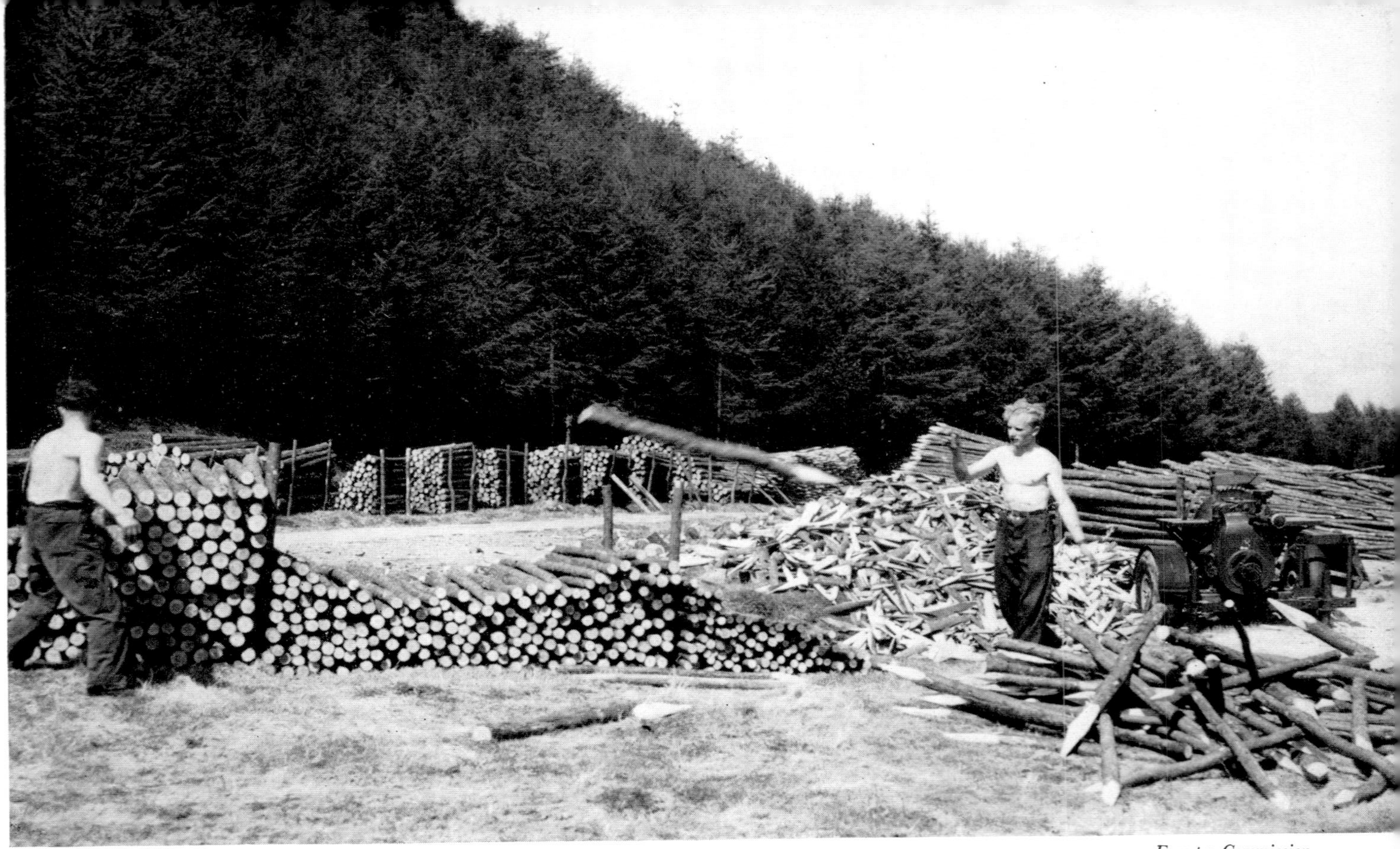

Forestry Commission

Plate 6. TIMBER EXTRACTION AT THINNING STAGE

Forestry Commission as a nursery for its developments at Fleet Forest. Cushatwood, on the estate, remains, however, in the possession of the family, this providing an historic link, as it was originally the Old Vicarage, when James Murray in 1799 set up a chapel and academy for the benefit of the English workers brought north by Messrs. Birtwhistle, and their children.   Mrs. Murray-Usher's own home is at Murrayton, mentioned in the previous Account.   Many other houses and farms also form part of the Cally estate, which has administrative offices in Gatehouse.

Three miles from the town, going up the left bank of the Fleet, lies the house and estate of Castramont, also belonging to the Murray-Usher family.   The densely wooded hill giving shelter from the north is one of the most prominent and delightful landmarks in the entire district.   The name, perhaps signifying 'fort of the hill', suggests the site of a Roman Camp, but no discoveries have been made to substantiate this theory.   A more probable derivation is Carstramon—the 'plain of the elders'.

Population

In 1755 the population of Girthon was given by Dr. Webster as 367. By 1841 this figure had risen to 1,872, the burgh of Gatehouse having come into existence about 50 years previously.   The landward portion claimed 495 people and the burgh 1,377.   At the census of 1931 the total population for the parish was 1,015, representing 363 for the landward area and 652 for the burgh (part).   The corresponding figures at the 1951 census were: parish, 875; landward part, 347; and burgh, 528. The decline in the burgh figure was accounted for almost wholly by the fact that town council building had been largely concentrated in the new suburb of Riverbank, in the Anwoth parish area.   All over, the burgh population is virtually static.

Administration

The Local Government (Scotland) Act of 1929 saw the passing of the parish as an administrative unit, as 1918 had seen its end as an educational unit or School Board area.   Anwoth and Girthon had then been administered together.   To-day certain delegated functions are controlled by the Western District Council, operating within the wider County Council.   On this Girthon has due representation.

The town council of Gatehouse consists of a provost, two bailies, dean of guild, honorary treasurer, and four councillors.   In recent years public interest in this work has not been high, whether because the burgh is too small for it to be easy to get away from parish-pump politics or because the former powers and duties have been severely curtailed by the Local Government Acts, it is hard to say.   Elections have been unknown for many years and co-option has had to be used to complete the council.   So far only one woman has shown herself willing to serve as a councillor.

L

Gatehouse has a police station, with resident constable, under Dumfries and Galloway Constabulary.

Water and Electricity

There is a good gravitation water supply from the reservoir formed by the Dalmalin burn on the land of High Barlay, one and a half miles from the town. Electricity is supplied to most parts of the parish by an overhead grid system of the South of Scotland Electricity Board. In Gatehouse every house is now provided with electric light. To the farms the provision of electricity has been an immense boon, particularly when the main form is dairying; refrigeration, water-cooling, milking by machinery, sterilising of utensils, are all made possible, so altering the whole basis of labour and production.

Roads and Cleansing

The main road from Dumfries to Stranraer passes through the southern part of the parish. In surface this highway is very fair, but its many twists and turns make it a rather difficult route for transport. Through Gatehouse itself heavy vehicles often speed at quite illegal rates. The bridge over the Fleet is now much too narrow for the volume of traffic, and though a bypass road has been planned through the grounds of Cally, it is not likely that this will eventuate, nor would it be favoured by local business people and hotel-keepers. Connecting roads are usually adequate for the amount of traffic, though care has always to be exercised owing to the many bends encountered. One of the finest of Galloway moorland roads is that which leads from Gatehouse 'over the hills' to Laurieston.

Allowing for the difficulties of isolation, public cleansing is efficiently carried out. A sewerage scheme for Gatehouse was started in 1914. At each house the burgh workers empty rubbish-cans twice weekly, and this is recognised as an adequate provision.

Health

In Gatehouse is a resident doctor, while the district nurse has her official residence there. Dental services have to be sought at Kirkcudbright, Castle-Douglas or Newton Stewart. The nearest cottage hospitals are at Kirkcudbright and Castle-Douglas. It is usual, however, for more serious cases to be treated in Dumfries and Galloway Royal Infirmary at Dumfries, this being the central institution for south-west Scotland. At both Castle-Douglas and Dumfries provision is made for the various clinics organised in connection with the National Health Service. The maternity hospital for Galloway is in the Cresswell Hospital at Dumfries. Tuberculosis cases are treated at Lochmaben and Laurieston Hall.

Housing

In general, for a rural area, the housing position may be called good. The demand is for less isolation and greater centrality, giving the chance of improved amenities and better educational and travel facilities, with the result that often the old wayside cottages are to be found unoccupied and falling into ruin. Here and there, however, are agricultural workers' houses which have been improved or wholly reconditioned.

No new houses have been built by the county council in the landward part of the parish, but in the burgh of Gatehouse there has been much building activity, mainly at Riverbank in Anwoth parish. The number of council houses put up since the end of the second world war at Memory Lane and Castramont Road on the Girthon side of the boundary is 12. All the houses, especially those of the cottage type, are of neat design and contrive to give Gatehouse an exceptionally tidy appearance. This is further enhanced by the tendency to restore old properties which would otherwise become unsightly derelicts. The pleasing effect of this is seen especially in Catherine Street. At the ancient clachan of Girthon Kirk a number of cottages have also been reconditioned, giving that place a strangely modern look.

Industry, Trade and Commerce
The main industry is still that of the oldest in the world, agriculture. In the landward area the majority of workers are connected with farming in some shape or form, be it as shepherds, dairymen, cattlemen, ploughmen, milkmaids. It is different, naturally, in the burgh. This is the shopping centre for a considerable area, and there is excellent catering for the public in this respect. Practically all necessaries can be procured in the main street of the town. Here there are several grocery establishments, a baker's, a home bakery and tearoom, a chemist's, a newsagent's, a tailor's, a millinery shop, a draper's, an ironmonger's, a jeweller's, a confectioner's, a fish and fruit shop, two butcher's, an ice-cream saloon, a dairy, and a boot and shoe store.

Gatehouse also possesses two banks, the Bank of Scotland and the former Union Bank of Scotland. These banking companies have been amalgamated for some years, and the Gatehouse branches are now under one manager, though separate premises are maintained, pending reconstruction. There are two hairdressing establishments—for ladies and gentlemen. And the various trades are well represented by four building contractors, two plumbers, two joiners, one painter and one blacksmith. Two garages maintain full repair services.

In the burgh, on the Girthon side, there are two hotels, the Murray Arms and the Angel and one licensed inn, the Masonic Arms. The Anwoth Hotel is across the river. The large Cally Hotel is only a mile away. The district has now developed into a considerable centre of tourism, and Sandgreen-by-Sea, a few miles off, with its safe stretch of sands, its attractive bungalows, and its well-serviced caravan Park, draws many visitors, both day and resident.

After agriculture and tourism, the third main industry is forestry Since the war ended in 1945 there have been extensive developments, particularly in Fleet State Forest. The number of people employed locally is 65, made up of 49 men, eight women, five boys, and three girls

Finally, as regards agriculture, it is interesting to find that, apart from several hilly sheep grazings which have been taken over for afforestation, all the farms and holdings listed in the *New Statistical Account* are still being actively carried on, if occasionally under a slightly altered form of name.

Ecclesiastical Affairs

Until 1818 the parish church of Girthon was situated about two miles from Gatehouse. With the rise of Gatehouse this proved inconvenient and a new and substantial church, capable of seating about 600 worshippers, was built in the town itself. The old building was unroofed and exists only as a ruin. It stands in the centre of the old burial ground. Beneath the church was the vault of the Broughton family. The Lennoxes of Cally also had a family tomb here, and one of their number, Robert Lennox of Drumrush, was a martyr for the Covenant, as a memorial stone testifies: 'Within this tomb lyes the corps of Robert Lennox, some time in Irelandtown, who was shot to death by Grieer of Lagg, in the parish of Toungland, for his adherence to Scotland's Reformation Covenant, National and Solemn League. 1685.' The new burial ground is about half a mile from the present church.

At one time the manse was situated in the immediate vicinity of the old church, but a new one was built towards the end of the eighteenth century about a mile nearer Gatehouse. This, though still known as the Old Manse, was sold by the kirk session in 1946 when a new manse was acquired only a short distance from the church.

The kirk session consists of 13 elders. The present incumbent is the Rev. J. B. F. Montgomery. In 1929 the Rutherford United Free Church elected for union with the Church of Scotland and on the death of the minister, the Rev. R. B. McGlashan, in 1932 this congregation was added to Girthon. The church was most usefully re-altered to form a main hall, with several smaller rooms.

The church maintains an active Woman's Guild of about 50 members. Total church membership is 425, with about 80 children attending Sunday school. Church services are in general well attended. On special occasions, such as Communion and Remembrance Day, most seats are occupied.

A bequest is administered by the kirk session and the minister for the benefit of the poor of the parish—the Minnie McKeand Bequest. This is of the value of £356, and is actually divided between Minnigaff and Girthon. There is also a considerable fabric fund from money left by James Carson. Other endowments are now administered from Church Headquarters in Edinburgh. These amount to £233 and go towards the stipend.

In Gatehouse there is also a Roman Catholic place of worship. There are not many Catholic families and services are taken by the resident priest at Kirkcudbright, Father Donnelly.

Education

There is now no school in Girthon parish.   All education is centralised in Gatehouse Secondary School, formerly known as Fleetside School, on the Anwoth side of the river.   A full account, therefore, appears under 'Anwoth'.   A relic of the old parochial system of education remains in the former Girthon School now used as the drill hall of the local company of the 5th King's Own Scottish Borderers.   This was in use until the extension of the present school in 1927.   It is a dingy building and gives a good idea of the kind of place long accepted for educational purposes.   Children of the parish and burgh, who wish to complete a full secondary course, do so at Kirkcudbright Academy, to which transport by a special school bus is provided.

Library

Gatehouse has a specific library building, in which formerly the upstairs section was used as a reading-room and for the holding of small meetings, while downstairs was the lending section, with a limited supply of books from various endowments.   The reading-room has been closed and the library now functions as a branch of the County Library.   Books are issued on two evenings and Saturday afternoon.

Voluntary Organisations

These are naturally centred in Gatehouse.   There are many of them, and it might seem that they would be maintained with difficulty. Occasionally some organisation goes to the wall, but a new one usually arises to take its place.   As one would expect, in view of the size of the place, the personnel is not very different in a number of the organisations.

One of the most popular and successful of all organisations is the local branch of the Women's Rural Institute, invariably known as 'The Rural'.   It has a large and enthusiastic membership, and the meetings in the Town Hall attract good attendances.   A Horticultural Society is in a thriving condition, and its annual show in the summer is rightly regarded as one of the most outstanding in the Stewartry.   A Music Society, with a membership of about 50, holds several concerts annually, introducing well-known local and outside singers and players. Gatehouse is also an enthusiastic centre of Scottish Country Dancing, with a club numbering over 40 which has gained high places in open festival competitions.   The town has a brass band, going under the name of 'I'll Mak Siccar', which holds weekly practices and has a special section for training juniors.   Performances are given on special occasions, such as Christmas Day and Gala Day, and in summer the band plays at Sandgreen and also visits neighbouring places.

The Burns Club, which is open to all residents in the district, holds its annual Supper in the Murray Arms Hotel, with its Burns Room, in which the bard is traditionally held to have written *Scots wha hae*.   The Supper attracts the full complement of 70 who can be accommodated.

Recently a dramatic club has been revived in Gatehouse, and is going actively ahead with the presentation of plays and sketches. It provides opportunities for young aspirants to receive training.

Youth organisations include active sections of the Girl Guides, Boy Scouts, Brownies and Cubs. All of them meet in the virtual community centre, the invaluable Rutherford Hall, belonging to the kirk session of Girthon. It also houses a youth club, founded or rather re-established in 1954, which caters for youths between 14 and 18. They have facilities for the playing of badminton, table-tennis, billiards and darts, together with drama and dancing sections. A Fellowship service is held on Sunday evening, and the club has a membership of from 40 to 50.

Carpet bowling is a popular game during the winter months, and a local club with a membership of 30 meets in the hall of the Masonic Arms. A badminton club, open to men and women, meets in the Town Hall. There is also a curling club, but the enthusiastic curler is hampered by the lack of opportunity to play on ice outside, and most competitions have to be decided at the Ice Rink in Ayr. The club, which has a membership of 50, holds an annual dinner for members and friends.

There are ample opportunities for outdoor sport in summer. An angling club, naturally, thrives in a district so well suited for disciples of Isaak Walton; it has a membership of between 40 and 50. A bowling club, whose green is situated at the Public Park, just within the lower entrance to Cally estate, particularly welcomes visitors. Inter-club games and championships and other competitions are held throughout the season, and the membership stands at 50. A tennis club, with courts in Laurieston Road, is open to all residing in the district, and special terms are arranged for visitors. On the sloping ground to the south of Laurieston Road a sporting nine-hole golf course is laid out, where regular competitions are held and matches played with other county clubs. The golf club, too, especially welcomes visitors. There is also a cricket club, which may claim to be virtually the county club, for its members are drawn from Castle-Douglas and other places in the county which do not cater for the game. Its chief sponsor has been Mrs. E. Murray-Usher, who made available an attractive ground, affording an excellent wicket, on the sylvan setting of Cally estate. Matches are played during the season on Saturday and Sunday afternoons, both with district teams and with special elevens from farther afield. Home games attract many spectators who come from a distance by car.

The Way of Life

The way of life in Girthon has perhaps changed somewhat less in the past few decades than in places nearer to a bigger town, such as Dumfries and Castle-Douglas. Despite improvement in transport, the area remains comparatively remote. Railway travel is no more.

Gatehouse station, nearly seven miles away, on the hilly back or 'chain' road to Creetown, was never really convenient. It is still maintained as a station on the Stranraer 'boat train' route for Ireland but is closed to passenger traffic. The nearest station, for practical purposes, is Kirkcudbright, eight miles away. Most travellers, however, prefer to use the bus services. On the main road to Dumfries these operate at two-hour intervals, with augmented services on Saturday. The time taken to do the 33-mile journey is almost two hours, a detour by Kirkcudbright being involved. It is clear, therefore, that while transport has been improved, it has in no sense been revolutionised, and the people of Girthon must still expect to do much business in Gatehouse and find their entertainment there. Fortunately, the town is just big enough to afford good shopping and banking facilities and has a population versatile enough to maintain most of the accepted community clubs and organisations, as listed above. There is also, for instance, a cinema show once a week in the Town Hall, given by an itinerant company. The town council frequently holds official dances and other entertainments there, as also a popular and well-patronised Gala Day on a Saturday afternoon during summer. Occasional concerts are also arranged under the auspices of the Arts Council through the agency of the Gatehouse Musical Association; and plays are presented by touring theatrical companies like the Perth Repertory Theatre. On Saturday evenings a special bus runs to Kirkcudbright for those who wish to attend the cinema there. The spreading sign of the television mast is an indication both of prosperity and of addiction to the latest form of sponsored entertainment for the home circle.

Gatehouse, and Girthon, the parish in which it is mainly situated, may be called a happy community. There is neither poverty nor flaunting of extreme wealth. The general standard of living is higher than it has ever been. Though the cost of living has increased enormously since the second world war, with its disastrous effect on Britain's vested wealth and general economy, wages have in the main kept pace, while the maintenance of a policy of full employment gives a feeling of security, formerly unknown to many workers, and creates contentment. While it would be untrue to say that there is no awareness of class divisions, owing to the survival of a remnant of the aristocracy who have been able to remain on their family estates, and the presence of retired people of wealth, giving Gatehouse a residential character, the absurdity of standing rigidly on these distinctions in a community of the size is freely recognised and there is an easy mingling of people of all classes, occupations and interests. In a word, there is something near the attainment of what democracy should mean. The middle-class is rather small, though it is possibly the section of the community most supplemented from outside, and, while the workers have reached much the same living standard, they do not show as yet similar ambition in the cultivation of the arts and the higher graces of life. On the other hand, it becomes harder to say what now constitutes the working-class.

It no longer exists on the old Victorian model, and it may be that, with the merging into middle-class standards, definition depends on what the individual cares to apply to himself through his own way of life.

We are constantly told that this is a selfish, materialistic age, and the charge is not without substance. Public service, for instance, is no longer greatly sought and leadership seems confined to the few willing to accept responsibility. Bureaucracy must shoulder a portion of the blame for the former state of affairs, but the individual could often help authority by showing greater co-operation instead of the 'couldn't care less' attitude, which belies all teaching and training. This is shown in such a seemingly small matter as scattering litter. In this respect our community is no better than the average British one. Special receptacles have been conveniently placed in the streets of the burgh, but too many adults and children alike continue to ignore them, scattering their rejected papers, cartons and cigarette ends on the pavements. On the other hand, much good is done, too, often in the most unobtrusive way. With lower infantile mortality and greater expectation of life, we face, as generally, an ageing population. Many old people, beyond caring for themselves, are, fortunately, helped as far as possible by others near at hand, and in this respect we live truly in a community of 'good neighbours'. There cannot be too much wrong with our parochial area when it reflects so Christian a spirit as this.

1956

CHAPTER 16

THE PARISH OF KELLS AND BURGH OF NEW GALLOWAY

by the REV. W. BRUCE YOUNG

The *Old Statistical Account* of this parish was compiled by the Rev. John Gillespie in 1793 and the *New Statistical Account* by the Rev. James Maitland in 1844, each being minister of the parish at the time. Since the latter date, the whole way of life of the people of the parish has been transformed, and in the main the transformation may be traced to two factors—the development of speedy and cheap transport, and the emergence in practice of the welfare state with the consequent centralisation and control of many aspects of the national life by government departments.

Transport

In transport there have been two major changes. The first of these was the building of the Dumfries-Stranraer railway line, on which lies New Galloway railway station, five miles south of the town. This opened up the whole district to visitors from other areas, especially from England, and also facilitated the transport of commodities which were brought to the station and then carted by the farmer, shopkeeper or coal merchant to their destination. The development of motor transport has been made possible by good roads. Buses are now used by passengers much more than the railway, and road haulage is increasingly replacing the railway for goods traffic. The buses from Ayr to Castle-Douglas pass through the north end of the parish on their way from Carsphairn to Dalry and later make a detour over Ken Bridge into New Galloway. There are four buses each day to Ayr, and six to Castle-Douglas; all these buses are double-decker. Ayr is reached in an hour and three-quarters, the fare being 6s 9d return; Castle-Douglas in three-quarters of an hour, return fare 2s 3d. A bus runs daily to Dumfries taking about an hour and fifteen minutes, return fare 3s 6d. These services are much used for shopping and for making the initial stages of longer journeys. The convenience of being able to board public transport at the door or at the road-end is obvious compared with the inconvenience of having to hire a car to get to the railway station. Many people, including most farmers and a number of shepherds, have their own private cars.

Similar considerations of convenience apply to the road haulage of goods, which can be delivered to the house or steading, or even to the field in which they are required, and both the writers of the previous accounts would have been pleased to see the lime-spreading lorries which not only deliver but spread the lime, and that on the hill-sides as well as on the flatter fields.   The railway goods-lorry delivers daily such goods of the lighter sort as may have come by train to the railway station.   There are two carriers in New Galloway, each of whom has several heavy lorries capable of bulk transport of coal, wool or stock, and at term times they also remove furniture.   Stock is carried to market in this way and the hogs, formerly driven to Ayrshire for wintering, now make the journey in autumn and return in spring by road, all in a matter of hours instead of the weary days formerly spent by sheep, dogs and men in walking the considerable distances involved.   A lorry also runs on Friday to Glasgow from New Galloway.   Fish merchants, grocers, drapers and general merchants run their own motor vans which bring the goods, either already ordered or for display and sale, to the door of the customer's house.

Agriculture

The application of machinery to farming also has made a considerable difference to agriculture.   Tractors have replaced the horse for haulage work and these powerful machines, which can also be used by means of a belt as a source of power to drive many other devices, are to be found on every farm of any size.   The power-driven milking-machine has made it possible for large herds of dairy cows to be milked speedily with little labour.   The byres, in accordance with modern ideas of clean milk production, are well-planned, spacious and well-ventilated, with adequate supplies of water piped in for self-operated drinking bowls for each cow and for cleaning purposes, while milk-coolers and steam sterilisers ensure that the milk, conveyed in large cans by lorries which lift it at the dairy or the road-end, arrives at the creamery in good condition. With these mechanical developments has come a lessening demand for labour, fewer people being employed about the farms than some years ago.   For seasonal needs men are obtained either among those resident locally or through the government's scheme of European voluntary workers.

In recent years the breeding of Galloway cattle has declined, but there are signs of reviving interest in this breed.   In the spring a bull bred in this parish at Knocknarling brought 1,000 guineas in the mart at Castle-Douglas.   The previous record price for a Galloway bull was 580 guineas.   The keeping of herds of attested Ayrshire cattle for dairying has become popular.   The Milk Marketing Board buys the milk from the farmer and probably the more regular and more frequent source of income has established the economy of many farms on a sounder basis.   The present shortage of meat and the new subsidies favouring the breeder of beef cattle, coupled with the interest of the government and the assistance given to those faced with the problems of farming marginal land, will be helpful, as most of the farms in the parish are of this character. Sheep are bred in large numbers on the hill land; but here the enormous extension of the lands planted by the Forestry Commission has led to a reduction of the area available for sheep farming. There are two poultry farms with blood-tested stock in the parish, and on most farms poultry-keeping is a profitable sideline. Eggs are bought and taken to a government packing station for grading. In the *Old Statistical Account* the price of eggs was 1d a dozen, now the price varies from 3s 6d to 5s a dozen seasonally, but feeding stuffs cost a great deal. The Glenkens Agricultural Society runs a cattle show at the beginning of October each year in New Galloway public park. The Young Farmers' Clubs do excellent work by lectures, visits, stock-judging competitions and social activities among the younger generation of agriculturists.

The filling up of forms for government returns of one sort and another, and the book-keeping required for income tax purposes, are sore trials to many farmers, but these burdens may be regarded as a permanent legacy of the recent war, which has also tended, by control of the individual farmer and his farming through the local Agricultural Executive Committees, to leave this essentially individualistic industry less free to indulge personal preferences in farming the land.

The advisory work done by the West of Scotland College of Agri-culture has been of great benefit. It is estimated that the average date of harvest has been advanced by about six weeks in this district, and that research on grass seed has extended the grazing season by about four weeks. While there is a strong movement in favour of the use of silage for feeding purposes, in the Stewartry as a whole, it has not been developed in this parish owing to the nature of the land and the stocking arrangements.

Forestry

Perhaps the most important development in the use of land within the last 30 years has been the planting of large areas by the Forestry Commission. The total area of the parish is 49,376 acres and of this some 15,000 acres have been or are to be planted. It has been estimated that this vast area may require between one and three men to each 100 acres, and when it is recalled that a hill shepherd might herd up to 2,000 acres it will be realised that great changes in the population are impend-ing. Like every innovation, forestry meets with much criticism, directed chiefly against the taking over of sheep land in a time of food shortage, or the neglect of hardwood in planting—the trees being mostly conifers. Sitka Spruce, Douglas Fir, Scots Fir, Japanese Larch are amongst the most commonly planted. There is some doubt about the long-term effect upon the soil of these plantations of softwood in possibly reducing fertility, and also about the possibility of wood being out-moded by the increasing use of plastics. To each criticism the forester has his answer, but in a survey such as this it may be of interest to note current opinions. Some anxiety is caused each year by the seasonal risk of fire, especially when the shepherds burn the old grass to make way for the young growth, as the spread of fire to the forest would cause great destruction.

Wild Life

Wild life abounds. There are herds of red deer on the hills. The writer has seen as many as 20 in a herd. There are also wild goats, picturesque black and white creatures. Adders are plentiful on some hills. Rabbits have been somewhat reduced but there are still too many. Foxes also are too plentiful and shepherds and poultry farmers prophesy gloomily about their multiplication once the woods grow up.

Trades

The ordinary trades show a great decline. There is only one firm of joiners with two master joiners and three tradesmen, one plumber and one apprentice, one mason, two stone-dykers, and one cabinet-maker and upholsterer in the parish; but all these are at work over a much wider area. It is difficult for the man with a small business to find time for the clerical work involved in dealing with forms and regulations. The incidence of taxation and the increase in wages have greatly reduced the number of tradesmen and labourers employed about the local estates. The business needs of the community are catered for by the bank referred to in the *New Statistical Account*. Established in 1837 as a branch of the Southern Bank, it has become, through the various banking amalgamations, a branch of the Clydesdale and North of Scotland Bank.

Commerce

In New Galloway there are the following shops: four grocers, including a branch of the Dumfries and Maxwelltown Co-operative Society; one butcher catering for a very large area extending from Carsphairn to Parton and including Dalry and Corsock; one shoe shop; and a very busy sub-post office and general store. A grocer's shop at Mossdale is the only other shop in the parish. There is no longer any market in New Galloway, the nearest being Castle-Douglas where Monday of each week is market day. There is an electrician and there are two garages, one of which is also a car hiring business. The two hotels in New Galloway are well patronised by visitors. Kenmure Castle has also recently become a hotel. Each year a number of summer visitors come to the district; some of them have been coming annually for many years. Many motorists stay for a night during touring. There is also an increasing amount of tourist traffic from bus tours, and an enterprising woman who has started a tea-room has built up a busy summer trade from these tours.

Royal Burgh

The population of New Galloway is 305 compared with 436 in 1844, and the affairs of the royal burgh are administered by the town council.

The rating value is small; 1d on the rates brings £10. The magistrates are seldom troubled. There is a resident policeman in the town but he also covers a large area beyond the parish.

Hydro-Electricity

In the early nineteen-thirties the rivers Ken and Dee were harnessed by the building of dams and power stations for the generation of electrical power by the Galloway Power Company. This has involved the formation of large dams at Clatteringshaws on the Dee, from which the water is piped through a tunnel down to Glenlee power station, and also at Carsfad and Earlstoun, these two dams having small power stations operated by remote control from Glenlee. The water from these power stations flows on into Loch Ken which in turn is controlled by a barrier at Glenlochar for the use of the power station at Tongland. Flooding still occurs, but it may be doubted whether the flood waters will retain the alluvial value referred to in the *Old Statistical Account* as creating the fertility of the meadows on Kenmure Mains.

The distribution of electricity has been a great boon to the district as most houses now have electric lighting, heating and cooking, while many use immersion heaters for supplying domestic hot water. Many of the farms also have electricity. Apart from this there has been the advantage of bringing into the district men of a high standard of technical education; though the wisdom of housing the staff in close proximity to the station is often criticised on the ground that the social effect of segregation in small groups of houses is not good nor conducive to contentment. It is regrettable that the Forestry Commission has shown the same tendency to build isolated groups of houses. The generation and distribution of electricity has recently been nationalised.

Leisure Activities

In the parish there is a wide range of leisure activities. The gardens are well cultivated and the Glenkens Society continues to run flower and poultry shows annually and presents scripture prizes in the schools of the four Glenkens parishes. Whist drives are frequent and with dances provide the most popular way of raising funds for a wide range of charitable objects. There is a branch of the W.R.I., with about 100 members, a Masonic Lodge with a large membership, a badminton club, a weekly film show, occasional amateur dramatic performances, and concerts. Most of these activities take place in New Galloway Town Hall; but social activities flourish in the reading room which provides facilities for carpet bowls and darts, and there is much social life in the outlying parts of the parish, in Polharrow School and at Mossdale, where a remarkable little community of about 20 households has raised almost £2,000 in a few years to build their own hall. A branch of the County Library has been established in the school at New Galloway, boxes of books are distributed through the schools, and a large mobile library van provides library facilities in the landward area. The people are hospitable and there is much domestic social life. Telephones are used not merely for business but for social purposes and provide a useful link with one's neighbour in so scattered an area. Every house has its wireless set which keeps even the isolated herding in touch with the wider world and provides varied entertainment and cultural facilities.

Outdoor recreation includes fishing (although the dams have had an adverse effect on salmon fishing, and fishing is mostly on the lochs or in the burns for trout, with pike in Loch Ken); golf on an excellent nine-hole course at New Galloway; a local football team of forestry workers; and the public park provides recreational opportunities for the children.

Education

Education is administered on a county basis by the county council. Within the parish there are three schools—Kells School, situated in New Galloway, has 44 pupils, Mossdale has 19, and Polharrow 8. A school at Clatteringshaws was closed a few years ago. These schools take the children up to the stage of the control examination and they are then graded by their examination results and their intelligence quotient into those who are likely to benefit from a practical course, a one-language course or a two-language course. The two-language pupils go directly to Kirkcudbright Academy, and all of the others go to Dalry Secondary School. To many this seems to be making a judgment with a certain finality on a child's capacity, at too early an age. The effect is to preclude from certain professions all those who at the age of 12 or thereby are deemed unfit to take a language course, and the system does not allow adequately for the personal reaction between teacher and pupil, so prolonged in rural schools, which may prevent a particular child from learning easily from a particular teacher. It is also objected to as giving the status of permanency to a passing phase of educational theory.

The children who go to Dalry live at home, but are transported to school by the education authority, as are all children under eight years of age whose homes are more than two miles from school, and children over eight whose homes are more than three miles distant. The children who go to Kirkcudbright live in lodgings and come home at the week-ends. Parents get a grant towards the expense of lodging. Some of the girls live in a hostel at Kirkcudbright and this is run by the Authority. The writer of the 1844 account would be heartened by the fact that 'the cauld kail blade' has ceased to be regarded as satisfactory sustenance and that all children even in the more remote schools have the opportunity at lunch-time of a cooked meal which is brought out by vacuum containers from the school kitchen at Dalry. The cost to the parents is 7d a meal.

The clauses in the 1945 Act relating to further education have not been extensively applied locally, though the county council provides evening classes in any subject for which there is a sufficient number of pupils. Recently classes have been held in embroidery, leatherwork, singing, beekeeping, country dancing and gardening.

Housing and Living Standards

Considerable development has taken place in housing within the last few years. The Forestry Commission has built 15 houses of the Swedish timber type at Woodhead, at the extreme northern end of the parish, and is building 21 brick houses at New Galloway where the town council has built six new houses and may build more soon. In addition to this new building, many of the shepherds' houses and farmhouses are being modernised with more economical cooking ranges, inside sanitation and bath, and in some cases electricity. The higher wages have led to a much more comfortable standard of furnishing and to more variety of diet, in spite of food shortage, and it is good to see the extra money being used in these ways in spite of increased costs. Drunkenness is virtually unknown, but there is very widespread gambling on football pools.

Health Services

There is a resident doctor in New Galloway, and the Castle-Douglas doctors also attend patients locally. The district nurse lives in Dalry and covers the Glenkens by car. There is an excellent cottage hospital in Castle-Douglas and most surgical cases are dealt with in Dumfries & Galloway Royal Infirmary in the burgh of Dumfries, where also the famous Crichton Royal Institution provides mental treatment. The majority of births take place in the maternity hospital at Cresswell also in Dumfries.

Religion

It may be said of the religious life of the parish that, while people do not attend church as frequently as in former years, yet most of those whose names are on the communion roll appear at the services from time to time. A service is held in the parish church each Sunday morning; from October to March there is a monthly evening service in the Town Hall in New Galloway. Services are also held as often as they can be arranged at Forrest Lodge in the north of the parish, and at Craigenbay on the west, while at Mossdale to the south there is an afternoon service on the first and third Sundays of each month. A well-attended Sunday school meets in Kells School before the church service and in the winter a Bible class meets at the manse on Sunday evening. There is a most active Woman's Guild with 100 members who run an annual and lucrative sale of work for church funds. A pipe organ was installed in the church about 1879. In 1911 the interior was reconstructed, the church being reseated with a capacity of 476. A baptismal font in memory of the seven men of the parish who lost their lives in the second world war has been placed in the church. Baptisms and weddings take place normally in church, the former 'in face of the congregation'.

The manse, built in 1806 and extended in 1836, is too large and the grounds too extensive for the conditions of to-day when domestic help is scarce and expensive. The stipend is £338, glebe rent £12, and there is a congregational supplement of £180. There is a small Scottish Episcopal Church in New Galloway, built about the beginning of the century.

Churchyard

The churchyard contains many interesting stones. In addition to the covenanting stone mentioned by Mr. Maitland there is the stone of John Gordon of Largmore who died 'January 6 1667 of his wounds got at Pentland in defence of the Covenanted Reformation'. Many stones show the skill of local craftsmen in the now vanished art of stone-cutting, notably the Adam and Eve stones, of which there are two, both dating from the opening years of the eighteenth century. They depict in relief the figures of Adam and Eve on either side of the tree of knowledge, round the trunk of which is twined the serpent, whose head appears among the branches. These older stones have been transported from the site of the pre-Reformation Church which stood on the lands of Achie some distance to the west. There is also a curious stone in memory of a keeper at Kenmure, showing in relief a dog, powder flask, a bird, a rod and a gun, with a quaint epitaph for which a prize of a guinea was offered by Mr. Gordon of Kenmure and won reputedly by Mr. Gillespie, then minister:

> 'Ah, John, what changes since I saw thee last.
> Thy fishing and thy shooting days are past.
> Bagpipes and hautboys thou canst sound no more:
> Thy nods, grimaces, winks and pranks are o'er.
> Thy harmless, queerish, incoherent talk,
> Thy wild vivacity and trudging walk,
> Will soon be quite forgot.   Thy joys on earth
> A snuff, a glass, riddles, and noisy mirth
> Are vanished all.   Yet blest, I hope, thou art.
> For in thy station well thou play'dst thy part.'

There is some excellent lettering on the stones both in the old and newer portions of the churchyard. A new burial ground has been opened about 300 yards to the north.

Population

The population of the parish is 756, but there is an undue preponderance of elderly people owing to the migration of the younger people. This is especially the case in New Galloway; but the balance may be corrected to some extent by the anticipated influx of forestry workers into the district. Such migration from the district as takes place is mainly on account of lack of employment for young men and women who wish to get training for a career. It is therefore more to the cities than overseas, and those who go keep in touch with their own folk.   The community as a whole may be regarded as one which after suffering a period of decline is in some respects recovering its vitality.

1951

CHAPTER 17

THE PARISH OF KELTON

by the REV. DONALD M. HENRY

and

THE BURGH OF CASTLE-DOUGLAS

by J. F. ROBERTSON

Boundaries

The boundaries of Kelton Parish remain the same as in the *New Statistical Account*. It is bounded on the north by Crossmichael; on the east by Buittle; on the south by Rerrick and Kirkcudbright; and on the west by the river Dee, which separates it from Balmaghie and Tongland. Since the year 1873, however, the civil parish has been divided into two ecclesiastical parishes. The two became Kelton proper, and Castle-Douglas *quoad sacra*. The boundary between the two is at the Buchan Bridge, which spans a canal from Carlingwark Loch to the river Dee. The bridge is situated a few yards from the Buchan hamlet towards Castle-Douglas.

Population

During the last two centuries the parish shows a great increase in population. The population in 1755 is given as 811. In 1792, the town of Castle-Douglas, most of which is in the parish of Kelton, became a burgh of barony. The following figures indicate the growth of the town. In 1801, the population of the parish was 1,905; in 1851, 3,186; in 1901, 3,734; and in 1911, 3,746. The census of 1951 gives the population of the burgh as 3,322 persons (1,524 males and 1,798 females). This increase shows the rise of Castle-Douglas from a mere hamlet into an important market town. The landward part of the parish has 729 persons (368 males and 361 females). Also in the landward part of the parish, besides the small hamlet of the Buchan, there are two villages, Keltonhill, now called Rhonehouse, and Gelston. Each of these has about 130 inhabitants.

Country and Town

The parish of Kelton provides in itself a striking example of how interest has shifted from the country to the town. For here we have the diminished importance of a once well-known village, and the rise of a market town. The village in question is that called Keltonhill. Two centuries ago, the parish had three villages, and no town. These villages were Gelston, Keltonhill and Causewayend. The parish church — now in ruins in Kelton churchyard, and near to where Kelton church now stands — was the natural centre for the whole population, and was about a mile and a half distant from all three villages. Of these three villages, Keltonhill was by far the most important. The parochial school was there, and the village was much renowned for its fairs, but especially for one of these, a horse-fair held annually in June. This Keltonhill fair is said to have been the largest of its kind in Scotland, but apparently the date of its origin has been entirely lost. The people of the village still talk of the fair, and even refer to the several houses that remain and once were inns, calling them by their old names, as for example, 'The Boar's Head', and 'The Crown', though these days are well beyond living memory. This village was destined to lose its glory.

The village of Causewayend — a name now almost forgotten — rose in importance. It had three successive names in so short a period as the second half of the eighteenth century. For during that time it passed from 'Causewayend' to 'Carlingwark' (after the loch of that name) and then finally to 'Castle-Douglas', after Sir William Douglas of Gelston Castle, when in 1792 it became a burgh of barony. Since those days, Castle-Douglas has gone on from strength to strength. The great horse fair was, nearly a century ago, transferred to Castle-Douglas from Keltonhill, and the importance of the village has passed away. The village has, however, found a place in local fiction, as when in S. R. Crockett's *The Lilac Sunbonnet* the half-witted Jock Gordon declares himself 'Laird o' Keltonhill an' Earl o' Clairbrand', and as when in *The Raiders*, by the same writer, Ebbie Hook describes his fears in these words: 'I misdooted I wad ever mair get merry at Stoneykirk Sacrament, as foo at Keltonhill Fair'.

Agriculture

There are 59 agricultural holdings in the parish, and of these some 35 are large enough to be reckoned as farms. The size of farm varies from less than 100 acres to as much as over 900 acres. A farm of average size is about 150 to 300 acres, and the number of farms which are owner-occupied is about 25. Where farms are let, the average rent is from 20s. to 22s. an acre. The normal length of lease is 15 to 20 years, with mutual breaks every five years. The land in the parish under tillage is 1,745 acres; under grass, 6,086 acres; and under rough grazing, 1,381 acres. The livestock is as follows: horses, 102; cattle, 3,594; sheep, 5,096; pigs, 238, and poultry 7,644. The cropping is based on fodder for cattle. The chief crops are oats and swede turnips. Oat straw is the most useful of all cereal crops for fodder. The land is not strong enough to grow wheat, and very little is grown, the last census giving only 10 acres. Potatoes are not much grown, the last census giving only 22 acres. The scientist and plant-breeder have greatly helped the farmer in selecting the more leafy types of grass.

Galloway used to be a cattle and sheep-rearing country, but now it is chiefly engaged in dairying. This change has been largely due to the advent of the motor lorry. Instead of the milk being manufactured into cheese on the farm, it is now collected and taken to the factories. These factories make cheese and also supply milk to the consumer. As in the rest of Galloway, very few farms in this parish now make cheese. The work of the dairy farm has also been greatly aided by electricity and modern improvements. Conditions of living on the farms have, in recent years, undergone great changes for the better. New houses have been built for farm workers, and old ones reconditioned; most of them now have electric light, water supply and bathroom. The growth and prosperity of Castle-Douglas are largely due to the mart. The chief market day is Monday of each week, but large sales now take place on other week days at different seasons of the year. In size, the mart is one of the largest in the south of Scotland, and ranks with those of Ayr and Lanark.

Transport

Castle-Douglas is the junction of three lines of railway — to Dumfries, opened in 1859; to Portpatrick, in 1861, and to Kirkcudbright, in 1864. Of late years, as in other places, the increase of road traffic and the advent of the motor-bus have resulted in the diminishing popularity of the railway and in the closing down of several small stations to passenger traffic. There are now from Castle-Douglas daily bus passenger-services to Glasgow, Stranraer and Dumfries. Because of its cheapness and convenience, the bus has largely taken the place of the railway for travel to the big centres. The roads around are good and cars for business and private purposes have become essentials of modern life. The horse-drawn vehicle now hardly exists, whereas less than a generation ago we had the horse-drawn station-bus in the town, the postman going his rounds in the country by horse and trap, and the farmer going to the market on the Mondays by the same means. So far as this parish is concerned, the landward area is for the most part away from the main roads, and is thus hardly served at all by the passenger bus.

Water Supply

There is a gravitation supply of water to Castle-Douglas from Loch Roan, which is situated about six miles distant near the village of Crossmichael. It was introduced in the year 1880, and there appears to be a sufficient supply of water. In this respect, there is much lacking in Rhonehouse and Gelston, but the lack is, at the time of writing, in process of being remedied. At present the village of Rhonehouse has no gravitation supply at all. A few houses have supplies of their own. Most of the inhabitants have recourse to the village pump, which stands conspicuously in the middle of the village at the junction of two roads, the one leading to Tongland, the other to Bridge of Dee. The village of Gelston fares better. There is a small gravitation supply leading from

Ingleston farm, but this is inadequate in dry weather. In the newer houses of the village the water is laid on, but in the older part most of the inhabitants have to carry water from an outside tap.

Electricity Supply

A generation ago electric light was very uncommon, but Castle-Douglas is now supplied from the national grid system, and electricity has been recently introduced into both villages. Most of the farms also have the main supply, but it does not reach some out-of-the-way farms and cottages, which depend on paraffin lamps. Besides lighting, the electricity is increasingly used for cooking, heating and other domestic requirements.

Recreation

Recreation is well provided for in town and villages. The villages have their own recreations, such as carpet bowling and badminton in the halls during the winter months. Both villages have halls. That at Keltonhill is of stone and was built some 50 years ago. The one at Gelston is of corrugated iron, wood-lined, and was opened in 1928; it is the larger of the two and seats 160 persons. Dramatic clubs in the villages during the winter have recently become a source of much interest. But the villagers also seek the town in which to use their leisure time, and special buses run from Rhonehouse and Gelston on Saturday nights to provide for a visit to the picture house. In town and villages the Women's Rural Institute is very popular. The membership in Castle-Douglas is about 300, and in Rhonehouse and Gelston, about 45 each.

Churches

The parish of Kelton is made up of the three united parishes of Kelton, Kirkcormack and Gelston. In the churchyard at Kelton, which is near the present manse and church, may be seen the ruins of the old church as rebuilt in 1743. This church was added to in 1783. Ruins of an old Church are also to be seen in Kirkcormack churchyard, situated on the bank of the river Dee, about five miles from Castle-Douglas, and in Gelston churchyard, lying southwards, on the old road to Auchencairn. The latter two churchyards are now hardly ever used as places of burial.

In the ecclesiastical parish of Kelton, there is but one church.[1] It stands just outside the burgh boundary of Castle-Douglas, and nearly two miles from Castle-Douglas railway station. It was built at a little distance from the churchyard on higher ground in the year 1806. It has undergone several changes. In 1821 and 1822 galleries were built to accommodate the worshippers, but in course of time these were found to be unnecessary, and they were removed in 1879. In its former state, with the galleries, the church had accommodation for 1,000 persons, but now, with the removal of the galleries and subsequent changes, the church holds about 500. Even so, it must be accounted too large, as the

(1) The churches of Castle-Douglas are described in the separate account of the burgh.

communicants' roll numbers some 380.   It may be noted that in 1880 the number of communicants is given as 435.   Session records inform us that in 1888 there was a proposal in the kirk session for 'the erection of a gallery', but we hear no more of this, and it was never carried out. A notable improvement was made to the church in 1895, when an organ chamber was built and a pipe organ installed.   The organ to-day remains without alteration and does good service.   Up to 1936 there was no Communion Table, but in this year the pulpit was removed from a high position, also the organ console to a lower, and a Communion Table — a memorial to the late Dr. George Galloway, minister from 1891 to 1915 — was placed in the church by the congregation.   In 1939 electricity was added for lighting purposes and also for blowing the organ. The church officer's house, situated on the glebe, was built in 1901 and, to meet a long felt want, a small hall was erected beside the church in 1925.   The manse, built in 1813, and just within the burgh boundary, has in course of time been considerably enlarged.

Schools

There are schools at both villages — Rhonehouse and Gelston.   The original parish school, as already stated, was at Keltonhill, and the great event in the school calendar was at one time the 'Candlemas Bleize', celebrated by a bonfire on 'the Hill'.   As it now stands, the school is a good building, having been enlarged and improved in 1929.   It has a headmaster and headmaster's house, two assistants, and about 75 pupils. The school is well equipped with cloakrooms, and has water and electric light and central heating.   A mid-day meal is provided, not cooked on the premises, but sent from a central kitchen at Dalbeattie.

The school at Gelston is completely new.   Built in 1932, it has a headmaster and headmaster's house, one assistant and about 50 pupils. It is equipped on the same lines as that at Rhonehouse.   The old school, standing beside the new, is used as a dining room for the mid-day meal. It has a kitchen and meals are cooked on the premises.   The meal costs 6d. and is taken by all the pupils.

School buses are used to convey children of over 12 years of age from the country to Castle-Douglas for secondary education, and also to convey children whose homes are situated at more than a reasonable walking distance from the village schools.

(For burgh schools, see CASTLE-DOUGLAS account)

Mons Meg

The cannon known as 'Mons Meg' is still on the ramparts of Edinburgh Castle, to which it was brought from London in 1829, largely through the influence of Sir Walter Scott.   Legend has connected its manufacture with this parish and with the siege of Threave Castle by James II of Scotland in 1455.   The well-known legend is to the effect that the cannon was manufactured by a blacksmith along with his seven sons at the Buchan hamlet, already referred to, on the banks of Carlingwark

Loch. It is possible that Joseph Train, the Galloway antiquary, is responsible for the perpetuation of the story. He was buried in Kelton Churchyard and his tomb may still be seen. In the *Old Statistical Account* this story is referred to as a 'tradition'. The *New Statistical Account* goes further and accepts the story as fact. Now, it does not seem possible to accept the legend of the birthplace of 'Mons'. It may be noted that in Harper's *Rambles in Galloway* the Galloway legend is not questioned. Sir Herbert Maxwell, however, in *A History of the House of Douglas* Vol. I, p.195, gives the note: 'Mons Meg was probably of foreign make'. We do not seem to be able to say much more than that, and the origin of this famous cannon remains unknown. Yet the legend dies hard, and as recently as September 1950 interest in the question was renewed, when during a repair to a house in the Buchan — the house nearest to Castle-Douglas — there was found in the gable-wall a chimney way, 6 feet 4 inches wide, which evidently must have been at one time a blacksmith's forge. The local paper, the *Galloway News*, naturally took note of it, and even *The Scotsman* made some reference to this discovery, reminding its readers that 'Local lore has always claimed that the cannon Mons Meg at Edinburgh Castle, used by the King's forces to subdue the Galloway Douglas's stronghold at Threave Castle, was forged at the Buchan'.

Castle-Douglas

Access to Threave Castle — in the parish of Balmaghie, and on an island in the river Dee — is to be had from Kelton parish. We may remind ourselves that Castle-Douglas does not derive its name from the Douglases of Threave, who for a period of 86 years, from 1369 to 1455, held sway in Galloway. The town had its name from Sir William Douglas of Gelston Castle — in this parish, but now falling into disuse — who died in the year 1809. From its situation, Castle-Douglas has now become the commercial capital of the Stewartry with many first-class shops. It is the normal centre, and it may be noted that while the Presbytery of Kirkcudbright sometimes meets in the county town, and once a year at Dalry in the Glenkens, most of the meetings are held in the market town. The Stewartry Education Committee also have their offices in Castle-Douglas.

The growing importance of Castle-Douglas was marked in the summer of 1950 by the celebration of its first 'Civic Week', during which various functions took place, reaching their climax on Saturday 15 July. On the afternoon of that day a tableau was enacted in Lochside Park of the scene which had taken place 158 years previously, in 1792 — the presentation of the original charter, creating the town of Carlingwark a burgh of barony. Great crowds witnessed the tableau and the procession through the town afterwards of over 60 decorated vehicles. These proceedings took place amid relentless rain and under leaden skies, but the holding of a Civic Week is an event which is likely to continue in the annals of the town.

This parish has its full share of natural beauty.   Its highest elevation is Screel Hill, 1,125 feet in height, which is easily climbed and commands a fine prospect.   The Loch of Carlingwark is a great asset to the town.   It is 100 acres in extent, most popular for curling and skating, a sanctuary for water-fowl, particularly swans, and may indeed be 'the pearl of all Southland Scottish lochs'.

1952

THE BURGH OF CASTLE-DOUGLAS

Physical Features

Castle-Douglas is the most central town and the commercial capital of the Stewartry of Kirkcudbright.   The main road and railway from Dumfries and Stranraer and the roads from Ayr, Dalbeattie, Kirkcudbright and the coast all converge on Castle-Douglas, making the town a natural route-centre.   In view of these excellent means of communication it is not surprising that Castle-Douglas, in the centre of a rich farming area, should have become one of the busiest market towns in the south of Scotland.

The boundaries of the town, which lies within the civil parishes of Kelton and Crossmichael, are fairly widespread, and the burgh actually covers an area of 1,000 acres.   But since the built-up area amounts to only 250 acres, there is an abundance of open spaces.   Although two belts of marshland lie to the west and south of the town, these are by no means obvious and do not mar the natural beauty of the town's surroundings.   Green fields, used chiefly for grazing, separate many of the built-up areas of the town, and the inhabitants of the houses which overlook these lovely tree-lined pastures are continually reminded that the country is never far away.

Carlingwark Loch, about 100 acres in area, lying wholly within the burgh boundary, is the home of great numbers of large pike and is frequented by a wide variety of bird life.   It is the permanent and picturesque domain of several score of swans and their families, which add to the beauty of the loch's natural setting.   Bordering the loch on one side is a 17 acre public park with great stretches of well-kept grass (for playing on, not keeping off!), avenues of ornamental trees, and flower-beds which are a blaze of colour all summer and autumn.

The loch and park are surrounded by some magnificent trees — oak, ash, beech, lime and sycamore — some of them over 70 feet in height. The Market Hill, another public park of nearly four acres in the centre of the town, is encircled with beautiful limes and chestnuts.   Much of the larger private properties on the outskirts of the town have several mature trees — giant Scots firs and copper beeches in addition to the varieties already mentioned — in their grounds, and some of the council housing schemes overlook, or are overlooked by, other picturesque belts of trees. In fact wherever one goes in Castle-Douglas open spaces and trees can be seen.

History

The earliest inhabited spot within the burgh boundary was the Buchan, which is still a picturesque and attractive hamlet on the edge of Carlingwark Loch. This community was in existence as early as 1353, when Edward Balliol's cavalry was stationed there. According to the well-known legend it was also at the Buchan that the famous gun, Mons Meg, was specially forged for the siege of Threave in 1455. The earliest village on the site of the present town was known as Causewayend at the beginning of the eighteenth century. Later, when marl, a popular fertiliser, was being quarried from the loch, the village increased in size and was called Carlingwark.

In 1792 Sir William Douglas of Gelston obtained a charter elevating this village to a burgh of barony and re-naming it Castle-Douglas, after himself and not the more famous family who had been Lords of Galloway and owners of Threave Castle. Sir William appointed and controlled the first town council and built a cotton factory which eventually failed. By 1800 the population of the burgh was about 1,000. After the death of Sir William a new charter, dated 1829, settled the affairs of the town in a more orthodox manner in the hands of a properly-elected town council. In 1861 the burgh boundaries were fixed as they are now, and in the following year the new town hall was erected on its present site.

During the first half of the last century Castle-Douglas was an important coaching town. Every day the mail coaches to and from Portpatrick passed through the burgh, and four other daily coaches plied between Castle-Douglas and Dumfries and Kirkcudbright. Perhaps the greatest event in the history of the burgh, because of its effect on the industry and commerce, was the opening of the railway from Dumfries in 1859, and the completion of the line to Stranraer in 1861. A century ago Castle-Douglas post office was the busiest in the south of Scotland, being second only to Glasgow in the number of sub-offices it controlled.

Notable Castle-Douglas figures during the nineteenth century included two writers and an inventor. In 1808 John Gladstone achieved a national reputation by inventing a reaping machine and by improving the design of the threshing mill. For these services Gladstone received from the Stewartry Agricultural Society an award of 100 guineas, a considerable sum in those days. Joseph Train, who died in 1852 and is commemorated by a plaque in the town hall, spent most of his life as an exciseman in Castle-Douglas and was renowned as an historian and antiquarian. He was a regular correspondent of Sir Walter Scott and provided that great writer with a wealth of material which was used in the novels *Guy Mannering*, *Old Mortality*, and others. S. R. Crockett, a popular novelist at the turn of the century, was born at Laurieston, but received his education from 1867-73 at schools in Castle-Douglas.

Population

The census returns since 1841 illustrate more clearly than anything else the steady rate of development of Castle-Douglas, particularly in comparing the burgh with the rest of the county.

Census Year	Population of Burgh	Burgh Population as Percentage of Total	
		County Population	Burghal Population
1841	1,847	4	22
1851	1,992	5	—
1861	2,261	5	26
1871	2,274	5	23
1881	2,565	6	24
1891	2,851	7	28
1901	3,018	8	29
1911	3,016	8	30
1921	2,801	8	31
1931	3,008	10	31
1951	3,322	11	32
1961	3,253	11	33

It can be seen that whereas in 1841 the population of Castle-Douglas was only 4 per cent. of that of the Stewartry, in 1961 it had increased to 11 per cent.   This trend may be shown another way by comparing the figures of 1851, when the county's population was at its greatest, with those of to-day.

	1851	1961	decrease/increase per cent.
Population of county	43,121	28,877	−33
Population of Castle-Douglas	1,992	3,253	+63

Compared with the total population of all five burghs in the county, Castle-Douglas has again increased its proportion, from 22 per cent. in 1841 to 33 per cent. in 1961.

Thus, while the county as a whole and most of the other burghs were suffering considerable depopulation, Castle-Douglas continued to flourish and increase both in population and importance.   As will be seen later, this was the direct result of the continuous development of the mart and of the industries and shops serving the farming community.

Industry and Commerce

As a market town Castle-Douglas is now internationally famous, and indeed its prosperity may be said to centre round the mart, with an annual turn-over recently estimated as being about £2½ millions.   It is through this medium that so much trade generally is brought to the town. The mart ensures not only the regular twice-weekly attendance of farmers and their wives from all over Galloway but also, for certain sales, a great influx of buyers from all over Britain and even from overseas. Attendance at the mart may be judged by the car-parking figures, which range from 200 to 300 cars at ordinary sales to nearly 1,000 cars on special occasions.

The first stock-market, an open-air one, was established in the burgh in 1819.   The town council, in 1857, erected the first enclosed mart on the Market Hill, on the site of what is now the Drill Hall, and leased it to Thomas Wallet. During this century the mart has been developed on its present situation, until to-day the premises extend to over 10 acres, with six sale rings and accommodation for 3,000 cattle or 20,000 sheep. The mart also owns some 55 acres of grazing ground within the burgh boundary.

Castle-Douglas is recognised as the principal centre and market for two important breeds of cattle. It provides the show place and the sale ring for the finest of Britain's Ayrshire dairy stock and holds the world record for a collective sale of this breed, when 1,500 head were sold for a total of £122,000. It is also the home of the beef-producing Galloway cattle which are rapidly becoming more popular with farmers at home and abroad. Castle-Douglas mart holds the record sale prices for Galloways with a top price of 13,500 guineas for a bull and 1,300 guineas for a heifer.

Castle-Douglas has several other local businesses directly connected with the farming industry. Two firms of agricultural engineers, founded in 1865 and 1876, serve over 2,000 farms in Wigtownshire, Dumfries-shire and the Stewartry, and give employment to approximately 60, of whom half live in the country. A local firm of grain merchants and manufacturers of animal feeding stuffs has about 1,000 customers among farmers and employs a staff of 25, of whom six live outwith the town. Five garages, with a labour force of over 50, owe much of their business to the farming trade. The Castle-Douglas branch of a Dumfries firm of building contractors employs about 100 men (about half of whom come from the country) and carries out work all over Galloway. A number of other smaller firms connected with the building trade are all assured of full employment throughout the year.

Castle-Douglas is unusually well provided with hotels, some of them quite large and luxurious in standard. There are nine of them— 8 licensed and 1 temperance—capable of sleeping 170 people. In addition the town has several boarding-houses and a growing number of places offering 'bed and breakfast'. The total accommodation provided by all these establishments, however, is quite inadequate for meeting the demands of the summer tourist trade or the tremendous influx of cattlemen during the special sales in winter.

The shopping facilities in Castle-Douglas are quite exceptional for a town of its size, and a great variety of goods of first-class quality can be obtained in many of the locally-owned shops. A number of multiple concerns have branches in the town. There are altogether over 90 shops in the town, and more than a quarter of them are engaged in the provision trade. Not only do they enjoy good business in their town premises but their vans are to be seen all over the county, serving villages, isolated farms and lonely cottages miles off the beaten track. Once again, in the larger businesses the proportion of employees who live outside the burgh is high—about 30 per cent.

The municipally-owned slaughterhouse brings considerable income, not only to the town council by way of dues but also to the town generally. In addition to killing for the retail trade throughout the county, a vast quantity of meat is exported to the English markets. The approximate numbers of animals slaughtered in a year—1,400 cattle, 1,400 pigs, 6,000 calves, 100,000 sheep—indicate the importance of this trade. To meet the needs of this ever-growing business the slaughter-house premises are soon to be still further enlarged.

The *Galloway News*, the local weekly newspaper, was founded in 1858, and three years later passed into the hands of John Hunter Maxwell. To-day the managing director is a great-grandson of that early proprietor, and for a hundred years the firm has been in the hands of a 'John Hunter Maxwell'. The employees number 47, of whom 14 are from the country.

An indication of the prosperity of the burgh is the presence of flourishing branches of all the Scottish banks. The Castle-Douglas Trustee Savings Bank (founded 1840) has now branches in Kirkcudbright and Dalbeattie, and the balance due to depositors is nearly £750,000.

Churches[1]

In the part of Kelton parish which is now the ecclesiastical parish of Castle-Douglas, there are two churches of the Church of Scotland. Lochside Church, as it used to be called—now St. Andrew's Church—the original *quoad sacra* parish church, was built in 1868, and is a good Gothic edifice, situated near the Common by the Carlingwark Loch. Since its erection many additions and improvements have been made. Built to meet the needs of the growing town, transepts and galleries were added in 1881, and in 1890 the tower was built. In 1931 the building was greatly enhanced by the addition of a very beautiful chancel and a fine oak pulpit, and in 1948 the chancel was further beautified by stained glass windows. There is a pipe organ and the church is capable of holding about 800 people. It contains a session room as well as a vestry and beside it stands the church hall. The roll of communicants is at present about 900. The manse is situated in St. Andrew Street.

The other Church of Scotland in the burgh of Castle-Douglas is in Queen Street, and is now known as St. Ringan's. Prior to 1923 there were three United Free Churches in the town. These were called Queen Street, St. George's and Trinity Churches. St. George's was always a Free Church. Trinity, up to 1900, was a United Presbyterian, and Queen Street was known to begin with as a Cameronian Church. Until 1876 its official denomination was Reformed Presbyterian. It then became a Free Church. In 1923 these three United Free Churches joined to form one congregation. The place of worship finally chosen was the Queen Street Church. Trinity Church was retained for hall accommodation; and St. George's was sold to be used as business premises. The spire was then removed and thus the town lost one of its distinctive landmarks. When the Queen Street Church was selected as the place

(1) Contributed by the Rev. Donald M. Henry.

of worship, its name was changed to St. Ringan's. It was, however, too small for the united congregation and was renovated and enlarged. The old gallery was retained, a chancel was added and also another transept. For the floor of the church, chairs, instead of pews, were provided. There is a stained glass window in the chancel, and the pipe organ has been completely overhauled and rebuilt. The church is now capable of holding 650 people, and the present roll of communicants is about 650. There is a session room as well as a vestry, and the church is well provided for in hall accommodation by the retention of the former Trinity Church buildings.   The manse is within the church grounds in Queen Street.

Apart from the Church of Scotland, there is a Scottish Episcopal Church (consecrated 1874) at the east end of St. Andrew Street, and a Roman Catholic Church (1867) at the west end of the same street.

Public Services

A century ago there were two schools in Castle-Douglas. The parish school, in King Street, moved in 1845 to a new building in Academy Street. In 1843 a Free Church School was opened in Cotton Street and later came to be known as 'Cowper's Schule' because of its headmaster, William Cowper (1861-72), who achieved considerable fame as a teacher, the novelist S. R. Crockett being one of his prize pupils. In 1872 the single-storey building in upper Cotton Street was erected; Cowper became its first headmaster and remained there until 1880 when he was appointed lecturer in English at New College, Edinburgh.   The rectangular two-storey school in Cotton Street was added in 1910. In 1934 a handsome new primary school, accommodating 400 and surrounded by 8 acres of playing fields, was erected, at a cost of £13,000, near the top of Queen Street.   The High School moved in 1958 from Cotton Street to new premises, with accommodation for 400, in Dunmuir Road, on the outskirts of the town.   Standing in 10 acres of playing fields, this magnificent building, which cost £210,000, has everything a modern secondary school should have—except, perhaps, a swimming pool.   The main Cotton Street building now houses the School of Commerce (full-time day classes) and the Further Education Centre (evening classes).   The old school (1872), which was damaged by fire in January 1957, was later rebuilt as a three-teacher school and occupied in August 1961 by St. John's R.C. Primary School.

Two departments of the county council have their offices in Castle-Douglas; the Education Offices (since 1920) and the Public Health Department (since 1950).   The county library, the first in rural Scotland to operate a mobile library van, also has its headquarters in the town. Carlingwark House, standing in lovely grounds on the bank of the loch, has been, since 1952, the county council home for some 30 old folk. The local cottage hospital, built in 1897, has beds for 34 patients and employs a permanent nursing staff of 14, of whom half are from the country.

Until 1880 the inhabitants of the burgh drew their water from three public wells.   A piped gravitation water supply from Loch Roan was introduced that year, and improved in 1924.   The first public drainage system came into operation in 1890, and a new sewage disposal plant, costing over £40,000, was completed in 1961.

Public lighting was first introduced to the town soon after 1843 when the Castle-Douglas Gas Company was formed with a capital of £1,000 in £5 shares.   Gas is still quite widely used for cooking in the burgh, and the local annual output amounts to 18 million cubic feet.   The headquarters of the Kirkcudbright District of the South of Scotland Electricity Board are situated in Castle-Douglas and give employment to 69 people, ranging from highly skilled engineers to labourers; of these one third reside outside the town.

The importance of the Castle-Douglas post office may be gauged from the fact that it has the main automatic telephone exchange for the area, 32 sub-offices under its supervision, and is responsible for mail services in the greater part of the county.   The post office has a fleet of 30 vans based on Castle-Douglas and employs 51 personnel.

Attention has been drawn, in this and the preceding section, to the large number of people who live in the surrounding district but work for firms in Castle-Douglas; these commuters represent about 30 per cent. of the total number of employed persons in the town.   This fact illustrates clearly the interdependence of the burgh and the country around.

Housing

Altogether there are 1,058 dwelling-houses in the town, of which 584 are privately owned and 474 owned by the town council.   Since the end of the war the council has built 267 houses, and of these 44 are two-apartment buildings suitable for elderly or single people.   Except for those small houses, which are in great demand, the council housing problem is nearly solved, although a number of houses have still to be built for key workers in local industries.

The situation, as far as privately-owned houses are concerned, is by no means satisfactory, for only 32 of these have been built since the war.   The chief difficulty has been acquiring land to build on.   A considerable number of privately-owned dwellings are now urgently required and the council will have to take action to requisition land for this purpose.

Cultural and Social Organisations

Although there are some who maintain that the townspeople of Castle-Douglas are more concerned with money-making than with 'culture', the musical, dramatic and educational activities are surprisingly well supported.   Last winter, for example, 230 students attended the Further Education Centre.   Evening classes leading to certificate examinations included those in commercial subjects, mathematics and science (up to

Ordinary National level) and English, mathematics and arithmetic for the O grade Leaving Certificate. Popular non-vocational subjects have been dressmaking, woodwork, art, welding, French, keep-fit and motor-mechanics. The Musical Society presents a light opera and an oratorio, and the Unity Players, who have their own 'little theatre', produce several plays every year. There are enthusiastic branches, senior and junior, of the Royal Scottish Country Dance Society and many pupils attend classes in both ballet and highland dancing.

The town council, with eight elections in the past ten years and an average poll of over 50 per cent., gives a lead to other local organisations by its continual efforts to improve the amenities of the burgh. Four years ago the town hall was renovated and enlarged at a cost of £15,000. The large hall, which has a magnificent built-in proscenium large enough to accommodate a full-scale opera production, can seat 500 in comfort. Also included in the building are a lesser hall (the burgh court), the council chamber, a suite of committee rooms, and a kitchen capable of providing a meal for several hundred people. During the past ten years the council has developed part of Lochside Park into a spacious caravan and camping site for 70 vehicles. The toilet accommodation includes wash-rooms, laundry, and spray baths with hot and cold water laid on. The council also provides boating on the loch, putting greens in each of the public parks, and well-equipped children's playgrounds in several parts of the town. In 1944 the late Miss Bessie Gordon Brown, sister of a well-known local ironmonger, left a bequest of £28,929 14s 10d to be administered by the town council and used for the common good. Since then the interest has supplied annual gifts of coal to some 170 townsfolk who are elderly or in straitened circumstances and has also been used in improvements to parks, playing fields and the provision of bus shelters.

Private sports clubs in the town include golf (a nine-hole course), tennis (two all-weather courts) and bowls. The municipally-owned football field has, in recent years, been improved by the addition of a pavilion, a covered stand and a concrete enclosure; these have been paid for partly by the council and partly by the supporters of a local team, Threave Rovers, who have raised about £1,000 for this purpose. There is excellent pike-fishing, and occasionally water-skiing on the loch. Earlier in this century cricket and quoits were popular games in the town, but have since died out.

The ladies of Castle-Douglas are enthusiastic supporters of their own organisations and the town has flourishing branches of the Women's Rural Institutes, Women's Voluntary Service and Red Cross. The Scottish Association for Mentally Handicapped Children is represented in the burgh by some 15 to 20 ladies, who do great work in holding classes for those unfortunate youngsters in the area who are ineducable by special school methods.

The biggest occasion of the year is undoubtedly Civic Week, celebrated during the second week of July for the past 13 years. A

committee of townspeople spend the nine months preceding Civic Week
in raising money required for staging a glorious week of non-stop
entertainment: over £2,000 is required annually. Civic Week reaches
its climax on the Saturday, Douglas Day, when the town's population
is swelled by over 10,000 visitors. The magnificent fancy dress procession of some 50 decorated vehicles presenting tableaux of various kinds
is followed by hydro-plane racing or gyro-boat demonstrations on the
loch, as well as a variety of other novel forms of entertainment. The
evening is rounded off by a searchlight tattoo and firework display in
Lochside Park.

A Lively Community

During the past hundred years, thanks to the wisdom and foresight of
its businessmen, Castle-Douglas has gradually achieved a reputation as
a prosperous and progressive market town. Its civic leader and its local
organisations have selflessly devoted their time and energy to improving
the amenities of the town and developing a lively social life among the
townspeople. All these efforts have not gone unrecognised. In 1962
the Saltire Society award was presented to the burgh of Castle-Douglas
as the most 'alive' community of its size in Scotland.

1962

CHAPTER 18

THE PARISH OF KIRKBEAN

by the REV. A. DICKSON

Physical Features

The parish of Kirkbean lies in the eastern district of the Stewartry of Kirkcudbright on the Solway Firth, four and a half miles south of New Abbey on the Dumfries, Dalbeattie and Castle-Douglas coast road. It is roughly six miles long by four broad and forms a compact area at the foot of Criffel (1,866 feet) 'the Sentinel of the Solway', by which it is bounded on the west. The parish is delightfully situated and from any point on the high ground there are magnificent views of the Firth, the Dumfriesshire coast and the mountains of Cumberland. In summer the countryside is lush and green with a great variety of wild flowers. Large numbers of wild geese winter on the coast and the area generally is an excellent one for the study of land and sea birds.

Apart from a thin band of limestone and sandstone in the north-west, the soil is alluvial and fortunately for the farmer has no connection with the granite mass of Criffel. In fact the parish can be described roughly as a spit of land washed down through the ages by the river Nith from the southern uplands of Scotland. From the fertility of the soil the parish is sometimes referred to as the 'Garden of Galloway'. It is a stronghold of the dairy farmer, for the mild and moist climate ensures good pasture for a great part of the year. Black-faced sheep are also grazed on the farms lying to the hills.

History

There are several interpretations of the meaning of the name 'Kirkbean'. The one we prefer derives the word from *Circ Beain,* Bean's Church. Bean or St. Bean was Bishop of Mortlach in Banffshire about 1012. Although the roll of ministers of the church goes back to 1585 we know little of the pre-Reformation history of the parish. The only ancient monuments are the ruins of Wraith's Tower, which belonged to the Earl of Morton and is said to have been visited by James VI, and the very interesting Market Cross of the old Burgh of Preston, which stands intact near the farm of East Preston.

The present era of the history of the parish may be said to have started towards the end of the eighteenth and beginning of the nineteenth centuries with the work of the noted agricultural pioneer, William Craik of Arbigland. He did much to improve the breed of cattle, drain the land and bring it into a better state of cultivation. At the same time, although to-day the parish is predominantly agricultural, we must note also its very close connection with the sea. During the eighteenth century the Solway port of Carsethorn was part of what was called the Port of Dumfries, having trading connection with America and the Baltic ports besides coastal towns like Liverpool and Whitehaven. The lighthouse at Southerness, the oldest in Galloway, is a reminder of the difficulties of navigation in the Solway when it was more used than it is to-day. Southerness—a corruption of Satterness or Salter's Point—is an interesting old village dating from the twelfth century. To-day with its golf course it is being developed as a holiday resort by Major R. A. Oswald of Cavens.

Another small centre in the parish is Preston Mill, which, as the name indicates, was the site at one time of an old estate meal mill. Kirkbean is a pleasant little village near Cavens House and is the present-day centre of the parish, with church and school. The church was built in 1776 in the time of William Craik and the Tower added in 1835 by Thomas Grierson, minister, writer of the *New Statistical Account* (1844). The manse dates from 1798 and there is a good glebe of nearly 13 acres. 'Teind' stipend amounts to £194 5s 6d, endowments to £54 1s 6d. The church, manse, glebe and glebe cottages were handed over by the heritors to the Church of Scotland General Trustees after the Union of 1929.

Notable Men

No summary of the history of the parish, however brief, would be complete without a reference to some of its better known sons. The most notable of these is the celebrated John Paul Jones, born in the gardener's cottage at Arbigland in 1747. He emigrated to America at an early age, became the virtual founder of the American Navy and fought on the American side in the War of Independence. He is a controversial figure who is, however, held in high regard in the U.S.A. as the 'Nelson of America'. During the second world war officers of the American Navy serving in Britain presented a baptismal font in his memory to Kirkbean Church.

As it happens, two other Kirkbean men have an intimate connection with the same period of American history. Dr. James Craik, born 1727, was the friend of George Washington and organiser of the medical services of the American Army during the Revolution. Richard Oswald, who died in 1784, an ancestor of the present Laird of Cavens, negotiated the Peace Treaty between the two countries after the war was over.

Admiral John Campbell, 1719-90, stayed at home to gain fame. He had a distinguished career in the British Navy and was a son of the Rev. John Campbell, minister of the parish. Dr. Edward Milligan, who died in 1833, was a distinguished lecturer in medical science in Edinburgh.

Land-owners

There are two estates in the parish, Cavens and Arbigland. Major R.

A. Oswald is proprietor of Cavens and Major C. W. S. Blackett of Arbigland.

Population

On the whole this parish has not suffered so much from depopulation during the last century as some others. The following census figures tell the story:—

1801	696
1851	982
1901	685
1911	711
1921	679
1931	560
1951	583

During the second world war the population showed a temporary increase through the influx of evacuees from centres threatened by air raids. There were 60 children from Dr. Barnardo's Homes billeted in Arbigland House during the war.

The causes of the decline in the rural population are well known. Since the first world war especially there has been a general tendency to drift to the larger centres of population. Families also are much smaller and fewer hands are needed on the farms since machinery came into general use. It is practically certain, however, that the population of this parish, with its excellent agricultural land, will remain more stable than that of others with less productive soil. Most of the inhabitants if not natives of the parish belong to the Stewartry of Kirkcudbright or Dumfriesshire. A few have come in and settled from England. A number of the dairy farmers came originally from Ayrshire.

The following analysis of age groups and occupations was made in 1947:—

Children under 5	boys, 28; girls, 25
Age group over 70	men, 18; women, 14
Children of school age (6-15)	boys, 53; girls, 44
Farm workers	men, 72; women, 10
Dairy workers	men, 24; women, 15
Landed proprietors	2
Farmers	18
Estate workers	14
Housewives	141
Tradesmen	17
Fishermen	6
Domestic Servants	6
Office workers	6
H.M. Forces	6
Professional	7
Miscellaneous	22
Total	548

Education

The schoolmaster has two assistant teachers. The number of pupils on the school roll has gone down recently from 120 to 73 since the raising of the school leaving age to 15. After the 'qualifying' class, pupils go on to the junior secondary school at New Abbey or to a course leading to the Scottish Leaving Certificate, at Dumfries or Kirkcudbright. Loaningfoot school at West Preston was closed some years ago. The endowments for Kirkbean and West Preston were good and are now incorporated in the Stewartry Educational Trust. The school is managed by the Education Committee of the County Council, the successor of the old Education Authority and, before that, of the School Board. The children are well looked after; they have their own electrically equipped kitchen and dining centre in the church hall, where they enjoy a two course mid-day meal at a cost of 6d a day. They also benefit under the Government's free milk scheme.

Housing

Since the pre-1914 or even the pre-1939 era the standard of housing expected in the country has greatly improved. Gone are the days of the 'but and ben'; working-class houses must now have a minimum of three rooms, and four is general, and for even the smallest cottage a bathroom and conveniences with hot and cold water are now deemed essential. This standard is being steadily pursued in this parish, although progress is not so fast as desired owing to the cost of material and labour and the difficulties facing proprietors. In general the laying on of water supplies is being taken up by the county councils. Practically every house has electricity supplied by the nationalised South-West of Scotland Electricity Board. Farm houses are on the whole very good and have been much improved especially by owner-occupiers who have benefited in recent years from government guaranteed milk prices. The local authority (county council) has just built a block of eight new houses at Preston Mill for agricultural workers. But the rate of building of new houses and the reconstruction of old ones does not keep pace with current needs. More houses might be built for general occupation, were the parish nearer Dumfries for work and recreation. The majority of the farm houses as well as a number of other houses are now owned by the occupiers, and only relatively few are rented. Most of the farm and estate cottages are still 'tied', although the present tendency is away from this system.

Agriculture

There are 21 farms in the parish, of an average size of about 250 acres. The biggest carry anything up to 130 Ayrshire dairy cows or more; the average is roughly 60 head attested, free from tuberculosis. Rents range from £88-£571, with £263 as the average.

Eight farms are occupied by rent-paying tenants but four of these are likely to be bought by occupiers in the very near future as part of Cavens Estate is being sold. Three are occupied by owner-farmers and the remaining ten, seven on the Arbigland Estate and three on Cavens, are farmed by the proprietors. The farm houses in this class are occupied by farm managers or dairymen. The proprietor turned 'multiple-farmer' is a new factor in country life. His advent makes one of the most important of the many changes which have taken place in the parish since the second world war.

Farming has of course become highly mechanised and the oil-driven tractor has taken the place of the horse. There is a grass-drying plant on the Arbigland farms and silage is also used for winter feeding. Turnips and mangolds are grown for the same purpose, but not to the same extent as formerly, owing to high costs of production. Because of the mild climate, grass pastures do very well and have a long season. There has just been introduced on the Arbigland farms the system of strip grazing using electrified fences. Cereals grown are mostly oats with some wheat and beans. There is no fattening of cattle for beef but the farms that lie up to the high ground have sheep which live on hill pasture. Egg production is carried on generally, and at one or two farms intensively by means of the battery system.

There is a certain amount of fishing for salmon, flounders and shrimps at Carsethorn.

The dairyman is a very important and essential member of the farming community. He looks after the cows only and does no other work on the farm. He hires his own labour and sometimes the dairy is a family concern. Usually he is not merely a wage-earner but has a percentage of milk receipts. Against this he may share in the cost of feeding stuffs. Milk prices are guaranteed by the Department of Agriculture's Milk Marketing Board. One or two of the farms still make a limited amount of cheese.

With regard to the incomes generally of dairymen, ploughmen and farm workers, they are incomparably better than they used to be. And the working week is much shorter. Apart from dairymen, who have no stated hours, farm servants work 48 hours a week in summer and 44 in winter. The average wage is about £5 weekly. Overtime in harvest and at other busy times is paid at higher rates. Compare wages 50 years ago in the south of Scotland: for example, a ploughman's wife had three shillings a week for milking ten cows twice daily and three shillings a day in harvest for a day of nine and a half hours. It is hardly necessary to say that milking to-day is all done by milking machines powered by electricity. At the same time, in reckoning real wages, we must remember that the purchasing power of money has declined.

Trades

The work that tradesmen used to do in the parish tends more and more to be done from centres like Dumfries. The country blacksmith has had to branch out in new lines; one of the two in Kirkbean has an up-to-date welding plant. The rural shoemaker and tailor have long since had their day and could not be expected to compete with the machine mass-produced products of the towns. Another fast disappearing member of the community is the domestic servant. Young girls to-day prefer to work in offices and shops or as bus conductresses, to mention only a few of the many alternative occupations open to them.

Public and Social Services

Public and social services have increased greatly in number and scope even since the second world war. In local government the place of the old parish council has been taken by the district council and the county council; for all practical purposes the county council, as the district council has very limited powers. Transport services have been revolutionised with the coming of the motor bus in the nineteen-twenties. The bus has opened up the country and given the countryman a more varied life than he ever had before, with a more frequent and convenient access to the towns. This parish was isolated in the old days as there was no railway station near and the horse-drawn bus went to Dumfries twelve miles away only twice a week. Farmers had a great deal of carting which is now done for them by motor transport. Potatoes were loaded on to boats at Carsethorn and coals taken off. There are many private cars in the parish and the farmer's 'shelt and gig' is now a curiosity.

The health services were nationalised in 1948 and for fixed contributions we have the services of doctor, dentist, optician and district nurse. The District Nursing Association, kept up by voluntary contributions, did excellent work up to its dissolution in 1948 and served the three parishes of New Abbey, Kirkbean and Southwick. The parish is served by two doctors, who work in close contact with the hospitals in Dumfries.

Educational developments have been noted above. Besides the work of the school proper, further education or continuation classes are encouraged by the authorities. This last winter (1949-50) in Kirkbean there have been very successful singing and sewing classes and also a class for country dancing.

Perhaps one of the greatest improvements during the last century has been in the lot of the poor. The poor used to be one of the main concerns of the kirk session; to-day they are cared for by the state. Old-age and widows' pensions, disablement and sickness benefits have freed the destitute from the fear of the poorhouse. This, of course, is not to disparage the excellent humanitarian work done by voluntary effort before the state took over. A further development to-day is the care of the aged in their homes rather than in institutions.

It would, however, be a bad thing for the parish if all responsibility for social service and welfare were handed over to the state, and happily this is not the case. The parish has a community council which concerns itself with all aspects of the good of the community. One of its main pre-occupations has been the building of a village hall, for which it has raised over £2,000. Unfortunately, owing to the economic state of the country, the council has been unable so far to get a permit for building a hall and this project must at present wait. Meantime the needs of local organisations are to some extent met by the use of the church hall, which is converted glebe property and also serves as a cooking centre and dining-room for the school children. It seats over 100. The Carsethorn Hall belongs to Major Blackett and when available is used by the Carsethorn Badminton Club. The Carsethorn Carpet Bowling Club meets in a loft belonging to the Steamboat Inn, while the Kirkbean carpet bowlers play in the loft above the Cavens Estate joiner's shop.

The Church

Although in changed conditions, the church still keeps her ancient place in the life of the parish. Apart from her main function, 'the conversion and sanctification of souls', she makes it her business, along with the school, to stress, whenever possible, the positive and constructive aspects of life, work and recreation. Church attendance is not what it used to be; the decline set in after the first world war. Sunday is not observed as in the past, while a number of the young people have formed the habit of going to the cinema in Dumfries on Sunday evenings. At the same time, there is a danger in painting too dark a picture. In a materialistic age the church is as live an institution for good as any. Communicant members number about 250 and of these approximately 190 come to communion once a year. The number of children attending two Sunday schools, one each at Kirkbean and West Preston, is 53. The old-fashioned Bible class on a Sunday evening with a membership of 9-12 still survives. In the winter time once a week the members of the Kirkbean Parish Youth Club, numbering 25-30, meet in the church hall. This club is led by the minister and the programmes consist mainly of games and social activities.

Cultural and Recreational Organisations

The local branch of the Women's Rural Institute plays an important part in the social life of the community, and its motto 'For Home and Country' denotes its aims. The Kirkbean Women's Rural Institute has been in existence since 1922 and during that time has done much to add interest and variety to the life of the country housewife. The Woman's Guild, a church organisation started in this parish in 1946, fosters the religious life of the church and interest in the church's work.

The whist drive is a popular form of social activity in the winter time. The dramatic society sometimes produces plays. As there is no parish hall there are fewer dances than there would otherwise be. Association football is the main summer game and the local team plays in the Kirkcudbrightshire Eastern District League. There is also a quoiting club at Carsethorn. In the winter time the ancient game of curling is played, but more often to-day at the ice rinks of Ayr and Glasgow than on Loch Kindar.

Way of Life

The way of life will appear from some of the facts given above. One or two additional observations may be made. The countryman does not have to work so hard as he did fifty years ago, as much more farm work is done by machinery. He is better clothed and better fed and has more money to spend; the conditions of work are also better. The amenities of country life have improved greatly with better transport, in the case of this parish to Dumfries, and more varied social activities. This perhaps has discouraged people from finding their own amusements at home. But we must not forget the difference the radio has made to all classes. Discipline in all walks of life, including the home, has been greatly relaxed since 1900. There was room for some change here if it is not carried too far.

Considering the disruptive tendencies of the last century the outward pattern of country life, being conditioned by the soil and the seasons, has not changed greatly. At the same time the attitude of the farm worker to his work has changed. He is not so closely 'thirled' to the land as formerly, and generally speaking he takes a less personal interest in the varied operations of the farming year.

With regard to the future of the parish the quality of the soil points to continuing farming prosperity, if world economic conditions remain favourable.

1952

CHAPTER 19

THE PARISH AND BURGH
OF KIRKCUDBRIGHT

by the REV. J. E. MOTHERSILL

Boundaries and Natural Features

The parish of Kirkcudbright, which occupies a part of the southernmost
extremity of the Stewartry, is clearly bounded on the south by the Solway
Firth; on the west by Manxman's Lake and the river Dee, beyond which
lie the neighbouring parishes of Borgue, Twynholm and Tongland; and
on the north by the parishes of Kelton and Rerrick, the latter forming
also the eastern boundary.

The land is, for the most part, undulating, with occasional flat fields
and pleasant valleys that extend into low arable hills. As one travels
northward from the Solway these hills tend to become more imposing
and more rugged, with stretches of moorland that are good only for
grazing purposes. It is everywhere a pleasant parish with an interesting
variety of scene that affords many lovely glimpses of hills and valleys,
water and woodlands.

History

The life of the parish centres very naturally in the old town of
Kirkcudbright itself. It is the county town; it possesses the only senior
secondary school in the Stewartry; it is also the seat of the Sheriff Court;
it is an excellent shopping centre, and a very charming old burgh, with
interesting bits of scene and story that carry one far back into the past.

The present parish comprises what was once three parishes—
Kirkcudbright, Galtway and Dunrod. In 1683 the two latter parishes
were annexed. Their churchyards still remain and are used occasionally.

It would seem that the Celtic name of the present royal burgh was
Caer-cuabrit, meaning a fortified place on the bend of a river, which
really affords an accurate description of the original town. In all
probability, the Church, on gaining possession of the land, remoulded
the name, the better to suit her own more saintly purposes, and the
present designation is generally taken to signify the Kirk of St. Cuthbert.
the patron saint of the town. Tradition relates that he founded the
original church, of which there is now no trace whatever, apart from
the burial ground, which lies to the east of the town and is believed
to have surrounded the first building. It is thought that St. Cuthbert.
on one of his missionary journeys, sailed up the Dee to Kirkcudbright.
Tradition affirms also that some two hundred years later his bones,

together with other sacred relics, found a brief but safe resting place in the community that was later to bear his name.

Present day Kirkcudbright retains few landmarks that date further back than the late sixteenth century. The old High Street, extending southward from the Mote, until it breaks sharply towards the east at the Tolbooth, retains its ancient line along the gravel ridge that witnessed the first settlement. The socket stones that bore the ponderous gate of the original Meikle Yett are still visible in the eastern portion of the street. The most inspiring building in the town is, doubtless, MacLellan's Castle, a venerable ruin, built by Sir Thomas MacLellan of Bombie in 1582. It is a splendid bit of masonry in which one can find most of the distinctive features of Scottish castles of that period.

Another landmark is the aforementioned Tolbooth, the quaint and lovely tower of which was built of stones brought from Dundrennan Abbey. The weather vane surmounting the spire represents a full-rigged ship of the seventeenth century. Begun in 1625, it was not completed until 1751. The 'condemned cell' so graphically portrayed by Sir Walter Scott in *Guy Mannering* is in the Tolbooth. In front of the Tolbooth is the well that, in olden days, supplied the town with water. A tablet with the following inscription still testifies to its ancient service.

> 'This fount, not riches, life supplies,
>   Art gives what nature here denies,
> Posterity must surely bliss
>   St. Cuthbert's sons who purchased this.'
> 'Water introduced 23rd of March, 1763.'

Near MacLellan's Castle, there stood once the Greyfriars Monastery, and on this hallowed spot, almost without intermission, Roman Catholics, Presbyterians and Episcopalians have worshipped in turn, since the middle of the fifteenth century.

The parish possesses several interesting relics even of the earliest days of our nation's history. In the Whinnieliggate area and on the farms of Bombie and Dromore one can readily distinguish the sites of various ancient camps. The British and Roman fortifications are easily distinguishable, both by their location and also by their differing forms of construction.

A visit to the present churchyard in Kirkcudbright will reward the visitor who is interested in the later history of the land. Among many ancient stones is one that marks the graves of two Covenanters who were captured, condemned and hanged by Claverhouse in 1684. The flat stone bears in its still easily decipherable inscription the full story of the tragic end of these two martyrs. Another curiously interesting stone marks the final resting place of the celebrated Gallovidian gypsy or tinker, Billy Marshall, who died in 1792, reputedly at the advanced age of 120 years.

Public Utilities

Since 1931 the town has been blessed with a most excellent supply of water from Loch Whinyeon, which lies some miles north-west of Kirkcudbright.

A few hundred yards beyond the parish boundary, in the parish of Tongland, is situated the headquarters of the Galloway Power Scheme. Since its inception in 1935, Kirkcudbright has enjoyed all the benefits of a good supply of electricity, which is used almost universally throughout the parish both for lighting and for power.

Gas is also in good supply from the local works, which were owned and controlled by the town council until the recent nationalisation of the service. The street lighting, which is adequate, is by electricity.

Communications and Transport

Lying as it does a little south of the main Dumfries-Stranraer road, the parish can boast no trunk road, but the secondary roads are kept in excellent condition, and communications generally are thoroughly good. Visitors to the royal burgh comment frequently on the very unusual wideness of the streets. The only explanation given locally is that when the streets were surveyed originally and pegged out accordingly for the contractors, a party of mischievous boys shifted the pegs by night, thereby serving posterity far better than they knew. The wide streets and open spaces have encouraged the town fathers to give due attention to the amenities of the place, and they can be justly proud of the several gardens of roses and flowering shrubs that have been laid out, even in the last decade.

The country roads which were formerly water bound and hardened by the iron-shod cartwheels and the hoofs of the horses, have been, since about 1914, of tarmacadam. The last war left its mark here, too, for between four and five miles of new reinforced concrete road, 20 feet wide, were laid down in the immediate vicinity of the extensive Armoured Fighting Vehicles Proving Establishment, known locally as the Tank Range, that occupies the south-east corner of the parish. Other roads were straightened, and the corners were concreted because of the heavy tank traffic.

Fifty years ago, of course, the chief means of transport was the pony and dog cart, with an occasional horse-drawn bus that plied between the town and neighbouring villages. Materials required for the farm were carried by the heavy horse and cart with iron-shod wheels. Because of the frequent hills, only loads to a maximum of 15 cwt. could be carried. Bicycles did not come into common use until between 1905 and 1910, by which date almost every farmworker possessed his own cycle.

Agriculture

At the beginning of the century, the landward portion of the parish was owned almost entirely by the laird of St. Mary's Isle estate. To-day some two thousand acres are owned by various farmers; the remaining farms are rented from the estate. The general appearance of the landward area has been changed considerably during the two wars through the cutting down of a great deal of timber. Up to date less than 25 per cent. of this area has been replanted. Some of this replanting was done, during the first war, by Belgian refugees, but most replanting has now been taken over by the Forestry Commission.

Nearly every farm in the parish carries a large dairy. These up to 1930 were all cheesemaking dairies. To-day, only two dairies in the parish produce cheese. This change came about largely through the policy of the Milk Marketing Board, which takes milk off the hands of the farmer at the farm. It was felt also that the Ministry of Food did not realise sufficiently the importance of quality, and so did not provide encouragement for the better cheesemakers. Of late years, too, very few young people have been willing to accept training as cheesemakers, knowing that it meant a seven day week job for from six to eight months of the year, whereas other farm workers now enjoy the week-end break.

Cheesemaking always demanded a high standard of cleanliness and sanitation; otherwise bad and inferior flavours would result. When, after the first world war, government control of dairies was introduced the parish of Kirkcudbright was therefore not ill-prepared. The attestation or testing of all bovine animals for tuberculosis was introduced locally 35 years ago. At first it was little welcomed, but by 1951 the parish was completely 'a free area', and the county itself was one of the first group of 'free' counties in Scotland. The Ayrshire is the popular breed locally.

About the beginning of the century the milking machine came into common use, and it is interesting to note that the first satisfactory milking machine was invented by Stewart Nicholson, of Bombie farm, in the parish of Kirkcudbright. As so often happens, this new invention was not, for many years, an unmixed blessing. It gave rise to a good deal of trouble amongst cows, in the nature of mastitis. Fortunately, trouble of this kind has been overcome, almost completely, by the use of penicillin, streptomycin and other modern antibiotics. Milk fever, too, which in early summer took a heavy toll of the farmer's choicest stock, is to-day under effective control through the use of modern drugs.

Great changes have taken place, particularly in the last decade, in methods of soil cultivation. In 1939 only two or three tractors were operating within the parish. To-day there are some 30, with the usual implements. For a time much of the work of transport and haulage was undertaken by the tractors, but of recent years most of the coal, artificial manures and feeding stuff is delivered to the various farms by merchant lorries.

While the use of the tractor enabled the farmer to overtake arrears of work, at certain seasons, it has not tended to reduce the supply of labour, since so much of the work about a farm has, of necessity, to be done by hand. The tractor has certainly eased the situation so far as week-end work is concerned, for there are now no horses to be attended to. Only the stockman is tied to his job for a seven day week. Most farmers have only one or two horses, and these are kept in the field, to be brought in for occasional work. In spite of the fact that the farms in this parish have a considerable outcrop of rock, which makes mechanical ploughing difficult and also makes for heavy wear and tear on machinery, the horse-drawn plough is seldom seen.

New methods often create new problems. Disc cultivation, which has become very popular, has been found to be responsible for the rapid spread of certain weeds, such as the dock, since the roots are cut in pieces, and thus multiplied. Sprays are used with hormone and other selective weed killers, with a good deal of success. Indeed, spraying is becoming fairly general for the control of annual weeds in oat crops and in pasture land, and particular attention is given to improved seeding, to strain grasses and clovers. Government assistance in providing 50 per cent. of liming costs has been very beneficial.

For the first quarter of the century, this parish was noted throughout Britain as the centre of the Clydesdale horse breeding industry. The farm of Banks possessed the biggest stud in Britain. But the advent of the tractor ruined the home market very quickly, and the overseas market fell away rather sharply as well, until by 1950 this thriving industry had faded out almost entirely. There has been comparatively little change in sheep breeding. Almost every dairy farm carries its quota of park or low ground sheep. In the past 20 years this parish has become known for an especially fine type of half-bred ewe lamb, produced from the north country Cheviot and the Border Leicester. These are exported to the Border district, where they top the market. Pig breeding has declined very considerably, with the loss of the by-product, the whey from cheese making.

Until recent years the parish has always been noted for its game. But since many farmers now own their farms, the number of game-keepers has been greatly reduced. Indeed, in the south-east area, game has almost disappeared, through casual snaring and shooting. There has been, unfortunately, a lamentable increase in the fox population, because of the plentiful cover afforded by the Tank Range, and also by the lands taken over by the Forestry Commission. A scheme has been organised, to which all farmers are expected to subscribe, for the eradication of the foxes, and a ten shilling bounty is paid for every brush produced to the local organisers. Apart from the number of animals killed by the Forestry Commission, an average of 850 are killed annually in the county.

Population

From the standpoint of population, the parish, in some respects, has shown comparatively little change throughout the years. This is reflected in the Census returns of the last 150 years:

1801	2,381
1851	3,555 (maximum ever recorded)
1901	3,309
1911	3,116
1921	3,054
1931	3,188
1951	3,316

This is explained, doubtless, by the fact that the parish is essentially an agricultural one. Apart from Kirkcudbright itself, there is no other settlement that might even be termed a village.

Occupations

In the town of Kirkcudbright there is a minimum of organised industry. For the past several years a small knitting factory has employed a score or more girls in the manufacture of high grade socks and gloves for export. Otherwise the inhabitants are employed in the various trades that minister to the needs of any small town and surrounding country district. It is a regrettable feature of the place that it offers so little for ambitious youth. Many of the most promising young people have therefore to look farther afield. Fifty years ago a good many of these went to Liverpool, because of the regular sea traffic between Kirkcudbright and that port. At that time, there was a thriving trade in coal, artificial manures and feeding stuffs for the farms. But the introduction of the railway, which was relatively late in this parish, and later the development of road transport, did away with this commerce by sea. In this connection, it is interesting to note that in 1952 Shell-Mex purchased five acres on the water front in Kirkcudbright for the erection of a water-fed distribution depot. The product would come in by water and would be distributed by road transport. This, it is hoped, will revive the life and worth of the port of Kirkcudbright.

Because of the mildness of the climate and of the acknowledged attractiveness of the town itself, as of the countryside round about, Kirkcudbright has, of recent years, acquired a good many people who have retired from business elsewhere in this land or abroad. Two-thirds of the population are native to the parish. In years past many Irish labourers were brought in for seasonal work on the land, and a few of these always remained here. To-day there are very few from that source. It is noticeable that more English people are coming into the parish, some to retire, and others to fill various positions, often in connection with nationalised services.

The greatest upheaval of life and population dates back to the recent war, when in 1942 an extensive area, lying to the south-east of the parish, and bordering on the Solway, was requisitioned by the War Department for military purposes. This has since developed into the aforementioned Armoured Fighting Vehicles Proving Establishment. Several of the finest farms in the south of Scotland, comprising in this parish 2,000 acres, were taken over partially or entirely, at very short notice. What was thought then to be a temporary arrangement has proved, unfortunately, to be a permanent one. This, naturally, has meant a loss to the parish, both in land and in people. From one farm alone the farmer, together with his workers, 30 in all, had to seek homes and employment beyond the parish. It meant a radical change, too, in the life of the town of Kirkcudbright, which has now a permanent element of so called 'troops'. Recently, houses, 18 in all, have been built within the town for officers and men of the permanent staff. A further six will be under construction in the immediate future. During the winter, of course, the range is quiet, and only necessary maintenance work is carried on. But in the summer months there is a never ending procession of troops and tanks passing through the town, and the loveliest of summer days are disturbed unhappily by the sound of gunfire on the range.

Housing

Throughout the parish generally housing conditions are good. The farm houses are commodious and comfortable, with all the convenience and attractiveness of town homes. All farm cottages have been enlarged, remodelled and modernised in the last 25 years. In many cases, entirely new cottages have replaced the old ones. Living conditions amongst farm workers are uniformly good, and the higher wages of recent years have made possible a much higher standard in the taste and in the degree of comfort with which these cottages are furnished. The same marked improvement is readily detected in the dress of agricultural workers, and in the food that amply supplies the family table. Nearly all dairymen, and a few of the so called 'cot folk' as well, possess now their own motor cars, and the taxi is a not infrequent indulgence for the week-end shopping or the too frequent visit to the local picture house.

In the town itself, the housing situation is less happy. The last two decades have witnessed the condemnation or the rebuilding of practically all the old houses in the burgh, which according to present day requirements had become unfit for habitation. Since 1918, houses erected by the local authority number 265. Certainly these have provided accommodation for many, yet the waiting list of those still requiring houses remains a very formidable one. Of the houses already built, ten are 'pre-fabs', while the rest are of traditional construction, containing two, three, four or five rooms, in fairly equal distribution.

Many of the finest houses in town, well built of local whinstone and freestone, with ample grounds and gardens, have become now a difficult problem for their owners. Servants for household work or for working in the gardens are almost nonexistent and the problem of heating and general upkeep, during and since the war years, has made life extremely difficult for a great many. Many of the happy and pleasant social contacts of a previous generation have had to be sacrificed. Apart from Christmas and the New Year there is comparatively little 'entertaining' done, and most of the spacious hospitality of former days has passed.

In its place there has been substituted the 'cocktail' party, which surely represents the most futile and superficial form of social intercourse that the world has discovered thus far.   Never was so little said by so many, with so much noise and confusion as on these occasions.

The complete destruction by fire during the last war of the home of the local laird, Sir Chas. Hope-Dunbar of St. Mary's Isle, deprived the parish of its finest residence and of one of the noblest homes in the land.   The contents, which included one of the best libraries in the south of Scotland, were a complete loss.   To replace a building of this kind, even were it desired so to do, would be quite impossible with prevailing restrictions on building, and the loss to the parish may well be a permanent one.   This house it was that experienced the rather unwelcome visit of Paul Jones on that occasion when he attempted to carry off the Earl of Selkirk as his prisoner.   The Earl happened to be from home, so, as a reward for his trouble, he made off with the family plate.   Later, this gallant seaman redeemed the plate, at a considerable sum, and returned it intact to Lady Selkirk.   Paul Jones is now hailed abroad as the Founder of the American Navy.

County Buildings

An outstanding event of recent date was the official opening in 1952 by the Secretary of State for Scotland, the Earl of Home, of the new Stewartry of Kirkcudbright County Council Offices.   The new building, situated at the rear of and connected by corridors with the former offices in High Street, is constructed of brick and roughcast, facing brick and artificial stone.   The large steel windows admit the maximum of light to all apartments.   The floors are laid in hardwood and the building throughout is equipped with intercommunication and post office telephones.   The various apartments are decorated in pastel shades, and the main staircase features a large crest of the county in full colour. The walls of the council chamber are panelled in waxed oak.   The principal table stands on a raised dais at one end of the chamber, and the surrounding panelling displays the crests of the five Stewartry burghs on either side of the county crest.   The dais table, the individual tables and chairs for members are made of oak, with green hide upholstery.   The erection of this building brought to an end a long-standing controversy as to whether the county seat should be in Kirkcudbright or Castle-Douglas.

Education

In the local Academy, Kirkcudbright possesses the only senior secondary school in the Stewartry.   It is a substantial building, beautifully situated in a quiet corner of the town that looks down the river Dee, towards the Solway.   The grounds which surround it are spacious and well kept, and are flanked by excellent playing fields.

On 27 August 1931 the Cochran Memorial Gymnasium was completed and officially opened by General Dawes, the American

Ambassador to Britain at that time. This gymnasium was the most generous gift of an American citizen, Thomas Cochran, in memory of his Kirkcudbright ancestors, and surely no gift could have proved a greater blessing to succeeding generations of youth throughout the county.

Centralisation of secondary pupils, commenced in 1946, was completed in 1947, when also the school leaving age was raised to 15. The operation of these two policies brought about changes in the roll of the Academy which were quantitative as well as qualitative. From being a selective secondary school, it became comprehensive, and now makes provision for the whole of the 12-15 age group. Classes are organised to suit the needs of all types of pupils, over the whole range of intelligence. In the early 1940's the secondary roll of the Academy was approximately 250: by 1953 the roll had grown to 457. A wide variety of courses leading to the Scottish Leaving Certificate, covering classics, modern languages, the sciences, domestic science and technical subjects, is now offered.

As a consequence of centralisation, the number of pupils who are conveyed daily by school transport, and the number who lodge in town during the week, have increased tremendously. Accommodation for about 20 girls is provided by a Girls' Hostel, associated with the Academy.

The school meals service has been a new development of great educational and social significance. In the session 1953-4, between 62 and 65 per cent. of the roll enjoyed each day a two-course meal, cooked on the premises, and served in a specially provided dining hall. From this central kitchen meals are sent out as well to the other schools in the parish.

The primary schools of the area, Kirkcudbright Johnston, Whinnieliggate and St. Cuthbert's R.C., have been maintained to a good standard. The school at Townhead was closed in 1942, when the Army took over much of the area which it had served. School rolls, which were tending to fall throughout the 1930s and 1940s, rose steeply in 1951-2, as a result of the increased post-war birth rate.

At September 1953 the numbers of staff and pupils in the various schools were as follows:

Secondary—Kirkcudbright Academy:
    The Rector, 28 secondary teachers and 457 pupils.
The primary rolls at the same date were:
    Kirkcudbright Academy Primary, 86 pupils—three teachers
    Kirkcudbright Johnston, 287 pupils—headmaster and eight teachers
    Kirkcudbright R.C., 39 pupils—two teachers
    Whinnieliggate, 19 pupils—one teacher

In this connection mention must be made also of the Kirkcudbright Summer School, which has functioned annually during the first two weeks in August since 1949. The time is so fixed because this is the only period at which Scottish and English schools are on holiday simultaneously. Each year the popularity of the school has grown until in 1953 the enrolment reached 100. These students were drawn from all parts of the country, and even from beyond our own shores. The Scandinavian countries have been well represented for the past two seasons.

The subjects studied are art (landscape, portraiture and still life), pottery and hand-loom weaving. No fixed time table is prescribed, and students may work in any medium. The tutors are distinguished representatives of the arts and crafts, both local and from farther afield. The school has now passed from the experimental stage, and is recognised to be a permanent and most attractive feature of the life of this ancient and royal burgh.

Artists' Colony

If one were to ask for what Kirkcudbright is best known, the response would be, in all probability, 'for its artists' colony'. This dates back to the life and work of the late E. A. Hornel, 1864-1933, the first local artist to gain international fame and recognition. Early in the century other artists were attracted to Kirkcudbright through the fame of Hornel, and also because of the beauty and variety of the local landscape. The extremely mild climate of this south-west corner of Scotland assures a very long season of foliage, which is a further attraction to the artistically inclined. There are always a dozen or more artists who reside here permanently, amongst them Chas. Oppenheimer and Phyllis Bone, the first and until recently the only female Scottish Academician. In the summer months the number is doubled because of visiting artists, who are drawn by the quiet charm of the old town, and by the simple and kindly hospitality of its people.

Community Life

One has no hesitation in saying that the artists have made a very definite impression upon the life of the place. They have been like a breath of fresh air that has redeemed Kirkcudbright from the stodginess of many a county town. Throughout the years their influence has been instrumental in raising the standards of taste and appreciation of the people generally. Local concerts and entertainments, music and drama, represent a very high standard, and all are well supported by the general public. For nearly half a century a Choral Society of some 70 members has functioned most successfully. Of late years an Audience Club has been formed, the members of which pledge themselves to bring the best possible Art, Music and Drama to the community, and to try to get others to attend on such occasions. The help and encouragement of the Arts Council have been invaluable in this regard. For those who are interested in debate, the town's Literary Society provides wholesome entertainment.

At his death, the late E. A. Hornel bequeathed to the town and county his former residence, Broughton House, together with its most valuable contents, and a very beautiful old-world garden. The outstanding feature of the house is a spacious gallery, which contains many of the artist's finest paintings, as well as many pieces of very beautiful antique furniture collected, for the most part, in the south of Scotland. The Hornel Library, too, is housed here, which, together with many most interesting and valuable early and first editions, contains also the finest collection of Galloway literature in existence. Broughton House is also the centre of the Kirkcudbright branch of the County Library.

Youth work has been rendered difficult here as elsewhere by the fact that so many young people were called up for National Service just when they began to be of value to the local community. For several years Kirkcudbright has reaped the benefit of a flourishing Community Centre. There are too the usual youth organisations, Scouts, Guides, and Boys' and Girls' Clubs, organised by the various churches. It has become increasingly difficult to secure efficient leadership for much of this work. Thanks to the Cochran Memorial Gymnasium, the physical and athletic needs of the community can be well catered for.

Apart from the work of the several churches, the chief interest of the women of the parish is centred in the Women's Rural Institute. The parish is blessed with several very active and thriving branches of this organisation, which has functioned for the past 32 years in this community, and has now a total membership of 300. The various branches carry on throughout the whole year, and thanks to excellent and devoted leadership and a loyal membership, they seem able at all times to provide an endless variety of programme. There is no doubt that the W.R.I. has met and satisfied a tremendous need in country districts. Not only has it created a wholesome and happy social life, through its choirs, country dancing classes and endless competitions, for many women who would otherwise be more or less isolated, but it is also introducing constantly new, stimulating and helpful ideas, that can be put into daily practice in the homes of the people. In that way it has made an incalculable contribution to the happy and wholesome home life of our country folk.

There has always existed in Kirkcudbright a very fine relationship between town and church. This relationship is highly esteemed and has been fostered and encouraged by the officials of the church, of the town council and of the incorporated trades of the burgh.

This latter organisation dates back to the very early days of the community, though not until 1681 were the Trades of Kirkcudbright incorporated. The present members, who number 300, are very proud of their privileges and conscious of their responsibilities in keeping alive in this, their native place, the best of the ancient traditions of their several trades. In 1953 a chain of solid gold, the craftsmanship of London's finest goldsmith, was given by Sir John M. Erskine and his two brothers to the Deacon Convener of the Trades, as permanent insignia of that worthy office. The Erskine brothers belonged originally to the town, and received their early education here. The gift was made as a memorial of a distant ancestor who, in his day, had filled worthily the office of Deacon Convener.

Religion

There are in all four churches in the parish. The Church of Scotland is represented by St. Cuthbert's, the parish church, and St. Mary's, a former U.F. church. There are, too, Greyfriars Episcopalian Church, and the Roman Catholic Church.

These various churches are fairly well attended at the morning service, but attendance at the evening service leaves much to be desired. There is a spirit of splendid loyalty on the part of many of the people, both old and young, to the church of their fathers, and one feels that the various churches exercise a great influence upon the life of the parish generally. At the same time there has developed, in recent years, a great deal of thoughtless indifference and almost complete lack of interest. Very few are entirely outside the church, and nearly all wish to have their children baptised, married, and in due time, buried by the church. But Sunday is becoming increasingly a day for pleasure and indolence, for motoring to visit friends or some nearby shore, or merely for the pleasure of the trip itself. The advent of the motor bus and of the excursion train has militated sadly against the local churches.

One has to record a definite decline in attendance at the Sunday school and at the Bible class, which in nearly every case can be accounted for through the lack of parental interest and discipline. Too many of our people are living on the spiritual capital inherited from their parents; for many it has ceased to provide interest any longer, and one is inclined to fear that the spiritual heritage of the next generation will be, in many cases, pathetically small.

Recreation

Great changes have taken place in the recreational life of the community. The devotees of golf and tennis have increased in number. The ancient and honourable game of quoits has almost disappeared, but its place has been pleasantly and effectively taken by the bowling green. Football is almost universally popular, and this parish, unfortunately, makes its full contribution to the Chancellor of the Exchequer, through its interest in the various football pools.

In the winter months, badminton and carpet bowling have a strong following. Curling, which never loses its popularity, is rather strictly rationed in this mild corner of the land through the scarcity of the natural ice and the complete lack of the artificial. The game of bridge is played a great deal, both in clubs and in the homes of the people.

Country dancing provides wholesome and hearty recreation for increasing numbers, both of the young and of the not so young. The pleasure of the public dance has been effectively killed for a great many by the ubiquitous bar, one of the sad and unfortunate features of social life bequeathed us by the last world war. In this corner of the land, as elsewhere, the local picture house flourishes the year round.

Amateur dramatics have made tremendous strides in the past 20 years, and the parish boasts several excellent clubs. Horticulture has always had an enthusiastic following locally, and each year a most successful flower and vegetable show is held in the town. On the part of a good many there is, too, a keen interest in homing pigeons and cage birds, and an annual show never fails to draw large crowds of interested spectators. Flourishing branches of the Red Cross and of the British Legion are responsible for much good work. As a method of raising funds for all sorts of good causes, the whist drive is ever popular and effective.

Fifty years ago the popular summer evening pastime was boating on the river Dee. One hired or owned a boat, and one's direction was dictated by the tide. The strains of music from the occasional fiddle or mouth organ aboard heightened the atmosphere of romance. All this has passed, and the river is now quite deserted.

The immediate environs of the town provide many lovely and interesting walks for those who, in this day of motor travel, retain still the ability to use their lower limbs. This is one old-time pleasure that can be, and is, richly enjoyed by many, in and about the town.

In 1950, on the occasion of the extension of the burgh boundaries, the ancient and picturesque custom of the Riding of the Marches was revived, and each year since a party of some 30 riders has provided a gallant and colourful picture that is greatly appreciated and enjoyed by the whole community.

An industry and sometime recreation that has declined sadly since the erection of the Galloway Power Station in the neighbouring parish of Tongland, is that of the Dee salmon fishing. Until the late 1920s, the fishing rights were owned and controlled by St. Mary's Isle Estate, but at that time they were acquired by the Galloway Power Company and have passed now to the British Electricity Authority. Before the Power Scheme began to function, the catch of salmon averaged about 1,800. In the past few years, the average has been less than 100. The reason for this marked decline has not yet been discovered, since every precaution has been taken to safeguard and encourage the normal development of the fish in the river.

Health

The health of the community is good, and for those who are in need of medical or surgical treatment a very efficient Cottage Hospital is maintained, equipped with a fine theatre, X-ray apparatus and modern equipment generally. This hospital, which originally was given and maintained by the local laird and his good lady, was later controlled by a Committee of Management, elected from the community and district, and supported voluntarily by the community that it served. It has now become a part of the national scheme.

In this department of the community's life, the most outstanding change that has come about is, doubtless, in the status of the 'family doctor'. The relationship between patient and doctor tends to become very impersonal, and one feels that this time-honoured and much loved institution is rapidly disappearing.

Another character that has passed with the years of this present century is that of the much loved 'worthy', whose ability to tell tall stories in a clever and amusing fashion never failed to provide him with an appreciative audience.

Way of Life

On the whole, life in this corner of Scotland has changed probably less than in most places, since the parish is comparatively isolated. We are cut off on the south by the Solway, and in other directions we are some 30 miles from Dumfries, the nearest town of any considerable size, while Glasgow and Edinburgh are about 100 miles away.

Life passes quietly and happily and its even tenor is reflected doubtless in the degree of longevity achieved by many of the inhabitants. The people are a loyal, kindly and intelligent folk, with a fine spirit of independence that has made them a more or less self-contained community. They are neither ultra-conservative nor provincial in their outlook and attitude to life.

It is felt by many that much of this spirit of independence and self reliance will pass with this generation. Present day youth are not easily catered for, and while much has been done for them by way of opportunities of self advancement, recreation and social advantage, there has been a very marked lack of appreciation on the part of the younger generation. The tendency is rather to take all for granted, with little thought of giving anything in return. One sees many a good effort, well begun, which soon fades out, through lack of ability to sustain the interest. Youth is restless and undecided, which is surely not to be wondered at, when one remembers the heritage from two world wars.

One can only hope that the next half century will deal as kindly with this pleasant parish and with this ancient and royal burgh, as has the last; that our splendid traditions will continue to be upheld, and that the faith of our fathers will continue to be cherished by an intelligent, industrious and happy community of souls.

1954

CHAPTER 20

THE PARISH OF KIRKGUNZEON

by ALAN W. LINDSAY

Boundaries

The Parish of Kirkgunzeon, lying between the burghs of Dumfries and Dalbeattie, is bounded by the parishes of Urr on the west, Lochrutton on the north, Southwick and Colvend on the south and New Abbey on the east. These boundaries are unchanged since 1792.

Natural Features

The parish consists of a shallow north-east—south-west valley five miles long and three miles broad. Through this valley runs Kirkgunzeon Lane which, as its name implies, flows, for a mile or two at least, through a straight channel (partly man-made) in the flat ground in the north-east of the parish. It is a good trout stream.

The high land in the parish lies roughly round the boundaries. On the southern side the hills are heather-clad, forming the slopes of the large granite batholith of Criffel. The opposite side of the valley lies on blue whinstone. The dividing line between the granite and the whin runs down the centre of the valley. The whinstone ground is considered to be stronger land and better able to hold moisture. Hence it grows better grass while the sharper granite-based ground produces better oats. Throughout the area much of the ground is uneven owing to small rocky outcrops here and there. The largest wooded area is Camphill, where there are perhaps 15 acres of rough coniferous plantation. Apart from this there are only occasional shelter strips, clumps and single trees, sufficient to prevent an impression of actual bareness.

Climate

The mild south-west climate of course prevails. Spring growth is slightly slower, and snow and frost linger longer, than in the seaside parishes five or six miles distant.

Agriculture

When the *New Statistical Account* was written in 1840 all the land belonged to persons residing outside the parish and was held by tenant farmers. To-day practically every farm is owner-occupied. In the two or three instances where this is not so, the land is managed for a farmer living in the vicinity.

In 1920 the Terregles estate, comprising 60 farms, was sold off. Over twenty sizeable holdings in Kirkgunzeon parish were included.

These passed for the most part to the sitting tenants. This process of owner occupancy has recently been completed.

Dairy farming is the principal activity of the parish. Out of 27 farms, 16 have commercial or pedigree herds of Ayrshire cows ranging from 30 to 90 head. Most of the commercial Ayrshires have lately been de-horned. In the 1920s there were only two or three dairies, but the number increased in the 1930s and rose sharply soon after 1939. There is a tendency at present for these also to engage in the rearing of beef cattle by crossing the Ayrshires with a Shorthorn bull. On the non-dairy farms, cattle for beef is the main concern but a small number raise Galloway cattle for breeding and beef. Some of these, from Congeith, have gained championships at the National Fat Stock Show in London. Only three horses are now used, compared with two hundred counted by the writer of the *Old Statistical Account*. Their work, and much of what used to be hard work, is performed by about 40 tractors. After grass, turnips or kale, oats and hay are the main field crops. About half an acre of potatoes is general. The acreage of turnips or kale together might be 12 to 20, hay the same, and oats twice as much. The making of silage in quantity is undertaken by two or three farms. For the past few years much of the oats has been cut by combine harvester and much of the hay baled.

Housing

Many new dwelling houses were built in Kirkgunzeon after the second world war. Out of 109 dwellings in the parish, 12 new ones and an equal number of extensively reconditioned buildings can be counted. Of these most are for agricultural workers, two or three for farmers, and two for persons not connected with farming. This does not include the county council housing scheme which stands by the church, across the burn from the original small village and the school. The ground which it occupies was part of the church glebe. Here there are 20 dwellings: a block of four steel houses, Athollbank, erected in 1945, and 16 brick houses, known as Kirkbank, erected in 1954. A small area adjoining is fitted up as a children's playground with swings and the like.

Church

There is one church, the Church of Scotland. The present building was erected in 1790 on the site of a former church. That this former building was very ancient may be deduced from the following facts. The author of the *Old Statistical Account* states that 'the roof is of a peculiar construction and is said to have been formed at Holmcultern in Cumberland and brought hither when the parish of Kirkgunzeon belonged to the Abbey'. As the monks of Holmcultern lost their property in Scotland in the reign of David Bruce, and Kirkgunzeon was given to Sir John Herries of Terregles by charter dated 7 June 1369, the old church must have been built some time before this date. This year, when the present church was being altered by the installation of electric heating and the conversion of the old hearse house into a vestry, it was noted that very old timber beams, which looked like roof beams, were supporting the floor.

In 1956, on the retiral of the Rev. R. L. Kirk after a ministry of 23 years, the church was linked to Dalbeattie Park Church and its minister, the Rev. S. M. Aitkenhead, assumed responsibility for both charges. As he lived in Park Church Manse, Kirkgunzeon Manse was sold. It is a large house adjoining the church and was built in 1804. The communion roll is 180. Morning services are held weekly and there are flourishing Sunday schools and Woman's Guild. The three Roman Catholic families worship in Dalbeattie.

Communications and Services
The adoption of the telephone began about 1920 and it is now in use in every farm house. Electricity for power and cooking is almost universally used; this dates from about the middle 1930s. Nowadays all farmers and most farm workers own a motor car for personal transport. Corra Garage, which was erected near the main Dumfries-Dalbeattie road about 1945, employs several mechanics. Bus services on this same main road have been maintained since 1928. About this date the old style macadamized road compacted with mud and sand gave place to the tarred surface on the main thoroughfare, and all side roads were similarly treated in the following decade.

With the establishment of the bus services the importance of the main line railway to the village declined. Kirkgunzeon station was first closed to passenger traffic. When the work of transporting cattle, feeding stuffs and manures to farms was undertaken by the more convenient cattle float or lorry about 1930 the railway station was shortly afterwards closed to goods traffic. At the start of the motor era farmers who had previously been in the habit of droving cattle to Dumfries took advantage of the new service.

Education
The present school building in the old village has served the parish area since the early nineteenth century. From the start of compulsory education in 1872 until 1945 instruction was provided for pupils up to the statutory school-leaving age. At that date it became a purely primary school. Pupils were transferred at the age of 12 years to Dalbeattie High School where a three years' course was available. From there they could proceed to Kirkcudbright Academy or Dumfries Academy for senior secondary education. Before the school was made a purely primary one, of course, progress to Dalbeattie, Kirkcudbright or Dumfries was open to pupils as an alternative to finishing their schooling locally. The provision of school meals was started in 1944. For many years around 1900 soup and bread were supplied to the school children at a penny for each family. For the last ten years 50 has

been the usual number dining each day. Living in the parish are 24 post-primary school children, one college student and one university student.

Occupations

Twelve men working on the railway reside locally; 17 men and 11 women travel daily to Dumfries or Dalbeattie to their employment. Apart from the blacksmith, three men who haul milk to the creamery, the two school teachers, and the half-dozen workers at the garage, all others are employed in farming. The total population is nearly five hundred.

Leisure and Recreation

The school is used in the evenings for country dancing, needlework, or arts and crafts classes. The newly formed Girl Guides and Brownies also meet there. In the well built and equipped public hall, given to the parish by the Maxwell family in 1911, various clubs function. The badminton club and the carpet bowling club make use of it for four evenings weekly. The Scottish Women's Rural Institute meetings are held every month.

Wild Life

In 1955 the rabbit plague, myxomatosis, cleared the parish of these animals, but they are beginning to return. The farmers are now organising a clearance scheme. Foxes are quite numerous and are kept down by fox shoots. Anything up to twenty guns may assemble for such shoots about half a dozen times in the year. Pheasants, grouse and partridges are seen occasionally.

The Name

St. Winnings Well near Kirkgunzeon Mill is marked on the 1909 Ordnance Survey map. Most speculations on the name of the village have linked it with a church named after that saint. The explanation of the letter 'z' in this name is no doubt the same as that given for the occurrence of that letter in such names as Menzies. At one time the alphabet as used in Scotland included a letter 'yoch' which was written like a flat headed 'g'. It sounded roughly like the 'z' in such names as Menzies, or Culzean. When this letter fell out of use it was mistaken for a 'z' and written as such. Hence it comes about that the name is pronounced Kirkgunnion despite its spelling.

Antiquities

At Torkirra Farm, Cowans Hill, and Camphill traces of old forts are to be seen. At Drumcoltran Farm a square sixteenth-century tower stands in good repair and is looked after by the National Trust. The remains of three massive walls of the much older Corra Castle still stand, but little trace of Barclosh Castle remains. Both adjoin the farmhouses of these names. The *New Statistical Account* states that in 1809 only three slated farmhouses existed in the parish. It is fairly obvious from their architectural style that Killymingan and Byrecroft farmhouses are two of these older buildings.

Local Government

Along with Lochrutton, Kirkgunzeon returns a member to the county council, and is represented on the district council by one councillor. A community council advises these councillors on local needs and also has arranged such things as old folk's entertainments, the provision of a car park at the public hall and equipment for the children's playground.

Kirkgunzeon forms a compact little community, almost unchanged in number over the years, hardly likely to attract many newcomers but always thriving enough to provide for the needs of its own people.

1959

CHAPTER 21

THE PARISH OF KIRKMABRECK

by the REV. C. V. A. MACECHERN

Boundaries, Climate and Natural Features

The crack of Doom will sound before the rival authorities come to agreement regarding the etymology of the name Kirkmabreck, saints and scenery competing for the honour. Until the Reformation the Church of Kirkmabreck belonged to the monks of Dundrennan. Early in the seventeenth century the parishes of Kirkmabreck and Kirkdale were annexed by the parish of Anwoth—the sphere of the ministry of Samuel Rutherford; but in 1636 a further division was made, resulting in part of Kirkdale being united with Kirkmabreck as a new parish, bounded by Minnigaff on the north, Girthon on the east, Anwoth on the south, and by the last few miles of the river Cree and Wigtown Bay on the west. Only a part of Cairnsmore (2,222 feet) is included in the parish, which claims, however, other lesser hills—the Larg, the Pibble and the Clints of Drumore among them. The six miles stretch of coast is flat and muddy, until about Kirkdale at the south end, where the shore is sandy and in places precipitous rocks rise to considerable height as at Ravenshall.

The climate is mild with a plentiful supply of rain, the prevailing winds being from the south-west and south. The winters are not severe, that of 1946-7 having been quite exceptional with 18-feet drifts of snow blocking the main road near Creetown. In that storm a milk train was completely buried in the snow a mile from the railway station, and a hundred men were signed on for clearing work. The phenomenal period of rainless months—June, July and August, 1949—occasioned a serious lack of water, despite the streams which flow down from the hills, and we became familiar, as in some former years, with the voice of the Creetown bellman going his rounds, announcing that no water might be used for the watering of gardens or the washing of motor cars with the hose-pipe.

The scenery, if not grand, is picturesque. The botanist finds the district a happy hunting ground, as both mountain and maritime plants appear to flourish. Some of the ferns are quite tropical and the landscape is particularly attractive in the springtime and in the autumn. Considerable areas are covered with natural wood, chiefly oak and ash. During the first world war and again during the second world war these were largely cut down for use as pit props and for the manufacture of gun-powder. Wood-felling on a large scale is now proceeding, but in certain parts the Forestry Commission is busily engaged in replanting.

Except at the eastward end of the parish, peat is no longer cut for fuel; and coal, which in 1844 cost 13s 4d a ton, is now priced at £5.

Population
A century ago, in 1851, the population of the parish reached its peak, and until recently it has steadily decreased. Here is the comparative table.

1801	1,212
1851	2,266
1901	1,859
1911	1,549
1921	1,333
1931	1,294
1951	1,301

Education
While a century ago there were five schools within the parish, the number is now reduced to two. There is a nine-teacher school, primary and secondary, in Creetown and a two-teacher primary school in Carsluith. To the former, senior pupils are brought by bus from Minnigaff, Carsluith, Palnure and Bargrennan. A school dining centre was built during the second world war where most of the pupils avail themselves of a two or three course dinner each school day at a cost of fivepence. The staff consists of five, including a highly qualified lady in charge. The hall is also used for other educational purposes by the mixed youth club, whose most popular activity is dancing.

A few years ago the village library was taken over by the county council. It is open on two days each week; but no one can claim that the local youth are book-minded.

Antiquities
In the earlier Statistical Accounts of this parish Cairnholy was given most space in the paragraph relating to antiquities. The mythical legend of one, King Galdus, was woven around this group of standing stones, the story being that in these beautiful and romantic surroundings the remains of the king lay. Research by some members of the Dumfries and Galloway Antiquarian Society confuted this mythological tale but in 1949 an excavation was carried out on the site of the two cairns. About ten skeletons were found, and from the bone structure it was deduced that they belonged to one family. Also taken from the tomb were stones with cup and ring markings, black pottery, a jet-black bead, shells, grain and knives. From these finds it can be realised what an elaborate burial ritual must have been observed by those early people. At first it was thought that the grain had played some part in the burial rites, but analysis revealed that the little store must have belonged to a modern field mouse, as it proved to be of recent origin! The date of the cairn is *circa* 2,000 B.C., and from a comparison with similar tombs in France, Ireland and other parts of Scotland, it has been deduced that the people who inhabited this part were either from Iberia or from

western France. It is interesting to note that agriculture and fishing, which are still important industries to-day, were in these far-off times the chief occupations of the people.

In 1945, on the farm of Garrocher above Creetown, two sand pits had been opened. The workmen had been informed that the site raised the possibility of pre-historic finds and after the lapse of a few months their interest was rewarded. High up on the face of the eastern sand pit a flat stone was revealed, and when the spade was inserted the stone came away, bringing with it a cinerary urn full of calcined bones. Unfortunately, the urn was broken, but the fragments were taken to Edinburgh and restored by an expert of the National Museum of Antiquities. The urn is made of coarse, gritty clay containing grains of mica and quartz, smoothed on the outside. Professor Childe gave the date as about 500-600 B.C. It was the first of this type to be found in Galloway. The makers of this kind of pottery were some branch of Celts, and it is assumed that they came from the continent during the trading in the bronze age. A similar urn has been found in Northern Ireland, and it is known that there was a regular trade route through Galloway between Ireland and Scotland at that period.

Life of the People

Creetown and Carsluith each possess a sub-post office, preference being given in the appointment of postmaster or postmistress to one who can provide a building suitable for an office. There are also several telephone kiosks within the parish. The post office is particularly busy on the day when the football pool coupons are dispatched; and it is strange that extremists who object to the possession of wealth by other people are not averse to spending an hour each week in their feverish endeavour to win a lucky twenty or thirty thousand pounds in the pools!

Motor cars and buses, both local and from other parts, have disturbed the erstwhile calm and peace of the weekly day of rest; but the local sports ground is not yet available for Sunday games. In 1948 the question of opening the putting green on Sunday was mooted and taken to a public plebiscite, when the proposal, to the joy of the kirk people, was substantially defeated. But, as one of the vanquished said, 'We shall live to fight another day', for 'it's comin' yet for a' that'.

Creetown, which is well lighted with electricity, has its own police station, with an officer in charge; but like many other such stations, it is earmarked to be scrapped, when the parish will be guarded by the mobile police. An occupant of the cell overnight is a rarity, and the parish provides few cases for the court in Kirkcudbright. Two well-equipped hotels and a number of boarding houses cater for the summer visitors, July being the peak month. For those who are not attracted by the surrounding hills other provision is made on the bowling green, the putting green and the two all-weather tennis courts. These are part of the King George V Playing Fields, opened in 1939.

On the social side of community life there are many activities, both in summer and in winter; but in these the most interested and active members are the women rather than the men. Among organisations are the Woman's Guild (which is the backbone of the church), the Women's Rural Institute, the Eastern Star, a youth club, a juvenile football club and a table tennis club. The proudest boast of the community is the possession of the Creetown Silver Band, instituted in 1881. It has won many trophies in open competitions and has performed as far afield as London. The local dramatic club has figured very successfully in the Scottish Community Drama Festivals.

During the second world war, when the local medical practitioner was on active service in the R.A.F., the parish of Kirkmabreck had a succession of no fewer than 20 doctors for longer or shorter periods. A permanent doctor is now serving in the parish.   On the local war memorial, built of native Creetown granite, and standing at the northern entrance to Creetown, the names of those who gave their lives in the two wars are inscribed.   The number who fell in the first war was 58;   the second memorial records 14 names.   Most of the young men served in the county regiment, the K.O.S.B., several in the R.A.F., and a few in the Royal Navy and Merchant Navy.

The Granite Industry

The parish of Kirkmabreck is rich in granite. Two quarries were opened over 80 years ago—the Fell Hill Quarry and the Silver Grey Quarry (Stewart and Co., registered in Aberdeen). The local granite combines all the essential and desirable qualities for high-class granite work: beauty, durability and freedom from defects and discoloration; and memorials made from it are found in all the principal cemeteries throughout the kingdom. Granite quarrying, engaged in by men of muscle, continues to be the main industry of the parish.

A New Enterprise

Creetown now boasts a new industry—the Solway Pre-cast Products Ltd. Within six months from the formation of the company in 1947, a factory was built on two acres of valuable agricultural land on Barholm Park, and production commenced. The pay roll of 35 has already been trebled, and despite its short life the company has established a wide business connection. Fifty tons of crushed granite from the famous Fell quarry four miles distant are brought to the factory daily. Two weeks later the finished product, in the form of prefabricated concrete components, is dispatched to various housing schemes all over the country. The factory, which employs entirely local labour, is fulfilling a long-felt want in Galloway and is a tribute to local enterprise.

A Novel Forestry Experiment

A novel experiment in forest regeneration is being attempted at Kirkdale. The idea is that, provided there are no enemies, trees will shed seed which will in time become trees.   An area of seven acres has been carefully fenced to ward off, principally, rabbits and deer.   In the course of a few years it is hoped young trees will have grown.   Indeed, it may be that many will become available for transplanting elsewhere.   When this happens, trees which are growing now will be cut down and removed for industrial use.

Fauna

The grey squirrel has not yet arrived in this area, but the red squirrel is quite common.   It is a timid creature but responds to human kindness. One which visits the manse daily has become tame enough to receive food out of the hand of the minister's wife, and on occasion even settles upon the arm of a study chair occupied by the minister.   During the long snowstorm three years ago the mavises in the garden became almost extinct.

Religious Life

The parish church still holds a real place in the life of the parishioners, but the old family pew is a thing of the past.   Few of the youths are interested in religion in an orthodox sense, and in many cases little encouragement has been given them by their home atmosphere.   The parish church, regarded at the time of its opening as the handsomest church in Galloway, dates from 14 December 1934, and is seated for about 600.   Since 1699 this parish has been under the Presbytery of Wigtown.   During the vacancy from 1934 to 1938 there occurred what came to be known as the famous Kirkmabreck case.   An attempt was made to unite the two parish churches, one of which had been formerly the United Free Church prior to the union in 1929.   Several interim moderators were appointed in succession before the union was effected, after which, under the present incumbency, harmony was soon restored. Since then the church has been improved and modernised with new heating and lighting schemes and the addition of electric power to the excellent pipe organ.   The former Trinity Church is now used as a parish hall, and the Mission Hall, which is also used for church purposes, is now about a century old.   A former Free church has become the possession of the Roman Catholic church, under the charge of the priest from Newton Stewart.   Regular meetings are also held by a loyal company of The Brethren in their little hall in Harbour Street.

General Observations

A century ago there were 57 paupers within the parish; to-day there are no poor.   But many of the houses are completely out of date, and the village pump is only now passing out of use.

There is a sprinkling of Irish ancestry among the inhabitants, as many of the local names suggest.   There is an authoritative warrant for the claim that beside the Shell Shore, south of Carsluith, dwelt the last of the cannibal tinkers in Scotland, a body of dragoons having been detailed to disband them or evacuate their camp.

In spite of much protest, both from the people of the parish and from the Gatehouse-of-Fleet community, the railway station of Gatehouse-of-Fleet has been closed down, both for passenger and goods traffic, leaving the farmers and shepherds six to nine miles distant from the nearest garage or bus route.

Without quoting the threadbare anecdote of Queen Victoria and her drive from Gatehouse to Creetown, we must put on record the charm of this area; but to see it at its best the visitor should come at the end of April, when the roadside and woodland are carpeted with colourful flowers, or in October, when the greenery is turned to gold.

1950

Chapter 22

THE PARISH OF KIRKPATRICK-DURHAM

by John Edwards

Physical Features

The parish lies west of Dumfries, Kirkpatrick-Durham village being about 13 miles by road from Dumfries and 5½ from Castle-Douglas, 1¼ miles west of Springholm, a village on the main Dumfries-Stranraer road. The extent of the parish is about ten miles from north to south and four and a half miles maximum from east to west.

About two-thirds of the area, lying north of the Crocketford-New Galloway road, is mostly rough moorland, rising to Darngarroch, 1,222 feet, Muil 1,135 feet, and other peaks in the north, and Milharay, 973 feet, in the south. In the section south of this road lies the arable farming country, where the elevation varies from 400 to 500 feet above sea level over most of the area, falling away to about 150 feet in the Urr valley at Old Bridge of Urr, and rising to 694 feet in the west at Bardarroch. Drainage is to the Urr Water, which forms the western boundary of the parish. There are several small lochs. Adjoining parishes are Dunscore in the north, Balmaclellan and Parton in the west, Crossmichael and Urr in the south, and Urr and Kirkpatrick-Irongray in the east.

Fauna and Flora

There are no reports of anything unusual in the parish, but foxes are said to be increasing in number, and roe deer may be seen sometimes near the Corsock-Crocketford road.

History

A most valuable addition to the earlier Statistical Accounts is a book by the Rev. W. A. Stark, published in 1903, *The Book of Kirkpatrick-Durham*. It records the history of the parish from the earliest times, and gives the origins of many local place names. P. H. McKerlie's *History of the Lands and their Owners in Galloway*, published in 1878, gives very full details of the parish in volume four. The significant change is that the large estates have been broken up into smaller farming units; there are now 64 farms and over two-thirds of these are occupied by the owners. The names of the families who were the large land-owners have disappeared from the parish.

Population
Census figures are as follows:—

1801	1,007
1851	1,508 (Maximum ever recorded)
1901	959
1911	914
1921	860
1931	783
1951	803

These statistics reflect the industrial development of the country as a whole and the mechanisation of farming. Post-war housing shortage may be the reason for the slight increase in 1951.

The greatest concentration of population in the parish is in Kirkpatrick-Durham village, where 87 houses are occupied, 53 by proprietors and 34 by tenants. The distribution of houses over the parish area is noted under 'Housing'.

The inhabitants of Kirkpatrick-Durham village itself are classified by occupations as follows:—

Agricultural workers	8%
Farmers	2%
Rabbit trappers ... ,..	2%
Motor vehicle drivers	5%
Artisans (masons, joiners, gardeners, etc.)	5%
Saw mill workers	3%
Labourers (general)	11%
Business proprietors (merchants, contractors, etc.)	10%
Domestic workers	7%
Others (ministers, teachers, Government officials, etc.)	11%
Retired people	36%

The large proportion of retired people will be noted. Widows and spinsters without occupation are included under this heading.

It is estimated that about 60-70 per cent. of the inhabitants of the parish are natives, whose forebears have belonged to the district. The remainder are immigrants or descendants of immigrants from other parts of the United Kingdom, with one or two of foreign origin, prisoners of war or refugees who have elected to remain in this country. Most of the older indigenous inhabitants have no desire to live elsewhere, but the younger people tend to migrate in search of wider economic opportunities, or to join the services.

Public Services
Since about 1948, most of the district has been connected to the main water supply from Lochenkit. A filtration plant for this supply is in operation at Areeming. Most of the more inaccessible farms and cottages are not yet connected. An electricity supply is now available to all the centres of population and nearly all the outlying farms are connected. There is still no mains sewerage system in the village but many houses have their own septic tanks. The standards of road maintenance and cleansing are high, and lighting is adequate in the village.

Education

There are two county council schools, one in Kirkpatrick-Durham village, and one at Crocketford. These are primary schools which take children up to eleven or twelve years old, until they proceed to the secondary school at Castle-Douglas. Present figures are, for Kirkpatrick-Durham, 78 pupils, three teachers, and for Crocketford, 60 pupils and two teachers. The school meals and transport schemes apply to these schools.

There is also Kilquhanity House School, now recognised and inspected by the Scottish Education Department. It is a boarding school, opened in 1940 by a group of pacifists. There is at present a staff of 12, and 35 boys and girls of all ages between 3 and 17 years. 'Difficult' children are catered for up to a ration of one to ten normal children. The headmaster (and founder) writes—'The school is viewed as an experiment in liberal education—an attempt to combine the traditional thoroughness of Scottish education with opportunities for wider activities and more responsibility for the pupil'.

Health Services

The local centre is Castle-Douglas Cottage Hospital, which is visited by specialists from the Dumfries & Galloway Royal Infirmary, Dumfries. Resident in the village there is a district nurse, whose services are highly valued. The nearest doctors are at Castle-Douglas.

Transport

The nearest railway station is Castle-Douglas, so that the bus services are the only means of local public transport. The main route of the nationalised buses between Dumfries and Castle-Douglas passes through Crocketford and Springholm, but a few buses in both directions take the route Springholm, Kirkpatrick-Durham, Bridge-of-Urr, Clarebrand, Castle-Douglas. There are ten regular buses daily on week days, with extras on certain days, and a Sunday service. Of these regular daily buses, four take the Kirkpatrick-Durham route, with extras on certain days. In addition, a privately owned service runs five buses daily between Dumfries and Corsock, and two to Dalry, with special services on Saturdays and Sundays.

Library

The introduction a few years ago of the Mobile Library van was a notable development. The van visits the village fortnightly with a good selection of books, and the service is a great boon to many people. There is of course an excellent branch of the County Library in Castle-Douglas.

Voluntary Social Services

The only youth organisations in the parish at present are those sponsored by the church and by the community council, but some girls belong to the Guides at Springholm. The Kirkpatrick-Durham branch of the Scottish Women's Rural Institute is very much alive, with a membership of about 40. A community council was formed at a public meeting in 1938, and money was raised for the purchase of the U.F. Church building as a community hall. The council fosters a number of clubs, including the following:—

Badminton Club	—	Membership approximately		30
Dramatic Club	—	,,	,,	25
Curling Club	—	,,	,,	12
Carpet Bowling Clubs	—	,,	,,	40
British Legion Club	—	,,	,,	16

There are 'The Walton Park and District Recreation Club' at Knockvennie, and the 'King George V Memorial Playing Field' at Crocketford. Country dancing classes are held in the parish.

Church

The parish minister writes as follows:—

'Since the publication of the *New Statistical Account* some changes have taken place in the ecclesiastical state of the parish. Since 1947 the parish of Kirkpatrick-Durham has been within the bounds of the Presbytery of Kirkcudbright, but still remains within the Synod of Dumfries. The church was completely redecorated and modernised in 1949. The part that was added in 1849, to provide additional seating to accommodate a larger number of worshippers, has been divided from the main body of the church and is now used as a church hall.

'In the year 1938 the two congregations in the parish, of the former United Free Church and the Parish or Established Church, were united. There is now only one church in the parish, that of the Church of Scotland. In most households there is at least one member of the church; in some cases all adult members of the family are in full communion. The number of Episcopalians is very small (five), but even they attend services in the parish church fairly regularly. There are no Roman Catholics living in the parish.

'There is very little evidence that the attitude towards religion has radically changed in the last few years. Attendance at public worship is certainly not on the same level as it was in former years, but this may be mainly because the younger members of the household are no longer forced to be present at every diet of public worship. The only group of people among whom one notices a different outlook concerning spiritual matters are the young people of school-leaving age'.

That strange religious sect, the Buchanites—described at some length in the *New Statistical Account*—is the subject of a book by John Cameron, published in 1904, entitled *The Buchanite Delusion, 1783-1846.*

In *The Book of Kirkpatrick-Durham*, by the Rev. W. A. Stark, the year 1863 is given as the date of 'the erection of Corsock into a *quoad sacra* parish'. It was formed from parts of the three parishes of

Balmaclellan, Kirkpatrick-Durham and Parton. The church, which is reckoned to be one of the most beautiful in the south of Scotland, lies outside the boundary of Kirkpatrick-Durham parish.

Housing

There are approximately 242 houses of all kinds in the parish area, distributed as follows:—

Kirkpatrick-Durham village	87
Crocketford	28
Corsock district	25
Bridge-of-Urr	12
Elsewhere	90

There is ample accommodation for the population of 803, and though many of the houses are small, there are very few cases of overcrowding. Five or six could be classed as mansion-houses, and the remainder, with the exception of a few of intermediate size, as country cottages. Nearly all have gardens of reasonable size, and most of the people make good use of their gardens and take pride in them.

Since 1918 ten houses have been built by the local authority, all at Crocketford. Just outside the parish boundary, near the main road at Springholm, several houses have been built recently as part of a scheme of some magnitude. In these circumstances, it seems unlikely that there will be much building of houses in this parish in the near future.

Agriculture, Industries and Commerce

Of these agriculture is of course pre-eminent. On this subject the County Agricultural Adviser has kindly contributed the following:—

'The type of farming is largely stock-rearing, since much of the parish consists of rough grazing, this area being almost double that of the arable acreage. A convenient division could be taken at the Crocketford-Corsock road, the area to the north being black-faced sheep and Galloway land, while dairy farming and dairy stock-rearing are largely confined to the area to the south of the better land.

'The farming methods in the area are similar to those generally prac-tised in Kirkcudbrightshire—the crops grown being oats, turnips, kale and a few potatoes 'for the house', these crops providing the winter feed for the stock, along with hay, which is generally taken in the first year after sowing oats to grass. No crops are grown for sale, so much of the arable acreage is down to rotation pasture.

'The changes in agriculture during the last hundred years could be said to follow the general county trend, with a swing from Galloway cattle to Ayrshires from 1850 onwards. Farm cheesemaking was the practice on dairy farms up to the 1930s, but this was ousted as a result of the formation of the Scottish Milk Marketing Board, which provided an efficient daily collection of liquid milk. The 1939-45 war increased the area under the plough, and thus rejuvenated much old grassland. This period also saw an improvement in husbandry with increasing use made of lime and manures, which in turn gave increased yield and increased stock-carrying capacity.

'The improved husbandry methods have gone hand in hand with increased farm mechanisation. There are now many tractors and ancillary implements, and few horses. The farm labour supply has also shown a diminishing tendency, which has hastened, or resulted from, the trend of farm mechanisation. On dairy farms the greatest change has been in milking methods, from hand to machine. There has also been a marked improvement in cattle housing and dairy hygiene.

'On sheep farms changes have not been so marked, but research work has solved problems and provided remedies for many diseases, which previously took their toll: pulpy kidney, lamb dysentery, liver fluke, worms and pine, to name only a few. The hypodermic syringe is now as essential to the shepherd as his crook.

'Future trends: At present there is a swing on stock-rearing farms from rearing dairy stock to rearing beef cattle. During the past few years there has been a large increase in the Galloway stock in the area, but whether this breed will replace Ayrshires remains to be seen. It is difficult to prophesy, but increased stock-carrying capacity on all farms may take place, if more use is made of grassland, both on low-ground farms, by better utilisation, and on hills when aerial methods of manuring are perfected.'

ACREAGE IN THE PARISH

Arable	6,140	acres		
Permanent Grass	817	,,		
Rough Grazing	10,239	,,	Total	17,196 acres

FARMS

Number of owner-occupied farms	45		
Number of tenant farms	19	Total	64

RENT

Arable 15s to £1 an acre	
Rough Grazing 2s 6d to 5s an acre	Total Rent £7,463 15s

NUMBER OF FARMS

0— 50 acres	19
50— 100 ,,	6
100— 150 ,,	13
150— 300 ,,	13
300— 500 ,,	3
500—1,000 ,,	6
Over 1,000 ,,	4
	64

The above figures are given by the Agricultural Adviser.

It is worthy of note that a poultry breeding business has been built up successfully at Newhouse, Crocketford, during recent years. Another new venture is a small tweed mill at Newbank. The old mill at Bridge-of-Urr is still in operation.

In Kirkpatrick-Durham village there remains but one inn; there are two shops which supply groceries and many other items, and a newsagent. There is a well-equipped joiner's shop. The last smithy closed down in 1951. Bakers, butchers and fishmongers (including the Co-operative Society) from the nearby towns send vans on regular rounds; service in this respect is considered satisfactory.

Way of Life

During the last half-century, the way of life of the people in this rather remote rural area, as in the rest of the world, has been strongly influenced by many changes. Two world wars have had profound effects. There has been the development of roads and road transport, radio, and the cinema. Although horizons of interest and thought have been widened enormously, and improved educational opportunities have raised the potential of most of the younger people, one hears expression of feeling by many that the world is not now their oyster; private incentive tends to be crushed by taxation and nationalisation. Nevertheless, in this farming locality there are still to be found a majority of people whose main interest remains in their work, and who do not count the hours of their labour. In this respect the parish seems to compare favourably with some of the industrial areas where a different spirit prevails.

The new social legislation, by relieving parents of some of their traditional responsibilities to their children, tends to reduce the importance of the family as the basic unit of the national life. The full effect of this change and of others which have been brought about by the development of the Welfare State, may come to light in a few more years.

Criminal offences, even minor ones, remain practically unknown in this parish; the people are generally quiet and law-abiding. There is a good range of occupations for their leisure time, as already noted in the paragraph on voluntary social services.

1953

CHAPTER 23

THE PARISH OF KIRKPATRICK-IRONGRAY

by the REV. W. B. AITKEN

Boundaries and Extent

The parish of Kirkpatrick-Irongray, in the Stewartry of Kirkcudbright and Presbytery of Dumfries, covers an area of 14,464 acres or 22.6 square miles. Measuring nine miles in length and varying from one to four miles in breadth, it is bounded on the east and south by the parishes of Terregles and Lochrutton, on the west by Kirkpatrick-Durham and on the north by Holywood and Dunscore. The natural boundary of the upper north march of the parish is the Cairn Water, which, when it is joined by the Old Water of Cluden, becomes the Cluden Water and continues as such to be not only the north march of the lower part of the parish, but also the boundary between Galloway and Dumfriesshire. The Barbuie Burn in the north-west of the parish marks the boundary with the parish of Dunscore. The Old Water of Cluden, running from south to north across the parish, separates the more level pastures of the lower end from the undulating and hilly ground that rises gradually to the moorland heights at the western boundaries, where Skeoch Hill (1,286 feet) is the highest point.

The Routin' Bridge, built across a waterfall dropping 32 feet into a deep leafy gully of the Old Water of Cluden, along with a ford near Midrig farm, are the traditional means of passing from the lower and eastern section to the upper or western part of the parish. There has been a bridge on the site of the Routin' Bridge since before 1590, according to Pont's map. At present there are other four bridges across the Old Water—at Shawbridge, Cornlea, Threepneuk and Barnsoul Mill. Within a few hundred yards of the church a fine sandstone bridge of two arches was built across the Cluden Water in 1856. Previous to that time the river was crossed by a ford which lay slightly to the east of the existing bridge.

Climate

The prevailing wind, as would be expected in this district, blows from the south-west, bringing a generally mild and damp atmosphere. This is particularly true of the low-lying south-eastern end of the parish, which is near the river Cluden, and which in the summer months is extremely relaxing. On the other hand, the western heights of the parish, the moors of Glenkiln, and the sheep pastures of the Shalloch, the Glen and Margreig, receive at most times of the year a clean, bracing ventilation that is highly invigorating. On these parts also the snow, when it comes, gathers deeper and lies longer than elsewhere. When the Cluden is in flood, the fields surrounding the eminence on which the church is built are often under water for days on end.

Wild Life

Roe deer and fox are occasionally seen in the district, especially during hard weather, and deer have sometimes been seen feeding on the glebe pastures. Since the advent of myxomatosis, the menace to the countryside of a surplus rabbit population has been overcome, but there are signs now that the animals which have succeeded in avoiding the disease are beginning to increase once more. The otter is an occasional resident, especially near the Cluden, while the mole, the hare and the hedgehog are particularly prolific in all parts of the parish. Weasels and stoats are common; the red squirrel has become scarce, none having been seen in the last five years.

In the winter months geese come in large numbers from Greenland, Iceland and Spitzbergen to winter on the shores of the Solway and are often seen on the wing over the parish. On occasion the banks of the Cluden provide a nesting-place for swans and the river is a favourite fishing place for the heron. In high summer it is a rare pleasure to see a kingfisher dart as a blue flash over the river. On the moors grouse hatch and are shot in season, while partridge and pheasant are also plentiful. There is a strange poignancy too, about the shrill plaintive calls of the curlews so familiar to Crockett and Stevenson—

'Where about the graves of the martyrs the whaups are crying
My heart remembers how.'

The Cluden provides excellent sport for anglers, with both salmon and trout, as does the Glenkiln reservoir with Loch Leven trout.

Name of Parish

In a charter by James III, granted in favour of Robert Herise, the name of the parish is spelt Earngray. In a sasine of David Herries dated 7 December 1484, it is found as Yrnegray. The inscription on the old Communion cups belonging to the church states that they were 'gifted for the use of the Paroch of Irengray'. The date of this inscription is 13 September 1694. There is every likelihood that the original form of the name was Errangreidh, signifying the cattle land. The place-names of the parish are largely Celtic in origin. There is also a strange predominance of tree-names, as for example—Bush, Oakbank, Peartree, Birkbush, Shawhead, Saughtree, Cogershaw.

Historical Associations

There is evidence of five British hill forts in Kirkpatrick-Irongray. Hallhill Mote is a good example of the British fort or earthen mound. It stands 350 feet above sea-level and is oval in shape, surrounded by a *vallum* except on the steep side. A cinerary urn containing a number of small bones, and belonging to a period long before the Roman occupation, was unearthed here in the 1870s. Another specimen of the early British fort is Ingleston Mote. Surrounded by a *vallum* with the addition of a fosse, it is almost circular in shape and is not raised above the level of the surrounding ground. Other not so obvious examples of this type of fortification are found at Barnsoul and at Chapelrigg.

In a later age, the parish has an interesting link with Mary, Queen of Scots, in that during her flight from the defeat of her army at Langside in May, 1568, she passed across the parish on her way to Terregles. The small party was led by Lord Herries of Terregles and came south by way of Sanquhar and Dunscore, crossing the Cluden at the ford near the present Irongray church on their way to Terregles House, where a night was spent. The next day they proceeded to Dundrennan and from there across the Solway to England.

The first Presbyterian minister was admitted to the charge of Irongray in 1601. From 1567 to that time the cure of souls in the parish had been in the hands of an exhorter and three readers. Irongray figured conspicuously in the struggle for religious freedom between 1662 and 1688. At the time of the Covenants, the minister of Irongray, John Welsh, was celebrated for his strongly anti-episcopal views. He was deprived of his living in 1662 and became one of the first of the field-preachers. Largely owing to his influence, a contingent of Covenanters (200 foot and 50 horse) set out from Irongray churchyard to march on Dumfries. Eventually this body of men joined with others, marched north and were routed at Rullion Green, Welsh narrowly escaping with his life. Though thereafter he was a hunted man with a price of £500 on his head, John Welsh was never captured and died in London in 1681; he was a great grandson of John Knox.

Relics of the stirring times of the Covenanters are still to be seen in the parish. On Skeoch Hill there are Communion Stones on which, in 1678, the ejected ministers dispensed the sacrament of the Lord's Supper to 3,000 people as they met in secret within the silence and safety of the hills. Within half a mile of the church a monument (sadly in need of repair at the time of writing) was erected in memory of two Covenanters, Alexander McCubine and Edward Gordon, who were hanged on an oak-tree which until several years ago overhung the monument.

In the kirkyard, which contains gravestones dating back to 1633, is buried a humble woman of the parish, named Helen Walker, who died in 1791. The courage and nobility of this person, who went on foot to London to ask a pardon for her sister condemned to death, caught the imagination of the 'Wizard of the North' and became the inspiration for his famous character, Jeanie Deans. The tombstone was erected by Sir Walter Scott in memory of the prototype of his heroine, and at all times in the year there are visitors who come from far and near to see the burial-place of this country woman whose deeds are immortalised in *The Heart of Midlothian.*

Monuments of many kinds are a feature of Irongray—an extra-ordinary one, erected on Glen Hill, is Turner's Monument. Johnny Turner wrote an acrostic based on his own name on the headstone and dug his own grave, in which he was later buried.

Visitors to the moors and the reservoir at the western extremity of Irongray are surprised to find examples of modern sculpture set up at various points in that isolated countryside. The local inhabitants are, of course, well acquainted with 'the statues', as they are familiarly called, and in general local opinion is rather sceptical of their artistic merit. Most of the sculptures are the work of Henry Moore and, as a recent article in *The Glasgow Herald* stated, 'all who know his work will appreciate the puzzlement of those who do not!' Among this collection there is also an Epstein figure called 'The Annunciation' and a bust by the French Impressionist painter, Renoir. All these works belong to the owner of the Glenkiln estate, whose fancy it has been to place them strategically among the bracken and the heather.

The Church

The name of the church implies that it was originally dedicated to St. Patrick, and there is evidence that it was founded as early as the twelfth or thirteenth century. In Bagimond's Roll of 1274, Kirkpatrick-Irongray was classed as a rectory and taxed at £3 6s 8d.

The writer of the *Old Statistical Account* says 'the walls of the church have been built time out of mind and are still firm and strong'. The present church of red sandstone, built in 1803 at the cost of £400, occupies the site of the pre-Reformation church which existed until then; the walls of that building are built into the walls of the present church. The church bell was re-cast from older bells which were cracked and broken. In 1872, when the building was repaired and extended, mullioned windows were inserted and two fine doorways in Norman style were constructed at the south and east. The substantial square tower was erected at the west end, providing a commodious vestry at ground level and an excellent belfry. The chancel arch inside the church was also built at this time. The cost of all these alterations and additions amounted to more than £700. The church has had no radical alterations since that time. In recent years, however, an electric heating system was installed in place of the hot-water pipes, and this provides a cleaner and quicker means of heating the building. On the few occasions when artificial light is required, the old hanging paraffin lamps are lit, but it is hoped to have electric lighting very soon. For the offering the traditional wooden ladles, more than a hundred years old, are still used, and provide some interest and amusement to visitors.

From the Disruption until 1934 there was also a United Free Church in the parish, situated within half a mile of Shawhead. The two churches were united in 1934, but divine worship continued in the Free Church building until 1949, when it was demolished and the site handed back to the superior. Since 1949 the Mission Hall in the village has been used for worship, services being conducted fortnightly for the benefit of those in the village who find transport to the church difficult.

Divine service is held at Irongray Church at 12 noon each Sunday. The Sacrament of the Lord's Supper is dispensed twice during the year, in May and November. The membership at 31 December 1958 was 391. There are several Episcopalians and two or three Roman Catholics in the parish—the rest of the community is Church of Scotland, and the church also draws a large proportion of its membership from the western end of Holywood parish, where the people live nearer to Irongray church than to Holywood. A few members residing in Dumfries or other neighbouring parishes are reluctant to sever family or childhood associations with Irongray kirk and continue to be fairly regular attenders. At Holy Communion, Harvest Thanksgiving and the Christmas services the kirk is filled to capacity, and the ordinary services are well attended too, though of course there is room for improvement! A chartered bus runs from Dumfries to the church by way of Shawhead to the Family Service once a month and to special services, and when the church bell rings out across this quiet corner of Irongray at noon on a Sunday there is always a fleet of cars—sometimes more than thirty—lining the road. Of the church's nine elders, only four active elders live within the parish, so that, unlike most country parishes, Irongray is not now able to employ a system of elders' districts for parish visiting.

The Woman's Guild, which for many years was in abeyance, was re-formed in 1958 and has some 30 members. The minister has two Sunday schools, with 14 pupils at Irongray and 25 at Shawhead.

Since the Reformation there have been twenty ministers in the charge, giving an average ministry of 18 years. Many of these ministers are buried at Irongray. A notable personality was Dr. A. K. H. Boyd, who in his first charge at Irongray began his literary labours, among them *The Recreations of a Country Parson*. Dr. Boyd, probably better known than any other Scottish clergyman of his day, spent most of his great ministry at St. Andrews and was Moderator of the General Assembly in 1890. It is interesting at this time to note that a century ago Dr. Boyd and his friend, Charles Kingsley, author of *Water Babies* and rector of Eversley, lamented the differences between Anglican and Presbyterian churches and strove for closer relations between the two.

Before this present century the Sacrament of Baptism was never administered within the church as part of the service, but took place in the home or in the manse. This practice has gradually altered during the last 50 years, and almost half the baptisms now take their rightful place within the public diet of worship in the church. The baptismal register shows other interesting social changes—during the last century there has been a steady decline both in the number of children in each family and in the illegitimacy rate. Families on the average comprise two or three children instead of the ten or twelve of a hundred years ago. In the years 1876-1900 10.7 per cent. (30 of 281) children baptised by the parish minister were illegitimate; in the first quarter of the present century 8.2 per cent. (21 of 255); 1926-50 illegitimacies amounted to 6.4 per cent. (17 of 264) while in the period 1951-8 there is a fall to 4.5 per cent. (4 of 90). One would hope that these diminishing percentages indicate an improvement in the moral behaviour of country people, but one feels that this trend is due more to general education, widening of interests, and perhaps a fear of social stigma, than to devout religious persuasion.

Marriage statistics, too, show that particularly since the end of the second world war there has been a sharply increasing tendency to marry within the church. From 1901 to 1925, of 83 marriages performed in the parish only 7 (8.4 per cent.) were celebrated in the church, while 14 were held in the manse. During the second quarter of this century 33 (26 per cent.) of the total 127 weddings were in Irongray kirk and 60 (47 per cent.) in the manse, while of the 49 marriages from 1951 to 1958 37 (76 per cent.) were performed in the church and 9 (19 per cent.) in the manse.

At funerals a short service is usually held at the deceased's home before the burial but it is no longer common practice to hold coffining services. The old kirk pad can still be easily traced over the hills between Crochmore and the church. On the steep slope of Hallhill the way has been cut into the hill to secure a safe footing and the crossing places over the dry stane dykes are evident from the large stone slabs forming stiles on which to rest coffins as they were being carried to the kirkyard for burial. The kirk pad meets the present road at Shop burn, which marks the boundary between the glebe and Hallhill farm. Local lore has it that a small shop beside the burn served the one-time village of Irongray, though there is no trace of such a settlement to-day when the church stands picturesque and quite alone amid the green pastures with but a handful of the parish community living within sight of it. Seemingly, it was so, too, in 1873 when Stevenson, in a letter written in Dumfries, tells how his father and he went for a long walk 'through a country most beautifully wooded and various, under a range of hills . . . there was the little kirk and kirkyard of Irongray among broken hills and woods by the side of a bright, rapid river'.

Education

No legal provision was made for the instruction of the children of Irongray until 1722. In compliance with the statute of 1696 the minister and heritors of the parish decided that 'ane sallary be settled upon a schoolmaster who may be thought qualified for teaching the youth in reading and writing, English, the Rudiments, Latin and Greek Grammars, Latin authors and Greek New Testament'. The salary was to be 100 merks Scots per annum. The first schoolmaster was John Kirkpatrick, son of the proprietor of Barncleugh. For the first year school was held in the church, then it was moved to a house at Drumclyer and again to Knockshinnoch. In 1755 the schoolmaster was required to teach the children for two years at Shawhead and then for the following two years at Townhead of Dalquhairn. In 1776 the school was transferred from Dalquhairn to Roughtree. Under the Schoolmasters Act of 1803 two schoolmasters had to be appointed by the heritors. In 1843 a new schoolroom was built at Roughtree, the cost being borne by voluntary subscription. This school was further extended and repaired shortly after 1872. Just before the first world war Roughtree School was closed, and during the hostilities Belgian refugees occupied both the school and the schoolhouse.

The schoolroom at Shawhead was completely rebuilt in 1862 at the cost of £450. Since then additions have been made to it in the form of a domestic science room, now used as a kitchen-dining room, and another classroom. A playing-field behind the school is equipped with swings and goal-posts. Pupils whose homes are two or more miles distant are transported by the school bus and have dinner in school. In 1877 there were 119 children of school age in the parish. In 1959 the number attending Shawhead school is 55. There are two teachers. Post-primary education for children of the parish is provided at Dumfries Academy or High School. At the moment Irongray can claim three students, two men and one woman, who are receiving full-time university education, two at Scottish universities and one at Cambridge.

Health Services

The district nurse for Irongray, Terregles and Lochfoot stays in one of the new council houses in Shawhead. There is no doctor resident in the parish, the nearest being at Dunscore or Maxwelltown. The doctor at Dunscore, with his assistant, attends most of the parishioners. Fevers, diphtheria, tuberculosis—savage killers of youth in the past, as headstones in the kirkyard show—are now almost unknown, and free immunisation from smallpox, and injections against whooping-cough, tetanus, diphtheria and poliomyelitis are given to every child. Almost all babies are born at Cresswell Maternity Hospital in Dumfries, where excellent ante- and post-natal care is given. The Dumfries and Galloway Royal Infirmary serves the general needs of the people. Since 1938 the Grove, a stately red sandstone mansion in the south-eastern corner of the parish, and once the home of the Maxwells, has been a hospital for 66 post-operative and orthopaedic cases. The minister, as chaplain of the Grove, pays regular visits to the patients and conducts a service in one of the wards each Sunday evening.

Public Services

The eastern end of the parish is poorly served with public transport; there is a bus service only twice a week from Dumfries along the road from Cluden Mill to the Routin' Bridge. The people resident in this part were previously served by the Dumfries-Moniaive railway, with a station in the parish of Holywood, within three-quarters of a mile of Irongray church. The line was closed to passenger transport in 1943, and remained in use for goods traffic until 1949 when it was completely closed and the track dismantled. A much better bus service runs to Shawhead from Dumfries *via* Terregles and the Grove. Buses run each morning and evening on this road, with additional services on Wednesdays and Saturdays.

Shawhead has a branch post office, and throughout the parish there is a daily postal delivery. The telephones in the north and easterly area are linked to Newbridge, while those on the south and west are on Lochfoot exchange. There is a public kiosk outside the post office at Shawhead. Electricity has been available since shortly before the second world war, though several homes are still without it, and use paraffin lamps and stoves. Most of the roads within the parish are classed in the Ordnance Survey map as 'other good roads', and certainly as far as surface and camber are concerned they are in good condition, though not always wide enough to permit easy passing for two large vehicles. A weekly refuse collection is made only in the village of Shawhead; the rest of the parish has to dispose of its refuse as best it can.

A revolutionary change in the face of the parish occurred in 1930, when work began on the construction of a reservoir at Glenkiln. The scheme, apart from Killylour filter station, which was not completed till 1937, came into operation in 1934, and now provides Dumfries with its water supply. The undertaking involved a reservoir with a capacity of 356 million gallons, situated on the upper reaches of the Old Water of Cluden, a road diversion of $1\frac{1}{8}$ miles and a conduit $4\frac{1}{2}$ miles long to conduct water to the filter station at Lochfoot. Into the reservoir flow the Shalloch, Marglolly and Muil burns, and the top water-level of this man-made loch extends to 68 acres. The villagers of Shawhead now have the amenity of water from the tap, instead of having to draw their supplies from the village well, as they did until the new scheme became operative.

Population

The population in 1801 was 730, and at various census dates since then the figures have been:—

1841 — 927	1921 — 648
1901 — 701	1931 — 602
1911 — 594	1951 — 586

In comparison with many country districts the population figures have declined very little in the past fifty years, probably because of the close proximity of the parish to Dumfries, which enables many of the young people to live in the country and work in the town, travelling the few miles daily by bus or car. The only concentration of population is at the village of Shawhead.

The War Memorial, erected in the churchyard in 1921, is in memory of 16 men of the parish who were killed in the first world war, and one soldier who lost his life in the second world war. It is indeed a commentary on the nature of those two great conflicts.

The Village

Shawhead, the only village of the parish, is 5 miles from Irongray church and 7¼ from Dumfries. The village may be approached from four roads, but the summer visitor on a Sunday afternoon invariably chooses the road which runs by the little brown and white church, up the valley close beside the Cluden to the leafy picnic haunt of Routin' Brig, and on through pretty, undulating countryside to the thick little wood which opens suddenly to the steep village street. Here old cottages fringe the narrow road which widens at the top of the hill to reveal a broad square with fourteen new council houses, and green fields beyond. Most of the cottages in Shawhead are at present occupied by elderly people, while the majority of the village children live with their parents in the semi-detached council houses at Braco Square. This housing scheme was built during the years 1952-5.

Except for the new villas at the top of the village, the outward appearance of Shawhead can have changed but little in the last hundred years, yet the profound social changes of this century, particularly in the last twenty years, have greatly altered the pattern of village and country life. Modern transport, telephone, radio and television enable everyone to keep in immediate touch with both local and universal events. Adequate sanitation, hot and cold running water and electricity have transformed the homes into convenient, pleasant and healthy living quarters, where smaller families thrive within the same walls which in former times witnessed the birth of ten or twelve children, few of whom survived childhood.

Farming

On the farms, which average about 300 acres, one no longer sees a pair of horses ploughing—tractors, combine harvesters, electric milking-machines and other devices perform the seasonal tasks; lack of suitable labour, and the high cost of that which is available, have greatly speeded up this mechanisation. In 1880, when the size and prosperity of a farm were reckoned locally by the number of scythes wielded in harvest-time, Ingleston (485 acres), the largest arable farm in the parish, employed 11 scythes, worked 13 horses and had 20 regular farm workers. At this time 100 acres yielded a corn crop, the equivalent of which is gathered from 40 acres to-day. Turnips and oats are the only crops now grown for sale; straw, hay and some oats are produced on the farms for the animals, but this is augmented by a large variety of concentrated marketed foodstuffs.

Although accelerated scientific research has greatly assisted the farmer, and artificial manures, selective weed-killers, better quality seeds

Q

and rotation cropping enable him to produce better harvests, the greatest single factor in transforming the land has been the heavy application of cheap lime. Land now carries twice the stock it did in 1900, and at present there are about equal numbers of dairy and beef cattle in the parish. Beef cattle are almost entirely cross-breeds. By Government regulation the dairy cows, mostly of the Ayrshire breed, are tuberculin-tested. Milk is collected daily and taken to the Carnation Milk Factory in Dumfries for processing into tinned milk. Only sheep farming seems to maintain the human touch, for the flocks are not large enough to warrant the expense of electric shearing facilities. The Glen is the largest sheep farm in the parish.

All farm workers have a higher standard of living than their fathers, with at least one full free day each week and two weeks' paid holiday in the year. On Wednesday, the market day in Dumfries, and on Saturday, the roads in the parish are busy with farmers travelling to town in their cars, and buses conveying the few shoppers who have no transport of their own.

Industry and Commerce

There has been no industry in the parish since a small glove factory at Rosebank removed to larger premises in Dumfries. Two old meal mills, one at Barnsoul and one at Cluden, have long been in disuse. The smithy at Nether Yett, where the Dragoons are said to have had their horses re-shod, has been transformed into a farm worker's cottage.

Irongray has no banking facilities and no police station, and tradesmen, except a joiner and a mason, must be sought outside the parish. There is no hotel, nor are there any licensed premises. The nearest is at Crocketford, Dunscore or Maxwelltown. Gateside farmhouse, half a mile from the church, was a public inn and toll, popular with cattle-drovers, until the Glasgow-Carlisle railway was built.

Resident servants are employed in only two mansion-houses; several large houses enlist a few hours' domestic help from the wives of farm workers, but most homes are now organised for maximum convenience and run very efficiently with the aid of electrical appliances that are clean, efficient and speedy compared with the implements and methods they replace. Shopping for food is done mostly from vans, other requirements being purchased in Dumfries, though many people do enjoy an occasional visit to Glasgow or Carlisle.

Social Life

In 1910 a village hall to seat 300 was erected in Shawhead, the money being raised by public subscription. The head-teacher and the minister are trustees, and a management committee is appointed at the annual general meeting each January. Improvements to the hall, which included redecoration and the construction of a new kitchen, were completed in 1958, greatly adding to the amenties. It is encouraging to note that despite the counter-attraction of television, which is now installed in most homes, many activities flourish in the parish and provide entertainment for the long winter evenings. Carpet bowlers and the Badminton Club each meet twice weekly in the hall, which also accommodates the monthly meeting of the Shawhead Women's Rural Institute, as well as dances and whist drives. Under the direction of the head-teacher both the Shawhead choir and drama group have been very successful in county competitions, and afford grand entertainment for appreciative local audiences. Another smaller but very useful hall has been made by putting a new floor, electric lighting and heating into the manse barn, and here in winter the Irongray Carpet Bowling Club meets bi-weekly, and the Irongray Woman's Guild and Steilston W.R.I. each meet once a month.

The oldest sporting club in the parish is the Irongray Curling Club. It is not known exactly when it came into being but a medal for an annual single-hand contest was presented to the club in 1845 by Thomas Biggar of Crochmore. In 1896 the Cluden below Irongray bridge was frozen and the club that year were able to hold their contests on the river. The losers in each game paid for half a ton of coal to go to the poor of the parish. Nowadays the club play regularly in the inter-area matches on the rinks at Glasgow or at Ayr during the season, and if the frost is sufficiently hard they have the opportunity of playing on outside rinks at Crocketford and Castle-Douglas. Shawhead has a football team which plays in district competitions, and the Dumfries team, Queen of the South, has many enthusiastic supporters in Irongray parish.

A pack of Brownies, comprising eight little girls, was started this winter, and it is hoped to increase their number and extend activities once the pack is well established.

The parish has no real poverty and no delinquency. When Irongray figures in the law courts salmon poaching on the Cluden accounts for what little crime there is, and the accused invariably dwell outwith the parish. The people of Irongray are, on the whole, community-conscious —generous, kindly, sociable, with a real affection for their parish and its historical associations. Most families are often represented at the church, and sales of work and all appeals for charitable causes evoke unstinted generosity.

Local pride is well founded, for, though the south-west of Scotland is known for its scenery, Irongray is particularly pleasant and beautiful. The irregularity of the hills, the long vistas over chequered farmlands, the profusion of great trees, the swift-flowing burns and the river, intensely clear and blue at Glenkiln, tumbling and leaping in white foam at Routin' Brig, deep and peaceful by Cluden banks—all these contribute to a variety and beauty second to none. The words of Dr. Boyd written at Irongray Manse over a century ago are still true: 'This is the true country, not the poor shadow of it you have near great and smoky towns. The sapphire air is polluted by no factory chimney. Green fields are all about; hawthorn hedges and rich hedgerows; great masses of wood everywhere. But this is Scotland; and there is no lack of hills and rocks, of little streams and waterfalls, and two hundred yards off, winding round the church-yard, a large river glides swiftly by. It is a quiet and beautiful scene.'

Our Covenanting forebears loved this countryside with passion and fervour, and no less to-day the parishioners of Irongray when they gather in their old church sing with feeling and sincerity the words that were so great an inspiration to their ancestors in this quiet land:

'I to the hills will lift mine eyes,
From whence doth come mine aid.
My safety cometh from the Lord.
Who heav'n and earth hath made.'

1959

CHAPTER 24

THE PARISH OF LOCHRUTTON

by JOHN HYSLOP

Physical Features

Lochrutton parish is of an elliptical form, and is computed to contain some thirteen square miles, being four and a half miles long from east to west, and three miles broad from north to south. It is bounded on the east by the parish of Troqueer; on the south by the parishes of New Abbey and Kirkgunzeon; on the west by the parish of Urr; and on the north by the parishes of Irongray and Terregles.

Lochrutton Loch, at an altitude of 502 feet, occupies one of the lowest portions of a remarkable basin of country, which stretches into the parishes of Irongray and Terregles, and, rising on the east, south and west, forms an undulating ring round Lochrutton in these parts. At the outlet of the loch, where a tiny tributary stream of the Nith emerges, stands the village of Lochfoot 'compactly built together'.

The parish, traversed by the old military road from Dumfries to Portpatrick and within five miles of the former town, although out of the beaten track of tourists and scarcely noticed in local descriptive works, is attractive in appearance.

History

One hundred years ago the finishing touches were being put to the great undertaking that was to bring the water of Lochrutton into the houses of Dumfries and Maxwelltown. The first pipe was laid on 16 January 1851, and on 21 October of the same year the water was turned on. Although the main source of Dumfries water is now at Irongray, over 2,000,000 gallons of water a day still leave the Lochrutton reservoirs for Dumfries. At the annual inspection of the waterworks, Dumfries Town Council always conclude their day's outing by visiting the Lochrutton plant, and have lunch in the old board room of the Dumfries and Maxwelltown Water Commission.

The greatest change in agricultural life in the parish during the last 30 years has been in the ownership of the farms. After 1918 a number of farmers bought their farms, especially in the south and west of the parish, where the land was in the ownership of the Terregles estate. There are 38 farming units, 28 of which are owned by their occupiers, and the others are held to a very great extent in security of tenure.

The most important changes in farming practice have been brought about by the general use of tractors and milking machines. The double furrow tractor plough is taking the place of the single furrow two-horse plough. Tractors are also used in drawing disc harrows, grubbers, mowers, binders, and in general transport about the farm. For 60 years the big mills for threshing have been taken from farm to farm by large steam engines, but heavy motor tractors are now used. A few weeks ago, a new rapid-cut hedge-trimmer was in operation in Lochrutton. Motor cars are universal and tractors are steadily replacing horses. In the course of a seven mile walk through the parish in the month of May, the writer saw 32 tractors and four pairs of horses at work. There are only 25 horses in the area, several of them old favourites grazing on 'some hain'd rig'.

The old parochial board, and later the parish council, were composed of local men of all ranks living side by side with their constituents. Under the present centralised scheme of administration, Lochrutton and its neighbouring parish of Kirkgunzeon send one representative between them to the county council. It is a curious fact that our present councillor, who is a lady, is neither a Lochrutton nor a Kirkgunzeon person. Each parish sends a representative to the district council, a body with very limited powers.

Church

The Kirk of Lochrutton, a plain unpretentious structure, occupies an elevation on the eastern slope of the parish. Surrounded by a small churchyard, in which there are some very old and interesting gravestones and 'throch stanes', its picturesque appearance is heightened by the clump of trees which shelter it. It is known to have existed before the Reformation. The present building was opened for worship in 1819. About 1887 during the incumbency of the late Thomas Crosby, who was minister for 39 years and whose memory is revered by the older residents, the kirk was reconstructed internally by the heritors to make it a commodious and comfortably seated church. On the gable a marble mural tablet tells of the men, 13 in number, belonging to the parish, who fell in the two world wars. The manse is a handsome erection and stands a little lower down the declivity from the church. Because of the distance of the church from the southern extremity of the parish, a considerable portion of the population in that area are connected with a church in another community, in which also their social activities are centred.

At the beginning of this century, with a regularity as unfailing as the ringing of the ten o'clock bell on Sunday morning, the road and paths leading to the church carried their quantum of people of all ages to the twelve o'clock service. To see so many of the parishioners meet in church on Sabbath was inspiring. Times have changed. The kirk bell has long ceased to toll at ten o'clock, and now, when the gathering bell has stopped at twelve o'clock, there is a slender proportion of the people in the parish at the service. There has been a general decline in church attendance and an increase in Sunday travel.

Most of the people in the parish belong to the Church of Scotland but, despite the united front it now presents since the Union of 1929, it cannot be said that the Church of Scotland, once the dominant institution, has retained its old position in Lochrutton. The minister holds the respect of the people and is ready to answer any call on him. Of recent years there has been a tendency to have baptisms administered within the church, and the same holds good in regard to the celebration of marriage. The number of members on the church roll is 189. There is an active Woman's Guild of 18 members, and a Sunday school of 30 children, with three teachers.

Historical Monuments

The antiquities of this parish are the ancient Tower or Castle of Hills, the crannog or lake dwelling, and the stone circle. They are fully reported upon in the *Old* and *New Statistical Accounts,* and have been listed in *The Royal Commission on The Ancient and Historical Monuments and Constructions of Scotland: Fifth Report and Inventory of Monuments and Constructions in Galloway. Vol. II—Stewartry of Kirkcudbright.* 1914. Their reference numbers are 330, 331 and 332 respectively. After being uninhabited during the nineteenth century, the Hills Tower, as it is commonly called, and house adjoining, have recently been repaired and are again being lived in.

Ancient Well

Lochrutton once possessed a healing well. The farm of Merkland Well, from which these waters issued, derived its name from the well. Some years ago, as a result of draining operations, the spring ceased to trickle.

Famous Native

In Lochrutton Manse, on 8 October 1774, was born the Rev. Dr. Henry Duncan, founder of the Savings Bank movement. He was the third son of the Rev. George Duncan, minister of Lochrutton from 1766 to 1807, and writer of its first *Statistical Account.* Dr. Duncan obtained, after great exertions, an Act of Parliament in 1819 establishing Savings Banks throughout Scotland, and in 1835 succeeded in procuring an Act for regulating them. He died on 12 February 1846.

Population

The population in 1801 was	514	
1851	726	(maximum recorded)
1901	497	
1911	484	
1921	559	
1931	453	
1951	527	

It is believed that the reason why the population at the 1851 census transcended the others is that a number of men engaged at the Dumfries water undertaking would be living in lodgings in the parish and would therefore be included in the Lochrutton census of that year. Documentary evidence of Sunday, 30 March 1851, reveals that 'Government in taking the Census for 1851 required to know the number of persons attending Divine Service on that day—Number in Lochrutton Church, 125'. With this comment, and recalling that the number of people at the census of 1790 was 528, a comparison of the figures shows that the population has not materially varied in the past 160 years. Lochfoot village has now a population of 183, or 35 per cent. of the parish. The increase of population by growth of Lochfoot balances the decrease of that of the farming community. The causes of the latter's decline are the uniting of small farms into one, and the attraction of the town. Over the area are to be seen the scanty remains of former farms and cottages, indicating a great farming population in the past. It is estimated that about 20 per cent. of the people of the parish are natives of it.

Housing

Housing has not been neglected in Lochrutton. A scheme of 30 houses in Lochfoot was finished seven years ago by the Stewartry County Council and the homes were fully occupied. These houses are of four apartments, built of brick, roughcast, and slated, four being of two storeys, and 26 of one storey. Along with the houses, all the normal services were provided, from electricity, water and drainage, to street lighting. They have a population of 128. These houses enjoy the appellation of the 'New Village', which is adjacent to and parallel with the old one containing 29 houses, varying from two to seven apartments. The population of the old village is 55, and 12 of the houses are owner-occupied. The tenants of the new housing scheme are in no way a group apart. Some of those living in them have been transferred from existing houses.

A public hall in the old village, taking the place of the public house of former days, is important as a community centre.

The crafts of weaver, tailor, mason, dyker, molecatcher, shoemaker, blacksmith, and others, are no longer practised in Lochfoot. Some of the houses occupied by these artificers have been demolished, and some, having been reconditioned and provided with the above normal services, are now comfortable homes of one storey. In the old village are three houses of two storeys each, two of them substantial and modern. One of these is the residence of the school headmistress, who holds the office of Registrar. The joiner's establishment in the village is the oldest business in the parish, having been carried on by grandfather, father and son for a hundred years. A post office fully equipped, a shop on a site advantageous for both villages, and seldom without a customer, a small church hall, an automatic telephone exchange, and a public telephone, are also to be mentioned. The planners of the site of the new houses did well to leave the school in isolation. In point of situation it, and the post office, grace the village's west end. The old village, with its variety of houses, and intersected by the military road, presents a pleasing appearance.

The farm houses, as stated, 38 in number, have nearly all been rebuilt or added to, and farm buildings improved, which reflects a healthier state of agriculture than that reported upon in the *Old* and *New Statistical Accounts*. Throughout the area of the parish, a further 52 houses, 14 of which are owner-occupied, bring the number of houses to 149—the total for Lochrutton. Since 1918 much renovation has been carried out on houses requiring attention, especially farm cottages. Much healthful rivalry exists among the neighbours, including farmers' women folk, as to what a garden, an adjunct to nearly every house, can be made to yield.

Water Supply

At the time the *New Statistical Account* was prepared it could only have been the manse and the mansions that had a supply of water within their walls. To-day the houses without this commodity are few and getting fewer. Lochrutton has no general gravitation supply of water. Spring water is plentiful and it has been brought in privately by most of the places over the area. The village and several houses on the Castle-Douglas road are served by the county council, under arrangement with the Dumfries Town Council, from their Irongray source.

Electricity

While the old paraffin lamps still shed a kindly light in several houses, electric light supplied by the South-West Scotland Electricity Board has been installed in the great majority. On the farms, with electric bulbs and tubes throughout the buildings, the new lights are considered by some to be a blessing next in importance to the tractors. Outwith the buildings, a couple of lamps in the right places throw helpful light over the farmyard, so that people can walk about with confidence. Electricity has certainly lightened the dark of Lochrutton. As power it is used to drive stationary threshing mills, milking and other machines.

Roads

The great road, which passed close to the church and the south side of the loch, is now a grass-grown right-of-way. In its stead, on the north side of the loch, is the old military road, already mentioned, having a branch a quarter of a mile long leading from Lochruttongate to the church. At a distance of half a mile from this main line to Lochfoot, the road from Dumfries to Castle-Douglas passes through the parish. There are two cross parish roads connecting the main roads. These are in good order and fully meet the requirements of the community. The practice of acquiring road metal from a large quarry ten miles distant has superseded the method of quarrying and breaking stones locally. Four road quarries in this parish stand unwrought.

Transport

The daily bus service introduced 25 years ago and carried on by an enterprising native of Lochrutton who has his premises on the military road, and the buses operating on the Castle-Douglas road, have settled many problems. They have greatly widened the area of employment for young people. Instead of having to find lodgings near their work, they can now stay at home, and many of them work in Dumfries.

The Royal Mail van arrives at Lochrutton from Dumfries at 8 o'clock a.m. At 12 o'clock the school dinners van arrives. There is a regular service of merchants' vans from the chief shopping centre, Dumfries, and farther afield. The extent of goods and livestock transport is impossible to measure. For the benefit of motorists and lorry drivers, an admirable idea has evolved and become the almost universal practice: that of having the name of each farm posted at some conspicuous place at the farm buildings, or at the entrance to the loaning leading thereto.

Education

The parish school, which is situated on the border of the village, was erected in 1861, and has since been enlarged. The staff consists of the headmistress, a native of Lochrutton, and another female teacher. The roll in 1952 was 42. Children for the most part come from the village, but several have a distance of one to two miles to travel. They attend the local school till the age of twelve and then proceed to secondary schools in Dumfries. The buildings are in good condition, water having been brought in, lavatories constructed, and electric light installed. The school is provided with a wireless set, a gramophone pick-up, and a film-strip projector. Full use is made of the juvenile books sent at regular intervals from the county library. The children are attended by a doctor yearly, and regularly by a nurse. They also receive dental care. Thirty-six pupils take the school dinners. Compelled as the children are to attend secondary schools in the town, they frequently lose much of their native attachment. The majority of children leave school at the earliest possible date and it is noticeable that few of the village children seek work on the land. Classes in further education are held each winter, supervised by the local schoolmistress. Subjects of a practical kind, such as dressmaking, are most popular.

Health Services

The parish is well served by the medical men in the neighbourhood, mostly from Dumfries, a quarter of an hour's run. A few families in the south and west areas require the services of a physician from Castle-Douglas, Dalbeattie, or New Abbey. The introduction of the telephone has facilitated matters in this respect. The hospitals in Dumfries, and the auxiliary hospital at The Grove, are easy of access. Some cases are treated at Castle-Douglas and Lochmaben. Although these places are at a distance there is ample bus service to them. A district nurse, who is a native of Lochrutton, serves the three parishes of Terregles, Lochrutton and Irongray; she resides in Terregles and is provided with a motor car.

Political Parties

The Galloway Unionist Association has a branch in Lochrutton, but the Labour Party has no organisation in the parish. Except on polling days, little interest is taken in either local or national government.

Agriculture

The 38 farms in the parish range in size from 16 to 700 acres, with an average of 196 acres, the average rental being 15s an acre. Animal husbandry is the main concern. With the returns for milk made sure by the Milk Marketing Board, more cows, mostly Ayrshires, are now kept than formerly. Broadly speaking, two-thirds of the farms carry on dairying in some degree and in many of them milking is by machine. The milk is lifted in cans and feeding stuffs are delivered, both by motor lorry. The drive to obtain tuberculin tested milk has led to a great improvement in byre accommodation. Some of the farmers rear their young stock to be sold as calving queys or store bullocks. On the non-dairying farms, which comprise the largest in the parish, stock is reared, bullocks and sheep are fed, and flocks of breeding ewes are maintained. In addition to sheep bred locally, many are brought in from other districts to be fattened; this is also the practice in regard to cattle. While the Ayrshire-Shorthorn cross bullock is a popular animal in this neighbourhood, some of the big feeders keep a herd of Galloways.

According to the figures supplied by the Department of Agriculture, the area of the parish, including the loch covering 160 acres, is 7,740 acres, of which 1,382 are under tillage, 4,696 in grass, 1,390 rough grazing, and 112 woodlands. Cropping is confined more or less to the requirements of the stock, very little fodder or grain being sold off. By the labours of improving and hard-working farmers, and the application of lime and manure, the land of Lochrutton has been brought into good cultivation, the harvesting of its crops being in due season and as timeous as that of any other places in the neighbourhood.

The chief crops are oats, turnips, hay and potatoes. Only a few of the farms grow potatoes for sale. The common rotation is oats, green crop, oats, hay and grass. In this district much attention is given to the management of grass and the making of good hay. A good many days are taken up with threshing. When the travelling mill comes round during the winter the spirit of co-operation exists of neighbour helping neighbour. Five or six farms join together to provide eleven or twelve men to do the threshing at each farm as the mill moves on. The farmer's wife cooks the large meals for the occasion, and has a very busy day.

Some of the farms in the parish are worked by the farmer, his wife and grown-up members of the family. The young folk begin full-time work on the farm when they leave school. Most of them seem to be quite happy in their occupation.

The keeping of poultry is an important adjunct to Lochrutton farming. Bees are kept throughout the parish, including the village, and in some years they thrive abundantly and good returns of honey are secured.

In the catastrophic epidemic of foot and mouth disease which affected more or less generally the whole of south-west Scotland during the summer of 1952, Lochrutton escaped. No outbreak occurred within the boundaries of the parish, although there were serious outbreaks immediately over its north-eastern border. Much anxiety, however, was caused among the farming community on account of closed markets, general restrictions of sale and movement of livestock, and veterinary inspection. Some of the older folk recalled the stories heard from their parents of the days when cattle were allowed to take freely of the disease and get better by nature's means, instead of the elimination of whole flocks and herds in pursuance of the policy of slaughtering.

Industry

The two mills in the parish mentioned in the *New Statistical Account* have been discontinued for many years. One of them is now the premises of an electrical engineer and plumber, and the other has been demolished. A new business in the form of a garage and filling station has recently come to the parish; it is situated on the Castle-Douglas road.

Farming and forestry do not go well together, but a farmer knows the value of shelter in moderation. Objections may be taken to trees because they keep away the drying winds in harvest, encourage rabbits, shade the land, and from the fact that their roots interfere with the plough. Lochrutton could, however, spare a little ground for shelter belts along the fields and round farm steadings so that men and crops and cattle might have a chance to get out of the wind. The children could be encouraged to respect trees, shrubs and other amenities by assisting in planting a row of trees on a waste space at the eastern entrance to the village.

Fauna

The starling has become the most numerous and noticeable of all land birds in this district. Of the migratory birds the cuckoo and swallow pay us an annual visit. The wheeple of the whaup or curlew is to be heard in the remote parts of the parish, but the peewit or lapwing, which used to be very common in the breeding season, is now scarce. Wild ducks are numerous on the loch, which is also the habitation of the stately swan. The loch with its wild life provides much scope for the children interested in natural history. Owls exist in small numbers

Rabbits are in abundance on the farms, and there has been a great increase in the number of foxes. The only wood of any extent in Lochrutton is at its eastern boundary on the military road and this plantation presents a picture of no mean beauty. The foxes are mostly found in this wood and many an effort is made to thin them out. Other pests include rats, moles, clegs or horse fly, grub, and May fly.

Way of Life

Lochrutton has sent out people far and wide and the majority of them keep up their connection with the parish. Many have sent to them the *Dumfries and Galloway Standard* as the medium between them and their native place, and many spend their holidays at the place where they were brought up. In November, 1950, Lochrutton held a reunion in its public hall of its natives and former neighbours, an event which was unique in the south-west of Scotland. Among those present were parishioners who had left the district at an early age to seek fame and fortune in other parts of the country. There were no fewer than 130 people in the hall, one quarter of the present population. A happier or homelier gathering it would be difficult to imagine, and the experience of meeting friends who had gone beyond one's ken for 40 or 50 years had a peculiar personal satisfaction.

So far as employment is concerned, apart from the farming community and three one-man businesses, the residents at work in the parish are two men engaged on road maintenance and three in charge of the waterworks. Every morning a considerable number of business people, tradesmen, transport employees, mechanics, forestry workers, shop assistants, office girls, and others travel to Dumfries and neighbourhood by bus, cycle or car for their day's work. To a certain extent Lochrutton has become a residential area for those who work beyond its borders.

There is no county family in Lochrutton. The two mansion-houses have been acquired by business men. Jobbing gardeners there are, but none full-time, and there are no gamekeepers. Many elderly people reside in the parish, among them a number of natives who have returned to the parish to end their days.

In Lochrutton considerable facilities for recreation are available. In the homes reading, listening to the wireless, sewing and knitting are the principal pursuits. A county council mobile library visits the village once a fortnight and full use is made of it. Books are also obtained from the circulating libraries in Dumfries. The *Dumfries and Galloway Standard, Galloway News, Glasgow Herald, Daily Record, People's Friend* and *Sunday Post* are the most popular papers. The farmers take the farming newspapers. A keen and intelligent interest is taken in farming topics and many individuals are too busy to be concerned with other than practical matters. In ordinary speech, the Scots is retained, the dialect of the natives being that of Dumfries district.

With Dumfries only five miles away and travel made easy by modern transport, an entertainment of the parishioners is the cinema. There is much interest in football and 50 per cent. of the adult male population go every Saturday to watch their favourites, the Queen of the South, at Dumfries, and farther afield. A popular carpet bowling club has an enthusiastic membership of 40, and a badminton club has 24 members. Whist drives and dances are also popular and there is keen competition for the whist drives. There is a local dramatic club and plays presented get good support. Mention must be made of the Women's Rural Institute which is in a flourishing condition, with approximately 60 members. The curling club was instituted over a hundred years ago, and, when the loch is frozen, skaters take full advantage of the opportunity to indulge in their sport. Football is played in the summer.

Most of the parishioners are now housed in modern dwellings and the result has been a great improvement in family life. The well cared for and well clad children are the best indication of a satisfactory home life. The ordinary husband recognises the need for outside interest for his wife, and keeps the house to let her out to her Guild and Rural meetings. Many of the inhabitants have come into the parish during the present century; a large proportion since the last war. Few now have their roots in Lochrutton's past but they adhere to the old traditions. The incomers for the most part naturally have their hearts in the districts in which they spent their early lives. Class differences are not altogether absent. A love for Lochrutton exists amongst its mixture of people and all sections are ready to co-operate in any movement for the common good. The parishioners as a body are entitled to be designated as an intelligent and well disposed community and in their intercourse with one another they are kind and neighbourly. There is no likelihood of any marked change in the life of the parish in the near future. By all indications, Lochrutton will continue to be a purely agricultural district as it is to-day.

1952

CHAPTER 25

THE PARISH OF MINNIGAFF

by DR. A. KELLIE BROOKE

Topography

The parish consists chiefly of vast areas of poor hilly land rising to 2,764 feet on its northern boundary at the Merrick, which is the highest point in the south of Scotland, and to 2,329 feet on its eastern boundary at Cairnsmore of Fleet. The land slopes down towards the west to the river Cree, its western boundary, and also down to the south with the Cree as it flows into the Solway Firth.

The hills are of granite, sparsely covered with sharp, stony soil except the flatter lower moors, which are of a peaty nature. There is a fertile plain of heavy clay along the last three miles of the river Cree. At this point the river is tidal, slow flowing and winding, and therefore tends to deposit any fine alluvial soil that has been washed down from the hills. The windings of the Cree are known as the Cruives of Cree. Formerly, for vessels of up to 80 tons, the Cree was navigable up to Carty, and its tributary, the Palnure burn, up to Palnure bridge.

Climate

The climate is damp, relatively mild and relaxing. From the records it would appear that the driest quarter of the year is April, May and June. Annual rainfall ranges from 40 inches in the lowland area to 80 inches in the hills. The parish often escapes the wintry conditions of snow and ice experienced elsewhere in Scotland and the northern half of England. Palm trees, in fact, have grown out-of-doors for many years in Bargaly Glen. This is probably due to the effect of the Gulf Stream and the proximity of the Solway Firth. One very severe winter occurred in 1895, but the worst one in recent years was 1947, when there was skating and curling on the river Cree for several days in the village of Minnigaff just above the Cree Bridge, that is within a quarter of a mile of the tidal portion of the river Cree. At that time curlers engaged in outdoor curling continuously for several weeks, and a heavy fall of snow about 15 March brought all road and rail communication to a standstill for some days. Although this delayed ploughing and the sowing of corn, the good weather that followed in the late spring and early summer brought crops on quickly and a dry August led to a quick, early, good harvest.

The moist, mild climate and the absence of extremes explain the pattern of agriculture: such conditions are conducive to good grass and pasture over a large part of the year, but they are not so favourable to grain production. The arable land on the lower reaches of the river

Cree is therefore given over to dairy farming, and only sufficient crops are raised to meet the fodder requirements of each individual farm. The nature of the climate is also one of the factors which has influenced the Forestry Commission to acquire such large areas of land for afforestation in the parish. In the higher hills in the north-east of the parish the average rainfall is much higher, 67-84 inches per annum, and this has been a factor in the siting of the hydro-electric power scheme dam at Clatteringshaws.

Afforestation

Up to the present day the chief industry has been farming, chiefly sheep farming. This picture is rapidly changing and very shortly the chief industry will be afforestation. This change has been brought about by several factors. The chief of these is probably the inability of landed proprietors to carry on their estates intact on account of death duties and greatly increased taxation; together with the increased costs of repairs, upkeep, and tradesmen's wages when there has not been a proportionate increase in farm rents. It is interesting to note that at the opening ceremony of the forestry village of Glentrool, Bargrennan, the Earl of Galloway stated that the rents he was receiving from the lands which had passed to the Forestry Commission were only 47 per cent. of the sum received by his ancestors in 1870, although taxation and maintenance expenses had risen very considerably during that period. It is only natural, therefore, that where a landlord receives a suitable offer for a large block of land from the Forestry Commission, it should be accepted in preference to selling isolated farms to tenants who might be in a position to purchase them. Secondly, the climate, notable for the absence of frequent severe frosts, is very suitable for afforestation. Thirdly, although the hills are composed chiefly of granite, their covering of soil is such that the percentage of plantable land is high. The area of afforestation in the parish may be divided into three —the Nursery at Daltamie, the plantations, and the National Forest Park at Glen Trool.

The Nursery

The nursery at Daltamie was begun in 1931. It now extends to 58 acres, and employs 90 men, 30 women and 24 boys at the height of the season in spring and summer. All the trees are raised from seed. The seeds are coated with red lead, sown broadcast in beds and covered with sand from the Palnure burn or Glenshalloch, which is particularly suitable for this purpose. As weeds germinate before seed, the beds are treated with a flame gun which kills off the first crop of weeds before the young seedlings appear. Thereafter the beds are kept clean by hand weeding, which is usually carried out by girls and schoolboys. The seedlings remain in the seed beds one to two years according to the size of plants. Thereafter they are 'lined out' in rows nine inches apart, with seven and a half inches between the plants. They may be

Plate 7. THE OLD KIRKCUDBRIGHT HARBOUR
With sailing ships.

Plate 8. SHELL FITTER
The first tanker to discharge a cargo of oil for the distribution depot at Kirkcudbright.

South of Scotland Electricity Board

Plate 9. CLATTERINGSHAWS DAM
The reservoir supplies water through a tunnel to Glenlee Power Station.

left 'lined out' for two years, after which they are suitable for planting out in the plantations at three to four years old. The nursery stock is at present approximately 18 million trees. From four to five million of these, at three or four years of age, will go out to the forests in this and other areas in Scotland, England and even Eire during the winter and early spring.

The Plantations

Planting commenced on a small scale on the hill ground of Kirroughtree estate in the year 1930-1, and it was only after the second world war that the scheme expanded to its present dimensions, when 53,216 acres were taken over from the Galloway estate. The main species to be planted are Scots Pine, Japanese Larch, Norway Spruce, Sitka Spruce, with small areas of hardwoods where the soil is suitable at lower elevations.

In choosing the type of tree to be planted in any area, the nature of the land, the soil and surface vegetation are taken into consideration. Generally speaking heather suggests pines, but rules out spruces; bracken-covered knowes are suitable for larches; spruces do best in damp flats and hollows where the soil is wet and peaty and there is a strong growth of blow grass or molinia. All wet areas must be drained and where possible this is done by drainage ploughs pulled by heavy diesel caterpillar tractors. The spruce firs do well planted on the upturned furrows of the drainage plough, or, if these are too far apart, on turves cut from the plough furrows. Trees are planted from four to six feet apart. Considerable labour is required for brashing—the removal of side branches when the canopy foliage has reached about ten feet from the ground—and for thinning. Thinning is carried out when the trees are at least 15 years onward. It is estimated that conifers will mature at 70-80 years and hardwoods at up to 150 years depending of course upon species, soil suitability, incidence of disease or pests and drought or frost damage. It is estimated that the labour required will be four to eight men for each 100 acres.

The following figures give some indication of the present extent of the scheme, which is still in its infancy.

Land in the parish held by Forestry Commission	59,585	acres
Plantable acreage (approximately)	25,480	„
Acreage planted to date	8,408	„

The Forestry Commission have built or possess ten houses at Daltamie Nursery and Kirroughtree Forest. At present the total number of employees in the parish is 187, but this must steadily increase as the young plantations grow up and thinning operations get into full swing.

The National Forest Park, Glen Trool

In the northern end of the parish lies the Forestry Commission's Glen Trool property which extends to over 40,000 acres of the most attractive, romantic, and least developed district of southern Scotland. In 1945 it was recommended that this be constituted a National Forest Park and made available, with almost unrestricted access, to ramblers, climbers, geologists, botanists, and all who find their recreation in hills and glens. The dangers of fire have made it necessary to restrict camping within the Forest Park to the Caldons, the only recognised camping site in the area. Here an ideal site has been laid out in the meadow below the farmhouse on the edge of the loch, and in the copse-wood bays adjoining. The land is level and well-drained, and suitable for camping under canvas or in caravans. There is an ample piped water supply and ablution facilities in suitable sheds; and water-flushed lavatories are available. This is probably one of the best camping sites in the country. The charge is two shillings a night or twelve shillings a week for each tent or caravan. Fishing is available on certain lochs, on permit, but not on Loch Trool itself which is private and strictly preserved.

A new village has been built in Glen Trool Forest, and called Glentrool village. It consists of 47 houses for forestry workers, a school and schoolhouse. The school is a two-teacher school built on modern lines. There are two classrooms, a dining-room and kitchen, indoor lavatory accommodation and a drying room. Central heating is maintained by an oil-burning plant. Most of the residents in the village are in the younger age groups, partly on account of the post-war housing shortage. The children are therefore in the younger age groups too. Pupils of secondary age are conveyed to Newton Stewart or Creetown. The houses are all of three or four apartments, brick-built, lit by electricity, and equipped with hot and cold water. Most houses are having television installed.

Wild Life

The parish has the usual run of birds common to the county. The Golden Eagle and Buzzard are seen on occasion and even the Osprey is claimed. Special mention should also be made of the Golden Pheasant and Amherst Pheasant and their hybrids, which were introduced originally to Cairnsmore by the Duke and Duchess of Bedford. Reeves Pheasants were also introduced, but these appear to be dying out. An occasional pair of Mute Swans appear on the river, but these never settle for any time, and only once have they successfully reared cygnets in the past 22 years.

Foxes are becoming more common and Otters are occasionally seen in the river. Red Deer and Wild Goats are disappearing from the hills as the Forestry Commission advance with their plantations. Four years ago the rabbits were practically wiped out with myxomatosis. The survivors, however, re-established themselves, but during the past year the disease has again taken its toll, although the infection has not been so virulent and there are more survivors.

There is excellent salmon fishing in the Cree, its tributary the Minnoch, and the Palnure burn. This fishing is all private and rents may reach up to £1,500 per annum. This is a change from 50 years ago when single shepherds residing with their employers sometimes had a clause in their bargain that they would not have salmon for their meals more than twice in any one week. The burns and lochs abound with trout. Some lochs are stocked with brown trout and rainbow trout. Many of the slower stretches of the rivers, and the lochs, contain pike. A recent venture has been the catching of eels by set lines and sending them to the market. In the lower tidal reaches of the Cree the salmon are netted in the pools. This is carried out at low water, six days a week, there being no fishing from 6 p.m. on Saturday until 6 a.m. on Monday. In the spring, large numbers of sparling come up into the lower reaches where they can be easily caught, even by small children. They are considered a great delicacy. A local angling association leases stretches of the river, and also lochs, for its members. Fishing is mostly by fly, but spinning is allowed when the water is at certain levels.

Good shooting is still to be had in the parish, although it has deteriorated with the breaking up of estates and the subsequent great decline in the number of game-keepers. There is a deer park on the Earl of Galloway's estate at Cumloden.

Organisations

There are branches of the Scottish Women's Rural Institute at Minnigaff, Bargrennan and Palnure. The Minnigaff Welfare Association and the Bargrennan Community Association look after the welfare of the community as a whole, entertaining the old age pensioners and children at Christmas, and also in the summer. These associations help to preserve the amenities of the parish, and arrange meetings throughout the winter of a social, educational and cultural nature. There is a detachment of the Red Cross. Scouts, Guides, Cubs, Brownies and Boys' Brigade are organised independently or in conjunction with Newton Stewart.

The playing field run by the district council includes a football pitch, putting green, swings, shute and pavilion. A juvenile football team functions in the summer time. A local golf club plays over a nine hole golf course at Kirroughtree. With the recent mild winters there has been little outside curling, but a very strong, enthusiastic club travels frequently to Ayr to play on the indoor rink. Carpet bowling is very popular and is played at Bargrennan and Palnure throughout the winter. Two bowling greens in Newton Stewart are well supported by Minnigaff players.

Religious Life

The majority of children are brought for baptism at about six weeks, whether or not parents are regular church attenders. Baptisms are in church in the face of the congregation at the weekly diet of public worship, except when the mother or child is ill. Only 15 per cent. of the births are in the parish; most mothers seem to be going into maternity hospitals. It is still a tradition that in the middle teens young people should 'join' the church. They are expected to show some real interest in the church beforehand and attend a special class of instruction run by the minister. Ninety per cent. of the adult population are members of some local church. Most are members of the Church of Scotland, but a few families belong to the Scottish Episcopal Church, the Roman Catholic Church or the Plymouth Brethren. Not all the adults are active church members; in the parish church there is an average weekly congregation of 120 out of a roll of 520. It is the present custom for most marriages to be solemnised in the church; only in exceptional circumstances is a religious ceremony performed in a hotel. A few couples go to a registry office to be married there. Thirty-five per cent. of the marriages are anticipated but it is noted that most of these couples get married, there being few unmarried mothers left to cope with bringing up children. No family, whether of church members or not, considers burying a relative without the presence of a minister of religion. A few coffins lie in the church, rather than in the home, awaiting the funeral; the service is then held in the church.

Monuments

There is a large granite cairn overlooking Loch Trool, erected to commemorate the victory of Robert the Bruce over the English in this Glen in 1307. A stone commemorates the death of the martyrs at Caldons in Glen Trool; it is said to be the work of Old Mortality.

Tenure of Land

In the past 20 years there has been considerable change in land tenure in the parish. The greater part of the parish was formerly held by five estates, Cumloden, Kirroughtree, Machermore, Cairnsmore and Bargaly. The Bargrennan and the Auchinleck areas of Cumloden estate have been sold to the Forestry Commission. All remaining farms have been sold to the tenants. The houses, with some of the surrounding land, are all that remain of these large estates. This has been brought about by death duties and heavy taxation. The mansion-house of Kirroughtree is now a hotel. Part of the surrounding park has been converted into a nine hole golf course and the remainder is farmed. The mansion-house of Machermore has been converted into an eventide home, run by the Plymouth Brethren.

Miscellaneous Services

The Health Services are provided by the Dumfries and Galloway Hospital Board, with the main centre in Dumfries. There is a General Practitioner Hospital in the neighbouring town of Newton Stewart, and also a clinic which is visited by consultants from Dumfries. The Public Health and Child Welfare Service is administered by the county council, the local health authority. A district nurse is resident in Minnigaff. The parish is served by five doctors, one of whom is resident in the village. Two ambulances serve the parish and surrounding district. Now that the police service has been regionalised there is no resident constable in Minnigaff. There is a fortnightly visit by a mobile library van although, with the coming of radio and television, reading is not so popular as it was. A new street lighting scheme has just been completed on the trunk-road, which is now considered one of the best-lit roads in the south-west of Scotland. There is a bus service at two-hourly intervals between Stranraer and Dumfries. The nearest railway station is in Newton Stewart whence there is also a thrice daily bus service to Glasgow *via* Ayr. The roads are all maintained by the county council, and on the whole are good. Household refuse is collected once weekly and taken out to a dump at Stronord. There is not yet any form of incinerator and the dump is open to vermin, cats and flies which may pass to neighbouring houses.

Industries

The chief industry in the parish is now forestry. The next industry is agriculture—dairy and arable farming on the lower banks of the Cree, marginal and hill farming on the higher ground. Another source of employment is a sawmill in the village of Minnigaff. The hand woven tweed mill has now ceased production. A number of the inhabitants find employment in the neighbouring town of Newton Stewart. The only mineral—lead—was mined at Blackcraig up to the end of last century. In Creebridge there are two hotels, Creebridge House Hotel, and Kirroughtree House Hotel, both licensed; with the Cree Inn—a six day licence. In Bargrennan there are two, the House o' Hill Hotel, licensed, and Garlies Lodge unlicensed. As this area is rapidly becoming a tourist centre, a large number of householders provide 'bed and breakfast' in the summer months. There is only one shop, a general store in Creebridge.

Education

There are three primary schools:—

Minnigaff	3 teachers	75 pupils
Glentrool	2 teachers	40 pupils
Stronord	2 teachers	35 pupils

A new secondary school to be erected in Minnigaff will provide for all the secondary pupils in the area up to the ordinary grade of the Scottish Certificate of Education. Pupils taking the higher grade course will transfer at the appropriate stage to Douglas Ewart High School across the river. A primary department in this new school will replace the present Minnigaff and Stronord primary schools.

Housing, Water and Drainage

Housing conditions on the whole are very good. Several new houses have recently been erected on the Race Green, Kirroughtree, beside the west or town lodge, by the Stewartry of Kirkcudbright County Council. These are financed partly by tenants' rents, local rates and exchequer grants. Practically all houses in the parish have a piped hot and cold water supply and flush sanitation. The greater part of the sewage from the village passes through a sewage purification scheme before discharge into the river Cree. Unfortunately, there is no such purification scheme for the neighbouring town of Newton Stewart, with the result that sewage is discharged in its crude form with gross pollution of the river below the village. The water supply is collected from the hills behind Barclye and Dranandow. It is all filtered and piped to the village. Most houses, including farms, have had electricity introduced in the past few years. While there has been a lull for many years in private building, several houses have been and others are being erected in the village. With the new housing scheme the centre of population is moving down to Creebridge, and the church and the present village school are no longer in the centre of the community.

Local Administration and Politics

The parish has one representative on the county council and one representative on the Western District Council, which embraces the parishes of Minnigaff, Kirkmabreck, Anwoth and Girthon. The Conservative, Liberal and Labour parties all have their supporters. The Conservative party has a very active branch, and the parish is predominantly conservative in its political outlook at present.

Parish Life and Prospects

With the advent of the Welfare State there is now little real poverty in the parish. Houses are well kept, people are well dressed and well nourished, and enjoy good health. General behaviour is good and there is little crime or juvenile delinquency in the parish. The chief cause for concern seems to be care of the elderly. The population is becoming longer-lived, with more elderly people. As the school meals service means that children need not come home for a mid-day meal, more mothers are taking a part-time or full-time job. In years gone by, neighbours often helped to look after old people, but they now seem to have less time and less inclination. More facilities for the care of the elderly, especially the sick, are badly needed.

It would appear necessary to attract industry to the district, to utilise the many square miles of timber now being planted. As Minnigaff is on the verge of this area, and has suitable sites, together with facilities for road and rail transport, it is quite possible that such development may take place in the parish. Regarding the more immediate future, as a result of mechanisation the farm labour force is being reduced. In the forestry nurseries large numbers are employed in hand weeding, but with the introduction of pre-emergence sprays it would appear that weeds can be controlled without weeding, with the consequent loss of another avenue of employment. The majority of children from this parish who take the Scottish Certificate of Education usually have to seek their fortunes and livelihood elsewhere.

1961

CHAPTER 26

THE PARISH OF NEW ABBEY

by H. DOUGLAS WALKER

Name

The parish takes its present name from the beautiful abbey built in the late thirteenth century (a ruin since the seventeenth century) called the New Abbey to distinguish it from the old abbey at Dundrennan, built about 1140. Both abbeys belong to the Cistercian Order. The old name of the parish appears variously as Lochkinderloch or Lockindeloch, the name being traced to Cendaeladh, a king who died in A.D.580.

Extent and Boundaries

The greatest length of the parish is nine miles, and its greatest width four miles. It is bounded on the north by the parishes of Lochrutton and Troqueer; on the west by Kirkgunzeon and Colvend; on the south by Kirkbean and on the east by Troqueer and the river Nith.

Topography

The western area of the parish consists of a range of hills running from Lotus Hill in the north-west corner to Criffell (1,866 ft.) in the south-west. A second, but lower, range runs parallel to the first from Lochbank Hill to Barlay Hill. Between these lies a pleasant valley leading down from the village of Beeswing to New Abbey village. The eastern area is low-lying fertile ground sloping to the channel of the Nith and facing Caerlaverock on the Dumfries side. A large extent of this part of the parish is merse, much used as pasture and a sportsman's playground during the shooting season when large flocks of geese and other birds are to be found. Two streams flow through the area: the New Abbey Pow from Kinharvie Hill, which passes just north of the village; and the Glen Burn, rising on Criffell and passing under the New Abbey-Kirkbean road at the southern tip of the village to join the Pow and enter the river Nith.

There are three lochs in the parish: Lochaber Loch and Loch Arthur in the north-west corner, and Loch Kindar one mile from New Abbey village. Loch Kindar is the largest of the three and probably the most interesting. It is a popular haunt of anglers who find its trout attractive both in flavour and in their elusiveness. This loch has other attractions, however. It is three-quarters of a mile long by half a mile wide and on it there are two islands, on one of which are the ruins of the old parish church, Kirk Kindar. Kindar Loch is the scene of many local curling matches, when severe weather makes outdoor curling possible.

Enthusiasm for the outdoor sport is dying out, however, and much use is made throughout the year of the indoor rinks in Ayr and Glasgow. It is a pity, for there is little to beat a crisp, keen afternoon on the loch when the sky above Criffell is blue and the keenness of the ice varies with the passing of a cloud overhead. The second island barely stands above the water's surface, and is much used as a breeding ground by sea-birds.

Soil and Climate

The soil of the parish, where it is cultivated, is composed for the most part of sandy, gravelly loam which is easily drained, but there are stretches, at Ingleston, where there is heavy clay which is much more difficult to work, especially during a wet harvest and when modern heavy harvesting machinery is used.

The climate is mild and moist, with a tendency to regular strong winds which blow up the Solway Firth.

Forests

Since the publication of the last account, the Forestry Commission has added to the wealth of the timber in the parish by planting 600 acres of fir, spruce, pine, larch, beech, oak and ash, and much more is to be planted. The forests belonging to the Commission lie on both sides of the New Abbey-Beeswing road and continue from the mature woods maintained by the Stewart family mentioned in the last account. The woods grown by this family now run to 611 acres and are situated at Lochbank, Craigend, at Kinharvie and on Criffell. The Kingan family also own extensive plantations in the parish extending in all to 130 acres.

Fishing

Some half dozen members of the community obtain at least part of their livelihood by fishing on the banks of the Nith, either by use of the haaf-nets for salmon, or by the stake-net for salmon and flounders. A thriving hatchery exists near the village, known as 'The Solway Fisheries', where trout of various kinds are reared, especially 'rainbow trout'. These are sold to angling associations throughout the country for re-stocking their waters.

Historical Monuments

The early history of New Abbey was the history of the abbey built by Devorgilla, wife of John Balliol. She was the mother of the well-known 'Toom Tabard', not his wife as has sometimes been stated. The edifice has been known for hundreds of years as the abbey of the *Dulce Cor*, or Sweetheart Abbey. Apart from enjoying the beauty of the country-side surrounding the village, most of the visitors to the area are there for the purpose of inspecting the picturesque ruins, which are maintained in their present state by H.M. Ministry of Works, which has issued an interesting and comprehensive brochure describing the remains of the building and giving its history. The Ministry of Works is engaged at the present time on some building work intended to preserve the fabric of the Abbey, using granite for the purpose. It is interesting to note that the material used in the original building is red sandstone which must have been brought from across the Nith, in Dumfriesshire, probably from Locharbriggs. A legend still exists in New Abbey that the sandstone was ferried across the river by women and this legend is enshrined in the wall of a cottage near the Abbey. A stone block is built into the house wall, close to the door, depicting a small boat being rowed by three female figures. It is thought that this stone came, as so many stones in other cottages have come, from the Abbey.

Within half a mile of the Abbey lies the ruin known as Abbot's Tower, of which little is left and that overgrown. The present parish church is built on a site that was originally part of the fish pond used by the inhabitants of the Abbey. In this pond they fished for pike and to this day it is known as the 'Ged' or pike loch, though it is now a field subject to flooding. The monks also had a fish pond at the other end of the village, where, it is reputed, they kept a stock of trout. This pond lay in the hollow directly across the public road from the little church at the end of Shambellie avenue. An old meal mill still exists complete with all its machinery and its mill pond, though it is no longer in use. This mill is mentioned in the two previous Statistical Accounts. The 'Ged' loch mentioned above, upon part of which the present parish church is built, was used as a dye pond for the tweed mill which functioned up to the end of the last century. Parts of the mill buildings are still in existence and are used for garage and other purposes by Kindar Lodge.

A building full of historical interest, which deserves much more attention than can be given here, is Abbey House. This ancient house was the home of the last abbot and possibly of his predecessors. Gilbert Brune, the abbot in question, died a centenarian in the early years of the seventeenth century. Abbey House became the home of the Stewart family, thereafter, their former home at Shambellie becoming a ruin of which nothing is left but an archway in the steading at Shambellie Grange farm. The Stewart family continued to live at Abbey House until they built their present home, Shambellie House, in 1856. Recent excavation has revealed a medieval drain in the garden of the house, which has been added to on at least two occasions since the original building of the abbots' days.

Only an archway on the lawn in the Abbey grounds is left of the original entrance to Abbey Yard, which at one time contained the former parish church (a lean-to against the abbey wall), the school and two cottages. Interesting etchings of the old church are to be seen in the Parish Hall.

On the Glen Hill overlooking the village stands a granite memorial known as the Waterloo Monument, built by the inhabitants of New

Abbey in memory of those of the neighbourhood who fell in that battle. It is 50 feet high and 16 feet in diameter and contains a winding stair leading to the top from which a splendid view may be obtained. The monument is falling into disrepair and may soon become dangerous.

Local Records

In the keeping of the minister of the parish at New Abbey are to be found the parochial records of baptisms and marriages and the kirk session records dating back to the beginning of the seventeenth century.

Place Names

One or two interesting place names in the parish are worth mentioning:—

Cullendeugh—a holly hollow (to this day much holly is to be found in that district).
Craigenfinnie—a little crag of the peats.
Criffel—raven or crow's hill (Scand. *kraka fjall*).
Kinharvie—wall head (ascribed to Gaelic, *ceann h-eirbhe*).
Shambellie—an old dwelling (*sean baile*).
Annatland—'annoid'—a church of a patron saint.

Land Owners

Among the chief land-owners in the parish is the family of Stewart of Shambellie. The name of Stewart of Shambellie has been associated with this area as far back as the year 1640. The present owner, Mr. A. McC. Stewart, has taken great pride in further increasing the large acreage of good forest land, the planting of which was begun as long ago as the time of Nelson.

Much of the land referred to in the last account as belonging to the Oswald family, of Cavens, Kirkbean, has now been sold to individual farmers in the parish and little is left in the hands of the present representative, Major R. A. Oswald.

A new name is now to be found among the land-owners, that of Kingan. This family has come to own much land and house property in the village of New Abbey, acquired during the last two generations; the family will be commented on later under the subject heading of 'Agriculture, Industries and Commerce'.

The Duke of Norfolk owns a large stretch of land in the parish, though this is mostly wild hill-country suitable for use as a game preserve. The estate runs to five thousand acres and includes the attractive area round Kinharvie mansion-house, recently sold by the Duke to the Marist brothers for use as a college.

Lord Perth owns the farm of Glensone, which lies between New Abbey and Beeswing.

Colonel Maxwell-Witham, of Kirkconnel House, who bears a name associated with the parish for hundreds of years, still owns some 800 acres of good arable land, some of it, Landis Farm, close to New Abbey village, and some, Trostan Farm, nearer to Beeswing.

Bequests

The following trusts and bequests are administered by the New Abbey kirk session or by the minister:—

The Gunning Bequest—to be expended by the minister on charitable or religious purposes.

The Hairstanes Bequest—administered by minister for charitable purposes.

The Thorburn Bequest—administered by kirk session for charitable purposes.

The Seton Bequest—kirk session expends on upkeep of family grave and balance on charitable purposes.

The Coupland Bequest—kirk session for charitable purposes.

The Lewis Trust—kirk session expends on grave upkeep and charitable purposes.

The Stitt Bequest—kirk session for charitable purposes.

The Graham Bequest—kirk session expends on grave upkeep and charitable purposes.

The Glensone Trust—half administered by county council and other half administered by kirk session of Lochend Church, Beeswing and New Abbey Church for charitable purposes.

The Walker Bequest—a grant administered by the headmaster of New Abbey Secondary School to provide prizes for dux scholars.

Population

The following were the census figures from 1901: 1901—957, 1911—742, 1921—779, 1931—728, 1939—837, 1951—790. Since then the population has continued to rise. The exceptional rise in 1939 was due to the presence of about 100 evacuee children from Glasgow and elsewhere.

Some of the present dairy farmers are incomers to the parish, Ayrshire being the birthplace of many. A transformation has taken place, probably related to some extent to this Ayrshire influx, in the type of farming carried out—as compared with fifty years ago dairy farming has superseded the raising of fat-stock.

Apart from the above exception, the population of the parish is composed for the most part of people born in the parish, though there is a regular exchange of farm servants with the neighbouring county of Dumfries and with other parishes in the Stewartry. Some signs of infiltration of immigrants from Ireland are to be found, but not to the extent noted by the writer in parishes to the north and west of the county, and not of first generation immigrants. There is evidence, too, of migration from the parish to America and even to New Zealand during the last hundred years.

Much of the prosperity of New Abbey village and its immediate surrounding area, and the steady increase of its population over the past few years, is based on the work provided by the firm of James Kingan and Sons, whose business covers a wide field, dealing in grain and animal feeding stuffs (including the milling of these), raising, felling, and sawing timber and selling pit props direct to the coal mines in Ayrshire and Dumfriesshire; and the cultivation of several farms. A further opportunity for employment is provided by another firm which supplies the local bus service. This firm maintains a fleet of over a dozen modern buses at its garages in the village.

With the improved transport of the last 20 years the villages of New Abbey and Beeswing are slowly developing as dormitory villages, providing labour, usually young people, for factories and shops in Dumfries. This has a deeply felt effect on the social life of the villages, where voluntary organisations suffer from the attractions offered by the town. The young folk, especially, naturally tend to form their circle of acquaintances around their place of daily work.

Roads

The parish is well supplied with good tarmacadam roads, maintained by the county authorities. A first class road runs through the parish on its east side entering at Martingirth in the north and leaving the parish at the southern tip near the Drum farm. A good road runs between New Abbey and Beeswing by way of the pleasant valley between Kinharvie and Auchenfad Hills. The surface of this latter road is not good all the way but is being improved.

Water Supplies

The village of New Abbey has its own water supply piped to all but a few houses from a reservoir in the Glen. This suffers from inferior filtration and is soon to be superseded by a county supply. This new supply, for which the mains are being laid through the county at the moment, will serve the farms and outlying cottages as well as the two villages. Some of the farms to the south of New Abbey village have their own private supply from the slopes of Criffell. The village of Beeswing is not so fortunate and is dependent still on private wells and pumps for its water supply.

Electricity and Gas

Electricity is supplied throughout the parish by an overhead grid system erected by the South of Scotland Electricity Board. Very few houses in the village are not connected to the grid, and all the farms make use of the power so provided. On the farms the provision of electricity has produced the most revolutionary change in the way of life. In a dairying area such as this the value of electrical power is manifest in refrigeration, water-cooling, milking by machinery, sterilising of utensils, bruising of corn and so on. No main supply of gas is available in the parish but many isolated crofts and cottages make use of 'Rural Gas' for cooking and lighting.

Sewage Disposal

Both New Abbey and Beeswing villages have septic tanks which deal with the effluent from the sewers running through each village. Some of the larger private houses and farm houses outlying from the villages have their own septic tanks for disposal of sewage.

Education

The parish is served by two schools, maintained at New Abbey and Beeswing villages by the Stewartry of Kirkcudbright Education Authority. Beeswing's is a primary school, whereas that at New Abbey, while providing primary education for the local children, acts as the central school for secondary education for the majority of the children in the area bounded by Mainsriddle on the south, the Dumfries burgh boundary on the north, and Beeswing and Drumsleet on the west and north-west. At the time of writing, the school roll at Beeswing is 33, while the primary roll at New Abbey is 80, with a secondary department of 80 also. Beeswing has two fully qualified teachers, and at New Abbey the primary department has three fully qualified teachers, while there are nine teachers qualified for secondary work, including part-time specialists in Physical Education and Domestic Science. In the secondary department of New Abbey school two main secondary courses are provided (a) the first three years of an academic course which may be completed at Dumfries Academy, and (b) a practical three years' course for the bulk of the scholars in the department, who leave normally at the school leaving dates after attaining the fifteenth birthday.

In the field of further education the Education Authority is always willing, where possible, to answer any demand for evening classes at New Abbey or at Dumfries.

A Marist 'House of Studies' has recently been instituted at Kinharvie mansion-house to train teachers of the Roman Catholic faith. It is not a public school and has a staff of five with 30 students.

Housing

There are 236 houses in the parish with a total of 1,037 rooms. As the population is almost exactly 800, the number of persons to a room is less than unity.

The problem of overcrowding, much in evidence elsewhere, is non-existent in the parish. Houses vary from mansions to small country 'but and bens', and average four rooms to a house. With one or two exceptions all the houses in the parish have gardens associated with them, though in New Abbey village some gardens are some distance from the houses to which they belong. In this village a number of the houses are owned by the proprietors of the sawmill, and are occupied only by employees of the firm and their families. The remainder, apart from council and agricultural houses, are privately owned. The whole aspect of New Abbey village has been altered by the erection by the county council of a total of 34 houses in a scheme known as Ingleston View, built in three stages, in 1937, 1952, and 1953. The first set of houses has been much admired by visitors to the district and recognised as a worthy model on which to plan other housing schemes. In addition to these houses, four Atholl type steel houses for agricultural workers have been built at the other end of the village.

The increase in the number of houses has had little effect on the sense of community. Many of the occupants of these newly built houses find their employment in Dumfries or at the I.C.I. works near Drumsleet, and take little or nothing to do with the evening activities of the village.

Health Services

The parish is served by two general practitioners, one working from New Abbey village and one from Mainsriddle. In addition, the area is served by a district nurse of the County Medical Officer's department who also acts as school nurse to the two parish schools. Hospital services are provided by Dumfries Royal Infirmary.

Churches

There are three churches in the parish in which regular worship takes place, two in New Abbey village and one in Beeswing. In New Abbey village the parish church, built in 1876, has a membership of 320. The present building, which supersedes that which lay next the Abbey and was mentioned in the last account, was built from stone taken from an old wool mill close by, no longer in existence. The site of the church was the dye pond of the mill and is reputed to have been originally the fish pond of the monks when the Abbey was still intact. The original parish church of the last account exists no longer as such, but the materials of which it was built were used to build what was, until the recent union, the United Free church. This building, until three years ago, housed evening services of the combined congregations, but, though kept in sound condition by the New Abbey kirk session, it has not been used since then for any purpose. It is smaller, and, with the building of the recent council housing schemes, not so central as the building at present in use. At the moment, attempts are being made to find some suitable use for the building.

There still exists a small chapel of the Roman Catholic faith, within the precinct walls of the Abbey and next to New Abbey school, but its membership, which varies from 30 to 40, is constantly dwindling. There is a resident priest.

Lochend Church in Beeswing was recently linked with New Abbey Church of Scotland under the one minister, who serves both congregations and lives in the New Abbey manse. It continues, however, to administer its own affairs under its own kirk session, to hold weekly services and assist in the upkeep of the New Abbey manse. The membership of the Lochend Church is 137.

Voluntary Organisations

In the village of New Abbey a Girl Guide company has been running for some years with a membership of up to 20, fed by a small Brownie troop. The New Abbey Church Sunday schools are thriving with memberships of (a) primary—35, (b) senior—40, and a youth fellowship meets weekly with a membership of 15. In Beeswing village there is a

Sunday school with a membership of 12 and a youth fellowship of six members.

New Abbey has a branch of the Women's Rural Institute (founded 30 years ago) with a membership of 50. The Woman's Guild connected with the church has a membership of 60. In Beeswing the W.R.I. membership is 48 and the Woman's Guild has 49 members.

Recreational and Cultural Societies

In New Abbey a village badminton club meets twice a week in the school gymnasium in the winter, while a football club functions throughout the summer months, as is the custom in the country. The men's club, which has its own premises, meets on several nights a week in the winter and provides carpet bowls and other games. There is a women's section of this club for the playing of carpet bowls. In Beeswing, the carpet bowling club has a membership of 22 and the badminton club has 20 members. In addition, a dramatic club has functioned most winter seasons in recent years, though drama has not proved a popular pastime in New Abbey for some time.

The New Abbey Flower Show Committee organises an annual flower show which is held in the school. The show is well supported by the horticultural enthusiasts of the parish, and entries for its open sections are received from far afield. The show, held on the first Saturday in August, is a red-letter day in the parish, and is usually combined with an open sports meeting.

A fishing association has also its supporters in New Abbey village and in the district around it. The association has a regular membership of 40, and is allowed to fish the length of the New Abbey Pow from the cauld at the sawmill to the point at which the Pow enters the estuary to the Solway.

Local Politics

In New Abbey a flourishing community council looks after local affairs and on several occasions in recent years has voiced, with effect, the feelings of the local inhabitants. It is annually appointed and is fully representative of all the activities of the New Abbey area. It serves as a useful link between the people and the district and county councils.

There is only one political organisation in the parish—a branch of the Unionist Association which has a membership at present of 102.

Agriculture, Industries and Commerce

It would be correct to say that the majority of the workers of the parish are connected with agriculture in some shape or form, though this is not true of the villages, particularly of New Abbey village.

New Abbey village has three main sources of employment—

(1) the sawmill, situated at Townhead on the bank of the New Abbey Pow, with its associated occupations of woodcutter and carter. Large forested areas in, and close to, the parish keep the mill plentifully supplied with raw material, though cutting is also undertaken

much farther afield and the timber brought home for processing. Power at the mill is supplied by a large steam engine;

(2) the firm of grain merchants, where animal feeding stuffs are ground and mixed, and feeding stuffs supplied to farms for miles around. This firm, already mentioned, has a very wide range of activities, which provide a livelihood for a large proportion of New Abbey villagers. The firm's bill-heads read as follows:—'Millers, Grain, Coal and Timber Merchants. Threshing and Baling Contractors. Lime and Manure Merchants'. The influence of this firm, both of the employers and the employees, is most marked in the community, in church and in social life. The movement in and out of workers, too, has its effect on New Abbey school roll from term to term;

(3) the omnibus firm, centred in its garages at New Abbey, employs drivers, conductors and conductresses who live in the village. Other sources of employment are:—

(4) the farms lying close in to the village;

(5) shops and factories in Dumfries;

(6) the I.C.I. works at Drungans, in the neighbouring parish of Troqueer, which manufacture, among other things, Ardil, an artificial fabric.

The landward parts of the parish are purely agricultural, with dairy farming providing the greater part of the employment and, to a lesser extent, some rearing of pigs and poultry. Beeswing provides its quota of workers who travel to town for their employment, but a larger proportion are employed on the farms immediately adjacent to the village.

It is of interest to record that whereas the *Old Statistical Account* lists over a dozen separate trades, there are now to be found only two joiners, one cobbler and one shop-keeper. New Abbey village has only one shop, a general merchant, while Beeswing has no shop. This one shop, whilst serving the village and its environs, maintains a mobile shop which travels far round the parish. Vans from Dumfries visit all parts of the parish regularly throughout the week, supplying every commodity but drapery. Among the vans supplying the parish in this way are those of the local co-operative society.

To conclude this section on commerce, reference may be made to the passing of a form of trade which was important to the parish until twenty years ago. This was the use of the New Abbey Pow to carry coals and lime into the district and farm produce and quarried granite from the quarry at Lochhill across the firth to England. Stories are still told of this cheap form of transport, which came to an end with the change of the course of the Nith away from the New Abbey shore.

There are two licensed hotels in the parish, both in New Abbey village.

The Way of Life

The change in the way of life which has taken place in and around New Abbey village in the last fifty years is directly connected, as must be the case in all similarly placed villages, with the improved transport situation. To read in the *New Statistical Account* of a coach to Dumfries every alternate week and compare it with seven buses daily to the town to-day, explains the great change in the outlook on life. New Abbey is no longer an out-of-the-way spot, though still unspoiled in its natural beauty. As it is easy for its inhabitants now to travel to all parts of the country, so it is equally easy for trippers and tourists to enjoy the beauty of the parish. The twisting road through the village, so picturesque and attractive, was adequate when vehicles moved in a leisurely fashion, but is now a cause for apprehension as hundreds of touring buses pass through in the summer. Such intermingling of visitors and natives has affected life in this hitherto remote community; while the radio, which is to be found in every house, and television, which already is to be found in quite a number of houses, are spreading new ideas and methods.

As mentioned already in this account, the regularity and efficiency of the bus service is tending to make New Abbey village increasingly a dormitory village, for more and more people are showing a desire to come to live there but to continue to work in Dumfries.

Through the continuous daily transport of produce of many kinds from the grain merchants and saw millers to the industrial regions to the north and north-west, the outlook of the New Abbey worker is no longer parochial, and his interests are more varied. To some extent, discontent with life in the parish community has shown itself, and has resulted in the departure of young people to the towns. This process has been aggravated and stimulated by the military service of the young men. It will be interesting to see just how much further depopulation of the rural areas will go as the number of houses available in the cities and towns comes nearer to saturation.

1954

CHAPTER 27

THE PARISH OF PARTON

by the REV. G. D. SUMMERS

Name

The name for more than 300 years past has been spelt Parton; and Parton, though possibly altered both in orthography and pronunciation from the Gaelic whence it is derived, is said to signify in that language the 'hill-top', which is perfectly descriptive of the situation of the place. It is set in one of the most beautiful parts of the Stewartry.

Boundaries

The parish is square in form, bounded by Balmaclellan and Kells on the north; by Kirkpatrick-Durham on the east with the Urr as boundary; by Crossmichael on the south; and on the west, separated by the River Dee, by Balmaghie. On this, the Parton side of the Dee, runs the main road from Castle-Douglas to Ayr, Kilmarnock and Glasgow. It is nowadays a busy highway for main traffic; not only is there a very good bus service, considerably increased in the last 15 years, to the city from Castle-Douglas and other neighbouring south-western districts, but also along the route there is the constant road transport movement in connection with the important agricultural market centre at Castle-Douglas. Parton village is on the main London to Stranraer railway line and has a station which is still open for passenger and goods traffic.

Estates and Mansions (West of Parish)

The parish is itself rural, and agricultural, with its four large estates and beautiful mansion-houses happily still occupied by members of the families whose names have been so long and so well known and honoured in the parish.

Airds, owned by the Henniker-Hughan family—Admiral Sir Arthur Henniker-Hughan Bart. commanded H.M.S. *Ajax* (1913-16) and was M.P. for Galloway from June 1924 until his death on 4 October 1925.

Parton House, formerly the home of the Glendonwyns, the original patrons of the kirk, is now the residence of the Murray family, who built the model village of Parton and in 1908 gave the parish its village hall. The church bell, also a gift of the family, was erected in the tower in 1901. Chairs of specially fine design, and made from local wood, were given to the kirk by the present Murray family.

Barwhillanty, the home of Mr. Yerburgh, whose father was M.P. for Chester. A member of the family, Lord Alvingham, is a most generous patron of Parton parish and church.

274

Glenlaggan is the residence of Commander Lyndesey Watson, who was a noted naval officer of the submarine service.

The change in the times is manifest in the estates, in the reduced staffs, now the enforced minimum—in some cases only one servant, whereas 24 years ago when the writer came to the parish there were up to ten males and females employed indoors. The reduction in staffs applies also to outdoor employees. This, in its measure, has led to the very considerable decrease in the population, which is due also to the drift from the rural way of life. The population at the 1951 census was 506.

Agriculture

There are in the whole parish 38 farms of over 25 acres and a fair number of smaller holdings. Many of the farms are now worked by the owners although some are still rented from the estates. Farmhouses and steadings throughout the parish have been modernised; almost all are now 'electrified', the majority of the electric installations having taken place since the war. Almost every farmer has the telephone, and houses and steadings, both inside and outside, show evidence of the 'new age' in all the up-to-date amenities enjoyed. In many farms the milking of the cows is done by electricity, and it is not only in the case of the farmer and his household that there are signs of higher standards of living and better and happier general conditions. So far as the lot of the agricultural worker is concerned, there have been reconstructions and reconditioning of houses everywhere for the material comfort of the people, who enjoy to-day not only a considerably higher standard of living and increased remuneration for their work, but so much more leisure time.

The ploughman with his pair of horses is seldom seen now—the horse and plough have given way to the machine, the pony and trap to the motor car. Twenty-four years ago, it was quite usual to see a queue of horses awaiting attention at the village smiddy and a pile of farm implements close by. In these days the smiddy was a favourite resort of the children on their way to and from school. The scene has changed and the smiddy is now a quiet place stocked with parts of bicycles, batteries for electric torches, modern tools and gadgets for motor cycles and cars. Every farm has its car; the tempo of getting about is accelerated for all; travelling, of which there is much more nowadays, is by bus or train if not by car. The school children, too, have car or bus supplied for the journey to and from home, when their age or the distance of the particular school attended makes it necessary.

Education

The school in Parton village is situated on the hillside about 100 yards from the main road. It was built in 1863 on ground given by Mr. Kennedy of Boreland, the farm now owned by Mr. Mungo Bryson, who recently purchased Boreland and Craigmore from the Parton estate. The building of the school cost £420 at that time. The arch-way, the entrance to the school, was erected in 1910 in memory of James Bell, a noted headmaster for 20 years, who was elder and session clerk in the church, as well as organist and choir-master. The school, now under the local education authority, has been equipped in modern fashion with electric lighting, central heating and other amenities; it is a two-teacher school. The parish minister, who is chaplain to the school, visits it regularly and a very happy and friendly spirit of co-operation exists between school and church in all the work amongst the children. Their numbers have, of course, in common with the parish's population, declined considerably in the last 30 years. The standard of educational achievement is high in our country school, which has a notable record on the part of past pupils. Only recently the local Stewartry paper, the *Galloway News,* remarked on the number of college and university students and graduates from our small community.

As in other communities the school children are in a very different case from their fathers and mothers in *their* school days, in the way their comfort is catered for not only in the school, but also in the present-day provision of a substantial mid-day meal. Anyone looking in at the hall where the meal is served must know how much the goodly fare is enjoyed, as well as the fellowship round the table. The benefit for the children in every way is obvious.

Community Life

It is in the village hall that the parish meets socially, whereas in the olden days functions were held in the school, the only available accommodation before the erection of the hall in 1908. The hall is set conveniently just off the main road at the end of the village and at the foot of the school brae. On the main doorway is the inscription *Floreat Partona.* Quite recently the hall was handed over to the parish, but previously it was owned by the Parton House family. It has its small body of trustees, including minister, schoolmaster and two farmers, and there is a managing hall committee composed of members of the different parish organisations, of which there are many—both church and secular.

For the men, there are curling and carpet bowling clubs, the membership of which includes most of the men of the parish, and in addition a football club for the younger men. The mixed church and secular societies are all very popular. For the women, there are the flourishing W.R.I. and the Woman's Guild. The nearest cinema, in Castle-Douglas, seven miles distant, does not have the attraction of the local clubs and activities (though there is an excellent and most convenient bus service). Organised whist drives are very well patronised and so too is the village dance, a special class sponsored by the education authority having stimulated interest amongst the adolescents. Dramatic productions are also popular, though in the meantime there is no club or class. There is, however, a choral class and a successful ladies' choir with musical festival competitions in view. The children in particular show a keen interest in, and enthusiasm for, choral and instrumental music. This is due in large measure to the work done in church and school as a result of the efforts and inspiration of the County Organiser of Music. In consequence, children's entertainments in the hall always mean a 'capacity house'. The hall is now in process of reconstruction. It will be lighted by electricity and will have an electric boiler in the ante-room. New, spacious and modern dressing rooms are to be added to the building. In this enterprise, as in all others in both church and parish affairs, there is the friendly family spirit characteristic of the rural community.

The Church

The simplicity and reverence which pervade the worship on Sunday manifest the fine spirit of rural church life. The body of members, though small in numbers, is devoted in loyalty to the 'Kirk of their fathers'. While the change in the times is not without its impact here as elsewhere, the attendance at public worship, the striking liveliness of youth organisations and Woman's Guild, and the facts that we have almost all the children of school age in Sunday school, and that every household in the parish contributes to the church by special book collecting, are encouraging and uplifting. There are five active elders on the session. Three successive ministers have covered a period of almost a hundred years. There is a fine manse, built in 1871 at a cost of £1,735 10s, modern in design outside and inside, set in a lovely site surrounded by the glebe, and overlooking the Dee to the hills beyond. Electricity was installed throughout in 1938. It has some spacious rooms which are suitable for accommodating youth meetings and gatherings of organisation representatives. It is often a social centre, as well as the desirable residence of the minister. If only the grounds, in these days of the non-existence of the 'minister's man' and the heavy expense of upkeep, were not so extensive! The glebe, 17 acres of pasture, is let to a local farmer.

The church, completed in 1834, is a characteristic example of the Scottish Kirk of that time. A straight-forward piece of construction, the building with its simplicity and its square tower has its own ecclesiastical dignity. The interior is plain, with cream walls and a purple narrow surround on the long windows. Pulpit and communion table with baptismal font and praise board are all of unpolished light oak. It still has its oil lamps for light, if required, though only on rare occasions is evening service held. It is hoped soon to instal electric lighting. Amongst the church's property are the communion silver at present in use—dated 1868; in pewter, three old communion cups, 1751; one flagon, and two trays, 1787; as well as 47 communion tokens dated 1717. The church, which has 322 sittings, and manse were redecorated in 1929 at a cost of £698 15s.

The war memorial in the church, and the stone of remembrance in the small square just outside the church's main gate, contain 19 names of the fallen in the first world war.

Close by the present church stands the ivy-covered ruin of the old church built in 1592. It has a very ancient bell in the turret, and on a stone in the wall below are inscribed the words *Laus Deo* and the date 1592. The old church is the burial ground of the Parton House family, and buried there also—with a stone marking the grave—is the distinguished scientist and physicist, with the parish's most illustrious name: James Clerk Maxwell, died 5 November 1879. In the same burial ground, his father, mother, and wife are laid. The brilliance of James Clerk Maxwell's achievements in physical science made him internationally famous. His genius was recognised by the nation when a memorial plaque was placed in Westminster Abbey.

1953

CORSOCK

The village of Corsock in the Upper Urr Valley is near the northern boundary, and has few links, social or economic, with the west of the parish. This pleasant upland village has a fine prospect over a wide sweep of moorland to the north; on the south-west it is sheltered from the prevailing winds by the higher and beautifully-wooded grounds of Corsock House. Two council houses built between the wars are the only houses built this century. The village is now even more isolated with the withdrawal of all public transport except for two return journeys on Saturdays between Dalry and Dumfries.

The village school, which became one-teacher in 1964, provides primary education; secondary pupils are conveyed by school bus to Dalry. Mid-day meals for the children are cooked in the school.

A general store and sub-post office, a joiner's business and an agricultural contractor cater for the needs of the village and surrounding district. The village hall is the centre of all the usual activities— W.R.I., Woman's Guild, bowling, badminton. Just below the village there is a memorial to A. C. S. Murray Dunlop, M.P., whose benefactions to the village included the Dunlop Church and the village hall.

Between 1863 and 1930 Corsock was a *quoad sacra* parish and had also, until 1930, a U.F. church, the Dunlop Church, which contrary to the normal pattern was surrounded by the kirkyard. In January, 1930, the two churches officially united and for a time the two buildings were used alternately. Later the attractive and more central Dunlop Church became the regular place of worship. Corsock Church is now linked with Kirkpatrick-Durham.

Although much of the surrounding land is marginal, it is suitable for hill-farming, mainly stock-raising with some dairying. In recent years much of the marginal land has been planted out as part of an extensive scheme of private afforestation.

1964

CHAPTER 28

THE PARISH OF RERRICK

by the late REV. ALEXANDER H. CHRISTIE

General Features

The parish of Rerrick is a seaboard parish, bounded on its landward side by the parishes of Kirkcudbright, Kelton and Buittle, and having a coastline washed by the waters of the Solway Firth for a length of nine miles from Mullock Bay to Auchencairn Bay. The physical features of the parish are as described in previous Statistical Accounts. Suffice it to say that in the north, dominating the whole parish, stands Bengairn which attains to the dignity of a mountain, 1,200 feet high. On either side are lesser heights, Ben Tudor and Suie on the one hand, and on the other the cone-shaped hill of Screel, which is in the parish of Kelton. Within the amphitheatre of these hills, and beautifully situated at the head of a bay of the same name, lies the village of Auchencairn, where S. R. Crockett lived for some years, and which he has pictured as 'the little, bright, rose-bowered, garden-circled seaside village of Auchen-cairn'. The attractiveness of the Auchencairn neighbourhood has induced many to seek a restful holiday here in recent years; and in this connection it may be proper to observe that, owing to the social and economic factors of the times, the mansion-houses of Orchardton and Balcary—both in the vicinity of Auchencairn—are presently in use as guesthouses or holiday hotels. Four miles south of Auchencairn is the older village of Dundrennan, clustering about the ancient abbey of the same name.

A feature referred to in both earlier Statistical Accounts as adding 'grandeur to the scene' was the number of the vessels ('upwards of a hundred') that might be observed on the waters of the Solway at the same time, the farthest away 'as if dropping out of the clouds'. The grandeur of this scene is less in evidence now. The introduction of the railways into the south-west of Scotland, and the more recent develop-ment of road transport have put most of the little ports round the Galloway seaboard more or less out of business. There is little coastal traffic nowadays. Three ports in Rerrick have been declared by statute to be 'free' ports—Balcary, Portmary (or Burnfoot) and Mullock—but they serve no purpose now as ports, and there is no harbour at any of them.

Name

The parish is named Rerrick in the previous Statistical Accounts, but Rerwick was often used in the nineteenth century. This latter form is based on a belief that the name is of Scandinavian origin. Chalmers in his *Caledonia* (1824) was among the first to give public support to this belief, observing that 'Rerrick is an abbreviated pronunciation of Rerwick, which was derived from a *wick*, or creek, at this place'. The writer of the *New Statistical Account* brushed aside this derivation as unsatisfactory.

The earliest record of the name discovered by the present writer is that in the *Register of Archbishop John le Romeyn*, where in 1282 a certain Adam de Rerik is referred to as one of the clerks of the Bishop of Whithorn. A Gilbert Rerik was a member of parliament in 1467. Adam Cutlare, 'vicar of Radeik', witnesses a charter granted by the convent of Dundrennan in 1544. In the Exchequer Rolls, 1562, mention is made of the 'parochia de Rerik', and in the Great Seal, 1571-2, reference is made to Reddik, and again in 1592 to the 'church of Redyk'. The act of parliament dissolving Dundrennan Abbey, 1606, makes mention of the 'kirk of dundrenane alias ririk'. Whether any 'wick' is latent in the name or not, a careful examination of State records issued in recent times and of books of local history and other evidence reveals no case in which the name is spelled with a 'w' before the close of the eighteenth century, with perhaps the single exception of the *Minute Book of the War Committee of Kirkcudbright* (1640-1) where Rerwick occurs two or three times. The original minute book is not now available for examination, but when it is remembered that the minutes were not printed and published till 1855 (when Rerwick was often used) it is possible that by a copyist's error this form may have found its way into the printed minutes, which have also the forms Rerik, Rerrik and Rerrick. In Church and State documents Rerrick is the form now in use, though Rerwick as the name of the parish has once again reappeared in the *Report of the Ancient Monuments Commission*, 1914, and in Sir Herbert E. Maxwell's *Place-Names of Galloway*, 1930.

Dundrennan, Monkton, and Munkland have also at times been in use as names for the parish, all of course deriving from the great religious house founded therein. They were probably popular designations, though it is worthy of note that on the sacramental cups still in use in the parish church there is this inscription—'This and another Communion Cup given by David Currie of Newlaw, one of the Heritors, to the parish of Rerick or Munkland, 1759'

Antiquities

The parish is rich in antiquities. These are carefully described in *The Royal Commission on The Ancient and Historical Monuments and Constructions of Scotland: Fifth Report and Inventory of Monuments and Constructions in Galloway. Vol. II—Stewartry of Kirkcudbright.* 1914 (pp. 228-42). Of forts or encampments, of which there are several kinds, the commissioners have identified no fewer than twenty sites, as large a number as in any other parish of the Stewartry. In the earlier Statistical Accounts reference is made to two Druidical circles. The commissioners make no mention of anything under such a name. What was in the mind of the earlier writers may have been certain cup-and-ring marked rock-surfaces, of which a good specimen is on Newlaw hill, and a less clearly defined group at Linkens. Perhaps notice should be taken here of what is not mentioned in the report, St. Glassen's Well, still in a good state of preservation and in regular use. St. Glassen (called also Glascianus and Makglastiane), whose date is put at 830, is described as a bishop and confessor of the early church. Perhaps it was the existence of this 'holy well' which prompted the building of a chapel at Kirkland, about 150 yards away, which subsequently served as the parish church for many years. Mention may also be made of the fact (unnoticed in the Commission's report) that there are on the Ordnance Survey map two localities marked 'Old Man', a name not infrequent in British topography. Whatever antiquarian interest they may have, nothing remains to mark the sites.

The chief object of historical interest in the parish is Dundrennan Abbey, now in the care of H.M. Office of Works, which has given a great deal of time and labour to the preservation of the ruins from further deterioration. In the process of work in the Chapter House in 1912 five grave-slabs of abbots of whose existence there was no previous record were recovered. The care with which the work has been done, and the well-trimmed lawns that now carpet the floor of the church and cloister-garth, add much interest and pleasure to visits paid to the ruins. The *Fifth Report of the Commission on Ancient and Historical Monuments* (1914) gives a very detailed account of the architectural features of the buildings, and a description of the surviving memorials, of which there is a goodly number. In the same year in which the Commission's Report was issued, the present writer published a new history of Dundrennan Abbey in which as much use as possible was made of facts recently brought to light in Calendars of State Papers and other official documents.[1]

For over four centuries the abbey dominated the parish. Nearly all lands within the parish passed into the possession of the monastery. Dundrennan was founded in 1142, the third of thirteen monasteries in Scotland belonging to the Cistercian Order. But it must have been one of the wealthiest of them, for when, in accordance with an Act of the Lords of Council (1545-6) the monasteries of the country were required to support the College of Justice according to the rate of taxation of their fruits, Dundrennan stood second highest in the list of Cistercian houses with its quota of £21 per annum, being exceeded only by Melrose.

The long history of the Abbey came to a close with its formal suppression by Act of Parliament in 1606, when what remained of its vast estate was erected into a temporal lordship and conferred on John Murray, a favourite of the King, who had already been appointed commendator of the Abbey, and was subsequently created Earl of

(1) A. H. Christie, *The Abbey of Dundrennan*, 1914.

Annandale. There is no reason to believe that Dundrennan suffered violence at the time of the Reformation (1560), for Leslie in his *Historie of Scotland* refers in 1578 to Dundrennan and certain other religious houses, that "standis zit haill'. As the monks left and disappeared, the buildings appear to have been allowed to fall into ruin, and eventually to serve the purpose of a quarry.

Population

In 1801 the population figure was 1,166. In the next fifty years it steadily rose to 1,725. A further increase was revealed in the census of 1871 when 1,911 was the number recorded. After that there came a gradual decline, and since 1901 it has been more or less about 1,300. The actual figure for 1931 was 1,228. The high figure of 1,911 reached in 1871 is partly accounted for by the fact that at that time there was a considerable amount of tree-felling being undertaken in the Auchencairn district, and the presence of wood-cutters, with wives and families, helped to augment the population. At the moment of writing (1950) the population is certain to be very considerably less than in 1931,[1] for a very wide area on the Dundrennan side of the parish was requisitioned in the late war for use by the military authorities, and from that area the entire community, comprising some fifty households, was evacuated.[2] There has been no return of this population. The evacuation has prejudicially affected all statistics of the Dundrennan area, and has resulted in a reduction of membership in church, school, and other organisations.

So far as the pedigree of the population is concerned, it may be said that the great majority are of Galloway stock. It is not easy to state in numbers how many were born in the parish, and how many without. A hundred years ago people moved little from their native place, but in the early half of this century there was a good deal of shifting of farm servants from one parish to another. On the other hand, several employees in recent years have been made the recipients of the Highland Society's long-service medals for having continued fifty or twenty-five years in service at the same farms.

Properties and Housing

The parish covers an area of 21,700 acres. After the dissolution of the Abbey, the monastery lands passed into the hands of individual owners. The *New Statistical Account* lists 27 land-owners. It is significant of the extensive changes during last century in the possession of

(1) The 1951 census revealed that the population had in fact fallen to 1,006.
(2) The wide area referred to, which was requisitioned by the military authorities during the war, has been retained by the War Office as a permanent tank range. It serves a twofold purpose. Five or six tank units attend camp here during the summer months to undergo annual training and local units have the use of the range for week-end tank-gun practice. In addition, the Ministry of Supply, by arrangement with the War Office, maintain an establishment of technicians who are engaged in research and testing tank equipment.

land that only one name in that list remains to indicate the continuance of the same family in possession of the old property. Largely owing to the heavy burden of taxation occasioned by war, the imposition of death duties and demands made for the furthering of schemes of social service, many proprietors in recent years have found it necessary to part with lands, more especially if they were not resident proprietors. Not only have properties changed hands, but large estates in all parts of the parish have been broken up. The tenants of farms were given the option of purchase, and most accepted the offer, so a large proportion of the land-owners now are farmers who are the owner-occupiers of their farms.

Most of the farm-houses are of fair size and good character, and through the operation of recent Rural Housing Acts much has been done in the way of reconditioning and improving the houses of cottagers. A survey undertaken by the county council of all houses within the county listed those that were below a certain standard for habitable occupation. These were 'condemned', and, if not adequately repaired, they remained untenanted. Thus, it may be taken for granted that all occupied houses are in a fairly good condition. At Auchencairn the county council has in recent years erected twelve new houses, and in Dundrennan, four. The total number of occupied houses in the parish is at present 280, but this number excludes all the houses in the area requisitioned by the War Department, which are now mostly uninhabitable. Many of the villagers are owners of the houses they occupy.

Industry

Farming remains the chief industry of the parish. The hill pastures are largely given over to the grazing of store-cattle and of sheep of the blackface breed, but at lower levels agriculture in all its branches is carried on at a high stage of development. Much land is brought under the plough and produces the usual rotation of crops in this district. The grain crop consists almost entirely of oats. Dairying is extensively followed, and some farms carry herds of dairy cattle to the number of 70 or 80. The Ayrshire breed of cattle is almost universally found in the parish dairies. In addition to the blackface sheep on the hill farms, most farms at lower levels carry their quota of sheep, these comprising in recent years Border Leicesters, Cheviots and Crossbreds. Store cattle are also fattened for the market. The chief auction mart for the district is at Castle-Douglas.

A hundred years ago agriculture, properly so called, was said to be not extending, and many of the finest farms were laid down in permanent grass. Black cattle were the 'staple commodity' by which the farmer paid his rent and made his living. Things are very different now, and the old native black cattle are less often seen. Horse-ploughs still do some service, but the tractor-plough is in general use. For the ingathering of the harvest two or three farmers have their own combine-harvesters, and others contract to have the work done by combines.

Rerrick farmers have often been well to the fore in matters agricultural. John McDowall of Girdstingwood, who early succeeded his uncle in possession of the property, and who for fifty years took a most prominent part in all parish business, was a noted flockmaster. For many years in succession Girdstingwood sheep won premier honours at the show of the National Fat-Stock Association in Edinburgh, and also at the Smithfield Show, London, Mr. McDowall won championship awards. For these successes a meed of praise is rightly due to his shepherd, William Henry, who served his master faithfully for over fifty years. Andrew Mitchell, who at the commencement of this century had a splendid herd of Ayrshire cattle at Barcheskie, did a large business as an exporter of the breed, and received commissions from several foreign governments for the supply of Ayrshires with a view to improving the character of foreign stocks. These he sent to Finland, Sweden, Canada, the United States, South Africa and Australia, and even to Japan. Quite a number of the younger members of the Rerrick community had a four months' journey to Japan and back with consignments of cattle for that country. At the opening of the century Castlecreavie farm was occupied by Stewart Nicholson, to whom belongs the distinction of having invented the first milking-machine for use in dairies. As far back as 1891 he had been awarded medals for his invention when exhibited at the Highland and Royal Society shows.

Other Industries
A century ago an iron-ore mine was operating at Auchinleck, and a mine of copper ore was wrought on Heston Island. Both have been long closed. Barytes has been mined at Barlocco even within recent years, but spasmodically and to a very limited extent.

Local Government
Since the passing of the Local Government (Scotland) Act, 1929, nearly all matters of local government are now the concern of the county council, to which Rerrick has the right of electing one member. Subsidiary to it there is a district council which exercises some small supervision of parochial affairs, and to this council Rerrick elects a member, the representative on the county council being also a member.

Schools
There are two schools in the parish—that at Auchencairn has 48 pupils on the roll, and that at Dundrennan 50. In these schools education is provided for children up to 12 years of age, and children between 12 and 15, the present leaving age, are conveyed at the public expense by motor bus or other means to the senior secondary school (the Academy) at Kirkcudbright. Some continue their studies to a later age. It is noteworthy that in 1873, after the passing of the Education Act of 1872 and the election of the first school board, the number of pupils in attendance at Auchencairn was 232, and at Dundrennan 172. That

was the time when the parish had reached its highest level of population, when families were larger than they are at present, and when all children of school age attended the local schools. The education rate imposed by the first school board was 3d in the £.

While directly the concern of the County Council Education Committee, the schools come within the province of a sub-committee which exercises supervision in certain matters; and a recently formed voluntary Parent-Teacher Association seeks to awaken a greater interest among parents in the work, and enables them to do something to contribute to the attractiveness of school amenities, not otherwise provided for. Thus, this year the Dundrennan school children had the advantage of a motor bus trip to the English Lake District.

Health Services

There is no resident doctor in the parish, but doctors visit from Kirkcudbright and Castle-Douglas. Very efficient cottage-hospitals (to whose support Rerrick contributed annually) were voluntarily maintained for many years in these towns, but they are now incorporated in the National Health Service. The same is true of the Rerrick Nursing Association, an institution which gave much-appreciated service for a period of about twenty years. Practically all the parishioners share in the benefits now guaranteed under the Health Service. Under the Education Committee the school children receive periodic examination at the hands of school doctors and dentists and are provided with a mid-day meal at a small charge.

Both the villages of Auchencairn and Dundrennan are provided with a public drainage system, and a public water supply, and a scavenging scheme is also in operation. The parishioners in general enjoy very good health, and there has been no serious epidemic for many years.

Fuel, Light and Power

There is no coal wrought in the parish. When the *Old Statistical Account* was written great hopes were being entertained of the discovery of coal. They came to nothing. In some places peat is still used as fuel, but it is rapidly passing out of use. While coal remains the chief source of obtaining heat and power, it has in recent years been meeting with rivalry, which will certainly increase. When about twenty years ago the Galloway Hydro-Electric Scheme began to function, the County Council of the Stewartry of Kirkcudbright were given the option of becoming distributors within the area of the county. They accepted that option, and immediately set themselves to the task of supplying electricity to the Stewartry. A main transmission line enters the parish about Overlaw, and continues through Dundrennan past Kirkcarswell and Culnaightrie, and after passing through Auchencairn leaves the parish in the direction of Dalbeattie. Nearly all houses within reasonable distance of this line have the benefit of electric power and light. The streets of Auchencairn and Dundrennan are illuminated from electric lamps.   From the main transmission line branch lines carry the current farther afield, and, among other uses, it is made available for the operation of milking machines in dairies.   Rerrick is now within the sphere of the South-West Scotland Electricity Board.

Public Assistance

There is practically no unemployment in the parish, and thus very little actual poverty.   In recent years only three or four names have appeared on the roll of those in receipt of public assistance.   The old age pension is a help to those in advanced years, and sickness and maternity benefits secured under the National Health Service are of aid in times of special necessity.   Though the cost of living is at present high, undoubtedly the position of the agricultural labourer has been much improved through increased minimum wages secured to him by authority of Agricultural Wages Boards.

Roads and Transport

The roads of the parish are the care of the Roads Committee of the county council.   The main classified roads, well-surfaced and rolled, are in first-class condition.   Secondary roads are also kept in good state. Only private or semi-private roads in some outlying regions are in a condition that calls for improvement.

No railway runs through the parish.   The nearest railway stations are at Kirkcudbright (seven miles from Dundrennan) and at Castle-Douglas and Dalbeattie (each about eight miles from Auchencairn).   A daily bus service (not too frequent) is maintained between Kirkcudbright and Dumfries, passing through Dundrennan and Auchencairn *en route*. There are bus services from Auchencairn to Castle-Douglas and Dalbeattie, and motor-hiring is also available at Auchencairn.   Many possess their own motor cars, and bicycles are in common use.

Ecclesiastical Affairs

The parish church of Rerrick was early 'appropriated' to the Abbey of Dundrennan.   Either the monks themselves may have served at its altar, or they may have supported a priest or vicar to minister to the religious needs of the community.   Indeed, one name—and only one name— survives of any pre-Reformation priest of the parish, 'Adam Cutlare, vicar of Radeik' (Rerrick) who in 1544 witnesses a charter granted by the abbot and convent.   No one can say where that old parish church stood.   It has been asserted that when it became ruinous, the abbey church was used as the parish church.   It may have been so, but there is no evidence in support of the statement.   But at Kirkland there was a chapel which seems to have served the purpose of a parish church in the latter part of the seventeenth century.   This church, undergoing reconstruction and addition from time to time, continued in existence as the parish church till 1865, when it was taken down and a new church of Rerrick was erected in the village of Dundrennan.   On its completion the kirk session expressed the congregation's indebtedness to the heritors, and especially to Ivie Mackie of Auchencairn and John McDowall of Girdstingwood whose contributions towards its erection were much in excess of what was legally required of them. In 1938 a handsome clock, the gift of William Fisher, Newark, a native of the parish, was installed in the church tower.

The old church at Kirkland was somewhat inconveniently located for the parishioners. It was a mile to the east of Dundrennan, and some four miles from an increasing community around Auchencairn. Indeed, for the greater convenience of parishioners in that part of the parish, it had already been found necessary to institute regular religious services at Auchencairn, and a resident missionary had been located there. More than that, mainly through the liberality of David Welsh of Collin and Miss Culton of Auchnabony, a church was built there in 1855. Finally, by decree of the Court of Teinds on 11 June 1856, this northern half of the old parish of Rerrick was erected into the parish of Auchencairn, with full and separate ecclesiastical jurisdiction. The beautiful stained-glass window in the south wall of Auchencairn church is in memory of John Gladstone Mackie of Auchencairn, and is the gift of his widow.

Meanwhile another factor had introduced a change into the ecclesiastical situation in the parish. After the Disruption of 1843 a body of Rerrick parishioners threw in their lot with the newly-constituted Free Church, and with commendable zeal they built for themselves a church at Auchencairn. For something like eighty years these two congregations in Auchencairn maintained a separate existence. But happily, all separation and division are now at an end. The long-sundered branches of the Presbyterian Church in Scotland united in 1929 to form one great Church of Scotland, and in 1932 the two congregations at Auchencairn were harmoniously united as one congregation under the ministry of the Rev. Walter R. Henderson, who had served as minister of the parish of Auchencairn since 1900.

Auchencairn Church has a membership roll of 270, but Rerrick Church roll has been most grievously affected by the evacuation of population on the Dundrennan side of the parish, and numbers only 165 at present. Sunday schools and Bible classes have been carried on, the latter perhaps with some difficulty. In each congregation there is a vigorous branch of the Woman's Guild of the Church of Scotland. Both congregations, through the holding of sales of work and other means, make very generous contributions to the support of the general work of the Church at home and abroad. The great majority of the parishioners is attached to one or other of the churches in the parish. They are careful in the observances of religion, and, if church attendance might be better, there is nothing approaching hostility towards religion.

As the old church of the parish, Rerrick is endowed from the ancient teinds pertaining to the parish. The standardised value of the teinds is

£515. In addition there is a glebe of 16 acres. Auchencairn is supported by modern endowments, which it has received at various times since its erection into a parish in 1856, by the generous and voluntary contributions of its members, and to some little extent out of general church funds. The stipend attached to it is £450.

Parochial Records

The minute books of the Kirk Session of Rerrick are in the custody of the minister at Rerrick Manse. They date from 18 December 1751, and there are very few blanks. The minute books of the Kirk Session of Auchencairn are in the custody of the minister at Auchencairn Manse. They date from the origin of the two churches (now united) in the middle of last century. The minute book of the heritors of Rerrick was retained in the office of Messrs. Lidderdale and Gillespie, Solicitors, Castle-Douglas, after the heritors had fulfilled their final responsibility for upkeep of the ecclesiastical subjects in accordance with the provisions of the Church (Property and Endowments) Act, 1925. Mr. Gillespie acted as treasurer to the heritors. The books of the former school board and of the former parish council are now in the custody of the clerk to the county council.

Community Life

While the old parish of Rerrick still remains the unit for all matters of civil government, it is right to observe that since the middle of last century there have been really two separate communities in the parish. one converging on Dundrennan and the other on Auchencairn. They have much in common of course, yet each lives its own life. Full account has to be taken of this fact.

Two handsome war memorials, commemorating the fallen in the two world wars, have been erected at Dundrennan, and at Auchencairn. Each of the villages possesses a post office. The telephone is found in a number of homes, and public telephone call-boxes are installed for general use. In each of the villages there is a hotel. In each there are grocery businesses, and in Auchencairn there is a bakery as well; but supplies of groceries, bread and butcher-meat are delivered through the parish by means of vans from neighbouring towns. At Dundrennan a joiner and a mason are in business, while at Auchencairn there are two joiners, a mason and a bootmaker. Salmon-fishing is carried on in the bays of Balcary and Auchencairn. The blacksmith's occupation is on the decline in rural districts. Where some years ago four or five separate businesses gave regular service, now only one family of smiths is resident in the parish.

Into many homes some daily newspaper is received, and into practically all there enters one or other of the local weekly papers. Wireless sets are common, and the B.B.C. news bulletins keep the people well informed. The Heughan Institute in Auchencairn—the benefaction of a native of the village—houses a reading room and library. The

J. Roman Rock, Edinburgh

Plate 10. **KIRKCUDBRIGHT ACADEMY**
Modernised 1958.

Adam Anderson, Castle-Douglas

Plate 11. THE STEWARTRY PROVINCE BONSPIEL
Curling for the Queenshill Cup on Carlingwark Loch.

Galloway News

Plate 12. SANDGREEN
A popular Solway shore.

Education Committee does a good service in providing a selection of books from the County Library for the schools. These are read not only by the children, but by adults in their homes. Both in Auchencairn and Dundrennan there are vigorous branches of the Women's Rural Institute. These by their monthly meetings have not only done much to brighten the lives of the women of the parish, but by competition which they encourage they are fostering an interest in the cultivation of arts and crafts. Not only so, but at open meetings to which all are made welcome they present plays, concerts, lectures, and other forms of entertainment for the community. As in all country districts dancing is very popular, as is also the whist drive; and when support is required for some local or charitable object generally one or other or both of these forms of entertainment is arranged. In Dundrennan there is a public hall, and in Auchencairn the Murray hall is available for general use. The parishioners have their political opinions or affinities, of course, but politics do not come too prominently to the front. Political meetings are infrequent, and political associations usually come to life only with the approach of each general election. Rerrick is in the constituency of Galloway, which for over 19 years has been represented in Parliament by Mr. J. H. Mackie of Auchencairn as a member of the Conservative Party. For many years a Horticultural Society existed in Rerrick, but recently it has come to an end. Not only for the residents but for visitors who sojourn there, Auchencairn has the advantage of possessing tennis courts and a bowling green. At Auchencairn a Community Council has leased a recreation field where football can be played, and where there is room for a children's playground. Other forms of amusement followed in the parish are carpet bowling, badminton, curling and quoiting.

There is much less monotony and drabness in rural districts than there used to be. People have a higher standard of living, and enjoy a fuller life. If a spirit of restlessness and a love of excitement are characteristic of this age, it is no wonder if some in our midst are caught up in the swirl, or that football-pool betting should have found a way in, with its insidious appeal for some whose hope it is to 'get rich quick'. On the other hand, owing to an improved standard of conduct not less than to the present high price of alcoholic liquors, drunkenness is very little in evidence and serious crime is hardly known. In spite of two world wars the people are well clad, and give evidence of an increased measure of material comfort. Taken all in all, our parishioners are a friendly and kindly-disposed people; they are happy in that they have work to do, and are diligent in the doing of it, and they are able to use such spare time as is theirs in ways that can promote both personal and social well-being.

1950

T

CHAPTER 29

THE PARISH OF TERREGLES

by J. M. HUTCHESON

Name

The name of the parish most probably derives from *treamhar eglais* (Gaelic), not, as suggested in the previous Statistical Accounts, from Latin *terra ecclesiae* or French *terre d'église,* though the meaning is in all cases the same—church farm—the territory of a chapel of ease. Compare the spelling of the name in a charter of David II, 1359, *Travereglis* and *Traveregliss.* The parish was originally within the bounds of the ecclesiastical establishment of Lincluden.

Extent, Boundaries and Natural Features

Terregles is 3.56 miles long on a line running approximately W.S.W. and E.N.E. through the manse, and the maximum breadth through the same point is 1.87 miles. The area is approximately 2,015 acres. The gross annual value at 15 May 1950 was £3,446 0s 8d and the rateable value at the same date £1,073 10s.

The boundaries are: on the north, part of the burgh of Dumfries and the parish of Irongray; on the east, Dumfries and Troqueer parish; to the south, Troqueer and Lochrutton; and on the west Irongray and Lochrutton. The western part of the parish is hilly and commands extensive views of the Nith valley and over the Solway Firth to the Cumberland hills. The general slope is from west to east. The only river is the Cargen, which forms part of the southern boundary and enters the Nith below Dumfries.

Agriculture

The land is largely sand and loam, the former predominating in the east end of the parish. The crops are the usual for this part of Scotland —oats, potatoes, turnips and hay. The mainstay of the farming community is dairy farming, most of the product being absorbed by the Carnation Milk factory at Lincluden. Four of the small holdings are registered poultry-breeding stations, with a good trade in day-old chicks, and there is a small but flourishing industry of market gardening, Dumfries taking the produce.

The number of farms of all types, including small holdings, is 89, ranging in extent from $1\frac{1}{2}$ acres to 193 acres. The area of tillage at the agricultural census of June 1951 was 837 acres, of grasses 2,044 acres, and of rough grazing $83\frac{1}{2}$ acres. It will be noted that there is a discrepancy between the total of these figures and the previously-given area of the parish; this is explained by the fact that the agricultural figures include about 900 acres now in the burgh of Dumfries, but still owned by the Department of Agriculture and included in their records for their Terregles estate.

Territorial Changes

During the past century there have been two outstanding changes in Terregles: its conversion, almost entirely, into small holdings; and the important reduction of its extent through the acquisition by the burgh of Dumfries of nearly half its area for future housing development.

Until after the first world war, the principal proprietors in the parish were the Herries-Maxwell family of Terregles, descendants of the ancient house of Nithsdale, though some minor properties were held by other owners. From about 1898 the Terregles House property and the immediate policies were leased to C. E. Galbraith. After the war, in 1920, the then Board (now Department) of Agriculture for Scotland bought the entire Terregles estate, together with several smaller estates, leaving as independent units the farms of Kirkland and Halmyre and the small estates of Terreglestown, Woodlands and Newton. The last two are now in the Dumfries area. In 1921 the Board divided their acquisition into small holdings for the resettlement of ex-servicemen. Terregles House and policies were sold to Mr. James Glenachan, who farms the land, though it was originally intended that this should be developed as an agricultural college. The extensive stabling of Terregles House was utilised for a short period after 1921 by a private company as a bacon factory, but this soon proved unprofitable. Under the Land Settlement (Scotland) Act of 1919 the Department provides the land for these small holdings, and grants a loan for buildings and improvements, only the latter becoming the property of the holder, who, however, has certain rights as to succession.

The division of the parish, which cut off most of its north-eastern part, took place by agreement between the Stewartry County Council and the Town Council of Dumfries, and was delimited by decision of the Sheriff of Dumfries and Galloway—not without protest. It took effect on 16 May 1948. The original ecclesiastical parish of Terregles persisted until June 1952 when the disjoined portion became the new area of Lincluden, for which a church is in course of construction.

Transport

There is one main road through Terregles, running roughly westward from Maxwelltown to Shawhead village in Irongray. Though so close to Dumfries, Terregles is singularly poor in public transport. On the Dumfries-Terregles-Shawhead road a bus operates on two days weekly, and on two evenings for the convenience of visitors to the Grove Hospital in Irongray. Several attempts to obtain an improvement in the service have failed, perhaps owing to the spread of the population, which is sparse to the west of Terregles. Modern conditions too, such as the use of cars and bicycles, have operated against the financial success of an increased bus service.

Water Supply, Lighting, Sanitation

The water supply is a property of the Department of Agriculture, and has its origins in the hills at the western end of the parish. By recent arrangement with Dumfries Town Council this is augmented, when local reservoirs are low, by the town's supply. In 1951 a large storage tank of 1¾ million gallons capacity was erected on the rising ground to the west. Fed from Glenkiln reservoir in Irongray, it is at present in use for the supply of water to the Imperial Chemical Industries factory at Drungans, in the parish of Troqueer. Electricity is in common use for lighting and heating in the area. Sewerage is mainly by septic tanks, the overflow draining towards the tributary burns of the Cargen. Refuse is collected weekly wherever practicable under county council arrangements.

Population

The population has remained fairly stable in numbers during the last century and a half. In spite of the nation-wide drift of the rural population towards urban districts, Terregles has, probably because of the steadying influence of its proximity to Dumfries, been able to resist this trend: this point is discussed later. The establishment of the small holdings, too, has meant a brisk upward movement in the numbers. The figures since the beginning of the last century are as follows:

1801	—	510
1821	—	651
1851	—	566
1901	—	454
1911	—	439
1921	—	428
1931	—	567
1951	—	448

The alteration to the parish boundary during the last intercensal period has, of course, affected the latest figures.

Historical Records and Monuments

Local records—principally those of the kirk session, which are in the custody of the session clerk and go back to 1714—are fairly comprehensive, but do not show a wide picture of the life of the parish, being largely concerned with the administration of 'discipline' by that body. Latterly, of course, with the creation of school boards and parish councils, kirk sessions were shorn of most of their influence over education and social service. The heritors' records are kept in the Register House, Edinburgh.

The principal monument in Terregles listed by the Ancient and Historical Monuments Commission, the Priory or College of Lincluden, has now passed into the Dumfries area and is thus removed from our

purview.   In the Kirkcudbrightshire volume of the Commission's cata-
logue there are noted in Terregles the following:

No. 432: Terregles 'Queir', originally attached to the nave of Terregles Church,
latterly a mortuary chapel of the Herries-Maxwell family.   With the
disappearance of this family from the district it is improbable that
there will be any further burials here.   The building is perhaps unique
in that a building of Roman Catholic use is at the same time joined
to a Presbyterian place of worship.
No. 434: Moat (supposed): Collochan Castle.   On the north side of Cargen
Water, quarter of a mile above Glen Mill.
No. 435: Fort, Beacon Hill, the highest point in the parish: now enclosed by
plantation.
No. 436: Lady Chapel Knowe and Well: since suggested to have a moat and
bailey—perhaps a hunting seat.
No. 438: Village Site: near Terreglestown House.

Church

There is one church in the parish—Terregles Church of Scotland—
rebuilt in 1814 on the site of a much older edifice.   It is situated, like
the school, near the geographical centre of the area.   The communion
roll contains 180 names, but attendance at the ordinary services is poor.
The manse, at some distance from the church, is substantial and commodious.   Both of these buildings are in good repair, thanks to the
vigilance of the kirk session.   Contrary to the report contained in the
New Statistical Account, the church is now dry, comfortable and well
furnished, with a finely timbered roof erected by local craftsmen.   It
contains a beautiful memorial window installed in memory of the parish
dead in the second world war by Terregles Social Service Committee.

Education

There is one school, placed close to the church.   The roll at present
fluctuates between 35 and 45, and there are two teachers.   Before the
recent war the school had three teachers, the roll being well over 60,
but rural depopulation and centralised education have had their effect
here as elsewhere.   The school now takes children to the end of the
primary stage only; thereafter, they proceed to secondary schools in
Dumfries, or to the only such school in the eastern part of the Stewartry
—that at New Abbey.

The only local endowment, the Nicholson Trust, is an educational
one, having been founded in 1849 to provide assistance in higher
education, principally for local students in Divinity.   Little use has been
made of this benefaction.

Housing

Apart from the houses—mostly constructed before 1860—existing before
the establishment of the small holdings and tenanted largely by tied
workers and employees, most dwellings in the parish were erected on
the holdings about 1921.   Some existing farm-houses were converted
into two homes, between two holdings.   Shortly before the last war the
local authority erected six houses near the centre of the parish (two for

roadmen), and in 1950 a block of four steel houses was erected under the scheme for the housing of agricultural workers. A beginning has been made with the building of a further 14 houses near the school, under county council auspices.

It is noteworthy that the number of new houses erected to date has been more than offset by the number demolished or allowed to become ruinous. There is much overcrowding. Lack of accommodation has caused many young people, on marriage, to move into rooms in Dumfries or elsewhere and this is likely to have potent influence on the age distribution of the population and on social life.

All the houses are good of their kind, with modern requirements as to water supply and sanitation, but many of the small-holding residences are small and ill-planned. They are all provided with gardens, but local authority houses are let at rentals which are high for the means of their tenants.

Health Services

Health services in the combined parishes of Terregles, Irongray, Troqueer and Lochrutton are in the care of a district nurse, under the jurisdiction of the County Medical Officer of Health. There is no doctor resident in Terregles, and Dumfries doctors are called on when required.

Voluntary Social Services

Terregles Youth Club meets in the school and has maintained a some-what precarious existence for about five years. Women's interests are adequately catered for by a branch of the Women's Rural Institutes—membership 60—and the Church of Scotland Woman's Guild, whose membership is small. Carpet bowling, a popular pastime in southern Scotland, and formerly a recreation with an enthusiastic following among the men of Terregles, has now fallen on evil days, and nothing has replaced it as a leisure activity for the male part of the population. Football, of a somewhat desultory nature, is popular with the younger men, and there is a good parish playing field, the property of the Eastern District Council. A flourishing badminton club operates during the winter months.

Two public halls provide ample accommodation for the social life of the parish. The larger of these, a fine brick, stone and timber structure, was given by the widow of the last laird of Terregles; it is administered by a body of local trustees. The other hall, smaller but sufficiently commodious, is situated near Maxwelltown Station, and was erected by the efforts of the small-holders at that—the eastern—end of the parish.

Political activity is almost completely confined to election periods, though a small Conservative Association carries on a quiet but continuous life.

Terregles Social Service Committee, already mentioned, is an organisation composed of the Civil Defence personnel of the parish from 1939 to 1945, who retained their entity as a group functioning in a broad manner for the good of the parish.

On the introduction of the National Health Service and the disappearance of the former voluntary parish nursing associations, a share of the existing funds was allotted to Terregles, and forms Terregles Benevolent Fund. This is administered by a popularly-elected committee to supplement informally and unofficially National Health Service benefits by providing additional comforts for the sick and aged and to aid cases of hardship not covered by official schemes.

The Way of Life

As has been said, small-holders and their families comprise the majority of the inhabitants of Terregles, but the work available to the parishioners is not confined to farming in its various branches. Several of the small-holders undertake additional work in or about Dumfries, such as agencies of various kinds. The Imperial Chemical Industries factory, already referred to, provides employment for an increasing number. There are two sawmills in the centre of the parish, one owned by a Larbert firm of timber merchants and drawing its raw materials from a wide area. The other is owned by the Department of Agriculture. It provides timber requisites, such as fencing, for the Department's small-holding settlements over the whole of south-western Scotland as far north as Cardross on the Clyde, and has extensive nurseries of young conifers for the afforestation practised by the Department. Each of these mills employs from eight to twelve men.

The majority of the younger people are employed in Dumfries itself, in shops, offices, mills and workshops. Thus the way of life in Terregles has been, to a very appreciable extent, conditioned by the proximity of Dumfries. Recreation, with the modern taste for dancing and the cinema, is amply catered for there, though local dances are well patronised by parishioners and are even popular among the townspeople. In this respect there has been a marked change in the relationships of family life in that the adolescent normally goes outside his home for his amusements. This has led to a deterioration of community spirit, a trend aggravated over the last 30 years by the influx from diverse parts of the country of small-holders who have no roots in the parish. It is true to say that such parochial consciousness as exists is fostered, and that to a limited degree, by the social organisations already mentioned. It will be noted from the nature of these that there is no wide-spread interest in intellectual pursuits, though individuals so inclined can cultivate such tastes in the excellent extra-mural classes held in Dumfries. Remoter parts of the Stewartry, under the compulsion of their isolation, have an advantage in being faced with the need of supplying their own communal requirements, but the factors outlined—

and perhaps of these the shortage of houses is paramount—have militated against a strong parish loyalty in Terregles. The tastes acquired during their post-primary education in Dumfries tend to make the younger people urban-minded, and it is doubtful whether, when the present generation of small-holders has passed away, their obligations to the land will, in many cases, be assumed by their children; alien hands will speed the local plough.

For the future, the prospects of prosperity, apart from the continuing industry of the farm, would appear to depend on the measure of employment offered by Dumfries, and its industries: and here the outlook is bright. Terregles tends more and more towards becoming a dormitory suburb of the town, though in a thoroughly rural setting. It is perhaps a good thing that this should be, even though it may mean nothing less than a peaceful revolution in spirit for the parishioners.

1952

CHAPTER 30

THE PARISH OF TONGLAND

by the REV. GEORGE TUTON

General Features

Tongland is a beautiful parish rich in all the unspoiled grandeur that nature can bestow, hills and valleys, burns and moorlands, rivers and glens. It is very near to the historic little town of Kirkcudbright, and but a few miles from the pleasant and prosperous market town of Castle-Douglas, while the main road from Dumfries to Newton Stewart runs through it. The manse is exactly 26 miles from each of these towns and this main road is the direct way from Portpatrick to London.

The parish has two rivers, the Dee and the Tarff, with excellent fishing. In winter a loch is artificially made on Meiklewood farm for the use of the local curling club and skating enthusiasts. One curiosity may be mentioned—a little loch on Meiklewood which is almost at the top of the hill and has no higher hills to feed it, yet has always an abundant supply of pure water, which must come by a subterranean passage from a distance of many miles.

The people are a happy, kindly, neighbourly class among whom it is a great joy to live and labour; no one could ever wish for better. There are no poor, and should anyone ever be in want, there are many who are ready and willing to assist and bring relief. There is not an unemployed person in the parish, and beggars and tramps are few and far between. The children are bright and happy, well clad and nourished, their gay smiles and cheerful greetings like the fragrant breath of a sweet summer morning.

The general health of the people is excellent, epidemics are unknown, there is very little tuberculosis and only three people suffer from chronic rheumatism.

Hydro-Electric Scheme

Tongland Electric Power Station plays an important part in the Galloway Hydro-Electric Scheme. The Galloway Water Power Company was incorporated under the Galloway Water Power Act, 1929, for the purpose of developing water power on the River Dee and its tributaries in the Stewartry of Kirkcudbright. It had long been known that small amounts of water power could be developed in the valley of the Dee and a station developing 400 h.p. for industrial purposes was installed at Tongland in the middle of the war period but it was not until 1923 that a scheme of public utility first came under consideration. At that time a small project was suggested by two Stewartry gentlemen, the late Major Wellwood Maxwell, then Convener of Kirkcudbright County Council, and Captain Scott Elliot, who consulted the late Colonel McLellan, a native of Dalbeattie, and a partner in a firm of consulting engineers. When the advice was given it was found that a far greater volume of power could be generated than could be absorbed in the Stewartry. This led to the development of a scheme involving the use of water for generating power from five reservoirs at different levels, the lowest, Tongland, being in this parish.

The Tongland aqueduct is constructed of reinforced concrete and is 3,335 feet long by 19 feet average diameter. The company has built three new houses at Tongland and three on the opposite side of the river Dee, and owns nine houses in the parish of Tongland. The whole scheme cost over £3,000,000 inclusive of all charges. As a result of the nationalisation of the generation of electricity, which took effect on 1 April 1948, the Galloway Scheme became nationalised and the control was transferred to the British Electricity Authority. It is of interest to note that, under the Galloway Water Power Act, the Board of Trade had the right to purchase the undertaking any time after the beginning of the year 2004.

The Dee is a salmon river and with the advent of the Galloway Power Scheme fish passes, or ladders, have been constructed at Tongland and other dams to enable the fish to make their way upstream. Tongland pass has to climb 70 feet in order to connect the river below the Dam with the reservoir above it. It consists of 35 pools, of which four are large resting pools. Each pool is connected to the next by a submerged orifice through which the water descends and the fish swim up. The pass is the highest in the British Isles and it has proved remarkably successful in practice, some 60 fish having been counted in the pass at one time when it has been closed at both ends for inspection.

Forty-eight people are employed at the power station, most of whom reside outwith the parish.

Religion

There are two churches in the parish, the congregations of which were united in 1932. Tongland, the original parish church, was built on the site of Tongland Abbey, founded in the twelfth century by Fergus, Lord of Galloway. There is only a very small part of the abbey, a doorway, now standing. The fabric was, for many years, looked upon as nothing more than a quarry from which stones were taken to build houses in the surrounding district and even used at times for dry stone dykes. That abbey doorway was built into a poor little church, the ruin of which is still standing.

Tarff Valley Church, formerly Tongland and Twynholm Free Church, and later the United Free Church, was built at the time of the Disruption in 1843. The people who came out from Tongland and Twynholm churches founded a new congregation and worshipped in a barn at Barncaple until the church was built. Tarff Valley church is built on the farm of Chapel, which derives its name from the fact that in olden times a church called St. Salvator stood there. The manse was Glenauld, but about 1879 a new manse, now the residence of the minister, was built at Tarff. It has a small glebe of two or three acres, and is beautifully situated with the river Tarff flowing through the grounds. In springtime the bank is clad with snowdrops, daffodils, and narcissi.

After the death of Mr. McFarlane, minister of Tongland congregation, the two congregations united as Tongland Church under the present minister, and it has been a very happy and successful union. Owing to the geographical situation, services and Sunday schools are conducted in both churches every Sunday, while evening services are held in Ringford six months of the year. The former manse and glebe of Tongland Church were sold by the General Trustees of the Church of Scotland to the Galloway Water Power Company. Electric lighting and heating were installed in Tongland Church in 1949 and in Tarff Valley Church in 1951.

All the organisations are very healthy, sharing a harmonious spirit. The services are well attended, the majority of the residents being keenly interested in all things pertaining to church life, and it is interesting to note that, at all three services, a third of the congregation is composed of children. Unfortunately, most of our young people, when school days are over, have to go away, because, apart from farm work, there are few openings for them. The children, almost without exception, who attend the Sunday schools stay on to the church services, and love to do so.

There are 102 Church of Scotland households, six Scottish Episcopal, one Jewish, one Roman Catholic, one Christian Scientist, and 26 have no church connection. This latter situation is largely accounted for by the fact that a considerable proportion of farm workers do not remain long in one district.

Notable Parishioners

The Rev. Dr. Thomas Brown, born at Closeburn, Dumfriesshire, in 1776, was inducted to Tongland in 1807, and called to St. John's, Glasgow, in 1826. Leaving the Church of Scotland at the time of the Disruption in 1843, he was appointed the first moderator of the Free Church at the General Assembly held in Glasgow in 1843. He took part in the opening of Tongland and Twynholm Free Church in 1844, and died in 1847.

Miss Annie Fisher, younger daughter of the Rev. Peter Fisher, a former minister, served for many years as a missionary of the United Free Church and later of the Church of Scotland, in India.

Tom Dobson was a missionary in Poona, India, where he was murdered. On his deathbed he requested that nothing should be done to the misguided youth who had mortally wounded him. He was born at Tongland, where his father worked as a baker in Gillone's bakery.

Later the parents removed to Glasgow where there were greater opportunities for their family.

Scotland's First Airman

Sir Walter Raleigh in his classic volume on 'The War in the Air' claims a first place for John Damian, the Abbot of Tungland, among the practical aeronauts of the world. It was at Stirling Castle in 1507 that John Damian made history by trying to fly. He was an Italian, a man of learning, who became a great friend of James IV. Both were keen students of medicine, chemistry, and various sciences, and spent much time together. Within a year of his appearance in Scotland James presented Damian with the Abbey of Tungland, but he was very much an absentee abbot and preferred to live at the royal court. For a long time he had thought it would be possible to fly, and he constructed a great pair of wings with which he attempted a flight from Stirling Castle. We are told that the King with his courtiers went forth to witness the flight which, unfortunately, ended in disaster, for Damian fell to the ground and broke his leg. The failure he ascribed to the fact that he had used hens' feathers in the construction of the wings and they yearned for the midden and not the skies.

Population

The population in 1952 was 536, the smallest so far recorded. The highest was 924 in 1851. There are 26 married couples with no family and 21 married couples with one child. The largest family is six.

While the old country trades have died out, we suffer from a scarcity of houses; no new houses have been built by the county council, although eight are now in the course of erection. Seventeen new houses have been erected in the last quarter of a century, all by private enterprise; ten have been demolished, and several have been completely gutted and renovated. Three new houses, built of wood, have been erected for workers by the Creamery company and are now ready for occupation.

Industry and Commerce

There are two post offices, one at Tongland and the other at Ringford; two grocery shops in Ringford; one builder; one joiner; and one garage. There is also the Tarff Valley Agricultural Co-operative Society.

The old established creamery, now a branch of the United Creameries, employs up to 40 people who mostly reside in the nearby village of Twynholm. Whey is brought from other factories, condensed and processed, then despatched to other branches for manufacturing purposes. A very large quantity of cheese is also handled and stored.

The West of Scotland Agricultural College has founded an experimental garden which is still successfully worked.

The last smithy in the parish, situated at Ringford, closed about 1947.

During the lifetime of some of the older inhabitants there was a very progressive business of varied enterprises at Tongland clachan. The founder, James Gillone, started with a starch mill making farina from potatoes. As time went on he added a meal mill, became lessee of the famous salmon fisheries, erected a gas works, and established a most progressive bakery. He gave employment to many men. Vans carried bread, biscuits and cakes over a very large area, and, it is said, the first machine-made biscuits in Scotland were manufactured at Tongland. At one time the firm supplied the Cunard Shipping Company with biscuits. It was a great loss to the community when the bakery closed.

The coming of the Galloway Power Company put an end to the lucrative salmon fishery on the river Dee; at the height of the season up to 100 prime fish were taken out of the doachs each evening. Four married men were constantly employed on this Tongland part of the river.

There are no inns or licensed premises in the parish, the last one, the Red Lion in Ringford, having been closed in 1927. In olden times, the stage coach drivers changed horses there. There was also a small place at Tarff bridge, until about 30 years ago. Another, the Pluckim Inn, was situated on Valleyfield Farm.

The School

The only school, formerly Tongland School, and now known as Ringford School, has but 36 pupils and two teachers. The children from the Tongland side now attend schools in Kirkcudbright. The previous school has been for many years Ringford Village Hall, where among other community interests it serves for bowling and badminton clubs. Women's Rural Institute, dances, Woman's Guild, and religious services.

Bridges

The main bridges in the parish are the railway bridge, the Telford bridge, and the old bridge crossing the river Dee, and the three crossing the Tarff. The foundation of the Telford Bridge was laid in 1804. The contract price was £2,420, of which £1,150 was raised by private subscription and the remainder paid by the county. In August, in a time of flooding, the whole structure, as far as it had proceeded, was swept away. Work was begun again in March, 1805, but the gentlemen of the county were worried by the incompetence of the contractors and relieved them of their contract. By this time £3,000 had been spent. A competent engineer was appointed to guide the work and in 1808 the bridge was finished, having cost, in all, £7,710.

The old bridge is about a quarter of a mile higher up the river. It is interesting to note that it was condemned in 1800, because of its tottering condition, but has been all these years in constant use and was only renovated in 1952. The beauty of the old-time structure has been preserved and the whole scheme is an excellent achievement.

One of the bridges over the Tarff is at the point where it joins the Dee. In 1832 a new bridge was thrown across the river to carry the new main road. The foundations sit on wooden piles 18 feet in depth. Soon after it was built it sank in the centre and it has remained in that condition ever since. About 20 yards farther down stands the old bridge, very old but still serviceable. In 1947 it was closed to vehicular traffic, because it was considered unsafe for heavy lorries. A stone wall was built across it, and it is used occasionally as a footbridge.

Tongland Quarry

This quarry has been operated by the county council since 1924. It has developed over the years and a scheme for improving the plant is at present under consideration. At the present time 25 men are employed there. The roads in the parish are kept in excellent condition, although there is room for improvement on some of the privately owned farm roads.

Land-owners

Many changes have taken place in recent years and houses and farms have new owners. Among the larger houses are Argrennan, Barcaple, Barstobrick, Bogra, Dunjop, Lairdmannoch, Largs, Valleyfield.

Agriculture

Farming is a highly specialised calling in this parish and while agriculturalists vary a little in method and ability there is not one who farms badly. On the other hand, it would be difficult to find any to surpass them in craftsmanship or results. Almost every farm is highly mechanised. Most have at least one tractor, although two farmers still do all the work with horses. All have not less than one motor car, while there are plenty of lorries, land-rovers, and labour-saving machines and implements. The general system of rotation is from four to seven years. Oats, beans, peas, turnips, kale, a little wheat, barley and rye are grown; potatoes are usually grown mainly for home consumption.

Most of the land is rich and fertile although much of it is hilly. Every farm is a mixed one; almost all have a regular flock of sheep and a dairy herd, and all are attested. While sheep raising, cattle rearing, and milk production are the main interests, poultry and pigs are kept in large numbers. Fattening cattle do well; pure Galloways and crosses are kept on many farms, while there is one herd of Aberdeen-Angus. Most of the sheep are of the blackface variety, a few Suffolk and Border Leicesters are bred pure, but apart from the blackfaces it is crosses that are bred for the most part. Suffolk, Leicester, Cheviot and Blackfaced are all crossed and make grand sheep for wool or mutton.

At Barncrosh, there is a stud of charming Shetland ponies, famous prize-takers in the show ring. Only three Clydesdale foals were born in Tongland this year, two at Barncrosh and one at Park of Tongland.

Two farms still make cheese, Langbarns and Barstibly.

All the farm workers are well housed with up-to-date amenities, such as sanitation and water, while many have bathrooms, with hot and cold water, and electric light. A few still have paraffin lamps.

Good working dogs for cattle and sheep are scarce and in demand, £12 to £15 being an ordinary price.

Historical Notes

On the upper lands of Kirkconnel farm there is an imposing monument erected to the memory of the Covenanters.   A panel thereon has the following words:—

> In testimony
> Of the feeling of the present generation
> on the 11th September, 1831,
> About ten thousand persons assembled here
> And after hearing an excellent sermon
> preached by
> The Rev. John Osborne
> From Psalm 74, verse 22nd
> contributed a fund for the erection
> of this monument
> To the memory of the martyrs
> (Alexander Murray, Esq., of Broughton
> having handsomely given the ground)
> Four of whom were carried to their respective
> burial places, but James Clement,
> being a stranger, was interred on this spot.

It is rather strange that the name of the donor of the poor little bit of moorland is blazoned on the monument, but the martyr is merely mentioned. The Rev. Dugald Stewart Williamson has some rather scathing remarks about the preacher: 'The name of the gentleman who conducted the service that day was Mr. Osborne. His discourse, which he printed, is an elaborate and strong performance, without the slightest reference either to times of religious persecution, or to the history of the martyr, James Clement'. The five martyrs so cruelly murdered on the orders of Grierson of Lagg were John Bell of Whiteside, David Halliday of Mayfield, Andrew McRobert, James Clement and Robert Lennox. The first two were men of position. David Halliday was laird of Mayfield and John Bell, particularly, occupied no mean station among the gentlemen of the Stewartry.

A conventicle was held at the Martyrs' Monument on Kirkconnel Moor on 21 June, 1931 under the auspices of the presbytery. It evoked great and widespread interest. A choir of about two hundred voices led the praise. In addition to local ministers, eminent churchmen from farther afield took part. There was a very large attendance and a collection taken for the repair of the memorial amounted to over £84.

At the head of Lairdmannoch Loch on Kirkconnel is a stone circle and cairn. The circle consists of eleven stones with another in the centre.

The estate of Queenshill derives its name from a tradition that Mary Queen of Scots on her flight from the Battle of Langside rested on a little knoll there and had a meal. Whether it is anything more than a tradition is questionable. Continuing on her journey she crossed the Dee at a narrow part of the river. The spot is still known to some of the oldest inhabitants as 'Mary's Brig', because it is said a wooden bridge was hurriedly thrown across for the Queen's accommodation. A well nearby is named 'Mary's well', for again tradition has it that she drank at its waters.

At Kirkconnel farm many years ago workmen came on a very old burying ground. With the exception of a varying colour of earth and divisions therein which resembled graves there was little else to prove that it was a burying ground. But in the centre of one of the grave-like divisions a gold ring was turned up with the following engraved writing in very old lettering, 'The gift and the giver are thine for ever'.

The Barstobrick Monument is a prominent landmark and can be seen for miles around. It was erected in 1928 in memory of James Neilson, the inventor of the 'hot blast' which revolutionised the iron smelting industry.

In such a delightful parish we have all God's blessing in great abundance for it is one of the happiest and most beautiful parts of Bonnie Galloway.

1952

CHAPTER 31

THE PARISH OF TROQUEER
(LANDWARD)

by the REV. J. L. MANGLES

The account offered here is, strictly speaking, the account of only that part of the parish of Troqueer which lies within the Stewartry of Kirkcudbright. In the reign of Charles II the eastern part of the now extinct parish of Kirkconnel was incorporated in the parish of Troqueer, but in the year 1928, when the burghs of Dumfries and Maxwelltown amalgamated, and the boundary of Dumfriesshire was extended across the Nith to include the former burgh of Maxwelltown, the parish became divided between the two counties.

Name

The name of the parish has been variously spelt throughout the years. For example, in the kirk session records of 1647 it is found as 'Troqueir', and in 1745 as 'Troquire', and many theories have been produced as to the origin of the name—some quite ingenious. The simple and likely explanation is that 'Troqueir' means 'the place of Quer'. On the farm of Barbush, about the centre of the parish, is a well which appears to have been a holy place and a place of pilgrimage for many years. This well is sometimes called St. Queran's well, St. Querdon's well, or St. Jargan's well. When in the 1870s the laird of Cargen had the well cleaned out, the coins (votary offerings) found ranged back to the early seventeenth century.

Antiquities

Besides Saint Queran's well on the farm of Barbush, there are many other antiquarian sites in the parish worthy of note. Behind the house of Castlehill and overlooking the Castle-Douglas road there is an earthwork almost entirely iron-age, with the possibility of dark-age and medieval occupations. Near St. Queran's well and in the midst of Mabie Moss there is an interesting site known as Pict's Knowe. On Butterhole farm, also near Mabie, a considerable area of iron bloomery slag suggests medieval iron workings, while around Mabie there are late eighteenth century and early nineteenth century copper and lead workings.

Boundaries and Natural Features

The area under our consideration is bounded on the north by the burgh of Dumfries and Maxwelltown; on the east by the river Nith; on the south by the parish of New Abbey; on the west by the parishes of Lochrutton and Terregles. The area is about 25 square miles.

A range of hills, running more or less north-south along the centre of the parish, divides it very effectively into two distinct portions. On the lower ground to the east runs the main road from Dumfries to New Abbey; to the west are two roads—one to Dalbeattie and the other to Castle-Douglas. The New Abbey road surmounts a spur of the higher ground by the Whinnyhill. The Dalbeattie road traverses the same range to the west by way of the Long Wood pass, which it shares with the railway, and the Castle-Douglas road follows the 'Glen', a valley still further north. On the eastern border of the parish along Nithside there is a considerable amount of merse land, which makes very good summer grazing. The central part contains a fair amount of moor and bog, but practically all the high ground, comprising about one-sixth to one-fifth of the total area of the parish, belongs to the Forestry Commission, who have large forests in the area.

Valuation

The most recent valuation roll before the re-assessment of 1961 gives the gross annual value of the parish as £63,052 8s 11d, which is greater than any other parish in the Stewartry and also than any of the burghs except the burgh of Castle-Douglas. This large rental derives from the large areas afforested, and in particular from the very large works of the Imperial Chemical Industries, situated at Cargenbridge. These works, which employ several hundred men and were built in the early years of the second world war, produce nitro-cellulose compounds and other chemicals used in the manufacture of paint. Until recently a great deal of their effort was directed towards the manufacture of man-made fibres, notably 'Ardil'. When this was abandoned that section of the works was converted to the production of plastics.

Agriculture

In 1791 the Rev. John Ewart records that there were in the parish four oat mills; one wheat mill; one walk-mill; one barley mill; two breweries and two malthouses. The rent of arable land was in general about 18s. an acre. There is now no mill of any kind in the parish and the rental of arable land must have increased five or six times. To-day almost all the farms in the parish are dairy farms, some with very large herds. Much of the milk produced goes for processing to the General Milk Products factory in Dumfries. Silage is used increasingly for winter feeding of cattle, with a consequent decrease in the acreage of turnips grown. Owing to the fact that more and more people take prepared breakfast cereals rather than porridge, the amount of oats sown in a countryside where there are hardly any horses continues annually to diminish. With a few exceptions, notably on the Kirkconnel estate, most farmers are their own lairds.

Ecclesiastical Affairs

The church of the parish is not in the Stewartry, but is situated just over the boundary, in the burgh of Maxwelltown close to the river. Although there is no ecclesiastical building in the area a Sunday school is carried on under the auspices of the church in Islesteps hall, and a monthly service is conducted there by the parish minister, who is also chaplain to the school at Cargenbridge. No other denomination conducts any service in the parish, and the parishioners are almost all presbyterian.

Schools

The Rev. William Thorburn, in the *New Statistical Account*, mentions that there were then three schools in the parish. Two of these were in that part with which we are now concerned, and until 1959 these two schools continued to function. The older of the two was Drumsleet school, situated at the junction of Lochfoot Road and Dalbeattie Road. This was a two-teacher school, and the direct descendant of the school at Doweel, which was erected in the very early years of the eighteenth century, with money left for this purpose by the minister of the parish, the Rev. Wm. Somervell, who died in 1698. Whinnyhill, the second school, was situated at Whinnyhill, New Abbey road, and was a single-teacher school. Both buildings are still in good order. In 1959 there was erected, near the hamlet of Cargenbridge, and just outside the Dumfries boundary, a secondary and primary school. When this very modern school was opened in October 1959 by the Earl of Galloway, Drumsleet and Whinnyhill became redundant. The primary section of Cargenbridge School serves as a parish school, drawing its 80 pupils from the landward parish of Troqueer. It provides secondary education for children from Troqueer and the five neighbouring parishes—from Kirkbean in the south to Irongray in the north. There are at present 144 children in this section of the school. The staff consists of three primary teachers, and 14 secondary teachers, including the headmaster. Pupils are prepared for their 'O' grade examinations at the end of the fourth year.

Population and Housing

Earlier accounts give the population as 2,774 in 1801, and 4,351 in 1841, and the comparable figure for 1951 is 9,875. Of this number 873 lived in the Stewartry. The extent of new building in the parish suggests that the population may have increased in recent years. Although a few cottages have lately become ruinous, notably on Whinnyhill and near Cargenholm, there have been very many more houses built in the last 10 to 20 years, most of these privately erected. At Mavisgrove, on the former path leading to Jock's Wood, there is a little community of some ten privately-owned houses, all erected during the past ten years. At Islesteps there are at least six houses built by the local authority, with as many more built privately. The community at Cargenbridge, on the Dalbeattie road, has been more than quadrupled by the erection of 36 local authority houses. Several of these are Swedish-type wooden dwellings. There are also small groups of dwellings, recently erected, on the Moss road and on the Castle-Douglas road at Castlehill. The Forestry Commission has provided houses for its workers on Mabie Estate.

Since practically all the people who reside in these recently-erected houses are employed in the town of Dumfries, it will be appreciated that the character as well as the appearance of the district has altered. In the *New Statistical Account* it was stated that in the parish there were the following mansion-houses: Kirkconnel, Dalskairth, Goldielea, Terraughtie, Carruchan, Cargenholm, Mabie, Mavisgrove and Cargen. It is worth noting that the first-named six of these are still occupied as family residences; that Mabie and Mavisgrove are still occupied, though by more than one family; and that only the mansion-house of Cargen is no longer habitable. Recently, after having been used for some years as a youth hostel, it was sold to the demolishers and is now without a roof.

Community Life

Although there is no place in the parish resembling a village in size or character, there are two quite definite and recognisable centres of community life. One of these is at Islesteps, on the New Abbey road, and the other at Cargenbridge on the Dalbeattie road. At each of these focal points community activities are enthusiastically carried on, at Islesteps in the Dudgeon Memorial Hall, and at Cargenbridge in the newly-acquired community centre in the former Drumsleet school. Each of these communities retains its rural character, and remains unaffected by the proximity of the large town of Dumfries, in which so many of the residents find their livelihood. The kindly, gentle, hospitable nature of the people of this parish is notable and deserves to be recorded.

1962

CHAPTER 32

THE PARISH OF TWYNHOLM

by the Rev. John Good

Name

The name of the parish has for long been spelt 'Twynholm', and, although no satisfactory explanation has ever been given as to its origin, the most commonly accepted theory is that it derives from an Anglo-Saxon source signifying two 'holms' or 'valleys'. Since the village, situated at the centre of the parish, is built at the confluence of two small burns which form the Twynholm burn, this suggestion is at least plausible. No changes in the limits of the parish have taken place since 1763.

History

The parish is not rich in historical interest and, although evidences remain of both Roman and Pictish occupation, very few attempts have been made to reconstruct a coherent story about these. In modern times few incidents of national import have occurred within the bounds. Sir Charles Hope-Dunbar, of St. Mary's Isle, still retains the land held by his ancestor, the Earl of Selkirk, in 1763. This land is now let as three excellent dairy farms and three grazing farms lying along the estuary of the Dee on the border of the parish. Cumstoun estate also remains intact and is owned by the Maitland family. The remainder of the farms in the parish are now, with the exception of two on Lairdmannoch estate, owner-occupied.

Agriculture

Since the end of the last century, there has been a gradual swing from pastoral and arable to dairy farming, and to-day, of the 25 holdings in the parish, 17 are chiefly dependent upon the production of milk as their source of income. Ayrshire cattle have been replacing the indigenous Galloways, although a number of the latter remain, and most dairy farms also carry a stock of breeding ewes. These are mostly North Country Cheviots which are crossed with Border Leicester rams, and the resulting half-bred ewe lambs are in great demand in the borders. The wedder lambs are usually kept and finished in the autumn, or kept to eat off turnips. On other holdings there are blackfaced ewes which are crossed with Border Leicester rams, and their cross lambs are a profitable source of income.

The emphasis on milk production has had a profound influence on the population during the last 50 years. At first the farmers who

309

changed to dairying were obliged to go to Ayrshire to obtain the services of experienced dairymen, whose descendants now form a very large proportion of the local population. So prosperous and thrifty were these men that many of them or their sons now farm a number of holdings on their own account. Originally milk was made into cheese on each farm, but the increase in the demand for liquid milk and the facilities for its transportation to the cities, provided by the Scottish Milk Marketing Board, have led the majority of farmers to sell liquid milk. Only two farms in the parish now make cheese.

There are two creameries within the parish—one owned by the Scottish Milk Marketing Board situated near Kirkcudbright, and the other on the main Dumfries-Stranraer road to the east of the village, operated by the United Creameries. The former handles the bulk of the liquid milk produced in the district. Some of this is sent daily by road to various towns in the industrial area, while in the peak of the season the surplus is manufactured into butter. As much as six tons a day is made during the summer months. Adjacent to this creamery is a factory, also owned by the Scottish Milk Marketing Board, which manufactures certain by-products and exports dried milk. The United Creameries business is with whey which is transported daily from other creameries manufacturing cheese. The whey is condensed here and is dispatched in barrels for further processing.

Farming practice in the parish has kept pace with the improved methods of modern times and the prosperity of the industry is reflected in the amount of machinery now used. Tractors have almost completely replaced horses. The amount of lime and artificial manure now used is greater than ever before, and the farmer becomes more and more dependent upon the scientific adviser.

Forestry

Some years ago the Forestry Commission bought the excellent sheep farm of Glengap at the north end of the parish, and this is presently being planted by them. Together with adjacent lands in Balmaghie parish, which have also been planted, this will form a forest of about 10,000 acres, and it is the intention of the Commission to build 20 houses for their workers at Glengap.

Occupations and Population

The social history of the parish in the last 50 years is similar to that of many rural parishes, in that the tailor, the drover, the farrier, the carter and the cobbler have disappeared. It remains essentially agricultural, and there is no industry apart from farming, and such ancillary occupations as the haulage and creamery work. A thriving haulier's business operates 30 lorries, practically all engaged in one or other branch of agricultural work. The creameries employ from 30 to 40 men and 15 to 20 girls.

At the 1951 census the population was 808, the highest recorded since 1861 when the figure was 815. Of the 28 parishes in the Stewartry only five, including Twynholm, have the distinction of showing an increase of population over the last 50 years. In the case of this parish the growth of Mersecroft, adjacent as it is to Kirkcudbright, would appear to be mainly responsible.

Public and Social Services

Twynholm claims with some cause to have been a progressive parish in the provision of social amenities. In 1900 a village hall was built by public subscription. This serves the community adequately and has been extended and improved in recent years. Trusteeship of it is vested in the Community Council, formed 20 years ago and representative of all the activities in the parish. This council has a written constitution, and meets regularly to deal with all questions affecting the life of the community.

The village claims to have been the first in Scotland to have street lighting when, in 1911, the late W. Stewart, merchant and owner of the former wool mill, operated a generating plant which supplied most of the houses and provided for a number of street lights. Likewise, a gravitation water supply was in operation from early in the century and this was sponsored and managed by a representative committee of the villagers. The system functioned until 1948 when the county council assumed responsibility for the water supply. There is a good sewage system which has recently been enlarged and improved. A regular bus service between Stranraer and Dumfries passes through the village. There is no resident doctor and the parish is served by various practitioners from Castle-Douglas and Kirkcudbright.

Education

There is a good primary school of four class rooms and at present an addition is being built to accommodate a dining room and kitchen for school meals. The staff consists of the headmaster and three lady teachers. Children over primary school age are transported daily to Kirkcudbright Academy where they remain until leaving. Few children stay on beyond the statutory leaving age of 15 and very few pursue an academic career. To the best of the writer's knowledge, the parish has not produced a minister since the son of the author of the *New Statistical Account*. He succeeded his father as parish minister. In 50 years, only one son and one daughter of the parish have become doctors. In this present generation, there is little to attract young people to the professions when their colleagues can with less blood and sweat, toil and tears, earn comfortable livings as hewers of wood and drawers of water.

Church

The parish church, built in 1818, is a stone building of simple design in excellent repair and adequate for the population. The interior is well furnished and has been improved by the installation of two memorial windows. The manse was built in 1835 and there is a glebe of 35 acres. The standard of church-going in the parish is perhaps better than the average for country parishes and the church holds its honoured place in the community. There is no other denomination in the parish.

Sports and Pastimes

The village hall is the centre for all communal life, and serves the needs of the various youth and recreational activities. There is a strong branch of the Women's Rural Institute. The indoor bowling association meets two nights a week and the badminton club two nights. During the winter months, there are concerts, dances and whist drives on Friday evenings. There is a curling club of national repute and a Burns Club. A branch of the County Library operates from the village hall and this is well patronised. There is a Girl Guide company of about twenty members.

Housing

Since 1947 the county council has built 26 houses to the west of the village on the Doon Hill. These are of four apartments, brick built and slated. The Council has also built 42 houses at Mersecroft, which is within the parish but so near to Kirkcudbright that the impact of this new development is not felt on this community. In general, the standard of housing is high and this in turn has had its effect upon the standard of living and well-being of the population.

Way of Life

A Scots word best describes the typical parishioner—'bien'. There is no poverty and there is a sense of well-being and contentment in the parish. In conformity with the national improvement in agricultural workers' wages, the farm worker is now comparatively well off and his conditions of service tend to make him realise his personality in a way which was impossible until recent times. The relationship between master and man is on the whole good. The experienced trustworthy man tends to stay in his place whilst the weak brother flits as a floating liability from place to place. There is a scarcity of the former type, and despite wages, modern houses and week-ends off, the industry is failing to hold men.

The people are warm-hearted, generous and neighbourly. There is still a sense of belonging to the parish in their outlook, and the parish is still their unit.

1955

CHAPTER 33

THE PARISH OF URR

by the REV. GEORGE G. CAMPBELL

Name, Boundaries and Extent

The origin of the word 'Urr' is unknown. On old communion tokens, which can be inspected in the Chambers Street Museum in Edinburgh, and in an old account of the parish, of 1627, the spelling is VR. On later tokens, and in the kirk session records up to 1777, the spelling is 'Orr'. The parish is still called 'Orr' or 'Ore' by the local inhabitants.

The boundaries have not changed externally, and Urr is bounded on the south by Colvend, the boundary stone being still visible in the Moss Road south of Dalbeattie; on the east by Kirkgunzeon and Lochrutton; on the north by Kirkpatrick-Durham and Crossmichael, and on the west by the river Urr and part of Crossmichael. The *quoad sacra* parish of Dalbeattie, of which a separate account is being given, has been carved out of the middle of Urr. Its boundaries are those of the burgh of Dalbeattie. The Mote of Urr, though on the Buittle side of the river, is in Urr parish, because, when the parish boundaries were defined, the river went round the other side of the mote, as it can do still in high flood.

The parish is therefore of very odd and inconvenient shape, being almost 15 miles long, never more than five, sometimes not more than one mile, broad, and with Dalbeattie parish inside it. The area is 14,631 acres. Thus the figure in the Old Account (1794) of 12,000 acres is surprisingly accurate, as the Scotch acre, presumably in use since the writer speaks of 'Scotch miles', was 1.27 English acres. The figure of 40 square miles in the New Account is thus a gross exaggeration, and it is difficult to explain the statement in the 1627 account that 'The paroche extends to eight myll off lenth and twa off breid consideratis considerandis', which would mean that the size of the parish was considerably increased sometime before the 1794 account was written. The gross valuation of the parish, excluding Dalbeattie, for 1950, was £18,700, with a rateable valuation of £7,614.

Rivers, Lochs and Woodlands

The only river of any size is the Urr, a shallow stream but capable of rising in flood very rapidly. In the flood of 2 September 1950 the old houses at Bridgend were inundated for the first time in living memory by the river, which rose to within a foot or so of the arch-top of the old bridge. The river is fished for trout, flounders (Stepend) and salmon, there being fewer of the last named than in former years. Poaching is very common, but villages of the parish still produce some very expert salmon fishermen, and, when a long-awaited 'rise' in the water takes place, all work that can be abandoned is immediately left, and a general move to the river is made. There are two fair-sized sheets of water in the parish, the lochs of Auchenreoch and Milton, both deep, and on both of which there is curling in suitable weather, the Vale of Urr cup being traditionally competed for on Auchenreoch. These lochs, with small stretches of water at Spottes and Edingham, and Richorn, add greatly to the beauty of the parish. One is compelled to add, however, that this beauty is greatly threatened by the persistent felling of standing timber. No one could grumble at this, since timber is after all a crop, but for the fact that little or no replanting is taking place and, where this is being done, it is of soft wood. Posterity is likely to pay dearly for this reprehensible policy. It has already ruined some beauty spots, and is having at least one other regrettable result, in the changes that are taking place in the bird life of the parish. Urr is an exceptionally interesting parish on account of its varied bird life.[1]

Population

The population of the parish (1951) is 4,485, of whom 2,147 are males and 2,338 are females. Of this total 3,228 live in the *quoad sacra* parish of Dalbeattie. Therefore the figure of 1,257 is given as the population of Urr *quoad omnia,* and this is an increase of 236 on the 1931 figure, which, in view of the prevailing trends, must be regarded as satisfactory. Not by any means all of the increase represents workers on the land, for a higher percentage of the working population nowadays lives in the parish but works in one or other of the neighbouring towns, travelling by cycle or bus. The number of children at the moment is increasing, and the sex distribution is unusual. In Haugh-of-Urr there are at the moment almost twice as many girls as boys, in Springholm the disparity in this direction is even greater, while in Crocketford the boy population very much exceeds the girl. However, from a study of the infant groups in the different villages it is clear that this will be rectified through time.

History

There are very few antiquities in the parish. Worthy of mention is a standing stone above Redcastle farmhouse, over nine feet high, of granite, very solidly embedded in the field. Why it is there no one knows, nor do the 1627 or 1794 accounts even suggest a reason. There are also the remains of a fort or lake-dwelling on a strip of land jutting into Milton Loch from its north-west shore. The place is called 'Green Island' locally, so it probably was one in the past. The fort

---

(1) Local names for birds: Jackdaw (Kyaw); Linnet (Heather Lintie); Chaffinch (Shelfie); Yellow Bunting (Yoit); House Sparrow (Spiug); Meadow-pipit (Mosscheeper); Wren (Cutty); Whitethroat (Nettle Creeper); Willow Warbler (Basket-hanger); Dabchick (Dooker).

measures about 80 yards by 24. The Royal Commission on Antiquities in the Stewartry published a report on it in 1914, but there have been no further excavations. Then there are the scanty remains of a fort at Waterside, facing the Mote, and almost obliterated. There is a sixteenth century castle at Edingham, of which one single ruined storey survives. It was obviously a keep of considerable size at one time.

The chief antiquity of the parish, however, beyond any doubt, is the Mote of Urr, the largest and most complete earthwork fortification in Scotland. It is now being properly excavated for the first time. (For a full report as to the dimensions of the Mote, see *Fifth Report and Inventory of Monuments and Constructions in Galloway. Vol. II—Stewartry of Kirkcudbright*, 1914, pp. 228-42.) Nothing definite is known as to its origin or age. Some claim that it occupies the site of Caerbantorigum as marked on Ptolemy's map (the same claim is made for other motes in the south-west). Then there is a legend relative to King Robert the Bruce's presence at the mote, so persistent that it may be based on fact. The story is told in detail in Dr. Frew's *History of the Parish of Urr*—'King Robert the Bruce, in the earlier part of his career, found himself in the vicinity of the mote, and there, though weary and footsore, was encountered by an English Knight, Sir Walter Selby, and compelled to give him fight. At the moment, the wife of one Mark Sprotte, who lived on the mote, was busy preparing a bowl of porridge, for her husband's breakfast. Seeing the King in danger, she rushed from the cottage, and coming up behind the Englishman, caught him by the hair, or some say by the knees, and brought him to the ground'. The story goes on to tell that the King refused to take advantage of his victory, and that, as friends, they repaired to the cottage for rest and refreshment. Dame Sprotte presented the porridge to the King but refused to give bite or sup to an Englishman. To get rid of her, and at the same time to reward her, the King told her to go out and run, and promised that when he came into his kingdom he would give her as much land as she could encompass while he supped the porridge. She made the best of her opportunity, and in due time was presented with 20 Scotch acres of land, the mote becoming known as the 'King's Mount'. 'The Sprottes of the Mount held this land for 500 years.' There is in existence a charter granted by Eustace de Balliol, and a witness to this charter is a 'Hugh Sprot, Burgensis De Hur'. If there was a burgh of barony located here it soon lapsed. As a Scottish historian has said, 'Many burghs of barony were due to baronial ambition only. A baron liked a burgh in his charter, even if it was a paper burgh with no real existence'. Excavations in the summer of 1951 have shown that the citadel of the mote was crowned by a large wooden structure of Norman type; and it is significant that in one of the inner trenches, of which a section has been excavated to its full depth, nothing earlier than the thirteenth or fourteenth century has so far been found. (See preliminary report, *Galloway News*, 1 September 1951).

There is also in existence, somewhere in the parish, although the site is lost, an underground cavern, presumably used for burial purposes in antiquity. This type of cave, which had a paved forecourt and of which a counterpart, now also lost, existed in Buittle parish, is described in the *Old Statistical Account,* vol. 17, page 120. The writer of that account, in the most exasperating way, casually remarks that a similar cave (to the Buittle one) 'can be seen any day in the neighbouring Parish of Urr, and that the Laird of Spottes will point it out to anyone desiring to see it on the lands of Auchenreoch'. A search has revealed no trace whatever, nor is there any tradition of such a place.

The parish contains a number of old roads and rights-of-way, some of them almost forgotten, as few of the parishioners walk nowadays if that can be avoided. Among the more important of these we have (a) a right-of-way from Hardgate, just above the former U.F. Church, crossing the old Milton-Dalbeattie road, thence through a field of Halmyre to Mosside (this unused right-of-way is now ploughed in places); (b) an old road: King's Grange—Bush o' Bield—Hermitage— across the old bridge (locally said to be Roman)—Bar of Spottes—West Glenarm—East Glenarm—Bridgestone—Milton (still lined by hedges much of the way); (c) an old road: Springholm—Hoggan's Hole—Fell— Lochside—Milton: (d) a very old road: from Buittle, across the Ford at Netheryett—through lands of Herriesdale—Townhead of Torkatrine— Meikle Culloch—Kingunzeon parish. Part of this road is now obliterated, and is not used; (e) Cowar Cottage (Kirkgunzeon)—Little Cocklick (Urr)—Alleyford (Kirkgunzeon)—branch through Craigley—Little Culmain — Milton. Other branch from Alleyford to Kirkgunzeon; (f) traces of an old road from Chapelton through Spottes, past Bridgend, over the ford—into Buittle. There is a strong local tradition that this was the coach road to Kirkcudbright.

Villages and Housing

It will be noticed that a number of these old roads led to Milton. This little hamlet, with about three inhabited houses, was once a burgh of barony with a market cross. The opening of the new trunk road to Stranraer spelt its doom, and gave corresponding life to Springholm and Crocketford. There was also a village of considerable size at Blackford, of which only two cottages remain. These have their backs to the Military Road, and face a street which no longer exists. On the opposite side of the Military Road, on the lands of Markfast, hearthstones are still occasionally unearthed by the plough. Blackford has preceded Milton to extinction, and for the same reason.

The other villages in the parish, Haugh-of-Urr, Springholm, Crocketford and Hardgate, are of more recent date and have more or less moved with the times, in matters of housing, sanitation, and lighting. In the Haugh 28 houses have been built by public authority within the last 14 years, and of these 24 are of pleasing design and well planned;

the other four, agricultural workers' houses, being inferior in construction and very ugly. All, of course, have modern sanitation and electric lighting. Crocketford, half in Urr, half in Kirkpatrick-Durham, has also benefited to the extent of ten or a dozen houses built between the wars in Kirkpatrick-Durham parish. But there, on the other hand, the Ministry of Transport has approved an order for the straightening of a small bend in the trunk road through Crocketford, by which most of the houses, including the smiddy and the garage on the south-east side of the village, will be demolished. The advantages to be gained by this action will be negligible, and as the houses in question are of stone construction and modern in every way, thus contributing to the pleasing appearance as well as the well-being of the village, the action proposed would, in the opinion of the whole parish, be of an appalling stupidity. Springholm has not yet benefited to any extent from the post-war housing programme, only four agricultural workers' houses having been built. But since the first world war, Springholm, which was then in almost derelict condition, has greatly improved in appearance, many old houses having been renovated, making the village a place of considerable beauty. It must be admitted, however, that very few of the houses have modern sanitation, nor, evidently, is a modern scheme possible, because of the level of the road. Building on a large scale has begun at the Castle-Douglas end of the village, and a new village is planned which will not only rehouse most of Springholm, but, it is said, the village of Kirkpatrick-Durham as well. Such a village will of course enjoy all modern housing benefits—a community centre is planned in this scheme—but it would necessarily lack the individuality of the present village, something of its beauty, and also the cheapness of its rents. Hardgate village, on the top of the hill above Haugh-of-Urr, is the most beautiful village of them all, enjoying all modern amenities, with no housing scheme and no housing problems.

Besides the county council's provision of housing schemes, most farmers, in the prevailing state of great prosperity, have either rebuilt old cottages or built new ones for their workers. This is partly due to a genuine desire that their workers should share in the present prosperity, or else, where this desire is lacking, it is seen to be a necessity if the farm workers are to be retained on the land. Most of the farm workers' cottages built recently are of bungalow type and of very pleasing design, some of them containing conveniences not yet found in the farms to which they belong. It should be stated also that both public and private builders have benefited, as has the general public, from the introduction of the county water scheme, and also from the extensive use of electric power on the farms.

Occupations

Naturally the greater part of the population is engaged in agriculture. There is, in all the villages, but especially in Springholm and Hardgate, a high proportion of elderly and retired people. There are now no shops in Hardgate or Milton, and but two in the Haugh, where there were once at least four, and one each in Springholm and Crocketford. Besides these general stores there is a long-established joiner's business in the Haugh, another in Crocketford, and a third, recently established, in Milton. Within living memory there were five blacksmith's shops in the parish, of which one, at Crocketford, remains. The blacksmith there, Corrie by name, is a water-diviner of oft-tried skill. Crocketford also contains a very able family of engineers, one of whom was recently responsible for the installation of an intricate electric heating system in the parish church. There are also found in the parish trappers, poultry-farmers, painters, market gardeners, and there is very little unemployment.

Agriculture

In 1950 in the parish there were 2,399 acres of tillage, 8,164 of grasses, and 2,657 of rough grazing. The farms are carrying 2,476 cows and heifers in milk or calf of dairy type; and a total of 5,523 cattle, 7,231 sheep, 449 pigs (the number now increasing rapidly) and 11,372 poultry. Only nine of the farms do not have dairies of considerable size. The usual arrangement between farmers and dairymen at present is that the dairyman gets one-sixth of the milk cheque and provides all labour; an alternative arrangement is to let the dairy at around £12 a cow. Dairying is a very popular branch of farming, and an extremely prosperous one, especially if the dairyman can supply labour from his own family. But, of course, the hours of work are trying. The average capacity of the parish would be roughly one cow to one and a half acres. As regards crops, a liberal estimate for a good year at present would be 38-40 bushels of oats to the acre; in a bad year 26 bushels may be harvested; potatoes, about six or seven tons to the acre; hay, about 30 to 34 cwt.; turnips, about 16 tons to the acre, depending on the weather.

A prominent farmer gives it as his opinion that the greatest single improvement in agriculture in this area was the introduction of wild white clover, for establishing new pastures rapidly, and storing up nitrogen for grazing crops when ploughed. The improved output is about 25 per cent. higher. The other factor that has changed the face of agriculture is of course the introduction of the tractor. At the time of writing one of the few remaining farms using horses only has gone over to the tractor, although some of the larger still maintain horses for occasional use with the plough, as this avoids the creation of a hard subsoil. Generally speaking, better ploughing is done by horses, or caterpillar tractor; but of course the time involved is nowadays a vital factor.

The increase in dairying has to a certain extent changed the outlook of the farmer. One learns that the tendency now is to maintain a settled stock, instead of frequent buying and selling. Ayrshires maintain their hold, though Friesians have made their appearance in the parish. There is some indication that beef cattle are beginning to come back into their own. One farmer, James Biggar of Chapelton and Grange, has an international reputation as an exporter and judge of Pedigree Shorthorn cattle.[1] His father enjoyed a similar reputation. There are very few pig-farmers at present in the parish, though a hundred years ago it is recorded that the drains in Haugh-of-Urr ran with blood at the annual pig-killing.

Beekeeping is almost ignored by the parishioners as either a hobby or a means of supplementing income, which is a pity as the parish is quite exceptionally adapted for this branch of agriculture. So well suited is the climate, in fact, as the writer has found, that with no effort at all in a good year one can obtain a surplus of 80 to 100 lb. of honey a stock. With proper attention this figure can be greatly exceeded. Even in a very poor summer it is possible to obtain a surplus of 30 lb. a hive. There is great need for instruction in this craft, and also for the introduction of the better disease-resisting strains. The Caucasian or French Black will be found to yield the best results; the yellow races are not so suitable. Unfortunately, most of the parishioners who keep bees have 'scrub' strains, though they would scorn to keep scrub cattle.

Education

There are at present three schools in the parish, at Hardgate, Milton and Springholm. Hardgate contains about 90 pupils, and will increase for a few years, probably reaching the record figure of 102 of 1878. There are three teachers. Milton is a one-teacher school, where numbers fluctuate rapidly. It was closed for a few years, but at present has 23 pupils. All 12-year-old children in the parish go to Castle-Douglas High School for secondary education. Springholm primary children go to Kirkpatrick-Durham school, to the displeasure of the Springholm parents; and the school at Springholm has for the past few years been used experimentally as a kind of Junior College of Agriculture, for boys and girls who have left school and wish a year's study of the subject before taking up agricultural work. A Diploma was awarded at the end of the course. This original scheme failed because of insufficient numbers, and at present a new scheme, whereby a one-day-a-week course in dairying is being provided for farm workers and farmers' sons who have left school, is being tried out. It must be admitted that the school has a precarious existence, nor will it do the good it might unless it becomes possible for boys and girls, still at day-school, and who wish to follow agriculture, to attend. Otherwise financial considerations force them to 'earn as they learn' on the farms.

It is worth noting that in 1876 Milton had 38 children and Springholm day school 53, both figures in excess of numbers to-day. In the early nineteenth century there were six private schools in the parish; two of these were in Springholm, and Kells Cottage, Hardgate, was

(1) His Galloway *Sovereign* was Supreme Champion, Royal Smithfield Show, 1964.

another.   There is no reliable information as to the remuneration of the schoolmasters of these private schools, and it is probably just as well, because in the early nineteenth century a salary of £11 2s 4d was divided annually between Hardgate and Milton Schools, Milton schoolmaster receiving £3.   There is mention of Milton School in the kirk session records of 1780.   Up till about 1850, the children brought a peat to school with them for the fire.

Whether education to-day is better than in former times is a frequent subject for discussion in the parish.   The general opinion, shared by the writer, is that it is certainly more varied but not nearly so thorough. One cannot probably have it both ways.   There is no doubt, however, when one compares the faces of children to-day with those on photographs of 50 years ago, that the children to-day not only look more intelligent, but also much happier.   The local inhabitants speak of the great improvement in the general appearance of the children since the inauguration of the school meals service, from which about 90 per cent. of them benefit.

Ecclesiastical Affairs

The Parish Church of Urr has the reputation of being one of the best-attended country kirks in the south-west, and so far as one can observe the reputation is justified.   There has always been a tradition of church attendance in the parish, and in this the farmers, with a few outstanding exceptions, give a good lead.   The situation of the church building means that a large proportion of the members are outwith walking distance, and the introduction of church buses has shown that lack of transport was a real hindrance to many, who do not possess cars.

Urr has the advantage of possessing an extremely beautiful church. The old building, foursquare with gallery, going back in part to the Reformation, and with its pulpit panel dated 1606, was crumbling to decay in 1914.   It was pulled down and the present building, of red sandstone inside and out, was erected on the site.   The architect was Dr. MacGregor Chalmers.   A bright and sunny building, it contains some very fine stained glass by Stephen Adam and Douglas Strachan, with one window by Alexander Strachan.   Most of the windows are war memorials.   The chancel is floored with Iona marble, and the organ, recently rebuilt and enlarged, is exceptionally good.   The church possesses some old silver communion cups, two dated 1734, the other two 1825.   The panel (from the old pulpit) already referred to, with the initials of the minister of the time, can be seen in the vestry of the new church.   It is worthy of note that this lovely building cost in 1915 less than £4,000.

Of the pre-Reformation churches in Urr, the site of the parish church at Meikle Kirkland Farm can easily be seen, with traces of the road that led to it, and the spring from which the monks drew their water. The burial ground was used after the Reformation, but fell into disuse by 1650, and about a hundred years ago, it is said, the old churchyard was ploughed over, and the lead from the old coffins sold by the tenant of the time. On the other hand, no trace at all remains of St Bridget's chapel at Blaiket, which was a very old foundation. The site had been lost even by 1627 when an old account of Urr was written. Nor is any trace to be seen of the chapel of Edingham, which cannot however have been part of the castle buildings. In the middle of the thirteenth century the lands and chapel of Blaiket passed to the monks of Holyrood,[1] as did also Edingham Chapel and St. Constantine's Church, the parish church, without their lands; all this to the great detriment of the religious life of the parish, because, instead of regular parish priests, vicars were appointed by the monks of Holyrood, and were paid a mere pittance, the rest of the wealth going to the Abbey. One result of this is that since the Reformation, when the church lands were restored to the local clergy, the stipend of Urr has been paid partly in vicarage, partly in parsonage teinds. Over and above these well known churches and chapels, there were probably private chapels at Chapelton, the location being unknown now, and Spottes, where some ruins in the glen are said to be those of a chapel. The present stipend, standardised at £475 plus glebe, present rent £30, is inadequate, not indeed to live on, but for the provision of transport for the proper supervision of the parish. There are 440 communicants.

Social Life

The social life of the parish has expanded rapidly with higher wages, more leisure, better transport. Each of the villages except Hardgate, which is near Haugh-of-Urr, has a hall; the parish hall, built in 1908, being in Haugh-of-Urr. There are community councils in the villages of Haugh-of-Urr, Springholm and Crocketford. The two latter have provided playing fields for the children of their respective villages, and the council in the Haugh is in process of doing so. There are Women's Rural Institutes also, with 110 members in the Haugh, 30 in Springholm, 40 in Crocketford. Each village has a carpet bowling club, that in the Haugh being particularly strong, with about 100 members. Often a money prize is played for. Each of the three villages has a badminton club, that in the Haugh again being the strongest, which is not surprising because the hall is the most suitable for the game. Milton Village has a small but good carpet bowling club, members travelling a considerable distance to it. All the villages have football clubs, some of which take part in various leagues, and the teams are followed from place to place by the supporters from their village; many from a genuine interest in the game, but many, it is feared, from a financial interest. There is a dramatic club in Crocketford, and there was formerly a good one in the Haugh, which at present is in abeyance. An attempt is being made to revive interest in bowling and, through the kindness of the late

(1) The charter by which Blaiket chapel was handed over to Holyrood is in the possession of the MacDowells of Logan in Kirkmaiden parish. The date was 1240 At the Reformation the Church of Urr became a Crown Presentation, which it remained until 1873, appointments until that date being made under the Great Seal of Scotland.

proprietor of Spottes Hall, a grass bowling green there, in use over a hundred years ago, is now once again played on.

As regards youth organisations, there are in Springholm a Guide company and in Haugh-of-Urr a Guide company and a Brownie pack; these have a total membership of 30 Guides and 20 Brownies. There is also a very old Scout Troop, which celebrated its 40th birthday on 1 April 1952. It has had various ups and downs during these years but has seldom been in abeyance. At present about 20 strong, it contains boys from all over the parish, some of whom come very long distances to its meetings. They have a hall of their own, in the Haugh, and own a considerable amount of equipment. Three ministers in the parish have been Scoutmasters of the troop. The Sunday schools meet in the manse (Primary); the church; Springholm Hall; Milton School; and occasionally in a farmhouse when that forms a convenient centre for a group of small children. There are about 130 children in the various Sunday schools.

Over and above these various diversions, a large proportion of the parish attends the cinema, more or less regularly, in the nearest towns, or even in Dumfries, especially on a Sunday. There are inter-village competitions between all the clubs; whist drives in different villages which the neighbouring villages support; likewise concerts, and dances ancient and modern. These functions are of such frequent occurrence that very little time, in many cases, is spent at home by either old or young, with the exception of the retired folk. Curling is popular among the farmers, many of whom travel to Glasgow and Ayr two or three times a week during the season. The ice on Milton or Auchenreoch lochs has seldom in the past 20 years been thick enough for the sport.

It will thus be seen that there is now ample opportunity for amusement and diversion in the parish, and in fact the people are, with the usual exceptions, friendly and companionable. There is not much drunkenness, which makes what there is all the more noticeable. Immorality is no higher than elsewhere, but Urr has suffered considerably from the fact that in it there has been a P.O.W. Camp, and the presence of a succession of Poles, Italians and Germans imprisoned there over the war years and after has been very detrimental to the moral life of the Haugh district, especially in 'careless' families. In the opinion of the respectable element in the district, very little of the blame can be attached to the prisoners, who, although living under unnatural conditions, behaved very well when left to themselves. However, it is hoped that the camp, at present occupied by Ukranians, is about to be closed. Gambling has greatly increased its hold on the local population, and it is fairly certain that two out of every three houses take part in the football pools. But so far there are very few homes in which this is carried on to such an extent that the family obviously suffers. The parishioners are, with very rare exceptions, law-abiding, and there is no resident policeman. On the rare occasions when one is called in, it is usually to deal with riff-raff of the neighbouring towns who have invaded a local dance. The local publican maintains that he could not carry on his business without a seven day licence, which is really a compliment to the parishioners, for it means that he depends for his livelihood on the *bona fide* travellers, so-called, from outside Urr.

Like most places, Urr is feeling the changes of the present day, but perhaps less than most. A prominent inhabitant, recently come to the parish, said that coming to live in Urr was like putting the clock back 50 years. He was not referring to the amenities of science, for Urr has these. But there is something in the way of life of the people, a steadiness, a cautiousness, and a humour, that is recognised in many parts of the country as belonging to the past. However that may be, it is a pleasure to notice it and appreciate it, in a parish where there is beauty, stability and faith.

1952

THE *QUOAD SACRA* PARISH AND BURGH OF DALBEATTIE

by R. M. HALLIDAY

Formation of Parish

When the *New Statistical Account* was written, over one hundred years ago, there was no *quoad sacra* parish of Dalbeattie. Prior to 1842 there were only two places of worship in Dalbeattie, the Roman Catholic Chapel in Craignair Street, and a Cameronian Meeting House in Burn Street. At this time the adherents of the Church of Scotland had to walk about four miles to Urr Church, and were dependent on the Rev. George M. Burnside (1839-55) for religious ministrations. As the population of Dalbeattie had increased to about 1,600, this arrangement was felt to be inconvenient. A parish church at Urr clearly could no longer meet the needs of Dalbeattie.

The matter was readily taken up by the community, and a Chapel of Ease was formed. The Cameronian Meeting House in Burn Street was purchased in 1842 and converted into a suitable place of worship. The following year an ecclesiastical district was assigned, and arrangements were made for securing the services of a minister. The first minister to the Church of Dalbeattie was the Rev. James MacKenzie, who was ordained on 2 March 1843. His ministry was of the shortest duration, as the Disruption in the Church of Scotland took place a few months after his induction, and he joined the seceding party and formed a Free Church congregation in the town.

On 6 July 1864, the means having been provided partly by local effort and partly by the Endowment Committee, the church was endowed and the district at length erected into a *quoad sacra* parish. So far as civil matters are concerned, it still forms part of the parish of Urr.

Extent and Boundaries

The new parish embraces the southern portion of Urr parish. It extends for about five miles from north to south, and one and a half to two and a half miles from east to west. It is bounded on the north by the remaining portion of Urr, on the west and south by the parish of Buittle, and on the south and east by the parishes of Colvend and Kirkgunzeon.

Natural Features

As a rule the soil is fertile and kindly, except on the east where there is a considerable extent of peat and moss land. The area contains a number of excellent farms, all of which are in a flourishing condition. The Ayrshire breed of cattle is the most popular, although some of the native Galloway breed may be seen on certain farms. The principal crops grown are oats, turnips and potatoes.

The river Urr, which rises in Loch Urr on the northern border of the county, has a course of 26 miles, and meanders through the beautiful valley of Urr and dewy pasture lands until it is joined by its tributary, the Dalbeattie Burn, at Dalbeattie Port, formerly known as the Dub o' Hass. It continues its course and empties its waters into the Solway at Roughfirth.

Climate
The prevailing winds are from the south-west, and bring with them rain clouds from the Atlantic. The climate generally is mild and genial.

Antiquities
Very little is to be found on record with regard to antiquities. In May 1832 a Roman tripod was turned up by the plough at Edingham, and in 1834 two Roman tripods were discovered at Richorn Moss.

The Town of Dalbeattie
The preponderance of population in the *quoad sacra* area is located in the town of Dalbeattie, the present population of which is estimated at 3,392.

There is little doubt that the town of Dalbeattie derived its name from the designation of the farms which formerly occupied part of its site and surrounding lands. This is borne out by Timothy Pont's maps in Blaeu's Atlas, published in Amsterdam in 1654. The accepted derivation of the name is from the Celtic, meaning 'the valley of the birches'.

For beauty of situation Dalbeattie would be difficult to surpass. The town nestles snugly in the picturesque valley of the Urr, encompassed almost entirely by pine clad hills. The Dalbeattie Burn flows through the town under a bridge with granite parapets, and unites with the Urr at Dalbeattie Port. Although Dalbeattie cannot lay claim to any palatial buildings, and does not aspire to the higher graces of architecture, the native stone has been used in its buildings and it presents a clean and attractive appearance. From the coigns of vantage on any of the surrounding eminences the view of the valley, with the windings of the river, never fails to give delight. The district is also rich in the variety of its flora and fauna, and forms a happy hunting ground for the naturalist.

Few towns of the size of Dalbeattie possess such extensive public parks. These parks, Colliston, Munches and the Rounal, are beautifully situated and are assets of which any town might be proud. Colliston Park was presented to the town in 1900 by the late Miss Copland of Colliston, and the credit of bringing it into its present condition, the erection of the bandstand, bridges over the burn, swings, joy wheel, pond, was due to what was known as the General Improvements Committee. Munches and Rounal Parks were given to the burgh by the late N. J. H. Maxwell of Munches.

In Colliston Park is placed the Memorial to the men of Dalbeattie who lost their lives in the first world war. Erected by public subscription, it is appropriately constructed of the native grey granite, and is in the form of a Mercat Cross. The column is surmounted by the Galloway lion in bronze, while on one of the side panels is the burgh coat of arms, also in bronze.

Every facility for recreation is found in the town, including golf, tennis, bowling, football, fishing and putting. A few years ago a committee was formed to raise money for the provision of up-to-date playing grounds. After untiring work the committee achieved its object, the completion of a first-class enclosed football arena and running track, with grandstand and dressing rooms, a hockey pitch and car park and three excellent all-weather tennis courts. The cost was in the region of £5,000 or £6,000. These were formally opened on 23 June 1951 by Sir Patrick J. Dollan, Deputy Chairman of the National Playing Fields Association.

The Granite Industry

The development of the town was to a large extent due to the initiative of Andrew Newall who introduced the work of granite hewing into Galloway in or about the year 1800. He afterwards commenced quarrying operations at Craignair in the neighbouring parish of Buittle. The Newall family were the pioneers of the granite industry in the town, and to their descendants falls the credit of the extension and development of the various branches of the trade which eventually became the staple industry of Dalbeattie. The art of polishing the stone had a humble beginning in 1841. In 1851, by hand labour and using a very primitive method, David and Homer Newall polished a stone which was sent to the Great Exhibition in London. Between that date and the sixties the granite trade boomed. Messrs. D. H. & J. Newall, whose fame extended far beyond the confines of the valley of the Urr, continued to expand their operations, and to adopt improved methods, until their works became the show place of the town. They had hewers and polishers as well as quarriers, and also sculptors who with wonderful patience and skill converted the stubborn rough-hewn blocks into works of art. Some very fine statues and monuments have been fashioned out of this unwilling material. An extensive business was also done in crushed granite, which was used for granolithic and other purposes.

It would take a volume to record the work for which Messrs. Newall have sent out the products of the everlasting hills. The grey granite of Dalbeattie has found its way into every continent of the world. The stone has been used in the streets of great cities, and may be seen in the edifices of the Bank of England; Municipal Buildings of Liverpool;

Manchester Assize Courts and Town Hall; George V Bridge, Glasgow; Mersey Docks; Thames Embankment; Eddystone Lighthouse, and the lighthouse at Point de Galle, Ceylon. It has also been used in many important memorials, on which the finest specimens of the sculptors' art were displayed. About 1924 Messrs. Newall transferred their business to the Improved Road Constructions, who carry on the various branches of the industry.

Other Industries

The granite industry has passed through many vicissitudes in its history, and several firms have come and gone. Indeed Dalbeattie, small though it is, has seen the growth and decay of many industries. The oldest at one time was a woollen mill, followed by a paper mill, in Mill Street. There also used to be two brick and tile works, but all these ceased to function some years ago.

Dalbeattie is well known in agricultural circles for the production of artificial manures and feeding stuffs. Messrs. J. Carswell & Sons, Barrbridge Mills, have been in existence since the year 1837, and still continue to carry on a large and increasing business. Messrs Thos. Biggar & Sons, the other firm of manure manufacturers, was established as long ago as 1840. This is also a firm with a flourishing and expanding business.

The Milk Marketing Board have a large creamery near the railway station which takes in great quantities of milk from the surrounding farms. There are also a large glove factory, two saw mills and two bobbin mills in the town. The I.C.I. munitions factory, which was in use during the war, is situated at Edingham, about a mile out of the town, and has been taken over by the Admiralty who employ a considerable number of local people.

Municipal Development

By 1858 the community had increased to such an extent that a movement was brought about for municipalisation. On 17 April 1858 a meeting of householders, held in the Maxwell Arms Hotel, unanimously agreed to adopt the whole provisions of the Police Act, and thus the town was elevated to the dignity of a police burgh. The first meeting of the newly constituted Police Commission was held in the Commercial Inn on 7 June of the same year. At this meeting Thomas Maxwell was appointed the first chief magistrate, and James McLaurin and David Paterson were elected junior magistrates. Since 1858 the burgh has had 21 provosts and 9 town clerks. James Little, father of the present town clerk, held office from 1879 till 1929 when he resigned, thus completing a period of 50 years' faithful service, which is a record unique in the history of Scotland for such an official.

During the first century of the town's municipal history the march of progress has gone steadily on. A gravitation water supply was introduced in 1880 which superseded the system of old wells. A proper sewage system followed and a great advance was made in the direction of improved sanitation. In 1893 the town council adopted a coat of arms, based upon the family arms of the superiors, Maxwell of Munches and Copland of Colliston.

Prior to 1852 there were no banks in the town. Now there are three. The Union Bank was established in 1852, the Commercial in 1889 and the Clydesdale in 1909. Before the advent of the railway in 1859 journeys to Dumfries and other neighbouring towns had to be performed on foot or in stage coaches. There were two coaches, the 'Perseverance' and the 'Victoria', between which it is said there was great rivalry. Heron's *Journey* of 1799 mentions the fact that there was navigation on the river at Dalbeattie, so that for considerably over a century small vessels, schooners and sloops, mainly in the coasting trade, have passed up and down the winding Urr to the Solway and the seas beyond. The harbour or port in those days was known as the Dub o' Hass. Alas! with the coming of the railway and modern road transport, to-day it is a port without trade, and a harbour without ships.

The Dalbeattie Gas Light Company was formed in 1858, and the town was among the first in the south of Scotland to be illuminated with gas. Another advance has been made as the town is now supplied with electricity by the South of Scotland Electricity Board. Among the many modern improvements carried out by the town council have been the installation of a mechanical filtration plant, the general improvement of the streets, including the paving with granite setts of Craignair Street, Maxwell Street, Station Road, and a portion of High Street. They have also introduced concrete pavements throughout the town, and have effected other improvements in many directions to keep in line with present day requirements. The provision of modern houses for the inhabitants has also been undertaken, and a large number of new houses have been erected under the Housing Acts.

There are several substantial buildings in the town constructed with the native granite. The Town Hall, situated in High Street at the north end of the bridge over the burn, is a fine granite structure surmounted by a square tower and illuminated clock. At the south end of the bridge on the left bank of the burn is situated the post office, also constructed of granite, and well equipped to meet all modern requirements. The granite drinking fountain in Maxwell Street was given to the town by the late Wellwood H. Maxwell of Munches. To commemorate the jubilee of Queen Victoria in 1887, a handsome fountain was erected at the Cross in High Street. Constructed of Dalbeattie and Peterhead granite, it is surmounted by a column with a lamp on top. The cost was defrayed by public subscription.

Schools

The citizens of Dalbeattie have always taken more than an ordinary interest in education. The parochial school, built in 1828, was situated

at Glenshalloch Place.   Shortly after the Disruption in 1843 the con-
gregation of the Free Church built a school in Mill Street adjoining the
church.   Several 'dame schools' were spread throughout the town.
There was a 'female school' at Lattimer Place in Southwick Road,
conducted by a Miss Johnston.   The finely appointed buildings of
Dalbeattie High School were opened on 7 May 1876.   In Maxwell
Street, in premises owned by the Roman Catholic Church, the Education
Authority maintains a primary school for Roman Catholic pupils.

Churches

The town is well provided with churches.   St. Peter's Roman Catholic
Church is the oldest place of worship, the present church having been
built in 1814.   Before the advent of St. Peter's in Dalbeattie, there was
a Roman Catholic Chapel at Munches which supplied the religious
wants of a very large district.   The family of Munches terminated in
an heiress who married into a Protestant family.   The Rev. Andrew
Carruthers, who was the priest in charge, was thus deprived of his
chapel, which was closed.   He was, however, generously treated by the
new proprietor, who granted him ground in Craignair Street to build
a chapel and parsonage.   The cost of its erection was defrayed out of
the fund left by Mrs. Agnes Maxwell to the Roman Catholic Church.
Father Carruthers was the last priest at Munches and the first of St.
Peter's.   Several of the priests who have passed through St. Peter's have
risen to high rank in the Catholic Church.   The Rev. Andrew Carruthers
ultimately became Archbishop of Glasgow.   The Rev. John Cowie
became Rector of Valladolid College, Spain.   The priest in charge from
1835 to 1857 was the Rev. John Strain, who rose to fill the position of
Archbishop of Edinburgh.

Towards the end of the seventies the population of the town had
risen to over 4,000, principally because of the influx of a large number
of quarry workers.   The membership of the Church of Scotland congregation had proportionally increased and the old parish church in
Burn Street had ceased to be large enough.   A site for a new church
in Craignair Street was given by the late Wellwood H. Maxwell of
Munches.   The memorial stone was laid by the late Mrs. Maxwell of
Munches on 24 December 1878, and the new church was opened for
worship on 27 January 1880.   It is built of granite with grey freestone
facings, and has a graceful spire rising to a height of 140 feet.

On 12 January 1895 instrumental music was first introduced by the
use of a harmonium, and a large pipe organ was installed in 1897.   The
practice of standing at praise was first adopted on 27 January 1880, and
the first hymn was sung in church on Christmas Eve, 1882.

At the union of the churches in 1929, Dalbeattie Parish Church
became known as Craignair Parish Church.   It is the largest and most
elegant ecclesiastical edifice in the town.   It is seated for 850, but it
can accommodate 1,000 worshippers.   Two years after the completion
of the church five stained-glass windows were placed in the apse in

memory of the Rev. Duncan Stewart. The windows represent the eleven Apostles witnessing the Ascension. A granite mural tablet was erected to the late Wellwood H. Maxwell of Munches, who was a benefactor of the church. In December 1954 a large stained-glass window was installed in memory of the Rev. Charles P. Grant, who was minister of the church for 22 years. The subject is taken from Holman Hunt's painting, 'The Light of the World.'

Shortly after the Disruption in 1843, the newly formed Free Church congregation built a new church in Mill Street. In 1882, during the ministry of the Rev. James A. Paton, the church was rebuilt. It is an attractive granite building with spire.

Prior to 1858 the members of the United Presbyterian denomination in the town had to travel every Sunday a distance of about five miles to a church at Hardgate. They worshipped in the Commercial Hall for three years before their church was built in John Street. The church was completed in 1861 and the manse in 1871. The first pastor was the Rev. David Kinnear who ministered faithfully to his flock for over 40 years till his death in 1903. Mr. Kinnear for a term held the position of Moderator of the General Synod of the United Presbyterian Church of Scotland.

The Congregational Church is situated in William Street and was built of granite in 1866, and enlarged in 1876. It is a neat little church.

About the year 1873 the granite trade was flourishing, with the result that it brought a large number of English granite workers to the town. They formed an Episcopal congregation and services were for some time held in a hall. Eventually Christ Church (Episcopal) was erected in 1875, on a site at the corner of High Street and Blair Street. Built of granite in the Early English style of architecture, it has seating accommodation for over 100 worshippers. Recently an apse was added to the church. It is the gift of Mr. L. M. Ellis and his family in memory of Mrs. Ellis, who was a devoted member. This has lent considerable beauty to the interior. At the same time a new vestry was supplied by the congregation.

Newspapers and Periodicals

It was not until 1889 that the town could claim a newspaper of its own. In that year *The Stewartry Observer* was launched. It carried on weekly for 65 years until December 1954, when it ceased publication.

With regard to the literary propensities of the inhabitants, Dalbeattie has produced its quota of poets and authors, several of whom are possessed of considerable genius. In the spring of 1899, Dalbeattie was the birthplace of the well-known provincial magazine *The Gallovidian*. It appeared regularly until the war years, when publication was suspended.

1955

ACKNOWLEDGMENTS

Contributions to County Account:

THE BACKGROUND

Geography, H. A. Moisley, Geography Department, University of Glasgow.
Geology, Professor T. Neville George, University of Glasgow.
Flora, Dr. H. Milne-Redhead, Mainsriddle.
Mammals and Birds, Donald Watson, Dalry.
Archaeology, A. E. Truckell, Curator, Dumfries Museum.
Early History, Rev. J. W. T. Dickie, Gatehouse.
Later History, David S. Graham, Edinburgh.

THE ECONOMY

Agriculture, Sir J. B. Douglas, C.B.E., Barstibly, Castle-Douglas.
I.C.I. Drungans Factory, Dr. J. B. Addison.
Forestry, J. A. B. MacDonald, Conservator, South Scotland.
South of Scotland Electricity Board
    Generation, G. W. Briggs, Stations Superintendent.
    Distribution, W. H. Wills, Manager, Dumfries.

GOVERNMENT AND PUBLIC SERVICE

Robert C. Monteath, County Clerk.
R. B. S. Gilmour, County Surveyor.
Dr. J. B. Shiel, County Medical Officer.

THE COMMUNITY

The Church, Rev. J. Ross Fulton, New Galloway.

Indexing and preparing bibliography

Mrs. M. G. Brown, County Librarian.

Abstracting statistics for section on agriculture

Ian Mitchell, County Advisor, West of Scotland College of Agriculture.

Typewriting and proof-reading

Miss C. E. Greggan.

Grateful acknowledgment is made to the following for the use of blocks:

Forestry Commission.
South of Scotland Electricity Board.
Scottish Milk Marketing Board.
Galloway News.
Shell and B.P. Scotland Ltd.
Galloway Cattle Society.

BIBLIOGRAPHY

This bibliography contains a selection of books of general interest relating to the Stewartry of Kirkcudbright. Lack of space has made it necessary to omit parish histories but material on the following is available through the County Library: Anwoth, Balmaclellan, Balmaghie, Borgue, Buittle, Carsphairn, Castle-Douglas, Colvend, Corsock, Crocketford, Crossmichael, Dalbeattie, Dalry, Gatehouse-of-Fleet, Girthon, Glenkens, Kelton, Kirkbean, Kirkcudbright, Kirkmabreck, Kirkpatrick-Durham, Minnigaff, New Abbey, New Galloway, Parton, Rerrick, Southwick, Tongland, Troqueer, Urr. Readers are also referred to: *The Statistical Account of Scotland, 1791-1799; The Statistical Account of Scotland, 1845-51; Transactions of the Dumfriesshire and Galloway Natural History and Antiquarian Society; Proceedings of the Society of Antiquaries of Scotland; The Gallovidian;* the files of local newspapers and magazines; valuation and voters' rolls; town and county council minutes and reports.

Agnew, Sir Andrew. *The hereditary sheriffs of Galloway.* 2 vols. Edinburgh, 1893.

[Aitken, James] (*A Gallovidian*). *Tales of the Solway.* Dumfries, 1873.

Biggar, James. *The Agriculture of Kirkcudbrightshire and Wigtownshire.* Dumfries, 1876.

Blake, Brian. *The Solway Firth.* London, 1955.

Christie, Rev. Alexander H. *The Abbey of Dundrennan.* Dalbeattie, 1914.

Corrie, John Maitland. *The "Droving Days" in the South Western district of Scotland.* Dumfries, 1915.

Crockett, Rev. Samuel Rutherford. *Raiderland: all about Grey Galloway: its stories, traditions, characters, humours.* London, 1904.

Cromek, R. H. *ed. Remains of Nithsdale and Galloway song.* Paisley, 1880.

Denniston, James. *Legends of Galloway.* Edinburgh, 1825.

Dick, Rev. Charles Hill. *Highways and byways in Galloway and Carrick.* London, 1916.

Fraser, William. *The Book of Caerlaverock.* Memoirs of the Maxwells, Earls of Nithsdale, Lords Maxwell and Herries. 2 vols. Edinburgh, 1873.

Fraser, William. *The Douglas book.* 4 vols. Edinburgh, 1885.

Gauld, William A. *Galloway: an introductory study, January 16, 1922. Agriculture and population in Galloway, October 15, 1922.* From, *The Scottish Geographical Magazine.*

Hare, F. K. *Kirkcudbright and Wigtown.* Report of the Land Utilization Survey of Britain. Parts 7-8. London, 1942.

Harper, Malcolm McLachlan. *The bards of Galloway, a collection of poems, songs, ballads, etc., by natives of Galloway.* Dalbeattie, 1889.

Harper, Malcolm McLachlan. *Rambles in Galloway: topographical, historical, traditional and biographical.* Edinburgh, 1876.

Hutchinson, Bertram A. *Depopulation and rural life in the Solway Counties.* The first report of an inquiry for the Department of Health for Scotland into the causes of rural depopulation. London, 1949.

Huyshe, Wentworth. *Grey Galloway, its Lords and its Saints.* Edinburgh, 1914.

Jolly, William. *On the evidence of glacier action in Galloway.* From, *Transactions of the Edinburgh Geological Society for 1867-8.* Edinburgh, 1868.

Learmonth, William. *Kirkcudbrightshire and Wigtownshire.* Cambridge, 1920. (*Cambridge County Geography, series*).

M'Andrew, J. *List of the flowering plants of Dumfriesshire and Kirkcudbright-shire. Compiled for the Dumfriesshire and Galloway Natural History and Antiquarian Society.* Dumfries, 1882.

McBain, J. *The Merrick and the neighbouring hills.* Ayr, 1929.

McCormick, Andrew. *Galloway: the spell of its hills and glens.* To which is added, *The geology of the Merrick region,* by R. J. A. Eckford. Glasgow, 1932.

McCormick, Andrew. *The Tinkler-Gypsies of Galloway.* Dumfries, 1906.

McDowall, John Kevan. *Carrick Gallovidian; a historical survey of the ancient lordship of Galloway.* Glasgow, 1947.

Mackenzie, William. *The history of Galloway from the earliest period to the present time.* 2 vols. Kirkcudbright, 1841.

McKerlie, E. Marianne H. *Pilgrim spots in Galloway.* London, 1916.

McKerlie, Peter Handyside. *Galloway in ancient and modern times.* Edinburgh, 1891.

McKerlie, Peter Handyside. *History of the lands and their owners in Galloway.* 5 vols. Edinburgh, 1870-79.

MacLelland, Thomas. *On the agriculture of Kirkcudbrightshire and Wigtown-shire.* From, *Transactions of the Highland and Agricultural Society of Scotland.* n.d.

MacTaggart, John. *The Scottish Gallovidian encyclopaedia.* London, 1824.

Maxwell, Sir Herbert Eustace. *A history of Dumfries and Galloway.* Edinburgh, 1896.

Maxwell, Sir Herbert Eustace. *A history of the House of Douglas from the earliest times down to the Legislative Union of England and Scotland.* 2 vols. London, 1902.

Maxwell, Sir Herbert Eustace. *The place names of Galloway: their origin and meaning considered.* [A revision of the 1887 edition]. Glasgow, 1930.

Maxwell, Sir Herbert Eustace. *Studies in the topography of Galloway.* Edinburgh, 1887.

[Maxwell, John Hunter]. *Maxwell's guide book to the Stewartry of Kirkcud-bright, from the Nith to the Cree.* Castle-Douglas, 1878. [Also subsequent editions].

Minute Book kept by the War Committee of the Covenanters in the Stewartry of Kirkcudbright in the years 1640 and 1641. Kirkcudbright, 1855.

Morton, Alexander S. *Galloway and the Covenanters.* Paisley, 1914.

Murray, Thomas. *The literary history of Galloway, from the earliest period to the present time; with an appendix containing notices of the civil history of Galloway till the end of the thirteenth century.* Edinburgh, 1822.

Nicholson, John. *Historical and traditional tales, in prose and verse, connected with the South of Scotland.* Kirkcudbright, 1843.

The Register of the Synod of Galloway from October 1664 to April 1671. Kirkcudbright, 1856.

Robison, Joseph. *Kirkcudbright Incorporated Trades, 1744-1799, being the Second of two lectures given to members of the Six Incorporated Trades.* 1920.

Robison, Joseph. *Kirkcudbright (St. Cuthbert's Town); its Mote, Castle, Monastery, and Parish Churches.* Dumfries, 1926.

Robertson, John F. *The story of Galloway.* Castle-Douglas, 1963.

Royal Commission on the Ancient and Historical Monuments and Constructions in Scotland. *Fifth Report and Inventory of monuments and constructions in Galloway.* vol. 2. *County of the Stewartry of Kirkcudbright.* Edinburgh, 1914.

Royal Commission on Tweed and Solway Fisheries. *Report of the Commissioners on the Fisheries of the Solway Firth.* Parts 1 and 2. London, 1896.

Russell, James Anderson. *The book of Galloway.* Dumfries, 1962.

Russell, James Anderson. *History of Education in the Stewartry of Kirkcudbright from original and contemporary sources.* Newton-Stewart, 1951.

Service, Robert. *The vertebrate zoology of Kirkcudbrightshire.* 1896. *The disappearance of the Chough from the Stewartry of Kirkcudbright.* 1885. *Mammalia of the Solway.* 1896. *The starling in Solway.* 1895. [One volume of collected papers].

Sloan, J. M. *Galloway.* Painted by James Faed, Jnr., and described by J. M. Sloan. London, 1908.

Smeaton, Oliphant. *The romance of the road: coaching in Scotland in the olden days.* A series of articles from cuttings made from a local [Galloway] newspaper. 1822.

Smith, Rev. Samuel. *General view of the agriculture of Galloway.* London, 1810.

Solway White Fishery Commission. *Report. Minutes of evidence and appendices.* Edinburgh, 1892.

Stewartry of Kirkcudbright Agricultural Society. *Report of the Stewartry of Kirkcudbright Agricultural Society for the year* 1810. With a short account of its institution in March, 1809. Dumfries, 1811.

Stewartry of Kirkcudbright County Council. *Survey report.* Prepared in accordance with Section 3 (1) of the Town and Country Planning (Scotland) Act, 1947, in respect of the Landward area of the Stewartry. 2 vols. Kirkcudbright, 1960.

Stewartry of Kirkcudbright Farmers' Club. *Average prices of farm produce during the years 1895-1903 . . . and consecutively 1906-1915. Reports and analysis of samples of manures and feeding stuffs . . . Seasons 1894-1914.*

Train, Joseph. *The Buchanites from first to last.* Edinburgh, 1846.

Symson, Andrew. *A large description of Galloway,* 1684. With an appendix containing original papers, from the *Sibbald and Macfarlane MSS.* Edinburgh, 1823.

Trotter, Alexander. *East Galloway sketches, or biographical, historical and descriptive notices of Kirkcudbrightshire, chiefly in the nineteenth century.* Castle-Douglas, 1901.

Trotter, Robert de Bruce. *Galloway Gossip eighty years ago.* Dumfries, 1901.

Webster, James. *General view of the agriculture of Galloway, comprehending the Stewartry of Kirkcudbright and the Shire of Wigton. With observations on the means of its improvement.* Edinburgh, 1794.

Wood, John Maxwell. *Smuggling in the Solway and around the Galloway seaboard.* Dumfries, 1908.

Wood, John Maxwell. *Witchcraft and Superstitious Record in the South-Western District of Scotland.* Dumfries, 1911.

THE COUNTY OF
WIGTOWN

PREFACE

FOR various reasons this volume is appearing later than was originally planned. Some of the chapters were written between 1947 and 1952 for publication in the comparatively early future, but conditions changed and there was a hiatus that lasted for a number of years. On activities being resumed most of the writing was completed in 1960. Since then a good deal of revision has been carried out and efforts have been made to give an account of Wigtownshire as it is today. One of the purposes of the *Third Statistical Account* is to provide posterity with a picture of the county at the middle of the twentieth century, but the book is also intended for present day reading and use. Accordingly, if some readers think that the text is not all quite topical they may reflect on the book's possible historical value in the distant future. Nevertheless, the sponsors hope that it will be of interest and considerable use now.

In the opening sections a general survey is given of the county as a whole, with all facets of Wigtownshire depicted, broadly in some cases and in detail where that seemed necessary. Subsequent chapters are devoted to the various parishes. The subjects described in the county account range from geology to modern customs and habits and in the course of the review reference is made to industry, communications, education, church work, housing and public services, trade and commerce, sporting activities, entertainment and many other aspects of the way of life in the Shire. Animal and bird life and wild flowers found in the Rhins and Machars are dealt with and there are also accounts of historical happenings.

Those responsible for the publication of the book are most grateful to all who have contributed to the contents of the *Account*. A great many people have given information and help to the various writers and without their assistance the enterprise would have been impossible. In this connection reference should be made to the writing of the geological section by Mr. R. J. A. Eckford, Moffat, who is specially qualified to deal with such a subject. One of his last assignments in his profession as a geologist was to carry out a survey of Wigtownshire and his study of the county from the geological point of view provided him with much of the material for his contribution to this volume. Appreciation should also be expressed of the aid given in various ways by the planning department and other county departments, whose assistance was of much value.

It is a matter for regret that several of the people who wrote parish accounts have died since their contributions were penned. They were: the Rev. James Thomson, Mochrum; the Rev. N. Elliot, Sorbie; the Rev. David Galloway, Old Luce; and Mrs. Grace N. Christison, Kirkinner.

M. C. ARNOTT

Stranraer.
March, 1964.

Part One

THE COUNTY

CHAPTER 1

THE BACKGROUND

NATURAL FEATURES

GALLOWAY, which at one time extended much more widely than it does today, consists of the counties of Wigtown and Kirkcudbright. With its constant defiance of the western seas, Wigtownshire wears a sterner aspect than its close neighbour, Kirkcudbrightshire, more often known as the Stewartry. For administrative purposes the two counties have only a few joint services—police and health. Together they form a parliamentary division, a comparatively recent development; during the middle ages the usual designation was the Lordship of Galloway.

From its boundary with Ayrshire in the west to the link-up with the Stewartry in the east, Wigtownshire is fringed with hills along the whole of the northern border, some sprawling and subdued, others rising to dominate the Southern Uplands. Unlike the Stewartry, it has a flat and empty look as seen from the main highways running east and west, with much rough pasture and marginal land, and some cultivated fields on the high ground that rises out of the bogland and peat mosses. There are clear reasons for the emptiness. The land is generally unsuitable for townships, while certain natural features have determined the location of the main centres of population near the perimeter of the county—Wigtown, Whithorn and Newton Stewart, grouped in the Machars district, and Stranraer in the Rhins along with most of the county's largest villages. To the east the boundary is mainly the Cree valley, consisting of forests and farmlands, which are shared with the Stewartry. In area Wigtownshire extends to 311,984 acres, or nearly 487½ square miles. A great deal of the county rises little above sea level. Most of the hills in the Rhins are low and they are dwarfed by the Merrick, Benyellary and other peaks to the east that dominate the Machars landscape. In the western district the only river of any size is the Luce, which rises among the hills to the north and empties itself into Luce Bay to the south. The Cree is a noted feature of the Machars, while the Tarff, some miles westward, if less famous, is popular with anglers, as is also the Bladnoch.

Deposits of blown sand are found on the coast along the head of Luce Bay. The prevailing current has brought about changes and has pushed the mouth of the Piltanton burn to the east side of the bay. Where the sand is free it is carried, during periods of strong winds, to Drochduil, Whitecrook and Mains of Park. Much of the sand is covered with heather, bracken and seasedge and if this vegetation is not maintained it is believed that effects of this blowing will become serious. This area, rich in archaeological finds, has provided a wealth of exhibits for the National Museum in Edinburgh.

In some parts of the coast erosion has taken place, notably on the west fringes of Luce Bay, where the sea has eaten away parts of the raised beach. Walls have been built north of Drummore along the main road to act as a bulwark and other protective measures have been taken in this area. A mile north of Cairnryan a thick plaster of morainic drift is mainly tree covered, but where trees have been removed erosion has set in and caused numerous landslides. Road widening work has recently been carried out here and the possibility of slides has been reduced. The River Luce has eroded part of the adjacent valley and the Cree at Newton Stewart has eaten into the banks, especially at a bend south of Machermore Castle. For the most part the soil is light and easy to work, but some districts have a stiff boulder clay. The Mull of Galloway, the most famous geographical feature of Wigtownshire, rises to a height of 287 feet and is separated from the main part of the Rhins by a narrow neck of lower land. At this part of the coast there are cliffs 200 feet high. Along the side of the lower reaches of the River Cree and at the head of Wigtown Bay the soil is alluvial.

Peat, now very little used, varies in quality and thickness throughout the county. Much of it is of the brown type and has little value as fuel. Between the hills and on the very flat ground peat of good thickness and quality has been found, particularly at the Moss of Cree, between Kirkcowan and Glenluce, and also west of Stranraer in the Larbrax district of Leswalt.

CLIMATE

Wigtownshire weather is milder than that of most other counties in Scotland. This is especially the case in the Rhins, apart from the parish of New Luce: from Cairnryan to the Mull, and at Stranraer, the winter often passes without more than a flurry of snow falling. The proximity of the sea is probably the reason for the long growing season and for the absence of undue summer heat. The district is subject, however, to periodical visitations of strong winds, especially in the late autumn. There is often a wintry spell in New Luce and in the hilly territory of the Machars while the rest of the county is getting off lightly, and the valley of the Luce provides more outdoor curling than any other part of the shire. There is a wide variation in the rainfall. At the Mull of Galloway the average annual fall is between 27 and 28 inches, while in the northern district, according to the readings at Lagafater, the figure is around 65 inches. Corsewall has 34.1 inches, Galloway House 41 and Kirkcowan 49.3 inches. (Fig. 1.)

GEOLOGY[1]

Wigtownshire geology is an epitome of that found throughout the Southern Uplands. As the terminal portion of the range where it is cut off by the sea, it is a greatly worn-down sector, much of it but the remains of denuded hills or mountains. The county is deeply eaten into by three bays, with the Rhins district nearly severed from the mainland. The rocks belong to the Ordovician and Silurian systems, and the two strata occupy nearly equal proportions in the county. The formations within the Ordovician range are Glenkiln Shales, at the top of Llandeilo and Hartfell Shales. Succeeding the Hartfell are the Birkhill Shales, the lowest of the Silurian formations, followed by the Tarannon. A remnant of the higher Wenlock formation, which forms part of the southern belt of the Uplands, is preserved at Burrowhead to the west of the Isle of Whithorn.

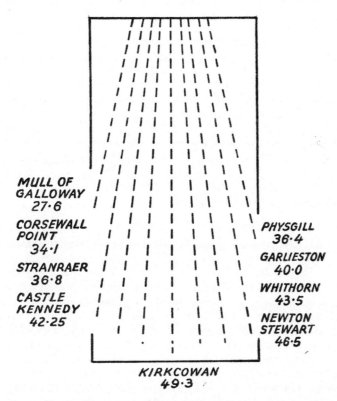

MULL OF
GALLOWAY
27·6

CORSEWALL
POINT
34·1

STRANRAER
36·8

CASTLE
KENNEDY
42·25

PHYSGILL
36·4

GARLIESTON
40·0

WHITHORN
43·5

NEWTON
STEWART
46·5

KIRKCOWAN
49·3

Fig. 1. Contrasts in the rainfall at different parts of the Shire are depicted in the diagram. The annual average fall varies by rather more than 21 inches, with the lowest at the Mull and the highest at Kirkcowan, in the centre of the inland area. A short distance over the Ayrshire boundary, at Lagafater, the annual fall is 64.8 inches.

[1] From material supplied by Mr. R. J. A. Eckford, Moffat.

By far the most common rock flooring in the county is greywacke, a type of indurated sandstone occurring in beds of various thicknesses. This rock was largely used as a building stone in former times, as can be seen in the towns and villages in the Southern Uplands; it has also proved a durable roadstone. Accompanying the greywacke are beds of shale, ranging from about an inch up to several feet. Wigtownshire is fortunate in having an extensive coastline with a splendid display of cliffs, as nearly all the west coast of the Rhins is cut across the folds, thus enhancing its geological importance. This coastline, forming the rampart of the whole region, bears the brunt of the prevailing gales, which lash the waves with fury against the resistant greywackes.

At the north end of the Rhins a massive conglomerate is to be seen around Corsewall Lighthouse, with boulders of granite and diorite up to a foot in length and smaller cobbles of lava, chert and limestone. Southwards, the beds become finer, pebbly and gritty bands being prominent. Within Dounan Bay, six miles south of the lighthouse, a marked change in the character of the strata produces a softer, more easily eroded, shaley type, while about the centre of the bay the major Southern Upland fault runs out to sea, having crossed the Rhins from Lady Bay on the east side after its course down Glenapp. This great fracture, extending from the North Sea to the Wigtownshire coast, appears to effect little displacement along its south-western sector compared with the few thousand feet by which the rocks along the north-western side have been lowered over most of its stretch. Its south-western sector appears to have split into three branches, the one disappearing in the sea at Dounan Bay being the southern branch. Nevertheless, it has exerted severe crushing, as witness the breccias (crushed rock) seen near the north end of the bay and the clay (probably crushed shale) which was formerly worked; iron ore is also associated with the crushed rocks.

Dounan Shales. Doctors Peach and Horne first drew attention to the mode of occurrence of the graptolite remains in the Dounan shales, named from this bay. They are found in black films and streaks in the coarser grey shales, which can be traced for many miles southwards along the coast, and the repetition of the same type of beds is due to the corrugations into which the strata have been compressed. The folding displayed is known as isoclinal, with the axes of the folds tilted at a slight angle to the north-west along this stretch of the coast. This gives the appearance of the strata all dipping to the south-east. Mostly it is only the limbs of the folds that are visible, the crests having been denuded off, but at some places, such as March Port, Broadport and Broadsea Bay, good examples of the crests can be seen where beds rise and turn over, then dip in the same direction. Most of the bays are excavated in the softer shaley material, while protruding cliffs are harder greywackes. Nodular limestone is fairly abundant in the strata along this part of the coast. At the south end of Broadsea Bay, on the skerries, an interesting, though small, exposure of volcanic rocks is recorded. Only a few exposures of lavas of doubtful Arenig age are found within the county.

The Dounan shales continue as far south as Killintringan Bay, still with the black seams often containing graptolites. A conglomerate, 30 to 40 yards in breadth, can be seen at Dove Cove, with boulders up to two feet in length; the most prominent are greywacke and limestone, the spongy appearance of the latter being due to weathering. From Killintringan down to Portpatrick the magnificent cliff sections have been excavated in greywacke. The cliffs continue in a south to south-east direction from Portpatrick to Morroch Bay, a distance of about a mile and a half. Here between high and low tide marks, for a distance of 450 yards, a fairly continuous section of Glenkiln and Hartfell shales with a high dip is exposed across the strike of the beds. At low tide the exposure along the strike stretches for a distance of over a hundred yards. Inland from the section a remnant of the former 25-foot beach is banked up against the old cliffs.

This is the best locality for graptolite collecting within the county and among the best within the Southern Uplands. Thirty-six species of graptolites, contained within thirteen genera, have been recorded from the shales exposed here. From the assemblage the top zone of the Glenkiln shales is well represented and, of the succeeding three zones of the Hartfell shales, the upper two are missing, or their types of graptolites have not yet been found. Cherts are exposed in the cores of some of the folds. Farther south along the coast the scenery alternately consists of cliff, heugh and bay, the cliffs representing greywackes, the heughs and bays generally the more shaley rocks. About a quarter of a mile south of Money Head, where a burn falls over the cliffs into the sea, the first of the monograptid graptolites has been recorded from the dark shales. This shows that the surface rocks are of the Silurian age and, in the lowest formation, Birkhill shales (more widely known as Llandovery) of that system. The provisional line separating the two systems, Ordovician and Silurian, has been drawn about a mile to the north of this locality.

It may be mentioned that the best locality for the Birkhill shales, where graptolites are easily found, is at the north side of Clanyard Bay, some three miles W.N.W. of Drummore. Here, besides exposures of the Birkhill shales with monograptids, the Hartfell shales apparently occupy the core of a large, steep fold; and similar strata are found on the south side of the bay.

Belt of Red Sandstone. From Jamieson's Point, northwards of Kirkcolm, a belt of red sandstone, with marls averaging half a mile in width, extends southwards along the western side of Lochryan to beyond Stranraer. It belongs to the Permian formation. Continuous with the red sandstone along most of its western side is a much narrower outcrop of Carboniferous (Millstone grit) sandstone, shale and fireclay. These deposits are but remnants of former widespread sheets. (Fig. 2.)

The intrusive rocks in the county occur in the form of minor masses and dykes, the outcrops of the former being small in comparison with the areas occupied by the major intrusions of Kirkcudbright. There are granite intrusions near Drummore, at Culvennan Fell and Glenluce. The Drummore mass occupies an area of approximately a square mile; the other two masses are more nearly rectangular in outline and the Glenluce mass makes an abrupt change in direction near its southern end. It is probable that these masses expand underground and that denudation has, so far, revealed only their upper portions.

Lesser exposures of porphyrite occur near Ervie, in the northern area of the Rhins, and east of Eldrig, in the Machars. In the southern district

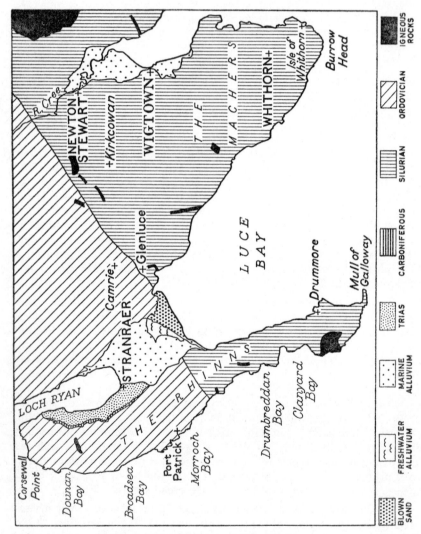

Fig. 2. The Geology of Wigtownshire.

of the Machars and conspicuous around the coast are lamprophyres, brownish coloured rocks showing large plates of glittering mica (biotite) set in a fine matrix of micro-minerals. The dykes along the west coast of the Rhins show many types of the lamprophyre group. Well over a hundred can be counted between Dounan Bay, to the north of Kirkcolm, and the Mull headland in the south. Their colours vary greatly, some pink, some light buff, others greenish from the hornblende they contain. They are easily spotted stretching up the cliffs and many make features inland, such as knolls, being more resistant to weathering than the surrounding strata. Good examples of long massive dykes of the diorite type are well exposed in the Gillespie Burn area, one stretching for a distance of two miles; also around Fell Hill, south-west of Culvennan Fell. A small mass that provides a lovely building stone, granitic in texture, is found near the Mark of Shennanton in the same district. The dolerite dykes of the Tertiary age are poorly represented throughout Galloway.

Like the solid geology, the glaciation of Wigtownshire is a replica of that of the Southern Uplands, except that the impact over most of the shire was more severe than that undergone by the rest of the southern area. Among the features attributable to ice action are the drumlins formed of boulder clay. They are believed to have taken shape under moving ice, the clay having been piled around some obstacle such as a knoll of rock or a concentration of boulders in the basement layer of the ice. Most of them are beautifully moulded and are probably the most conspicuous of the glacial relics to be seen in the lowlands of the county, some forming minor hills. Between Newton Stewart and Glenluce and to the west of Wigtown they are particularly impressive.

Boulder Clay. Boulder clay is widely spread, varying greatly in thickness and being deepest in the depressions, where it may amount to many feet. Other features attributable to ice action include spreads of sand and gravel, lochs, lochans and quaking bogs. Ice planed and tore off rock in some places; in others it deposited and moulded. The topography of the county, therefore, has been greatly modified by the work of ice. In dealing with glaciation, mention must also be made of the former beach strands, frequently referred to as raised beaches. There are remnants of the 100-foot, the 50-foot and the 25-foot strands along many parts of the coast. On the east side of Lochryan the three platforms can be well seen in the stretch of slope through which the Several and Beoch burns have cut ravines. The platforms mark the fluctuations of sea level during and following the ice age.

The economic products yielded by the rocks are negligible. The veins of hematite in the Dounan Bay stretch appear to be thin and not-far-reaching. Copper ore at Tonderghie seems to have been worked out, while fireclay found along the west side of Lochryan gives poor quality bauxite.

There are brick clays at Carty, Newton Stewart, and at Terally, to the north of Drummore. At Carty the tile works started many years ago are still operating. Similar activities were carried on at Terally for a long period, but the brick works have now been closed down. Quarrying of building stone in the county ceased some years ago and of the road metal quarries only that at Boreland Fell, near Kirkcowan, is still in use.

FLORA[1]

Of the great number of wild flowers to be found in the area, the species mentioned here are those which are rare in Wigtownshire or exhibit some peculiar characteristic and which, at the same time, are representative of habitats of all types except Alpine (over 2,000 feet). The place names indicate one or two of several localities where the plant has been found.

The extensive coastal areas of the county provide suitable climate and environment for a rich and varied maritime flora. Common on all shores where they are periodically saturated with salt spray are colonies of Glasswort, Sea Purslane, Saltwort, Sandwort, Scurvy grass and Sea Milkwort. To be met with occasionally on the wet sand are Sea Kale, Sea Rocket and Sea Beet and on muddy ground Sea Lavender (*Statice limonium*)—Wigtown and West Tarbet. On the dry sand and shingle are some interesting but less common species, typical maritime plants with their glaucous foliage, including Sea Holly (*Eryngium maritimum*)—Cailiness Point; Morroch Bay; Horned Poppy (*Glaucium flavum*), one of our most spectacular wild flowers—Kirkmaiden; abundant on Portwilliam shore; Sea Lungwort (*Mertensia maritima*) occurring more frequently than is generally supposed—plentiful on Portwilliam shore; West Tarbet. Farther inland the following are of interest:—Sea Bindweed (*Convolvulus soldanella*) on sand dunes associated with Marram Grass—Port Logan; Monreith; Scotch Burnet Rose (*Rosa spinosissima*)—Morroch Bay; widespread on Portwilliam shore; Lovage (*Ligusticum scoticum*)—Lady Bay; Finnarts; Vernal Squill (*Scilla verna*)—abundant locally on grassy places at Monreith and cliff tops at Portpatrick; Bitter Sweet (*Solanum dulcamara*), poisonous, climbing on Blackthorn—Stairhaven; Ardwell Bay; Common Nightshade (*Solanum nigrum*) very local, poisonous—Sandhead; Samphire (*Crithmum maritimum*), once common on rocks at Laird's Bay, now rare, also found at Mull; Stag's Horn Plantain (*Plantago coronopus*)—Portpatrick; Sea Buckthorn (*Hippophae rhamnoides*)—near Portlogan Fishpond; Tutsan (*Hypericum androsemum*)—St. Medans; rocks at Lady Bay; Skull cap (*Scutellaria minor*) and Sea Stork's bill, found on shingly turf at New England Bay and Garlieston. Thorn Apple (*Datura stramonium*), very poisonous; rare; reported from time to time on the shores of Wigtown Bay.

The rivers, lochs and numerous ponds, burns and ditches provide habitats for a variety of aquatic plants. A few of the more striking are Bulrush (*Scirpus lacustris*), frequent on edge of lochs—Aird Moss; Globe flower (*Trollius europeus*), local—River Tarff. Frequent on water's edge are Meadow Rue (*Thalictrum flavum*), Bur-reed, Water Plantain, Great Spearwort (*Ranunculus lingua*) and Arrow Head, together with Water Figwort and Water Scorpion Grass; the Crowfoot (*Ranunculus fluitans*)

[1] Notes on flora were kindly supplied by Mr. J. G. Hay, Stranraer.

flourishes in running water; Yellow Water Lily (*Nuphar luteum*); White Water Lily (*Nymphaea alba*), occasional in lochs; Hemlock Water Drop-wort (*Oenanthe croccata*), common in ditches and burns, poisonous to animals, consequently eradicated from most farmlands; Heart-leaved Valerian (*V.pyrenaica*)—Lochnaw, edge of loch; Bog Bean (*Menyanthus trifoliata*), one of the loveliest of our wild flowers; occasional in ponds and bogs. A striking colony of this plant may be seen on Limekiln Loch.

Plants of unusual interest of the fields and woods, waste places and waysides include Meadow Saxifrage (*Saxifraga granulata*), a distinctive plant, local—Rocks of Garchrie and Monreith; Greater Celandine (*Chelidonium majus*) in large clumps on waste ground—Bridgebank; Greenfield near Piltanton; Bloody Cranesbill (*Geranium sanguinium*), local, dry rocky places—Stairhaven; Cordyne Cliffs; Dusky Cranesbill (*Geranium pheum*), rare in Wigtownshire—Corsewall Wood on Kirkcolm shore; Tongue Glen; Purple Milk Vetch (*Astragalus hypoglottis*), occasional, dry pastures—Drummore; Hemlock (*Conium maculatum*), poisonous, fairly frequent on roadsides and waste ground; Winter Helio-trope (*Petasites fragrans*), seldom found—Jackie's Lane and banks of burn north of Gallowhill; Sweet Cicely (*Myrrhis odorata*)—spreading widely on roadside near Wigtown; Challoch Farm; Gromwell (*Lithospermum officinale*), rare—near Glenluce Abbey; Giant Hogweed (*Heracleum giganteum*), magnificent plant, an escape—Stairhaven Road near Glenluce; Moschatel and Wood Sanicle—both frequent in shady places; Aaron's Rod, a handsome plant, usually solitary—Garlieston shore; roadside near Portwilliam; Henbane (*Hyocyamus niger*)—on sandy waste ground, poisonous, rare—Garlieston Bay; Low Torrs; Purple Oxytropis (*Oxytropis uralensis*), a rare plant, recorded at Mull; Toothwort (*Lathraea squamaria*), saprophytic on roots of Hazel—rare in county—Banks of River Luce; Penninghame Woods; Indian Balsam, an alien—Ardwell Mill dam; Welsh Poppy (*Mecanopsis cambrica*)—Cree Valley, fairly widespread; *Claytonia alsinoides*—Garrochtrie; road to Blairs Park, Newton Stewart; Solomon's Seal (*Poligonatum multiflorum*)—Colfin Glen; islands in River Cree; Lords and Ladies (*Arum maculatum*), locally abundant—Creechan shore; Dunskey Glen.

Striking features of the landscape are the extensive heath and moor formations. Plants found there grow on acid humus, covering mostly a sterile subsoil. Exposed to high winds and periods of drought, their foliage shows such adaptations as reduced surface (as in Whin, Broom and Heather) or a hairy undersurface, as in Creeping Willow, Thyme and Cat's Foot (*Antennaria dioica*). Large associations of Bracken are present in many districts while Blaeberry (*Vaccinium myrtillus*) occurs locally in smaller units. Apart from these, a few plants of note, typical of the heath and fairly common, are Harebell, Milkwort, Tormentil, Bedstraw, Grassy Stitchwort (*Stellaria graminea*), Bent Grass, Hawkweeds, Sheep's-bit Scabious, and, less common, Slender St. John's Wort (*Hypericum pulchrum*), Cowwheat, a peculiarly local plant favouring damp localities, and Cranberry (*Vaccinium oxycoccus*) on moor at Loups of Kilfeddar.

Hemi-parasitic on the roots of heath grasses are Eyebright (*Euphrasia nemorosa*), Yellow Rattle (*Rhinanthus*) and Red Rattle (*Pedicularis sylvatica*). Numerous species of the moorland grow also, of course, in the bogs and marshes.

The true bogs, marshy tracts of wet Sphagnum peat, that form yet another feature of the county, are in many instances interspersed with such shrubs or trees as Bog Myrtle (*Myrica gale*) and the various willows. To be found there along with Marsh Marigold, Flag Iris, the Spearworts, the Rushes and the Sedges are the Marsh Valerian (*V. dioica*), Bog Bean, the not too common Water Dropwort (*Oeanthe fistulosa*) and here and there wide expanses of Cotton Grass. Plants of particular interest, all requiring a wet peaty soil, are Bog Speedwell (*Veronica scutellata*); Wild Rosemary (*Andromeda polifolia*)—on moor near Gass; Eldrig; the hemi-parasitic Lousewort (*Pedicularis palustris*); Grass of Parnassus (*Parnassia palustris*)—wet slopes at Larbrax; moor at Glenwhilly, and Marsh St. John's Wort (*Hypericum elodes*). Typical bog plants, growing mostly on spongy peat, are the insectivorous Sundew and Butterwort, the rarer varieties *Drosera longifolia* and *Pinguicula lusitanica* growing on the moor at Kilfeddar Loups. In the same locality are Bog Pimpernel (*Anagallis tenella*), Bog Asphodel (*Narthecium*) and Clubmoss (*Lycopodium clavatum*).

Varieties of the Orchis family are much sought after. Apart from the common Early Purple O., the spotted O. and the Marsh O., the following may be noted—Butterfly O. (*Habenaria bifolia*)—Dunskey Glen; White Butterfly O. (*H.albida*), occasional—on dry ground, Dinduff Glen; Frog O. (*H. viridis*), much less common—Loch Ochiltree area; Tway Blade (*Listera ovata*)—frequent on moist humus in Aldouren Glen; Tongue Glen; *Listera cordata*, rarer—on moor by River Luce; Bird's Nest O. (*Neottia nidus-avis*), rarely found, saprophytic on beech humus—woods at Castle Kennedy; *O.pyramidalis*—frequent on dry ground. Of the many attractive and distinctive ferns, one of the most intriguing is Moonwort (*Botrychium lunaria*), purely local, thriving on Glenluce golf course.

BIRDS[1]

Of the birds to be found in Wigtownshire the majority belong to the species that prefer the open spaces to the sheltered areas. Great numbers of sea-birds inhabit or visit the long stretches of coastline and quite frequently dominate the countryside in the vicinity of the shore. A recent happening of great interest to ornithologists is the return of the Fulmar, which had deserted these parts but in recent times has been regularly seen south of Portpatrick and around Ardwell Bay. Nowadays they follow the fishing boats into the North Channel as the vessels head for the North of England ports, for, since the fish are gutted and processed on board, there is an abundant supply of food for the Fulmars and their companions. A feature of bird life in Luce Bay that appeals to the many but is visited by the few

[1] Material kindly supplied by Lieut.Commander H. Inglis and Mr. John McQuaker, Stranraer.

is the Gannetry on the Scar Rocks. The number of Gannets is reported to have increased recently, belying the fears that were felt when the Royal Air Force began to carry out bombing practice in the bay more than twenty years ago. Other birds that inhabit the Scars include the Rock Pipit, Peregrine Falcon, Cormorant, Shag, Common Gull, Herring Gull, Great Black-backed Gull, Kittiwake, Razorbill, Guillemot and Tern. In point of numbers the Gannet comes third to the Guillemot and the Kittiwake. There are more Guillemots than all the other species put together, and it may be added that there is a colony of Black Guillemots at Portpatrick Harbour. Grebes nest annually at Finnarts Bay, near the mouth of Lochryan.

Among the geese the commonest is the Grey Lag. Others found in different parts of the county are the White-Fronted Goose, Pink-Footed Goose and the Barnacle Goose. The Grey Lag, introduced at Lochinch a few years ago, has grown largely in numbers and the flock has become a feature of the gardens.

Enormous numbers of sea ducks populate the inshore waters and many swans winter in the area. A colony of freshwater Cormorants, known locally as 'Mochrum Scarts', is an unusual feature of bird life at Castle Loch, Mochrum. It is sometimes said that Golden Eagles have been seen in the eastern district of the Machars and such reports may be true, as a pair nested a few years ago in the vicinity of Murray's Monument. The Corncrake has almost disappeared from the county, but Lapwings are more numerous than they were a few years ago, and Buzzards occur in both the Rhins and the Machars, while Peregrines, possibly from the Scars, are found in Kirkmaiden. and there are reports of the Chough having been seen in the same parish. Ravens are fairly common in the western districts and nest almost yearly in moorland near Corsemalzie. The Kestrel and Sparrow Hawk are often to be seen in parts of the Rhins, and the Kingfisher occasionally. Large flocks of Widgeon and Mallards frequent Lochryan and Soulseat lochs, while Mergansers and Goosanders are fairly regular visitors. Migrant Muscovy ducks sometimes make their appearance in Lochryan and Golden Eye ducks at Garwhadie lochs. The numbers of Grouse are very much smaller than they used to be. In addition to the species that are common in most parts of the country, the shire attracts immense numbers of Wheatears and Fieldfares. Stonechats and Whinchats have a habitat to the west of Luce Bay and the Reed Warbler occurs in the same locality. The Waxwing makes frequent appearances, as does the Redwing. The Short-eared Owl is common and there are large numbers of carrion crows, but the real 'hoodie' greyback is not often seen. Magpies have increased in number. Snow Buntings were seen in February 1960 at Markdhu, Glenwhilly, and Redstarts in October 1959 near Cairnerzean and at Gass, Glenluce. About that time, too, the Pied Fly Catcher was seen on the outskirts of Stranraer near Auchtralure. A rare visitor was found at Portpatrick during the severe snowstorm in January, 1963. This was a Bittern in an exhausted state which was carefully tended but died a few days later.

OTHER FAUNA[1]

All three native species of deer are found in the county. Roe Deer are relatively common wherever there is woodland, small numbers of Fallow Deer are to be found in the east, especially round Newton Stewart, and Red Deer, probably strays from the Kirkcudbrightshire hills, are found in the Rhins, even beside Lochryan. Both Brown and Mountain Hares are common. The Mountain Hare can be found all over the moorland in the north of the county, though its numbers fluctuate greatly. The Brown Hare has become commoner since myxomatosis drastically reduced the rabbit population, though rabbits are coming back in some parts. Otters are more numerous than is usually thought, while foxes are widespread, especially in the cliff edges of the Mull of Galloway. Stoats and Weasels are both in the county in fair numbers. The Pine Marten is almost certainly extinct. Grey Squirrels have not yet reached the county, so far as one can gather, but Red Squirrels can frequently be seen, especially in the Cree Valley. Despite the numbers killed on the roads, there are many Hedgehogs in the shire, and Badgers are present in large numbers, especially near Glenluce. Moles are abundant. The Common Shrew, the Short-Tailed Vole and the Field Mouse are common in arable areas, as is the Water Vole where conditions are suitable. Both Bats occur, but the Pipistrelle is much the commoner of the two. The Common Seal can usually be found in small numbers off the coast. Adders are locally abundant, as are Slow-worms. Frogs are very much commoner than Toads. Both Lizards and Newts can easily be found if one knows where to look.

In the rivers and lochs the fish include salmon, grilse, seatrout, herling, brown trout, grayling, roach, perch and pike. Flounders are to be found in the estuaries and in a few places lampreys can be gathered. There are a great many eels. Trout as heavy as ten pounds have been caught in the lochs at Lochinch and in this area efforts are regularly made to clear the waters of pike: these are often found in the River Bladnoch, in the Machars.

HISTORY[2]

Although there are Roman remains in Kirkcudbrightshire there are no traces of the occupation in Wigtownshire. That is the position at present but for a long time there was a firm belief that there had been Roman settlements in the county. Among the sites mentioned in many publications were Rispain, near Whithorn, and Innermessan, at the head of Lochryan. These and others have been ruled out as Roman outposts, but archaeologists are convinced that Wigtownshire must have housed contingents of the invaders at some period of the occupation. The Wigtownshire Antiquarian Society has been told on several occasions by men of standing to 'go out and find the Romans'. The view of most authorities is that the Romans would not stop their incursion into Galloway at Gatehouse-of-Fleet, the most westerly location at which Roman constructions have been found. In some quarters the opinion is held that Stranraer may be covering

---

1 Mr. Ian Murray, Beoch, provided information on other fauna.
2 Historical notes were kindly provided by Mr. A. E. Truckell, Dumfries.

the site of a Roman settlement and that, if a thorough excavation were carried out, remains of the occupation might be brought to light. There have been finds of Roman coins and small personal belongings in the Luce Bay area; the coins, dating from the middle of the third century until about 360 A.D., suggest active trade.

The traditional date of 397 for St. Ninian's landing at Isle of Whithorn has been subjected to challenge, but he certainly was established at Whithorn within a few years or so of this date. It seems likely that his mission was to combat heresy in an already partly Christianised area and to introduce monasticism rather than to make a first introduction of Christianity to a pagan area. The little mid-fifth century oratory excavated in 1949 at Whithorn, with the great Whithorn series of sculptured crosses, testifies to the historicity of the site. Irish crofter-fishermen were settling on the western coast of the Mull by 450, but the shire remained Brythonic-speaking until the seventh century, when the Irish came in such numbers that the earlier place-names were almost supplanted by those introduced by them: the Irish annalists of this period treated Whithorn as being in Ireland. Chapel Finnian, on the east side of Luce Bay, the hermitage on the island in Castle Loch, Mochrum, and the lost monastery from which several sculptured cross fragments found around Elrig must have come, all seem to be linked with the name of St. Finnian of Moville, who studied at Whithorn, and dedications to Irish saints are legion.

During the period of Scoto-Norse dominance in the tenth and eleventh centuries, the region experienced a prosperous phase. From about 1120 Fergus, Lord of Galloway, brought Wigtownshire into the mediaeval comity, with the re-establishment of the bishopric, the founding of Soulseat Abbey at Inch and of Glenluce Abbey, and the settling of the Anglo-Norman lords in the numerous castles of the county. His son Uchtred continued this Normanising policy, but the strong 'national' feeling in the area led to a revolt by his brother Gilbert and the death of Uchtred. Those of the line of Fergus were able to act throughout almost as independent kings: their prestige can be judged by the marriage of Fergus to a daughter of Henry I of England. With the extinction of the main line most of the Galloway lands passed through Devorguilla to the Balliols and were forfeited to the Douglases because of the stubborn Balliol support of the English cause in the Edwardian wars. In 1372 Archibald Douglas, lord of Galloway and later third Earl of Douglas, purchased the earldom of Wigtown and in 1426 Wigtownshire, with the rest of Galloway, passed at last under the general Scottish law. The native race had not taken kindly to the rule of Robert I and the south-west remained longer than the rest of lowland Scotland in a rude, unsettled state. The Douglases ruled until the middle of the fifteenth century, when James, ninth Earl of Douglas, was condemned for rebellion and his estates were forfeited. About the same time Sir Andrew Agnew of Lochnaw was created hereditary sheriff by James II. During the Covenanting troubles of the later seventeenth century, Graham of Claverhouse and his brother successively became sheriffs; the people of the shire who supported the principles of the Covenant were severely persecuted by Claverhouse and several were put to death. To this period belongs the traditional tale of the drowning in Wigtown Bay of Margaret McLachlan and Margaret Wilson. At the Revolution settlement Sheriff Agnew was restored to office and the honour remained in the family till the abolition of heritable jurisdictions in 1747.

On the downfall of the Douglases the Kennedy family, the Adairs and the McDoualls came to the fore, followed in the mid-sixteenth century by the Vaus family of Barnbarroch. It is said that all these families benefited materially by the Reformation, though they had already had a firm grip on the local ecclesiastical establishment for fifty years.

The Kennedy family dominated the scene for many years, their chief residence in the shire being at Inch, near Stranraer. Although damaged by fire, their castle is still a prominent feature of the Castle Kennedy grounds. In course of time the Dalrymples of Stair acquired the estate, where Lochinch Castle was built in 1869. The first Viscount Stair married Margaret, eldest daughter of James Ross, of Balneil, Old Luce; after his retiral he took up residence at his wife's estate at Carscreugh, and here he wrote the book that made him famous, *The Institutions of the Law of Scotland* (1681). The second Earl held high office under Marlborough on the Continent, and later devoted much attention to improving the land and introducing the cultivation of potatoes and turnips in the open fields. The seventh Earl of Galloway, whose family had been active in many enterprises in earlier times, was also a notable improver; about 1760, before his succession to the title, and while he was styled Lord Garlies, he founded the new village of Garliestown, near Galloway House in Sorbie parish. Nowadays the name of the village is generally in Galloway spelt Garlieston.

The burghal history of the shire goes back to the late thirteenth century, when Wigtown is recorded as a king's burgh, though its first surviving royal charter is that of 1457. Whithorn became an ecclesiastical burgh in 1325 and a royal burgh in 1511. Innermessan, now smaller than a hamlet, but a place at one time of much importance, was a burgh as far back as 1426. Stranraer became a burgh of barony in 1595 and a royal burgh in 1617. Portpatrick was erected as a burgh of barony in 1620 and Newton Stewart in 1677. Other nominal 'erections' failed to take effect 'on the ground', but these half-dozen burghs for a time, at least, fulfilled their mission as market centres. Wigtown, Whithorn and Stranraer survived as royal burghs, while Newton Stewart became a police burgh in 1861: all four are now classed as small burghs.

Galloway News

Plate 1. MULL OF GALLOWAY LIGHTHOUSE

The Mull of Galloway Lighthouse stands on the most southerly point of Scotland and dates back to 1828. The rocks rise to a height of 269 feet above sea level and standing sentinel on the top is the lighthouse, 60 feet high. Those who visit the Mull and climb to the balcony of the lighthouse for the view are rewarded with what is frequently described as a thrilling experience. To the east stretches Luce Bay, with the two Scars (rocks) a good many miles off shore giving a home for large numbers of Gannets, and to the south can be seen the Isle of Man, if the day be clear, rising in the Irish Sea. To the west is the North Channel, beyond which can be discerned the hills of Northern Ireland.

Galloway News
Plate 2. DUNSKEY CASTLE

Galloway News
Plate 3. ISLE OF WHITHORN

Galloway News
Plate 4. CASTLE KENNEDY
The lily pond and the ruins of the old castle in the grounds of Lochinch near Stranraer.

CHAPTER 2

THE ECONOMY

AGRICULTURE

WHILE Stranraer appeals for new industries, the oldest industry of all continues to provide Wigtownshire people with a flourishing means of livelihood. Farming, as always, is a strong and firm basis on which the county economy is built and the industry has never been in better heart than it is today. Through the years that have elapsed since agriculture began to be developed on scientific lines, the farmers of Wigtownshire have aimed at keeping up-to-date in their methods and have often turned new ideas to good account. The quest for advice and information took some of the farmers into England during the later part of last century and they brought back knowledge of new methods that was used to advantage. These related mostly to cheesemaking and in course of time this branch of farming was extensively followed throughout the length and breadth of Galloway, less in the Machars District than in the Rhins, as cattle feeding receives more attention in the lower end of the county than in the west. Cheese-making and milk production were closely bound up with the breeding and rearing of dairy cattle and, the old nondescript cow having gradually given way to the pure-bred animal, many Ayrshire pedigreed herds ultimately made their appearance. By the turn of the century farming had come a long way in a relatively short time. In dairy farming ideas from abroad were likewise reaching the people of Galloway during the same period, especially that of milk recording. The basic principle was that if a correct record were kept of the individual cow's output the milk production of the herd could be increased by deleting the poor milkers and by adopting a system of selective breeding. The value of milk recording was recognised by some of the shire farmers and their example in giving it support was gradually followed until the system had become general.

Difficult Times. Improvements in technique and in the quality of cattle, however, did not bring the farmers overwhelming financial reward. On the contrary, the economic position of the industry caused a great deal of concern. The situation became progressively worse after the 1914-18 war. In the early post-war period the Corn Production Act was passed and one of the steps taken under this measure was the appointment of county agricultural officers. There were fears that the Act meant the imposition of some form of Government control and direction. Without much being said by the politicians the Act was allowed to disappear and the county officers never did a day's work, though possibly the dairy farmers might have been better off if the measure had been put into operation. What is certain is that dairying fell on evil days in the 1920-30 period. Prices dropped so low that farmers received as little as 3d. a gallon for milk. An effort to organise a voluntary pool among the farmers did not meet with much success, for in those days farmers did not look with favour on co-operative effort. Within a short time it became obvious that something would have to be done on a national scale if dairy farming was to be saved, and the Milk Marketing Boards were set up in 1933.

For reasons not easily fathomed many of the farmers did not take kindly to the new régime despite all the advantages that it offered. They

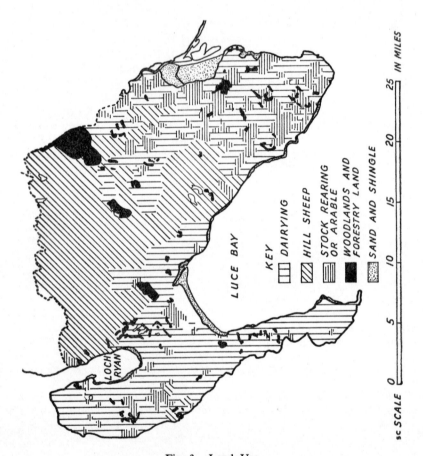

Fig. 3.   Land Use.

were critical of the measure, but in time they realised the benefits that were being conferred on the industry. For some years, however, the subject of analysis was the theme of many protests until eventually the local authority set up a laboratory in Stranraer. Prior to that Rhins farmers complained that as the milk samples were often delayed before they reached the analyst in Dumfries the procedure was unfair. While this aspect of dairying was creating a furore, another aspect of the industry was also receiving attention. This was the eradication of tuberculosis among cattle in the county. By the spring of 1960 the objective had been finally achieved. Just prior

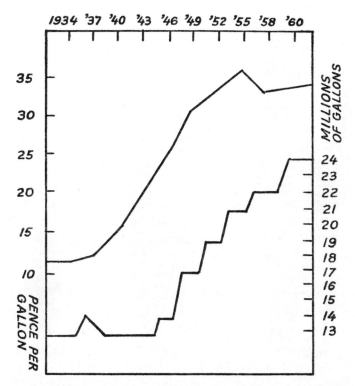

Fig. 4. Variations in the price of milk and in production since the Milk Marketing Board began operations in 1934 are shown in this diagram. The figures on the left give the weighted average pool prices. The actual price for 1960 was 34.93d., but this included the T.T. Premium of 2d., so in effect, the comparable figure with those of previous years is 32.93d., as shown. The broken line shows how production has increased during the same period.

to the clearance date the number of cows in milk throughout the county was 31,094, and in calf 7,753—a total of 38,847. Creameries at Stranraer, Sandhead, Portwilliam and Sorbie were among those taken over by the Scottish Milk Marketing Board on its institution and they handle most of the milk in their respective areas. Cheese is also manufactured in the various creameries and Wigtownshire exhibits gain leading awards each year at the London Dairy Show. The few remaining farmers who continue to make cheese at the farms also collect prizes in London and there is still a good section for cheese at the district shows. For many years dairy shows at Castle Douglas and Kilmarnock aroused widespread interest and attracted enormous entries, but they collapsed as farm cheesemaking declined. (Fig. 5.)

Fig. 5. Farm cheesemakers are on the point of disappearing from the Wigtownshire scene. In 1934 they numbered 131. By 1938 the total had dropped to 83. In 1942 there was a drop to 49 and in 1961 only eight remained.

Tractor Supplants Horse. Instead of expansion in the Clydesdale world, contraction almost to the point of disappearance has been recorded. Mechanisation on the farm began during the first world war, but did not make much headway until about ten or twelve years afterwards. Even then the number of tractors and other contrivances rose only slowly and it was only in the post-war years of 1945-55 that the horse began to disappear quickly from the scene. In that decade mechanisation made tremendous strides and the Clydesdale faded out. This eclipse of the horse was often referred to with regret by some of the older generation who could remember the great days of the Clydesdale in Galloway. In the closing quarter of the nineteenth century a large number of shire farmers devoted great attention to the breeding and rearing of horses and many famous animals were bred in the county or brought in for stud purposes. Numerous leading prizes were gained at the national shows every year by local exhibitors and some remarkable records were set up for awards and prices. Among the last studs to survive the onslaught of mechanisation were the famous Clydesdales at Bridgebank and South Boreland. The most important now remaining is at Glasserton Mains, in the Machars.

This transformation from horses to machinery, one of the greatest changes in the industry during the present century, has taken place without any resistance or fuss. The complete change-over may not have been to the liking of some, but after a certain stage had been reached its course was inevitable. Now, horses and harness, which at one time bulked so largely in the farm worker's conception of his work, are a thing of the past. The daily routine has undergone a radical change and a generation is growing up that knows nothing of the old days, with the grooming, watering and feeding that horse teams entailed.

Wigtownshire's cattle population is dominated by the Ayrshires, but the native breed of Galloways is still well represented, and there is a well-known herd of 'Belties' at the Old Place of Mochrum; there are a few Herefords and a number of British Friesians. Cross-bred cattle are brought on for the fat stock market at numerous farms in the Machars and to a lesser extent in the Rhins, where the practice fell away as the emphasis was placed by the Government on milk production in the early post-war years.

Around the sheltered stretches of the coast great attention is now paid to the growing of early potatoes. This branch of farming has been developing since the turn of the century, and for a long time farmers and merchants have competed keenly to achieve the distinction of being first in the market with their potatoes and to get the benefit of the highest prices. This rivalry has perhaps been a little less noticeable of late as a result of a marketing arrangement among the growers. In recent times the shire farmers have taken exception to their crops being termed 'Ayrshire potatoes' in broadcasts and newspaper reports, and efforts are being made to let the public know that usually the earliest potatoes of the season come from Wigtownshire, which was later in getting into this particular field than Ayrshire, but is now making up the leeway. Some planting may start in the middle of January, but many farmers contend that March is an early enough date, holding that growth is very slow earlier in the year and that actually no time is lost. Normally, the first week in June is the time when the earliest potatoes reach the market. The first supplies make high prices, sometimes as much as £100 a ton, but the figure drops very quickly and within a few days of the arrival of the first consignments the price may be down to £50 or less. Most of the early potato growing is carried out in the Rhins but it is also a feature of the farming on raised beach land in Glasserton and near the coast in Whithorn.

Hill Sheep Farming. The northern part of the shire, known as the Moors, is used for hill sheep farming, the flocks consisting of Blackface and Cheviot breeds. The total number is normally in the region of 160,000 sheep. Some beef cattle are also raised in this moorland district. A feature of the autumn season is the disposal of lambs and rams; large sales are held at Newton Stewart and attract buyers from many parts of Scotland.

In the inter-war period the Department of Agriculture for Scotland acquired a number of farms in the shire by buying Dunragit estate. Part of the land was formed into small holdings, part was let as larger farms and another part was kept in the hands of the department as a home farm. The department also owns the farm of Broadwigg, near Whithorn. In addition to those at Dunragit there are small holdings at Culreoch, near Stranraer, North and South Balfern, Kirkinner and Carsduchan, at Barrachan, in the Machars.

During recent years the employment of squad labour has spread all over the county. The squads are brought in for turnip singling, hay-making, potato lifting and the grain harvest. They are conveyed by motor lorry from the towns and villages and brought home in the evenings. Many of the workers are women and during the summer young people take part in the work. Large numbers of Irish workers come over for the potato lifting and in many instances they are provided with living accommodation at the farms. The number of farm workers living in villages and clachans goes on increasing and the days of the bothy are over.

The numbers of people employed in farm work at midsummer, 1958, totalled 3,146 and included the following workers engaged full-time:— Males, 65 years old and over, 89; males, between 20 and 65 years of age, 1,567; males, 18 years old and under 20, 186; males, under 18 years old, 194; women and girls, 325. Part-time workers comprised 69 males and 172 women and girls. Casual and seasonal workers included 290 males and 254 women and girls. The number of hired workers among the regular farm staff was 1,535.

Recent Changes. Among recent arrivals on the agricultural scene is the combine-harvester. Although the general view at first was that this machine could not be widely used in the county, 'combining' has become a regular feature of the grain harvest and far larger quantities of crops are being cut and bagged at the same time than was thought feasible. The introduction of the combine set up a whole series of new problems. The millers at once became involved, as they had to extend their premises to enable them to handle the large quantities of grain that were coming in from the farms within a matter of days and requiring immediate space for drying. When the milling was over there was plenty of space to spare for everything. The situation called for a co-operative spirit on the part of the farmers and millers and the problems were resolved within a very short time. Other mid-century developments have been the construction of a grass-drying factory at Dunragit and the establishment of an artificial insemination centre for Ayrshire cattle.

For many years one of the events of the winter was the parish ploughing match. All over the county contests were held and they created keen interest in the districts, but few now survive. The most important nowadays is the Wigtownshire open championship match, which was inaugurated during the war, when the proceeds were given to the Red Cross. When the first competition was held in 1943 the swing and digger ploughs drawn by horses were numerous, but the tractor has now completely displaced the horse. Wigtownshire ploughmen and farmers were loth to part with the horse for ploughing, but they had to capitulate. There is also a district match in the Machars each year. The only parish society now functioning is in Old Luce, where the match is a recognised New Year event.

Egg-grading centres, established at Newton Stewart and Stranraer after the war, were initially conducted by a local company, but they are now owned by a large farming organisation with headquarters in Cumberland; there is also a centre for the raising of broilers at Portwilliam. Market gardening is not carried out on a large scale, but there are several nurseries at both ends of the county.

WOODLANDS. Since the second world war a good deal of attention has been given to forestry in the shire, as in other counties throughout Scotland. A census of woodlands taken by the Forestry Commission in 1947-48 showed a total area of 8,351 acres. Of this 1,343 acres were scrub, 1,873 acres felled woodland and 123 acres devastated. Most of the high quality beech has been felled. All the good ash for which the county was well known and most of the oak have also been cut. There is a unique small plantation of Monterey Pine at Ardwell and another unique Monkey Puzzle feature can be seen at Monreith Estate. Monkey Puzzle trees also form an attractive avenue in Lochinch policies. The Forestry Commission have acquired the following areas:—At Penninghame, 5,430 acres; Kilsture (between Kirkcowan and Sorbie), 511 acres; Bareagle, at Dunragit, 1,116 acres of hill land; and Bareagle nursery, 57 acres on lower land; Fell of Loch Ronald (Kirkcowan), 969 acres; Knockinaam (Portpatrick), 75 acres; Torrs Warren (Luce Bay), 473 acres. Trees being planted at Torrs Warren will, it is expected, stabilise the blowing sand.

FISHING. Although a maritime county, Wigtownshire for some reason has never developed an extensive fishing industry. When the *Old Statistical Account* was written fishing was reported to be on the decline and since then there have been many ups and downs in the affairs of the fishermen. In general the tendency has been downwards and nowadays few boats are engaged locally in the industry. A few drifters come early each year from the north-east and fish out of Stranraer for a few months. At one time a fleet of fishing boats shared in these activities but now the number is usually no more than three. Each summer Portpatrick is visited by a fleet of east coast boats, which catch herring in the Irish Sea from about midsummer until the autumn. The construction of a factory in Northern Ireland has affected the landings at Portpatrick, as many of the catches are marked down for processing. At one time the many little harbours round the coast were quite busy; there is still occasional activity at Cairnryan, Drummore, Portwilliam, Isle of Whithorn and Garlieston, but none at Kirkcolm, Portlogan, Glenluce or Sandhead. In 1900 the number of local boats was 144 and this total had fallen to 42 in 1954. The number of fishermen in 1900 was 255 and in 1954 the figure was 62. A Stranraer firm, however, owns vessels that engage in fishing off the west coast and have their headquarters at Lochryan. Some people in Stranraer still recall an extraordinarily heavy catch of herring in Lochryan shortly before the first world war: there were so many fish that it was impossible to handle them, according to the old folk, and many were allowed to go to waste. Since then the loch has been deserted by the herring, say those people with long memories.

The Lochryan oyster beds which have lasted for centuries are at present under the care of the Scottish Marine Biological Association. In post-war years it was found difficult to run the fisheries economically, as supplies of young oysters could not be procured in this country and shipments from French waters were very expensive. With a view to putting the industry on a better footing and perhaps carrying out a programme of expansion, experiments are being carried out, and the outcome is awaited with much interest. Many years ago the oysters were very numerous and the Lochryan beds were regarded as a regular source of food supplies.

Salmon fishing is an historical vocation on the Cree that is still followed with profit. Netting of salmon also helps to provide a living for fishermen at Innerwell (Garlieston), Stairhaven, Ardwell and Kirkcolm. Lobsters are brought ashore at Portlogan, Drummore, Portpatrick, Kirkcolm, Stairhaven and the Isle of Whithorn.

Anglers, fishing the various rivers, normally grass many salmon each year, but they had a disappointing season during the fabulous summer of 1959 when the waters fell so low that the fish were unable to get up the rivers. They contracted disease and eventually were hauled on to the bank and put out of their misery. Scores of salmon were thus dealt with near the mouth of the Luce. It was a sorry experience for the anglers, who had been denied a season's sport, not for lack of fish but an over-abundance of sunshine.

MANUFACTURES. The manufactures carried on in the county are in the main allied to the staple industry of agriculture. Newton Stewart has the one woollen mill in the shire. Local wool was at one time the chief form of raw material, but changes have taken place in the course of the years, and wool is now obtained from abroad and from the Scottish sales. A substantial export trade is carried on in addition to manufactures designed to meet demands of the home market. At one time a smaller mill at Kirkcowan provided work for local people in the making of tweeds and blankets, but manufacturing ceased in 1950. There are sawmills at Newton Stewart, Garlieston and Castle Kennedy. The owners buy and fell timber throughout the county and cut it up at the mills into suitable sizes for collieries, railways, case-making and agricultural work.

In Stranraer three mills produce animal feeding stuffs and one of these also makes oatmeal and porridge oats. Feeding stuffs are manufactured at a Garlieston mill. Oats grown locally are used in these mills as well as imported materials.

A post-war development at Stranraer was the setting up of a knitwear factory which has provided work for a number of local people. A few years ago the owners transferred their premises from Dalrymple Street to a commodious structure that had been a Church of Scotland canteen during the war.

CAIRNRYAN. During the second world war a military port was constructed at Cairnryan and the installations included a branch line from the main line near Stranraer station. The harbour was used extensively by the United States forces in bringing in weapons and material from America. These were transported by road and rail to England in preparation for the invasion of Europe and for a long time the quiet roadways of Galloway echoed to the sound of strange tongues and strange noises as the convoys forged their way southwards. After the war the harbour was used by the Government for various purposes. In the autumn of 1945, for instance, old ships were brought in, loaded up with obsolete shells and taken out into the Atlantic, where they were scuttled, a destroyer taking off the crew after the seacocks had been opened. In the course of time the supply of old ships gave out and the useless ammunition was taken out to sea on landing craft and dumped overboard. For a time the harbour installations were used by the Ministry of Supply as a centre for ship-breaking. A firm from Clydeside carried out the work and among the battleships that were reduced to scrap were the *Ramillies* and the *Valiant*.

The depot ship *Sandhurst* lay at the harbour during the early post-war period, when a fleet of U-boats which had been surrendered by the Germans were anchored in the loch. Ammunition dumping went on intermittently for years after the war, with the Navy, Army and R.A.F. all sharing in the activities. By the spring of 1959 the work of the Services came to an end and about 300 civilians who had been employed at the port were gradually dismissed. The closing of the war-time harbour raised the number of workless to a high figure and Stranraer was classed as a development area. Efforts were made in many directions and by many people to have the harbour taken over by a private firm and this was eventually done. In the early part of 1960 a start was made with the changeover, but little had been done by the end of 1962 and disappointment was being felt at the long delay.

FLYING BASES

In contrast to the war-time activities, there is now not one operational R.A.F. station in Wigtownshire. There is, however, an important base at West Freugh, close to Luce Bay. This station comes under the Royal Aircraft Establishment, Farnborough, and is mainly

staffed by civilians.   During the war the Rhins district was dotted with
air stations and Baldoon, near Wigtown, was for a long time an important
centre.   West Freugh was the largest of the installations in the war years,
and there were also stations at Castle Kennedy, Wig Bay, Corsewall, North
Cairn and Stranraer.   For a time two squadrons of flying boats operated
from Stranraer and they took an active part in the early stages of the Battle
of the Atlantic.   For ten years after the war Wig Bay was utilised as a
base for Sunderlands, mostly by an aircraft firm, Short Brothers and
Harland, of Belfast.   Many of the craft that had become unserviceable were
disposed of as scrap.   Others were fit for further service after repairs had
been carried out and took off for many parts of the world, especially for
South-East Asia and the Far East.

"COMMERCIAL CAPITAL"

Stranraer is often referred to as the commercial capital of the shire, as
it is by far the most important centre.   Several firms have branches in the
outlying villages, such as Glenluce, Portpatrick and Ballantrae, while a
company of motor agents conduct business in Stranraer and Newton
Stewart, and this firm also has an ironmonger's shop in Stranraer. A recent
change in the local bakery business has been a large increase in the import
of supplies from Ayr and Glasgow, along with the cessation of bread-
baking by several firms in Stranraer.   As a shopping centre Stranraer
meets the needs of a wide district and is able to hold its own against strong
opposition.   In 1961 Messrs. Woolworth opened a branch in part of a
new block of buildings in the town, and it is understood that several outside
firms may occupy parts of the building, thus adding to the number of
multiple companies represented in Stranraer.

A system of one-way traffic was recently introduced in Stranraer, as
the number of motor vehicles on the streets was leading to much loss of
time and long delays.   In the old days lorries took out supplies to the
country districts two or three times a week and many people did not visit
Stranraer except at long intervals.   Nowadays a constant stream of vans
and cars goes in both directions.   Buses provide a good service for those
who do not own cars, but the number of such people is decreasing every
year.   In addition the motor cycle has attained great popularity among
the young of both sexes.

PROFESSIONS

Teachers are by far the most numerous professional people in the county
and in practically all parishes take an active part in community life.   A
recent survey showed a total of 250, with a large proportion on the
staff of Stranraer schools.   In most cases the head teachers were men, but
some women had charge of small rural schools.   Of the medical profession
there were 23 general practitioners in the county, with the largest group
in Stranraer, where the medical officer of health and his assistant were
also resident.   Most of the dozen lawyers practised in the Stranraer area,
and others were resident in Newton Stewart.   With all the Scottish banks

represented in Stranraer, there were six managers in the burgh, besides four
in Newton Stewart, two in Whithorn, and one each in Wigtown, Portwilliam and Glenluce.   There were six practising dentists in the county
and two on the county council staff. Chartered accountants numbered three,
but several others undertook accounting work.   At the same period there
were three full-time estate factors in the county and six part-time, two of

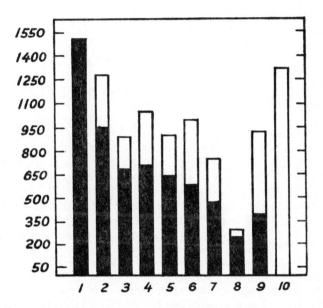

Fig. 6.   People in employment during 1960 in the Shire numbered
approximately 9,788.   Of the total 6,048 were in the Rhins and
3,740 in the Machars. The diagram depicts the numbers in the
various industries and services, with those in the Rhins indicated
in black and the Machars totals white. Columns 1 and 10 refer
to agriculture, forestry and fishing; 2, distributive trades; 3, transport and communications; 4, professional and scientific services; 5,
construction; 6, miscellaneous services; 7, food, drink and tobacco;
8, public administration; 9, others. The drawing is based on information supplied by the Ministry of Labour, who, for official purposes,
include Creetown as part of the Machars area.

the full-time men residing in the Rhins and the third in the Machars.
Ministers in every parish continue their historic mission.   Stranraer has
four Church of Scotland congregations, a Reformed Presbyterian church,
a United Free church, a Roman Catholic chapel and an Episcopalian
church.   In Newton Stewart there are four ministers.   Inch parish
(including Cairnryan) has two, while the Sandhead-Ardwell area has
one minister for two churches.

TOURISM AND HOLIDAYMAKING

Parts of the shire have been popular with holidaymakers for many years, but of late efforts have been made to develop the tourist industry on a much bigger scale than before. Newton Stewart has been a holiday centre for a long time and the villages along the coast have attracted many visitors for more than half a century. Portpatrick has been a recognised resort for longer than that, but the holiday features of the village have been extended in more recent times. A large hotel, built about sixty years ago, is a dominating landmark, towering on rising ground above the rocky shore and overlooking the harbour. There are numerous smaller hotels and boarding houses in the village, which is one of the most picturesque in the South-West.

Since the end of last century efforts have been made to attract holidaymakers to Stranraer and these are being continued today with greater success than ever before. Stranraer suffered in a way by the intensive advertising of the short sea route to Ireland. Early in the century the strenuous campaigns to induce people to go to Ulster by way of Stranraer proved only too successful, but Stranraer is now endeavouring to provide attractions that will retain more holidaymakers on this side of the North Channel. All records were broken in 1959 and this was a direct result of the activities of the recently formed Stranraer and District Development Association in arousing local interest and in arranging numerous summer events. Many in the town think there is scope for making Stranraer a much more important holiday centre than it has been in the past. An ironic touch was given to the situation when, just as the flow of holidaymakers into Stranraer began to increase, the largest hotel in the town—the Auld King's Arms—was sold; early in 1959 it was razed to the ground. On the site a block of shops has been built.

Drummore, the most southerly village in Scotland, continues to attract holidaymakers as it has done for many years, without doing much in the way of advertising or organising summer programmes, although in recent years special weeks have been set aside for parades and dances. There was at one time a popular regatta each year, but this was not revived after the second world war. Many people call at Drummore on their way to the Mull of Galloway and until quite recently they wondered why the road that leads to the Mull and the lighthouse had been allowed to become so bad. The question of responsibility was discussed time and again until agreement was reached in 1962 and the road was put into proper order.

Portwilliam, Garlieston and Isle of Whithorn are favourite village resorts in the Machars and many who spend their holidays in these parts have done so every year for a long time. Tourism has lately been encouraged by the Galloway Publicity Association, whose efforts have met with success, to which, of course, the new approach to holidays in industry has contributed.

ECONOMIC ORGANISATION

The farmers and landlords rely upon each other for the success of agriculture and throughout the county relations have for long been friendly and helpful. In most of the shire the land is let to tenants and management is in the hands of practical farmers. On most estates there is a home farm on which a close eye is kept by the owner. Labour relations on the whole are pleasant, for conditions have improved greatly in recent times; the countryside knows more happiness and fewer financial worries than used to be the case.

As for urban conditions, there is a thriving co-operative society in Stranraer, with three blocks of premises in different parts of the town; self-service has recently been introduced at two of the grocery shops. The directors include tradesmen and railwaymen; the dividend is usually about 2s. in the pound. There is a society on a smaller scale in Wigtown. In addition, the Scottish Co-operative Wholesale Society has creameries at Stranraer and Whithorn, and a margarine factory at Bladnoch. The Stranraer society conducts a funeral undertaking service and another department provides spectacles under the National Health Service.

CHAPTER 3

GOVERNMENT AND PUBLIC SERVICES

PARLIAMENTARY REPRESENTATION

PARLIAMENTARY representation in Galloway has undergone a number of changes over the years. For a long time the county returned a representative to Parliament while Wigtown, Stranraer and Whithorn, along with New Galloway in the Stewartry, formed the Wigtown Burghs and sent one member to Westminster. All that was changed after the first world war. The counties of Wigtown and Kirkcudbright were brought together as the single constituency of Galloway, and, after a period of changing fortunes, John McKie won the seat for the Conservatives in 1931 and retained it until his death at the end of 1958. In the by-election that followed in April 1959, Mr. H. J. Brewis succeeded as Conservative member and he again topped the poll at the General Election in October 1959.

LOCAL GOVERNMENT

In the realm of local government the most important body is the county council, to which the education committee is responsible. Great changes have taken place since the county councils came into being, some seventy years ago. Burghs, however small, looked after their own affairs and parish school boards were in charge of the educational facilities. Now many of the burghs' services are carried out by the county council, with the town councils responsible for raising the sums required in rates. Although the county council is often under criticism and carries out much work in the public interest, there is difficulty in finding sufficient candidates to fill the vacancies at the triennial elections, and it is seldom that there is a contest for a seat. Some of the duties that have to be undertaken in the country areas are discharged by district councils. The services are not expensive and the councils have not much latitude. The position is different from what it was down to 1930, when the district councils were responsible for the upkeep of roads and for some aspects of the public health.

There are four town councils in the county and since the second world war their chief occupation, like that of the county council, has been the provision of houses. At one time the county council held meetings at Stranraer and Wigtown alternately, but the routine has been changed; since the county acquired premises in Stranraer, all meetings of the committees and the full council have been held there. Additional buildings are being purchased by the county council in Stranraer, where all the official work will be carried out in the not far distant future.

POLICE

Early in 1948 an amalgamation of the police forces in the three southern counties was carried out, with Mr. S. A. Berry, from Edinburgh, as chief constable. Previously there had been three forces, but now the whole of Galloway, Dumfriesshire and Dumfries burgh have the one force, with headquarters at Dumfries. The Galloway division has headquarters at Stranraer, where new police buildings were built a few years ago, and there are sub-divisions at Kirkcudbright, Newton Stewart and Stranraer, with staff utilising part of the new building. The authorised strength of the force is 202 and the actual total at the end of 1962 was 183. Of the seven policewomen employed two are at Stranraer.

Radio is used to a large extent and motor patrols are a regular feature of the service. The withdrawal of policemen from most of the villages was not received favourably, but the new system is now generally regarded with satisfaction. Since the institution in June 1951 of the Police Long Service and Good Conduct Medal, 67 members of the force have received the award and of that number 21 were serving in the force at the end of 1962.

LAW AND ORDER

The Lord-Lieutenant of Wigtownshire is the Earl of Stair, who succeeded his late father, the 12th Earl, in 1962.

There are sheriff courts at Wigtown and Stranraer, with sittings on alternate Tuesdays. The sheriff substitute is Mr. S. A. Lockhart, who also presides at the Kirkcudbright court. Miss Margaret H. Kidd, Q.C., was appointed sheriff principal in 1960, the first woman in Scotland to hold such a position. Justice of the Peace courts are held each month in Stranraer and in the Machars when occasion demands. Police courts are held in each of the four burghs, with sittings in Stranraer generally once a month. The numbers dealt with in the various burghs during 1960 were:—Stranraer, 451; Newton Stewart, 99; Wigtown, 25; Whithorn, 47. The number of cases of crime made known in Wigtownshire in 1959 was 362, compared with 365 in 1958. Miscellaneous offences numbered 870 in 1959 and 737 in the previous year, giving totals of 1,232 for 1959 and 1,102 for 1958. The number of juvenile offenders in the Dumfriesshire and Galloway area in 1959 was 328, an increase of 85.

HOUSING

In common with other parts of the country, Wigtownshire had still a housing problem in 1960, though it was not as serious as in some other places. The steady rise in population during the period from 1821 to 1851, when it doubled to 43,389, was not maintained and in the present century it has lapsed to around 30,000. Though families were smaller and there was a big loss by emigration, house building failed to keep pace with the demand. Movement was towards the larger centres. Stranraer attracted many agricultural workers who had been living on the farms, until in 1959 the major part of the population was centred within a ten mile radius of the town.

In Wigtownshire in 1959 there were 8,697 inhabited dwellings, of which 4,635 were in the landward area. Of the remainder 2,671 were in Stranraer, 685 in Newton Stewart, 378 in Wigtown and 328 in Whithorn. Thirty years earlier there were 6,934 houses in the county, of which 4,279 were in the rural districts. Many of these were much below the living standards of the time and 897 were recommended to be demolished, 645 were stated to be capable of improvement and 97 were suggested as needing replacements. These were almost entirely agricultural cottages situated on the farms and for the most part on tenant-farms; despite the introduction of gravitation water, many were without proper sanitation facilities. Water closets were lacking in a large number of those recommended for demolition; 4.9 per cent had no conveniences at all and 8.6 per cent of the occupants shared a water closet. Almost half of the private houses had no fixed bath.

While a quarter of the population lived in houses of six rooms or more, 6.7 per cent lived in either one or two-roomed dwellings. Indicative of the smaller families was the fact that 89.7 per cent lived not more than two persons to a room. In the burghs 7.9 per cent lived more than two in a room and in the landward area 12.1 per cent, with the highest figure in Whithorn, where it was 12.2 per cent compared to Newton Stewart's 4.9 per cent. Almost one-third of the private houses contained only one person or two. Whithorn took advantage of the gravitation water supply and reduced the number of houses without an indoor supply in the years after 1950. Stranraer had still almost 500 houses without a fixed bath, but improvements had been made in the town from 1931 onwards.

Electricity became available in 1931, and in 1950 gravitation water was extended to certain parts of the outlying districts in the county. At the outset, however, more emphasis was put on proper facilities for the dairy cow than for the household, no doubt because that was the main source of income for the large part of the population. Improved facilities offered by the towns and the consequent gradual change-over of population led to many tenant farmers, particularly in the lower end of the Machars, applying for and receiving grants under the various Improvement Acts. Estate owners were slow to follow suit and it was only after the second world war that the county council tackled the task of re-housing the population, especially in the clachans or agricultural villages, some houses being erected solely for agricultural workers. The resistance to change of many tenants was no doubt caused by the fact that the rents hitherto paid were either nominal or non-existent on the farm, £4 being about the usual, whereas the council houses were let at rents up to £104 a year.

To meet the demand for houses, Stranraer boundaries were extended in 1935 and Whithorn's in 1948. A further extension of Stranraer burgh area was carried out in 1960. The drift in population was shown by the drop at Kirkmaiden of 500 from 1921, of 380 at Mochrum, 250 at Glasserton, 280 at Old Luce, altogether 1,800 in the landward areas in thirty years. The burghs more than held their own in that time and, of the four, Stranraer made most progress with the re-housing of its citizens. In 1935, the county council built their first scheme of houses to stem the flow from Drummore, Garlieston, Isle of Whithorn, Portwilliam, Glenluce, Kirkcolm, Portpatrick, Sandhead and Glenstockadale. In all 142 were built, but from 1946 onwards 710 were erected. Stranraer and its own environs were most popular. A new village was erected at Dunragit, an almost new village at Castle Kennedy, and additions made at Leswalt, Lochans, Kirkcolm and Cairnryan, while a new area alongside Stranraer Town Council's scheme to the east of the town came into being at Bishopburn. More than half of the total were 'traditional' houses.

Of the 50 houses at Dunragit, ten were built for forestry workers employed at a new seeding station nearby; at Kildrochet and other places houses were erected for agricultural workers only. Portwilliam with 50 and Garlieston with 48 were the largest schemes in the Machars. Eight were built at Carty and four at Culwhirk for farm workers and tile workers, and 34 were constructed at Kirkcowan to replace what were undoubtedly the worst houses in the county. These schemes fortunately saved some of the smaller villages from extinction but Knowe, Grange of Bladnoch and Glenwhilly were dying or dead. Portlogan, however, was given a new lease of life with a scheme of neat storey-and-a-half houses, such as had proved popular at Dunragit and Kirkcowan. The latest scheme at Glenluce had the distinction of being given a leading award by the Civic Trust.

While lack of adequate water and of suitable drainage and sewage schemes had proved very serious obstacles to house building, the presence of nearly 2,000 sub-standard dwellings in the landward areas caused concern to sociologists. Up to 1959 only 117 houses had been demolished and 146 new houses had been completed, including 29 by private enterprise, in the rural areas. Of 1,383 houses occupied by farm workers, 763 were considered unfit, and of these nearly 500 were not capable of improvement, while 267 were stated to be in need of replacement. It was considered necessary to rebuild *in situ* in all districts, as the population had tended to drift away from the villages to larger centres, and many of the unfit houses were occupied by elderly people who were loth to move; thus the increased rent may have been only a small factor in the dislike of change.

Meanwhile in Stranraer, where the population had greatly increased, the town council had shown a realistic attitude. By 1959 slightly more than a quarter of the county's population was resident in the town itself and in Stranraer there were 2,671 of the 8,697 houses in Wigtownshire, while within a ten-mile radius of the town 500 others had been built, mainly by the county council; thus 36 per cent of all the houses stood in and around Stranraer. The village of Castle Kennedy was created to remove the hutted camps where people had squatted in the years following the war, but Sandhead, Portpatrick, Lochans and other villages retained their attraction and required more houses. Building went on in various areas, but still the demands continued and in 1962 the county council set in train plans for many more houses in the Rhins and Machars.

2A

Stranraer's first real attack on the slums in the burgh was made under the terms of the 1931 Act and created a new housing area to the south of the old town. By its construction tenants were removed from cul-de-sacs off Dalrymple Street, known as Sloss's Close and Rankin's Close, which had consisted of one-storey dwellings about 14 feet high with a communal water spigot and toilet. All the houses were in a row, dingy and most unattractive, and were tenanted in the main by a class of people whose habit it had been to spend only the winter in the confines of a house, removing in the spring and living in caravans and tents, a gypsy form of life that died away. Following the removal of these blots the town council tackled the centre or old part of the town, where, it was said, the houses had been huddled together for shelter from incursions of invading Irish. These houses lacked proper facilities and were old and derelict, and as late as 1955 outdoor water closets were quite common and these were shared by various tenants; a few years later, however, each house had an indoor w.c. Nevertheless a number were still without bathrooms and the immediate concern of the council was to rehouse tenants with families.

By 1959 the county had built 1,500 houses. While the municipal schemes were under way, new residential estates arose in Leswalt High Road, to the south and to the west of the town and along London Road to the east. The long-term plan was to clear the centre of the town of houses, leaving it for business purposes only, but nearly 100 families remained to be re-housed by 1959, while road-widening proposals added another 600 to that figure. Because of the failure of individuals to ask for and obtain grants for modernising their houses, the responsibility fell on the council. An indication of the spread from the centre was the fact that only 140 houses were planned for it, compared to 300 in the Sheuchan area and 400 at Rephad, the population being reckoned at 2,300 in the west, 4,300 in the centre and 2,600 in the eastern district.

In addition to the council schemes private building went on and almost 200 new bungalow-type houses were erected, but the municipal houses far outnumbered the private dwellings. An indication of the progress being made with housing was that of the houses in the burgh, 1,530 were council houses and 203 recently built private houses. Stranraer's thousandth council house was let in 1953 and in 1959 the oldest house in the burgh, Clenoch Cottage, dating back to the 1700s, was demolished.

HEALTH.

Wigtownshire is the only county in Scotland with a health centre, constructed soon after a centre had been built in Edinburgh (at Sighthill). The Department of Health was responsible for the provision of both of these centres, but they are run by local practitioners. The health centre adjoins the Garrick Hospital and this development has appealed both to the public and to the doctors. The medical men have their consulting rooms at the centre for patients coming under the National Health Service and the centralisation of the work and the facilities has proved very satisfactory all round. Private patients are dealt with at the various doctors' own consulting rooms as they existed prior to the setting up of the health

centre.   The Garrick Hospital, which dates back to the latter part of the
last century, accepts patients from all parts of the county, but many are
passed on to larger hospitals in the South-West of Scotland—Ballochmyle,
Killearn and Hairmyres—where specialist services are provided.   There
is also a maternity hospital not far distant from the Garrick and this recent
addition to the health service has proved of much value.   A small hospital
in Newton Stewart provides a very useful service.   Doctors are resident in
all the burghs and in five of the villages.   Dentists in Stranraer and Newton
Stewart have consulting rooms in the other burghs.   Health visitors undertake a helpful service under the supervision of the Medical Officer of
Health and in addition there are district nurses in the burghs and many
of the parishes.

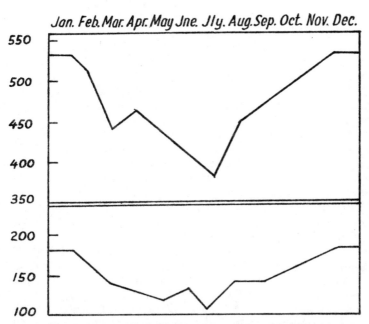

Fig. 7. Variations in the number of unemployed in the county
during 1960 are shown in this diagram, based on information provided by the Ministry of Labour. The trends in both districts bore
a close resemblance. Figures for the Rhins are outlined in the
upper panel and the other deals with the Machars.

PUBLIC ASSISTANCE AND SOCIAL WELFARE.

Since 1960 a serious problem in Wigtownshire has been the high rate of
unemployment, especially in Stranraer and district, due mainly to the
closing down of Cairnryan port.   By the end of 1962, however, there were
hopes of an improvement taking place as a result of Government action
and private enterprise.   A permanent source of expenditure falling on

the ratepayers is the high incidence of illegitimacy. In discharge of their functions under the Children Act the county council levy the highest rate in Scotland for this purpose—1s. 5d. in the pound. Most of the amount raised is spent in the interest of illegitimate children: the remainder is expended on helping families in need of aid. Two homes have been provided by the county authority for children and a large number of young people are boarded out. Much attention is also given to the aged and infirm, many of whom go to the Waverley House at Stranraer; and a 'home help' service is proving of considerable value. Quite recently homes for elderly people were opened at Newton Stewart and Stranraer. Over 7,700 free meals are provided at schools throughout the county each year and, of course, free milk is supplied to all school pupils.

PUBLIC UTILITIES

A transformation in the county supply of water has taken place within recent times. For a long time a number of villages and rural areas were badly inconvenienced during spells of dry weather. Various schemes were planned but it was not until after the second world war that the problem was tackled thoroughly. As part of the comprehensive scheme, a dam was constructed at the Penwhirn Burn, to the north-west of New Luce. The reservoir, officially opened in the summer of 1955, has a capacity of 450 million gallons and the catchment area has a safe yield of 3,000,000 gallons a day. Already a large area has been provided with an adequate supply and schemes are going forward for housing and other developments that were not previously feasible. The county scheme has been a boon to many residents in such districts as Kirkcowan, Portpatrick and Kirkmaiden.

By charter granted in 1826 gas had been introduced to Stranraer and the streets in the town were lit ten years later. Subsequently the service was extended to Wigtown and Newton Stewart, and for nearly a hundred years this form of lighting held, the output growing from five million cubic feet to about forty million. Wigtown Gas Works were, however, closed down in 1955 for economic reasons. In 1931 electricity was taken to Wigtownshire on a county basis; an earlier supply had been provided in Portpatrick by private source. In 1960 there were 10,000 consumers of 50 million units and 900 farms were served. All the burghs and main villages were lit by electricity. Gas, however, held its own for cooking purposes in the towns.

TRANSPORT SERVICES

The railways took away a great deal of the traffic that was at one time carried by coastal shipping and road transport is now detaching from the railways a substantial part of their traffic. Although the railways did reduce the amount of seaborne traffic, they brought benefits through the building of the East Pier at Stranraer, which provided a valuable link with Ireland. In addition, Stranraer had direct rail connections with Central Scotland and many parts of England.

Portpatrick Railway was opened in 1862, traversing the county from east to west and extending into the neighbouring Stewartry with a length of line running 61½ miles to Castle Douglas. It entered Wigtownshire at Newton Stewart and terminated at Portpatrick. The railway stations on the line were Newton Stewart, Kirkcowan, Glenluce, Dunragit, Castle Kennedy, Stranraer, Colfin and Portpatrick. Wigtownshire Railway, opened in 1875, branched from the Portpatrick line at Newton Stewart and ran 16 miles southwards to Garlieston. The stations served were Newton Stewart, Wigtown, Kirkinner, Sorbie and Garlieston. The Girvan-Portpatrick junction railway was opened in 1876 and ran a distance of 31½ miles from Portpatrick to Girvan, in Ayrshire. It served Castle Kennedy, Dunragit, New Luce and Glenwhilly.

A suggestion to have a branch line from Dunragit to Drummore never materialised. Several amalgamations took place before the system was integrated into British Railways and, because of lack of support from the travelling public whose habit had changed, the branch lines from Newton Stewart were closed for passenger traffic and the line from Stranraer to Portpatrick was lifted altogether for economic reasons. This took place about ten years ago. Diesel-powered trains were introduced on the Stranraer-Glasgow run late in 1959.

From 1911 steam coaches were run by the railway company as a road service from Stranraer to Drummore and small district bus operators ran services until 1927, when the Caledonian Company took over the area; at that time the company's operations extended from Newton Stewart through Stranraer to Portpatrick and also from Stranraer to Cairnryan, and thence out of the county to Ballantrae and on to Glasgow. The company soon had command of all road services, apart from the short run from Stranraer to Drummore, and on nationalisation it became part of the Western S.M.T. Company. But travel fashions continued to change and many more motor cars came into use, so that by 1959 the bus companies in rural Wigtownshire were thankful for the £20,000 per annum they received for the conveyance of school children. Without that additional revenue it is doubtful if even a reasonable service could have been maintained.

A few figures will give an idea of the development of motor traffic. In 1926 (the earliest year for which county details are available) the number of cars licensed was 746. By 1946 the total had risen to 1,807 and in 1962 the figure was 4,056. Goods vehicles licensed in 1926 numbered 249; by 1936 there were 369 and by 1962, 892. The number of motor cycles reached the peak figure of 691 in 1930. In 1946 there were only 300, but by 1962 the total had increased to 577. Hackney licences have dwindled with the growth of private transport from 204 in 1926 to 32 in 1962. The drift away from horses on the farms is reflected in a great rise in the numbers of tractors. Only 14 were licensed throughout the shire in 1926. By 1946 there were 484 and by 1962, 1,606. Over all there has been an increase in the number of motor vehicles from 1,750 in 1926 to 7,198 in 1962. In 1946 the figure was 3,019. Thus the total has more than doubled within the last seventeen years.

An effort to establish a civilian airport in the county did not achieve much success. In 1955 Silver City Airways acquired ground at Castle Kennedy, which had been an R.A.F. station during the war, and started up a service for passengers and vehicles between Galloway and Northern Ireland. Three years later the enterprise was discontinued.

Wigtownshire has a spendid road system and most of the highways are remarkably level. In recent years many improvements have been made; numerous bends have disappeared and narrow stretches have been widened. There are 33 miles of trunk roads and the mileage figures of the others are as follow:—Class one, 109; class two, 99; class three, 143; unclassified, 186. In some of the rural areas the number of roads is an occasional source of confusion to strangers, but they are all required to service the needs of a scattered community.

COMMUNICATIONS

The growth of the postal service has been swift. By 1959 more than 110,000 letters were delivered weekly in the county and nearly 4,000 parcels. Outgoing mail extended to 77,000 letters and 2,000 parcels each week, while the staff numbered 190. Pensions payments per annum totalled 190,000, besides 73,000 family allowances and 55,000 other allowances. Some 5,500 C.O.D. parcels were delivered, 500,000 postal orders were sold and 70,000 postal orders were paid. Savings Bank transactions amounted to 45,000. The licences included nearly 6,000 for television and more than 2,000 for sound, and there were 3,368 telephone subscribers. An automatic exchange was in preparation, as was a new post office at Stranraer. The telegraph service had almost completely vanished. Telephone wires were all underground on the main lines and the district wires were being put underground.

PLANNING

A comprehensive report has been prepared for the County Council on present conditions in Wigtownshire and plans have been put forward for future developments, especially in the burghs. The survey was undertaken by Richard E. Moira and B. L. C. Moira, planning consultants, in conjunction with Robert M. Clive, county architect and planning officer. The final report was expected early in 1961, but changes had to be made and its appearance was delayed.

EDUCATION

Facilities for education have been greatly improved in recent times. Many people have left the rural areas and come into Stranraer, with the result that new schools have become necessary. At the same time there has been a movement towards centralisation. Between 1939 and 1959 the number of children attending Stranraer schools rose from 1,791 to 2,030. The Roman Catholic population showed slight annual increases and the total number of children attending St. Joseph's School was 131. The school roll in Wigtownshire at the end of 1959 was 5,355, of whom 1,768 were over twelve years of age. Locally it was a matter of pleasing comment that Sheuchan School, which had been handed over by the Presbytery in 1872, was remodelled and kept in being after having been closed for a number of years prior to the second world war. Stranraer provided all the senior secondary education for pupils in the Rhins. With the general prosperity and larger bursaries there was a tendency for parents to keep their children longer at school. In the fourth, fifth and sixth years at Stranraer High School there were 112 scholars out of a total roll of 409. In 1959 a fourth year's course was started at Stranraer Academy for junior secondary pupils and 35 children attended. This was the first real attempt to bridge the gap between the school leaving and gainful employment stages for pupils not academically minded. Boys received instruction in

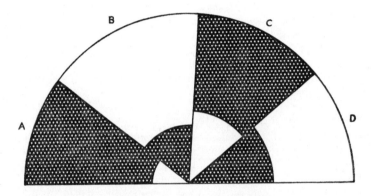

Fig. 8. SCHOOL LEAVERS

On leaving school to go into industry more young people enter the retail distribution trade than any other. The diagram indicates the percentages who went into the various industries during 1961. A —agriculture, 20 per cent; B—shops, 31 per cent; C—skilled trades, 28 per cent; D—unskilled trades, 21 per cent. The shaded portions represent boys and the clear portions girls. The analysis refers to the whole of Wigtownshire.

the internal combustion engine, electricity and mechanisation, while the girls were taught nursing, housewifery and needlework. Tuition was also given for national certificates in engineering. In addition pupils were encouraged to prosecute their studies, so that, in addition to the larger exodus of scholars to colleges and universities, there was an increased flow from junior secondary schools of girls who wished to follow a nursing career and of boys whose bent was for mechanics or engineering. Facilities were made available for those who remained at home to obtain further education at evening continuation classes, but these were not in the main well supported; the largest classes were those for Scottish country dancing.

A feature of school life was the part played by itinerant specialist teachers, who brought to the smaller rural schools a knowledge of music, art, woodwork, domestic science and physical education. The importance of the services rendered by these specialists was reflected in the fact that at Glenluce there were three resident teachers and eight visiting teachers. An innovation at Glenluce was the introduction of classes based on the ability of the pupils rather than on their age, with a special leaning towards agriculture, in which the majority of the scholars intended to seek a livelihood. Another development was the inauguration of classes for handicapped children; two such classes were held at Stranraer and in addition there was a small class for uneducable children.

As in the Rhins, the centralisation scheme was carried out in the Machars from about 1935. The first completely central school was established at Newton Stewart, in the Douglas Ewart school, itself an amalgamation of the Douglas school for boys and Ewart school for girls. Whithorn school lost Latin, and in course of time was shorn of its senior secondary department; Wigtown had already lost this department. The pupils travelled to the Douglas Ewart school, which in 1956 became a comprehensive school, with a roll of 405, of whom 85 were in the fourth, fifth and sixth years.

Closing of Small Schools. By 1960 a number of rural schools had been closed and the total number at the end of the year was 44. Glenwhilly was the first single-teacher school to be closed: the roll had fallen to six. Grange, Portlogan and Dhuloch followed. Further closures were effected and within two years 16 schools were closed. There was general regret at the closures, particularly in the case of Portlogan, which during its 78 years of existence had had on its roll 37 boys who in course of time became sea captains. The reasons for the closing of such schools included staffing difficulties and the deterioration of the buildings; the cost of bringing them up to modern standards was regarded as prohibitive. There was opposition by some to the closing of schools, but others felt that centralisation was a good thing for the children and for education generally. Among the larger primary schools, excluding those in Stranraer, where there were three with higher rolls, were Penninghame, Newton Stewart, which had 228 pupils, Lochans with 114, and Portpatrick with 112. It had been thought at one time that Portpatrick would become a junior secondary school, but the scheme was dropped.

Library and Museum

In the post-war years the County Library service grew quickly and by 1959, in addition to the centre in Stranraer, there were more than sixty branches throughout the county. In the early days the book stock was under 3,000 and the annual expenditure amounted to £350; by 1959 there were 53,000 books in circulation and the yearly cost was £8,000. The library buildings now in use were a war-time British Restaurant and in recent years a museum has been built up. Pleas have been advanced for additions to the accommodation and extensions have now been planned. The nucleus for the museum was provided by gifts from the late Rev. R. S. G. Anderson, Castle Kennedy, who also bequeathed a large collection of books. Earlier, the late Mr. James Muir, Newton Stewart, had presented the library with a notable selection of books and the two gifts were formed into the Galloway Collection. Many local people have given articles and relics in the past few years and the museum has created more and more interest as the number of exhibits has continued to grow. The formation of the Wigtownshire Antiquarian Society in 1955 has led to numerous additions to the museum, for which a great deal has been done by Mr. A. E. Truckell, curator of the Dumfries museum. There is a museum at Whithorn, with a splendid collection of interesting objects recovered from the site of the ancient church. There is no permanent art gallery in the county. A display of pictures by school children is arranged at intervals at Stranraer and Newton Stewart.

CHAPTER 4

THE COMMUNITY

POPULATION

RURAL depopulation has affected Wigtownshire substantially since the middle of last century. The number of people in the county reached its peak in 1851 when the total was 43,389. It has now declined to 29,107 (a density of under 60 persons to the square mile), as revealed in the census taken in April 1961. Only once, in 1951, has an increase been recorded during the intervening period.

The fall became perceptible in 1861, following increases in the first half of the nineteenth century, when the population rose from 22,918 to nearly double that number at the start of the "Hungry Forties". In the decades 1861-70 and 1871-80 the birth rate and the death rate both rose, from 29.2 per thousand to 31.4 and from 18.3 to 19.6 respectively; thereafter both fell gradually. The birth rate fell by 10.7 from 31.4 in the years 1871-80 to 20.7 in the years 1931-50, and the death rate fell by 6.2 from 19.6 in the years 1871-80 to 13.4 in the years 1931-50. This relationship meant that the natural increase fell from 10.9 in the years 1861-70 to 7.3 in the period 1931-50. The actual natural increase exceeded 4,000 in 1890 and 2,000 in 1920, and stood at 1,944 in the period 1921-30. In the period 1931-50 there was an increase over previous intercensal periods, as 2,575 was the natural increase figure for 1941-50. This was due, however, not only to the increased birth-rate following the second world war, but also to the presence of some 1,400 servicemen and women stationed in Wigtownshire during the years 1939-50, notably at Cairnryan and West Freugh. In addition there was a large group of Irishmen at Wig Bay seaplane base, employed by Short Brothers and Harland (Belfast) on the repair and maintenance of Sunderland flying boats. By April 1961 both Wig Bay and Cairnryan harbour were completely deserted, while the number of people at West Freugh aircraft establishment had been very much reduced. Thus whereas in 1951 the county population was 31,620 as compared with 29,331 in 1931, by 1961 the total had dropped to 29,107, showing that the century-old trend had been resumed after the departure of servicemen and others engaged on Government work.

Only at one census period did the number of males exceed the number of females, and that by a mere 156. This was in 1951 when the males reached a total of 15,888 while the females numbered 15,732. From the beginning of last century up to 1951 the females had generally been in the majority of about 2,000. The change was due, of course, to the presence of troops and workmen from outside areas.

378

And the presence of such transients affected the migration figures to some extent, though the loss had been steady since 1861. The percentage migration exceeded 10 except for the periods 1911-20 when it was 8.8 and 1931-50 when it was 9.6. In the periods 1861-70, 1881-90 and 1891-1900 the loss by migration exceeded 15 per cent. From 1951 to 1959 the loss by migration, however, was less than that of the natural increase. There were two causes for that: one was the number of service personnel in the district from 1935 to 1950 and the other the number of prisoners of war from Germany, Italy, Poland, Yugo-Slavia and other countries. The fall in population caused by migration from 1861 to 1951 was therefore halted because of the unnatural increase of persons normally resident elsewhere. Then, too, the economic factors which forced many to leave the country-side changed after the second world war, when many were induced to stay in their native place. At one period, 33.4 per cent of the population were born outwith the county; by 1959, the numbers of these had declined to about one in five. The presence of former prisoners of war did not appreciably affect the numbers but did lead to a changing pattern and had an effect on the outlook of the people in general. Not all the additional people were former war prisoners, or war-time personnel; many came to reside in the county from other parts of Scotland and elsewhere. Most of these were of the professional classes and they too had their effect on the general way of life. Most of the incomers came from Glasgow or from Ayrshire, Kirkcudbrightshire and Dumfriesshire and they were supplemented by the English members of the Services who remained to make their home in the district.

A point of interest about recent shifts of population is that although the total was down in 1961 by 2,513 as compared with the 1951 figures, the burghs showed a net increase of 274. In three of the burghs a decrease was noted, but the number of Stranraer's inhabitants had risen by 612. The total was 9,249 compared with 8,637 ten years previously. Males numbered 4,451 in 1961, an increase of 290, and the numbers of females were 4,798 and 4,476 respectively—an increase of 322. Newton Stewart's total dropped by 81. In 1951 the figure was 2,061 (927 males and 1,134 females) and by 1961 the population had dropped to 1,980—males numbering 894 and females 1,086. A larger decrease was reported in Wigtown. There, the 1951 total of 1,376 (656 males and 720 females) fell by 175 to 1,201, comprising 573 males and 628 females. These figures show a drop of 83 and 92 respectively. In Whithorn a fall of 82 took place in the ten-year period. The total population numbered 1,068 in 1951 (495 males and 573 females). By 1961 the figure had dropped to under a thousand, 986 in all, consisting of 450 males and 536 females.

The rise in Stranraer's numbers was due to a large extent to the movement into the town of workers, mostly farming employees, in search of better amenities. Many of them continued to work on the land, travelling to and fro by bicycle or, in numerous cases, by car and bus. As a result the number of people resident in the Rhins district went down by 2,034 in the decade. The total in 1951 was 11,762 (6,345 males and 5,417 females), while the overall figure in 1961 was 9,728, of whom 4,901 were males and 4,827 were females. This was an unusual ratio and marked one of the rare occasions when the number of males was greater than the female population. In the Machars the position was rather different. There was no drift into the burghs in the eastern area, but the population went down by 753. This must have been accounted for by people leaving the shire for other areas. The 1951 figures showed a total of 6,716 (3,304

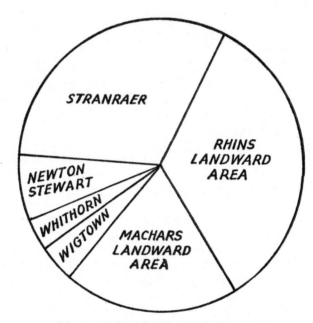

Fig. 9. POPULATION DISTRIBUTION

At the 1961 Census the population was 29,107. The number of people in Stranraer was 9,249, in Newton Stewart 1,980, Wigtown 1,201, Whithorn 986, Rhins Landward Area 9,728, Machars Landward Area 5,963.

males and 3,412 females); and the 1961 Census revealed that the total had fallen to 5,963 (2,972 males and 2,991 females).

So far as age structure is concerned the trend in Wigtownshire has been pretty much as in the rest of Scotland. In 1959 there were 263 children under 15 years in every thousand, a slight decline since the beginning of the century, and 99 persons in every thousand were over the age of 65, a slight increase. The average age of the population was 33.1 years, slightly under the national average. Numbers of old people in Wigtownshire compared with those in the rest of Scotland, but in 1959 there were at least four who were approaching the century mark, besides 30 other nonagenarians, twenty female and ten male.

The number of males had increased with the rise in the population to just under 49 per cent and of these 4,000 were under 15 years of age; 8,708 were aged from 15 to 64; and the remainder, 1,218, were over 65 years of age. In both latter groups the males were outnumbered by the females, totalling 9,837 between 15 and 64 and 1,513 over 65. This number would have been substantially increased but for the migration of young women to the cities because of the lack of suitable employment in the county. Another feature common to the county as a whole was the fact that 57.8 per cent of males aged 16 and over were married as compared with 52.1 per cent in 1931, and the rise in the married rate for females over 16 was even more emphatic, 56.5 per cent compared to 42 per cent in 1931. Females, that is to say, married younger than in former times.

Following recent census results a good deal of concern has been expressed in different quarters about the continuing decline in Wigtown-shire's population. There was a time, not so long ago, when it was contended that the people might remain on the land if better housing was provided and if transport facilities were improved. In the post-war years the county council has undertaken extensive housing schemes in practically all parts of the rural districts and the bus companies have extended their services to cater for people in out-of-the-way areas, but the downward trend in population has not been halted. As a result of modern development in farming, the number of workers has gone down and the countryside is undergoing a gradual change. Although the population is less, the prosperity of the farming industry has not faded; indeed, the opposite is the case. On all sides there are signs of a prosperous age in agriculture.

RELIGION

Religious ordinances do not now receive the attention that was accorded them up to the first decade of this century. Church-going began to fall away during the first world war and that trend has continued, though in some churches the congregation has increased. As in other parts of the country, Sunday is often devoted to sport of various kinds and the old-fashioned day of worship has disappeared. Large numbers of people give little thought to religion, but on the other hand evangelistic campaigns and special schools conducted by ministers and lay preachers have in the past few years aroused much interest—mostly among church-goers, however. The Church of Scotland, naturally, is by far the largest of the denominations, with a congregation in every parish and more than one in several of them. As the shire has a near neighbour in Ireland, it is not surprising that a substantial number of Roman Catholics are included in the population of Western Galloway or that many of the Presbyterian ministers come from Ulster. There are Episcopalian Churches at Stranraer, Portpatrick and Newton Stewart; the Stranraer and Portpatrick congregations come under the same minister. Stranraer has one Reformed Presbyterian Church, the only one in the county, and in recent times it has had a succession of Irish ministers. Stranraer has many Roman Catholics and there are large attendances at St. Joseph's Church. A group of Sisters of Mercy reside in the vicinity of the chapel and spend much time in the diligent discharge of their duties. A new church was dedicated in the autumn of 1960 at Whithorn, while a priest who resides at Newton Stewart regularly visits Wigtown and other parts of the Machars. St. Ninian's cave on the Glasserton shore is the venue of pilgrimages each year. This practice is a revival of customs that were in vogue in earlier times, but were banned about 150 years ago.

VOLUNTARY SERVICES
People in all walks of life devote much of their time to voluntary service Some of the organisations have been in existence for a great number of years; others are comparatively young. Hospital committees date back to last century and still function, but now as part of the National Health Service. In addition to the Dumfries and Galloway Hospital Board, which has taken over the work of local committees, there is the Galloway Health Executive Committee, and on both of these bodies are representatives from Wigtownshire and the Stewartry. A new organisation is the Hospital League of Friends, which originated in Dumfries and has now a helpful branch in Stranraer. One of the older organisations, the Red Cross Society, undertakes a variety of services throughout the county in addition to training members in first aid and in dealing with requests for attendance at public gatherings where help may be needed. There are Voluntary Aid Detachments at Stranraer, Newton Stewart, Kirkcowan and Whithorn while the cadet unit has a large membership. More recent bodies are the W.V.S., and those devoted to Civil Defence. The newest committee of all is being organised to aid the Cheshire Home at Carnsalloch, near Dumfries. Active service is given on behalf of the Societies for the Prevention of Cruelty to Children and to Animals, the Shipwrecked Mariners' Society, the Royal National Life-boat Institution and the Victoria League. There are old folk's committees in the various parishes with central committees in the two districts—the Rhins and the Machars. Another committee gives help at the Waverley Home (formerly the poorhouse) and in Newton Stewart a committee provides service at the Girls' Home. In Stranraer a committee attends to the needs of defective children and another gives advice on family planning.

In a different field, enthusiastic service is given on behalf of the Stranraer Development Association, which was formed a few years ago to attract holiday-makers to the town. The Galloway Pageant calls for much voluntary service each year in Newton Stewart and a Wigtown committee carries out the arrangements for the annual Riding of the Marches, which came into existence in its present form only a few years ago. Portpatrick has a vigorous Improvements Committee and at Portwilliam an energetic committee sponsors summer events. Although they cannot be described as voluntary bodies in the same sense as those already mentioned, numerous organisations give aid to people who are in need. These include the Rotary Club, Inner Wheel, British Legion (which has a strong Women's Section in Stranraer) and the Business and Professional Women's Club. Services are also rendered by the Women's Rural Institutes, the Woman's Guilds, the Savings Committees, the Girl Guides, the Boy Scouts, the Girls' Guildry and various musical and dramatic associations.

CHARITY AND PHILANTHROPY

With the advent of the Welfare State and nationalised services some of the charitable and philanthropic bodies of earlier days have disappeared. On the other hand new organisations have arisen, most of them to fill gaps in the services taken over by the Government. Stranraer Town Council administers two funds from which disbursements are made at the Christmas season. In December 1960, 287 people received gifts of money from these sources. At one time there was a coal fund, but this was wound up when rationing was introduced during the second world war. The Stranraer Rotary Club, although not a charitable institution, according to the movement's constitution, distributes parcels of food to elderly people at the festive season and provides an outing for old folks in the summer. The Inner Wheel Club, whose members are the wives of Rotarians, also provides gift parcels and sends clothing to homeless people on the Continent.

Many committees in the county arrange entertainments and outings for elderly folk; and in Stranraer there is a club for members of the senior generation who care to avail themselves of its facilities. Social gatherings are held frequently and are well attended. Branches of youth organisations are numerous and in many parts of the county community associations include entertainments for young and old among their activities.

ENTERTAINMENT

Television soon made an impact on Wigtownshire. By reason of its geographical situation, the Drummore area has enjoyed excellent reception since the earliest days of TV. Aerials sprout from every roof and remind one of the appearance of villages in the vicinity of Kirk o' Shotts. In other districts the Scottish programmes cannot be satisfactorily received and many pleas have been made for better service. The programmes from Northern Ireland come in quite clearly, but their content has very little of a Scottish flavour, which gives rise to many complaints. On some football occasions there was an exodus of followers from the Stranraer area to Drummore and Sandhead, where the Scottish team could be seen in action and the match followed in full detail. As in other places, television has brought about changes in the social life of people in Wigtownshire and the old-time emptiness of the evening has disappeared. The wireless and the cinema had previously provided entertainment and filled blanks that had long existed in the lives of country folk, whose diversions had consisted mainly of a visit to the nearest town on the fair days. The introduction of bus services and the coming of radio brought a new outlook, but television has made a much greater impact and the phrase in "wanted" advertisements, "Near bus route", has almost disappeared. The picture houses are not attracting the large attendances of a few years ago, though they are still doing fairly well at Stranraer, Newton Stewart, Wigtown and Whithorn; smaller concerns at Glenluce and Drummore have closed down.

Sport

Rural counties are as a rule rather backward in the realm of sport and this shire is no exception. A refreshing feature of recent times, however, has been the development of sea sports for which there is plenty of scope around the coast. Yachting clubs have been formed in several centres and craft are raced all through the summer on Lochryan and on stretches of Luce Bay. Inter-club contests are becoming more numerous and some time ago an association was formed to co-ordinate local activities and to promote competitions. At one time Stranraer could boast of having regattas, which, under the patronage of the Prince Consort, formed one of the most fashionable events of the summer. Interest waned when almost the whole of the prize money went to yachtsmen coming from a distance. The later regattas, on a less expensive scale, were popular features for a long time. Between the wars the number of craft fell away, but after 1945 there was a revival of interest in sailing. Since then the sport has attracted large numbers of devotees, many of whom have constructed their own craft.

Water ski-ing, a somewhat startling form of marine sport, made its appearance quite recently. For a time it was confined to the Drummore area, but demonstrations are frequently given at Stranraer, Portpatrick and various places along the Machars shore. One of the achievements that caused a stir in the early days was a Kirkmaiden youth's crossing to Ireland and back on water skis in less than three hours.

Nothing attracts so much interest, however, as football, and the Stranraer club has its place in the Second Division of the Scottish League. At one time local games aroused wide enthusiasm, but Stranraer's admission to a higher sphere has brought many changes and district matches has lost their appeal. Clubs in Newton Stewart, Whithorn, Wigtown and Kirkcowan have felt the effect of the changed conditions and financially they are in a continual struggle. When Stranraer first took part in the Second Division matches large crowds flocked to Stair Park, but the novelty has worn off and the attendances are hardly sufficient to keep the club in a sound position. Donations from organisations associated with the club are required to eke out the income, and the financial situation is frequently the officials' major worry.[1] In this respect, of course, Stranraer is not alone; the majority of the clubs in the Second Division are in a similar plight.

Interest in rugby is confined to a very small circle. Wigtownshire Rugby Club, based on Stranraer, consists mainly of men who learned their

[1] Despite what is here said, it is still noteworthy that Stranraer finished Season 1960-61 in fourth place in the Second Division (which comprises 19 clubs) — immediately ahead of Queen of the South, from Dumfries, the only other team from the South-West in the competition. In 1962 Stranraer were leagueleaders for a time.

Galloway News

Plate 5. STRANRAER
The west end of the burgh, looking towards the entrance to Lochryan.

Galloway News

Plate 6. PORTPATRICK

Galloway News

Plate 7. THE CREE BRIDGE AND WEIR, NEWTON STEWART

Scottish Sunday Express

Plate 8. PENNINGHAME OPEN PRISON, NEWTON STEWART

rugger at school in Edinburgh. At the helm and on the committee are those whose playing days are over, while the younger element constitute the playing members. The home matches are usually attended by only a handful of spectators, but the enthusiasm of the few reaches a high peak. The only opposition from the southern counties is provided by the Dumfries club, as the Stewartry no longer has a team and Langholm is in a far different class; most of the matches are therefore with clubs in Ayrshire, Lanarkshire, Glasgow and Larne.

Badminton has gained a wide hold in post-war years, with leagues in both districts of the county and clubs in nearly every parish; in addition to friendly and league matches, there are championship and inter-district fixtures. The county has not so far produced a player of national calibre, but the game has certainly done much to establish closer social ties among the people from the various areas. Table tennis enjoyed a vogue for some time and after a lapse is again popular.

Bowling greens are to be found in most parts of the county and two clubs have been in existence for more than a hundred years. Wigtown club, formed in 1854, is the oldest in the county, and next in seniority comes Stranraer, which dates back to 1859. There are district, county and Southern Counties titles to play for, besides the national competitions, which culminate in the Scottish finals at Queen's Park; some clubs have done well in the finals, but have not yet carried off any of the championships. Carpet bowling has devotees in the rural parishes and local clubs take part in the international matches as well as district tournaments. New Luce Club has gained distinction in the wider fields.

With six courses in various parts of the county, golfers are well catered for both in the Rhins and the Machars. The latest to be added to the list is Wigtown, where the town council took steps in 1959 to provide a course and the ground is now in good playing order.

Stranraer golfers lost their original course during the second world war. Their ground was taken over for military purposes and for something like ten years those who wished to have a round of golf had to travel to Portpatrick or farther afield. Some time earlier a large area of farmland at the Drums and Creachmore had been bequeathed by Major Garroway to the town council as a golf course. The will did not become operative without a long delay and various legal and other difficulties, but eventually James Braid laid out the new course: it was one of the last he planned. The course, which borders Lochryan for some distance, has many natural beauties and attracts golfers in large numbers from some of the best-known clubs on the Ayrshire seaboard. This new course is now the venue of all the important matches and competitions played in Wigtownshire. The old course, to the east of the town, ceased to be used for golf in 1940, and it is now the site of a primary school and of a large municipal housing scheme. It is expected that in the near future the remainder of the site will be utilised for more school buildings and playgrounds. There are good seaside links at Portpatrick, Glenluce and Monreith, while Newton Stewart has a pleasant inland course.

2B

Curling has assumed a new significance as a sport among the farming community. In the early days of the ice rink at Ayr, interest was rather half-hearted, but in recent years enthusiasm for the game has grown tremendously and women as well as men make frequent visits to the rink. Inter-club, inter-district and inter-county games provide about as much curling as the average player wants, but there are those who take part in international fixtures and world championships. Visits of teams from abroad, mostly Canada and the United States, create a furore and the Test matches arouse interest all over the country. Gone are the days when curling depended on the vagaries of the weather and when the games were played on a loch or pond, with all amenities improvised when it was seen that the ice was "bearing". On a few ponds in the county games are still occasionally played: New Luce has a long tradition in this respect and Logan sometimes comes into the reckoning. In times of really hard frost matches are held at Castle Kennedy and Craichlaw, which is the venue of the inter-county game when play takes place on open ice.

THE WAY OF LIFE

Wigtownshire has seen great changes within the past two decades. Early in the century people living in the country districts had an isolated existence. Workers on the land rarely left the neighbourhood of the farms between terms and other people, apart from farmers, paid only occasional visits to the nearest town in the course of a year. The farmer, in accordance with established custom, went to town every market day and on occasion was accompanied by his wife, with a horse and gig as the main form of transport. Some ploughmen and other farm workers had their cycles, but travelling about the countryside was limited to short distances except when there was a strong magnet in the form of an agricultural show, a sports meeting or a circus. Life in the country was dull and drab for most folk. Preparations for the ploughing match or cattle show gave the farm employees a spice of excitement, but for the women there was little to occupy their attention after their day's work was over. The formation of Women's Rural Institutes, begun soon after the first world war, introduced a new note and gradually the movement took a firm hold all over the countryside. "Rural" activities are now numerous and varied and have given many a countrywoman a new interest, though there is still a proportion of the women in each parish to whom they have no appeal. The younger generation devote much of their leisure time to dancing, often travelling long distances to dance to their favourite band.

The motor car and the bus altered customs and habits, while radio and television brought even greater changes, and life in the country is now vastly different from what it was not many years ago. A great deal of attention is devoted by all classes to entertainments, amusements and sport. Modern contrivances have made farming conditions easier and shorter hours, higher pay and better housing have substantially improved the lot of the rural workers. In general they are happier than they used to be and enjoy the new opportunities for a wider social life that have come about in recent times.

People who reside in the towns have also had their horizon extended by modern developments, especially in the realms of sport and recreation. Holidays abroad—including air travel to the Continent or Channel Islands —are becoming more popular every year among town and country people alike and trips to America are also fairly numerous.

As for the more serious things of life, much greater interest is shown in national and international affairs than in the pre-war years. This is no doubt due to a large extent to radio and television. On the other hand, interest in local government activities has declined: town and county council elections create very little stir, and the number voting nowadays is usually around 33 per cent.

Church-going has not undergone much change in the past thirty years, but had already declined from the closing quarter of last century or even earlier. Church unions have been effected in the Rhins and the Machars, often because of falling membership. Of late laymen have been taking a more active part in congregational work and in the western part of the county there is a branch of the Office-bearers' Association; this is an aspect of church work that has assumed importance both in the larger communities and in the rural districts. As in other parts of Scotland, a union of presbyteries has recently taken place. The presbyteries of Wigtown and Stranraer have become one.

A serious blot on the shire's reputation is the high rate of illegitimacy. This has been a source of concern for many years and the subject of grave consideration as well as widespread publicity. Up to now the steps taken to curb this social evil have not been very effective.

1961 CENSUS FIGURES

RHINS PARISHES

	Persons	Males	Females
Inch	2,070	1,021	999
Kirkcolm	1,019	493	526
Kirkmaiden	1,106	562	544
Leswalt	821	409	412
New Luce	226	117	109
Old Luce	1,778	900	878
Portpatrick	1,062	515	547
Stoneykirk	1,701	888	813

MACHARS PARISHES

	Persons	Males	Females
Glasserton	492	248	244
Kirkcowan	695	341	354
Kirkinner	857	436	421
Mochrum	1,174	561	613
Penninghame	704	368	336
Sorbie	1,109	541	568
Whithorn	737	366	371
Wigtown	203	107	96

Part Two

THE PARISHES

CHAPTER 5

THE PARISH AND BURGH OF WIGTOWN

by the REV. GAVIN LAWSON

History of the Local Community

Wigtown, the county town, lies near the eastern border of Wigtownshire and on the west shore of Wigtown Bay. It is an ancient burgh, certainly in existence before 1292; James II gave it a new charter in 1457, while in 1662 Charles II confirmed and extended the burghal privileges in another charter, whereby one of the additional rights conferred was that of levying dues on all sheep, cattle and wool crossing the river Cree, which is entirely outwith the boundary. While much of the extensive land that once belonged to the burgh has been alienated and such privileges as the cutting of peat on the burgh moss and the maintenance of a ferry between Creetown and Wigtown have been lost, the burgh still holds the crossing of the Cree and British Railways now pay it £20 per annum for the right to carry sheep, cattle and wool across the river.

The parish of Wigtown runs west from the town for nearly 5 miles; its greatest breadth is about 4½ miles, while its area is 9,633 acres, of which 1,793½ acres are foreshore and 34¾ water. In 1905 there were 26 heritors; today there are 45. After the first world war the Earl of Galloway disposed of his land in the parish and almost all the farmers became proprietors. The largest resident landowner is Sir Thomas A. W. Whyte, Bart., Torhousemuir.

The modern spelling of the name 'Wigtown' serves to distinguish it from 'Wigton' in Cumberland. The meaning of the name is not known with certainty; it has been interpreted as 'the town on the hill', 'the town on the bay', 'the town washed by the sea' and 'the town of the castle'. The castle of Wigtown, situated on the banks of the Bladnoch, south of the town, at a place where in ancient times the river fell into the bay, was among those that were delivered into the hands of Edward I pending a decision between the competitors for the crown of Scotland, and it was handed over to John Balliol to become for a time a royal residence. Wallace took it in 1297. The outlines of this fortress were traced by Captain Robert McKerlie in 1830, but today even the fosse which was plainly discernible in 1849 has been completely obliterated.

The same has to be said about the Dominican monastery on the ridge above the castle, which was founded in 1247 by the mother of John Balliol, Devorguilla, daughter of Alan, last of the ancient Lords of Galloway. By 1648 its very stones had been carried away, probably to be used by the parishioners for the building of houses, so that the monastery survives today only in place names, such as Friarland, Monk Hill, Friar's Well and Bell Yett. There was evidently a cemetery connected with the monastery, for human bones have been dug up on the site from time to time, while in the old churchyard nearby there is a broken tombstone to an unknown monk; it may be that this ancient burying ground was part of the cemetery of the monastery and that here we have the dust of the monks mingling with the dust of martyrs.

Memorials of the Past

The Wigtown Martyrs were not natives of this parish, but were put to death in 1685 in Wigtown. Margaret Wilson and Margaret Lachlane, who were drowned, came from the parishes of Penninghame and Kirkinner, while William Johnston, John Milroy and George Walker, who were hanged, also belonged to Penninghame. Their tombstones once stood close to the north wall of the old church, but when that church was taken down about 1850 they were removed for safety a few yards in a northerly direction and an iron railing was put round them. Other stones from different parts of the churchyard are now pinned against the ruins of the old church, where they were set by the parish council to preserve them from destruction —a fate that has befallen some of these relics of historical interest during the past 30 years. In 1948, however, a cist with a holed coverstone was discovered during ploughing on Redbrae Farm about 900 yards east of the standing stones of Torhouse. By the intelligent action of the farmer, Mr. James Cannon, in reporting his find, and guarding it until it had been examined by experts, this interesting memorial of a past age was preserved and it is now in the National Museum of Antiquities in Edinburgh.[1]

In 1858 there was erected at Windyhill by public subscription, as a monument to the memory of the martyrs, a handsome obelisk terminating in a cinerary urn; and in 1936 a stone erection was placed in Wigtown Bay on the spot.

Beside the old churchyard stands one of the most handsome war memorials in the county. This fine structure, fittingly placed, is built of granite from across the bay, and bears the names of 54 men from this parish who made the supreme sacrifice in the first world war. On Remembrance Day, November 1948, one of the panels, inscribed with the names of 14 men who gave their lives in the second world war, was unveiled by Mrs. James Clark, who lost her husband and her brother in the war, and was dedicated by the Rev. Gavin Lawson, who served as a combatant in the first war.

Within the old churchyard are the remains of a pre-Reformation church, the older portions of which date back to the twelfth century. The

[1] See Mr. R. B. K. Stevenson's article in the *Transactions of the Dumfries and Galloway Natural History and Antiquarian Society*, Vol. XXVI.

original church belonged to the priory of Whithorn, but later became a free rectory of which the King was patron. The patronage was acquired by the Earl of Galloway in 1650. The church on this site, rebuilt in 1730, repaired in 1770 and re-roofed in 1831, continued to be used as the parish church until the middle of the last century, when the new church was built on adjoining ground to the east.

Modern Buildings

The new church, in the Gothic style, was evidently designed to be cruciform, but the west transept was never built. The Earl of Galloway, who as the largest heritor bore the major part of the cost of the building, generously presented the two beautiful windows that adorn the north and south gables, and gave two of the three stained glass windows erected in 1866 to the memory of the Rev. Peter Young, who ministered in Wigtown for 65 years. This was surely one of the first *country* parishes in Scotland to have a pipe organ, for such an instrument was introduced here in 1877. Extensive alterations, begun in 1914 and interrupted by the war, were completed in 1925. An organ chamber was built and the organ modernised by the addition of several new stops and pneumatic action. A generating plant was installed in a new building at the rear of the church to provide electricity for the blowing of the organ and the lighting of the church. The furnishings were replaced by a new pulpit, elders' seats, a new communion table and a baptismal font. The vestry was enlarged and the church heated for the first time by hot water pipes. Ten years later the church hall was built for work among the young and for other social and religious activities, and here for a number of years films were used for religious instruction.

On the south side of the town, opposite the centre of the Square, is the first Roman Catholic Church built in modern times in the Machars: it was opened in 1879. Previous to that, Roman Catholics in Whithorn, Sorbie, Kirkinner and Wigtown had to travel to Newton Stewart. Designed by Garden-Brown, a London architect, the church is early English in style and consists of a nave, apse, north and south transepts and sacristy.

Forming the chief architectural ornament of the burgh, the County Buildings stand at the eastern end of the Square and occupy the site of an older building of the same nature erected in 1756. This fine Tudor structure, completed in 1863, gained the approval of John Ruskin, who occasionally visited friends in the town. It contains a court-room with the usual side rooms, the offices of the sheriff clerk, the public library and a large assembly hall. On the sides of the main entrance the arms of Stranraer and Whithorn are carved and the initial letters of the other principal places in the county appear on the keystones of the arched windows. Over the side entrance is an imperfect representation of the burgh arms, and on the wall to the left is a slab with the royal arms, taken from the court-house that formerly stood there. The tower belonging to the old building has been faced by new stonework, but the old Tolbooth beneath it has been preserved intact with its iron door and massive bolts. In the Council Chamber are to be seen the capacious punch-bowl presented to the burgh by Queen Anne, a wooden drinking cup, five infitting beakers, a wine gallon, a quart, six bell-shaped and two circular weights, a three-legged bushel measure and other interesting relics. In the tower hang three bells dated respectively 1633, 1777 and 1881. The earliest bell bears the inscription, 'O GOD LET WIGTOUNE FLOURISH BY THY WORD IN CHRIST, WHO IS OUR ONLIE HEAD. ANNO 1633.'

The well-trimmed grass of the bowling green and the red blaes of the tennis courts, facing the County Buildings, give an unusual charm to the town; but the beauty of the scene has been marred, and the Square given a bare appearance, by the cutting down of the tall and stately chestnut trees that formerly graced it. On a path between the courts and green stands an ornate dial, bearing quotations from the poets and inscribed with the name of John McMurray, Stranraer, and the date 13 October 1807. Beyond them to the west are a large circular flower bed and the old and new Mercat Crosses. The new cross, an elegant octagonal column of granite fully 20 feet in height, was erected in 1816. The old cross, which 200 years ago stood at the other end of the present Square, had been taken down for safety during building operations and was lost. When found it was set up to the west of the new cross, but it was later removed to the east of it, where it now stands. It has been described as 'a fine specimen of the pillar crosses with which many of our Scottish burghs were adorned. A columnar monolith, about 10 feet long and 18 inches diameter, rests perpendicularly on a square base and is surmounted by a square stone on which dials are carefully sculptured. For finial it has a pomegranate carved in stone'.

The first building to catch the eye of visitors arriving by rail is Wigtown Prison, built in 1848 and only recently closed; outwardly it has the appearance of a miniature castle with well-kept grounds.

Local Customs

Until 1867 fresh salmon could be caught in Wigtown for 3d. or 4d. a pound. From time immemorial the inhabitants had fished in the bay and in the rivers Bladnoch and Cree. There was no railway then to convey the fish to a wider market and the supply of flounders and salmon exceeded the local demand; the period of plenty, however, was not to last. In 1867 the council, inspired perhaps by reference in their charter to the rights of fishing, or by the success of their other ventures about this time, and hoping no doubt to increase the revenue of the burgh, raised an action of declarator and interdict against the fishermen in the Court of Session. The action drew the attention of the Earl of Galloway, who thereupon claimed that the fishings belonged neither to the inhabitants nor to the council, but to himself. His claim was upheld by the court and the fishings were thereafter let at such a rent as made cheap salmon a thing of the past.

Up to the middle of the last century the loyal inhabitants were wont to assemble in the Square once a year to drink from the town's large punch-bowl to the health of the reigning sovereign. This bowl made its last public appearance on 20 May 1931, when the new water supply was turned on. Until recent years New Year's Eve brought a large number of the inhabitants from their homes to gather in the wide open space around the Mercat Cross.

The one really big day in the parish is the first Wednesday in August when the Wigtown Agricultural Society holds its annual show, and old Wigtonians and their friends from all parts of the county and beyond make their way to the town and crowd the show field to the number of over 9,000. A new popular annual event is the Riding of the Marches.

Forty years ago it was customary in the parish to invite the minister to what was called the 'coffining'. Friends were gathered in until the kitchen or parlour was packed, a dram was handed round and when the undertaker had placed the corpse in the coffin a portion of scripture was read and a prayer offered. This custom, evidently a remnant of the 'wake', has died out, but it was deeply rooted, especially among the old folks, and no little tact was needed to change it. The minister, recognising the appropriateness of a religious service at such a time, expressed his willingness to meet the relatives and friends, if asked to do so, on an evening prior to the day of burial, and this is now the custom.

Until recent years very few baptisms took place in face of the congregation. In some cases there was a good reason for this, but even when the child was born in wedlock it was impossible to insist on baptism in church. Sometimes poverty meant the lack of the clothes supposed to be needed on such an occasion; some of the mothers had to milk cows to within a few days of the birth and had to return to their work within a few days after it; neighbours might be kind, but 'You could not be asking too much from them'; or there was no conveyance, so that the child had to be carried. All this has happily changed and baptisms in private houses are now rare. The improved conditions of the workers have also led to a large increase in the number of church weddings, followed by a reception for the numerous guests in the new tea rooms or in the hotel, and perhaps a dance afterwards in the Town Hall.

Population

In 1801 the population of the parish was 1,475. By 1851 it had increased to 2,824. The causes of this remarkable growth are not far to seek. The new harbour was opened in 1817, and during the next 50 years Wigtown flourished as never before. The Irish potato famine of 1845 and 1846 drove many impecunious peasants into this, the nearest county, and a large number found their way to the county town. These two events account for the doubling of the population within a short period. The opening of the Wigtownshire Railway in April 1875 was hailed with delight (the school children were granted a holiday for the occasion); but the jubilation proved to be premature. The harbour, which could not compete successfully with this new rival, struggled on for a number of years, was finally closed, and now lies derelict. Wigtown ceased to be the busy market town it had been. It is not surprising therefore that there has been a decline in the population. At the 1961 Census the total was 1,201 (573 males and 628 females), a drop of 175 from the 1951 figure. There were 83 fewer males and 92 fewer females. The rateable value of the burgh was £15,256 in 1962, when the total figure for Wigtownshire was £396,181.

In the last *Statistical Account* it is stated that the inhabitants, with the exception of the Irish settlers, were nearly all natives either of the burgh or of the county. On a rough estimate not more than half the present inhabitants were born in the parish; of the remainder, 30 per cent were born in the county and 20 per cent outwith the county. The descendants of the 'Irish Settlers' cannot today be distinguished from the other inhabitants by speech, condition, or behaviour.

A certain leakage of population there always will be, for the most intellectual, ambitious and enterprising natives are compelled to leave a small country town to find scope for their energies and abilities in the large cities. Very few leave the parish for foreign lands or our colonies; but for at least 50 years, and in spite of the Bladnoch Creamery which opened in 1899 and gives employment to 44 males and 25 females residing within the burgh, many of the young people of the parish have had to seek work in other parts of Scotland or across the border. Their places have been taken by old folks who have made a competence and find Wigtown a quiet and healthy spot in which to spend their declining years.

Public Services

About 1910 the burgh's water supply was inadequate and bad: all but the fortunate few who had private wells had to depend on rain water collected in barrels or on water drawn from street pumps, some of which was unfit for domestic purposes or even contaminated from the sewers. Nevertheless, there were those who held that the town could not afford the enormous cost of bringing water from Cairnsmore, a distance of eleven miles. After a plebiscite, one well was sunk and it proved very useful. However, the Cairnsmore scheme was carried out in 1930 and is still functioning, but there are plans afoot for adding to the supply.

With the new water supply came also a new sewerage system, so that dry closets, germ laden refuse pits at back doors, and frequently polluted streets became things of the past. The householders collect refuse in buckets which are regularly emptied by scavengers who convey the refuse to a dump outwith the town.

When many larger towns were in darkness or lighted by oil lamps, the streets of Wigtown and many of its shops, offices and houses were lit by gas. The gas works, erected in 1816 by a private company, was taken over by the town council about 1920 when the company was about to close it. The debit balance grew rapidly and the gas works soon became a heavy burden on the ratepayers. Under the Gas Act, 1948, it was taken over by the Minister of Fuel and Power and was subsequently closed.

In 1931 the Wigtownshire Electricity Company began to function, and many of the houses in the parish were soon wired for this new lighting. The parish church, which generated its own electricity for 16 years (the first in the county to be so lighted), is now on the grid, as are also the county buildings and all the shops and offices in the town. The streets of the town and of Bladnoch village are lighted in the same way.

The main roads in the parish are wide and well kept. They bear much of the heavy traffic and most of the passengers once carried by the railway. The station was closed to passenger traffic some years ago, since when only goods have been handled. In the town itself the streets are remarkably wide, a relic of the old days when they had to be able to hold the horses, sheep and cattle after they had been gathered in and made safe by the closing of the ports at the east and west ends of the Square. In 1845 the magistrates and council, with commendable foresight and enterprise, purchased and pulled down a large property in the centre of the town and opened to the north what is now known as the new road.

Education

At the time of the *New Statistical Account* responsibility for education was shared by the town council and the heritors. From a petition to the council by the schoolmaster of the grammar school, we learn that he received a salary of £45, besides collecting £22 10s. in fees and receiving New Year's gifts and Candlemas offerings worth £13 10s. A new schoolmaster appointed in 1852 had his salary adjusted according to the number of pupils on the roll. His appointment was confirmed by the first school board, elected in May 1873. The six schools in the parish at this period were all fee-paying, the fees varying from 5s. 3d. a quarter to 9d. a quarter in the charity school.

The year 1895 saw the establishment of a secondary department in the school, which, however, was not recognised as such until after the old schoolmaster had resigned and his successor had been appointed in 1898. In 1919 the administration of education became a county responsibility. Until 1935 pupils who passed the control examination might choose to remain for three years at Wigtown, where they were given an academic course including a foreign language. In 1936 the education committee decided that all qualifying pupils should proceed direct to Newton Stewart, and that Wigtown should be a primary school with an advanced division. The school now has infant, primary and junior secondary departments; this last offers a domestic science course for girls and a technical course for boys. The total number of pupils in 1960 was 262. Extensive repairs were completed in 1960. About 100 meals, prepared at Newton Stewart and conveyed by motor van, are served daily at the school. About 130 pupils take advantage of the free milk scheme. In the winter months continuation classes in cookery, dressmaking, country dancing and choral music are all well attended. There is a Roman Catholic School with 15 scholars on the roll.

Health Services

Wigtown and District Nursing Association, formed in 1908, maintained a nurse whose services were free to such householders in Wigtown and Kirkinner as became members by paying a nominal fee annually. A door-to-door collection was made each year in the two parishes, donations were received and money was raised by entertainment, so that the association never lacked funds. In addition to paying the nurse's salary they provided a motor car, house and telephone, and made allowances for necessary outlays. When the association ceased to function there was a credit balance of £700. Its work has been taken over by the county council under the National Health Act.

The district hospital board has provided accommodation at Newton Stewart, where surgeons, oculists and other specialists may be consulted by people from the surrounding parishes. Surgical and other cases are treated at Dumfries, 54 miles away, or at the Garrick Hospital at Stranraer, 26 miles distant. An ambulance is available.

Ecclesiastical Affairs

Fifty years ago there were in Wigtown four churches and two sects of the Plymouth Brethren; the Brethren ceased to meet about 1911, while of the churches only the parish church and the Roman Catholic church remain. The Free Church and the United Presbyterian Church, by a union in 1903, became a branch of the United Free Church, worshipping in the old U.P. church, and using the old Free church as a church hall. Within a few months trouble arose and the United Presbyterians left the church which their fathers and they had built, and became members of the parish church. In 1929 the United Free Church congregation, which continued to worship in the old U.P. church, decided to become a branch of the Church of Scotland, and the building became known as the West church. In 1948 the minister of the parish church resigned to facilitate union, and the united congregations now worship in the parish church. Four ministers served this church from 1799 to 1948—a period of almost 150 years—although one of these remained only 3½ years. The membership is about 550 and the Roman Catholics number about 100.

Voluntary Services

Youth organisations include the Sunday School, a Bible class, junior choir, a company of the Boys' Brigade, Lifeboys and Girl Guides (with members in Wigtown and Bladnoch). A Youth Fellowship has disappeared in recent times, but there is a very strong badminton club. The women's organisations comprise the Woman's Guild, with a large membership, and branches of the Women's Rural Institute in Wigtown and Bladnoch. At one time there was a choral society, but it is no longer in existence and a pipe band had a short life; the silver band formed over 70 years ago has not been making public appearances of late, but a fresh effort is being made to increase the number of bandsmen and to arouse more interest. The Wigtown Players cater for those who are interested in drama. By their efforts they raise at least £100 annually for a winter entertainment and a summer trip for the old folks of the burgh, and freely give their services for charitable objects in neighbouring parishes. There has been a public library in Wigtown since 1794.

Bowling, golf, tennis, badminton and football all have their followers and organised clubs, while a quoiting club and recreation club at Bladnoch give further scope to the energetic. Wigtown Bowling Club, formed in 1830, is one of the oldest in Scotland. The local branch of the

Oddfellows, formed in May 1873, has at present 102 members. The lodge of Freemasons was opened in 1903. There was a lodge over a hundred years ago, when the foundation stone of the new Mercat Cross was laid. The 92 employees of the S.C.W.S. creamery at Bladnoch are all members of one or other of six different trade unions. The 16 local men and women employed by the Scottish Motor Traction Co. are members of the Transport and General Workers' Union, but there is no branch of the Farm Servants' Union in this parish, where there are 99 farm workers. A branch of the British Legion was formed here in 1945 with a membership of 150. The hostel built for the Women's Land Army was purchased and altered internally to provide a house for a caretaker and ample room for recreation and other activities.

Local Endowments
Some of the gifts and bequests made to Wigtown in the past 80 years have been substantial. Sums amounting to £1,200 were given by William Ross in 1871 and 1873 for educational purposes and the relief of the poor, who likewise benefit from the McWilliam bequest of about £6,000 (1882). A capital sum of over £7,000 came into the hands of Wigtown Town Council in 1943, to be expended, under the terms of John Beddie's will (1914), on the public utility. The aged and needy of Wigtown (especially those deemed to be of the old Celtic stock) shared with those of Kirkinner, Sorbie and Whithorn an interest in the McKerlie bequest, which, transferred to trustees in 1947, yields an annual income of £135. The minister and kirk session, as trustees, administer 14 smaller funds for the behoof of the parochial poor, for missionary and other work in the church, and for the upkeep of certain burial grounds.

Housing
There are 462 occupied houses, 400 in the burgh and 62 in the landward part of the parish, and 127 are owned by their occupiers. Many of the latter are small houses belonging to manual labourers, but the farm houses are substantial and commodious buildings: at least 35 of them are houses of six apartments or more, with well-kept gardens.

The town council, who until lately were the proprietors of only seven habitable dwellings, have now provided additional houses for 124 families. The new council houses have two, three or four bedrooms, with living room and kitchenette. Thirteen blocks are of one-storey and semi-detached type, 39 blocks are two-storey semi-detached type. Five blocks each accommodate four families. All are constructed of bricks and rough cast, except ten blocks which are prefabricated (Cruden) houses. The tenants take a commendable pride in them, not only furnishing them tastefully within, but making their gardens a delight to the eye. The cottages for farm workers in the landward part of the parish may still leave much to be desired, for few farm proprietors have so far made any extensive alterations to their cot-houses, and the town may no longer be the 'quaint auld farant town' beloved by Crockett, although still 'combining the bracing air of the hills with the balmy air of the sea'. Wigtown, with its modern sanitation, its wide and well lit streets, and a good water supply, is a delightful place to live in and any house offered for sale finds a ready buyer.

Agriculture and Industry[1]

Many changes have taken place in the crops raised and in methods of cultivation since the *New Statistical Account* was prepared, and mechanical implements then unknown are in common use on all but the smallest farms. Oats are the main crop, 981 acres being sown, with turnips and swedes using 220 acres, and other crops bringing the total to 1,470½ acres. There are 1,173 acres of clover and rotation grass, 2,391½ acres of permanent grass, and 2,274 acres of rough grazing. The parish contains 1,612 dairy cattle, 735 beef cattle, 3,858 sheep, 27 pigs and 4,598 poultry, and there are still 144 horses. Farming cannot be regarded as an unprofitable occupation, in spite of the large increase in the wages of farm workers, but it is not to be wondered at if there is a grave shortage of skilled labour on the land. Better houses and better wages for fewer hours of labour are bound to attract farm workers to other occupations. At present there are 99 at work on farms in the parish, 84 men and 15 women.

The distillery has resumed production after a brief closure and barley is being grown again. The potato preserving factory has been demolished, and this may account for the comparatively small acreage devoted to this crop.

The Scottish Wholesale Co-operative Society's creamery at Bladnoch is on the borders of the parish, and of its 92 employees 83 reside in the burgh—62 men and 21 women—including motor drivers, engineers and joiners. The milk handled in 1903 (the earliest figures available) amounted to 633,437 gallons, compared with over a million gallons today.

There are five licensed premises, including one hotel, in the parish, or four fewer than in 1900; these employ six men and eighteen women. Apart from these, 21 shops (grocers, butchers, bakers, ironmongers, confectioners, chemist, newsagent and hairdressers) cater for the needs of the community and employ 42 men and 35 women.

Fourteen women are employed in the wool mill at Newton Stewart, 10 men and one woman in the pre-cast factory at Creetown, and 30 men in forestry. Fourteen men work on the roads, 14 men and one woman on the railway, 6 men and 7 women in the post office, and 13 men and 3 women on omnibuses. The local picture house gives employment to 4 men and 3 women. There are 35 general labourers, 11 joiners, 11 domestic servants, 10 mechanical engineers, 10 clerks, 8 teachers, 8 motor drivers, 4 bricklayers, 4 masons, 4 painters, 4 hawkers, 4 veterinary surgeons, 3 electrical engineers, 3 gardeners, 3 caretakers, 3 insurance agents, 2 ministers of religion, 2 factors, 2 linesmen, 2 gas workers, 2 coal distributors, 2 scavengers, 2 distillery workers, 2 policemen, 2 cobblers, 2 wood merchants, 1 blacksmith, 1 chemist, 1 chiropodist, 1 chimney sweep, 1 grave-digger, 1 motor hirer, 1 haulage contractor, 1 plumber.

[1]The statistics in this section were recorded in 1949.

1 saddler, 1 scrap merchant, 1 tinsmith, 1 R.A.C. patrolman, 1 dealer,
1 gamekeeper, 1 burgh surveyor, 1 dressmaker, 1 doctor, 1 excise officer,
1 sheriff clerk, 1 bank manager, 1 nurse and 1 registrar.

The Way of Life

The palmy days of the parish seem to have been during the 25 years on
either side of the middle of last century.   One cannot but mark with
admiration the courage and foresight shown at that period by the local
representatives in launching out on large and costly enterprises for the
welfare of the town and parish, and the ready and generous support that
was given to their plans at a time when money was none too plentiful. If
today the town has a beauty and a charm all its own it is because of the
civic pride that inspired and united all the inhabitants. And if today the
parish stands among the foremost in all that pertains to agriculture the
credit is largely due to the Wigtown Agricultural Society, which from the
day of its inception encouraged the more enlightened proprietors and
tenants with praise and prizes and held them up as an example which they
hoped would 'convert the great body of the farmers to a system of
husbandry so intimately connected with their own interest and the general
prosperity of the country'.

Civic pride is not so evident today. One example of its decline is to be
found in the lamentable condition into which the old churchyard with its
historical monuments has been allowed to fall. When a representative of
the Royal Commission on Ancient Monuments visited the parish in 1911
he complimented the parish council on the way in which this ancient
burying ground was kept, but no one could truthfully praise its modern
custodians. Recently, it is true, an effort has been made to tidy up the
churchyard, but its present state still leaves much to be desired.

The people, in general, are industrious, thrifty, generous, bitter
opponents but loyal friends, intelligent and well-informed. The writer
was much gratified to learn from one of the managers of the I.C.I. factory
at Carsegowan during the war that the most satisfactory workers there
were local men; and no more contented employees could be found anywhere than those at the creamery at Bladnoch. The large amount of shares
held by members of the Co-operative Society, the money collected weekly
for savings certificates and the fact that so many of the working people
own their houses, all testify to the thrift of the inhabitants. The public
library, established in 1794, had in its latter years 60 subscribers and made
over 2,360 issues annually. It was merged recently with the County
Library and this arrangement is working satisfactorily.

Drunkenness is not so prevalent as it was forty years ago, but the
drinking of alcoholic beverages is more widespread among both men and
women and it is not confined to those of mature years. There is some
gambling but the sums involved are small. The majority of the inhabitants
are better housed, better fed, and better clothed than ever before, and the
provision of school meals has already made a marked improvement in
the health and appearance of the children. Galloway hospitality has long
been proverbial. There was a time when the farm worker lived a lifetime

on one farm, took as much interest in the land and the stock as his employer, reared a large and healthy family on a small wage, owed not any man and never came to want. Today many of them seem to spend little time in one place but keep wandering from one farm to another and from one parish to another.

With bicycles, motor cars, Sunday buses and television sets, few are lonely and the social instinct no longer reinforces the call to public worship. Nevertheless the vast majority in this parish still have a real devotion to the church, and their religion finds expression in deeds of neighbourly kindness, in voluntary work among the young, and in liberal support of a great number of charitable objects, ecclesiastical, parochial and national. One particular scriptural injunction has registered itself in their minds: they are not forgetful to entertain strangers (Hebrews XIII, 2). The shorter the period of a man's existence in the parish the surer his chance of being nominated as an elder of the kirk or of being elected to the town council; and the writer cannot conclude his account of the place he has learned to love without expressing the hope that one day they will be rewarded by the appearing of the angels.

Written 1949
Additions made 1963

CHAPTER 6

THE PARISH OF PENNINGHAME

by the REV. JOHN ROSS

Penninghame parish extends from the Ayrshire border for some fourteen miles in a roughly southern direction. It is bounded on the east by the River Cree, which separates it from the Stewartry of Kirkcudbright, and to the west the boundary is the Water of Bladnoch, which also forms the larger part of the southern boundary. The neighbouring parishes are Kirkcowan on the west and Wigtown on the south; a small part of Kirkinner also touches Penninghame. The width of the parish varies with the windings of the Cree and Bladnoch but the average is about four miles with a bulge to the south.

The main centre of population, in fact the only populated part, is the market town of Newton Stewart, formerly a burgh of barony, with a charter granted in 1677. The town lies north and south of the bridge which carries the main Dumfries-Stranraer road across the Cree and along another man road from Ayr to Whithorn. The main railway line from Stranraer to London also passes through it and it was a terminus of the Whithorn branch line. Its position has made the town of some importance as a centre for business and shopping for the Machars district of Wigtownshire and part of the western district of Kirkcudbright.

Population

The maximum recorded population of the parish was in 1851. By 1901 that figure, 4,155, had dropped to 3,356, by 1911, to 3,059 and by 1921 to 2,839. There was a slight increase recorded in 1931. At the 1950 election 1,602 were entitled to vote in the burgh of Newton Stewart and 628 in the landward area, a total of 2,230 persons of twenty-one years of age and over. In 1951 the population was 2,803, so that there had been no marked decrease in the preceding thirty years but the falling off continued during the next decade. The figure for the burgh, as distinct from the parish, in 1961 showed a decrease of 81. The total was 1,980 (males 894 and females 1,086).

Public Services

Newton Stewart has a good water supply and an efficient sewage system, which discharges into the tidal waters of the Cree. Most of the houses are lit by electricity and some are also served by gas. The main streets are lighted to Ministry of Transport standards. In the landward area, most of the farmhouses and buildings have electric power and light. Most cottages, too, have electricity though a few in outlying areas are still

2c

dependent on paraffin lamps. The lack of a piped water supply is the greatest disadvantage suffered by the cottage housewife. The majority have still to depend on outside pumps and in one part of the parish water had to be taken from the nearest creamery. There are some rocky farm roads in the parish, but other roads are in good condition and the streets in the town are well paved. The town affords adequate parking space for cars, and there is a small shelter for bus passengers.

Five doctors practise in the parish, and two of these are resident in the town. Because of centralisation the public health department, which for many years was located in Douglas House, has removed to Stranraer and only a small number of officials remain. Douglas House became a Civil Defence centre in 1962. The duties of the former District Nursing Association have been taken over by the public health department. The new area hospital board has recently opened a clinic in Newton Stewart to which specialists come to see patients, thus saving the patients a journey to Dumfries or Lochmaben. Part of the infectious diseases hospital near the town was recently given over for the reception of general cases and this has proved a boon to older people. A mansion house was recently bought by the county council and converted into an Eventide Home. In cases of serious illness, patients are taken by ambulance to Dumfries, fifty miles away, or on occasion to Castle Douglas. The nearest maternity hospital is at Stranraer and some patients also go to Dumfries. There is a great need for a cottage hospital or a maternity hospital.

Education

Of the two landward schools Loudon has been closed and the future of Challoch is uncertain. In the burgh Penninghame school was some time ago reduced to a primary establishment, to which Corsbie Infant School is now linked, and there is a small Roman Catholic school. Douglas Ewart High School, the only comprehensive school in the county, was recently renovated, enlarged and modernised and serves the Machars and a part of the western district of Kirkcudbright. Well staffed and equipped, it takes all the senior secondary pupils from the area and all the junior secondary pupils from the immediate surroundings. Under successive rectors it has gained a high reputation in the educational world. It is also the centre of continuation classes held during the winter months. Dramatic plays, country dancing festivals and the like are held in the spacious hall of the school. Work on a new building to replace Penninghame school is now under way.

Ecclesiastical Affairs

There are six places of worship in the parish, five of which are in Newton Stewart. The Scottish Episcopal church, the Roman Catholic church, the Christian Brethren and Penninghame Old Parish and St. John's (both Church of Scotland) are in the burgh and there is an Episcopal church at Challoch, two miles to the north. Since the Union of 1929 the parish has been divided between Penninghame and St. John's for pastoral purposes.

Previously the northern part of the parish had formed part of the *quoad sacra* parish of Bargrennan established in 1862 and the people of that area remain in the pastoral charge of the minister of Bargrennan and attend that church, which is, however, in the civil parish of Minnigaff. Minnigaff parish church itself lies across the Cree from Newton Stewart, and some who reside there attend it, while a number of residents of Minnigaff attend the Newton Stewart churches. Cordial relations exist between the people and the ministers of all the denominations, and on occasions like Remembrance Day the rector of the Episcopal church shares in the services with the Church of Scotland ministers.

Youth organisations established in the district include Boy Scouts, Girl Guides, Boys' Brigade, Army Cadet Force, Air Training Corps, a Youth Fellowship Club and Church of Scotland Youth Fellowship. The Boy Scout Headquarters are in the village of Minnigaff across the Cree, but the majority of the boys come from the town. Village and town, although in different parishes and counties, are in fact very closely linked, and most of the voluntary organisations draw their members from both.

Women's organisations include the Church of Scotland's Woman's Guild, Scottish Women's Rural Institute and the Eastern Star. A retired men's club, sponsored by the town council, but run by the members themselves, has recently been opened, and there are lodges of Freemasons and Oddfellows and a branch of British Legion in the town.

Penninghame Fellowship Association, connected with Penninghame Old Parish Church, is an old-established literary society. The two bowling clubs and Penninghame Curling Club were all founded early last century and of more recent date are the tennis, golf, badminton and carpet bowling clubs. The golf course in Minnigaff was for a time an eighteen holes course but has recently been reduced to a shortened circuit of nine holes in wonderfully wooded country (formerly part of the Kirroughtree estate). The local angling association has fishing rights on parts of the Cree and other waters in the district. There are half a dozen lochs, the largest of which are Ochiltree and Black Water, situated in the northern end of the parish, and there is some excellent fishing there. Newton Stewart Football Club employs a professional team and plays in the South of Scotland League and other competitions with varied success. There is an active supporters' club.

The McMillan Hall, in Newton Stewart, is the largest public hall in Galloway and as such has become the recognised centre for musical festivals, concerts, dramatic entertainments, flower shows and other events of a similar nature. There are musical and dramatic clubs in the town, as well as other associations, which draw their members from the surrounding district. Penninghame has been fortunate in her children who have prospered in life; the McMillan Hall, Douglas Ewart High School, and bequests to town improvements are some of the abiding evidence of their remembrance of their native town and parish.

An event which roused much interest and speculation, not only locally but much wider afield, was the establishment in 1954 of an open prison at Penninghame House, four miles north of Newton Stewart. There was objection from local people when plans were made known in 1952, but despite the opposition the Home Department went on to establish the first open prison in Scotland. In the years following its opening the fears of the townspeople were so completely removed that many of the inmates were made welcome into the communal life of the district. They attended church regularly and took part in sporting activities and in amateur dramatic productions.

The lack of a proper water supply is possibly one of the reasons why there has been little local authority building in the landward area. Some farm cottages were improved between the wars, and since the last war, and a small number of fine cottages have been built and others improved. A small scheme of agricultural workers' houses was completed near Carty, and in the town of Newton Stewart the council has undertaken various building projects. Apart from farm workers it is the rare exception for a newly-married couple to have a house to themselves; the great majority have to live with relatives or in furnished rooms. The needs of old couples and single persons are also clamant and indeed this lack affects all classes directly or indirectly.

Agriculture

Penninghame is an agricultural parish and most of the residents depend on that basic industry. Formerly the rearing of cattle and sheep was the chief occupation of the farmer and his workers; it still is in the higher moorland parts, but, in the lower end where the land is better, many of the farms have gone over to dairying. There are several large herds and most of the milking is done by machinery. The landed proprietors of former days have almost disappeared and most farmers now own their farms. The majority were formerly tenant farmers, farmers' sons or farm workers, but lately farms have been bought and are being worked by men new to the industry and the district. Machinery plays a large part in the work, the tractor almost everywhere taking the place of the horse, the motor car of the gig, and the milking machine of men and women. Whether the complaint of the old ploughman that 'tractors are ruining the Moss o' Cree' may prove to have been well founded one cannot say, but it is evident that, if only because of the shortage of labour on the land, the change could hardly have been avoided. Under the new conditions, farm work can be done more quickly, greater advantage can be taken of better weather, and farmers and workers alike can enjoy more leisure. As a class the farm workers still frequently change their place, but on the other hand many farms have workers with twenty, thirty or forty years' service, while in one at least there is a worker who is in the same employment as were his father and grandfather before him. This speaks well for both master and man, and the close relationship which has developed between the two in good times and in bad is of great benefit to both. At present times are good for the agricultural worker, and he has an advantage over the townsman in that there is a house with the job even though the dwelling may lack modern conveniences.

There are some estate workers, gardeners, gamekeepers and labourers but their number is decreasing. Forestry and saw-milling give employment to others and there is prospect of more work in the large afforestation schemes that are at present on foot. At the now disused port of Carty a small tile works has recently been rebuilt and it may expand in future.

In Newton Stewart the number employed in shops, banks and offices is more than the average for a place of the size, possibly because of the town's remoteness from any city and the fact that it is a centre for a fairly wide area. The head post office of the district, the offices of the Ministries of Labour and National Insurance, five banks, several law and business firms, give employment not only to the people in the town but to others living outwith its bounds. A number are employed in the manufacture of woollen goods at the Cree Mills, but work on the railway has decreased with the closure of the branch lines. A monumental sculptor and printing works, contractors, builders and allied tradesmen employ men in the town and district, while a sawmill and a pre-cast factory, though outside the parish, obtain their staff in Newton Stewart. There is a co-operative store but the other shops are owned by independent traders. On the weekly market day, Friday, and on Saturdays, the town is very busy and in summer months is the centre for tourists, for good hotel accommodation and restaurant facilities are available. Much more might be done in this regard, for Penninghame is not as well known as it deserves to be for its scenery, climate and historical associations.

The Way of Life

While most of the people are natives to the parish, and many of the families are related to each other and to others in the surrounding districts, there have been infiltrations from all parts of Scotland, from England, Ireland and Wales and from Italy, Germany, Poland and other European countries. These incomers have been assimilated into the way of life. Of some eight hundred communicants in Penninghame Old Parish Church, two hundred had surnames beginning with 'M', the 'Macs' running from McAvoy to McWhirter. Fewer Scots words are in use than in the north east, for example, and the voices are soft and pleasing. The local newspaper, *The Galloway Gazette*, plays an important part in maintaining the close link that exists between the people at home and their relatives now living in other parts or abroad. The healthy community spirit is fostered by the town council, and by such events as the Galloway Pageant, held in Newton Stewart each summer, when a Queen of Galloway is crowned and events and characters from local history are depicted. S. R. Crockett described the town as 'the natural gateway to the enchanted land of Galloway', and H. V. Morton said, 'Someone has set an inhuman standard of cleanliness and integrity to which the town faithfully adheres'. While the majority take their church connection lightly, in all churches there are faithful men and women who can be relied upon, and to whom the Church owes a great deal. More interest is, however, shown in the television programmes and the 'pictures', and dances are popular, as are whist drives and concerts and evening classes. Whether with all their advantages the people of today are as happy and as contented as they were in former days is a moot question. Perhaps every generation as it grows old asks the same question, or it may be that, having lived in the aftermath of two world wars, we have lost our peace of mind, that peace of mind which our forefathers possessed in harder but less unsettled times.

Written 1950
Additions made 1962

CHAPTER 7

THE PARISH OF KIRKCOWAN

by the REV. HUGH TOLLAND and A. E. TRUCKELL

'Out of the world and into Kirkcowan'—and indeed there is some justification for the old saying, for Kirkcowan, the most inland Wigtownshire parish, much of it marginal moorland, has preserved to a greater degree than other places the Wigtownshire dialect and characteristics; even Kirkcowan village itself, seen from the air, preserves—except for a recent housing development—the typical 'croft-and-toft' pattern of a mediæval strip village.

The parish is bounded to the east by Penninghame, to the south-east by Kirkinner, to the south by Mochrum, to the west by Old Luce and New Luce and to the north by Ayrshire. It is one of the few Wigtownshire parishes that does not touch the sea at any point.

Climate

From its inland and mainly upland situation, the climate of the parish is scarcely as mild as the normal for the shire, but even so it is far from severe. It has the heaviest rainfall in the county.

Population

The parish of Kirkcowan has changed considerably from that described in the *New Statistical Account*. A large part of the population has gone, the causes of depopulation being similar to those found in many other parts of the country, namely rural poverty, the attraction of the towns, the lack of opportunity and of amenities. One hundred years ago there were many small farms scattered throughout the parish, but most of these have now merged into larger units. With the advent of mechanised traction the number of people employed in agriculture is substantially less than it was even 25 years ago. The present population of 869 is only slightly more than it was in 1801, when it was said to be increasing. It reached its peak in 1851 at 1,541.

Agriculture

Along with a marked decline in population, there has been an immense improvement in agriculture. A number of sheep farms still exist in the north end of the parish, but, whereas in the *New Statistical Account* mention was made of the splendid herds of Galloway Cattle to be found in the parish, now most of these stock farms have been turned into dairy farms and the Ayrshire has ousted the Galloway. To support these dairy herds a large acreage previously used as pasture land is now cultivated and is producing good crops of oats and turnips. Crops are generally good, for much drainage work has been undertaken, and large quantities of lime and artificial manures are used annually on the land. Thus during and since the war there has been a great measure of prosperity.

Industry

The old woollen mills, established in 1882 and giving employment to many workers occupying tied houses, were forced to close down in 1950 owing to the high cost of wool. The blankets that were made were sold locally as well as being exported. Fortunately, however, the county council opened a stone quarry at Boreland Fell in the south end of the parish about two miles from the village. The quarry, now the main source of supply of road materials to the county, employs about 50 men. Most of the adults and adolescents commute to Newton Stewart for employment, some even travelling as far as Minnigaff to work in the sawmills and under the Forestry Commission. There are in the village a blacksmith's shop, garages, joiners, builders, a sub post-office and grocers' shops.

Housing

The village of Kirkcowan changed little over the years and for more than 50 years not one single new house was erected by private individuals. However, with the coming of the gravitation water supply from Penwhirn an almost new village grew up alongside the old, to the north-east on the Newton Stewart road. The houses built by the county council are of one and a half storeys and present a pleasing appearance. A sewage and drainage scheme was introduced to the old village and many improvements have been carried out in recent years. The introduction of electricity in 1936 was a great boon. Many of the houses formerly occupied by mill workers have been torn down and more houses are to be built by the county council.

Farm houses are generally in a good state of repair, many are now supplied with electricity from the grid and about 80 per cent have telephones. Almost all farmers possess motor cars. Unfortunately farm cottages are not in such good condition as farm houses, and in some instances farm labourers have had to give up their employment on account of bad housing. Yet, apart from poor housing, it is becoming increasingly difficult to get farm labourers and their families to reside in remote areas away from public transport and the communal life of a village or town. Moreover, modern methods of farming do not always necessitate a farm labourer living close by his employment.

Social Life

The village itself lies in the heart of a district of dairy and sheep farming. It is remote from any large centre, but its proximity to the main Stranraer-Dumfries road and railway makes it a lively community. The parish church is situated at the north end of the village; the former United Presbyterian church is now linked to the parish church. A doctor and a nurse reside in the village. The school, reduced to primary status, has a roll of 75. The children come from a wide area, six miles to the north-west and four miles to the south-west. School meals are provided daily. Secondary pupils travel to Newton Stewart.

The parish has its Community Association, and around it are grouped numerous organisations. The village hall is the meeting place of many societies and organisations, and there are branches of the W.R.I. in the parish. For over half a century Kirkcowan has had a musical society, whose annual choral concert is patronised by music lovers throughout the county. During those 50 years the society had as its conductor John Crozier, who was also precentor and organist in the parish church for 64 years. There are football, badminton and table tennis clubs and a good bowling green; a fine spirit of co-operation and comradeship exists in all these varied societies and recreations. Life in the village and parish is vigorous, for the people are energetic and enterprising.

Geology
The greater part of the parish is made up of Silurian Shales and Slates; but there is an outcrop of granite in the north central part and dykes of porphyrite and felsite in the south. Much of this is veiled by the universal cover of boulder-clay—though, even where invisible, rock is never far below the surface.

Pre-historic Remains
The record of human occupation in Kirkcowan seems to begin in 2,000 B.C.; for several polished flat stone axes of this period—as also several perforated stone axe-hammers of the Middle Bronze Age—have been found in the parish. Further confirmation of early human habitation is provided by the concentration of large circular cairns which date to the end of the Neolithic and the succeeding Early Bronze Age covering at the fullest stretch the period 1900-1400 B.C. Shennanton Cairn, for instance, in the angle formed by the junction of the roads to Newton Stewart from Glenluce and from Kirkcowan, now almost entirely removed, yielded a pottery vessel which the finder took home to his cottage, set up on the garden dyke and destroyed by stoning! The nearby cairn at the north end of a cultivated field on the north side of the Glenluce/Newton Stewart road, about half a mile west of Shennanton, has likewise been circular, with a diameter of about sixty feet; though much of the stone work has gone, the cist may still survive. At Barhoise, in a field by the roadside about a mile north of Kirkcowan village, a dilapidated circular cairn has had a diameter of about seventy feet. On the lowest slope of the ridge facing east, above half a mile south by east of the Fell of Loch Ronald farmhouse, is a cairn of 35 feet diameter which has at some time been excavated. In the centre the remains of a large cist or chamber can be seen.

On the top of a slight swelling on the moorland, some 200 yards west of the upper end of a wood N.N.E. of Airies farmhouse, is a well-preserved circular cairn 35 feet in diameter and seven feet high. 'Wood Cairn', 50 feet in diameter and still standing six feet high, stands on the summit of Eldrig Fell; it seems to be untouched. The White Cairn, Boreland, lying in the angle formed by the junction of two roads on Boreland Farm, opposite the cottage at Spittal, is now reduced to two feet in height, with a diameter of about 80 feet; on the south is a shallow trench which is visible, about twelve feet in width, while the situation is at the foot of a slope in cultivated land.   One definite short-cist is recorded on the summit of a gravel knoll at the end of a cultivated field which runs to a point about ¼ mile to the south of the ruins of the Mains of Loch Ronald. Four thickish slabs rest on the gravel and the cist measures interiorly two feet in length, 1 foot 6 inches in breadth and 1 foot 11 inches in depth, while the covering slab, still in place, is 3 feet long by 7½ inches thick.   The main axis of the cist lies E. and W. and a fragment of unburnt bone was found in the cist. If the two standing boulders a quarter mile south of Boreland farmhouse, in cultivated land, are indeed part of a circle, this would date to the same period as the large round cairns and the short cist inhumation burial.

A change of climate from a drier Continental type to the wetter conditions of today and the last two millennia may well be the reason for the paucity of the remains of the periods succeeding the Middle Bronze Age.   The only likely Iron Age hill fort is that at Doon Hill, Boreland, on the elevated southern end of Boreland Fell.   Though much destroyed by cultivation, two concentric ramparts are visible on the south side; this might suggest a bivallate fort of say 0-60 A.D.   As for crannogs, one of the two islands on Loch Heron is certainly a crannog of a type similar to those occupied in the first two centuries of our era elsewhere in the shire; and the other island is said to be a crannog also and if so would be of the same date; but it must be emphasised that this type of crannog had a very long life, up to the seventeenth century at least.   The hut circle group with adjacent small field clearance cairns just north of the summit of Fell of Loch Ronald, and the thirteen or fourteen field clearance cairns near the centre of the eastern slope of Eldrig Fell, may also be of the Iron Age, but they, too, could date to much later.

Nothing Roman is recorded from the parish, though it seems likely that the main road westwards from the postulated fort at Newton Stewart would follow approximately the line of the modern road. In the post-Roman period, it seems likely that the striking fortified island in Loch Maberry, with its massive drystone wall—6 feet 7 inches thick and 7 feet high—enclosing a roughly boat-shaped area with several small rectangular drystone buildings set against the inside of the enclosing wall and a larger building 28 feet by 11 feet, interiorly, with mortared walls and with causeways to an islet and the nearest neighbouring island, was first built—so far as the drystone construction goes—in the Viking period.   That would be in keeping with other boat-like forts with rectangular drystone buildings—that in the White Loch of Ravenstone, that in Loch Ochiltree, or that in Loch Urr, and like the impressive boat-shaped and apparently palisaded fort of Green Islands on Milton Loch.   The reputed chapel on the south bank of the Tarff Water, some three miles by road south of Kirkcowan, of drystone masonry, may well have been founded in the Dark Ages, as may the old church site and the graveyard at Killgallioch near the drystone dome-covered 'Wells of the Rees', while the cross slab at Low Eldrig may be of late Dark Age or twelfth century date.

Historical Notes

Boreland Moat—not the significant 'Boreland' which, like 'Ingleston', often indicates the nearness of a motte—situated close to a roadside just beyond the entrance to Boreland Farm, near the Bladnoch River, though somewhat altered by cultivation, is a reasonably typical twelfth century motte, a predecessor of the Keep of Craighlaw, built shortly after 1500 in the time of William Gordon, son of John Gordon of Lochinvar, who bought the lands of Craighlaw in 1498 from Andrew Muir. The Keep still survives as part of the modern mansion.

The old boundary crossing the hill ¼ mile N.E. of Loch Derry may be mediæval, while the standing stone in the path leading to Craighlaw House from the north-west known as the 'hanging stone', taken from a spot nearby where it lay, might be mediæval also, though it could of course date back to the early Bronze Age.

The Gordons of Craighlaw, typically energetic and colourful Borderers, provide most of the little history the parish has during the sixteenth and later centuries—though it is highly likely that a close investigation would reveal traces of the old farming system which prevailed down to the eighteenth century.

Written 1950
Additions made 1962

CHAPTER 8

THE PARISH OF KIRKINNER

by the late MRS. GRACE CHRISTISON

Kirkinner, on the eastern side of the Machars of Wigtownshire, is roughly square in shape. The eastern side lies along Wigtown Bay and the northern along the River Bladnoch, which separates the parish from Wigtown and Penninghame. In area, it is approximately 25 square miles and it includes 52 farms and several smallholdings. Kirkinner village is in the east and Whauphill, much smaller, is more central. The main roads divide the parish into three. A large wood cut down during the war years has been re-planted by the Forestry Commission to the south of the parish.

Transport

Since the *New Statistical Account* was written, the railway, the building of which was a great event, has come, had its day, and gone. Travellers all proceed by road. Farmers and tradespeople have their own cars and the pedal cycle is a popular form of transport for others.

War Damage

On the flat seaboard land of Baldoon, a large aerodrome was built during the second world war. A training school for navigators, it housed around two thousand men. Now the aerodrome has closed but the demolishers have left an unsightly ruin: the ground is spoilt for agricultural purposes and is fit only for grazing.

Population

From its peak of 1,914 in 1851, the population, as in other rural areas, has declined until now it appears fairly stabilised around one thousand: smaller families, the introduction of machinery to the farms and emigration are the reasons for the decrease. The peak year for emigrants was 1912, when a number of young people went to Canada; they still keep in touch with their old home and some have made return visits. A small percentage keep drifting to the towns, but with modern transport many who might otherwise have gone to the cities work in the towns and live in the country. In a few instances former prisoners of war and displaced persons remained.

Education

Educational reforms have also wrought large changes. Two of the three schools—Malzie and Longcastle—have recently been closed. Kirkinner school remains and is served by a head teacher and three assistants. In 1920 a serious fire destroyed Kirkinner school and a new building was

erected in 1924.   School meals and milk at morning break are supplied.
The daughter of a former schoolmaster of Kirkinner—Miss Mantle—
bequeathed a sum of money to Kirkinner school to provide a grant,
tenable for three years by a child going on for secondary education.   For
senior secondary education the children go to Douglas Ewart, Newton
Stewart, and for junior secondary education to Wigtown.   They travel in
hired transport to and from the schools.   The Queen's English is now
more generally spoken, the doric used only colloquially.   One of the sad
features is that some of the more delightful words—yestreen, clachan,
yaul, bien—are being lost.

Public Services

Where once the postman walked many miles in all weathers, now the
mail is delivered by motor vans.   The new method is not always an
improvement.   There are two collections daily, Sunday excepted.   The
parish is well supplied with telephones; almost every farm and business
has one and there are public boxes at Kirkinner and Whauphill.
Gravitation water has been brought to Kirkinner and Whauphill, and has
been supplied to many farms.   Scavenging schemes are in operation in
the villages and electricity is now in general use throughout the parish.
Vast changes are also apparent in health services.   For the general practitioner in his gig, assisted by the village mid-wife, there are now general
practitioners in motor cars with lady assistants, district nurse, school
doctor, school dentist and health visitor, all with their own method of
transport.   At Newton Stewart, where there is a clinic, patients may see
specialists of all kinds.   An ambulance is provided in case of need.
Maternity hospitals for the area are at Stranraer and Dumfries.

Social Life

There is only one church in the parish—the Church of Scotland at Kirkinner.   Compared with fifty years ago, attendance is poor though the
membership, at 325, is good.   The usual youth organisations are connected
with the church but these are difficult to maintain, as the young people
leave the district to prepare for the future.   For the last fifteen years there
has been a very flourishing Woman's Guild.   There are three branches
of the Women's Rural Institute, at Kirkinner, Whauphill and Longcastle;
Whauphill is of recent date.   Singing, country dancing and drama are all
practised, as well as the homelier crafts.   Kirkinner has a branch of the
Order of the Eastern Star and also of the British Legion.   In Kirkinner
village there are a bowling club and tennis club as well as a badminton
club, which meets in the Public Hall, a substantial stone and lime building
erected by public effort in 1894.   Whauphill has a hall built in 1938, a
comfortable wooden structure where whist drives are held and which
houses the Carpet Bowling Club.   The tarmac curling rink at Whauphill
belongs to the Machars but the parish has a strong club centred on Barnbarroch Loch.   Most of the games are, however, held indoors at Ayr or
Crossmyloof.

Housing

In the villages, most of the houses are of substantial stone and lime and the inhabitants take a pride in them, keeping them comfortable, neat and tidy; recently built houses are of brick. The villagers are served by travelling vans—the grocer, butcher, baker, fishmonger, milkman and ironmonger all call regularly. In Kirkinner there are three grocer's shops, two hotels, a post office and a joiner's shop, while Braehead has a joiner's and a meal-mill. The two smithies have been closed down, for the advent of the tractor meant the departure of the horse. There are, however, two smiths, one at Whauphill and the other at Malzie, who serve the surrounding area, and at Whauphill there is an agricultural engineer; Whauphill also has a grocer's shop, joiner's shop, hotel and post office, while Malzie has one joiner's shop.

Agriculture

Within the last fifty years all the farmlands have changed hands. The two main landlords were the Earl of Galloway and Colonel Vans Agnew of Barnbarroch, but increasing taxation forced them to sell. One by one the farmer tenants became owners and the heritors of the church are now all farmers, each with their portion of stipend to pay. In 1941 the only mansion house, Barnbarroch, was completely destroyed by fire and the wife of the owner, Colonel Vans Agnew, lost her life. A firm of wood merchants purchased the policies and the woods disappeared. In 1933, the farms of North and South Balfern were purchased by the Government and broken up into holdings, each averaging about forty acres; in all eighteen families are accommodated and all are engaged in dairying. Since the end of the last century dairying has become general, Ayrshires being the favoured breed. Cheese and butter making has disappeared and the milk is sent to Kirkinner or Sorbie creamery or to Portwilliam; the milk is collected and some local people are employed. Fixed prices for milk gave stability to the farmer and resulted in increased wages for the workers. It has become general to pay a cash wage and not to include benefits such as free coal and meal. Mechanisation and electricity led to improved conditions and much labour saving. The dairy cows are milked mechanically and the milk is tuberculin-tested. Grain is cut by binders and elevators and much of the drudgery of harvesting and haymaking has been removed. One or two farmers still feed for beef and some rear young stock, while a substantial number of sheep are raised. Farm cottages have been improved, water and electricity have been installed, and a number have had bathrooms added, but in most cases the cot house requires modernisation. Council houses have been built for agricultural workers, one block at Kirkinner and another at Whauphill, and the trend appears to be towards clachans: it is impractical, however, to have dairymen living away from the farm. The high rents of the council houses are a deterrent to many, being as much as six times as large as that charged for cot houses.

The Way of Life

Improved roads, modern transport, more leisure and more money have all had a marked effect on country life. Saturday half-holidays are general and the workers visit the nearest towns. The annual event of the year is Wigtown Cattle Show in August and in post-war years there was quite a craze for mounted sports. Motor cycle racing became more popular and it was disturbing to find that in many cases these noisy events were held on Sundays. Womenfolk have been released from their thraldom and have more leisure than was once thought possible. It is noticeable that many young people are not following their parents on the farm, but seek the comforts of the town-dweller.

Written 1952
Additions made 1962

CHAPTER 9

THE PARISH OF SORBIE

by the late REV. N. ELLIOT

Sorbie is an amalgam of three parishes—Sorbie, Kirkmadrine and Cruggleton, each of which had its separate church. It is bounded on the east by the Bay of Wigtown which includes the smaller bays of Garlieston and Rigg. On the south is Whithorn and on the south-west Glasserton while to the north and west is Kirkinner. Its total area is 16 square miles; in length it is about 4½ miles and in breadth 3½ miles, so that it is small and compact. Until recently it was well wooded but extensive felling has cleared Eggerness and other small hills. There are no high hills, only gradual rises, and the sea retreats outside Garlieston Bay, where it is possible to wade a considerable distance. South of Rigg Bay high cliffs face the bay. Eggerness peninsula is a tangle of rocks and wild vegetation. The rocks are generally of metamorphic geological formation and slate-like, projecting at strange angles into the sea. There is a wealth of wild flowers and fauna; brambles are very common. Swans are present all year in Garlieston Bay and water hens are plentiful in the streams. Foxes and weasels are numerous. Pheasants are seen during the day and owls are heard at night. The climate is mild and pleasant except for an occasional cold east wind. The more than average rainfall is compensated for by more hours of bright sunshine than is normal in Scotland. There are several springs in the parish.

Ecclesiastical Affairs

The Disruption affected Sorbie parish in as much as the Rev. A. Forrester, one of the two parish ministers responsible for the *New Statistical Account*, was one of those who demitted office and led a number away from the national church; the senior minister remained. In 1877 the old parish church of Sorbie was closed by the Earl of Galloway, who however provided a very handsome church at Millisle; a cartoon of his Lordship removing the church hangs in Millisle vestry. In 1912, 38 years after the removal of patronage, the parishioners elected the Rev. Oliver S. Rankin, who was later appointed to the chair of Hebrew at Edinburgh University. In 1937 the former United Free church of Sorbie, latterly termed Sorbie West church, united with Sorbie parish church; an area around Broughton Mains and Cults farms was disjoined from the ecclesiastical parish of Whithorn and added to that of Sorbie. A membership of 359 worships at Millisle and Sorbie; only annual services are now held at Cruggleton. A Congregational church in Garlieston which had a long connection with the parish was closed in 1962 owing to the falling-off in numbers. Its members joined Sorbie parish church congregation. Sunday work on the farms prevents many from regular attendance, and it seems that the majority of the community have no church connection at all, except for funerals.

Industries

When the *New Statistical Account* was written, the damask industry in Sorbie was at its zenith. The industry declined; there was a fire in the premises, and the looms could not compete with the more elaborate machinery used elsewhere, and finally the industry collapsed. A small sawmill operates on Galloway estate ground at Rigg Bay and a main sawmill in Garlieston has a substantial number of employees. The Innerwell fisheries specialise in salmon and sea trout; cod, mackerel and plaice are sold locally and herring shoals occasionally visit Wigtown Bay. The new estates of the Forestry Commission are developing into a handsome ornament to the countryside. At Garlieston harbour a large mill for converting grain into flour is in use; manure, cement and lime are brought in and on occasion sailings are still made to the Isle of Man, while cargoes of wood sometimes come from Norway and Germany. In Sorbie the main source of livelihood is the United Creamery, though cream has not been manufactured since 1940; cheese is made in summer and the whey is transported for pig feeding. Farming is the main work in the parish. Oats is the principal grain, but some barley and wheat are also grown; fields are rotated in turnips and pasture. Few sheep are reared, but there are some pigs. Dairy farming is prosperous, but there is little prospect of increased employment in agriculture or any other industry. Most of the farms are owned by the occupier. The Earl of Galloway, formerly the heritor, sold many farms to the McEchern family. In some cases grieves look after the farms. Great improvements have taken place in wages and housing conditions, but much remains to be done with regard to the latter.

Population

As in other parts of the county, there has been a steady decline in population from 1851, though since 1921 the figure has not dropped very appreciably. Most of the 1,117 inhabitants are natives, but farm servants keep moving from one farm to another. When the railway was being made many Irish workmen were employed, and a number of these settled down and were absorbed. Children under five have declined in numbers and females outnumber males slightly, particularly among the old. Garlieston attracts elderly people who have chosen to retire in the neighbourhood because of the pleasant climate. Many of the young people emigrate to the cities to follow business or one of the professions.

Public and Social Services

There is now a good water supply in the area, thanks to the county gravitation scheme. Sorbie for many years suffered the lack of this amenity. Electricity is common in both village and farm, though no gas is available. Many of the farm workers have still primitive sanitary

2D

conveniences, and this fact may have been responsible for the outbreak of infantile paralysis in 1947. The main roads are satisfactory, but the side roads are in need of improvement. Of the two schools, one at Sorbie and the other at Garlieston, each has three teachers; domestic science and general subjects are taught. Older scholars proceed to the junior secondary school in Whithorn or to the senior secondary at Douglas Ewart. Wireless talks supplement instruction. The medical and nursing services are adequate, but the dental service is not used much. There is a Life Boy movement in Garlieston, but difficulty was experienced in keeping the Boy Scouts and Boys' Brigade going through lack of leaders. The Girl Guides and Brownies are more fortunate. Youth clubs function in both villages. Sorbie parish church has a branch of the Woman's Guild and there are branches of the Women's Rural Institute at Sorbie and Garlieston. Football teams are connected with Garlieston Youth Club and Sorbie Youth Club; a tennis court and a bowling green are in use at Garlieston. A branch of the British Legion was formed after the first world war and revived in 1948 and a local Unionist Committee holds occasional meetings. There is a branch of the Transport and General Workers' Union in Garlieston. The only public libraries are at the schools and a few people take advantage of the service.

Housing

Before the second world war, several old houses in Church Street, Garlieston, were closed and new homes with modern conveniences took their place in Randolph Crescent. About half of the houses in both Garlieston and Sorbie are owner-occupied. In the main the houses are adequate for the population. There is no single-apartment house in the whole parish.

Archaeological Notes

When in 1863 Sir William Maxwell of Monreith cut through a barrier of rock at the east end of Dowalton Loch and drew off the water, beaches of different elevation, islands, piles and bones were revealed. Other finds are now in the museum at Edinburgh. The old parish church of Cruggleton has a Norman arch dating from the twelfth century. St. Ninian is believed to have erected a church there. The present building was restored by the Marquess of Bute in 1892. The old church of Kirkmadrine, now an ugly ruin, may also have been built out of the ruin of a church built by St. Ninian. Little is to be seen of Cruggleton Castle. Old shrines and churches at Eggerness and on the site of the present Millisle church were also in existence. The ruins of Sorbie Tower still occupy a prominent place in the landscape, and in recent years a move has been made to restore the ancient dwelling-place of the Hannays.

The Way of Life

The second world war had not the same profound effect on the parish as had the first. Returning ex-servicemen settled down and, apart from a few cases, family life is happy. Of juvenile delinquency there is none. Newspapers are in every home and Sunday newspapers have a wide sale. Football pools constitute a great interest. The community is law-abiding apart from occasional quarrels among men under the influence of drink. The people are of a friendly and hospitable disposition and generally support all good causes; there is seldom, if ever, any industrial dispute and their leisure is generally well occupied. The parish presents an appearance of well-being and prosperity, for there are no ragged persons and the children are well and tastefully dressed. Many of the residents take a pride in their gardens and grow their own fruit, potatoes and vegetables, while some cultivate roses, dahlias, lupins and other flowers. It is true that some of the older retired people conceal straitened circumstances under an appearance of tidiness, cleanliness and cheerfulness; a few of the aged live alone and need a helping neighbourly hand, which is always forthcoming, but they resent any suggestion of a move to a relative or to a home. There is need of playing fields at both Sorbie and Garlieston.

Written 1949
Additions made 1962

CHAPTER 10

THE PARISH OF WHITHORN

by the REV. JOHN G. SCOULAR

Area and Surface

The parish is upwards of eight miles in its extreme length from north to south and five in its extreme breadth from east to west. It is bounded on the north and east by the parish of Sorbie, on the south-east by Wigtown Bay and the Solway Firth, on the south by the Irish Sea and on the west by the parish of Glasserton. The surface of the parish is generally level. Much of the land is good and fertile but there is outcrop and gravel in almost all parts. An area of moss and peat land lies to the west. The coastline is everywhere rugged and rocky. A stretch of cliffs runs from Tonderghie round Burrowhead to Morrach and is continued at Isle Head and Stein Head.

Geology

The rocks of the parish are mainly of Palaeozoic age and belong to the Silurian system. Of that system they include two divisions, the lower of Tarannon age (flooring most of the parish) and the upper of Wenlock age, forming a narrow band at the Burrowhead. Later than the rocks described are the numerous vertical sheets of dykes of intrusive igneous rock well seen in the coastal cliffs but generally concealed inland by later superficial deposits. They are considered to be of Lower Old Red Sandstone age and may be connected with the great granitic intrusions of the Galloway region. During the glacial period the area was swept and ground by an ice sheet which moved generally from north to south. Evidence for this view is seen in the smoothing and rounding of rock exposures. Boulder clay, which is abundant, often takes the form of ridges trending in the direction of ice movement. Later than boulder clay are the spreads of fluvio-glacial sands and gravels into Kames. A conspicuous sheet of these sands and gravels is crossed by the road from Whithorn to Isle of Whithorn.

History

The history of the local community is bound up with the two chief centres of population—the burgh of Whithorn and the village called Isle-of-Whithorn. The latter was the port of Whithorn and the harbour dues at one time went to Whithorn Town Council. The priory church from which the burgh and parish are named has again come into prominence owing to the publication of several books on the subject of St. Ninian and to recent excavations undertaken by the Ministry of Works under the leadership of Professor Ralegh Radford. (A full account of these is given in the

420

Whithorn volume of the *Transactions of the Dumfries and Galloway Natural History and Antiquarian Society*.)

It is highly probable that the present priory is on the original site of *Candida Casa* ('the White House'), which was probably founded and dedicated to St. Martin of Tours by St. Ninian about 397, and consisted of a group of small, simple buildings enclosed within a fence or bank. At Whithorn the heart of the monastery lay on the small rounded hill west of the modern street, on which the ruins of the mediæval cathedral now stand. The small dry-stone building at the east end was one of the principal churches of the Celtic monastery. Its outer face, daubed with white plaster, recalls Bede's description of the 'White House'. The monastery founded by St. Ninian became a famous seat of learning known throughout the Celtic world. Scholars from Ireland resorted there in the fifth and sixth centuries. Later the monastery came under the control of Northumbria and the first of a succession of Northumbrian bishops was Pechthelm, who was consecrated shortly before 731. Most of, if not all, the buildings would be destroyed by the Viking invasion. Viking rule must have come to an end soon after 1100 since some twenty years later we find Earl David receiving dues from Galloway. The province was then or shortly after under the rule of Fergus, a member of David's court, and he re-established the old Anglican bishopric at Whithorn. A Romanesque cathedral was erected in the time of Bishop Gilla Aldan, *circa* 1128.

The arrival of the reformed monastic orders in Galloway marks a further stage of ecclesiastical re-organisation and led to the foundation of the Premonstratensian house at Whithorn about 1177. Some time before 1280 the great church of the thirteenth century was built for the Premonstratensian canons. In the sixteenth century the greater part of the church and other buildings were allowed to fall into decay. They were not destroyed by the people but became ruinous because of neglect of those on whose lands they stood. Early in the seventeenth century the nave was restored as the cathedral of the Protestant bishops of Galloway. The present parish church, built in 1822, is understood to be on part of the site.

Shortly after the founding of the Premonstratensian monastery and until the year 1581, when they were forbidden by the General Assembly and Parliament, pilgrimages in quest of physical and spiritual good were made from all parts of Scotland, England, Ireland and the Isle of Man to the shrine of St. Ninian. Thereafter Whithorn suffered decline as a religious centre. Its importance as the cradle of Scottish Christianity has become more widely recognised in recent times.

The Burgh of Whithorn

Whithorn's first charter was granted by Robert I in 1325 and the existing charter granted by James IV in 1511 confirms all privileges conferred by previous charters. The burgh is governed by a provost, two bailies, a treasurer and six councillors, and prior to the Redistribution Act of 1885 it united with Wigtown, New Galloway and Stranraer in returning a member to Parliament.

Visitors to Whithorn cannot now approach the burgh by the way taken by kings and queens of old times. To reach the royal route now called King's Road, formerly Route de Roi, they would require to come across the fields from the coast. If they could come by the pilgrims' way they would not see the grievous spectacle of a handsome church at the north entrance to the burgh turned into a garage and bearing the name of a commercial firm on its tower.

The general appearance of the burgh has improved considerably during recent times. Old accounts describe it very unfavourably as a place where dunghills lay before almost every door and swine fed on the luxuriant herbage in the street. In the modern town there are many substantial buildings, including the Town Hall, opened 1885, the offices of the Clydesdale and National Commercial Banks, the Post Office, the Station Road Hotel and the Grapes Hotel. Historical buildings in the main street are the Gateway to the Priory, known as the Pend, which was built by Bishop Vaus, Prior of Whithorn from 1482 to 1508, the old Town Hall, built in 1814 to replace a Tolbooth and steeple which occupied the centre of the street, and the War Memorial, which gives the names of the men of the burgh and parish who fell in the two world wars and is built on the lines of the old Mercat Cross. A memorial plaque to the late Mrs. Jeanie Donnan, the Galloway poetess who died in 1942, rests on the wall of the house in George Street which was occupied by her. Some distance along the narrow roadway leading to the Priory is a house which was formerly the school, bears the date 1731, and is now used as a museum.

The appearance of the main street has been much improved since the county authorities took over the maintenance of the roads in 1930. The whole extent of George Street, which probably formed the ancient burgh, is now paved with tarmacadam. The North and South ports still remain, the roadway at both ends being dangerously narrow. Successive housing schemes have provided additional accommodation for the increased population but the housing needs have not yet been met. Trade in the burgh is good and the various shops are well supported by both burgh and country residents. The railway station at the north end is now used only for goods traffic.

Isle of Whithorn

The Isle of Whithorn village is the other main centre of population and is also a place of great historical interest. Near the harbour stands the ruin of a little church which has been claimed as the original site of *Candida Casa*. This is not likely but the church may have stood on the site of an earlier chapel, built in honour of St. Ninian or to commemorate his landing on the coast or simply as a chapel serving the religious needs of the people in that part of the parish. The ruins of the chapel now stand in private property but the site has been taken over by the Ministry of Works and access for the public is assured.

Seawards from the church is the public park handed over to the community by the late Admiral Johnston Stewart of Glasserton. The district council have the custody of the ground and it is a popular resort for visitors and residents alike. At the highest point of the park stand the ruins of an ancient fort, one of a ring stretching completely round the coast line of the parish from Tonderghie to Dinnans. They may have been associated with the Viking invasions of Galloway in the tenth and eleventh centuries.

Another of Isle of Whithorn's historical buildings is the castle standing on rising ground to the north of the main street. It is an L-shaped building with a large staircase in the re-entrant angle. On a stone panel are the initials PH MG with the date 1674, the initials being those of Patrick Houston of Drummaston and his wife, Margaret Gordon. At the west end of the village stands the War Memorial, unveiled in 1921 by the late Sir Herbert Maxwell of Monreith, on a little hill above the bowling green. About three miles to the south, near Burrowhead, a large military camp was used in the second world war, and at Portyerrock Bay, one and a half miles from the Isle, part of Mulberry harbour was constructed and tested with the skilled assistance of Chief Coastguard John Maguire. There is no longer a lifeboat at the Isle of Whithorn; it was taken away in 1920 because of lack of crew and was replaced by an auxiliary coastguard station. The harbour was built by the monks, who levied dues for its upkeep, and was later taken over by Whithorn Town Council but is now the property of the Isle of Whithorn Harbour Company. It was formerly a busy and prosperous place: trading vessels were built and launched near the Old Ha' and also at the Black Rocks. Around 1880 a fleet of oyster fishing boats from England operated off the coast, storing their catches in a marine pond at the Blue Hole. A considerable cattle trade was maintained with Liverpool. The trade almost ceased when the railway came in 1877 and since that time there has been very little activity at the harbour, which has only been used by inshore fishermen, visiting yachts and an occasional seine-net fishing boat. Recent years have seen increased yachting and in summer much good sport is witnessed in the bay.

The other parts of the parish contain much of interest for archaeological and historical study, including a fort at Rispain, near Whithorn, which was excavated in 1901 and was probably constructed between the fifth and eleventh centuries. The most valuable early records were, however, lost in the fire which destroyed the priory church in 1280.

The principal land-owner in the parish is Mr. R. H. Johnston Stewart of Glasserton and Physgill. The Earl of Stair sold his farms and most of the farmers own their land.

Ecclesiastical Affairs

Great changes have taken place in the ecclesiastical state. At the beginning of the last century there were five churches representing different denominations, and now there are two. The Reformed Presbyterian church has become the headquarters of the Territorial unit in Whithorn, the U.P. church is now a garage, and the Free church a hall for the parish church. The Roman Catholic denomination opened a new church in the autumn of 1960. The Isle of Whithorn church, now united with Glasserton, has authority over the southern half of the parish.

Population

The population, after reaching its peak of 3,001 in 1851, has not varied much since 1901, though there has been some migration towards Whithorn from the landward parts, so that more than half the inhabitants—986 in all—reside in Whithorn burgh. There are over 400 houses in the burgh and close on 100 in the Isle. House building continues but the high costs have prohibited the town council from proceeding as quickly as they would wish with new dwellings. The average cost rose from £370 a house in 1935 to £1,770 in 1951. There are 157 houses in the landward area but these are not all occupied.

Industries

Agriculture is still the principal industry in the parish. Improved methods of cultivation, a regular crop rotation and the production of milk have led to increased prosperity. Whithorn Creamery, opened in 1902, began on a basis of 900 liquid gallons a day and now handles more than 4,000 gallons a day. There has been a falling away in the production of beef and mutton and a recent development has been the growing of early potatoes, started in 1934. Mechanisation powered by electricity in the byre and tractors on the fields have taken much of the hard labour out of the work. Horse-breeding continues, however, on a small scale. Wages have reached a high peak and skilled men such as dairymen and shepherds are better paid than the ministers of the parish. A number of workers reside in Whithorn or the Isle of Whithorn and travel daily. Farmers have spent substantial sums on building improvements, mainly to the byres and to their own dwellings, but much could still be done for the farm cottages if these are not to disappear altogether. There is now only one blacksmith's shop, in Whithorn. Numbers engaged in fishing are very small. Milling has ceased; at one time there were mills at Portyerrock, Isle of Whithorn, Whithorn and Caulside. Most farmers have bruising machines. Catering trades have benefited from the advent of many visitors during the summer. Shopping is done in Whithorn and in the Isle of Whithorn and the shopkeepers have gained from the improved conditions of farm workers. Motor cars and tractors are repaired at the various garages.

Education

Changes in education are remarkable. At one time there were five schools in Whithorn and three in the Isle. Today there are two and the prospects are that shortly there will be only one. Whithorn Junior Secondary school was at one time an Academy; built on the present site between 1860 and 1865, it was added to in 1895, 1899, 1907, 1910, 1934 and 1958. It takes in all post-primary junior secondary pupils from Garlieston and the Isle of Whithorn; the roll is 321. The roll at Isle of Whithorn, where the school is on the site of the old parochial school, is 40 and has been declining of late years. The building is in much need of improvement and plans for changes in the future are uncertain.

Social Services

Whithorn receives part of its water supply from the county scheme and the Isle has a good gravitation system from Boyach Loch. Many parts of the landward area are still in need of a more adequate supply. In the drought in 1959 the county authorities made temporary arrangements. Whithorn was lighted by coal gas from 1852, and a change was made to acetylene gas in 1903. Electric lighting started in 1935 at both Whithorn and the Isle. A sewage system was completed in Whithorn in 1937, to replace the earlier and primitive arrangements, and a sewage scheme followed at the Isle in 1940. Scavenging arrangements were made by the county in 1950. Roads have greatly improved but there are still bottlenecks at Whithorn. Side roads to farms can still be very bad in poor weather. Health services are efficiently maintained under the National Health Act and medical practitioners from Whithorn and Portwilliam have consulting rooms in Whithorn and the Isle. The services of a trained nurse are available. The school medical service is excellent and the schools meals system of great benefit.

Voluntary Service

A troop of Boy Scouts was founded in Whithorn in 1920 and a company of the Girl Guides a year earlier. The Women's Rural Institute, started in 1933, has a membership of seventy. There are sixty members at the Isle of Whithorn. Whithorn has a long record of musical attainments: as far back as 1841, the Whithorn Total Abstinence Instrumental Band came into existence, a brass band was founded in 1911, and a male voice choir was formed in 1952. Amateur dramatic performances are given by a local group as well as by the W.R.I. Whithorn Football Club was founded in the later years of last century. The town has a badminton club and public tennis courts, but its nine-hole golf course disappeared during the war. A bowling green was laid out in 1873. The curling club unites with Glasserton. Isle of Whithorn has a bowling green, but the golf course there too has disappeared and the tennis courts were lost during the second world war. A carpet bowling club is run by the Whithorn and Isle British Legion. A Good Templar Lodge, begun about sixty years ago, was responsible for the building of Belmont Hall, now used as a fire station in Whithorn. The Shepherds existed for about thirty years, but the Lodge is now defunct. Whithorn Homing Society has an annual show and a flower show is held by the Rural Institutes. Community work in Whithorn was done successfully by the Town Improvement Committee and by the Village Improvement Committee at the Isle. The British Legion is active in Whithorn.

The Way of Life

This sheltered corner of the country has many advantages and some disadvantages. The natural surroundings are of great beauty and this is the cradle of Scottish Christianity. To some the privilege of living here is inspiring; to others it has little value. Churchgoing has fallen away, though most families claim a connection, but their real interest lies elsewhere. The Roman Catholics have improved their position and their political influence has increased. Greater prosperity has not been an unmixed blessing; the place of the lairds and landed proprietors has been taken by the farmers, who have not always the same public spirit, and have still to learn that material wealth carries responsibilities; they have not yet realised the importance of leadership in the community. Farm servants, better off financially than ever before, do not often know how to make the best use of their improved position. Big wages have not brought blessing to many; in some cases the higher cost of living has nullified the increases and, where there are extravagances in the use of stimulants like tobacco and drink, there is destitution and want. The consumption of drink and pool betting are widespread. Home life has suffered, for many are out every night in the week and the moral tone has been lowered. The incidence of illegitimacy, always high, has been a source of anxiety and worry to many. The centres of population, it is true, show some signs of a better social outlook, for, while the last fifty years have brought times when the civic spirit was notably absent, recent years have seen a change for the better. The prosperity of the district is assured for some time to come, but a greater effort needs to be made to live up to the traditions of the past. Many visitors come to Whithorn because of its historic importance, but the people must realise that they themselves have a share in these traditions. Until they do so and apply them to their way of life, there will be no hope of a religious or social revival. Once the centre of religious pilgrimage from lands near and far, Whithorn will regain her former splendour as a real centre of faith and of true devotion.

Written 1952
Additions made 1962

CHAPTER 11

THE PARISH OF GLASSERTON

by the REV. JOHN G. SCOULAR

The name Glasserton is said to be derived from the old Gaelic words, glas airtein, stream of the pebbles or flints, or from the British word, glastir, meaning green land.

One of the most southerly parishes in Scotland, Glasserton is bounded on the west by Mochrum, on the north by Sorbie and Kirkinner, on the east by Whithorn, and Luce Bay is on the southern boundary. Rugged sea coast with some fine cliffs and headlands, an expanse of moorland, hills from which wonderful views seaward can be obtained, make the parish a delightful natural place. From the Carleton Fell and other hills can be seen, in favourable weather, the Isle of Man, the coast of Cumberland and the peaks of the Lake District, and, to the south-west, occasionally the outlines of the Mountains of Mourne in North Ireland. To the north-east, Wigtown Bay and the Stewartry hills are almost always in evidence.

On the coast two specially attractive places are Physgill Glen which leads to the cave of St. Ninian, scene of annual pilgrimages, and Monreith shore, visited by many from far and near in summer time. There are sandy beaches at Kirkmaiden and Monreith. For the antiquarian, geologist, botanist and naturalist, there is much material. In shape, the parish is long and narrow, eight miles in length, and varying from one to three in breadth. The surface is hilly, and on the coast line there are cliffs, known locally as 'heughs'. The best of the land is to the south and to the west. Along the coast farmlands are not level and the outcrops of rock are covered with whins and bracken, while in places the docken causes much concern to the farmer. Wooded land is sparse.

Agriculture

Cultivated land has increased through the impetus of the two world wars and the enthusiasm of the local farmers. Early potato growing started about 1934 and now extends to over one hundred acres. Dairying has developed and the area under cultivation is much extended. Whilst Ayrshire cattle are most popular, one or two farms carry Holstein or British Friesian breeds. Hill farms pasture sheep and cattle. Around the north boundary much has been done to reclaim the wasteland on the moors of Ravenstone, Balcraig and the Fell of Barhullion. Farmers and workers have adapted themselves to the new methods following the introduction of machinery. Workers go out daily from Portwilliam and Whithorn to the farms, possibly because in the villages and towns they

427

have better housing, but the consequence is that they carry a mid-day 'piece' and their working capacity is perhaps thereby diminished.

The Local Community

Several crannogs in the Dowalton and White Lochs were uncovered when the water was drained and there also existed at one time groups of standing stones on Glasserton Hill, Blairbuy and Balcraig. Remains of castles, camps and forts have been found in the heughs and inland. It is worthy of note that the present parish church stands on the site of an earlier church and on the floor was discovered, in 1896, a portion of an ancient Celtic cross. A partly ruined church of Kirkmaiden, dedicated to St. Martin, stands on the shore of Kirkmaiden in Fernes, now united with Glasserton. A full list of historical monuments is given in *The Inventory of Monuments and Constructions in the County of Wigtown.* To that may be added the War Memorial at the main gate of the entrance to Glasserton House; a granite column, with the names of the fallen in the two world wars, it was dedicated by the late Sir Herbert Maxwell in 1920.

Traces of local history occur in the names of fields: at Kidsdale, one is named the Angel and a knoll is termed Angel Hill, while at Glasserton Mains a field is termed Kirkland, and others are Sleeping Man and Man-Wrap. On Carleton Fell, the name of a rocky plateau is Kirk o' Drumatye, traditionally the meeting place of the Covenanters.

Sir Aymer Maxwell of Monreith and Mr. R. H. Johnston Stewart of Physgill are the principal heritors. Sir Aymer succeeded his grandfather, Sir Herbert, who died in 1937 after a distinguished career as a politician, man of letters, scientist, historian and artist. Mr. Johnston Stewart succeeded in 1940 when his father, Admiral Johnston Stewart, died; his home, Glasserton House, has been partially reconstructed and given an award by the Saltire Society.

Following the general trend, the rolls at the local schools have been steadily decreasing. Glasserton was closed and the pupils were taken to Whithorn. Later, both Ravenstone and Knock schools were also closed. School meals, the provision of milk in schools and the general health service have done much to improve the physique of the scholars, and the horizon of the older pupils has been widened by travel to Whithorn and Portwilliam. The outstanding event in the ecclesiastical sphere was the union of Glasserton parish church with the charge at Isle of Whithorn, carried out after much controversy; since that union, Monreith village and hall have been included in Portwilliam parish area.

Population

In 1851, as in many another parish, the population reached its peak (at 1,487); since then it has declined until the figure in 1959 was 591, and this decrease argues a drift from the land that has been encouraged but not caused by the introduction of much farm machinery. In summer visitors swell the population, but there is no immediate prospect of a settled increase.

Public and Social Services

Apart from the villages, the parish has no public water supply, though the county gravitation scheme will in time serve all the area. Supplies come from local wells and a dry spell brings danger of drought. Few of the cot-houses have water laid on but electricity is now available; sewage is a difficult problem. The standard of roads has greatly improved in recent years and means of communication have been made easier, though, regrettably, the inland road from Whithorn to Portwilliam is not a regular bus route. Voluntary social service has become a feature; some of it stemmed from the use of Physgill as a convalescent hospital during the first world war. Youth organisations have been developed and a branch of the Women's Rural Institute was started in 1921; its aim is to raise the standard of the domestic arts, especially cookery, housekeeping, and care of children, while on the educational side it has created interest in music, drama and literature.

Recreation

Glasserton Curling Club, instituted in 1842 and admitted to membership of the Royal Caledonian Club in 1914, is one of the oldest and strongest in the county. Golfers use a beautiful little course at Monreith, opened in 1905, but the game was earlier played at Kirkmaiden for several years. There are carpet bowling clubs at Glasserton, Monreith and Ravenstone. The Quoiting Club at Glasserton Mains is no longer in existence and the tennis courts at Kirkmaiden have also disappeared.

Housing

With the decline in population cot-houses fell into disrepair or were used as feeding sheds for cattle. Many of the remaining houses are quite inadequate, lacking water and sanitation. Almost all the farm houses have been reconstructed, mainly because most farmers in the parish own their farms. Farm workers take a pride in their gardens and their interest is stimulated by the local horticultural show. Though they share in the general prosperity, the homes of many of the workers are much in need of improvement. As an instance of the changing circumstances, it is noteworthy that there are now no blacksmiths in the parish, though at one time there were three, at Craig Croft, Clarksburn and Glasserton. Plans for better housing are about to be put into operation.

The Way of Life

Community centres at Glasserton, Monreith and Ravenstone give young and old the opportunity for healthy recreation, social gatherings and educational meetings. Farmers' sons and daughters are now sent to university or to agricultural or training college, but family life suffers in some respect through the type of work. High wages have had their effect, for the sums spent on food, tobacco and recreation are much greater, while the gambling habit has taken a firm hold. Material prosperity has not been an unmixed blessing. Recent years have brought the passing of the old aristocracy and the break-up of landed estates. In their new prosperity, farmers appear more concerned with their present privileges than with their responsibilities. The community need is for leadership. There is grave danger of a secular way of life and possibly the infiltration of communistic principles. The Church is facing a great task and is ill equipped, for, though many parishioners remain loyal to the Church and its principles, it is true that, were it not for a devoted band of school teachers, the new generation would grow up entirely ignorant of the Christian faith. Life has changed greatly during the last century, with still greater changes in prospect, and these must be accompanied by an enlightened community sense and a readiness to sacrifice selfish interests for the good of all.

Written 1949
Additions made 1962

CHAPTER 12

THE PARISH OF MOCHRUM

by the late REV. JAMES THOMSON

There are several theories of the meaning of the name, Mochrum. If we consider, however, that in Celtic Magh means 'Open ground near the sea' and Rum means 'Ridge' and reflect further that Mochrum Fell is the highest hill in the Machars, we may reasonably conclude 'Hill in the plain by the sea' to be the meaning.

Mochrum is bounded by Luce Bay on the west, and by the parishes of Old Luce, Kirkcowan, Kirkinner and Glasserton, successively from north to south. The many masses along the sea boundary—that at Chippermore rises to 200 feet—are, according to geologists, composed of moraine detritus and are a legacy from the Ice Age. The total length of the parish is eleven miles and its average breadth five. Moors, mosses and flows occupy a third of the total area and predominate in the north end. In the north end are also situated nine of the eleven lochs, whereof Mochrum Loch and the Castle Loch, just west of it, are both nearly a mile long. Mochrum Loch is close to the Old Place of Mochrum. Near it of old stood the parish mill, a place of general and frequent resort, as mills were wont to be; hence aforetime the polite proverbial way of telling an inquirer to mind his own business, 'I'm going to the Old Mill of Mochrum'. The Castle Loch is so named from an ancient ruin on an island which is said to have been the residence of the Dunbars before they built the Old Place. This loch is notable for cormorants with whose nests the islands are covered. The cormorant was formerly known as the Scart, whence a native of the parish used to be spoken of as a Mochrum Scart.

From the Castle Loch, the Craignarget Burn runs to the sea. This is the scene of the ballad, *Fair Margaret of Craignarget* (1750; Maidment Collection, 1868). She refuses to marry sons of three historic Wigtownshire families, is won by an outlaw and robber from the Isle of Man, is cursed by her father, and is drowned along with her lover immediately on setting sail. Other lochs of importance are Elrig Loch, near the village of that name, and the White Loch, in the policies of Monreith House, at the south end of the parish; it is a bird sanctuary. The only hill of any significance is Mochrum Fell, a table land of 646 feet. Rivers there are none. Trees are scarce, save by Mochrum kirk in the Monreith policies.

Antiquities

On Drumtrodden farm seven groups of Cup and Ring markings are under the care of the Ministry of Works. In the vicinity are a group of three standing stones, two erect, measuring roughly ten feet in height. The

431

carlin stone, at the eastern end of Elrig Loch, five and a half feet in height and three feet at the base, is said to have stood at the centre of a stone circle. Remains of crannogs have been found in five of the lochs. There are over a dozen funerary cairns; the most notable of these, a megalithic structure at the top of Mochrum Fell, is marked on Pont's Map, 1590, but was ruined fairly recently by serving as a base for a bonfire. Place-names, generally Gaelic or Celto-Norse in origin, have suffered some corruption and meanings are often obscure. The following, however, are probable— Auchengallie (field of the gallows); Alticry (wild country); Chang (headland); Chippermore (hill of the shepherd); Chilcarroch (rocky woodland); Clone (meadow); Corhulloch (Cross on the hillock); Corsemalzie (Cross on rising ground); Druchtag (Druid's death); Drumtrodden (hill pasture); Landberrick (shepherd's hut).

Twenty forts or entrenchments have been traced; the most outstanding are at Barsalloch Point, Doon of May and Chippermore. They vary in type but the fact that they are adjacent to the sea seems to indicate that they were directed against Norse invaders. On the lawn at Monreith House stands a tenth century cross, seven and a half feet high, the face disc shaped with central boss and a shaft of interleaved work. The cross, presumed to be the work of a Galloway school founded by a Yorkshire sculptor, known as the Master of Whithorn, is the only complete specimen of the type. There are motes at Crailloch, Myrton and Druchtag. At Myrton a castle or tower has been built and at Crailloch there is but little trace. That at Druchtag near Mochrum village is an Anglo-Norman structure dating probably to the period 1185-1200. The name 'Philip and Mary Point' appears to suggest a ship of that name being washed ashore following the Armada.

Ecclesiastical Affairs

On the Glenluce road, by Corwall Port, and just over the wall, is the earliest relic of Christianity in the parish, Chipper Finnian or the Well of Finnian. By this well, St. Finninan (who died in 576) baptised and taught. Finbar or Finnian studied under St. Ninian's successors at Candida Casa. Thence he founded the monastery of Maghbile (Moyville) in County Down, whither he took with him a copy of St. Ninian's copy of the Gospels and Psalter. At Maghbile, Columba made a copy thereof and King Diarmid gave judgment in favour of Finnian when he claimed it. Columba raised an insurrection, was defeated and sailed in exile to Iona. Thus was Mochrum's own saint responsible for the coming of Columba to Scotland. Adjacent to the House of Elrig, at the foot of Mochrum Fell, is Barrhawble, Hill of the Chapel, on the same pattern as the Well of Finnian. Excised crosses and slabs may be seen built into farm buildings in the district. A mile off, opposite Chang old steading, traces of two vanished villages are to be found on the moor; nearby is an eminence on which tradition says a fair was held.

Of chapels adjacent to the 'Norman' motes, that at Crailloch cannot now be traced, that of Myrton is still extant and that of Druchtag developed into the parish church. The building of the original parish church, in the Norman style, resembled Cruggleton and is dedicated to St. Malachy, who passed through in 1139. Monumental crosses and carven slabs, now in the National Museum at Edinburgh, are said to be of an earlier date and, if that be so, the Gospel may have been preached in Mochrum for a thousand years.

The present kirk (1794) was presumably a direct successor to that of the twelfth century. Originally it was a plain oblong without galleries, with a lairds' loft facing the pulpit. Galleries were added in 1835 and in 1876 the arch facing the pulpit was pierced; this is now the central area of the church. *The Old Statistical Account* reports the manse as recently covered with slates (1794). Part of the manse still remains. Additions were made in 1822 and in 1901, and now there are 13 rooms and ten out-houses in three-quarters of an acre of ground. In the spring the display of purple crocuses is a notable sight. The kirkyard contains one seventeenth century stone, and the family commemorated thereby have been identified as being on Claverhouse's examinable list. Three families were on the black list—Airyolland, Airiequhillart and Chilcarroch; two were deported and Chilcarroch was hanged. He was the parish's only victim. In 1760 Seceders at Clantibuies were scattered by the laird on horseback: he had made a bet that he would 'skail the byke'. After forming the Relief congregation at Portwilliam, they became the United Presbyterian Church in 1847 and united with the Free Church in 1900, but the United Presbyterians later withdrew. The building of Portwilliam Free Church began in 1863 and the manse and hall were added during the closing years of the century. Roman Catholics, given in the *New Statistical Account* as numbering thirty-five families (mostly belonging to imported Irish labourers at Elrig Mill), are now almost unknown. In 1929 Port-william United Free church became part of the Church of Scotland and union was effected between Mochrum and Portwilliam a few years ago.

Families

The history of the parish is closely bound up with three families. First we may deal with the Dunbars of the Old Place of Mochrum. In 1368 David II bestowed the lands of Mochrum on the Earl of March, whose family name was Dunbar. Till they built the Old Place the Dunbars resided, so it is said, in a castle whose ruins may still be seen on an island in the Castle Loch. For approximately 300 years Dunbars were to hold and reside in the Old Place; this consisted principally of two towers, whereof the less ancient part was built in the closing years of the fifteenth century by Sir John Dunbar, whose arms and monogram could be seen upon it. James Dunbar (who succeeded in 1675) was made a Knight-Baronet by King William in 1694, the patent bearing that he had suffered much 'because he did not give his concurrence to a very great number of measures carried on under former governments.' This explains why he sold so many of the lands, with crippling effect on the estate. Sir James was a man of colossal proportions, a literal 'giant'; hence anything notably outsize used to be called in Galloway 'a Mochrum', from a monster potato to a thundering lie.

Gavin Dunbar, son of the Sir John aforesaid and a daughter of Sir Alexander Stewart of Garlies (ancestor of the Earls of Galloway), was the parish's most famous son. He became successively Dean of Elgin Cathedral, Prior of Whithorn, tutor to young James V, Archbishop of Glasgow, and Lord Chancellor of Scotland. He was also founder and first President of the Court of Session, and member of the Council of Regency during the King's absence in France. He it was who led the opposition when the Scottish Parliament sanctioned the Bible in the vernacular (1543). Till the Reformation the Church presided over our Universities, which accounts for the Archbishop's arms being displayed by Glasgow's old college buildings; after these buildings were abandoned in 1870 the arms were transferred to Mochrum Park and are built in there.

Towards the end of the eighteenth century the Old Place was sold to the husband of the Countess of Dumfries and through her it passed to the Bute family. After a century's dilapidation it received (1911) at the hands of Lord Bute a restoration which is a gem of its kind, the towers being renovated according to individual purpose and Scottish pattern and the whole finished with a courtyard whose buildings conform.

The ruins of Myrton tower are situated within the policies of Monreith House by the side of the White Loch. On this spot the McCulloch family had for early home a mote or stockaded hill and they subsequently built a tower towards the year 1500. They shared with the McDoualls of Logan the honour of being among the oldest Celtic families in Galloway. In 1338 Patrick McCulloch appears as owner of Myrton. He and his family, however, having been supporters of Balliol, had to seek refuge in England for a time; and it was not until 1363 that he was suffered to come home at the price of part of the estate.

In 1511 James IV on pilgrimage to Whithorn stayed he.e with Alexander McCulloch who was his Master Falconer and whom he made a knight. At Flodden James IV had ten men dressed 'lyk unto his awin present apparell, amongis whom was twa of his awin guard who wer baith verrie lyk in makdome to the King'; Alexander McCulloch was one of these two. The last of the McCullochs was Godfrey who sold Myrton to Sir William Maxwell in 1683. Dissolute and wild, and having parted with his heritage, he took life, fled to England, returned, and was recognised and executed (1697).

The Maxwells of Monreith first appeared in 1481 and settled at the Moure, which is beyond Mochrum boundary in Glasserton parish. Here they resided for 200 years; Dowies farm shows evidence of their occupation. In the seventeenth century father and son supported the Covenanting side, and the former was the hero of the meal-chest story; said the Edinburgh gudewife to the pursuing soldiers, 'Ye're welcome to search the meal ark an' see if ony o' ye can hide in't withoot giein' a hoast'. The son fought at Rullion Green (Pentland Hills, 1666) and owed his life to his good steed which bore him safe home; thereafter that good horse was turned loose for all time, and his field at Dowies bears the name of Pentland to this day.

William Maxwell, the founder of the family's fortunes, was a shrewd lawyer who seized the numerous opportunities of wadset that offered themselves at the close of that troubled century. He was made a baronet in 1681 and purchased Myrton in 1683. Jane, Duchess of Gordon, daughter of the third baronet, has a lasting place among famous Scotswomen. She was a mainspring of politics under Dundas, the brilliant leader of Edinburgh fashionable society, an acquaintance and patroness of Robert Burns, and she took a hand when the Gordon Highlanders were first raised, bestowing on each recruit a kiss. William, fourth baronet, is commended in the *Old Statistical Account* as a progressive agriculturalist. He built the Church and Monreith House; he also built the original harbour and gave his name to Portwilliam. William, fifth baronet, lost an arm at Corunna with Sir John Moore; he won the St. Leger in 1815 with Filho da Puta. William, sixth baronet, was an antiquarian of note and drained Dowalton Loch, discovering a crannog (1863).

Herbert Eustace (1845-1937), seventh baronet, was M.P. for Wigtownshire, Scottish Whip, Lord of the Treasury and Privy Councillor, chairman of the Royal Commission on Tuberculosis, president of the Society of Antiquaries of Scotland and chairman of the Royal Commission on Scottish Historical Monuments, historian, essayist, novelist, naturalist, lover of trees, botanist and painter of flowers, Lord Lieutenant of Wigtownshire and Knight of the Order of the Thistle: a man as beloved as he was distinguished.

The Community

From a total of 828 in 1755, the population rose to 2,946 in 1851 and thereafter dropped steadily until it is now about 1,280. There has been a gradual move from north to south, Elrig dropping to under a hundred and Portwilliam rising to 700, largely because of the county council's housing schemes and the number of people who retire to the village by the sea, which is the headquarters of public services, having a school, post office, bank, police station and several garages, a doctor and a district nurse. The Maxwell Hall is the centre for communal activities; after being vacated by the United Presbyterians, it was adapted by public subscription. The harbour, built by the Maxwell family, is now almost deserted; the last ship to unload cargo was in 1942. The Haig Institute, a converted army hut, is the centre for the British Legion activities. There are two licensed hotels in Portwilliam and also an inn. Lodge Myrton (Freemasons), No. 539, whose consecration dates from 1873, has 71 brethren in good standing. Mochrum, the nominal capital of the parish, is a village in whose outward appearance (enhanced by the great trees in the manse grounds) the inhabitants take local pride. The population is 95 and the village has a school and a post office. Barrachan has a population of under 300 and Elrig under 100. Once a busy centre, Elrig has declined: the Farina Mill closed in 1850, the bone-meal mill in 1904, and the oatmeal mill in 1913, while the school also has now been closed.

Industries

Smuggling was once a major industry, ending abruptly in 1894, when a floor on Clone Farm collapsed, revealing a commodious cellar. The Close Brethren, who subscribed to all good causes, also lost their ship and all their finance. There are normally about six one-man boats engaged in fishing; three joiners' shops employ seven men; at the mill there are three employees. There are still two smithies employing four men, and electricity and the motor trade give work to others. Agriculture of course dwarfs all other industries. There are about sixty farms; half of these are owner-occupied and there are four small holdings. Peat was once cut in quantity. The ploughing match has faded out in face of the tractor, and the annual horse and foal show has also disappeared. A remote parish, Mochrum benefited by the tarmacadamised road and the internal combustion engine. The parish possesses a creamery for the dairy farmers' produce. Started by local effort in 1921, it was burnt down ten years later and re-opened by the Scottish Milk Marketing Board. It employs 25 men and women and has a peak output of about 6,000 gallons daily. There has recently grown up a productive broiler and bacon industry on the shores of Portwilliam.

Recreation

Football is played in Maxwell Park, but cricket has never been popular. Golfers travel to St. Medan's, in Glasserton parish. A tennis court and bowling green dating from 1874 are situated in High Street. There is also a quoiting pitch, but the club has not resumed since 1939. Rod fishing is available on Elrig Loch. Mochrum Curling Club (1838) is one of the strongest in the county and is referred to as the 'Mighty Men of Mochrum'. There are two billiard tables in the Haig Institute and three carpet bowling rinks. Carpet bowls are also played at Mochrum, Elrig and Culshabbin. Portwilliam Dramatic Society boasts that it was the first in the district to play to the public (1914). Rural Institutes meet at Mochrum, Portwilliam, Elrig and Culshabbin. A weekly film show was at one time popular, but nowadays the fans travel to Newton Stewart or Whithorn.

Written 1950
Additions made 1962

CHAPTER 13

THE PARISH OF OLD LUCE

by the late Rev. David Galloway

In 1646 the former parish of Glenluce was divided into Old Luce and New Luce as they exist today. The derivation of the name Luce is uncertain, but a possible interpretation is *Vallis Lucis*, the Valley of Light. Another view, widely held, is that the name originally meant the place of herbs. The parish covers more than 30,000 acres and is bordered to the north by New Luce, on the west by Inch and Stoneykirk, and on the east by Kirkcowan and Mochrum; to the south lies Luce Bay. It contains some good arable land, some rough pasture, hilly areas and some stony or rock-covered hill pastures. It is bisected by the river Luce, which provides excellent sport for anglers during the summer and autumn. The highest point, the Knock of Luce, is approximately 700 feet high; Craig, The Ronald and Camrie Hills are all about 400 feet high. The best land is that which is on the banks of the river.

Archaeological Treasures

If the parish had no archaeological sites it would still be unique, because it contains the treasure-house of Luce Bay sands, whence tons of material, from the Middle Stone Age onwards to the eighteenth century, have come to enrich the museums of Britain and which continues to yield up its treasures to whoever has time to seek. Conversely, if the parish did not have the sands, because of its astonishing concentration of sites, from the Neolithic through the Bronze and Iron Ages, the Dark Age and the Middle Ages—29 cairns, 7 crannogs, 6 hill-forts, 24 groups of huts or individual huts and their field-stone heaps, crosses and chapel sites, Glenluce Abbey, peel towers and seventeenth century mansions—it would still be one of the richest parishes in Scotland. Taking the two together, it is unique. Something over 25 stone axes from the Neolithic period, including the beautiful translucent axe of pyroxene jadeith imported from Brittany and found at Glenjorrie, come from the parish.

Glenluce Abbey

The outstanding antiquity of the parish is Glenluce Abbey, since 1932 in the hands of the Office of Works, whose officials have cleared all debris, revealed the ground plan and preserved the existing masonry. This abbey was founded by Roland, Lord of Galloway, in 1190 and was inhabited by the white monks of the Cistercian order. To judge from the ruins, which cover over an acre of ground, it must have been a splendid edifice, and, long after the destruction of the other abbeys in Scotland, it was in use in its entirety; as late as 1646 it is mentioned in the presbytery records as having been in very good order, and, indeed, this is still true of the chapter-house. This portion of the abbey is supported by one freestone pillar, divided into eight arches, which are built into the surrounding walls; the centres of the arches are ornamented with a variety of figures wrought in the facing stones.

The last Abbot or Commendator of this monastery was Thomas Hay, the paternal ancestor of the Dalrymple-Hay family, who at one time owned Dunragit estate, now taken over by the Department of Agriculture. This family had the right, which they used till 1932, to have burials within the precincts of Glenluce, but the privilege was withdrawn when the abbey was taken over by the Office of Works.

Population
Unlike the neighbouring parishes, Old Luce has largely retained its population: the percentage decrease has been much smaller than in most rural areas and the inhabitants number close on two thousand. This stability is due partly to the acquisition of former estates by the Department of Agriculture, which has set up many small holdings in the area, partly to the establishment of a modern village (the first in the south of Scotland) at Dunragit, based on the presence of a Nesmilk factory, large afforestation schemes, a building contractor and a tractor repair shop, and to a lesser extent to the provision of a dry grass plant; the strategic situation no doubt suggested these developments and of course encouraged the population to remain. In Glenluce, the largest village in the county, too, there was a strong inducement for the residents to remain because of the building of council housing schemes, which have almost transformed the village and have enhanced the comfort and well-being of the people. The latest scheme was accorded a high award by the Civic Trust. There are several persons over 80 years of age. The one centenarian, Miss Agnes Rusk, who celebrated her 102nd birthday in the summer of 1962 and who was the oldest person in the county, died in 1963. The population is fairly evenly divided between the sexes with males slighly predominant. A few young people have emigrated to lands overseas during the past few years, most of them going to relatives, and all seem to be prospering.

The Local Economy
Stair Estates are the principal heritors in the parish, but the Department of Agriculture, having taken over the estates of Park and Drochduil, own many small holdings which give a reasonable living to the smaller farmer. There are a few owner-occupied farms in the parish. Dairying is the principal occupation and a few farmers have gone over to the Friesian breed of late. Pig-rearing is carried on at several farms and there are hill pastures for sheep and rough ground for black cattle.

Ancillary trades employ fairly large numbers—engineering and tractor repair work, mainly in connection with farms, as well as school renovations and the maintenance of farm buildings, carried out by a local contractor. Moreover, the Forestry Commission, with a nursery at Bareagle, has expanded its work in the last decade and now controls 1,546 acres, which are in course of being re-planted; the nursery is one of the most important in the South-West. Nearly 500 acres have been taken over from the Air Ministry at Torrs Warren for planting; this ground had been used in connection with the bombing trials in the Bay of Luce. These trials interfered to some extent with the fishing, but few local men have been engaged in this industry for some years. The oyster fishery has also been closed and the former harbour at Stairhaven is now derelict. Many travel from Glenluce to Dunragit to supplement the local workers at the creamery there and the firm who own the creamery have been largely instrumental in improving the amenities of Dunragit village, in which the new housing scheme presents a pretty picture to the traveller on the main road.

Situated on the main Stranraer-Gretna Road, Glenluce is a well-kept village with a good post office, public hall, police station, three hotels, railway station, a primary and junior secondary school, a well-appointed garage, electrical engineers, haulage contractors and many shops. A few years ago, Lady Stair gave a park in the village for football and children's sports and each year are held in Balkail Meadow the only games in the Rhins district. A tennis court and bowling green have their devotees. The supply of water is plentiful, sewerage is satisfactory, electricity is used for street lighting and domestic purposes, and communications are excellent.

Ecclesiastical Matters.[1]

There are two Church of Scotland churches in the village, besides the Plymouth brethren. The old parish church, dating from 1636 but rebuilt in 1814, is a whinstone building with three outside stairways leading to the galleries. Connected with it are a Sunday School, the Boys' Brigade, Girl Guides and Woman's Guild, all well supported. Ladyburn church, a former U.F. church, is an attractive freestone building, pleasantly situated near the Lady Burn. Services are also held in the community centre at Dunragit, an old building renovated and modernised in 1952, which has since proved so popular that extensions have had to be made. Dunragit is a thriving village with 60 houses, two shops, a railway station, and office buildings. Other community associations are at Glen of Luce and in Glenluce, but Dunragit is probably the strongest.

The Way of Life

The village of Glenluce has an excellent Dramatic Society, which has reached the final stages of the South-West Community Drama Association competition, and a strong branch of the British Legion with a membership of well over 100. The youth club is well-patronised and the three branches of the Rural Institute, at Glenluce, Glen of Luce and Dunragit, enjoy good

[1]It was with deep regret that news was received of the death of the Rev. David Galloway soon after he had revised his account of Old Luce parish. Mr. Galloway was minister of the old parish church and after his death the two congregations in the village were united. The united congregation now worship in the old parish church. The future of Ladyburn is at the moment uncertain.

support and do much valuable work. The County Golf Club, the oldest in Galloway, is stronger than at any time in the last thirty years, while Glenluce Curling Club, amongst the oldest in the country, was instituted in 1839; one of its rules is, 'It shall consist of members of unexceptional character, resident in the district or neighbourhood.' The Ploughing Society is also a well-established association, dating back to 1847, though there are now no horsemen competitors. With so much that is of interest within their bounds, the parishioners are closely-knit around their respective community centres, and their way of life is quiet and almost untroubled by petty crimes or legal offences: the few law-breakers are usually transient travellers. The great majority have at least some interest in religion and the welfare of the community.

Written 1952
Additions made 1963

CHAPTER 14

THE PARISH OF NEW LUCE

by the REV. F. J. CHAMBERS

Geography and History

New Luce, the most northerly parish of Wigtownshire, is part of the Moors. Roughly 60 square miles in extent, it is bounded on the north by the parishes of Colmonell and Ballantrae in Ayrshire, on the south by the parish of Old Luce (with which it was joined until 1646), on the east by Kirkcowan and on the west by Inch. Of the opposing theories as to the meaning of Luce, one is that (spelt *Lus* in early charters) it meant a place of herbs; certainly the valley of the Luce river from the hills in the north to the Bay of Luce abounds in countless varieties of herbs, some of great medicinal value. The other view is that the name is derived from Saint Lucy of Sicily, or else from a virgin, Saint Lucy of Scottish origin, who died in 1100. The parish is thinly populated; its vast acreages include tracts with no population at all, while the small village of 55 houses contains about a third of the whole population. Locally the district is known as Nineveh but for what reason is difficult to discover. The parish is remarkable for the number of cairns, many raised by pilgrims on their journey to St. Ninian's relics at Whithorn, and many names have the prefix *Kil*, indicating Chapel.[1] The only outstanding historical figure is Alexander Peden, the Covenanter, for three years minister of the parish, who became known as Peden the Prophet and died in 1686 at the age of 60. The secular affairs of the parish are in the hands of the county and district councils, while ecclesiastical affairs are governed by the seven members of kirk session. An excellent village hall was built by local subscription after the first world war, as a memorial to those who had fallen.

Population

The population, like that of all other parts of rural Wigtownshire, has been steadily declining, and now numbers under 300, whereas in 1851 it was 791, the highest ever recorded. Apart from agriculture there is no work whatever for the young people, who therefore leave the district for the towns at the first opportunity.

[1] The parish offers much of interest to the archaeologist; few can equal it in respect of chambered cairns, long and round, and even the smaller, late cairns with cists seem abnormally plentiful. A fair number of flat polished axes show Neolithic occupation; and the numerous relics of the croft and shieling economy are particularly important. In between, two Iron Age forts and some at least of the many hut-circles show that at the beginning of the Christian era the parish was by no means empty.

Education

At the fine school in the village, the head teacher, assisted by an infant mistress, takes charge of some 50 pupils. Built in 1870, it has been altered, extended, re-equipped and brought up-to-date. The earlier school was in a one-roomed dwelling now known as Church cottage, which stands at the entrance to the church, and the roll was then 100. Each child was obliged to bring peat to the school, while water was carried from a well 200 yards distant. Great progress has been made in educational amenities, but whether the pupils of today are any better equipped for facing life is another matter. It is clear that few people in the parish read anything but portions of the daily newspaper, some of them not particularly edifying. The classical works, which were enjoyed and appreciated by a generation whose education cost the ratepayers little or nothing, now lie mouldering and neglected, along with the Bible.

Ecclesiastical Affairs

The present church, erected on the site of the former building, known as the Moor Kirk of Luce, was erected in 1821 to seat 200 worshippers. The manse is beautifully situated on the banks of the Cross Water of Luce and is surrounded by a glebe of 25 acres now let to a grazing tenant. It is unfortunate that, as in many other places, the congregation is dwindling, yet the church still remains the centre of village and parochial life. A flourishing Sunday School keeps the children in touch with spiritual life, there is a fine band of enthusiastic and helpful teachers, and the elders enjoy the regard and respect of the whole community. The average attendance is, however, between 50 and 60 in the summer and in winter but 30; at Communion, held twice a year, the attendance is about 85. These figures compare most unfavourably with those of thirty years ago. A remarkable feature is that, while the attendance of the farmer and his family is good, the labouring classes, as a whole, have drifted away from the church; while in no way hostile, they absent themselves from the church worship and its way of life, and this constitutes a serious problem in rural communities.

Recreation

There are many amenities for the promotion of social intercourse in the parish. Chief of these is the Women's Rural Institute, started in 1929 with a membership of about 50; its members, together with those of the badminton, carpet bowling and bridge clubs, all use the village hall, where are also held whist drives, dances and other entertainments. A strong curling club enjoys more outdoor games (on Loch of Larg) than do other clubs in the county, for there is ice on the loch when outdoor ice is not available elsewhere.

Local Services

It would be wrong to say that housing in New Luce is inadequate. With the falling population, many cottages are unoccupied and have become dilapidated and ruinous. Even in the village the housing is in a sense adequate though most of the dwellings, small cottages, are in a sad state of disrepair. Outside they are maintained in a clean and tidy condition but the high cost of repairs is the trouble. Few of them have modern sanitation for their condition was such that, even when the gravitation water scheme from Penwhirn, just outside the northern boundary, became available, the houses could not take advantage of this improvement; many of them have been declared unfit. The problem is that, with the dwindling population and the high rents necessarily imposed for council houses, only eight of these have been built; there is no further demand, for most people prefer to remain where they are in their old-fashioned cottages with low rents.

There is no resident doctor or policeman. Medical service is provided from Glenluce or Stranraer, and treatment for more serious cases is available at Stranraer, Ayr, Dumfries and Glasgow. Tradesmen too have almost entirely disappeared; the parish is without a slater, blacksmith, plumber or mechanic of any sort, while the two joiners are semi-retired. The ancient occupation of mole trapper is, however, still pursued, for the whole countryside is overrun by the 'moudie'. There are two shops, and, in place of four public houses, one well-conducted hotel; cases of drunkenness are very rare.

Agriculture

The parish is completely agricultural but contains only 25 farms. The northern portion consists almost entirely of sheep farms, but the southern portion is arable and given over to dairying. Some horse breeding continues despite the farm tractor. There are three heritors, the Earl of Stair, Major-General McMicking and Mr. David Frederick, of whom the last resides in the parish. With so many sheep farmers, the annual event of importance is the Sheep Dog Trials held at Airyolland. Farmers have to fight a more destructive pest than the mole, as the field vole does immense damage to growing plants. Adders and grass snakes are found in abundance; a small lizard known as the 'ask' is harmless. Rabbits are still very common, hares are numerous and so are badgers and otters; the parish, indeed, abounds in wild life.

The Local Community

Undoubtedly, the living standards of farm servants, with higher wages, more leisure and more time for recreation, are much better than they were fifty years ago. The River Luce abounds during the season in sea-trout and salmon, and there are usually large numbers of herling and brown trout; moreover, a large stretch of the Cross Water is available for parishioners who are anglers. Pheasants and partridges are numerous. Thus life can be pleasant in this rural setting.

Radio and television have been a great boon to people in the outlying districts. The roads to Stranraer and Glenluce are good, but the farm roads to the north are very bad for motor traffic. The restriction of the bus service to one day a week means that people who do not have cars must stay at home a good deal. Severe snowstorms were experienced in 1940 and 1947; in the second of these the railway was blocked at Glenwhilly for several days and passengers underwent some hardship. Normally, however, the weather is bracing and invigorating.

Written 1952
Additions made 1962

CHAPTER 15

THE PARISH OF INCH

by the REV. HARRY GALBRAITH MILLER

Natural Setting

In Pont's map in the *Theatrum Scotiae* the White Loch which lies near the centre of the parish of Inch is called the 'Loch of the Inch', that is, the Loch of the Island, and it is probably from this that the parish takes its name. In local speech the name, more often than not, has the definite article, and you will be assured, for example, that 'they're strange folk at the Inch'.

The parish, part of which is in the burgh of Stranraer, falls into two parts: the northern is moorland, rising to over 840 feet, while the southern is a low undulating plain, seldom as high as 100 feet, and is rich agricultural land. The northern half is drained by the river Luce, which bounds the parish on the east and flows south into Luce Bay. In the level plain to the south there are four principal lochs. The White and Black Lochs lie side by side in the policies of Lochinch Castle, and drain northwards into Lochryan. Roughly a mile further south are Loch Magillie, locally reported to be 'bottomless', and Soulseat Loch, only 40 feet above sea level and draining southwards into the Piltanton burn, which is the southern boundary of the parish and itself flows into Luce Bay not far from the mouth of the Luce.

There is good salmon and trout fishing on the Luce. The Black Loch is well stocked with brown trout, perch and roach, and sea trout are also taken. Loch Magillie used to be stocked with trout, but has been almost emptied by poachers, and it is not thought worth the trouble and expense to restock it. Soulseat Loch is infested with pike: there is record of one weighing 40 pounds having been caught in it. The Stranraer Angling Association, with the assistance of the Royal Engineers then stationed at Cairnryan, attempted to destroy these by blasting in May 1954, with a view to stocking the loch with trout; the effort was unsuccessful but subsequent measures proved more effective.

Otters are to be found in the Black Loch, Soulseat Loch, the Luce and the Piltanton Burn. A badger was killed in the parish some 25 years ago. Adders infest the northern moors, and it is not safe to leave a baby in its pram near to a stone dyke in summer time. Hawks, both kestrel and sparrow, are not uncommon. Pheasant and other game birds used to be reared in large numbers on the Lochinch estate, but now for the most part they breed wild. The lochs and marshes abound with many kinds of duck. During a hard winter an occasional deer finds its way down to the level pasture land from the moors.

During the late war, when great numbers of troops were stationed in the countryside, the rabbits were very much reduced and myxomatosis has practically cleared them away. Moles are a serious pest, while the rats are kept under only by the efforts of the farm cats. Stoats and weasels are common, and the fox is beginning to increase.

Midges and (recently) mosquitoes make life a misery on summer evenings out of doors. The clouds of small gnats remarked on in the *New Statistical Account* are still to be seen on a summer evening hanging like smoke over Soulseat Loch. Shortly after coming to this parish, the present minister, alarmed to see what looked like clouds of smoke arising from the manse, ran home only to find these little creatures dancing with a shrill, piping noise above the trees around the house. More beautiful are the glow-worms which on dark nights gleam in their hundreds on the moors towards New Luce.

The lower part of the parish is tolerably well wooded, but neither soil nor climate is favourable to the growth of the finest timber. Ash trees, in particular, grow to a reasonable size only to begin to rot at the heart and decay. The storms of 1953 worked great havoc among the plantations.

Ecclesiastical Matters

The parish church referred to in the previous *Statistical Account* was built in 1770; its roofless ruins, standing on the shore of the White Loch, about half a mile up the main avenue to Lochinch Castle, still serve as the burial place of the Earls of Stair. The present church was built at the main entrance to the castle in 1861-62, in the ministry of the Rev. James Fergusson, author of the account of the parish in the *New Statistical Account*; he died on 1 January 1862, and only entered his new church feet first, as it was expressed. This church was struck by lightning and burnt out on 29 December 1894; the communion vessels and tokens and the harmonium were destroyed, but the Session records, dating from 1730, were saved and are still in the custody of the parish minister, with their outer leaves charred. The church, as rebuilt in 1896, has an unusually fine barrel-vaulted roof in pine, and the chancel is also panelled in pine. Above and behind the chancel is the old laird's pew. The north transept is the Stair Pew, decorated with the arms of the Earl of Stair, and containing a typical Victorian stained glass window. There is a pleasant chancel rail of wrought iron. A conspicuous object is the White Ensign from H.M.S. *Rodney* which took part in the sinking of the German battleship *Bismarck* in the Atlantic on 27 May 1941. It was presented to the church by Admiral Sir Frederick H. G. Dalrymple-Hamilton, who commanded the *Rodney* during the engagement; the admiral is a member of the congregation, and a cousin of the late Earl of Stair. The present communion plate and the font were the gift of Sir Hew Hamilton Dalrymple, uncle of the late Lord Stair, and for over 46 years an elder in the church.

The organ that was destroyed in the fire had been the centre of great controversy when first introduced. Many walked out of the church when it was first used. The minister had to defend his action before the Presbytery, which he did with great vigour, declaring that he had 'sought' to tear the lion's skin from an ass of superstition which has too long terrified and disgraced the church'. The controversy is long since dead, and the church now has a pleasant little pipe organ. The graveyard surrounding the church is peaceful and beautifully kept by the county council. Here are buried Captain James Ferguson and other officers of the *Princess Victoria*, which was lost with 128 lives in the North Channel on 31 January 1953, during one of the worst storms within living memory.

In 1846 a Free Church, manse and school were built at Castle Kennedy. The congregation was united with the parish church in 1932, and the old church building is now in a state of disrepair. It is used mainly by the Inch Badminton Club, but occasional functions such as sales of work and whist drives are held there. The school is now part of the county system, and the manse is a small private hotel.

The numbers attending the parish church today are small, ranging from 30 to 140. During the war so few attended that sometimes the vestry was large enough to contain the congregation. The most popular service of the year was that on Christmas Eve, when carols were sung by candlelight, but this has been discontinued since a change of ministers took place. The number of communicants is 260, but, as many parishioners are members of churches in Stranraer, it is not possible to give accurate figures of the number of baptisms or marriages in the parish. In 1953 there were 32 baptisms in the parish church, but the probable number of children baptised in the parish may be estimated at 60. No record of marriages performed by a minister is kept; a rough guess puts the number about twenty. A few are married by the registrar in Stranraer, but most still prefer to seek the services of the minister; one wedding in four is in the church, while others take place in the village hall and some are held in Stranraer and also in the manse. A minister is considered all but indispensable at a burial, and a service is frequently held in the church beforehand. It is a rare thing for any ladies to attend a public funeral, though a short service is generally held for them beforehand at the dead person's house. It is now unusual for silk hats to be seen at a funeral: these are worn only by the minister and the undertaker, and few people change into black before attending a funeral.

In 1841 a church was erected at Cairnryan—a building of no special interest. In 1858 the parish of Lochryan was disjoined from Inch, and in 1941 it was united with the parish of Glenapp which lies in the county of Ayr. Services at Cairnryan are well attended, and there are some 160 communicants in the Lochryan section of this parish; eight baptisms were recorded in 1953. The minister of Lochryan and Glenapp was chaplain to all troops stationed at Cairnryan with the exception of members of the Church of England, who were served by the priest-in-charge at the Episcopal church in Stranraer. Services are also held regularly in the Public Hall at Lochans.

There are under a hundred Roman Catholics in the parish, and the majority of these are Irish.

Lochinch Castle

Castle Kennedy, the ancient home of the Kennedy family, was acquired by James Dalrymple (later first Viscount Stair) sometime about 1670. The castle was accidentally burnt in 1815 and has never been rebuilt; it is the most imposing antiquity in the parish. In 1867, the present mansion house of Lochinch at the north end of the White Loch was completed; it is in the Scottish Baronial style and is pleasantly dignified. The glory of Lochinch lies, however, in its gardens. Owing to the drastic reductions in staff that are today inevitable the acres of velvet lawns have disappeared, but the architecture of the gardens remains magnificent. All the avenues radiate from the ruined castle, that composed of araucaria, the monkey puzzle tree, being for the ordinary person the most spectacular. There are some 200 different species of conifers in the pinetum, and the rhododendrons are world famous. Within recent years great numbers of embothrium have been imported from the Argentine, and these, when in flower, suggest trees covered with scarlet honeysuckle. The Earl of Stair, whose seat Lochinch is, also owns the estate of Oxenfoord in Midlothian, but he resides permanently at Lochinch; he owns most of the land in the parish. The other principal landowner is Malcolm Wallace of Lochryan House, who is also resident in the parish.

Antiquities

The main antiquities of the parish have already been described in the *New Statistical Account*. They include the standing stones of Glenterrow, the stepping stones of Glenterrow, the moat at Innermessan (in excellent preservation) and Craigcaffie Castle (which is no longer inhabited, but is still in a fair state of preservation, though the doors and windows of the top storey are blown in). The moats at Gallowhill and at Cults disappeared before the plough at the beginning of the century, and are now only names on the map.

Soulseat Abbey, according to St. Bernard of Clairvaux, was founded about 1125 by St. Malachy, Archbishop of Armagh. That was doubted by some. It is certain that in 1148 it was settled with white canons from Prémontré, and so became the mother house of the Premonstratensians in Scotland, an order which counted amongst its houses Whithorn, Holyrood and Dryburgh. The *New Statistical Account* speaks of a few remains being visible, but nothing is now to be seen except a rising mound which probably marks the site of the Abbey Church. In 1911, some excavating was attempted under the guidance of the late Sir Hew Dalrymple, but nothing was then discovered. The site might well repay scientific excavation. It is at present a disused and somewhat derelict graveyard. In 1891, John Paton of H.M. Register House in Edinburgh, father of the then minister of the parish, dug up in the manse garden the bronze matrix of the seal of the priory of Whithorn. This is now in the Museum of Antiquities in Edinburgh and a facsimile has been sent to the museum at Stranraer.

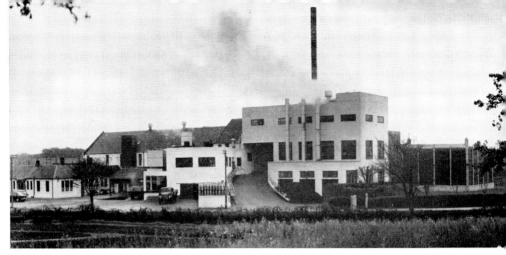

Plate 9. GALLOWAY CREAMERY, STRANRAER

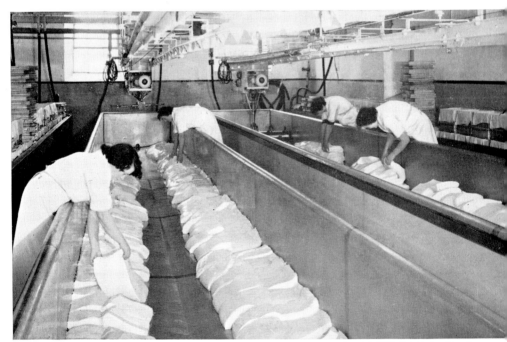

Plate 10. CHEESEMAKING AT THE GALLOWAY CREAMERY
The creamery, which was built in 1898, is soon to be replaced by a larger and more modern
plant.

F. H. McCarlie, Stranraer

Plate 11. A THATCHED COTTAGE NEAR THE MULL OF GALLOWAY

G. J. Edwards, Newton Stewart

Plate 12. NEW HOUSING, GLENLUCE
This scheme received a Civic Trust award.

In 1873, Charles E. Dalrymple discovered that the island in the Black Loch was artificial; it is 180 feet long and 135 feet broad at the widest part. A full description of this crannog can be found in the *Proceedings* of the Society of Antiquaries (Old Series Vol. 9, page 389).

In the museum of the County Library in Stranraer is a small collection of exhibits presented by the late Rev. R. S. G. Anderson, the last minister of the U.F. Church, Castle Kennedy, which includes some Bronze and Stone Age objects found in the parish. It also includes a pitchpipe used to 'set the tune' in the parish church in the early nineteenth century, and two collection ladles from Castle Kennedy U.F. Church. At Lochinch Castle and Lochryan House there are many interesting historical objects.

Population

Part of the parish of Inch falls within the burgh of Stranraer, and it is therefore not easy with the figures available to give completely accurate figures of the trend of the population since 1801. An increase in population from 1,577 to 3,122 at the beginning of the nineteenth century was probably due to improved methods of farming and the draining of marshland, resulting in more labour being employed on the farms, and to the influx of Irish immigrants. The decline after 1911 from 4,000 to 2,440 may fairly be attributed to the results of the first world war, to the burden of taxation on the great country houses which naturally led to large reductions of staff, both outdoor and indoor, and to the beginnings of the mechanisation of the farms. The decline in the size of families at this time must also be taken into account. The gradual rise from 1931 was due to the building of housing schemes, largely to accommodate the overspill from Stranraer. The mechanisation of farms continues, and families tend to remain small. Among the farmers, families of more than four are very uncommon, and families of one and two are common. Among the farm workers larger families do occur, but more than six is most unusual. There are, of course, exceptions, but generally speaking large families tend to show a low level of mentality, some of the children being little better than half-witted. Very few people pass the age of 84. In six years the parish minister has buried six infants of under 18 months.

Housing

There is no real centre of unity in the parish. Formerly Lochinch Castle would provide the needed focus point, but, with the decline of the great houses through taxation, and with the growth of Stranraer, the parish has tended to split into unrelated fragments. The village of Cairnryan, in the north west, has 133 houses, is now a parish *quoad sacra* and has a separate existence of its own. The village of New Luce spills over the boundary from the neighbouring parish on the north-east, and tends to attract to itself the life of the northern part of the parish. The village of Dunragit, lying across the Stranraer/Newton Stewart road, just outwith the parish, draws off the interest of that part which lies to the east. On the south-west, the flourishing community of Lochans, with 156 houses, and lying in the three parishes of Inch, Stoneykirk and Portpatrick, has a life and vigour of its own. A new council scheme of 50 houses at Bishopburn, on the fringe of Stranraer, is largely occupied by professional people who work in the town, and inevitably considers itself a residential suburb of Stranraer. The village of Castle Kennedy in the centre of the parish, consisting until recently of some twenty houses, was not strong enough to hold the parish together; recently, however, the county council has erected new houses here, and perhaps this virtually new centre of population will give the parish a sense of unity and individuality.

Fifty per cent of the population are native to the parish, 30 per cent come from neighbouring parishes, 12 per cent come from other counties in Scotland, seven per cent are English and one per cent are foreigners; these figures are approximate. Many of those who came from neighbouring parishes, and even from further afield, were squatters attracted by the army huts available after the war. With the pulling down of these huts, the number of these incomers has fallen greatly, but many have now obtained permanent houses in the parish; the other incomers have married local people and settled in the district. Most of the English have settled here through marriage, in many cases through being stationed here during the war, or through marrying some local men stationed in England. The foreigners (who are regarded with a certain suspicion by the natives) are either refugees or ex-prisoners of war. Most of the weekly shopping is done in Stranraer. The three little shops in Castle Kennedy do no more than a fraction of the local trade. The same is true of the shops at Lochans, and, perhaps to a lesser extent, of those at Cairnryan. The people of the parish go regularly into Stranraer to the two picture houses there. The Stranraer football ground draws in the men of the parish every Saturday afternoon. Many attend one or other of the Stranraer churches regularly. On a normal Friday afternoon you can find all the farmers of the parish in Stranraer, partly to do business, but partly to meet their friends and exchange news. With the exception of a new hotel at Cairnryan, there are no licensed premises in the parish, and it is to Stranraer that people go, more or less regularly, to have a drink.

Housing itself is in process of revolution. Many houses are most tastefully furnished, equalling in interior decoration anything to be seen in the most fashionable parts of a city. They are of medium size, eight apartments being the average. The cottages range from excellent to miserable. Many have recently been reconditioned and have electricity and hot and cold water but too many still have no adequate sanitation; most are well and cleanly kept, but a few are sordid to a degree. They are usually of two or three rooms; in some cases two cottages have been made into one good house. The new county council houses are uninteresting in appearance but are modern and convenient, and with few exceptions are excellently looked after. The village of Castle Kennedy thirty years ago was a picturesque beauty spot, its cottages in the summer smothered in climbing roses. Today it is drab and sadly in need of painting, and an air of decay hangs over it, though reconditioning is being carried out.

The village of Cairnryan was also once noted for its beauty as it nestled between the hills and the waters of Lochryan; thanks to the building of the railway from Stranraer to a military port there, it assumed the look of a railway siding.

During the war many army and air force camps were built throughout the parish, and one of these, that at Cairnryan, was occupied by the army until a few years ago; the others were taken over by squatters who appeared out of the blue. The history of one may be given as typical of all. At first, in 1947, the squatters were decent and respectable people who could get no other accommodation, and the village of huts was pleasant and cleanly. As the original squatters obtained permanent houses, their places were taken by others, but, as the huts were continually deteriorating, each change was for the worse, until only a few decent families were left in a community of wasters who were content to live in filth. These camps were gradually demolished, and none now remain in the parish.

Public Services

With the introduction of the county supply, water is now available in many more parts of the parish than it was up to a few years ago. Some farms have wells and also a piped supply and the benefits of the county project are reaching the cottagers throughout the parish. Electricity is the rule, though some forty per cent of the farm cottages are still lit by paraffin lamps. Coal and wood are the common fuel, but peat is still dug in the north of the parish.

The parish is served by ten doctors resident in Stranraer and one resident in Glenluce, while there are dentists, opticians, chiropodists and chemists in Stranraer; the hard-working and invaluable district nurse lives at Lochans. The usual arrangements for the medical examination of school children obtain. A general hospital of some thirty beds is located in Stranraer, and a maternity hospital has recently been opened there. Serious cases of illness are frequently sent to Ballochmyle Hospital in Ayrshire.

No policeman is resident in the landward area of the parish, which is patrolled by police cars from Stranraer and Glenluce; the fire station is in Stranraer.

Fifty years ago even the main roads from Girvan and Newton Stewart were rough metal with numerous pot holes. Today all are excellent in surface, but the secondary roads are often too narrow and have many dangerous bends and blind corners. Many of the private farm roads are still very bad. The frequent bus services from Cairnryan, Dunragit, Lochans and (on certain days of the week) New Luce have helped further to disintegrate the parish, but they have undoubtedly been a great boon to the country cottages; many people, however, still have a mile or so to walk to the nearest bus route. Grocers' and bakers' vans call once and in some cases twice a week at even the most isolated houses.

Education

There were five schools in the parish—at Inchparks (3-teacher), Castle Kennedy (1-teacher), Cairnryan (1-teacher), Lochans (7-teacher) and Rephad (7-teacher). Both Castle Kennedy and Inchparks were in need of modernisation and have now been replaced by one establishment. This new school is nicely situated at Castle Kennedy. The school at Lochans has recently been modernised. The school at Cairnryan was demolished when the military port was constructed at the beginning of the war. At first the children were housed in a wooden hut provided by the army, but later, because of the dumping of ammunition at Cairnryan, they were taken by bus into Stranraer; now the younger children are taught in the Y.M.C.A. building which has been purchased by the education authority.

The standard of education in the country schools tends to be low, largely because the level of intelligence is low. Few children pass the control examination and proceed to the High School in Stranraer; the majority attend the junior secondary school in the burgh. Handwriting is bad, spelling is shaky, history and geography are rudimentary. When the children of one school were questioned recently, it appeared that none (the maximum age being thirteen) had read any novels by Dickens or Scott; none had read any Shakespeare; *Robinson Crusoe, Alice in Wonderland* and Hans Andersen's and the Grimms' *Fairy Tales* were unknown. One boy aged twelve had started to read an abridged version of *Waverley*, but had found it too dull to finish. In country lore, however, they are knowledgeable. When the minister asked once in the Sunday School about an unusual bird song that he had heard, it was immediately identified for him. The children have on an average 2s. 6d. or 3s. a week for pocket money, and in addition their parents appear to buy them two and sometimes three comics a week. Innumerable ices and bags of potato crisps are also bought for them.

The usual youth organisations throughout the parish flourish or languish according to the leaders available. At the moment they languish, because of a dearth of people with the time or interest, which is not entirely due to a lack of public spirit, but is also due to the extremely hard-working character of the farming community, who exhaust their energies on the land. The former U.F. church building at Cairnryan was occupied during the war by the army, but in 1946 it was opened as a community centre, one of the first in the county. The flourishing Sunday Schools at Cairnryan, Inch and Lochans are well staffed with teachers, but the children drift away after they reach the age of twelve.

Agriculture and Industry

Some two hundred years ago most of the parish seems to have been poor land, but by the energy of the second and fifth Earls of Stair the level southern part of the parish was gradually transformed into rich agricultural land. The process has been continued during the last hundred years, and today many rich farms carry valuable dairy herds. The soil is, however, light with an underlying bed of gravel, and a long dry spell in the summer will burn the pasture brown. There is a saying in the district that 'The parish of Inch needs a shower every day and a wet day on Sunday'. There are 66 farms in the parish; 150 to 200 acres is an average size, but six of them are very small. There are seven small holdings. The herds of Galloway cattle, at one time almost universal, have disappeared, being replaced by other breeds which give a higher milk yield—particularly the Ayrshire. There is very little hand milking, most farms using machinery. The average yield is 700-900 gallons a year; a cow giving only 700 is considered hardly to earn its keep. In the north end of the parish sheep farming is mainly practised, and the common breed is the Blackface. There has been a great decline in cheesemaking; thirty years ago many farmers specialised in cheese, but it is now a rare thing to find a farmer who makes any at all. The result has been a decline in pig rearing, for the pigs were fed on the by-products of the cheese; some farmers still keep pigs, and the common breed is the Large White cross, but there is little pedigree breeding.

The parish shares with the rest of the country in the revolution worked by the tractor: except in the hill country horse ploughing is now a rare sight. The introduction of artificial fertilisers has added to the productivity of the land, and they are used intensively. The use of wild white clover has largely replaced the older grasses for pasture land, the nitrogen released by the roots of the clover being a valuable addition to the mineral content of the soil. Poultry are kept on all the most up-to-date systems.

Owing to the high cost of draining, much acreage, particularly on the farms of Aird, Deerpark, Mahaar, Mark and Barsolus and on the church glebe, is marsh; some of this was once good land. One field which before the war would bear a heavy crop of the highest quality is now a bog, the haunt of wild duck and the breeding ground (owing to the sewage from neighbouring farms running into it) of mosquitoes, which in the summer are often a vicious nuisance for several miles around.

While agriculture is the main employment and there is no other industry in the parish, some find employment in the creameries at Dunragit and in Stranraer, while many are employed on Lochinch estate as game-keepers, gardeners, foresters, domestic servants and tradesmen, though the estate staff is a skeleton of what it was fifty years ago. Some work in shops and offices in Stranraer, others at a sawmill at Castle Kennedy, and the new water scheme at Penwhirn also provides employment. Only two blacksmiths' shops are left in the parish, but a number of garages have opened in recent years and are flourishing. One lady recently started the manufacture of furniture in the finest traditions of craftsmanship, and employed two female assistants, but marriage ended this venture.

Culture, Manners and Morals

Few people read serious literature; their number is not likely to be more than thirty. The minister once noticed a volume of the poems of Donne among the books in a farmhouse, but it looked very new and was probably a wedding present. Novels are more widely read, but few of these are bought, most being obtained from the County Library, though a few people are members of one of the well-known book clubs. Newspapers, including the Sunday papers, are read universally, and the local paper, *The Galloway Advertiser and Wigtownshire Free Press*, finds its way into every house. Music is scarcely practised. Singing, in the schools and in the church, is painful to an educated ear, and only a few, chiefly among the older people, still play the fiddle admirably for dancing. Wireless sets are to be found in almost every house, but it is hard indeed to discover anyone who listens to the Third Programme. Television sets are present in large numbers.

There are many keen gardeners, principally among the cottagers. Most farmers have an efficient knowledge of modern science in its application to agriculture. The baking of the farmers' wives is superb, and an invitation to tea at a farmhouse leaves the city dweller speechless (in every sense). The younger women in the farm cottages do not appear to bake so much, perhaps because they are often out at work in the fields, and among them shop-bought cakes are more common than formerly. It is astonishing, however, that such magnificent baking is still produced by the older women, even in old-fashioned range ovens which are heated by a small fire kindled underneath them.

The amusements of the younger people are dances, the cinema, and, for the men, the football match in Stranraer on a Saturday afternoon. Bowls are popular and there is a green at Castle Kennedy. Indoor bowls are played in the Castle Kennedy Hall. Curling is a favourite game in the season, sometimes on the curling pond at Castle Kennedy, but mostly at Ayr. Badminton is played at Castle Kennedy, but tennis seems to attract few. Whist drives are highly popular.

The very noticeable class distinction between the farmers and the farm workers may be partly explained by the fact that farms remain in the same family for several generations, whereas the workers tend to shift from year to year and do not grow the same roots in the countryside. Moreover, it must be admitted that the poor housing and the economic conditions of a past age have left their mark, for the best type of worker left the district to better himself. Farm workers now dress excellently, and plough-men may be seen wearing a silk shirt and a suit of impeccable cut.

As is the case in the rest of the county, fornication is so common as to pass almost unremarked. Out of 32 children baptised in the parish church in 1953 six were illegitimate. Adultery seems to be rare. Swearing is widespread, and even children scarcely able to speak will use language that is foul. Poaching is very common. Yet, while these are things that may catch the eye of any visitor, those who live in the parish become aware that the people as a whole are hard-working, kindly and thrifty, and have a stubbornly ingrained, if often shadowy, Christianity.

In a past age the parish seems to have had many worthies, but this is no longer true; nor is it easy to discover any old or remarkable proverbial sayings still in use. One of the most astonishing features of the parish, however, is the rapidity with which rumours, arising apparently nowhere, spread over the entire countryside. As one man said to me, 'Half the lies they tell at the Inch aren't true'. There is even a famous case of a gentleman enlivening the weary hours of a slow recovery from illness by reading the letters of condolence which, somewhat prematurely, had been sent to his supposed widow. The rumour-monger is irrepressible, and, to quote another local saying, 'A bowl o' meal wouldna' stap the moues o' them that say that'.

Famous People

The parish has its share of famous men. John, sixth Earl of Cassillis, who used to 'retire himself betwixt sermons' to a little island in the White Loch, was one of the commissioners to the Westminster Assembly of Divines. James Dalrymple, first Viscount Stair, was perhaps the greatest jurist that Scotland has produced. The lives of many others of the Dalrymples of Stair are interwoven with the history of their country. Mrs. Dunlop, the charming correspondent of Burns, was the daughter of Colonel Agnew of Lochryan. Sir John Ross, the intrepid Arctic navigator, was born at Soulseat Manse on 24 June 1777. The Rev. James Aikman Paton, minister of the parish from 1879 to 1916, was well enough known in his day as the cultivator of many new varieties of potatoes. Mrs. John B. Chalmers, till the untimely death of her husband resident at Aird Farm, but now returned to her native New Zealand, is a cousin of Sir Edmund Hillary, the conqueror of Mount Everest.

Written 1954
Additions made 1962

CHAPTER 16

THE PARISH AND BURGH OF STRANRAER

by M. C. ARNOTT

Parish and Burgh

Stranraer parish is actually only the core of the burgh and extends to a mere 59 acres of the 917 acres included within the town's boundaries; the remainder are fairly evenly divided between Inch and Leswalt. For all practical purposes, however, the Inch and Leswalt portions are under the jurisdiction of the burgh authorities. Until a few years ago the residents of these two areas enjoyed a slightly lower rate (usually ½d. in the £) than was imposed on the Stranraer parish inhabitants, but now all ratepayers in the burgh are treated alike. The electoral roll still differentiates between the burghal and landward areas of Inch and Leswalt, but otherwise the portions of these parishes in the town are part and parcel of Stranraer. From the time of the Reform Act of 1832 until 1935 the burgh covered an area of 387 acres. In the summer of 1935 the boundaries were extended to bring in other 238 acres and in 1960 an additional acreage of 292 was included.

Population

Since the housing schemes began, many of the people who resided in the heart of the burgh have removed to new quarters in the Inch and Leswalt burghal areas and so the population of Stranraer parish has sharply decreased. The Census figures for this part of the town show that for the first thirty years of the present century there was little change in numbers, but since 1931 the drop has been very marked. The comparative figures are as follows:—In 1801—1,722; 1851—3,877; 1861—4,022 (maximum); 1901—2,856; 1911—2,866; 1921—2,723; 1931—2,802; 1951—1,465. In Stranraer burgh the total population in 1961 was 9,249 compared with 6,635 in the smaller area that belonged to it before the boundaries were first extended.

At one time the Irish element was conspicuous in Stranraer and district, but it is nowadays less evident. There is a resemblance between the local accent and the Irish tongue: strangers frequently comment on the fact and many local people have been asked from what part of Ireland they come. The natural inference is that the presence of large numbers of Irish folk in the district a century and more ago left its imprint on the language. When Stranraer people go to Ireland, however, they are quick to note the difference of accent.

Marriages between Scots and Irish are still recorded, but the number is not large. Although many of the residents are descended from Stranraer families, a large proportion come from other districts. Nearly all the professional people hail from counties or towns outside Wigtownshire and there is a leavening of 'outsiders' amongst the shopkeepers and trades-people. In recent years the number of residents from England has increased, chiefly as a result of war-time exigencies. There are three Italian families. People with an Ayrshire connection are numerous both in the town and in the farming areas around. The North of Scotland is well represented and natives of most parts of the country are included in the burgh's population.

During the latter part of the last century there was an exodus of Stranraer people to Canada and the United States. This trend continued into the present century and the stream of emigrants still goes on, to America, South Africa, Australia, New Zealand and to a less extent to the Orient. Scarcely a year passes without someone coming back to old haunts and old friends and the 'exiles' who return are able to speak of success achieved overseas. At one time many Stranraer men went to sea, but there are fewer nowadays, although the Royal Navy attracts a number of recruits each year, many local men serve on the cross-channel service, and others are to be found in the Merchant Navy.

The Impact of War

Like many other towns, large and small, Stranraer underwent a trans-formation after 1939. Greater changes have been witnessed in the past decade than in the preceding sixty years. The town has taken on a new appearance and the people have become more sophisticated, more cosmopolitan, less Gallovidian. Before the war had long begun soldiers and airmen were arriving in small groups, which grew into battalions and squadrons as the months and years passed. By the summer of 1940 a transit camp had been established on the outskirts of the town and the golf club lost its course to meet military needs. For six years the former links accommodated men from many of the allied countries, with British and American troops predominating. In all, over a million men passed through the camp.

Squadrons of R.A.F. flying boats were stationed at Lochryan, which laps the burgh's western fringe; airfields spread themselves around the environs of the town; army camps sprang up; and very quietly No. 2 Military Port at Cairnryan began to take shape. By the spring of 1942 this project had been completed by the Royal Engineers and the Royal Pioneer Corps and the first ship to leave the harbour—a destroyer—conveyed the late King George VI and Queen Elizabeth to Northern Ireland in secret. The port was closed in 1959.

In the interval the town and countryside around had seen many changes and Stranraer had assumed a new character. Many of the serving officers were occupying houses or rooms and there was a continual coming and going of troops who were billeted for brief periods on householders, in addition to the soldiers who were quartered in camps. Americans came to swell the number of strangers and later prisoners were brought in large numbers—Italians and Germans. At one stage a contingent of Poles arrived in the district, but this was after hostilities had ceased.

This immigration of new people with their own distinctive attitude to life, their habits and customs, made the Stranraer people realise that there were places and things in the world that had not hitherto come within their ken. Friendships sprang up, ideas were exchanged and horizons were widened. Many of the men found the attractions of the Stranraer girls irresistible and war weddings became frequent. After the war a proportion of the erstwhile sailors, soldiers and airmen who had left their wives in Stranraer returned to take up residence in the town, if not permanently, for long enough to influence the atmosphere of the Galloway seaport and to imbue many of the inhabitants with a less parochial outlook.

By now the tide of immigration has subsided, but the burgh has still a substantial quota of people from other parts. Wig Bay seaplane base was occupied mostly by men from Northern Ireland employed by a Belfast firm on the maintenance of Sunderland aircraft and the Irish brogue mingled with the distinctive accent of the Gallovidians. This establishment was closed in 1957 after 16 years as a flying boat base.

Housing

The accession of married couples to the town's population intensified the demand for housing, already acute, and affected in other ways the affairs of the community. Pressure on school accommodation was greatly increased, demands on the welfare services rose and the provision of playing fields and facilities for recreation presented problems that had to be tackled with vigour.

The town council had in the inter-war years carried out a good deal of building, but the slowing down of operations during the war and the heavy demands for accommodation after 1945 created new difficulties. The county council were also involved, as they had to provide houses for many of their officials on the outskirts of the burgh, as well as for people resident outside the town but employed in Stranraer. Restrictions on the quantities of material available handicapped the councils in their efforts to meet the urgent demands and it required much energy, patience and diplomacy to deal with the situation. Traditional houses up to the limit allowed were planned and built, prefabricated dwellings were erected, and, after a descent on camps by 'squatters', the occupation of huts was brought within the official ambit.

At the end of January 1953, the thousandth permanent house provided by the town council was opened, but the community's housing needs have not yet been met and there is a long waiting list. At the end of 1962 there were 2,772 houses in the burgh. Of these 1,593 were owned by the town council and 1,179 by other proprietors. The council's share included 70 prefabricated houses. Over 700 houses are owner-occupied and there are 209 shops. Whole areas have been brought within the municipal orbit. To the south are Murrayfield, Dick's Hill, Moorefield, Belmont, Sheuchan Parks and Parklea schemes. There are several schemes at the west end; to the east there are groups at Royal Avenue and Marine Gardens; and nearer the centre of the town are Broomfield Gardens. The appearance of many parts of the town has been transformed and people returning from abroad after a long absence are struck by the change. Shops and other business premises in the heart of the town have also been undergoing a process of alteration and improvement in conformity with modern ideas. But throughout the town there still remain old properties that detract from the appearance of the streets, some of them derelict and others used as stores.

Many of Stranraer's main streets are narrow and irregular, and the traffic problem has caused the local authority and the police much concern. There are several bottlenecks, where strict control has to be enforced, and to ease congestion unilateral parking, introduced in the autumn of 1952, proved beneficial, though not to the liking of some tradesmen who have on alternate days to carry their goods across the street when loading or unloading is in progress. This was followed in 1960 by the imposition of one-way traffic in the town centre. Comprehensive plans for future development have been prepared by the planning authority for the county, in conjunction with an Edinburgh consultant.

Local Services

As Stranraer is a small burgh, many of the public services are administered by the county council and the apathy that marks the municipal elections suggests that the ratepayers do not take as much interest in local affairs as they used to do. The town council has a strong representation on the county council, but many feel that the administration of the services is something remote.

Welfare work by the local authority has expanded. The former poorhouse, now known as Waverley House, is regarded as a benign and comfortable institution, where the modern approach has brought about many improvements and where much kindly care is bestowed on the aged and frail. A children's home has been set up in London Road, where a former boarding house was transformed for the purpose, and a home for old folks has been provided by the county council.

Stranraer has now a plentiful water supply and is in fact able to assist the county authority in providing for the needs of people in districts adjacent to the burgh. The sewerage system has been improved in recent times, but with the growth in population and the construction of new housing schemes the needs of the town in this respect have not yet been fully met. The town council are faced with heavy expenditure in their efforts to provide adequate facilities. Flooding during heavy rain was a recurrent problem. Expensive schemes to overcome the trouble were carried out, but more remains to be done under the development plan.

An important addition was recently made to the gas works, which were in the hands of a local company before the industry was nationalised. As a result the supply has been perceptibly improved, and the service is regarded as most satisfactory. All public and nearly all private lighting, however, is carried out by electricity; the current comes from the Grid and is generated in Kirkcudbrightshire. Occasional trouble arises when the overhead cables are damaged during storms and the supply is interrupted. A private company provided the electricity prior to nationalisation and the staff now operate under the South of Scotland Electricity Board.

Parts of ten farms are included in the burgh area. In all 95 acres are under cultivation and 78 acres are in permanent grass. The annual rent for the farmland is around £2 an acre and the ground is feued to the holders by the proprietors, Stair Estates, and the Sheuchan Land Company, mostly on a 14 years' basis.

All the municipal housing tenants are provided with gardens and most of them tend the plots with care. In the summer months some of the surroundings are ablaze with colour. Other tenants concentrate on vegetables. To encourage the keeping of tidy and artistic gardens the town council offer prizes from time to time. For several years the council organised a horticultural show, and then a horticultural society was revived under the guidance of the council. Lectures and 'brains trusts', arranged by the society, have proved popular ventures during the winter.

Education

The housing question has impinged on the realm of education. A difference of opinion arose between the town council and the education authority as to whether certain ground should be utilised for educational purposes or for houses. Both sides held firmly to their view and to have the problem solved the council appealed to the Secretary of State for Scotland, who decided in favour of the claims of education.

In 1936 a new primary school was opened and two outmoded establishments were closed—Lewis Street and Sheuchan (Madras) schools. Within a short time the Lewis Street building was taken over as a Labour Exchange, and it is now modernised. For some years Sheuchan was left empty, but after the outbreak of war it became a centre for instruction in air raid precautions; the building was recently improved and re-opened as a school, with open spaces left for playing fields in the vicinity. It was at this point that the two local authorities came into conflict. At the same time, to meet the needs of the quickly growing population in the east end, a new single-storey primary school was erected at Rephad. Thus the town pattern was determined, and the zoning of the children to the primary school nearest their area was carried through with the minimum of fuss.

The oldest school in the town is the Academy which, dating back to 1844, is now the centre for junior secondary education; close by is the Annexe which comes under the same headmastership as the Academy. In the near vicinity is the High School, where a five years' secondary course is provided and the pupils who pass the Leaving Certificate examinations may qualify for entrance to the Universities. In 1962 the education authority after much deliberation decided to construct a building consisting of a high school and an academy to take the place of the two existing schools. The cost was estimated at over £750,000 and work was begun in November of that year.

Primary instruction is given at Park School, Sheuchan, Rephad and St. Joseph's R.C. School. At the end of 1960 there was a total enrolment at the Stranraer schools of 2,000, the highest on record: 368 pupils at the High School, 374 at the Academy, 577 at Park, 273 at Rephad, 276 at Sheuchan and 132 at St. Joseph's. Among the scholars at the High School are a number of children from the surrounding rural districts. Under a recent centralisation scheme, pupils are brought in to the Academy from Cairnryan, Inchparks, Lochans, Castle Kennedy and Portpatrick, and this development has raised the school population.

In the junior secondary school stress is laid on practical work, such as woodwork, gardening and metal work, with domestic subjects for the girls. Encouragement is given to the pupils to take part in corporate activities: there are school choirs, instruction in dancing and team sports. Free choice periods are included in the curriculum, the list of subjects comprising sewing, handwork, drama and leatherwork, while pupils are given guidance in the use of the school library.

Motor transport brings the children from the outlying districts to school and home again, so that the school buses are a regular feature of the daily arrivals and departures in the town traffic. There is no doubt that inter-mixing of the young people outside the walls of the school and the trips through the countryside have sharpened the wits of the children and dispelled the 'countrified' atmosphere that used to characterise rural groups when the young folks were more or less isolated and their vision was limited to a small part of the parish.

Many of the High School pupils come from the small villages or farms and they reside in the town for the greater part of the week. At one time this arrangement did not receive general approval, as some parents were of the opinion that their children's welfare might suffer, if the adolescents were for most of the time away from home. Such objections are rarely heard now, as it has been found that the supervision of the teachers and the care shown by the landladies are such that the behaviour and health of the children are not impaired and, indeed, that the experience is beneficial. It is noteworthy that the juvenile delinquents dealt with in the courts very rarely include children from the outlying districts attending the town schools.

There is a virile High School Former Pupils' Association, whose annual reunion is the occasion for recollection and reminiscence and whose activities include the provision of prizes for leadership. With a membership of 90 the association is representative of the younger generations of former pupils; veterans of the old days form only a small minority. Much is heard of schools being different from what they used to be, but it is still a fact that the date to which most pupils look forward is their last day at school. Continuation classes attract only a small number of young people in search of further education, and the most popular of these classes are those devoted to country dancing and dressmaking, which are attended for the most part by married women. Tuition in the dramatic art is also given and in this branch the 'under twenties' are prominent.

Cultural Activities

For a long time Stranraer had a vigorous literary and debating society, which was revived recently after a moribund phase, when many of the members were on war service or otherwise fully engaged. In the intervening period, the W.E.A. courses of lectures and discussions attracted large attendances, especially in the immediate post-war years, but interest faded and these activities have ceased. There has, however, been a revival of concern with music. The Wigtownshire Musical Association was formed while the war was in progress and soon afterwards the Stranraer Musical Association came into being. A little later the Education Committee, spurred on by these associations, appointed a musical organiser for the county and fostered a quickening of interest both in vocal and instrumental music. Oratorios are given occasionally, concert versions are presented of such operas as *Merrie England* and *Maritana* and occasional 'popular' concerts are arranged. In earlier days the Choral Union gave performances of Gilbert and Sullivan operas, which are still recalled with pleasure; but the 'Choral' is now only a memory.

A recent development is a music and verse-speaking festival for young people, promoted by the county education authority. Held in Stranraer, the festival attracts boy and girl entrants from all parts of the county, but especially from the surrounding district, while the singing, instrumental music and verse-speaking are judged by adjudicators with a national reputation. One of the curious and disappointing features of the festival is that it fails to attract an audience of adults, despite the most cordial invitations. It is only when the closing concert is held that the older people attend; and, although large numbers of children are interested in music when at school, few of them continue to sing or play in later years—but this appears to be a national habit.

An Antiquarian Society was formed in 1955 and has a membership of about a hundred. Monthly meetings are held throughout the autumn and winter and many people of note in the field of archaeology have given lectures on local subjects and national themes. Under the auspices of the Scottish Community Drama Association, local amateur theatrical productions began to take the place of professional performances, and within a few years the district drama festivals jumped into public popularity. In Stranraer they frequently ran for three nights, but recently the number of entries has fallen away. Stranraer has for long had at least one amateur dramatic club (for a time there were two societies) and plays were presented regularly. In addition performances are given under the aegis of the Arts Council, in conjunction with the musical association and the W.R.I. The first ballet performance in current memory was given in the town towards the end of 1952 and was witnessed by a crowded house. Occasional classes are arranged for drama producers and for instruction in stagecraft, but these have a specialised appeal.

For entertainment outside the home, however, nothing approaches the films in the estimation of Stranraer people, and the two picture houses in town have come to be regarded as the regular source of diversion and amusement. Many people visit them twice or thrice weekly, and the effect of film going on feminine fashions, on idiom, and on subjects of conversation, is readily apparent. Finally, within the short period of eight years, television so jumped into popularity that by 1960 two out of every three houses in the town had this form of indoor entertainment. A new craze swept the town in 1962 when 'bingo' made its appearance and the weekly sessions attracted hundreds of participants.

Sport and Recreation

Rivalry on the football field among Wigtownshire clubs dates far back and Stranraer could boast at one time of several teams. Local matches were events that are still recalled with relish by those who participated in the games of forty and fifty years ago. Nowadays Stranraer is represented in senior football by an all-professional team and rarely does the eleven contain more than one local player. It might be thought that this would tend to reduce public interest, but the reverse is the case. Attendances are now counted in thousands as compared with hundreds in earlier years, for Stranraer F.C. compete in the Second Division of the Scottish League, and the crowds converge on the enclosure from miles around, coming by bus, cycle and car. And during the week football takes its place above all others as a topic of conversation.

Across the way from Stair Park is the Rugby pitch, on the site of the old Cattle Show field. Here are played the home matches of the Wigtownshire Rugby Club, a vigorous organisation, which, however, has but a small following; attendances are dwarfed by the crowds who flock to the 'soccer' matches. The players are practically all ex-public school pupils, who learned the game in Edinburgh or Glasgow. The others are mostly former High School pupils.

Besides the senior club, numerous soccer teams consist of youths who take part in organised local competitions, and the school leagues bring boys from a wide district, extending from Drummore to New Luce, into Stranraer on Saturday mornings to play in matches under the discerning eyes of their teachers. School pupils also take part in hockey, rugby and netball matches, and their fixture lists include matches with their opposite numbers in Girvan, Newton Stewart, Kirkcudbright and other schools.

With the coming of indoor ice rinks, the age-old game of curling has entered a new phase. Prior to this latest development Stranraer had a tarmac ice rink and for a time the more enthusiastic curlers foregathered there for a game when the lochs in the neighbourhood were only thinly coated with ice. But, when a rink with facilities for curling all through the autumn and winter was constructed at Ayr in 1937, a decisive change was brought about. Games can now be arranged without reference to the vagaries of the weather and bonspiels are organised on the definite understanding that play will go on. Curlers were quick to recognise the advantages of having a rink within motoring distance and now hardly a week passes from October to March without an exodus to Ayr either for a competition or for a 'bounce' match. Some of the younger people visit the rink to skate, but the number is small, as Stranraer's winters are generally mild and skating is not a sport at which many of the residents excel. They can hold their own, however, at such winter indoor sports as badminton and table tennis, both of which have attained great popularity in recent times, with numerous clubs in the town taking part in league contests and cup competitions.

Quoiting, once a popular sport, has died away, probably because of the change-over from horse-power to mechanical power on the farms. Cricket is enjoying a mild revival with an eight-a-side league, but there is little likelihood of a resumption of the scale of the years between the wars. Outdoor tennis has a large following in the summer months; indeed, the courts provided by the town council and those of the Sun Street club are taxed to their uttermost at the height of the season. There have always been good swimmers in Stranraer but the annual regatta ceased some years ago. Sailing on the loch has recovered some of its popularity, although the great days of yacht racing, around 1880 and 1890, have not since been paralleled. Perhaps this recession of interest has been due to the advance of golf. In the early days of the century a course was laid out to the east of the town, along the shores of Lochryan, and from small beginnings the membership increased and expansion was continuing, when in 1940 the course was requisitioned as the site of a transit camp. From then until six years after the war ended, Stranraer golfers had to journey to Portpatrick to enjoy a game. By 1951 a new course had been constructed and it was formally opened the following year, the ground having been bequeathed by the late Major Garroway. With the opening of this 18-hole course at Creachmore, stretching along the western shores of the Loch and regarded as potentially of championship class, there has been a remarkable accession to the ranks of golfers in the town and the game has touched a new peak of popularity.

There are two bowling greens in the burgh. The centenary of the Stranraer Club was celebrated in 1959, while the other, the West End Club, was formed in 1925, when much of the constructional work was carried out by a group of artisan members. Though there is keen rivalry on the greens when the clubs are in opposition, a spirit of sportsmanship and camaraderie exists among bowlers and this pleasant atmosphere has become more apparent in recent years.

Among indoor recreations, dancing is predominant; country dancing enjoys a vogue, but it is the modern type that evokes real enthusiasm, and no sooner are new dances introduced on a national scale than they become a feature of the local programmes, which are carried out with the accepted ritual of the day. The cult of the American Square Dance was short-lived. Almost as popular as dancing are whist drives, which appeal most to the senior generation, with women players usually in the majority, and which are very effective methods of raising funds for local charities. At the several Bridge clubs, the atmosphere is less care-free than at the whist drives, while league matches and occasional tournaments lend variety to the activities of the players, who mostly concentrate on weekly games confined to club members.

Pigeon-racing has increased in popularity and there are two homing societies in the town. A poultry, pigeon and cagebird society has since the war held well-supported annual shows, including large numbers of budgerigars; a budgerigar society was formed a few years ago and the members are enthusiastic exhibitors. Since 1945 dog shows have been held regularly by the Canine Club and these attract entries from many parts of the South-West. Stranraer Harriers have a fair membership of young athletes; and the Wheelers have a programme of cycling events in the course of the summer. An archery club was started but it had a short life; the members were mostly drawn from the Post Office. But another organisation, the Car and Motor Cycle Club, has maintained its position as a social organisation.

Youth Activities

Much has been done of late for the youth of the town. Shortly before the outbreak of war a Boys' Club was established, commodious premises were acquired, and enthusiastic young men strove to provide lads just out of school with attractive recreations and hobbies. These activities were curtailed when the premises were taken over for service purposes, but were resumed after the war. About the same time the Education Committee appointed a youth organiser. Week-ends for the training of leaders were instituted and youth work took on a new aspect, with a youth panel in general control. At the moment more is being done for the welfare of young people than ever before and in time the results should be highly beneficial for the community. There are, of course, groups of the national and international organisations in the town—Boy Scouts and Cubs, Girl Guides and Brownies, a company of the Boys' Brigade, a unit of the Army Cadet Force, a squadron of the A.T.C., a company of the Girls' Guildry and others.

Emphasis is placed on team games in the work among the youth and in recent years groups from Stranraer and district have been taking part in inter-county sports. Facilities for recreation have recently been expanded by the opening of a King George V Playing Field, situated between two of the largest housing schemes, on a site formerly known as Archie's Bog and part of the old Trotting Track; towards the costs a grant of £3,000 was received from the trust. Open spaces and playing fields have been provided in various parts of the town. Not long before the King George V Field was opened Agnew Park had been laid out at the west end, consisting partly of reclaimed ground and bordering Agnew Crescent Bay—for long known as the Clayhole. Reclamation work went on at the bay during the inter-war years and ranked for unemployment relief grants; the partial filling-in of the bay was the subject of controversy, but as the work proceeded criticism ceased and ultimately Agnew Park emerged.

2G

It is really a children's playground with swings, paddling pool and a putting green. More ambitious plans reached fruition in 1962 with the opening of a marine lake in the same vicinity.

Stair Park, divided from Agnew Park by almost the whole length of the town, is the most imposing and decorative of all the public parks. Presented to the town in 1905 by the Earl of Stair, the enclosure is extensive and attractively laid out, with rows of trees lining some of the paths, spacious flower beds, a bandstand, a putting green, tennis courts with pavilion, and a paddling pond (constructed on the site of a war-time emergency supply tank). With its wrought iron gates and railings framing a wealth of rhododendrons and other shrubs, Stair Park provides a pleasant approach to the town from the east.

Organised Labour

There are few tradesmen or artisans who are not members of trades unions. Railwaymen are numerous in Stranraer and they are highly organised, as are the road transport employees. There is a Trades Council, but the public hears little about its activities.

Politics

At General Elections the Labour Party is vigorous, organising the local campaign on the recognised lines. Their activities reached a peak in the immediate post-war years. For a time official Labour candidates took part in the municipal elections and returned members; only the Labour Party did so and this innovation died away a few years ago. As part of Galloway, Stranraer was represented by a Conservative M.P. (John McKie), who held the seat from 1931 until his death in 1959, when he was succeeded by Mr. John Brewis, Ardwell. A Junior Unionist Association is the most active local section of the Conservative and Unionist organisation; between elections the seniors hold occasional meetings and social gatherings. After a quiet spell the Liberals are again active and fought hard in two 1959 campaigns.

Farming

Amid the changes that have taken place, Stranraer has not altered much industrially. Farming is its life-blood, and market day, with all that it means in a country town, is still observed. As main developments in farming during the past sixty years, dairying and the growing of early potatoes have forged ahead to such an extent that they now dominate the life of the community. In the parishes that surround the town and those that extend southwards to the Mull of Galloway, the dairy herds contain some of the cream of the Ayrshire breed. Only a few years ago the highest price ever paid for an Ayrshire Bull—9,000 guineas—was given for a stirk by a farmer in the Dunragit district, some five miles from the town; conversely, cows and bulls bred in the Rhins of Galloway frequently make top prices at the stock sales, many going into England or overseas. Rather curiously, Stranraer itself is not an important centre for the sale of Ayrshire cattle. Castle-Douglas and Ayr have become recognised venues and so Wigtownshire stock is transported to these markets in large numbers. For many years there were two auction marts in Stranraer, but the only auctioneering company now represented in the town has its headquarters at Ayr and the staff journey south to Stranraer for the weekly markets and special sales.

Herds of Ayrshires numbering from 60 to 100 cows, with followers, are common and an enormous amount of milk is produced, mostly for delivery at the two creameries in the town, where it is tested and bulked for dispatch to the cities. These creameries handle anything up to 90,000 gallons of milk a day and are fitted with all modern equipment; a proportion of the milk is retained for conversion into cheese or milk powder. Until the advent of the Scottish Milk Marketing Board in 1933 the manufacture of cheese was carried on regularly at over three hundred farms in the county, but this practice has now virtually died out. A substantial price is paid for milk by the board and this changed the farmers' attitude: rather than face the risks and costs of cheese-making, they decided that sending off the raw milk was a better economic proposition and acted accordingly. The scarcity of labour during the war also affected the situation and most farmers—though not all—have given up cheese-making. The quality of the cheese made at the creameries on a large scale is reflected in the many prizes gained at the London Dairy Show and other exhibitions; that the farm cheese-makers are also expert in their art is borne out by the fact that they too continue to receive leading awards at the shows. Under present methods no part of the milk is regarded as unusable. There was a time when whey at the factories was put into the sea, but now it is converted into casein, which is used extensively in the manufacture of buttons, umbrella handles and other articles. Whey butter is also manufactured and compares well with other types. On the farms in earlier days whey was given as food to the pigs and pig-rearing played an important part in the economics of dairy farming. Many pigs are still reared in the district and there are two factories which handle thousands of animals each year. The older of these factories was set up in the early years of the century and is now completely controlled by farmers, with a manager carrying out the work according to the wishes of the company directors. The other was established after the war and operates under private ownership.

Early potatoes are grown from the shores of Lochryan all the way down to Kirkmaiden, with such success that supplies from the Rhins of Galloway are invariably first on the city market—sometimes in the closing days of May, but mostly in the opening days of June. Several of the early farms are near the town. Expert knowledge is required for the successful growing of early potatoes and the farmers engaged therein spend many a worrying day during the spring. Frost is the enemy of the crop and May frosts are dreaded most; some farmers during the critical stages place braziers in the fields, as smoke and warmed air drifting over the fields give effective protection. There are two chief methods of marketing the potatoes: in one case the merchant buys the crop as he sees it and pays an agreed acreage price, and in the other the farmer sells the potatoes on a tonnage basis. During the lifting season large squads of workers go out from Stranraer to the farms to raise the crops. Both men and women take part in the work, adults receiving £1 a day in wages and the young people only a little less. Turnip-thinning is now carried out in the same way by contractors. At one time large numbers of men and women came from Northern Ireland to assist in the harvesting operations and during the war the contingents increased in size. In many cases they were provided with living accommodation at the farms. Within the past few years their numbers have decreased.

The introduction of new varieties of oats has led to earlier harvesting. Nowadays the cutting of grain sometimes starts in the first week of August and it is very often well under way by the middle of the month. In an average season the harvest is well over by mid-September, whereas many people remember the days when the 'hairst' was not completed until October was well in. The shortening of harvest time has brought, according to men of knowledge, a tendency to rush the operations: they contend that a slower process is preferable, that in the pre-war days the grain was given a better chance to dry, and that present practices lead to heating and deterioration of the crop. That applies to 'binder' harvesting. The arrival of the combine harvester has brought about important changes and one of these is that the millers have to deal with a heavy inrush concentrated into a few weeks. Oats, potatoes and turnips are the chief crops. More barley is now grown than formerly, but very little wheat is produced.

Farm work has been transformed since the appearance of the motor tractor over thirty years ago. The pace of the change was quickened during the second world war, when labour became scarce, manufacturers produced far more tractors, and the use of machines was officially encouraged: within a few years the farming community had become mechanically minded. This attitude owed something to the changed outlook of the young men returning from the forces, with knowledge and skill in mechanics, and a strong preference for machines, which could accomplish much more in a given time than was possible with a team of horses; in addition, when the day's work in the fields was over, no grooming or feeding was required. Farmers who were slow to turn to tractors found difficulty in hiring men, who had become accustomed to handling machines instead of horses.

Every year the number of horses shows a decrease. At one time the Rhins of Galloway was noted as a horse-breeding district and the streets of Stranraer echoed to the clop of horses and the ring of shoe metal. Today the street sounds consist mostly of the rumble of tractors and the beating of motor engines. The last of the railway horses disappeared ten years ago. Time was when they brought from the station into the town most of the supplies that had come by rail and hauled loads as far as Drummore in one direction and Glenapp in the other; now their places have been filled by motor lorries. Horses are retained at the farms for certain purposes, but mechanisation has developed to such an extent that the number is only a fraction of what it used to be. A few breeders remain and Clydesdale classes are still important on a small scale at Stranraer show. At the ploughing matches, three of which are still held in the county each year, the tractors dominate the field, but the traditional custom of giving prizes for best decorations and best-kept harness continues: the 'old fashioned' ploughman and his employer hang on grimly to the glories of the past.

There is still one 'smiddy' located in the burgh, but only very occasionally is the blacksmith seen in his shop at the age-old job of shoeing horses. In recent times a practice has grown up of making the shoes in the 'smiddy' and going out to the farms by motor to complete the task there, instead of the farmer bringing the horses to the blacksmith. So great, however, has been the falling-off in the number of horses that the blacksmith has now very little to do. In one of the 'smiddies' which was formerly regarded as the largest in the South-West, 300 horses came regularly to be shod from the farms, hotels, bakers, grocers and others; today there are no horses in the town and the smith's job has almost disappeared, for odds and ends are not enough to keep the forge going.

Stranraer Cattle Show has long been a feature of the summer season. There were several occasions about seventy years ago when the show had to be cancelled as a result of cattle diseases and this trouble arose again in 1952, when a foot-and-mouth outbreak in the Machars district led to cancellations. For many years the show was held on the ground that became the transit camp in 1940, and thereafter various locations were used until a so-called permanent site was found on a Bridge of Aird field, a short distance from the old show field; this, however, is the area that has been chosen for two schools. Fortunately, the original field has now been made available once more.

Transport

Motor transport has greatly changed life in the districts. In many areas at one time the people made few visits to Stranraer, as railways were lacking and the passenger services on the roads were meagre. Schemes for constructing a railway from Stranraer to Drummore never materialised. The 17-mile stretch of countryside between the two places is thinly populated and Drummore for a long time drew supplies of coal and other necessities by sea. For seventy years Stranraer and Portpatrick were connected by rail, but the development of traffic by road led to the railway being largely ignored and the line was closed over ten years ago. Protests were raised by the Portpatrick people, but Stranraer was nearly silent on the subject and the closure was carried out according to plan.

From Stranraer to Portpatrick and Drummore there are excellent bus services and practically all the goods are transported by motor lorry from Stranraer to these villages and the hamlets by the way. The development of road services has led to a new outlook among the country people. Children are conveyed to and from school by bus, and adults make frequent visits to the town, to do their shopping or to go to the 'pictures', football matches and other entertainments. Indeed, farmers have difficulty in obtaining workers if road travel is awkward, and one of the inducements often mentioned in advertisements is that the farm is situated near a bus route.

Fishing

As a fishing centre Stranraer has receded far from the position it once occupied. In the *Old Statistical Account* mention was made of fishing as being one of the chief industries, but not what it used to be, while the industry had gone back further by the time the *New Account* was written and since then the fishing has gradually dwindled. There are people in the town who remember much activity and heavy catches, but during the past fifty years these have suffered from the introduction of the seine net: the local fishermen used what were known as small lines, which were so outmoded by the seine nets that competition against the new method was useless. The Stranraer men turned to other things and now very few fishermen remain. Each winter a fleet of drifters comes to Stranraer from the north-east: at one time between 40-50 boats would put in and use the harbour for the first three months of the year, but nowadays only 5 or 6 vessels come. Fishing with great lines, they bring in catches of cod, conger, hake, dog fish, haddock and 'rocker', all of which are purchased by a Stranraer merchant and sent off to the large centres.

Lochryan has the distinction of having the only oyster fishery in Scotland. For many years oysters were fished from the beds lying between the Cairnryan side and the Kirkcolm shore, and were taken to the purifying tanks, where they remained for 24 hours before being dispatched to Glasgow and the south. That was the procedure for a long time, but the oysters grew scarcer and re-stocking became so expensive that a change had to be made and at the moment an experiment is being carried out by the Scottish Marine Biological Association to find out how the industry may be restored.

Sea Transport

Shipping has through the years been a recognised industry of the town, with much traffic to and from Glasgow, the Ayrshire ports and Northern Ireland, but the coming of the railways from Glasgow and Dumfries led to a gradual recession of the coastal traffic. Vessels with supplies of cement from Northern Ireland may still be seen at the harbour and ships from Antwerp bring in cargoes of fertilisers, though the visits of these vessels are not numerous.

It is as the Scottish terminus of the short sea route between Scotland and Ireland that Stranraer is now best known in shipping circles. For long Portpatrick was the point of departure and arrival, but a change was made to Stranraer over seventy years ago. The transfer was strongly opposed by those who had interests in the Portpatrick route, but the postal authorities were adamant in their decision that Stranraer should be the

Scottish port for the mail traffic. Stranraer has thus become firmly established as a link in the chain of shipping that connects the two countries. For a long period there was only one daily run, except in the summer months, but with the coming of the *Caledonian Princess* two trips each day became the normal practice in 1962.

Over the years the vessels plied between the two ports without serious mishap until 31 January, 1953. On that day of wild weather the *Princess Victoria* was involved in one of the greatest sea tragedies in British waters for a hundred years. Setting out in a north-westerly gale, the vessel developed a technical defect after she had cleared Lochryan and became unmanageable. Urgent messages for assistance brought out lifeboats from Portpatrick and Northern Ireland and a destroyer dashed all the way from Rothesay, while ships in the area made with all speed to render aid, but before any of the vessels reached the spot the *Victoria* had disappeared beneath the wild waters. Radio messages sent out from the ill-fated ship during her last tragic hours became more and more urgent in their appeal and poignant in their import, until at last they ceased.

Of the 172 people on board 128 lost their lives, including 39 members of the crew of 49 and 89 passengers. A large proportion of the officers and the crew had their homes in Stranraer and the catastrophe plunged the town into mourning. The bringing home of the bodies and the funerals of the victims engraved the saddest page in the history of Stranraer. On one day ten burials took place and the attendance at the funeral of Captain James Ferguson, master of the ship, was the largest the town had ever known. Among the victims of the disaster were 16 men from Northern Ireland who had been employed at Wig Bay aircraft base with a Belfast firm engaged on work for the Royal Air Force.

There are two piers at Stranraer harbour—the East, belonging to the railway authorities, and the West, owned by the town. Traffic into the town pier has been considerable since the war, during which the facilities were extensively used by the Royal Navy and the Royal Air Force. Until the war years the whole of Lochryan was claimed by Stranraer Harbour Commissioners as coming within their jurisdiction. This claim was contested when the first ship to bring in material to be used in the construction of the docks at Cairnryan discharged her cargo of timber. In the end a small *ex-gratia* sum was offered by the owners and was accepted by the commissioners, who have not subsequently received any financial benefit from the shipping traffic at Cairnryan. The railway pier was acquired from the local authority by the railway company towards the end of the last century; the commissioners derive revenue from this source in the form of a standard payment and a percentage of the dues paid for certain types of traffic.

The loch has now no aircraft quartered off the Kirkcolm shore; seaplanes flying over the water and its surroundings were for a quarter of a century a familiar sight. For a period during the war operational squadrons used Lochryan as a base and the people became accustomed to seeing and hearing flying boats landing and taking off at all hours.

Wig Bay was retained as a base after the war by the R.A.F., but, as already indicated, it is now closed and most of the large hangars have been demolished. A small harbour was constructed near Innermessan by the military authorities while Cairnryan docks were being built, but it was not used very much and vessels have not been seen in the vicinity since the war ended.

A Natural Curiosity

Near the edge of the loch there still exists what is thus described in the *Old Statistical Account* (1791):—'The only natural curiosity in this parish is St. John's Well, considerably within high water mark. It is flooded every high tide by the sea; and in five minutes after the tide retires it boils up in a copious spring of excellent soft fresh water'. The well is still there, but the piping, which must have been put in after the foregoing paragraph was written, is not functioning properly and the water is running to waste in the sand. Until recently people in the vicinity drew their supplies of water from the well when the tide was out. Now they have supplies laid on and the well is only approached by visitors to the shore, though its presence in such surroundings is the subject of frequent comment.

Local Amenities

In keeping with a practice followed for many years, wandering tinkers used the eastern shore of the loch as a site for their caravans and the appearance of this locality was not improved by the dumping of rubbish from building sites. The amenities of what should be an attractive adjunct to the town were spoiled by unsightly heaps of discarded household articles, but changes for the better have now been made. To prevent the sea water undermining Cairnryan Road, a good deal of concrete work has been carried out and the task calls for constant supervision.

The Churches

Church-going in Stranraer is, as in many other places, not what it used to be. Slightly under half the population maintain a regular church connection. The four Church of Scotland congregations have a total membership of about 2,566. In addition there are a United Free, a Reformed Presbyterian, a Scottish Episcopalian and St. Joseph's R.C. churches. There are also two groups of Brethren with mission halls. Stranraer has a substantial population of Catholics and large congregations attend the chapel. The R.P. church is well attended, as is the U.F. church, though their membership is smaller than that of the Church of Scotland congregations. After an effort to unite St. Margaret's with St. Andrew's failed, the congregation of St. Margaret's in 1956 joined with that of Sheuchan to be the High Kirk of Stranraer. In all about 4,000 people in the town attend the church services, many of them only occasionally. During twenty years the membership has slightly increased, though it has to be remembered that the population of Stranraer has gone up in the same period.

Many people give little thought to the church or what it stands for and spend their Sundays reading newspapers, working in their gardens or visiting friends. Motor bus runs attract large numbers of passengers in the summer months and party outings are numerous.

Community Life and Spirit

Things of the spirit do not appear to receive much thought in many quarters and material enjoyment is the quest of a large proportion of the population. Cultural activities are not prominent in Stranraer. Dances, concerts, the cinema and whist drives absorb a great deal of the people's leisure time in the winter months, with football and other forms of sport occupying attention on Saturdays. Though the latest 'song hit' or dance tune is often heard from groups in the streets, good music appeals only to a small minority, despite the efforts of the musical organisations. A popular modern dance band visiting the town will attract a packed 'house', but it is only occasionally that a serious concert is well attended. Television has brought changes and altered some customs and habits.

In recent times public interest in municipal affairs has fallen away. There used to be crowded attendances at the local election meetings, but since the polling was altered from November to May these meetings are a mere echo of the former robust and lively gatherings. General elections still stir up interest and are conducted locally with as much vigour as in the old days.

Although Stranraer has no Women's Rural Institute of its own the movement has a following here, and the branches in the adjoining parishes have amongst their members many womenfolk from the town. The 'Rural' has had a profound influence on social life in the country districts and the townswomen like to share in the activities. The amount of work undertaken is remarkable, and there is no doubt that the new crafts and the revival of the old, the cookery and 'work' demonstrations, have contributed a great deal to making the housewives' lives brighter and happier. The gatherings have enriched the life of the community and, with the Institutes' interest in welfare, housing and kindred subjects, the women have been given a wider horizon.

One of Stranraer's recent acquisitions is the County Library, maintained by the Education Committee. Before a permanent building was found, the library was located in various temporary quarters, which restricted its scope. Now it is housed in the former British Restaurant in London Road, which was adapted for its new purpose and provides excellent accommodation. Since the extension of the service the number of people making use of the library has increased enormously and there is now a book stock of 59,000. Schools in all parts of the country are supplied regularly and efforts are made to stimulate interest in good literature. Stranraer readers take out books of fiction far in excess of other forms of reading, but biography, tales of travel and books on crafts are also in good demand. A feature of the library is the 'Galloway Collection', consisting of books dealing with the province. The Library building includes a room laid out as a local museum, containing numerous relics of ancient days and several instruments and other equipment which were used by Sir John Ross, of Stranraer (1777-1856), the Arctic explorer, on his voyages. The house he built close to the harbour and named North-West Castle is now a hotel.

Stranraer has an excellent hospital service, including the only health centre outside Sighthill, Edinburgh. Among the facilities are consulting rooms for all the doctors in the town. The convenience of having X-ray investigations and opinions, surgical advice and anaesthetists always available has proved an enormous boon both to doctors and patients, and this is true too of the dressing-room, with a nurse in attendance, and of the clerical and telephone assistance. The centre has been built on to the east side of the Garrick Hospital, which, dating back to 1898, has, after several extensions, accommodation for 28 patients; the average number under treatment is 23, while over 200 out-patients are treated each week. Ex-Provost Garrick provided a sum of £1,200 towards the provision of the original hospital, which took the place of an earlier 'cottage' hospital in Dalrymple Street. A short distance from the Garrick is the Clenoch Maternity Hospital, which was opened about ten years ago; this building was formerly a fever hospital and was reconstructed for its new purpose after the National Health Service came into operation. If specialist treatment is required, patients are conveyed to Dumfries, Ballochmyle, Killearn and other hospitals.

An aspect of life that has undergone changes is the attitude to Sunday labour and sport. For a time a good deal of building work was done on Sundays, following a half-holiday on Saturdays. Much transport work is also undertaken on Sundays and many youths engage in football while others go golfing. Moreover, an attempt to hold motor-cycling races on Sunday afternoons brought a protest from the local newspaper and this was followed by objections to the innovations from Stranraer Presbytery; as a result the promoters did not persist with their original plan.

Buildings and General Appearance

Stranraer has not many architectural features of note. The front as viewed from the harbour or a steamer has a utilitarian appearance. A row of red-tiled bungalows along Cairnryan Road gives the eastern fringe of the town, along the loch side, a more attractive aspect, but generally the shore is less inviting than strangers expect. The High Church is a landmark seen from far distances to the west, whence the town has its most satisfying appearance. One of the most ornamental buildings in the burgh is the New Town Hall, with accommodation for some of the county staff and the sheriff court. The main hall is small for a town of Stranraer's size and, indeed, there is a dearth of hall accommodation in the burgh. When a Community Association was formed in the autumn of 1945, one of the projects discussed was a commodious centre, but the plan did not come to fruition and later the association was dissolved. In addition to the Town Hall there are the Temperance Institute, Masonic Hall, St. Mildred's

Hall, Drill Hall and halls in the three primary schools, but none of these can hold a really large audience.

The Old Castle of Stranraer is almost hidden by adjoining buildings, but its tower gives an old-world touch to a busy part of the town. The castle has been scheduled under the Ancient Monuments Act, but is owned and maintained by the town council. It dates back to the end of the fifteenth century and is in a good state of external preservation. One of the apartments was until recently used as a bandroom and during the war the building was a fire-guard centre; last century the burgh authorities used the building as a jail.

The offices of the local newspaper, the *Galloway Advertiser and Wigtownshire Free Press*, extend into part of the castle. The Stranraer paper is the oldest in Galloway and the first issue appeared in 1843, shortly before the Disruption. No other newspaper is published in the town, but the *Galloway Gazette*, published in Newton Stewart, and the *Galloway News*, from Castle-Douglas, also circulate in the district, in addition of course to the national papers.

For many years the question of drawing holiday-makers to Stranraer has been discussed, but it was not until recent years that a sustained effort was made in this direction. A development association held open air dances and other events to attract summer visitors, and in the past few years their efforts have been highly successful. They are backed by the town council, who have helped with the provision of parks, flower gardens and sports. While Stranraer may remain a commercial centre, with summer visitors regarded as incidental, there is scope for increased vigour in these efforts, and this has recently been shown by the inauguration of 'Scottish Week', with a varied and comprehensive programme.

Written 1953
Additions made 1963

CHAPTER 17

THE PARISH OF KIRKCOLM

by JAMES G. LITTLEJOHN

Situation and Characteristics

Kirkcolm parish is a small peninsula with Lochryan to the east and the North Channel to the north and east. The only neighbouring parish is Leswalt to the south. Lochryan runs practically north and south, and the most severe wind comes up through the gully in the loch from the south-east, whence come also the heaviest snowstorms. The climate, however, is favourable and extremes are rarely experienced. The coastline is rocky, and sand appears only in short stretches at the Wig Bay and Lady Bay. Erosion has become a serious matter. Farmers with ground on the shore could formerly graze their beasts on a grassy margin, but this has been replaced by boulders and sand, and at one time at the Boat Bank there was a football pitch which has now disappeared. From the high promontory called Clachan Heughs, round Jamieson Point, Milleur Point and Corsewall Point and along the coast to the North Channel, no perceptible change has taken place. Three bays, Wig Bay, Lady Bay and Dally Bay, used to be havens into which vessels came to unload cargoes of coal and lime, but there is now no coastal traffic. Transport of these commodities is from Stranraer or the place of manufacture.

As regards local customs and traditions, it is noteworthy that the words and phrases in common use have been affected by the proximity of Ireland, for many Irish potato workers come over for seasonal work and each year some stay.

Local Services

Gravitation water is supplied from a well sunk at the north end of the village, but the council houses erected in 1950 are supplied from Stranraer. Paraffin lamps have given way to electricity. Few houses are without bathrooms and fewer without flush lavatories. Street lighting, which up to 1936 was by paraffin lamps, is now by electricity. Of the two church buildings, one was built in the village in 1924, and from it the buttresses have been removed, while the other, at Ervie, was built by the Dissenters; these were joined in the union of 1951 and services are now held in each. The population remains fairly static though in 1851 it was 2,018 and it is now 1,635. The occupation of the council houses by young people with families restored the age balance in the village and the school population remains fairly steady around 200

Education

There are now only two schools in the parish, Kirkcolm junior secondary, raised to that status in 1951, and Mahaar. Dhuloch, by reason of its falling roll, was closed and the children were transferred. Mahaar school, reckoned the oldest in the county, was erected about 1819. The original building was one long room and the fees charged ranged from 1s. to 2s. 6d. a month. The schoolmaster's salary in 1824 was £17. The fees of a number of the children were paid for by charitable folk, Mrs. Moore of Corsewall among them. An alphabetical list of paupers in the parish in 1856 shows that the place of birth of 41 out of 110 is given as Ireland; Irish immigration has continued ever since in a small way. Dhuloch school, opened in 1866, was closed down in 1960; the original register was in use throughout. The roll at the commencement was 67 and it dropped fairly steadily until it was under twenty. Kirkcolm junior secondary school, built about 1872, has still the original school as a class room. It was erected by the Misses Moore of Corsewall as an alternative to Mahaar, which was the old parish school. When pupils reached the age of eight or nine they went on to Mahaar, until in 1910 Kirkcolm school was raised to a two-teacher establishment; gradually, as numbers increased, so did the accommodation, until a former Women's Land Army Hostel was taken over to make a junior secondary department for instruction in technical and domestic subjects. A head teacher, three assistants and an assistant for English form the permanent staff and itinerant teachers of specialist subjects attend almost daily. Few people under the age of thirty make use of the County Library branch. Readers are in the main women of an older generation and fiction forms the greater number of books borrowed.

More than fifty years ago, Kirkcolm had the reputation of a sea-going community. The love of the sea was in all probability due to the teaching of one John Wright who was termed the 'Whaleback Dominie'. He went to the South Sea whale-fishing and also sailed amongst the Japanese islands, and when he went into retirement he had sufficient knowledge of seamanship and the science of navigation to become a very good instructor to youths with ambitions for sea-faring. He opened his first school in Kirkcolm parish, a two-roomed house with the smaller children in one end and the older ones in another and for the sum of 1s. 6d. a quarter, with the addition of a peat fire, he gave instruction in the three R's and taught navigation. His fame spread and pupils were boarded out in neighbouring farms. A Portpatrick man, he was born in 1797 and died at Dally in 1884.

Agriculture

There are 27 farms and farm-houses in the parish belonging to Stair Estates, eleven farms and farm houses belonging to Colonel David Richard Carrick-Buchanan, Corsewall, and others owned by the farmer occupier. All of them are mainly devoted to dairy farming. Few sheep are reared, and cheese-making has almost disappeared, only one farmer continuing the old practice. Most of the land is arable and cultivated, the crops being oats, turnips, hay and early potatoes; barley and wheat are occasionally grown, but there is not a big yield. Methods have changed with the advances in scientific research. Tractors and tractor equipment have superseded the horse, which is, however, still used on soft land. A smithy at Knockcoudie was built by the farmers, and another was added at Ervie in recent years. Of the cottages, 21 are empty and three ruinous. Parts of three farms, Salchrie, Glenside and Clendrie, were taken over for a large seaplane base during the second world war and a jetty was built at Glenside for air-sea rescue work. This continued until 1959 when the base was finally closed and the ground returned to the former owners. Much of it, however, remained to be cleared and this constituted a blot on the landscape.

Recreation
Following the erection of a public hall in Kirkcolm in 1928 various youth organisations sprang up and many different functions were held. The hall, built on the site of an old stable, comprises one main room with balcony and platform, kitchen, dressing room, cloak rooms, and a smaller hall. The building, erected by public subscription, was intended for the purposes of physical and mental recreation, and social, moral and intellectual development through the medium of reading and recreation rooms, library, lectures, classes, recreations and entertainments. Boy Scouts, Girl Guides, Woman's Guild and the Women's Rural Institute are centred here and in 1947 a Community Association was formed. Dramatic productions are staged; badminton games, whist drives and dances are also held. A playing field is mooted. A recreation centre was formed in the Dhuloch area in 1953. The local football clubs play in summer and there is of course a bowling green. A very strong curling club, Loch Connel, is known throughout the curling world, for one of its skips played in a rink that became world champions in 1958; most of the curling is done indoors at Ayr.

Ecclesiastical Affairs
The old parish church, built in 1824 on high ground on the west side of the village, is a substantial building in good repair, and can accommodate 650; with a gallery it could accommodate 300 more. The manse had additions made to it about 1890; these made it very large, but it has since been sold to a farmer. After the Disruption, the Free Church built a church and manse at Ervie in 1845, which later joined with a church in the neighbouring parish and ultimately, after that link was broken, became part of Kirkcolm, under the name of Ervie-Kirkcolm (1951); the Ervie manse became the residence of the minister. The glebe extends to ten acres, part of it rented by a farmer for early potatoes and part for grazing; the rent forms part of the minister's stipend. Church attendance is very good and probably amongst the highest in the county.

Antiquities
In the garden of Corsewall House stands a stone which was a lintel of the old church. It is a grey whinstone, carved on one side with armorial

bearings, but the figures are not at all clear and can only be conjectured. The house, belonging to the only resident laird in the parish, Lieut.-Colonel David Carrick-Buchanan, is a commodious building, commanding a view of Lochryan and the adjoining countryside. The wooded grounds are laid out to show the British formation at the battle of Corunna, in memory of Sir John Moore, whose brother had been bequeathed Corsewall by Robert Carrick, a banker in Glasgow. In the northern part of the parish, near Corsewall point and within a mile of the sea, stand the remains of Corsewall Castle, now ruinous. It is a tower with walls of great thickness, built of irregular stones with small slits for windows and mortar now as hard as the stones. A silver plate with an inscription, a gold ring and some coins were found about a hundred years ago. Marian tower stands on a high part of Drumdow farm.

The Way of Life

The fishing industry has all but disappeared: only one salmon fisher remains, but cod, haddock and whiting are found in the loch in large quantities and several men who fish for pleasure distribute their catches in the villages free of charge. Crabs and lobsters are also found. There are three grocer's shops in the village, but butcher meat and other items are brought by van from Stranraer. A good bus service runs from Stranraer to Ardwell Shop. There are 34 owner-occupied houses and two hotels with accommodation for guests, each with a seven-day licence. Over-crowding was relieved by the council housing scheme, which started in 1935 with six houses. Since then other schemes have been carried out. Many of the houses are occupied by agricultural workers, an extension of the clachan system now prevailing. Each house has a garden for flowers and vegetables. There are no private buildings. Housing conditions in the parish have improved and many cottages have now modern conveniences. In the absence of a resident doctor, medical service is provided from Stranraer. In 1932 a District Nursing Association was formed, but it was dissolved under the National Health Act in 1948. In general it may be said that the people are hard-working and take a pride in their surroundings. They have a strong community sense and are fiercely loyal to the area. Their partisanship is widely known, particularly in the field of sport.

Written 1954
Additions made 1962

CHAPTER 18

THE PARISH OF LESWALT

by J. S. BOYD.

Leswalt is bounded on the west by the North Channel, on the east by Lochryan; to the north is Kirkcolm and to the south Portpatrick. It is approximately eight miles square and the most populated part lies within the burgh of Stranraer. There is little activity around the coast. Soleburn, on the Lochryan side, was at one time used extensively by coastal steamers, but is no longer in commission and the bay at the Clayhole, which was once the haven for fishing boats, has long since been superseded by Stranraer East Pier. The ground slopes gently down to the lochside on the west, but on the east rocky cliffs drop down to the channel. In the landward area are large tracts of barren moorland and in other parts are gentle rolling meadows. Of the several lochs at Lochnaw, one laps the castle walls and forms with the building an outstanding scenic feature.

Population

No clear picture can be obtained from the population trend, which has risen steadily because of the increased house building in the town part of the parish. In 1831 the population numbered 2,636, of whom 328 were in Hillhead and 462 in the Clayhole. These former villages are now included in the burgh of Stranraer and, because of extensive council house building, the population of the parish has risen to 5,197, an increase of 119 per cent compared with the figure of twenty years ago. The town dwellers have little in common with their country cousins, though many of them maintain a connection with the village from which the parish takes its name. In the village the majority of the remainder of the population reside, for the landward area contains only some 450 electors. The population for the most part is native, but there is a fair sprinkling of descendants of Irish workers.

Agriculture

With the improvement in husbandry, the agricultural population has remained fairly static and is now much more comfortable than in former years. Within its small confines are almost all types of farming. On all but the worst of the hinterland, where the ground is boggy and marshy with many areas which cannot even accommodate the hardy blackfaced sheep, farming is extensive. The better farms lie towards the lochside, where the ground is more easily cultivated; despite what has been done, there is much room for improvement in farm buildings and in farm cottages. Dairying is the chief branch of farming and opportunity has

Plate 13. LAST OF THE PORTLOGAN LIFEBOATS
The *Thomas McCunn*, which went out of service in 1928. The first lifeboat on the station
was the *Edinburgh and R. M. Ballantyne*, which was commissioned in 1866.

F. H. McCarlie, Stranraer

Plate 14. THE PORTPATRICK LIFEBOAT
The changes that have taken place in the design of lifeboats over the years are exemplified
in this picture of the Portpatrick boat, *The Jeanie*, after the naming ceremony in 1961.

Plate 16. T.S.S. *CALEDONIAN PRINCESS*
The new British Railways vessel plying between Stranraer and Larne.

Plate 15. THE FIRST *PRINCESS VICTORIA*
This paddle steamer was engaged in the cross-channel service between Stranraer and Larne
from 1890 until 1904.

recently been taken to introduce new methods of feeding and milking. Early potatoes are grown fairly extensively on the ground close to the shores of Lochryan, where the mildness of the climate proves excellent for the crop. Some 35 years ago, however, many farmers suffered serious loss as a result of frost and to this day some favour a 'hat' of straw placed on the foliage of the tubers; fortunately this is not very often necessary. When the crop is raised early in June the potatoes are in much demand in the cities. There is still a lot of permanent pasture, though many old pastures were ploughed up during the war years. The area is almost completely denuded of rabbits, partly because of myxomatosis and partly because of the enthusiasm for poaching that prevailed in the district. Through its proximity to Stranraer many of the residents obtain employment in ancillary work, with the Wigtownshire Creamery, at the grain mill, or as agricultural engineers.

Ecclesiastical Matters

The village church, erected in 1826, was renovated and redecorated in 1953, when the service was taken by Rev. Dr. A. Nevile Davidson, minister of Glasgow Cathedral, whose family had been responsible for the building. In the old churchyard stands the crypt of the Agnew family dating back to 1455. Following the union of the Churches in 1929, the former United Free church, Leswalt West, was linked with Ervie in the neighbouring parish of Kirkcolm. The link remained until 1937 and some bitterness ensued before a final union took place between Leswalt and the remnants of the former Leswalt West; Ervie, at this juncture, became part of Ervie. Kirkcolm church in Kirkcolm parish. The other congregation of the Church of Scotland is the High Kirk of Stranraer, the result of a recent union between a former Free Church, St. Margaret's, and Sheuchan. For some years services were held by the Christian Brethren and at intervals up to thirty years ago revivalist meetings aroused much interest in the landward and burghal areas. The Roman Catholic population, high in numbers compared to most other parts of the county, Whithorn excepted, have their place of worship in Stranraer outwith the bounds.

Education

In addition to the village school, there are three other primary establishments which are attended by children resident in various parts of the parish—two in Stranraer and the third, at Larbrax, on the south boundary. Sheuchan school, the oldest in the district, was recently renovated and converted into a single-stream primary school, after it had been closed for some years. The extension was built on ground used during the war by the services and was only obtained by the education authority after a public inquiry, when Stranraer Town Council opposed the scheme for housing purposes. Park school, the largest primary building in the county and, like Sheuchan, located in the burghal part of Leswalt, also draws pupils from the parish.

2H

Recreation

No doubt because of the proximity of Stranraer, few sporting activities are carried on in the landward area. Centred on the village hall, which was erected by public subscription to the memory of those who fell in the first world war, there is a Community Association of recent date. Dances and whist drives are almost the sole winter pastimes, though a curling club, without a home, plays all its games at Ayr. At one time there were a cricket club and a football club. In the burghal portion, of course, there is more activity and the football team there has for long been a feature. The Women's Rural Institute, the largest numerically in the county, meets in the Public Hall but draws most of its members from Stranraer. The Institute promotes a flower show each summer and this event creates keen interest throughout the district; it has also encouraged more amateur gardening than was formerly the case.

Local Services

The parish is almost entirely dependent on Stranraer for its services. There is no local resident doctor, dentist, midwife, nurse or policeman. No tradesmen are based on the village, but recently an agricultural engineering establishment has been set up. There are no licensed premises in the landward part but three in the urban district, as well as an off-licence. In addition to the sub-post office in the village there is another in the Clay-hole. There are only two shops in Leswalt; the ubiquitous van from the grocer, the butcher, or the baker supplies the needs. A modicum of home baking is still practised by both farmer's wife and cotman's wife. The village has been almost entirely rebuilt: the majority of the rural dwellers are in council houses, but many of the farm cottages are still in poor condition. Both water and electricity are available. There are no resident landlords in the parish. A holiday centre on a large scale is reported to be at the planning stage and is to be located near Lochnaw.

Local Features

Dominating the parish is a monument erected in 1851 on Craigoch Hill to Sir Andrew Agnew, whose seat, Lochnaw, is the only building of note apart from Knock House. Lochnaw Castle dates back to the fourteenth century. The castle was captured and burned by Archibald Douglas, Lord of Galloway, but was restored to the Agnew family in 1426. On several occasions reconstruction work was carried out and the castle has now been given the aspect of the building as it was in the early years of last century. It is still in the hands of the Agnews and is now mainly used as a Common-wealth Club for overseas visitors, although a number of local people are members. Within the grounds are the remains of a fort known as Kempés Graves and there is a sea-king fort at Larbrax in a strong defensive position; these are possibly Viking and certainly Dark Age or Medieval.

Other ruins are those of Galdenoch Castle, a sixteenth century building which has fallen into decay, but still shows signs of the corbelling supported by a turret; it is said to have been the home of pirates, and is now part of a farm. A tale is told of its being haunted and of the minister from Kirkcolm in a loud voice chasing away the Devil; the probable truth is that the pirate residents resented interference. Galdenoch was built by the Agnews at some time between 1547 and 1570. At Dally Bay is a house formerly occupied by smugglers, who followed a lucrative calling at one time.

Dindinnie Reservoir and water works, belonging to Stranraer Town Council, serve the parish. The Ministry of Aviation maintain a radio station at Larbrax and use it in conjunction with Prestwick Airport to guide trans-Atlantic planes. There are no public works, however, though there is very little unemployment. Some greywacke stone and red sandstone are to be found, but no quarries are worked. The parish has yielded several Neolithic flat stone axes of some 4,000 years ago. The cairn on Cairn Hill of Balgracie may well be of the Bronze Age and the comparatively large score of promontory forts of the Iron Age and Dark Ages is understandable.

The Way of Life

For the most part the parishioners have an urban rather than a rural way of life. They go into Stranraer for almost all their pleasures. They were fortunate a few years ago when the Stranraer Golf Club constructed their course at Creachmore, but few of the people from the landward part evince much interest. The standard of intelligence, if the control examination is taken as the yardstick, cannot be high, for few pupils proceed to senior secondary education. The occasional outbreak of petty crime in the area around the village is probably due to the absence of the restraining influence of a resident policeman or the lack of the influence of any of the professional classes.

Written 1960
Additions made 1962

CHAPTER 19

THE PARISH OF PORTPATRICK

by JOHN MUIR

Situation
The parish of Portpatrick lies rather nearer the northern than the southern extremity of the peninsula bounded by Lochryan, the North Channel and Luce Bay. It is approximately rectangular, having a western coastline of four miles on the North Channel and stretching about four and a half miles towards the isthmus formed by Lochryan and Luce Bay. The adjoining parishes are Leswalt to the north, Inch to the east and Stoneykirk to the south, the only natural boundary being the small Piltanton Burn which separates Portpatrick from Inch.

Name and History
Legends link Portpatrick with Saint Patrick of Ireland but no historical connection is known. Portpatrick became a parish in 1628, having previously been part of Inch and known as the Black Quarter of the Inch. The new parish was given the ancient and present name of the harbour, although the latter was sometimes also called Port-Montgomerie after the Montgomeries, Lords of Ardes in Ireland, the proprietors for a period before and after 1628. The village, too, was generally known as Portpatrick, having been made a burgh of barony by a royal charter of 1620.

Geographical Features
The surface of the whole parish is elevated. Ascending abruptly from the sea in the west to over 100 feet, the land continues to rise gradually for three miles and then slopes downwards to the eastern boundary. There is practically no level ground, the whole surface being irregularly undulated. Only a few of the slopes are too steep for cultivation, but outcrops of rock are frequent on the higher parts. Some of the higher hills or fells are almost conical. From the summit of Cairnpat, the highest hill in the peninsula, a magnificent view of land and sea can be had on a clear day. The streams are all small and rapid, their whole length lying within the parish, with the exception of the Piltanton, which forms the eastern boundary and runs into Luce Bay. The coast consists of jagged rocks and cliffs or heughs rising steeply from deep water. In some places the cliffs are perpendicular to a height of 130 feet. The only beaches are in six small bays, two of which mark the boundaries of the parish. Equidistant from these is the bay containing the harbour of Portpatrick and about half a mile to the north of the harbour are two small bays separated by a rocky ridge. About a quarter of a mile to the south of the harbour

the ruins of the old castle of Dunskey stand 100 feet above the sea on a promontory and overlook another small bay.

Population

Portpatrick is the only village in the parish. At the census of 1801 the parish population was 1,090, and in 1831 it had risen to 2,239, the highest recorded. This huge increase was due to the number of men employed in constructing a new harbour. By 1851 fewer men were employed at harbour construction and the population had decreased to 1,963. In 1901 the population was 1,136 and it has remained fairly steady as the following figures show:—1,495 in 1921; 1,101 in 1931; 1,063 in 1951. The high figure for 1921 may be attributed to the presence of summer visitors, the census having been taken in June that year. Although the parish population has remained steady there has been an increase in the village and a corresponding decrease in the country district.

Housing

The *New Statistical Account* (1838) gives the number of inhabited houses as follows:—village, 120; country, 177; total, 297. The corresponding figures today are:—village, 230; country, 133; total, 363; these returns showing clearly the drift from farm to village or town during the last 100 years. A survey map published in 1894 shows only three houses built near the rim of high land encircling the village. Today over 30 houses overlook the bay from the north-west rim, including Portpatrick Hotel, which has an imposing site above the harbour. The county council built 18 houses above the eastern rim between 1937 and 1939 and ten years ago they built 30 houses to the north-east. Apart from these schemes the period of greatest activity in building was at the beginning of this century. Mr. Charles Orr Ewing became proprietor of Dunskey Estate in 1898 and was responsible for the building of Portpatrick Hotel, which was completed in 1905. He also built 16 houses in Hill Street to accommodate the fishermen, whose houses in Blair Street were demolished and replaced by the present houses of Blair Terrace.

Farming

Farming is the staple industry of the parish. Practically all the farms are stocked with Ayrshire cattle, the chief aim being milk production. In 1838 the cattle were mostly Galloways, and a few of this breed are still reared on the rougher grazings, where some sheep are also found. The chief crops are oats, hay, turnips and potatoes. The work on the farms has become almost completely mechanised, the farm-horse of former days being rarely seen, and not one smithy is left in the whole parish. The farmers in the western part of the parish are mostly tenants of Dunskey Estate, while in the eastern part they are tenants of Stair Estates, but a number of the farms are now owner-occupied.

Dairy cattle at June 1960 numbered 2,118 and beef cattle 1,035, a total of 3,153. There were then 4,468 sheep, 237 pigs, 16 horses and 5,326 head of poultry. People employed on farms included men, full time, 65; part time, 8; women and girls, full time, 10; part time, 9; casual workers, 3— a total of 95. Approximately 1,200 acres were under crop:—oats, 760; barley, 66; wheat, one; first early potatoes, 40; main crop and second early potatoes, 21; turnips and swedes, 270; mangolds, 19; kale and cabbage, 16; vegetable for human consumption, 3. Grass accounted for 3,723 acres and rough grazings for 2,485 acres.

Creamery

Colfin Creamery, the only factory in the parish, is owned by United Creameries, and was built by them between 1916 and 1919 beside the Portpatrick railway about three miles from the village. At that time this company owned creameries at Dunragit, Sorbie, Tarff and Campbeltown. Colfin Creamery was built for the reception of milk from the Portpatrick and Stoneykirk areas, either to manufacture into cream, butter or cheese at Colfin or to send in bulk to Dunragit. The creamery was opened in 1919, a fleet of horse-drawn lorries being used to collect the milk from the farms. A few years later those vehicles were replaced by motor lorries. The main activities have been the production of various types of cheese, cream and milk powder. In past years large quantities of milk were dispatched by 3,000 gallon rail tanks to London, Newcastle and Edinburgh, but, because of the expanded milk production around these cities, this is no longer necessary. The creamery has expanded to deal with the increased milk supplies of the district, the production of milk having risen by over sixty per cent in the last forty years. Moreover, cheesemaking on the farms has practically ceased, the milk going to the creamery, where as much as 18,000 gallons has been made into cheese in one day.

Fishing

Although quantities of fish are still landed at Portpatrick, very little fishing is done by the local inhabitants, only one motor fishing vessel and one very small boat being employed. Over 100 years ago at least 20 local boats were in use and 70 years ago about 12, but the number has gradually dwindled. Cod were caught from November to April, flat fish and lobsters during the other months. Very few local boats fished for herring. During and after the second world war, when rationing was in operation, large quantities of white fish were landed, mostly by boats from Ireland or the east coast of Scotland. In 1944 up to 25 seine-boats were operating from Portpatrick, the heaviest landing in one night being 70 tons of fish. This type of fishing still continues in winter, six to eight boats being normally engaged. The usual herring season is from late June until September, when the boats come from Ireland and the Firth of Clyde. From 1930 onwards heavy landings have been made, the peak period being from 1946 to 1952, when over forty drifters were operating. The largest recorded catch for one day was 3,043 crans. The opening in 1957 of fish-meal factories in Northern Ireland and the Isle of Man has affected the landings at Portpatrick. The 1960 season, however, was the best for some years, good catches being landed from a fleet of about 20 boats.

Harbour

The history of the harbour provides a tragic story since the time of the *New Statistical Account*, wherein we may read a glowing description of a fine new outer harbour being constructed under government orders for the better accommodation of the steam packet-boats carrying mail and passengers to Ireland. In 1849, even before the north pier was completed, the Irish mail ceased to pass through Portpatrick and in 1862 the packet-boat service was transferred to Stranraer. In 1874 all government interest in the harbour ceased. Before many years had passed the walls of the new piers had been breached by the heavy seas and today only jumbled masses of huge blocks of stone and concrete remain. The small natural inner harbour, sheltered by the Dorn Rock (McCook's Craig), remains intact and is used by a few fishing boats during the winter months and in summer by the herring fleet, by a few visiting yachts and in very recent years by two or three speedboats engaged in water ski-ing. It also provides accommodation for the Portpatrick Lifeboat. In 1954 a sea wall was built on the north side of the harbour to stop coast erosion, the sea having gained 30 or 40 feet within the last 50 years. During the seamen's strike in 1960 many stranded holiday-makers were conveyed to and from Northern Ireland by fishing boats.

Education

The only school in the parish is in the village of Portpatrick. This school has four teachers with an average roll for the past few years of 110 pupils, and provides primary education for children living in the western part of the parish. Most of the children in the eastern part attend the primary school at Lochans, which is just outside the eastern boundary, but a few go to Stranraer. All secondary pupils are now transferred to Stranraer, the junior secondary pupils having been transferred from Portpatrick and Lochans in 1952. Transport to Portpatrick is provided for children living in the Killantringan area and school meals, brought daily from Stranraer, are available. The present school, built over 80 years ago, will require to be reconstructed or replaced to comply with modern standards. In recent years further education classes in dressmaking and country dancing have been held in school.

Churches

At present there are three places of worship in the parish, all situated in the village. These are Portpatrick parish church, St. Ninian's Scottish Episcopal church and the Christian Brethren's Gospel Hall. The present parish church was built in 1842 but all the internal woodwork and furnishings were renewed in 1932. At the Disruption in 1843 the minister, the Rev. Andrew Urquhart, seceded to the Free Church but continued to live in Portpatrick. In 1887 Trinity Free church was built and continued as such until the union of the Churches took place in 1929. After being employed for various purposes this building was purchased by the parish church in 1953 and is now in use as a church hall. Portpatrick parish church has approximately 400 members. Its organisations include a Woman's Guild, a Sunday School, a Bible class and a youth club. St. Ninian's Scottish Episcopal church, built in 1937, is only 39 feet long and 17 feet wide. Services are conducted by the Scottish Episcopal minister from Stranraer and at present the membership is about 20. The Christian Brethren acquired their present hall in 1936. Built in 1909, it had previously been the property of Portpatrick Workmen's Club. The Brethren have about 26 members and about 50 children attend their Sunday school.

Transport

In 1838 horse-drawn mail coaches left Portpatrick daily for Glasgow and Dumfries, the packet-boat also leaving daily for Ireland. The mail coach service ceased in 1849 and the packet service in 1862. A railway was laid between Stranraer and Portpatrick between 1856 and 1861 and a branch line to the harbour in 1862. The branch line was out of action before 1880 but trains continued to run between Stranraer and Portpatrick until 1951, when, despite petitions by the local inhabitants, the service was stopped and the rails were lifted between Portpatrick and Colfin. About four years ago the goods service from Colfin to Stranraer was also stopped and the rails were lifted. Motor bus services between Stranraer and Portpatrick started in 1924 and today there is an adequate service, no part of the parish being far removed from the bus route.

Public Services

In 1955 the county water supply became available for most of the parish. Before that the village supply came from a reservoir built at Enoch in 1903 at the instigation of Mr. Charles Orr Ewing, who shared the cost of the construction with Wigtown County Council on the understanding that the council would be responsible for maintenance. Because of the increased water consumption this supply proved inadequate in dry seasons and temporary expedients had to be found. Electricity is available throughout the parish from the South of Scotland Electricity Board. Portpatrick can boast of having the first supply in the area, for in 1903 a dam was erected at the Craigoch Burn by Mr. Charles Orr Ewing. Under county council auspices, refuse is collected twice a week. A district nurse is stationed in the village, her services being available for the parish. Portpatrick has had a coastguard station since 1863. It was under the control of the Admiralty until 1923, when it was transferred to the Board of Trade; the Ministry of Shipping took it over early in the war and control later passed to the Ministry of Transport. Originally on the south side of the village, the station now has a commanding site on the north cliff and a continuous watch is kept over the North Channel. Four coastguards are employed, and they are relieved at times by local auxiliaries; a fifth house is being erected at the station, the others having been built in 1933. The district officer for South-west Scotland is also stationed here. When the south pier began to disintegrate more than 70 years ago the lighthouse, built at its point in 1835, was taken down stone by stone and rebuilt at Colombo in Ceylon. It was replaced by the small lighthouse which still stands to the south of the harbour and which operated until 1900, when the present lighthouse at Killantringan came into use. For several years the small lighthouse supplied light to the harbour and neighbouring streets, the seaward side being shuttered and acetylene gas burners supplying the light. A post office in the village gives two postal deliveries daily, the rest of the parish having one.

Portpatrick Radio Station, under the control of the Post Office since 1921, maintains continuous watch for shipping in distress, a well co-ordinated safety communication service, including free medical advice, always being ready. Commercially the station handles telephone calls to and from shipping, in addition to telegrams by radiotelegraphy or radio-telephony. The station, standing on the north cliff, is dominated by two transmitting aerials 120 feet high. Inside the station are three transmitters which can be used for radiotelegraphy or radiotelephony, with a range of 300 miles, three operating positions equipped with modern receivers and a direction finder. The staff, consisting of one overseer and ten radio operators, handles on an average 100 communications each day and maintains a constant vigil over shipping in the north-western approaches and in the Irish Sea. In 1950 a Carrier Telephony Repeater Station came into operation at Merrick Farm to form a link between Ulster and the mainland in the communication system, and, with the laying of additional submarine cables across the North Channel, helped to extend the British Post Office telephone trunk network.

Another radio repeater station was installed at Enoch Hill in 1959 by the Post Office. This was one of a number of stations erected to form a micro-wave radio link between Carlisle and Belfast and extended the I.T.A. national network to Northern Ireland, making Ulster commercial television possible. It also further developed the Post Office telephone trunk network.

Voluntary Organisations

Since 1877 a lifeboat has been stationed at Portpatrick. During the past 70 years the crew has saved 200 lives and one silver and two bronze medals have been awarded for gallantry. A new vessel, the Jeanie, two years ago replaced the former boat, Jeanie Spiers. There is a volunteer crew of eight, a local committee looks after the interests of the Lifeboat Institution, while the Life-Saving Association has been in operation since 1863. Many rescues have been effected of the crews of ships grounded on the rocky shore of the North Channel and of people and animals marooned on the cliffs.

Portpatrick Improvements Committee has been active for almost 60 years in making the village more attractive and comfortable for the inhabitants and summer visitors. In 1926 Portpatrick Public Hall was built with funds raised by the inhabitants and has since then been the venue of most of the local functions. Portpatrick Advertising Committee looks after the interests of the proprietors of the boarding houses and produces a brochure each year. This committee developed from a work party of ladies who raised money during the war for charities and later held sales of work on behalf of the British Sailors' Society. A small committee of ladies raises money to give the old folks of the parish an outing each summer. Other organisations at present active in the village are the Women's Rural Institute, Girl Guides, Brownies, Cubs and those already mentioned under *Churches* and *Education.*

The Way of Life

Living conditions have naturally improved greatly both in the village and in the country since the 1838 account was written. The poverty depicted then is no longer in evidence today. The people seem well contented with their lot in life, especially if they are allowed to go their own way, for there seems to be little desire for communal life. A Community Association was started about ten years ago but was dissolved a few years later, and public meetings are generally very poorly attended. Church attendance could be much better, but most of the children turn out regularly to the Sunday schools.

The main interest of the villagers is catering for summer visitors. Portpatrick developed as a summer resort about 60 years ago and it is still a popular spot for those who seek a quiet holiday. In addition to private hotels, boarding houses and five licensed hotels, many houses now display a 'Bed and Breakfast' notice. Bowling and tennis facilities have been available since 1892, golf since 1903 and putting since the war. Many touring 'bus parties come to the village, the busiest time being Sunday afternoon, when they are joined by people from the surrounding district. Although a number of the residents are retired people, lack of work in the village makes it necessary for many to travel daily to Stranraer for their employment. The winter months pass quietly, the majority of people being content to find their entertainment at home. A branch of the County Library is well patronised. Apart from the organisations already mentioned, activities are limited to a weekly dance, an occasional concert or whist drive, a bridge club and a badminton club. The local curling club celebrated its centenary in 1959; the curlers play mostly on indoor ice at Ayr. The nearest cinema is eight miles distant in Stranraer. Because of their proximity to Lochans, the residents in the eastern part of the parish naturally go there for their social activities.

Written 1960
Additions made 1962

CHAPTER 20

THE PARISH OF STONEYKIRK

by the REV. ARCHIBALD L. MELROSE.

Stoneykirk parish, one of the largest in the Rhins of Galloway, is bounded on the north by the parish of Inch, on the north-west by Portpatrick, on the west by the North Channel, on the south by Kirkmaiden, on the east by Luce Bay and on the north-east by Old Luce. It is irregular in shape, extending to some nine miles in breadth in the north and tapering gradually till it is no more than 2½ miles broad in the south.

Topography

The parish is divided into two geographical regions with the central axis as the dividing line. To the east the ground is low-lying and forms part of the isthmus that lies between Lochryan in the north and Luce Bay in the south. The soil is light and dry and along the shore of Luce Bay is definitely sandy. To the west of the axis the ground rises steeply to a green ridge which attains a height of 450 feet at Meoul Hill, although in the south of the parish the elevation is more even from east to west. For the most part the western seaboard is formed of cliffs indented by a number of bays, one of which once harboured fishing vessels but is now the habitat of the sea fowl.

From the peninsular nature of the parish and the prevailing south-west winds bringing abundance of rain, the atmosphere is moist and many years ago was suitable for the flax industry which thrived in the parish. In his book, *Highways and Byways in Galloway and Carrick*, C. H. Dick speaks of the mildness of the climate and its suitability for sub-tropical trees and plants.

The parish is cut up into sections by burns which have their origin in the high ridges running north and south. Some of these burns flow west and rapidly empty themselves in the North Channel, while others flow more gently to Luce Bay. The only lochs worth mentioning are at Kirkmabreck and Ardwell House.

Of the plantations, those at Knockinaam, Balgreggan and Ardwell help to break up the barrenness of the surrounding countryside.

History and Antiquities

From the remains that have been discovered here and there, indications are that the parish was thickly populated and heavily afforested and that the people were of Celtic origin, their religion 'Druidism', with seemingly more than one place of worship.

491

For the lover of history and the antiquarian the parish provides a wealth of material: its antiquities are described, with illustrations, in the *Report on the County of Wigtown* (1912) of the Royal Commission on the Ancient Monuments of Scotland. The ruins of the ancient castle of Killaser on Ardwell Estate, the evidences of old Balgreggan Castle near the shores of Luce Bay, the site of Garthland Castle with its square tower dated 1274 whose stones have since been used for farm-buildings, all speak of the ancient clans of McDoualls, McCullochs and others now gone from their ancient seats of Killaser, Garthland, Freugh and Balgreggan.

Around 1900 were discovered the remains of subterranean dwellings of the early Picts on the farm of Low Mye not far from Stoneykirk village, and these are similar to those found in other parts of Scotland and Orkney, which suggest the common origin of the early inhabitants of Galloway with those of the rest of Scotland. Very complete motes or forts are still to be seen at Ardwell, Caldons Hill and Balgreggan. The last of these (used constantly during the second world war by the members of the Royal Observer Corps) is 460 feet in circumference at the base and 60 feet in height and is surrounded by a fosse or ditch. Many relics of the Stone Age have been found at Culmore and among the sand dunes at the head of Luce Bay. On the lands of Low Culgroat stand the remains of an old windmill, erected about 1670 by a McDouall of Logan, in order to augment the few water-driven mills of the district.

Although all traces of the church of the old parish of Clayshant, before it was merged with Stoneykirk and Toskerton, have disappeared, yet the boundary of the burial ground can still be traced on a field belonging to Clayshant farm between the road and the shore. In a field at Kirkmabreck farm known as Toskerton Knowes are traces of dwelling-houses. On the road to Kirkmadrine is a huge monolith about which history and tradition are silent, but from its form it would appear to be of 'Druidical' origin. Kirkmadrine, most famous of all the antiquities in the parish, is traditionally situated on the site of an ancient 'Druid' temple. Three old inscribed stones, now preserved within iron gratings at the church, had been used at one time as gateposts; the last to be found was discovered by the minister, the Rev. Philip Robertson, in 1917. According to Dr. R. C. Reid and other authorities, they are fifth century stones and bear the names of three bishops of the early Celtic Church—Viventius, Mavorius and Florentius. The present church, modelled on Cruggleton, is a late nineteenth century restoration on the site of the old building.

In a plantation behind the Lodge on the Ardwell Estates, a large unhewn block of stone, with the single word MURDER deeply cut in its upper surface, is the subject of many local traditions, but the nearest to historical facts is to be found in *The Gallovidian* of summer 1907.

Land-Owners

A comparison with the *New Statistical Account* (1840) shows many changes in the ownership of the land. The old land-owners in the accepted term of that word are gone, victims of high taxation, the lapse of some families, and the re-distribution of wealth. In 1840 the whole parish seems to have been in the hands of eight heritors, whereas today the bulk of the land belongs to the Ardwell Estates (the McTaggart Stewart family), Stair Estates, Balgreggan and Freugh (Miss Helen Stuart Weir). Besides these, about 20 individual families own their farms.

Population

The figures over the years have remained remarkably steady, with a slight decrease, since the beginning of the century, following the mechanisation of agriculture and the normal drift of population to the larger centres; the present population numbers 2,284. There is much movement from one district to another within the shire, though not a great deal out of it, on the part of the farm-workers; it is true that a number of the farmers have come into the area from other parts, especially from Ayrshire. In 1855 there were 95 births, 36 deaths, 18 marriages and 8 illegitimate births, and in 1950 the respective figures were 36, 17, 8 and 4. The county as a whole is unfortunately still notable for its illegitimate births.

Public and Social Services

The main arterial road between Stranraer and Drummore, running through the villages of Stoneykirk and Sandhead, is in first-class condition and well up to the standard of such roads. Another road, narrower, more tortuous and hillier, runs along the west side of the parish connecting Portpatrick, Port o' Spittal, Meoul, Cairngarroch and the Float district with Ardwell. A network of roads interconnects these two routes, all in good condition. For a rural area, indeed, the parish is well served with roads, and easy access can be got to most parts of the area. Thus, the advent of the internal combustion engine and of improved road surfaces has brought a great advance in transport facilities. There are no railways in the parish, but it is only six miles to Stranraer, where connection by rail may be had with Glasgow in the north and with London *via* Dumfries in the south, and by steamer with Northern Ireland *via* the shortest sea route between Britain and Ireland.

Education

The three primary schools in the parish are situated at Stoneykirk, Meoul and Clachanmore,[1] and a combined primary and junior secondary school at Sandhead, with accommodation of the latest design, was completed just before the outbreak of war in 1939, so that it conforms to the Education Department's scheme for centralisation and therefore takes in most of the scholars of post-primary age from the parish. After the control examination stage at 12 years, primary scholars pass on to the junior secondary school at Sandhead or to the High School in Stranraer. The number of scholars attending primary schools in the area is approximately 330, and the number at the junior secondary at Sandhead is about 50; in addition,

[1] Moreover, some Lochans pupils attend school in Inch parish.

about 20 pupils are conveyed by special bus to Stranraer High School, and a few go to a junior secondary school in Stranraer.

Health Services

For many years there has been a resident doctor in Sandhead, but a number of the parishioners call on the services of doctors from Stranraer and Drummore. The Garrick Cottage Hospital in Stranraer provides hospital facilities for most medical and surgical cases, though some go to Balloch-myle, Ayr, Glasgow or Dumfries. Maternity cases are given attention by the local nurse in the homes or at the Maternity Hospitals in Stranraer and Dumfries.

Voluntary Services

The Youth Clubs at Stoneykirk, Meoul and Ardwell offer country dancing, athletics, table tennis and other forms of recreation. At Lochans, which lies within the three parishes of Stoneykirk, Portpatrick and Inch, there are companies of Rangers and Girl Guides and Brownies as well as a troop of Boy Scouts and Cubs, whose numbers are partly drawn from Stoneykirk parish. Stoneykirk church has a junior choir.

Of the two branches of the Woman's Guild, one is attached to each church, Stoneykirk with 14 members and Ardwell-Sandhead with 20. The Scottish Women's Rural Institute has five branches in the parish, at Stoneykirk, Meoul, Ardwell, Sandhead and Lochans. Of the two Community Associations, one at Lochans serves the three parishes, and the other at Ardwell meets in the old coachhouse attached to Ardwell Estates. The British Legion, which meets from time to time in the hall at Sandhead, has been raised in recent times from a sub-branch of Stranraer to the full status of a branch; the membership comprises about 25 ex-servicemen from the first and second world wars.

The Church

The Church of Scotland has two congregations, each with its own minister, dividing the parish between them: the northern part is the concern of Stoneykirk congregation, and the southern that of Ardwell-Sandhead congregation. The *quoad sacra* charge of Ardwell-Sandhead is a union of two congregations, Ardwell worshipping in its own lovely little church built in 1902, and Sandhead in the Old Free Church built in 1847; the two congregations were united in 1955. A new church has now been built at Sandhead. Large contributions towards meeting the cost have been made by Miss Stuart Weir, of Freugh and Balgreggan. There is also an assembly of the Christian Brethren, who recently erected a hall in Sandhead village.

Weather and distance play their part in church attendance. At Communion the church is well-filled, though at other times it may be very thinly attended. For the church organisations, such as the Woman's Guild, Sunday School, Bible Classes and Youth Clubs, a hall would be of great benefit in the life of the community. In Stoneykirk church a pipe organ with an electric blower has been installed, and the church has been re-seated and re-decorated; Ardwell church recently got electric heating, and both the churches are electrically lit.

To assist members to attend, the kirk session of Stoneykirk church have arranged for a bus to travel *via* Lochans, Meoul and Cairngarroch to the church and to return after the service on the first Sunday of the month, and on the occasions of Communion and the Christian festivals.

When a minister conducts a funeral service, he does so most frequently from the door of the house, so that the personal mourners and the public may take part together. It is the custom of the men of the area to turn out almost to a man to show their respect at a funeral, so that few homes could accommodate all for a service indoors.

Recreations

Badminton is very popular, with clubs at Stoneykirk, Sandhead and Lochans; the membership of each is in the region of 30-40. Carpet bowls has its devotees in Stoneykirk and Sandhead. The followers of 'the Roarin' Game' play locally when conditions permit, and at Ayr Ice Rink at other times. For the bowling green and tennis court in Sandhead, the membership is drawn from people of all parts of the parish. Several people have their own little boats and enjoy the amenities of Luce Bay, which is generally regarded as safe for bathing, while line fishing is also indulged in. A Small Bore Rifle Club, with headquarters at Culmore, has competitions with other clubs in the area from time to time.

In each of the schools branch libraries are operated voluntarily by the schoolmaster, but the people of the parish on the whole do not make as full use of these facilities as they might: they are not a great reading population and many of them seem to be content with the daily newspaper, which is frequently delivered by post straight from the Glasgow offices, and with the popular Sunday newspapers.

Housing

There are four large houses in the parish: Ardwell House on the Ardwell Estates, Balgreggan House on the Balgreggan Estates, Knockinaam House in the Bay of that name on the North Channel and situated on the Dunskey Estate, and Kildrochat House on the Balgreggan Estate. Of houses under £45 rental there are 386 and of these 158 are sub-standard and unfit for human habitation according to the County Sanitary Inspector. In the village of Stoneykirk there are 50 houses of which 35 have water connections; 22 of these are recently built houses with all modern conveniences, including hot water, bathroom and electric light. They consist of one living room and kitchenette and bathroom downstairs and three bedrooms upstairs. At Kildrochat there are twelve modern houses of four apartments built solely for agricultural workers. Sandhead has 46 houses in the village, of which there are 12 semi-detached permanent houses at Stairmount, near the new school. Generally speaking, farm workers' cottages are in poor condition, having neither water nor drainage facilities; sometimes water is drawn from a well by hand pump, and otherwise, though to be regretted, from an open hole very inadequately protected. The cottages conform to a type of room and kitchen with a small bedroom sandwiched between. There are no sculleries and the grates are poor; this type of house is tied to the farm and goes with the job. Within recent years, however, there has been a tendency to improve dairymen's houses, and bathrooms and sculleries have been introduced along with modern grates and hot-water systems. The farm-houses almost without exception have been kept abreast of modern standards and are generally fairly commodious two-storied houses. All houses have their gardens, and many of these are well cared for, though there are others that are left derelict. In the housing schemes there is friendly rivalry over the gardens, and many of these show a love of gardening and ingenuity of design.

These county schemes are a departure from the universal practice of the tied houses. This is all to the good; for apart from the dairyman there is no reason why the farm worker should live on the farm. With the gathering together of the people there is created a far greater spirit of community, and, moreover, the children do not have great distances to travel to school. The establishment of these clachans has meant a great deal of adjustment for the people living in close proximity. Many have been used to relative solitude, and are now surrounded by their neighbours with whom they may or may not be on good terms. This readjustment will take time, but will be accomplished by the younger generation if not by the older, when the full benefits of the schemes are realised.

Industries and Commerce

The staple industry is farming. There are 6,208 acres under tillage, 7,168 acres are rotation grass, 2,030 acres are permanent grass and 1,151 acres are rough grazings. There is some sheep-rearing, pig-breeding, fat stock rearing and growing of early potatoes. The farms are well cared for and rotation of crops is universally practised. There is very little wheat, if any, grown in the parish; the main cereals are oats and some rye. Turnips, kale, mangolds, carrots and cabbages are all grown and most of these are for cattle consumption. A number of farmers devote a few fields to the cultivation of early potatoes. The seaweed that is driven up on the shore of Luce Bay by certain winds acts as the best of manure, and with the addition of processed potato manure a very good crop of early potatoes can be obtained. The seed potatoes used are invariably 'Epicure'.

The number of hand milkers is greatly reduced and on most farms they are non-existent. Many of the farmers have their own mill for threshing the corn, but others prefer just to work with the millers, of whom there are a number in the area. Electricity is extensively used for power, heat and light, replacing peat, coal and paraffin. A whinstone quarry is situated on the Balgreggan Estate. There are two small engineering establishments, one in Stoneykirk village, and the other on Ardwell Estate, and there are also two garages, one in Stoneykirk and the other in Sandhead. These serve the needs of the farming community around, maintaining, over-hauling and renewing all sorts of farm machinery including tractors, binders, reapers, ploughs and combined harvesters. On most farms the tractor has largely replaced the horse, though there are still plenty of jobs which the horse can do when the tractor is beaten. There is a small sawmill at Ardwell which deals with locally grown timber as well as with what is imported from Germany and elsewhere, most of which is used up locally. Fishing is carried on in Luce Bay and the North Channel for commercial purposes, but it is on a very small scale. Burn fishing is almost unknown. There is, however, on Ardwell Estate a good loch with considerable resources of salmon and trout.

The creamery at Sandhead receives the milk from the farmers and converts it into dried milk or cheese. In the parish there are only a small number of farms where cheese is now made, whereas in times past it was part of the regular farm work. There are four joiners in the parish, including two brothers, one at Stoneykirk and the other at Culmore; there is also one at Ardwell and one at Sandhead. These men, along with some of the joiners from Stranraer, including the Co-operative Society, perform undertaking duties. There is a blacksmith at Meoul who repairs the farm implements in that area as well as doing what horse-shoeing is required. At Knockinaam young game is reared for shooting.

The community is served throughout its length and breadth by a few shops, each of which has vans that tour the parish and beyond. There is one combined general store and sub post-office in Stoneykirk village. Another shop is at Awhirk. In Sandhead there are two shops and a sub post-office, the postmistress there being also the district registrar of births, deaths and marriages. Ardwell has its own shop and sub post-office. In Stoneykirk village there is also the local shoemaker's shop.

There are two market gardens and nurseries: one is at Balgreggan and the other is at Lochans. Pig-breeding and rearing is carried on in Sand-head, near Low Mye, and at Cairngarroch.

Way of Life

There can be no doubt that the century has seen great changes in the way of life of the people of even a rural area like Stoneykirk parish. Mechanisation of farm work both outside and inside the farm steading has revolutionised the industry, speeding up the work to such an extent that fewer hands are required, and much of the drudgery and back-breaking effort has been banished. The proportion of the population who go to town at least once a week for entertainment and recreation is now considerable.

Along with the advent of wireless and television in the home it is not too much to say that the modern ease of travel has had an effect on the musical ability of the people. Not the same number can put their hand forward to a musical instrument, be it piano or violin or even accordion, as in days gone by. Dancing forms a perennial source of entertainment if not recreation.

Amongst the farmers and their families, who are much more localised than the farm workers, there is a certain pride in belonging to the parish. There is little of it amongst the farm workers, because, it would appear, of their habit of going from one job to another within a comparatively short time. It would be truer to say of the farm worker that he has a sense of loyalty to the county rather than to the parish.

The last century has known considerable changes in the social life of the people. Formerly the family was the focal point of the individual's life and, apart from his work and the church, there was little else to take up his time. Today the individual's interests may be spread over a host of activities, including not only the home, work and church, but also youth groups or Women's Rural Institutes, reading, films, arts and crafts, and many others. The people have more opportunities of meeting each other and with the advent of the telephone there is a very close link between homes where that facility is available.

One can sometimes feel a certain strain between farmer and farm servant, which is presumably a reflection of the feeling between employer and employed that exists in other departments of industry and commerce, though this is not common to all. A happier feature of modern times is that with the incentive of ownership many of the farmers have improved their land so that today it is yielding greater crops than in former years.

Written 1954
Additions made 1962

CHAPTER 21

THE PARISH OF KIRKMAIDEN

by the REV. J. I. ANDREWS

A Maritime Parish

Kirkmaiden, the most southerly parish in Scotland, is almost an island. The boundary by land measures about two miles across the peninsula from Luce Bay to the North Channel. For the rest the twenty square miles of the parish are enclosed by the sea. A radical change in the local way of life has been effected by the construction of modern roads and the development of road transport. The nearest railhead is at Dunragit, 14 miles from Drummore, which was a long haul for the horse and cart, and until the arrival of motor lorries Kirkmaiden continued to use the older highway of the sea. In earlier times the vessels were beached at various places suitable for unloading at low tide. The building of a quay at Drummore led to a change, but the practice was continued even after small steamers had replaced the schooners. In 1862 John Marshall settled in Drummore and started a business as miller and grain merchant. He took over the quay and the stores and for many years handled practically the whole trade of the parish. In 1934 the business was sold to a large firm operating throughout Dumfries and Galloway. Other changes were taking place: the motor lorries were already on the road and the shipping days were almost over. The business passed into new ownership in 1950 and the management of the Drummore branch became centred in Stranraer. Now the quay is deserted and the harbour is silting up. So Kirkmaiden has moved away from the island way of life.

There are now only short spells of fishing activity, mainly by boats from Stranraer, Portpatrick, Ballantrae and Ireland. They visit Luce Bay during the flat-fishing season and make Drummore their base. A little fishing is done at Portlogan, mostly for lobsters. It is in Portlogan Bay that herring are caught by the unusual method of 'jigging'. Two thin metal spars (the spokes of old umbrellas are much favoured), about ten inches long, are bound together to make a cross, which is attached by its centre near the end of a weighted line, and two more such crosses are placed at short intervals above that; unbaited hooks are attached at each of the twelve ends of the spars. In the summer evenings, when the shoals of herring come into the bay, the fishers go out in rowing boats with these 'jigs' and try to come amongst the fish, when the whole contraption is dropped into the shoal and jigged up and down by means of the line; if the shoals are packed tight, large quantities of fish are caught up on these twelve hooks. The skill lies in working fast and keeping above the shoal: 'a night at the jigging' means something different from the usual

499

connotation of the words in other parts of Scotland and can often result in a remarkable catch of herring—which, needless to say, are held to possess quality and flavour never to be found in fish caught by the more orthodox way.

The Mull of Galloway lighthouse, built in 1828 and standing high above a rocky shore where there is always a whirl of thundering tides, marks the extremity of the Scottish coast. The last mile of roadway was for a long time very rough, but it has now been resurfaced and complaints have ceased. There is a Coastguard Station at Drummore and observation posts are located at Cailiness Point, on the east shore, and at Crammog Head on the west; Crammog also has an automatic light and fog signal. At one time large numbers of local men went to sea and many became captains, but nowadays sailing has lost its appeal and Kirkmaiden is almost wholly an agricultural parish. And so we leave the sea and turn to look at the land. The first and lasting impression of Kirkmaiden is a green land.

Agriculture

Around Logan House, fairly extensive woodlands give shelter to many tropical plants; but beyond that are only a few thin plantations much harried by the wind and the whole of the southern portion of the parish contains not a single tree of any size. The farming economy centres on the dairy herds and it is the extent and quality of the grass fields which give the lasting impression of a green land. Fields are usually four years under grass, then three years under the plough; the universal cereal crop is oats, providing the best straw for fodder, but a large acreage of turnips provides the third part of a feeding system that has seen little change for the best part of a century. Change, however, is on the way. The mechanisation of farming methods has been rapid, combine harvesters are becoming more numerous, silage-making is on the increase, butter-making has ceased and cheese-making is following suit: only at two farms is cheese now made. The milk is taken by lorries to the creameries at Stranraer and Sandhead and recent times have seen a new method of transport, the carrying of milk in bulk: tankers call at the farms and the milk is taken away and delivered with the minimum of handling. A creamery at Drummore, which was started in 1900 by a group of farmers on a co-operative basis, is now a grain merchant's store; and many of the old cheese lofts have been altered to provide additional dwelling space for farmer or dairyman. With the decline in farm cheese-making came a reduction in the number of pigs and the trend continues.

In a parish once noted for the breeding of Clydesdale horses the sight of a foal is a rarity. Ploughing is still done on a very small scale in the traditional manner, but the tractor has almost completely replaced the horse. There has been a great improvement in farm steadings over the past 25 years, and particularly since the end of the war. Concrete has been extensively used for floors, stalls, and even many of the farm courts; others are laid in tarmacadam. The older buildings, including dwelling houses, are of random rubble construction, with slate roofs. (There is one thatched cottage in the parish, near the Mull smithy.) Recent building is of brick, with asbestos-cement roofing for byres and sheds. The cothouses suffered most by the long period of neglect between the wars, but in recent years many of them have also been much improved. Electricity is now in general use throughout the parish and the county water supply, inaugurated in 1955, has brought about a tremendous change for the better.

Prior to the second world war, there was one owner-occupied farm in the parish, and the rest of the land was shared by Logan Estate, Stair Estate and Ardwell Estate (which owned three farms in Kirkmaiden). Since the end of the war, the Ardwell farms and nine of these on the Logan Estate have been sold. Logan now holds 25, including two small holdings and the five small farms created on the land of Low Currochtrie in 1914 by the Department of Agriculture. Stair owns 12 farms and one small holding; and the remaining 13 farms are owner-occupied. It is a pity that the 1914 experiment on Low Currochtrie was not repeated on more farms, for those five 'family-sized' farms show a total stocking and prosperity far beyond that of the single holding. It is a serious matter that there are so few small farms in this district: the days are past when a thrifty dairyman or even a thrifty ploughman might hope at some time to set himself up in a place of his own.

Although the great majority of farm workers still live in tied houses on the farm, this is no longer essential since the tractor replaced the horse, except for the dairymen and byremen. An increasing number of men prefer to live in the villages and travel to work on the farms either on bicycle, or in some cases, by their own cars. The average size of the family is smaller, but it is no longer the case that young people, leaving school, will automatically find employment on the farm where their father is working. They must often leave home to find employment in other areas; and the tendency is towards earlier marriage. Farms are not the self-contained units they once were, and the men are content to be doing a job of work, rather than participating in the life of a miniature community; for example, every fair-sized farm formerly had its own quoiting rink, where the men and boys spent a great part of their leisure, but quoiting is never seen today. While the parish population has dropped by one-third since 1901 (1,943 in 1901 and 1,257 in 1951), it is reckoned that the population on the farms has decreased by more than half; only in Drummore village has the number of homes increased over that period.

Drummore Village

Of the 138 dwellings in Drummore village, 54 are owner-occupied, 44 are rented (from owners mainly resident in the village, and none of them from the large estates), while the other 40 houses are owned by the county council. The first scheme of 24 houses was built in 1936-1939 and the second scheme of 16 was completed in 1952.

No milling is now done at Drummore mill, the buildings of which are chiefly used as stores for coal and feeding stuffs; the principal machine is that used for cleaning and dressing seed oats, and electrical power has replaced the old water wheel.

For outdoor recreation Drummore offers a safe, sandy beach, three good tennis courts made in 1928, and a bowling green which was inaugurated in 1907.   One serious lack is a proper playing-field, with football pitch and playground space for children.   For indoor social occasions there are the Church Hall, a small Masonic Hall and the King's Hall, owned by a group of local men and used for the larger public gatherings.   In 1946 a Community Association was formed for promoting the good of the village.   A disused barracks hut vacated by the R.A.F. Air-Sea Rescue Unit was opened as a Community Centre, but after only three years it had to be handed back to the R.A.F.   The Association has now purchased property in Main Street and converted this into a recreation centre which should be a permanent asset to the village.

Portlogan

The village of Portlogan now gives its name to a lovely bay, originally called Portnessock, on the west shore of the parish.   The houses are in two parallel rows, one at shore level and the other a short distance up the hill.   In recent years the county council has carried out a housing scheme and brought a water supply that was very much needed.   The quay, which was built by Colonel Andrew McDouall of Logan in 1820, is now almost completely broken down; the seaward end with its little light-tower still stands and the tumbled blocks of stone make an effective breakwater. But the boats that were to repay the laird's investment never tied up at that quay and only a handful of rowing boats now shelter behind it.   There was a lifeboat station at Portlogan for many years.   The lifeboat was brought into use in 1866 and much of the money was raised by the efforts of R. M. Ballantyne, the writer of boys' stories.   Edinburgh people subscribed most of the money that was required and the vessel was named the 'Edinburgh and R. M. Ballantyne'.   When the boat was required in Luce Bay it was taken overland on a wooden carrier drawn by a team of horses.   The last trip was made by the lifeboat in 1926, and thereafter the boathouse became the village hall.   A reading room and recreation room were provided by the laird in the nineteenth century; in place of the original library there is now a branch of the County Library, while the other apartment is used by the carpet bowling club.

In a large circular hollow among the rocks on the northern side of the bay Colonel McDouall constructed the famous Logan Fishpond. Originally intended for the ready supply of fresh fish for the Laird's table, the pond ultimately became a showpiece in the neighbourhood and the fish are so tame that they will come at the sound of the keeper's voice and rise to take a limpet out of his hand.

The proportion of men from Portlogan who have followed the sea and risen to high rank is remarkable.   For generations the village provided officers for the mercantile marine, captains for small ships and large ships, who were pioneers of trade in Eastern waters and some of whom settled in Australia and New Zealand and others in Canada. Within living memory at least twenty men have made a name for themselves and have become almost legendary figures. In one case three brothers rose to the highest rank. Not so many are going to sea now, but a number of the villagers do retain an association with shipping and trade at home and abroad.

The Other Hamlets

Half a dozen houses near the parish church are all that remain of the village which bears the parish name of Kirkmaiden. Within the old kirk-yard are the ruined walls of what was once the parish school. Across a field, sheltered among trees, stands the Manse, built in 1837, in which presumably the Rev. John Lamb wrote the *New Statistical Account* of the parish in 1839. Sites of ruined cottages and farm buildings serve to show that this was once a more populous centre.

Damnaglaur is another small group of houses at a cross-roads a mile south of Kirkmaiden. On a corner site, which lay for years littered with the accumulated scrap of the forge, an old man created a thing of beauty— a little garden, complete with a tiny burn running through it and blooms for every season of the year.

There is no village at the Mull but the parish's third active blacksmith has his smithy here and a general builder has his yard not far away. Recently there was formed the Mull Community Association with the main purpose of erecting a Community Centre and this project has been accomplished.

Logan Estate is the only large property in the parish. The McDoualls of Logan have claimed to be one of the oldest families in Scotland, with a charter from John Balliol in 1295 and a claim to be settled on the lands of Logan long before that date. This long historic line is now ended. The last of the name, Andrew Kenneth McDouall, died in 1945; his younger brother, Nigel Douglas, had died in 1943, and they were both unmarried. The estate was inherited by a relative, Mr. (now Sir) Ninian Buchan-Hepburn, and Logan House, with the world-famous gardens, was sold to Mr. R. O. Hambro, who died in 1961. Logan Gardens Trust are now the owners. Sir Ninian has made his home in Chapel Rossan which was formerly the factor's house. In the prosperous Victorian days, around 1870, extensive additions were made to the original Logan House, giving it an entirely new frontage. After acquiring the house Mr. Hambro demolished these additions, restoring and modernising the original eighteenth century house. The gardens are still maintained with the care they merit and the gardeners' cottages have been modernised. These, with a small staff of estate workers, form a community which is much reduced, indeed, from the great days of Logan, but which has yet come to have importance again in the life of the parish.

The parish seems to have an unusually large percentage of old folk living on to their eighties and nineties. Indeed, Mr. James Blackwell, Longrigg, Ardwell, reached the age of 100 in 1960. He died in the following year.

Recreation and Social Life

Drummore is the location for most affairs organised on a parish basis—
one notable exception being Kirkmaiden Flower Show, which is traditionally held each August in Portlogan School. The smaller village is
jealous of its separate identity and works hard to preserve its own
community life. Activities in the Mull area depend upon a certain amount
of support from Drummore district so that there is some reciprocal partici-
pation between these two. Three branches of the Scottish Women's Rural
Institute have been making a valuable contribution to the life of the parish
for more than 30 years. On the men's side the Freemasons' Lodge, St.
Medans, maintains a strong membership, but a fair portion of this is drawn
from furth of the parish. Young people's organisations fluctuate according
to the leadership available. The Girl Guides and Brownies have usually
been more successful than the Boy Scouts, twice started and twice
disbanded after a few years; many potential scout leaders were obliged to
pursue their careers elsewhere. A Saturday night Youth Club, with a
membership of 20 to 25, was run in Drummore for a time by the minister.
This has been succeeded by a similar club which meets three times a month
and has a membership of 30-40. For those with an inclination towards
training and instruction, the adult education programme of the education
committee has provided classes in dressmaking, china painting, handloom
weaving and country dancing, all of which have enjoyed their season of
popularity; the one enduring affection of the parish is for amateur
dramatics, and on two splendid occasions in the past a team from Drummore has been selected from the Wigtownshire Festival to compete in the
S.C.D.A. area finals in Glasgow. Very few homes are without a radio set
and the same may almost be said about television: Drummore village
bristles with aerials and reception is excellent.

Local Lore

Most of the place names, and of the older field names, are obviously Gaelic
or Celtic in origin, with the usual mixture of old Scandinavian, but the
spoken language for many centuries has been a rather distinctive form of
lowland Scots. It is true that the tongue, like the people themselves, is
often referred to as Galloway Irish and many of our people, when they
move into other parts of Scotland, are taken to be Irish. Yet an authentic
Irish tongue is every bit as distinctive in Kirkmaiden as a true Highland
tongue is in Glasgow. Today the Scots flavour is preserved in the
pronunciation and idiom, in the turn of a phrase, rather than in the use
of peculiarly Scots terms. It comes out plainly, for example, in the
unaffected use of 'ocht' and 'nocht'; in the broad 'gaan' for either going
or gone; in 'sawin' and 'mawin' for sowing and mowing (the latter term,
incidentally, refers exclusively to the use of the scythe).

Chief among the parish antiquities is Saint Medan's Cave, situated
on the east shore, which is mentioned in most histories and guide books
dealing with the district, and is treated at some length in the Wigtownshire
volume of the Reports of the Ancient Monuments Commission. Close

at hand is a so-called healing or wishing well. In the Old Kirk of the parish is a church bell that seems to have been cast in 1534. The bell is said to have come into the possession of the Gordons of Lochinvar and from them to have passed to the Gordons of Clanyard, on the west side. They in turn gave it over to be the parish bell and it rang at the top of the hill for 250 years. For a time it was at Logan House, but after the death of the last of the McDoualls it was handed over to the Kirk Session of Kirkmaiden. Other antiquities include a panel on which is inscribed Patrick Adair's prayer and which is said to have come from the old Castle of Drummore held by the Adairs from about 1484 until the beginning of the seventeenth century.

Another item of interest in the old kirk is a copy of one of the early English versions of the Bible. Parts of it are missing, but it has Coverdale's renderings of Judges IX 53, 'and brak his brainpanne', and Jeremiah VIII 22, 'Is there no treacle in Gilead', and is probably a copy of the great Bible. A printed page has been inserted giving 'The descent of Barncluiths family from the House of Hamilton about or before the year one thousand four hundred and seven', followed by a genealogical table. The Bible was brought to the parish towards the end of last century by a farmer who came into the district from Ayrshire. Mention may also be made of 'William Todd's History'. Todd was schoolmaster in the parish from 1798 until 1843 and his book is a valuable record of happenings in the parish, especially during the early part of the nineteenth century.

Ecclesiastical Matters

The Rev. John Lamb, who wrote the parish account for the *New Statistical Account*, came out at the Disruption, taking with him four of his elders and 200 of the congregation. At first they worshipped in the open air on the green at Low Drummore, but before long Lord Stair, although he was patron of the parish church, granted them land on which to build their own place of worship. A Free Church was opened in November 1843 and in the following year work was started on a school. The architect was William Todd and the total cost was £500; much of the construction was done by voluntary labour. After the congregation had become part of the United Free Church in 1900 a new church was built and was opened in August 1903. In the old kirk on the hill the Rev. William Williamson, who succeeded Mr. Lamb in 1843, was the last to be appointed to Kirkmaiden under the system of patronage, which Parliament abolished in 1874. Mr. Williamson ministered until 1881 and was succeeded by his son, the Rev. David Williamson, who retired in 1914, but continued to live in the parish for more than 25 years. The two congregations were united in 1931, after the national union had taken place.

The present minister is the Rev. John I. Andrews, a native of Houston, Renfrewshire, who was ordained and inducted in 1943. For the few Roman Catholics in the parish, the nearest place of worship is Stranraer. A small group of Plymouth Brethren have their gospel hall in Drummore. The average attendance of 100 at the principal diet of worship at the parish church is comparable to the general situation in Scotland today, but, to a greater degree than in industrial areas, it could justly be claimed that the church still has a large place in the life of the parish. There are very few in any real sense hostile, either to the minister or to religious ideas. The 'Kirkmaiden Chronicle', a monthly news letter produced by the congregation since 1948, is circulated to 270 homes. The Sabbath, for most, if not actually a day of worship, is still a day of innocent leisure. Only at the pressing seasons of turnip singling and harvest do the farmers have recourse to Sunday work in the field and then even some of the elders have begun to count it a work of necessity.

The Way of Life

Kirkmaiden is sufficiently remote from any large centre to have preserved a strong corporate life. The parish insularity, however, is now rapidly breaking down. More people, especially the young folk, are participating in affairs on a country-wide basis—sports, dances and Young Farmers' Clubs. In the last generation, few of the farmers, and practically none of the farm workers, married outwith the parish, but today about 80 per cent of the farmers' sons are bringing their brides from elsewhere. A unit of the R.A.F. Air-Sea Rescue Service was stationed in Drummore throughout the war and provided husbands for ten local girls, but only five have remained in the district. Four German prisoners of war, working on the farms, have found their wives in Kirkmaiden and three of these have settled here. The lack of work for young people leaving school is not yet an immediate problem but in time families may have to leave the district. The bus service to Stranraer is as frequent as such an area could expect, but the timetable is not suitable for a person living in Drummore and working in Stranraer. Young people must take lodgings in some town or else the whole family must move. This is one of the less admirable features of what is, in the main, a happy, contented and prosperous parish.

Written 1956
Additions made 1962

ACKNOWLEDGMENTS

The late Professor George S. Pryde, of Glasgow University, played a leading part, as general editor, in the planning and preparation of this volume and in the subsequent stages. To the deep regret of all associated with him he died suddenly in April, 1961, while on holiday in Cornwall. He was succeeded in the position by Mr. J. B. S. Gilfillan, also of Glasgow University, who has carried out the task that fell upon him with marked competence and in a spirit of kindliness to all concerned. It was largely due to their efforts and guidance that the book became a reality.

Mr. J. G. Kyd, former registrar general, provided valuable assistance at the beginning of the enterprise.

The County Council staff kindly co-operated when information was sought Officials who gave their aid included Mr. D. R. Wilson, county clerk; Mr. R. M. Clive, county architect, and Mr. L. Girgan, of the Planning Department; Mr. J. F. Jamieson, road surveyor and water engineer; and Mr. D. A. Aitken, former county clerk.

Information relating to the burgh of Stranraer was helpfully supplied by Mr. R. McInnes Wilson, former town clerk; and Mr. A. Y. Barbour, burgh surveyor. Mr. Wilson was also kind enough to draw the diagram for the section dealing with cheesemaking.

In other parts of the county the local officials were most helpful in aiding the writers of the parish accounts.

On the subject of education Mr. H. K. C. Mair, director of education, and Mr. D. G. Gunn, assistant director, gave kind co-operation.

The local officials of the Ministry of Labour supplied figures on which several diagrams are based. Postal service details were provided readily by the Stranraer postmaster, Mr. W. W. McDougall.

The Scottish Milk Marketing Board not only gave the use of blocks, but also provided figures relating to milk production and prices and to cheesemaking, details of which formed the basis of diagrams.

Farming statistics came to us from Mr. J. Thorburn, county agricultural adviser, and some of the fishing information from Mr. Alex. McMillan.

Mr. A. E. Truckell, curator of Dumfries Museum, with customary helpfulness, wrote on the archaeological aspect of some parts of the county and, as indicated elsewhere, Mr. R. J. A. Eckford, Moffat, contributed the section on geology. The references to Portlogan lifeboat are based on information kindly sent by Miss Galloway, Portlogan, who also lent pictures, and Mrs. Sheila Gorman, Drummore.

Splendid assistance was given in the matter of research and in other ways by Mr. J. S. Boyd and Mr. W. J. Kyle. Mr. A. Wilson, county librarian, and his predecessor, Miss E. McCaig, gave valuable service on numerous occasions.

In the field of natural history we were fortunate to have contributions from Mr. J. G. Hay, Mr. Ian Murray, Mr. John McQuaker and Commander H. A. Inglis.

Grateful acknowledgment is made of the kindness of the proprietors of the *Galloway News* in giving gratis the use of a considerable number of blocks for illustrative purposes.

A special tribute is due to the writers of the parish accounts for carrying out their exacting and difficult task with so much care and diligence. Thanks are also due to many other people for their help and co-operation.

BIBLIOGRAPHY

Old and *New Statistical Accounts.*

Wigtownshire Survey Report, prepared by Mr. Richard E. Moira and Mrs. Moira, planning consultants, in conjunction with Mr. R. M. Clive, county architect and planning officer.

Reports from Marine Station, Millport.

Dumfries and Galloway Police reports.

Scottish Census reports.

Wigtownshire Free Press files.

Department of Agriculture reports.

Ministry of Labour reports.

Rev. William Mackenzie, *History of Galloway from Earliest Times,* 1851.

P. H. McKerlie, *History of Lands and their Owners in Galloway,* new edition, 1906.

Æneas J. G. Mackay, *Memoir of Sir James Dalrymple, First Viscount Stair,* 1873.

William Learmont, *Kirkcudbrightshire and Wigtownshire,* 1920.

Gordon Fraser, *Wigtown and Whithorn,* 1877.

Sir Andrew Agnew, Bart., M.P., *A History of the Hereditary Sheriffs of Galloway,* 1864.

Rev. Charles Hill Dick, *Highways and Byways in Galloway and Carrick,* new edition, 1938.

Sir Herbert Maxwell, Bart., *Dumfries and Galloway,* 1896.

APPENDIX I

STEWARTRY OF KIRKCUDBRIGHT

STATISTICS OF LICENCES FOR MOTOR VEHICLES AND DRIVERS

Number of Motor Vehicles licensed during the years:

1954	5,619
1955	6,114
1956	6,228
1957	6,484
1958	6,746
1959	6,874
1960	7,996
1961	8,220
1962	8,658

Analysis of 1962 Total:

Motor Cars	5,327
Motor Cycles	850
Goods Vehicles	734
Tractors	1,647
Hackney Vehicles	47
Exempt Vehicles	53
	8,658

The rapid increase in the use of motor vehicles is shown clearly from the above table. The break-up of the total vehicles for 1962 into categories shows the growing importance of tractors in an agricultural district.

No. of Driving Licences valid during the years:

1904	90
1914	312
1924	1,092
1934	3,390
1944	3,475
1954	7,370
1959	8,610
1962	9,312

It would appear from the above table that about half the population who are of age and physically able to drive are in possession of current driving licences. This underlines the importance of a car as a means of travel in an area where public service transport is limited and tending to diminish.

APPENDIX II

Civil Parish	1901	1911	1921	1931	1951	1961
Anwoth	651	688	611	555	658	611
Balmaclellan	634	559	557	627	550	437
Balmaghie	802	770	764	650	681	659
Borgue	1,045	1,023	990	990	936	752
Buittle	879	825	799	778	764	692
Carsphairn	351	360	365	355	248	238
Colvend and Southwick	1,171	1,143	1,430	1,128	1,026	901
Crossmichael	1,231	1,196	1,231	1,160	1,731	1,775
Dalry	826	807	860	843	775	752
Girthon	1,209	1,174	975	1,015	875	838
Kells	878	847	803	848	756	759
Kelton	3,734	3,746	3,438	3,621	3,396	3,145
Kirkbean	685	711	679	560	583	522
Kirkcudbright	3,309	3,116	3,054	3,188	3,316	3,131
Kirkgunzeon	527	497	548	487	467	446
Kirkmabreck	1,859	1,549	1,333	1,294	1,301	1,240
Kirkpatrick-Durham	959	914	860	783	803	643
Kirkpatrick-Irongray	701	594	648	602	587	532
Lochrutton	497	484	559	453	527	510
Minnigaff	1,309	1,202	1,127	1,144	1,251	1,342
New Abbey	957	742	779	728	790	773
Parton	613	593	597	548	506	395
Rerrick	1,356	1,293	1,332	1,228	1,012	883
Terregles	454	439	428	567*	448*	380
Tongland	693	751	704	669	575	532
Troqueer	6,599	7,050	6,870	768*	873*	731
Twynholm	718	758	751	720	808	987
Urr	4,736	4,536	4,063	4,032	4,482	4,260
Total of County	39,383	38,367	37,155	30,341*	30,725*	28,866

* Extension of Dumfries Burgh.

SMALL BURGHS

Burgh	1901	1911	1921	1931	1951	1961
Castle-Douglas	3,018	3,016	2,801	3,008	3,322	3,255
Dalbeattie	3,469	3,357	2,998	3,011	3,285	3,105
Gatehouse	1,013	1,032	893	888	877	822
Kirkcudbright	2,386	2,205	2,101	2,311	2,499	2,439
New Galloway	376	352	348	307	305	327

INDEX

THE STEWARTRY OF KIRKCUDBRIGHT

A

Abbeyyard, 143
Adam, Stephen, 320
Agnew, Col. David, 74
Agricultural Wages, 72, 154, 197, 242, 286
Agriculture, 28-29, 32-34, 71, 82, 89, 99, 100, 103, 111-113, 121-2, 127, 139, 152-3, 163, 170, 179, 196, 203-5, 215, 230, 241, 245, 251, 271, 275, 278, 283, 290, 302, 306, 309, 318; see also Cattle, Farmers' Co-operatives, Sheep, Stewartry Agricultural Society
Aitkenhead, Rev. S. M., 217
Alan, Lord of Galloway, 26, 108, 143
Alexander II, King, 26
Alvingham, Lord, 274
Angling, 73, 146, 155, 166, 174, 234, 258, 271, 313; see also Fishing.
Antiquities, 31, 74, 79, 86, 99, 108, 135, 142-3, 147, 218, 247, 280-1, 293, 304, 305, 315, 325; see also Archaeology
Anwoth, 66-77, 158
Archaeology, 30-1, 79, 85-6, 99, 110, 111, 135, 142-3, 147, 218, 221-2, 234, 235, 247, 280, 305, 315, 325; see also Antiquities.
Ardwall, 68, 69, 71
Armoured Fighting Vehicles Proving Establishment, 206
Art Galleries, 54, 55; see also Broughton House, Harbour Cottage.
Auchencairn, 28, 279, *passim*
Auchenskeoch Castle, 136
Ayr Bank, 27

B

Bagimont's Roll, 236
Baird Trust, 134
Ballads, 71
Balliol College, Oxford, 108, 109
Balliol, Edward (d. 1367), 185
Balliol, John, King, 143
Balliol, John, of Barnard Castle (d. 1269), 26, 108, 109, 264
Balmaclellan, 78-84
Balmaghie, 85-96
Banks, 28, 40, 163, 172, 328; see also Ayr Bank
Savings Banks, 188, 247
Bannatyne, Sir William, 79
Barbour, J. G., 147
Barbour, James, of Bogue, 148

Barbour, Miss M., of Glendarroch, 148
Bargrennan, 256, 261
Barnbarroch, 127
Beekeeping 319
Beeswing, 272
Bell, James, 276
Bell, John, of Whiteside, 303
Benedictine Nunnery of Lincluden, 134
Bibliography, 332-4
Biggar, James, of Chapelton, 319
Blackett, Major C. W. S., of Arbigland, 195
Blackford, 316
Bone, Phyllis, 210
Borgue, 98-107
Bothwell Brig, 147
Boyd, Rev. Dr. A. K. H., 237
Bridge-of-Dee, 85, 180
Bridgend, 132
Bridges, 301-2
Bristowe, Ethel, 79
Bristowe, Sidney, 79
British Electricity Authority, 138
Broughton House, Kirkcudbright, 54, 211
Brown, J. Douglas, of Roberton, 99
Brown, Rev. Dr. Thomas, 299
Brown Bequest, 191
Bruce, David, King, 216
Bruce, Marjory, 160
Bruce, Robert, King, 17, 260, 315
Brune, Gilbert, Abbot of Sweetheart Abbey, 265
Bryson, Mungo, 275
Buchanites, 229
Buittle, 108-120
Buittle Castle, 108
Burghs, 41-2, 56-60
Burns, Robert, 148, 160
Burnside, Rev. George M., 324

C

Cairnholy, 30, 221
Cairnsmore of Fleet, 220, 255
Campbell, Admiral John, 194
Campbell, Rev. John, 194
Cardoness Castle, 67, 68
Cargenbridge, 306, 307
Carlingwark House, 189
Carlingwark Loch, 30, 184
Carnation Milk Factory, Lincluden, 242
Carruthers, Rev. Andrew, Archbishop of Glasgow, 329

Carsethorn, 194
Carsfad Dam, 48, 146, 173
Carsluith, 221, 222
Carson, James, 164
Carsphairn, 121-4
Castle-Douglas, 29, 42, 142, 178, 180, 183, 184-192; see also Crossmichael, Kelton.
Castle-Douglas Cattle Market, 28, 38, 186, 187
Cattle, 27, 71
  Ayrshires, 28, 90, 101, 127, 170, 187, 204, 216, 230, 241, 251, 283, 309, 318, 325
  Galloways, 28, 71, 101, 127, 153, 216, 251, 302, 309, 325
  Belted Galloways, 28, 170, 187, 230
Caulkerbush, 127
Causewayend [Carlingwark], 179, 185
Chalmers, Dr. MacGregor, 320
Chapelton Row, 105
Charles II, King, 305
Charles Edward Stuart, Prince, 29
Children's games, 119
Church of Scotland, 27, 61-3, 87, 134, 138; see also Churches, Covenanters, Religion
Churches, 74, 82, 86, 87, 105-106, 115, 123-4, 134, 143, 154, 164, 175-6, 181, 188, 199, 212, 216, 224, 229, 246, 260, 270, 277, 278, 286-8, 293, 298, 307, 311, 320, 324, 329, see also Communion plate
Cistercian Order, 263, 281
Clachanpluck, see Laurieston
Clarebrand, 141, 145
Clark, David, 70
Clark-Kennedy, Col. William H., 124
Clatteringshaws Dam, 173, 256
Clement, James, 303
Climate, 19-20, 159, 215, 220, 233, 255, 264, 325
Clubs, see Voluntary Organisations
Cluden Water, 233
Cochrane, Thomas, 209
Colvend and Southwick, 125-136
Communion Plate, 87, 115, 277, 280, 320
Congregational Church, 63
Copland, Miss, of Colliston, 325
Corsock, 229, 278
Covenanters, 27, 78, 79, 86, 87, 110, 144, 147, 164, 176, 202, 235, 260, 303
Cowan, Jean, 148
Cowie, Rev. John, 329
Craik, Dr. James, 194
Craik, William, of Arbigland, 27, 193
Crawford, Duncan, of Netherskeldon, 68
Creetown, 28, 29, 220
Criffel, 193, 263
Crocketford, 316

Crockett, Samuel Rutherford, 17, 87, 88, 179, 185, 279
Crosby, Rev. Thomas, 246
Crossmichael, 30, 137-45
Currie, David, 280
Cutlare, Adam, 280

D

Dalbeattie, 29, 31, 37, 42, 112, 114, 126, 324-330; see also Urr
Dalbeattie Port [Dub o' Hass], see Dalbeattie
Dalry, 146-156
Damian, John, Abbot of Tungland, 299
David I, King, 25, 74
David II, King, 26, 290
Dawes, General, 208
de Morville, see Morville
de Quenci, see Quenci
de Rerik, see Rerik
Devorgilla, 26, 108, 109, 143, 264
Distributive and Service Trades, 39, 75, 83, 124, 129, 152, 163, 172, 187, 232, 242, 272, 280, 300
Dobson, Cowan, 148
Dobson, H. J., 148
Dobson, Raeburn, 148
Dobson, Thomas, 299
Donnelly, Father, 164
Douglas, Archibald "The Grim", Third Earl of Douglas, 26, 86
Douglas, William, 147
Douglas, Sir William of Gelston Castle, 179, 183, 185
Douglas Hall, 127
Drumstinchall, 132
Dry stane dykes, 76, 90, 104, 153
Dryburgh Abbey, 98
Duchrae, 86
Duff, Mary, 139
Dumfries Town Council, 27, 29, 37, 291-292, 305
Dumfries and Galloway Development Association, 37
Dumfries and Galloway Standard, 253
Dumfries News, 40
Dunbar, Major Basil D. Hope-, 99
Dunbar, Sir Charles Hope-, of St. Mary's Isle, 208-309
Duncan, Rev. George, 247
Duncan, Rev. Dr. Henry, 247
Dundeugh, 146
Dundrennan, 279
Dundrennan Abbey, 135, 286

E

Earlstoun, 146, 173
Earlstoun Castle, 147

Education, 51-54, 69-70, 81, 92-3, 105, 116-7, 130-1, 141, 151, 165, 174, 182, 189, 195-6, 208-9, 217, 221, 228, 238, 250, 258, 261, 269, 275, 278, 284, 293, 301, 307, 311, 319, 328; see also Libraries, Meals in schools
Further Education, 53-4, 174, 190, 198, 209, 218, 250
Edward I, King, 31
Electricity, services and distribution, 49-50, 76, 104, 130, 140-1, 150, 162, 173, 181, 190, 203, 249, 268, 285
Elliot, Captain Scott, 298
Ellis, L. M., 330
Enclosures, 27, 76, 86
Entertainment and recreation, 64-5; see also Voluntary Organisations
Episcopal Church, 63, 96, 135, 154, 176, 189, 212, 260, 330
Erskine, Sir John M., 211
Ewart, Rev. John, 306

F

Faed, John, 159
Farm Industries; see Agriculture, Industries
Farmers' Co-operatives, 38
Farming; see Agriculture
Fauna, 22-4, 89, 99, 136, 147, 172, 218, 224, 226, 234, 252, 258; see also Game
Fergus, Lord of Galloway, 26, 86
Ferguson Bequest Fund, 134
Fisher, Annie, 299
Fisher, Rev. Peter, 299
Fisher, William, 287
Fishing, 38, 99, 103, 197, 264, 301; see also Angling
Flora, 20-2, 89, 99, 146, 220, 226
Forestry, 29, 34-5, 71, 146, 163-4, 171, 223, 256, 257-8, 264, 278, 310; see also Woodlands
Forestry Commission, 34-5, 83, 90-1, 114, 121, 126, 128, 161, 171, 204, 205, 220, 256, 260, 264, 310
Forrester, Adam, 148
Frew, Rev. Dr. David, 57, 315

G

Gaelic, 25, 88
Galbraith, C. E., 291
Gallgaidhil, 25, 31
Gallovidian, The, 330
Galloway, Randolph Stewart, 12th Earl of, 256, 307
Galloway, Rev. Dr. George, 182
Galloway Hydro-Electric Scheme, 48-9, 80, 285, 297
Galloway Nags, 28, 39

Galloway News, 28, 39, 188, 253, 276, 315
Galloway Publicity Association, 40
Galloway Water Power Company, 49, 138, 140, 173, 213, 297, 301
Game, 76, 78, 146, 147, 205, 218, 258; see also Fauna
Gas, services and distribution, 47, 81, 190, 203, 268, 328
Gatehouse, 28, 29, 30, 42, 67, 158; see also Anwoth, Girthon
Gelston, 180
Geology, 17-9, 85, 108, 215
Gillespie, Rev. John, 169
Gillone, James, 301
Girthon, 67, 158-68
Gladstone, John, 185
Glenachan, James, 291
Glenkiln Reservoir, 240
Glenlee Power Station, 48, 80, 173
Glenlochar, 30, 85, 143
Glen Trool, National Forest Park, 17, 256, 257
Glen Trool Village, 258
Gordon, Alexander, of Earlstoun, 147
Gordon, Edward, 235
Gordon, John, of Largmore, 176
Gordon, John, Viscount Kenmure, 75
Gordon, William, of Earlstoun, 69, 147
Gordon, Sir William, 107
Gospatrick, Gilbert, 136
Gospatrick, Thomas de Culwen, 136
Gourlay, William Robert, 148
Grant, Rev. Charles P., 330
Grant, Rev. James R., 115
Greyfriars' Monastery, 202
Grierson, Sir Robert, of Lag, 164, 303
Grierson, Rev. Thomas, 194

H

Halliday, David, of Mayfield, 303
Hannay, Col. Frederick Rainsford-, 68, 69, 76
Harbour Cottage, Kirkcudbright, 54
Hardgate, 316
Haslam, Oliver H., 135
Haugh-of-Urr, 316
Hayward, R. Curtis-, 148
Health and health services, 43-4, 81, 131, 141, 150, 162, 175, 178, 213, 223, 228, 239, 250, 260, 270, 285, 294, 295, 311; see also Hospitals, Water and drainage
Henderson, Rev. James Bell, 98
Henniker-Hughan, Admiral Sir Arthur, 274
Henry, William, 284
Hepburn, William, A. F., 88
H.M. Office of Works, 265, 281
Heron, Robert, 328
Herries, Sir John, of Terregles, 216

Heston Island, 284

History, 25-9, 78, 85, 108-110, 111, 137, 149, 159, 179, 183, 185, 193, 201, 226, 235, 245, 264, 292, 303, 309, 314; see also Antiquities, Archaeology

Hope, David, 134

Hornel, Edward Atkinson, 54, 210, 211

Hornsby, George Faed, 71

Horticulture, 38

Hospitals, 43, 81, 141, 162, 175, 213, 239, 250

Housing, 44-5, 72-3, 82, 91, 103, 118, 124, 142, 149, 162, 175, 190, 196, 207, 216, 230, 248, 261, 269, 282, 293-4, 307, 312, 316-7

Hughan, Henniker-, see Henniker-Hughan

I

Industries, 28-37, 91, 118, 129, 139, 187, 206, 242, 252, 261, 327; see also Occupations
Agricultural Industries, 204
Barytes, 36, 284
Bobbin Mill, 37
Coal, 28
Copper Ore, 284
Cotton manufacture, 28
Denim overalls, 37
Granite, 28, 35, 114, 223, 326
Imperial Chemical Industries, 36, 272, 295, 306
Iron ore, 28
Lead, 28, 36
Marl, 27, 185
Nobel and plastics, 36-7
Pre-cast concrete, 36, 223
Quarrying, 128, 302
Saw-mills, 38, 271
Shipbuilding, 129
Steel radiators, 37
Timber processing, 38
Uranium, 36

J

James II, King, 26, 182
James III, King, 234
James IV, King, 300
James V, King, 149
James VI, King, 193
James VII, King, 27
Jameson, Andrew, Lord Ardwall, 69
Jardine, W. G., 19
"Jeanie Deans", see Walker, Helen
John, Bishop of Whithorn, 74
Johnston, John, 88
Johnston, Rev. John, 138
Johnstone, Rev. John, 87
Jones, John Paul, 194, 208

K

Kells, 169-77
Kelton, 178-92
Kendoon Power Station, 48
Kenmure Castle, 79
Kennedy, Clark-, see Clark-Kennedy
Kinharvie House, 266, 269
Kinnear, Rev. David, 330
Kippford, 126, 127
Kirk, Rev. R. L., 217
Kirkandrews, 98
Kirkbean, 193, 200
Kirkcudbright, 26, passim, 201-214
Kirkcudbrightshire Advertiser, see Galloway News
Kirkdale, 220
Kirkgunzeon, 30, 215-219
Kirkmabreck, 67, 220-25
Kirkpatrick-Durham, 30, 226-32, 317
Kirkpatrick-Irongray, 30, 233-43
Knox, John, 51

L

Landsborough, Rev. David, 148
Laurieston, 85, 88, 91, 94
Laurieston Hall Hospital, 94
Law and order, 42-3, 119, 123, 131, 222, 243
Learmonth, Professor Sir James, 70, 159
Learmonth, William, 70
Lennox, John, 160
Lennox, Robert, 164, 303
Levellers; see Enclosures
Libraries, 54, 93, 117, 131, 141, 155, 165, 173, 189, 211, 221, 228, 250, 253, 260, 288, 312
Local Government, 41-2, 151, 161, 219, 246, 262, 284; see also Education, Health and health services, Housing, Roads, Stewartry of Kirkcudbright County Council
Loch Arthur, 263
Loch Doon, 48
Loch Fleet, 158
Loch Grannoch, 158
Loch Ken, 23, 48
Loch Kindar, 199, 263
Loch Knockman, 146
Loch Knocksting, 146
Loch Lochaber, 263
Loch Reglund, 146
Loch Roan, 180
Loch Skerrow, 159
Loch Whinyeon, 159
Lochenkit, 46
Lochfergus, 26
Lochinvar, 46, 146
Lochinvar Castle, 147, 148
Lochrutton, 245-254

Lorg Hill, 146

M

McCubine, Alexander, 235
McCulloch, Agnes, 68
McCulloch, Sir Alexander, 69
McCulloch, David, of Ardwall, 68
McCulloch, Gilbert, of Cardoness, 68, 69
McCulloch, Sir Godfrey, 69
McCulloch, William, of Myreton, 69
McDowall, John, of Girstingwood, 284, 287
MacEwan, Elspeth, 79, 148
MacGill, David, 79
McGlashan, Rev. R. B., 164
McGowan, Rev. A., 148
Machermore Eventide Home, 260
McKeand Bequest, 164
MacKenzie, Rev. James, 324
McKerlie, P. H., 226
Mackie, Ivie, 287
Mackie, John Gladstone, 287
Mackie, John H., M.P., 143
McLellan, Colonel, 298
McLellan, Sir Thomas, of Bombie, 202
McLellan Trust, 138
MacLellan's Castle, 202
McMichael, Prof. John, 159
McMichan, Rev. John, 147
McMillan, Rev. John, 86
McRobert, Andrew, 303
McTaggart, James, 76
Mainsriddle 30, 127
Maitland, Rev. James, 169
Malcolm III, King, 25
Malcolm, John, 147
Manxman's Lake, 201
Marist Brothers, 266
Marshall, Billy, 202
Martin, Rev. Samuel, 87
Mary, Queen of Scots, 303
Maxwell, Major General Sir Aymer, of Kirkennan, 117
Maxwell, Commander D. Herries, (R.N.), of Munches, 117
Maxwell, Sir Herbert, 98, 280
Maxwell, James Clerk, 278
Maxwell, John Hunter, 188
Maxwell, N. J. H., of Munches, 326
Maxwell, Major Wellwood, 298, 328, 329, 330
Maxwell, Rev. William, 69
Maxwell-Witham, Col., 266
Maxwelltown, 29, 305
Mears, Sir Frank, 72
Meiklewood Loch, 297
Melville, Dr. Frances, 148
Merrick, 19, 255

Milk Marketing Board, see Scottish Milk Marketing Board
Milking-machine, invention of, 204, 284
Milligan, Dr. Edward, 194
Milton, 316
Milton Loch, 30, 314
Minnigaff, 28, 30, 255-262
Mitchell, Andrew, of Barcheskie, 284
Mons Meg, 182, 185
Montgomery, Rev. J. B. F., 164
Moore, Henry, 236
Moray, Regent, 79
Morville, Sir Hugo de, 98
Mossdale, 173
Murray, Alexander, of Broughton and Cally, 67, 160, 303
Murray, Rev. George, 80
Murray, Rev. George, 80
Murray, Rev. George, 159
Murray, James, 160
Murray, John, Earl of Annandale, 281
Murray, Richard, 160
Murray, Dr. Thomas, 159
Murray-Usher, Mrs. Elizabeth, 68, 160
Museums, 54, 55

N

National Assistance Board, 51
National Forest Park, see Glen Trool
National Playing Fields Association, 326
Neilson, James, 304
Neilson, William, 88
Netherhall, 94
New Abbey, 135, 263-73
New Galloway, 29, 42, 199, 172; see also Kells
New Statistical Account, 28, 56, 67, 75, 98, 101, 106, 121, 126, 127, 137, 141, 142, 159-60, 164, 169, 172, 178, 194, 215, 218, 229, 249, 252, 279, 293, 307, 308, 311, 313, 324
Newall, Andrew, 326
Newall, David, 326
Newall, Homer, 326
Nicholson, John, of Kirkcudbright, 87
Nicholson, Stewart, of Bombie and Castlecreavie, 204, 284
Nicholson Trust, 293
Norfolk, Bernard Alan-Howard, 16th Duke of, 266

O

Occupations, 83, 91, 103, 124, 129, 139, 152, 163, 172, 195, 197, 206, 218, 227, 242, 253, 272, 295, 300-1, 310, 317-8, 327
Old Bridge of Urr, 142
"Old Mortality," see Paterson, Robert

Old Statistical Account, 101, 138, 139, 160, 169, 171, 173, 216, 247, 249, 279, 285, 313, 316
Oppenheimer, Charles, 210
Orchardton Tower, 110
Orkney, Earldom of, 25
Osborne, Rev. John, 303
Oswald, Richard, 194
Oswald, Major R. A., of Cavens, 194, 266

P

Palnackie, 108, 117
Parishes, 56-60
Parliamentary representation, 29, 41; see also Political parties
Parton, 274-8
Paterson, Robert, "Old Mortality", 79
Paton, Rev. James A., 330
Paul, John, see Jones, John Paul
Pentland Rising, 79, 147
Place names, derivations of, 25, 78, 86, 88, 98, 108, 121, 136, 137, 158, 201, 218, 220, 263, 266, 274, 279-80, 290, 303-4, 305, 309, 313
Political Parties, 29, 41, 75, 133, 155, 251, 262, 271, 294
Poole, Rector, 105
Population, 28, 42, 56-61, 76-7, 93, 104, 115, 122, 127, 139, 149, 161, 172, 176, 178, 186, 195, 205, 218, 221, 227, 238, 240, 247, 267, 282, 292, 300, 307, 311, 314
Portling, 127
Portowarren, 127
Postal services, 129-30, 185, 190, 222, 240, 248, 288
Pritchard, John, 70
Professions, 40; see also Occupations

Q

Quenci de, Earl of Winchester, 26

R

Railways, 28, 68, 81, 133, 145, 180, 185, 225; see also Transport
Rainy, Thomas, 105
Ravenshall, 220
Reid, Prof, H. M. B., 86
Religion, 25, 26-7, 61-3, 115, 116; see also Church of Scotland, Churches, Cistercian Order, Episcopal Church, Roman Catholic Church
Rerik, Adam de, 280
Rerik, Gilbert, 280
Rerrick, 279-89
Rhonehouse, 180
Richmond, Prof. I. A., 143

Rights-of-way, 316
River Cree, 255
River Dee, 23, 30, 38, 63, 85, 98, 140, 173, 201, 213, 297, 298
River Fleet, 67, 98
River Ken, 146, 173
River Nith, 23
River Tarff, 297
River Urr, 109, 117, 133, 313
Roads, 27, 50, 51, 68, 81, 92, 162, 185, 203, 240, 249, 268, 286, 316; see also Rights-of-way
Rockcliffe, 126, 127
Roman Catholic Church, 63, 96, 117, 135, 154, 164, 189, 212, 224, 260, 270, 329
Rough Island, 136
Rutherford, Samuel, 74, 220

S

St. Constantine, 31
St. Cuthbert, 201
St. John's Town of Dalry, see Dalry
St. Joseph, Dr., 143
St. Lawrence's Chapel, 135
St. Mary's Isle, 208
St. Ninian, 25
St. Patrick, 236
Salmond, George, 70
Saltire Society, 192
Sandgreen, 163
Sandyhills, 126, 127, 132
Satterness, see Southerness
Savings Banks, see Banks
Scaur, The, 126
School Meals Service, 53, 105, 117, 131, 182, 199, 209, 217, 221, 276
Schools, see Education
Scott, Sir Walter, 79, 147, 182, 185, 202, 235
Scottish Milk Marketing Board, 100, 111, 128, 170, 197, 204, 230, 251, 310, 327
Scottish Woodland Owners' Association, 38; see also Woodlands
Selby, Sir Walter, 315
Selkirk, Earl of, 208
Senwick, 98
Shankfoot, 85
Shaw, Robert, 69
Shawhead, 239, 241
Sheep, 101, 112, 171, 205, 231, 242, 283, 302, 309
Blackfaced sheep, 27, 83, 90, 193, 230
Shennan, David, 69
Shipping, 27, 28, 39, 67, 117, 133, 206, 279, 328
Sinclair, Archibald St. Clair, 16th Baron, of Knocknalling, 148
Sloan, George, 135
Slogarie, 93

Smith, Rev. Samuel, of Borgue, 76, 98
Smuggling, 27, 119-20, 125
Solway Firth, 47, 67, 98, 125, 193, 201, 255, 279
Solway Hatcheries, 38, 264
Somervell, Rev. William, 307
South of Scotland Electricity Board, 49, 130, 150, 162, 249, 268, 286, 328; see also Electricity, services and distribution
Southerness, 194
Southerness Lighthouse, 194
Southwick and Colvend, 125-36
Springholm, 226, 316, 317
Sproat, George G. B., 71
Sprot, Hugh, 315
Sprotte, Mark, 315
Stark, Robert, 69
Stark, Rev. W. A., 226, 229
Statistical Accounts of Scotland, see New Statistical Account, Old Statistical Account
Stevenson, Robert Louis, 64, 234, 238
Stewart, A. A. McC., of Shambellie, 266
Stewart, Alexander A., 70
Stewart, Rev. Duncan, 330
Stewart, Rev. J. D., 138
Stewart, J. Douglas, 138
Stewart, Sir John, 160
Stewart, Sir Mark J., M.P., 134
Stewart, Mitchell B. A., 138
Stewart, William A., 138
Stewartry Agricultural Society, 185
Stewartry Observer, 330
Stewartry of Kirkcudbright, 17, 26, passim
Stewartry of Kirkcudbright County Council, 41-2, 208, 291, 298
Strachan, Alexander, 320
Strachan, Douglas, 320
Strain, Rev. John, Archbishop of Edinburgh, 329
Stroanfreggan, 151
Sweetheart Abbey, 109, 110, 143, 264

T

Tarff, 29
Tarff Valley Agricultural Co-Operative Society, 300
Templetown, Henry Upton, 5th Viscount, 79
Terregles, 290-5
Thomas, Bishop of Galloway, 110
Thomson, John, 69
Thorburn, Rev. William, 307
Thorfinn, the Mighty, 25
Threave Castle, 26, 86, 182, 185
Threave School of Gardening, 38
Tongland, 173, 180, 297-304
Tongland Abbey, 300
Tongland Power Station, 48, 297

Topography, 67, 78, 85, 98, 108, 121, 125-6, 146, 158, 178, 184, 193, 201, 215, 226, 233, 245, 255, 263, 274, 279, 290, 297, 306, 313, 324
Tourism, 40, 128, 163, 172, 187, 191, 222, 258, 261
Townhead of Greenlaw, 140, 142
Trades, see Distributive and service trades, Occupations
Train, Joseph, 185
Transport, 39, 120, 133, 145, 150, 169, 180, 185, 198, 203, 217, 228, 239, 250, 261, 268, 274, 286, 291; see also Railways
Troqueer, 305-7
Trotter, Dr. A., 146, 148
Trotter, James, 148
Trotter, R. de Bruce, 148
Trotter, Dr. Robert, 148
Tungland, see Tongland
Twynholm, 28, 309-12

U

United Creameries, 300, 310
Urr Parish, 313-23; see also Dalbeattie
Usher, Murray-, see Murray-Usher

V

Village Halls, 81, 119, 132, 145, 198-9, 248, 277, 278, 289, 294, 308, 311
Voluntary organisations and services, 63-4, 73, 74, 81, 94-5, 106-7, 119, 123, 132, 144, 155, 165-6, 173, 181, 191, 199, 210, 211, 223, 228, 242, 259, 270, 276, 289, 294, 312, 320-2

W

Wages, see Agricultural wages
Walker, Helen "Jeanie Deans", 235
Wallets Marts, see Castle-Douglas Cattle Market
War office, Tank Range, 282
Washington, George, 194
Water and drainage, 46-7, 80, 91, 104, 130, 140, 150, 162, 180, 190, 203, 227, 240, 245, 249, 261, 268, 285, 292, 311, 327
Waterloo Monument, 265
Watson, Donald, 148
Watson, George P. H., 70
Watson, Commander Lyndesey, 275
Way of life, 65-6, 72, 83-4, 95, 96, 97, 106, 145, 156, 166-8, 200, 214, 232, 253, 262, 272, 289, 295, 308, 312, 323
Welsh, David, of Collin, 287
Welsh, Rev. John, 235

West of Scotland College of Agriculture,
  38, 171, 300
Whinnieliggate, 30
Whithorn, 26, 149
Wigtownshire, 26
William the Lion, King, 86, 108
Williamson, Rev. Dugald Stewart, 303

Witchcraft, 79, 148
Witham, Maxwell-, see Maxwell-Witham
Women's Rural Institutes, see Voluntary
  organisations
Woodhall Loch, 85
Woodlands, 34-5, 71, 103, 113-4, 264
Wraith's Tower, 193

INDEX

THE COUNTY OF WIGTOWN

A

Abbeys, 351, 367, 421
Accent, local, 456, 504
Adair family, 352
Adders, 443, 445
Age structure, 380
Agnew family crypt, 481
Agnew monument, 482
Agnew Park, 465
Agnew, Sir Andrew, of Lochnaw, 351
Agriculture, 353-9
Agriculture, Department of, 438
Airfields and army camps, 362, 423, 457
Airport, civil, 374
Air-sea rescue service, 478
Aliens, 379, 506
Alluvial soil, 340
American troops in shire, 457
Ammunition dumping, 361
Angling. See Fishing
Animal feeding stuffs, 361
Animals, wild, 350
Antiquarian Society, 462
Antiquities, 351, 390, 410, 428, 432, 448, 482, 492, 504-5
Aquatic plants, 346
Archaeology, 409, 410, 437, 492. See also Antiquities
Archie's Bog, 465
Ardwell House, 495
Area of Wigtownshire, 437
Army camps, 423, 457
Artificial insemination, 358
Artificial loch, 449
Auction Mart, 467
Ayrshire cattle, 357
Ayrshire, immigrants from, 457

B

Bacon industry, 467
Badgers, 443, 445
Badminton, 385, 495
Bakery industry, 362
Baking at farms, 454, 482
Baldoon air station, 362
Balgreggan House, 495
Ballantyne, R. M., 502
Balliol charter, 503
Balliol support for England, 351
Barrachan village, 435
Belted Galloways, 357

Bible, early, at Kirkmaiden, 505
Bingo sessions, 463
Birds, wild, 348-9
Birkhill shales, 343
Bishopburn housing scheme, 369, 450
Bittern, 349
Black and White lochs, 445
Black Quarter of Inch, 484
Blacksmiths, 469
Bladnoch Creamery, 398
Blown sand, 339-40
Boating in Luce Bay, 495
Boglands and peat mosses, 339
Bombing trials, 439
Boreland Fell quarry, 408
Bothies disappear, 358
"Bottomless" loch, 445
Boulder clay, 345
Boundaries extended, 368
Bowling clubs, 385
Brewis, Henry John, M.P., 366
Brick clay, 345
Bridge clubs, 465
British Friesian cattle, 427
British Legion, 383
Buchan-Hepburn, Sir Ninian, 503
Budgerigar society, 465
Bungalows, 370
Burghal history, 352
Burns, Robert, 435, 455
Burrowhead military camp, 423
Buses, 373, 461, 495
Business and Professional Women's Club, 383
Bute family, 434

C

Cailiness Point, 500
Cairnpat, 484
Cairnryan military port, 361, 451, 457
Cairnryan village, 451
Caledonian Bus Company, 373
Candida Casa, 421
Canine club's shows, 465
Carols by candlelight, 447
Carrier-telephony repeater station, 489
Cartoon in Millisle vestry, 416
Carty tile works, 405
Cassillis, Sixth Earl of, 453
Castle Kennedy, ruin and grounds, 448
Castle Kennedy village, 450

Castle of Drummore, 505
Castle of Wigtown, 388
Catholic population, 381-2, 472
Cattle in the county, 355-7
Cattle mart, 467
Cave of St. Ninian, 382, 427
Celtic monastery, 421
Cement from Northern Ireland, 470
Chapel Finnian, 351
Charity and philanthropy, 383
Cheesemaking, 355, 467
Cheshire Home, 352
Children's homes, 372, 459
Children's playgrounds, 466
Choral Society, 462
Christian Brethren, 488, 494
Church attendance, 381, 387, 442, 472
Church bell cast in 1534, 505
Church bus, 495
Church closures, 416
Cinemas, 384, 463
Cistercian Order, 437
Civic Trust award, 438
Clachan system, 479, 496
Clanyard, 343
Class distinction, 454
Claverhouse, 351, 433
Clayhole, 465
Climate, 340
Close Brethren, 436
Closing of small schools, 376
Clydesdale horses, 356-7
Coast erosion, 340
Coastal shipping, 372
Coastguard stations, 488, 499
"Coffining" ceremony, 393
Coins, Roman, 350
Columba, 432
Combine harvesters, 358, 468
"Commercial capital", 362
Commonwealth club, 482
Communications, 374, 425, 459, 489, 493
Community associations, 382-3, 439
Community drama, 462, 504
Commuters, 408
Comprehensive school, 402
Continuation classes, 376, 411
Corn Production Act, 353
Corsewall House, 478-9
Corsewall old castle, 479
Corunna, 435, 479
Cottages unoccupied, 442
County council's responsibilities, 366
County town, 388
Covenanters, 351, 428, 434
Craigcaffie Castle, 448
Craighlaw, 411
"Craignarget, Fair Margaret of", 431
Crammog Head, 500

Crannogs, 428, 432
Creachmore golf course, 464
Creameries, 355, 467
Cree, Moss of, 340
Cree, river, 340
Cree salmon fishing, 360
Cree Valley, 340
Crimes and offences, 367, 483
Crockett, S. R., 405
Croft-and-toft pattern, 407
Cross Water of Luce, 388
Cruggleton church, 418
Culvennan Fell, 344
Cup-and-ring markings, 431
Curling, 386, 436, 442, 454, 463
Customs, local, 392-3, 475

D

Dairy herds, 353, 466
Dairying difficulties, 354
Dalrymples of Stair, 352; burial place, 446
Dalrymple, Sir Hew Hamilton, 446
Dalrymple-Hamilton, Admiral Sir Frederick, 446
Dalrymple-Hay family, 438
Damask industry, 417
Damnaglaur, 503
Dancing, 386, 454, 464
David II, 433
Debating society, 462
Deer, native species, 350
Delinquency, juvenile, 367
Depopulation, rural, 369, 378
Development Association, 364
Devorguilla, 351
Dhuloch School's record, 477
Dialect, local, 413, 456, 504
Diesel trains, 373
Dindinnie reservoir, 483
Disruption of 1843, 505
Distillery re-opens, 398
Donnan, Jeanie, Galloway poetess, 422
Douglas Ewart School, 376
Douglas family, 351
Dounan shales, 342
Dowalton Loch finds, 418
Drama, 462, 504
Dress, 454
Drinking more widespread, 399
Drochduil estate, 438
Druidism, 241, 491
Drumlins of boulder clay, 345
Drummore Castle, 505
Drummore Community Association, 502
Drummore quay, 499
Drummore village, 502, 504
Ducks, Muscovy, 349
Dumfries, Countess of, 434
Dunbar family of Mochrum, 433-4

Dunlop, Mrs., friend of Burns, 455
Dunragit estate, 438
Dunragit new village, 369,437
Dunskey castle, 485

E

Early potato growing, 357, 467
Economic organisation, 364
Economy, 353-365
Educational developments, 375, 402, 460
Egg grading centres, 359
Election apathy, 473
Electricity, 368, 372, 460
Elrig village, 435
Emigration, 457, 520
Employment statistics, 363
Enoch Hill, 489
Ensign of H.M.S. *Rodney*, 446
Entertainment facilities, 383
Erosion, coastal, 340
Eventide homes, 402
Ewing, C. A. Orr, 485
Export of manufactures, 360

F

"Fair Margaret of Craignarget", 431
Farm building improvements, 424
Farm employees, 358
Farm ownership, changes in, 404, 414
Farm size, 501
Farm work transformed, 468
Fauna, 348-50
Fergus, Lord of Galloway, 352
Festivals, 462
Field voles, damage by, 443
Films' appeal, 384, 463
Fish desert Lochryan, 360
Fish landings at Portpatrick, 359, 486
Fishing at Kirkcolm, 479
Fishing at Sorbie, 417
Fishing industry changes, 359-60, 470, 499
Fishing, river and loch, 350
Flat fishing season, 499
Flax industry at Stoneykirk, 491
Flooding problem, 459
Flora, 346-8
Flounders, 350
Flour mill at Garlieston, 417
Flying boat stations, 362
Football rivalry, 384, 463
Forestry Commission areas, 359
Forestry Commission's nursery, 438
Forestry work at Sorbie and Old Luce, 439
Fortified island in Loch Maberry, 410
Forts or motes at Stoneykirk, 492
Foxes, increase of, 350, 446
Fulmar's return, 348

Funeral customs, 393, 447
Funerary cairns, 432

G

Galdenoch Castle, 482
Galloway Advertiser and Wigtownshire Free Press, 475
Galloway cattle, 357
Galloway Collection in Library, 473
Galloway family, 352
Galloway Gazette, 405
Galloway Irish, 504
Galloway, Lordship of, 339, 352
Galloway Pageant, 405
Galloway Publicity Association, 364
Gambling habit, 429
Gannetry at the Scars, 349
Garlieston founded, 352
Garlieston industries, 417
Garrick Hospital, 474
Gas and electricity, 372
Gasworks improved, 459
Geese, 349
Geography of the county, 339-40
Geological map, 344
Geology of the county, 341-5
George VI, 457
Gifts and bequests, 397
Glaciation effects, 345
Glasserton House award, 428
Glasserton Parish, 427-30
Glenapp, 342
Glenluce Abbey, 367
Glenluce, last Abbot of, 438
Glenterrow standing stones, 448
Glow worms, 446
Gnats, 446
Golden Eagles, 349
Golden Eye Ducks, 349
Golf clubs and courses, 385, 464
Gordon, Duchess of, 435
Gordons of Clanyard, 505
Gordons of Lochinvar, 505
Graham of Claverhouse, 351
Granitic intrusions, 420
Graptolite collecting, 343
Grass drying factory, 358
Grass snakes, 443
Gravitation water supply, 368
Grebes' nesting place, 349
Grey Lag Geese, 349
Greywacke, 342
Grouse, 349
Guillemots, 349

H

Haig Institute, 435
Hall accommodation, 474

Hambro, R. O. Logan, 503
Handicapped children, 376
"Hanging Stone", 411
Harbours, 360, 423, 470, 487, 499
Harbour traffic, 360, 470
Harvesting, earlier, 468
Hay, Thomas, abbot of Glenluce, 438
Health Centre, 370
Health Executive Council, 382
Health services, 371
Heath and Moor formations, 347
Hillhead and Clayhole, 480
Hill sheep farming, 358
History of the shire, 350-1
Holiday centres, 364
Holstein cattle, 427
Home baking, 454, 482
Home farms, 365
Home help service, 372
Homes for elderly people, 372, 402
Horse-breeding, 356, 468
Horses, railway, 469
Horticultural society, 460
Hospital board, 382
Hospital League of Friends, 382
Hospital services, 474
Houses in poor condition, 368, 442-3, 495-6
Housing in Stranraer, 458
Housing problem, 367-70, 404, 458

I

Ice Age, 345
Illegitimacy, 372, 426, 454, 493
Immigration, 351, 405, 456, 457, 468, 477
Imports, 470
Inch parish, 445-55
Industrial relations. See Labour Relations
Industries, 345, 358, 398, 417, 456, 467. See also Occupations
Infantile paralysis, 418
Inhabited dwellings, 368
Innermessan as burgh, 352
Innermessan harbour, 472
Innermessan Moat, 448
Innerwell fisheries, 417
Intelligence level, 452
Intrusive rocks, 343, 456
Irish accent, 456, 504
Irish element, 456, 476
Irish farm workers, 468
Irish immigration, 351
Irish in Kirkcolm, 477
Irish scholars, 421
Isle of Whithorn, 422
Isle harbour changes, 423
Isle's ancient buildings, 422-3
Itinerant teachers, 376

J

James IV, 434
"Jigging" for herring, 499
Johnston Stewart. See Stewart.
Juvenile delinquency, 367

K

Keep of Craighlaw, 411
Kempes Graves, Leswalt, 482
Kennedy family, 352
Kennedy family's castle, 352
Kildrochat House, 495
Killantringan lighthouse, 489
King George V Playing Field, 465
Kirkcolm curlers, 478
Kirkcolm parish, 476-9
Kirkcowan antiquities, 408
Kirkcowan Musical Society, 409
Kirkcowan parish, 407-11
Kirkinner parish, 412-15
Kirkmadrine stones, 492
Kirkmaiden antiquities, 504-5
Kirkmaiden (Glasserton) ruined church, 428
Kirkmaiden parish, 499-506
Kirk o'Drumatye, 428
Knockinaam House, 495
Knock of Luce, 437

L

Labour relations, 365, 399, 404, 466, 498
Lady Bay, 342
Laird's bet to "skail the Byke", 433
Lamb sales, 358
Lamprophyres, 345
Land ownership, changes in, 404, 414
Land transformation, 452-3
Land use, 354
Landed proprietors disappear, 404, 414
Landslides, 340
Language changes, 413, 504
Lapsed burghs, 352
Law and order, 367
Leswalt parish, 480-3
Library and museum, 376-7
Lifeboats, 489, 502
Lighthouses, 489, 500
Litigation over fishing rights, 392
Living standards, 443
Lobster fishing, 360, 499
Local government services, 366
Loch fishing, 350
Loch Maberry, 410
Loch Magillie, 445
Loch of Larg curlers, 442

Loch of the Inch, 445
Lochans village, 449, 494
Lochinch Castle, 352, 448
Lochnaw, 480
Lochnaw Castle, 482
Lochryan, 360, 470, 471-2
Lochryan and Glenapp church, 447
Logan's famous gardens, 503
Logan fishpond, 502
Logan House and estate, 500, 501
Lordship of Galloway, 339, 352
Luce Bay sands, 339-40, 437
Luce, Knock of, 437

M

Maberry, Loch, 410
McCullochs of Myrton, 434
McDoualls of Logan, 434, 503
Machars, 431
Magillie, Loch, 445
Mail link with Ireland, 471
Manufactures, 360
Marian Tower, 479
Marine lake, Stranraer, 466
Maritime flora, 346
Market Gardening, 359
Marriages, early, 501
Marriages with foreigners, 506
Martyrs' graves, 390
Maxwells of Monreith, 434
Maxwell, Sir Aymer, 423
Maxwell, Sir Herbert, 435
Meoul Hill, 491
Mercat crosses, 392
Mica, 345
Micro-wave radio link, 489
Midges, 446
"Mighty men of Mochrum", 436
Military camps, 451, 457
Military Port, Cairnryan, 361, 451, 457
Milk analysis, 354
Milk Marketing Board, 355
Milk production and prices, 354-5
Milk recording, 353
Milk transport in bulk, 500
Milling dwindles, 423
Mochrum Curling Club, 436
Mochrum lochs, 431
"Mochrum scarts", 349
Moles, 443
Monastery, lost, 351
Money Head, 343
Monkey puzzle features, 350
Monolith, Stoneykirk, 492
Monreith, Maxwells of, 434
Monterey pine plantation, 359
Moor Kirk of Luce, 442
Moore, Sir John, 479

Morton, H. V., 405
Mosquitoes, 446, 453
Motes in Stoneykirk, 492
Motor traffic development, 373
Mulberry harbour, 423
Mull of Galloway, 340, 500
Mull's low rainfall, 340
"Murder stone", Stoneykirk, 492
Muscovy Ducks, 349
Music and verse speaking festivals, 462
Musical associations, 409, 462
Musicians, amateur, 497
Myrton Tower, 434

N

National Museum, Edinburgh, 340
Natural features of the county, 339-40
Neolithic stone axes, 483
Nesmilk factory, 438
New Luce old school, 442
New Luce, parish, 441-4
New Luce sheepdog trials, 443
Newspapers, 405, 475
Newton Stewart, burgh, 403-4
Newton Stewart, burgh of barony, 352
Newton Stewart as tourist centre, 405
Newton Stewart, ram and lamb sales, 358
Norman motes and chapel, 432-3
"Normanising" policy, 351

O

Oatmeal production, 361
Observation posts, 500
Occupations, 362, 375, 439, 469, 486
Ochiltree and Black Water lochs, 403
Office of Works, 437
Old Luce archaeological treasures, 437
Old Luce parish, 437-40
Old Place of Mochrum, 431, 434
One-way traffic, 362
Open prison at Newton Stewart, 403-4
Organ controversy, 446
Organised labour, 466
Orr Ewing. See Ewing
Otters, 443, 445
Outside pumps, 402, 429, 496
Ownership of land, changes in, 404, 414
Oyster fishery, 360, 470

P

Packet boat services, 448
Paddling pools, 466
Palisaded fort, 410

Parishes amalgamated, 416
Park estate, 438
Parliamentary division, 366
Peat, 340
Peden the Prophet, 441
Penninghame open prison, 403-4
Penninghame parish, 401-6
Penwhirn water supply, 372
Permanent pasture, 481
Persecution by Claverhouse, 351
Philanthropic organisations, 383
"Philip and Mary" Point, 432
Picture houses, 384, 463
Pig rearing, 467, 497
Pigeon racing, 465
Pike infestation, 350, 445
Pilgrimages to St. Ninian's shrine, 421
Piltanton burn, 484
"Place of herbs", 441
Planning developments, 374
Plantations. See Forestry
Ploughing matches, 359
Poachers, 445
Poisonous plants, 346
Police, 367
Political activities, 366, 466
Population distribution, 380
Portlogan lifeboat, 502
Portlogan quay, 502
Portlogan village, 502
Port Montgomerie, 484
Portpatrick as burgh of barony, 352
Portpatrick harbour, 487
Portpatrick Hotel, 485
Portpatrick radio station, 489
Portpatrick railway closure, 488
Portpatrick's ruined pier, 487
Portwilliam, 435
Postal services, 374
Potato growing, 357
Potato marketing, 467
Pre-historic relics at Kirkcowan, 409-10
Premonstratensians, 421, 448
Presbyteries united, 420
Pride, local, 498
"Princess Victoria" disaster, 447, 471
Prison, Penninghame, 403-4
Prisoners of war, 379, 457
Professions, 362
Promontory forts at Leswalt, 483
Pump wells, 402, 429, 496
Punchbowl presented by Queen Anne, 391-2

Q

Quarrying at Boreland Fell, 346, 408
Queen Anne's gift to Wigtown, 391-2
Quoiting, 464, 501

R

Radford, Professor Ralegh, 420
Radio station, Leswalt, 483
Radio station, Portpatrick, 489
R.A.F. flying boats, 457
R.A.F. stations, 362
Rail schemes dropped, 469
Railway construction, 373
Railway pier, 471
Railway services, 372
Rainfall statistics, 340-1
Raised beaches, 345
Ram and lamb sales, 358
Rankin, Rev. Oliver S., 416
Reclamation work, 465
Recreation. See Sport
Red Cross Society, 382
Reformed Presbyterian Church, 382
Regattas, 339, 384
Re-housing schemes, 369
Religion, 381-2
Restoration of Old Place of Mochrum, 434
Revivalist meetings, 481
Rispain fort, 433
River fishing, 350
Rivers in the shire, 339
Road system, 374, 493
Road transport services, 373
Robert I, 351
Rocks, 341-5
Rodney's ensign, 446
Roman Catholics, 381-2, 472
Roman coins found, 350
Roman settlement doubts, 350
Romanesque cathedral, 421
Ross, Sir John, Arctic explorer, 455, 474
Rotary club, 383
Royal Air Force. See R.A.F.
Rugby matches, 463
Rullion Green, 434
Rural depopulation, 369, 378
Rural schools closed, 376
Ruskin, John, 391

S

St. Columba, 482
St. Finnian, 351, 432
St. John's well, 472
St. Malachy, 433
St. Martin of Tours, 421
St. Medan's cave, 504
St. Ninian, 351
St. Ninian's cave, 382, 427
Salmon fishing, 360, 392
Sand carried by winds, 339-40
Sandhead combined school, 493
Scholars from Ireland, 421

School buses, 461
School changes, 460
School closures, 376
School leavers, 375
School meals, 372
Schoolmaster's £17 a year, 477
Scoto-Norse dominance, 351
Sculptured crosses, 351, 432-3
Sea ducks and swans, 349
Sea-going community, 477, 502
Sea-king fort, 482
Sea sports, 384
Sea transport, 470
Seaweed as fertiliser, 496
Seceders dispersed by laird, 433
Seine net fishing, 470, 486
Sheep farming, hill, 358
Sheepdog trials, 443
Shells, disposal of, 361
Sheriff courts, 367
Sheriff, hereditary, 351
Sheriff-Principal, 367
Sheriff-Substitute, 367
Sheuchan school, 374-5
Shifting population, 379
Ship-breaking, 361
Shipping, 372
Short Brothers and Harland, 362
Short sea route, 364, 470
Silage making, 500
Silver City Airways, 374
Slum clearance, 370
Small farms experiment, 501
Small holdings schemes, 358, 414
"Smiddy" changes, 469
Smuggling, 436
Snakes, 443, 445
Social relations, 454, 506
Social services, 382-3, 429
Soil of the county, 340
Sorbie parish, 416-19
Sorbie tower, 418
Soulseat abbey, 351
Soulseat loch, 445
Southern Uplands fault, 342
Sport and recreation, 384-5, 463-5, 487, 495
Squad labour, 358
Squatters at Inch, 450, 451
Stair, first Viscount, 352
Stair Park, 466
Stairhaven harbour, 439
Standing stones at Torhouse, 390
Steam coaches, 373
Stewart, R. H. Johnston, 428
Stoats, 446
Stone axes, 437
Stone quarrying, 346, 408
Stoneykirk castles, 492

Stoneykirk parish, 491-8
Storm damage to plantations, 446
Stranraer Academy, 460
Stranraer burgh and parish, 456-75
Stranraer castle, 475
Stranraer cattle show, 469
Stranraer High School, 374
Stranraer High School F.P. Association, 461
Stranraer housing, 370, 458
Stranraer Musical Association, 462
Stranraer's "Scottish Week", 475
Sub-standard dwellings, 369
Subterranean dwellings, 492
Sunday labour and sport, 474, 506
Sunderland flying boats, 362
Supplies by sea and road, 469
Swans, 349
Swearing, 454

T

Table tennis, 464
Tarff river, 339
Television's impact, 383, 463
Thatched cottage, 501
Thrift, 399
Tied houses, 501
Todd, William, 505
Topography, 339-40
Torhouse standing stones, 390
Torrs Warren, 439
Toskerton Knowes, 492
Tourism and holidaymaking, 364
Tractor supplants horse, 356
Trade Unions, 396, 466
Trades Council, 466
Traffic problem, 425, 459
Transit camp, 457
Translucent axe, 437
Transport services, 372, 469
Trotting track, 465
Tuberculosis, eradication, 353

U

U-Boats in Lochryan, 361
Unemployment, 371
United Creameries, 486
United States Forces, 361

V

"Valley of Light", 437
Vaus family, 352
Viking rule, 421
Village resorts, 364
Volcanic rocks, 342

Voles, damage by, 443
Voluntary milk pool, 354
Voluntary services, 382-3, 429

W

Warships broken up, 361
War-time developments, 361, 457
War weddings, 458
Water ski-ing, 384, 487
Water supplied from wells, 402, 429, 496
Water supplies transformed, 372, 501-2
Waverley Home, 459
W.E.A. lectures, 462
Weapons from America, 361
Weasels, 446
Weather, 340
Welfare work, 459
Wells, 402, 429, 496, 505
Western S.M.T. Co., 373
West Freugh R.A.E. station, 361-2
"Whaleback Dominie", 477
Whauphill, 413
Whey butter, 467
White and Black lochs, 445
White monks, 457
Whithorn as ecclesiastical burgh, 352
Whithorn burgh and parish, 420-6
Whithorn Museum, 373
Whithorn pilgrimages, 421
Whithorn said to be "in Ireland", 351

Whithorn's associations with St. Ninian, 421
Whithorn's musical attainments, 425
Whithorn's Priory Church, 420
Whithorn's sculptured crosses, 351
Wig Bay air base, 362, 458
Wigtown agricultural show, 393
Wigtown burgh and parish, 388-400
Wigtown Castle, 388
Wigtown customs, 392
Wigtown martyrs, 352, 390
Wigtown's ancient history and relics, 391
Wigtown's burghal privileges, 388
Wigtownshire Musical Association, 462
Wild animals, 350
Wild birds, 348-9
Wild flowers, 347
Winds, 340
Wireless stations, See Radio stations
Wishing well, 505
Woman sheriff, 367
Women's emancipation, 415
Women's Rural Institutes, 473
Woodlands, census, 359

Y

Yachting clubs, 384
Youth activities, 455, 504
Youth organisations, 465

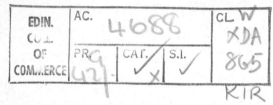